The Supreme Refuge

The Supreme Refuge

Durgā's Transformation into the Hindu Great Goddess

Hillary P. Rodrigues

SUNY PRESS

Published by State University of New York Press, Albany

EU GPSR Authorised Representative:
Logos Europe, 9 rue Nicolas Poussin, 17000, La Rochelle, France
contact@logoseurope.eu

For information, contact State University of New York Press, Albany, NY
www.sunypress.edu

Publication of this book was made possible in part by the generous support of the University of Lethbridge.

Library of Congress Cataloging-in-Publication Data

Names: Rodrigues, Hillary, 1953- author.
Title: The supreme refuge : Durgā's transformation into the Hindu Great
    Goddess / Hillary P. Rodrigues.
Description: Albany : State University of New York Press, [2025] | Series:
    SUNY series in Hindu studies | Includes bibliographical references and
    index.
Identifiers: LCCN 2025016910 | ISBN 9798855804690 (hardcover) | ISBN
    9798855804713 (ebook) | ISBN 9798855804706 (paperback)
Subjects: LCSH: Durgā (Hindu deity)
Classification: LCC BL1225.D8 R63 2025 | DDC 294.5/2114--dc23/eng/20250505
LC record available at https://lccn.loc.gov/2025016910

To my teachers

yac ca kiñcit kvacid vastu sadasadvākhilātmike /
tasya sarvasya yā śaktiḥ sā tvaṃ kiṃ stūyase tadā //
Whatever thing exists and wherever, you [O Goddess] are the power of all that, in the innermost self of the whole of reality, manifest or unmanifest; how then can you be praised?

Contents

Illustrations

Preface and Acknowledgments

My academic interest in the goddess Durgā began with my doctoral studies under David Kinsley in the late 1980s. At the time, aside from a chapter in his influential *Hindu Goddesses*, few detailed studies of Durgā existed, mostly limited to journal articles or book chapters. David once confided that he might have occasionally conflated the Mahādevī with Durgā — a common occurrence in Hinduism scholarship and generally unproblematic after the 8th century CE — even though he had wisely assigned them separate chapters in his book. A comprehensive study of Durgā was clearly needed, but the scope was daunting. My doctoral research had focused on contemporary Durgā worship in Banāras but persistent questions over the years led me to examine her cult more broadly and examine its historical evolution. This two-volume work is the culmination of that decades-long inquiry.

I extend heartfelt thanks to Rosalind Lefeber and Phyllis Granoff, my first Sanskrit teachers, and to John Arapura, Krishna Shivaraman, Paul Younger, Graeme MacQueen, and Yun-hua Jan, who were key mentors in my early studies of Asian philosophies. In India, Pandits Vagish Shastri and Hemendra Nath Chakravarty, and Om Prakash Sharma deepened my understanding of the living tradition of Durgā worship. Thomas Coburn, the external examiner for my doctoral dissertation, offered invaluable insights, and revised portions of that work, primarily from its appendix, were later published as *Ritual Worship of the Great Goddess* (SUNY Press, 2003).

My understanding of Durgā was enriched by exchanges with Clifford Geertz (on the symbol complex circumscribed by Durgā), Alf Hiltebeitel (on the *Mahābhārata*), Patrick Olivelle (on dating the Dharmaśāstras), R. Nagaswamy (on temple iconography), J. N. Tiwari (on early goddess cults in South India), and Madhuvanti Ghosh (on the goddess Nanā), among others. Particularly valuable were discussions within the Navarātri and Durgāpūjā in South Asia working group, led by Ute Hüsken, which united scholars studying Hindu goddess festival traditions.

I am grateful to museum curators, including Sarojini Chanchlani, Superintendent of the Hawamahal in Rajasthan, and the delightful faculty at the Chandraketugarh Sahidullah Smriti Mahavidyalaya, in Berachampa, for their guidance through their collections. Susan Trink and her mother, Bruni Cawi, kindly assisted with German translations of H. Stietencron's work. And special thanks to my student assistants, Ralph Pollock and J'Lean Koinberg, for their labors in the early stages of this research, and to Forrest Freihaut more recently.

This project benefitted greatly from the constructive feedback of anonymous reviewers, although any errors remain my own. Generous funding from the Social Sciences and Humanities Research Council of Canada (SSHRC), the Community of Research Excellence Development Opportunities (CREDO) at the University of Lethbridge, and the School of Graduate Studies at McMaster University supported this work over the past four decades. I owe a special debt to James Peltz, the acquisition editor at SUNY, for his patience and guidance in navigating the project's challenging early phases.

Abbreviations

AniH	-	Aniruddha's Hymn
AV	-	*Atharva Veda*
BCE	-	Before the Common Era
BaudhDhS	-	*Baudhāyana Dharmasūtra*
BG	-	*Bhagavad Gītā*
BGŚS	-	*Baudhāyana Gṛhyaśeṣasūtra*
BṛDe	-	*Bṛhad Devatā*
BU	-	*Bṛhadāraṇyaka Upaniṣad*
CE	-	Common Era
CII	-	*Corpus Inscriptionum Indicarum*
DevīP	-	*Devī Purāṇa*
DM	-	*Devī Māhātmya* (aka *Durgā Saptaśatī*)
DS	-	*Durgā Saptaśatī* (aka *Devī Māhātmya*)
DStv	-	Durgā Stava
DStv*	-	Durgā Stava (or unknown variant)
DStv+	-	Durgā Stava (with frame verses)
DSto	-	Durgā Stotra
DSto+	-	Durgā Stotra (with frame verses)
EI	-	*Epigraphia Indica*
HV	-	*Harivaṃśa*
KālP	-	*Kālikā Purāṇa*
KRām	-	*Kṛttivāsa Rāmāyaṇa*
l.	-	line(s)
MārkP	-	*Mārkaṇḍeya Purāṇa*
Mbh	-	*Mahābhārata*
PN-s1	-	Praise of Nidrā (First Stratum)
PN-s2	-	Praise of Nidrā (Second Stratum) (i.e., Āryā Stava)
PradH	-	Pradyumna's Hymn
Rām	-	*Rāmāyaṇa*
RV	-	*Ṛg Veda*
RVKh	-	*Ṛg Veda Khila*
ŚDS	-	*Śaṅkhalikhita Dharma Sūtra*
SP	-	*Skanda Purāṇa* (Critical Edition) (i.e., Old *Skanda Purāṇa*)
SP (Bh)	-	Old *Skanda Purāṇa* (edited by Kṛṣṇaprasāda Bhaṭṭarāī)

SkP	-	*Skanda Purāṇa* (i.e., *Veṅkateśvara* Press version)
SV	-	*Sāma Veda*
TA	-	*Taittirīya Āraṇyaka*
TB	-	*Taittirīya Brāhmaṇa*
v.	-	verse(s)
VāmP	-	*Vāmana Purāṇa*
VarP	-	*Varāha Purāṇa*
VasDhS	-	*Vasiṣṭha Dharmasūtra*
VDŚ	-	*Viṣṇu-dharmaśāstra* (*Viṣṇu-smṛti*)
VRām	-	*Vālmīki Rāmāyaṇa*
YV	-	*Yajur Veda*

A Note on Transliteration

Conventional diacritics are used when transliterating Sanskrit words. Apart from diacritics for a few city names, such as Banāras, Vārāṇasī, and Mathurā, contemporary spellings are used for living people's names and most geographical locations. So, you will read Maharashtra and Odisha instead of Mahārāṣṭra and Oḍiśā. Tamil words are rendered using common Sanskrit equivalents and most Central Asian terms follow widespread conventions; so, one will see Śiva instead of Śivaṉ, and Šapur instead of Shapur. Alternate transliterations are often provided in parentheses at the first occurrence of a word.

A Note on Abbreviations

The full title for a book or hymn is used in its first occurrence in a chapter, with subsequent occurrences using an assigned abbreviation. If the title has not been used for a long stretch, the non-abbreviated form may reappear for the convenience of the reader.

Introduction

Amid the vast Hindu pantheon, Durgā stands as one of the most revered goddesses. Navarātra, the vibrant nine-day celebration honoring the Great Goddess, is commonly called Durgā Pūjā, reflecting her widespread identification as the Hindu Great Goddess. In countless depictions, from Central Asia and India to Bali and Vietnam, Durgā is portrayed wielding the weapons of the male gods with her many arms, riding a great lion, and triumphantly vanquishing the Buffalo Demon, Mahiṣa. But who is this remarkable divinity? How did she come to be so passionately venerated? What can we uncover about her captivating persona and myths? These questions form the foundation of this study.

Although Hinduism features innumerable goddesses, its Śākta sectarian stream envisions a feminine supreme deity, who is routinely addressed as Devī (Goddess), Mahādevī (Great Goddess), or simply Mā (Mother). Other sects, such as the Śaivas or Vaiṣṇavas, may use the terms Devī or Mahādevī to refer to a supreme goddess, but not the supreme deity in the Hindu pantheon. The widespread identification of Durgā as the Mahādevī has often led scholars to treat them as synonymous. While this is mostly unproblematic in contemporary contexts, it has complicated our understanding of her historical development because Durgā's name has been prematurely or erroneously applied to early mentions of the Mahādevī, or to goddesses resembling her.

This two-volume study places Durgā at its core. Volume 1 meticulously traces how she became identified as the Great Goddess, while volume 2 explores her worship's spread throughout South and Southeast Asia, culminating with a focus on its expressions in the sacred city of Banāras. Following J. Z. Smith's (1988) assertion that "religion" is an academic construct defined by researchers, this study defines Durgā as its subject — a boundless and intricately shaped one. This volume works through textual and material evidence, cautiously distinguishing Durgā from the other goddesses with whom she has been conflated. It traces her rise from the earliest literary mentions and possible iconographic depictions to her eventual status as Mahādevī, the supreme deity of the Hindu pantheon from the Śākta sectarian perspective, at the historical point Thomas Coburn (1984) called "the crystallization of the [Great] Goddess tradition." Surprisingly, despite her prominence, Durgā had not been rigorously examined in this way before.

Bihani Sarkar (2017) finally dealt in substantive detail with Durgā worship in ancient and medieval Indian kingship, primarily through a rigorous examination of inscriptional evidence. It has proved to be a critical resource in this work. Thomas Coburn's (1984) study of goddess epithets in the *Devī Māhātmya*, and his subsequent translation and commentary (1991) have been invaluable. Yuko Yokochi's (2004, 2013) works on the myth-cycle of the warrior goddess Kauśikī-Vindhyavāsinī in the old *Skanda Purāṇa* provided rich insights, as did J. N. Tiwari's (1985) study of early South Indian goddess cults, particularly Korravai. M. Seshadri (1963), H. Stietencron (2005), and Doris Srinivasan (1997) helped to clarify the iconography of the buffalo-subduing goddess, as did the works of Gary Tartakov and Vidya Dehejia (1984) and Charlotte Schmid (2002, 2011). Michael Shenkar's (2014) and Mary Boyce's (1975, 1979, 1982) studies on ancient Iranian cults were equally valuable for my understanding of those regional influences.

My theoretical and methodological approach is eclectic. Rather than adhering rigidly to any single theory or method, I align with W. C. Smith's (1975) perspective that these must remain subordinate to the subject matter. Utilizing a toolbox approach, I begin with textual hermeneutics to identify the earliest scriptural references to Durgā and their contexts. I then integrate iconographic and inscriptional evidence with the textual content to establish a firmer chronology. This process reveals exciting correlations. A central contribution of this study is its compilation of the most significant early textual and iconographic evidence on Durgā's cult, offering a foundation for future research. By correlating this material, I propose a revised chronology for key texts and for the evolution of Durgā's worship. Some of this aligns with and supports the more recent work of other scholars, although it derives from the study's distinctive focus on Durgā and related goddesses.

As Clifford Geertz (1993, 87–125) asserts that religion is a cultural system constituted of symbols, I seek a holistic interpretation of the symbol complex that is Durgā, situated within its historical, geographical, social, political, economic, and related contexts. I explore tendrils of her worship within and beyond the Indian subcontinent. The second volume examines the consolidation of her cult in contemporary India, particularly in Banāras, and its historical and modern configurations in Nepal and Southeast Asia.

In this study, I translate Sanskrit verses only when their phrasing reveals distinctive meanings, relying otherwise on well-regarded translations. I paraphrase texts as needed, occasionally citing Sanskrit or other languages to clarify nuances. The chapter on the *Devī Māhātmya* paraphrases my translation of the scripture, although I primarily cite Coburn's (1991) version and verse numbering system. While excellent studies on aspects of Durgā's cult exist, this work offers alternative chronologies, challenges prevailing opinions, uncovers overlooked evidence, corrects errors, and proposes new hypotheses. Regardless of whether my interpretations are embraced, the data presented should enable researchers to explore alternative formulations.

A key argument of this study is that Durgā has always been worshipped as a refuge, growing ultimately into the supreme refuge, accessible to all in their most desperate needs — not solely to kings or in martial contexts. Furthermore, I argue that Śākta theologians have configured Durgā not merely as the supreme goddess, but into the supreme deity of the Hindu pantheon. I contend, however, through Śākta metaphysics as expressed in the *Devī Māhātmya*, in particular, that Durgā is intentionally receded into the background to sustain a polytheistic framework that counters monotheistic or monolatrist theologies.

Readers may occasionally feel led into seemingly obscure analyses of philology and iconography, but these are essential for addressing academic questions rigorously. I have, however, aimed for accessibility, even for novices with limited familiarity with the subject. Beyond my primary arguments, I address questions that have intrigued me and likely others studying the Hindu Great Goddess, such as: When does Durgā's name first appear in literary sources, and what traits does she exhibit? What are the earliest symbolic depictions of Durgā or a closely related goddess? Which textual sources align with these depictions or with her modern worship? Why is she portrayed with many arms and weapons, and when did this motif emerge? How did the lion become her vehicle and why does she battle a buffalo demon? Were her attributes influenced by other goddesses, either within or beyond the Indian subcontinent? How does the buffalo demon myth develop into one involving shapeshifting? What are some of the enigmatic items that she holds in early iconography? Were there antecedents to her myths in the *Devī Māhātmya*? Why does Durgā's victory over Mahiṣa overshadow Skanda's attribution to the same victory? What earlier stories might have shaped the tale of a powerful female warrior defeating an arrogant emperor? How is Durgā related to other goddesses, such as Pārvatī, Kālī, Kauśikī, Nidrā, and Jayā, or gods such as Indra, Viṣṇu/Kṛṣṇa, Agni, and Śiva? When did the epithet Mahiṣamardinī become common, and what is the symbolic meaning of "crushing" (*mardana*)? When was the *Devī Māhātmya* composed, and how does it relate to the *Caṇḍīśataka*? Finally, what historical factors might explain the *Devī Māhātmya*'s composition, and its rise to prominence in Śākta traditions?

Astonishingly, many of these questions have been addressed inadequately or not at all, while others have been obscured by prematurely conflating Durgā with the Mahādevī. By focusing primarily on Durgā, some answers to these questions may surprise even those well versed in the study of the Hindu Great Goddess. In some cases, I reach the same conclusions as previous scholars — such as proposing a later date for the *Devī Māhātmya* than older works suggest — but through a different route, thus reinforcing those positions. In other cases, I offer intriguing possibilities, such as suggesting that the goddess depicted with weapon hairpins depicted in early Common Era plaques may be the river goddess Kauśikī. These proposals aim to spark further research. I hope this study enlightens those who share my curiosity, and provides compelling evidence to refine our understanding, helping us move past old errors. With this foundation, we will be better positioned for further explorations into the world of the Great Goddess.

Initially, I wrote this book heuristically, laying out early hypotheses and revising them as I worked through the material. However, this approach proved confusing to some reviewers of earlier drafts. Consequently, I have revised the structure, providing a clear outline of the book's sequence of topics and main contents in this introduction. Although this introduces some repetition, each chapter now includes introductory paragraphs alluding to some of its content and key arguments for the reader's benefit.

Chapter 1 examines the word *durga* and its variations in early sources such as the Vedas, Āraṇyakas, Dharmaśāstras, and pre-epic literature. We note that *durga* initially refers to inaccessible places of refuge appearing in the masculine form in the *Ṛg Veda*, and in the feminine form in the *Atharva Veda*, although not as a goddess. By the 1st century CE, the *Vasiṣṭha Dharmasūtra* mentions Durgā in mantric formulae, such as the Durgā-Sāvitrī — possibly a variant of the Gāyātrī *mantra*, although details are unclear. Earlier occurrences in the *Taittirīya Āraṇyaka* and *Bṛhad Devatā* may include insertions from a later period. Verses from late appendices (1st to 3rd century BCE) of the *Taittirīya Āraṇyaka* could represent the earliest known mentions of the goddess. The most detailed early material on Durgā appears in the Rātrī Khila, part of the *Ṛg Veda Khila*, a *Ṛg Veda* supplement. It is very likely an insertion, arguably composed around the 1st century BCE, and preceding the *Mahābhārata* hymns to Durgā. By the early Common Era, texts such as the *Baudhāyanagṛhyaśeṣasūtra* indicate rituals to Durgā, affirming her persona as a refuge — a theme that permeates this study.

Chapter 2 explores hymns to Durgā in the *Mahābhārata* and the *Harivaṃśa*. The goddess Durgā appears within the Durgā Stava and Durgā Stotra of the *Mahābhārata*, as well as within the *Harivaṃśa*'s Second Stratum of the Praise of Nidrā, Aniruddha's Hymn, and Pradyumna's Hymn. While the First Stratum of the *Harivaṃśa*'s so-called hymn to the goddess Nidrā is often regarded as the earliest of these paeans, I suggest it may have been preceded by the *Mahābhārata*'s Durgā Stava or a similar variant. The *Mahābhārata*'s Durgā hymns are generally seen as late insertions, which may be true. Separating the hymns from their framing verses reveals their likely earlier origins and the sectarian motivations behind the framing.

The framing verses reveal clear efforts to assimilate the goddess within a Vaiṣṇava framework, through allusion to the Kaṃsa myth in which she is the sister of Kṛṣṇa, thereby subordinated to Viṣṇu/Kṛṣṇa. The hymns portray Durgā as linked to buffalo sacrifice, victory, and defeating enemies through associations with such goddesses as Jayā, Vijayā, Kālī, Kātyāyanī, and Kauśikī. Early hymns highlight attributes such as peacock feather bracelets and standard — which later disappear — while her lion emerges in later hymns. These details connect with iconographic evidence, helping to establish chronology. I argue that the First Stratum of the Praise of Nidrā is not a proper hymn per se, but an attempt to subordinate a prominent goddess of substantial repute, likely Durgā, Kālī, or Kauśikī under Viṣṇu, by portraying Nidrā/Kālarātrī as dependent on Viṣṇu's largesse.

Chapter 3 investigates early post–Indus Valley iconography of female deities, aligning these depictions with textual references tentatively dated earlier than mainstream scholarship suggests. Central to this analysis are plaques featuring goddesses adorned with hairpins resembling weapons, primarily from Chandraketugarh in West Bengal but also found across northern India. Often labeled as *yakṣīs*, I argue these likely represent a specific goddess, due to their consistent attributes. Two examples, a plaque from New York's Metropolitan Museum of Art and the Tamluk Yakṣī at Oxford's Ashmolean Museum reveal parallels with descriptions in the Durgā Stava and Durgā Stotra of the *Mahābhārata*, and the First Stratum of the Praise of Nidrā in the *Harivaṃśa*. Distinctive features, such as plump arms, peacock feather bracelets, ornate earrings, coiled hip-belts, a wondrous diadem, a peacock standard, and *bhūta* attendants, suggest a fusion of Durgā/Kālī and Nidrā/Kauśikī, although the Praise of Nidrā does not explicitly mention Durgā/Kālī. Kauśikī, with her riverine attributes, is possibly the goddess represented. Her traits parallel the Near Eastern goddess Arədvī Sūrā Anāhitā, praised in the *Avesta* hymns, such as Yašt 5. These connections are instrumental in the last chapter's thesis that the *Devī Māhātmya* addresses perennial tensions between iconism and aniconism, and monolatry and polytheism.

Chapter 4 examines early depictions of the goddess subduing a buffalo, one of Durgā's defining exploits. Using M. Seshadri's classification of buffalo-subduing goddess images, which may be rendered as Theriomorphic (T), Victorious Goddess (V), Anthropomorphic (A), and Emergent Demon (E), we trace these types from an Indus Valley example to Kuṣāṇa period plaques showing a multi-armed goddess overpowering a buffalo. The buffalo, a symbol of untamed power, is linked to Zoroastrian motifs of slaying demons (*khafstra*), where initial representations show the goddess defeating the buffalo with her hands or feet. The lion, associated with Durgā in later depictions, finds precedents in figures such as Kybele, the lion-headed Egyptian goddess Sekhmet, and Nanā of the Kuṣāṇa pantheon. Nanā, a sovereignty-conferring goddess with ties to Inanna-Ištar, provides critical context for interpreting Durgā's symbolism in early iconography, particularly her association with power and divine rule. The chapter concludes with reflections on the emergence of multiple arms when depicting the goddess.

Chapter 5 continues this iconographic exploration, focusing on Gupta-era depictions of the buffalo-subduing goddess. Examples, such as a Rājghāṭ seal and a panel from the Bhumarā Śiva temple, depict the goddess pressing the buffalo's head with her foot while spearing it. In several images at the Udayagiri caves in Madhya Pradesh, the goddess is depicted with multiple arms, holding various weapons, and spearing the buffalo. A puzzling object held aloft by the goddess, interpreted as a serpent, drum, or garland, is argued here to represent her self-coronation with a particular diadem — a symbol of divine supremacy referenced in the epic hymns.

Chapter 6 links these iconographic elements with textual descriptions, enabling re-interpretation of mischaracterized items in Kuṣāṇa and Gupta art (e.g., shields, quivers) as peacock feather standards — a sovereignty symbol central to Durgā's depiction. This connection illuminates the Peacock Goddess

(Mahāmāyūrī) in Buddhism and parallels with China's Xi Wangmu, the Sovereign Mother of the West. The chapter underscores interregional cultural exchanges across South Asia, Egypt, Mesopotamia, Central Asia, and China, emphasizing that South Asia was deeply interconnected through trade and ideology. Ideological pressure to look only at South Asian sources as the basis for all features of South Asian religious culture has often stymied scholarship. The extended discussion of symbols of sovereignty, such as self-coronation with the diadem and association with the peacock banner, are essential to illustrate Durgā's assertion of supremacy in the Hindu pantheon. They are crucial to the thesis presented in the final chapter, which argues that the *Devī Māhātmya* (discussed in chapter 9) skillfully nuanced the theology of the Great Goddess as Supreme Deity.

Chapter 7 focuses on the evolving imagery of the goddess stepping on the buffalo and the emergence of the term Mahiṣamardinī, emphasizing the concept of *mardana* (crushing). This term is absent in early literature, likely originating in Śaiva sectarian texts around the 7th or 8th century CE. I propose limiting the use of Mahiṣamardinī to post-7th century images where the goddess is depicted with her foot atop the buffalo demon. Bāṇa's *Caṇḍīśataka*, composed in the 7th century, glorifies this motif and introduces Caṇḍī as a synonym for Durgā. The chapter also examines references to human sacrifice in Xuanzang's travelogue and fictional accounts such as Bāṇa's *Kādambarī*, the *Mālatī-Mādhava*, and the *Gauḍavaho*, linking these rituals to Durgā, Kālī, and Cāmuṇḍā. The *Mahābhārata* attributes Mahiṣa's defeat to Skanda, offering scant details about the buffalo demon. We delve into Skanda's cult and its gradual displacement by Durgā, a topic further explored in the concluding chapter, which highlights theological tensions and the *Devī Māhātmya's* unifying vision of the Divine Feminine.

In chapter 8 the focus is on the *Devī Māhātmya* (DM), without doubt the seminal text establishing the Hindu Great Goddess (Devī) as the Supreme Deity and Supreme Reality itself. This is a departure from our proposed chronological sequence, in part because earlier scholarship had placed the DM's composition as early as the 5th or 6th century CE, which is why it is discussed here. Chapter 12 examines occurrences of Durgā or a related buffalo-slaying goddess in the *Varāha*, early *Skanda*, and *Devī Purāṇas*, which appear in episodes that we suggest pre-date the DM. The strategy is to compare these against the DM and in tandem with iconographic parallels. Embedded within the *Mārkaṇḍeya Purāṇa*, the DM is analyzed for its three main episodes, hymns of praise, and frame narrative. Particularly crucial is the second episode, detailing the goddess's destruction of Mahiṣa, which shaped the enduring iconography of the buffalo-slaying goddess. The DM's identification of the goddess as Durgā solidifies her role as the Hindu Great Goddess, with the text's ritual recitation ensuring its influence through the ages. Near the end of the DM, the goddess predicts her future manifestations, likely reflecting earlier goddess cults assimilated into the Devī's persona.

Chapter 9 explores these predicted manifestations, including Śākambharī, Bhimā Devī, and Durgā, which enrich the salvific, nurturing, and compassionate aspects of the Devī's persona. These examples demonstrate Durgā's evolution beyond associations with sovereignty to encompass broader protective and life-sustaining roles. Together, these chapters trace the integration of diverse regional and sectarian traditions into a unified vision of the Great Goddess.

Chapter 10 examines Victorious Goddess (V) images, where the goddess stands atop a buffalo head. These depictions, prevalent in South India during the Pallava and Coḷa periods and in Southeast Asia, are analyzed alongside South Indian texts such as the *Cilappatikāram*, which identify Korravai as an early Dravidian goddess. We extend J. N. Tiwari's argument that Durgā/Kālī assimilates fierce regional goddesses such as Korravai, the nude Koṭavī, and Caṇḍamārī, adorned with human limbs. The chapter concludes with the concept of "Durgā-fication," the process of merging regional goddesses into Durgā's persona, evident since the Kūṣāṇa period.

Chapter 11 delves into the iconography of the Anthropomorphic (A) and Emergent Demon (E) types, primarily from the Pallava, Cāḷukya, and Rāṣṭrakūṭa territories. Key examples from Māmallapuram, Pattadakal, and Ellora are analyzed to correlate their features with textual descriptions, providing evidence to place the composition of the DM in the mid-8th century CE.

As mentioned above, chapter 12 examines Purāṇic accounts — likely composed earlier than the DM — of a goddess battling a buffalo demon. Here we seek to identify elements later developed in the DM while noting the absence of key DM features. For instance, the *Varāha Purāṇa* portrays the demon Ruru driving the gods from heaven, leading them to pray to Raudrī (also known as Kālarātrī), who, with her entourage and Rudra's assistance, defeats the demon. Similarly, the early *Skanda Purāṇa*, as detailed by Yuko Yokochi, recounts Kauśikī's defeat of Sumbha and Nisumbha (early variants of Śumbha and Niśumbha) and Mahiṣa. The *Devī Purāṇa* credits Umā/Vindhyavāsinī with vanquishing the buffalo demon Ghora. These accounts, while highlighting the goddess's power, simultaneously subordinate her to male deities: Raudrī is empowered by Rudra, Kauśikī is a manifestation of Pārvatī (and thus subordinated to Śiva), and Umā/Vindhyavāsinī shares a similar fate. The DM counters this trend by depicting the Great Goddess as supreme, independent, and the ultimate refuge for the gods.

Previous scholarship (e.g., Coburn 1984 had identified the DM as marking the "crystallization of the Goddess tradition," establishing the Great Goddess as the source and manifestation of all other goddesses. However, our close examination of Durgā's persona and worship, through the textual and iconographic materials available, reveal a process spanning thousands of years were we to trace the earliest resonances of the lion riding goddess, via Nanā, to ancient Sumer. Chapter 13 deals with the development of the theology of the Great Goddess (*thea-logy*, if we adopt the neologism for reflections on the Divine Feminine), as it culminates in the DM, which tackles millennia-old tensions between a range of dualisms. These include iconism versus aniconism, monotheism or monolatry versus polytheism, and political versus religious imperialism.

To fully appreciate the enduring Goddess tradition, it is essential to situate South Asia in a broader context, extending from the Roman Empire to China. Unlike neighboring regions that embraced religious monotheism or secular ideologies, India has preserved a vibrant polytheism with a central role for the Divine Feminine. As Bharat Mā, India continues to maintain this rich tradition, ensuring the relevance of the Great Goddess in the modern world. Weaving together the evidence, I argue that the Goddess's central mythic exploits symbolize her triumph over monotheism and monolatry, represented by Mahiṣa's aspiration to supreme divinity. The Devī does not defeat Mahiṣa to claim sovereignty herself but restores the gods to their rightful places in the heavens, reinstating a balanced polytheistic order. She reverts to a primordial role, existing beyond the gods and serving as their ultimate refuge. This primacy also explains her ascendancy over Skanda, whose monolatrist claims echo the male gods' competition for supremacy within the polytheistic pantheon.

I further propose that the *Devī Māhātmya's* (DM) popularity grew during periods of tension for Hindu polytheism, particularly with the advent of Islam in South Asia during the 7th and 8th centuries. Similar pressures had earlier come from Buddhism and, before that, from the Achaemenid promotion of Ahura Mazda's aniconic worship. These historical contexts highlight the DM's role as a theological bulwark, reasserting the vitality of polytheistic traditions. This theme reemerges during the decline of Mughal and British rule, paralleling the rise of the Durgā Pūjā, a historical progression to be explored in volume 2.

The Appendices include Coburn's translation of the Rātrī Sūkta hymn from the *Ṛg Veda*, central to the arguments in chapter 1. Additional material explores the cult of the Peacock Goddess among the Yezidi, which may have roots in South Asia. I also retell Herodotus's narrative of Tomyris of Massagetae, who defeated the Achaemenid emperor Cyrus the Great. Such an account may have influenced the story of Durgā's victory over Mahiṣa. An extensive timeline summarizes the main chronological events proposed in this study.

Chapter 1

Durgā in Pre-Epic Literature

A suitable starting point for studying Durgā is to trace the earliest appearances of the Sanskrit word *durga* in the literary record. Early meanings may shed light on key aspects of the goddess's character, while the term's application to a goddess could mark the beginnings of Durgā worship. Our analysis begins with occurrences in the Vedas, Hinduism's oldest scriptures, specifically the *Ṛg Veda Saṃhitā*. The oldest core of this text, encompassing books 2 to 7 of its ten *maṇḍalas*, was likely composed between 1500 and 1200 BCE, with a conservative dating around 1250 BCE (Witzel 1989, 249).

This chapter argues that references to Durgā as a goddess may date as early as the 3rd century BCE, appearing in *Taittirīya Āraṇyaka* 10.1.7 (as Durgī) and 10.2.1 (as Durgā), or a few centuries later in the Rātrī Khila of the *Ṛg Veda Khila* 4.2. The latter is cited in a ritual litany to Durgā in the *Baudhāyana Gṛhyaśeṣasūtra* 3.3, likely from the early centuries CE. The name Durgā also occurs in the *Vasiṣṭha Dharmasūtra*, dated to the 1st century CE, in connection with the Durgā-sāvitrī, invoked for expiating sins. While the nature of the Durgā-sāvitrī is unclear, it suggests that mantric verses or hymns of refuge linked to Durgā were significant enough to merit mention in Dharmasūtra literature. Additionally, the growing worship of Durgā, likely among non-Brahminic communities, prompted insertions of her name into earlier Vedic texts, such as the *Bṛhad Devatā*, and inspired hymnic elaborations of her salvific powers, as seen in the *Ṛg Veda Khila*, to secure her acceptance within Hindu orthodoxy.

In the *Ṛg Veda*

In the *Ṛg Veda* (RV), *durga* — with the short final vowel "a" — functions as an adjective or a noun, always in the masculine or neuter forms, never feminine.[1] Karl Friedrich Geldner's (1951–1957) German translations interpret *durga* as Bergfeste (5.34.7), Engweg (7.25.2), Fährlichkeit (7.60.12), and Gebirge (8.27.18). These terms suggest "mountain stronghold," "narrow path," "danger," and "mountain range," respectively. Ralph T. H. Griffith's (1889–1899) English translations offer: "wide stronghold" (5.34.7), "hard to traverse" (7.25.2), "peril" (7.60.12), and "a sloping path" (8.27.18). Stephanie W. Jamison and Joel P. Brereton's (2014) recent translation renders *durga* as a "(place) of no exit" (5.34.7, 7.25.2), "difficulties" (7.60.12), and "difficult going" (8.27.18).[2] While none of these instances suggest anything feminine or a goddess, *durga* consistently conveys foreboding. As a path, it is steep, narrow, perilous; as a place, it is mountainous, lofty, and challenging to reach or escape.

In the *Atharva Veda*

The *Atharva Veda* (AV), the fourth collection of Vedic hymns (*saṃhitā*), survives in two recensions (*śākhās*), the Śaunakīya and Paippalāda. As the earliest Vedic text to mention iron — whose presence in South Asia archaeological studies date to around 1200 to 1000 BCE — the AV can reasonably be placed within or after this period. The first feminine occurrence of *durgā* appears in AV 12.4.23:

> *ya evaṃ viduṣe 'dattvāthānyebhyo dadad vaśām |*
> *durgā tasmā adhiṣṭhāne pṛthivī sahadevatā //23//*

The verse concerns the proper offering of a sterile cow to Brahmins. Maurice Bloomfield (1897, 176) translates: "He that refuses [to give] the sterile cow to him that knoweth thus, and gives her to others, difficult to dwell upon [*durgā*] is for him the earth [*pṛthivī*] with her divinities." Here, *durgā* is associated with the earth (*pṛthivī*) and her deities (*sahadevatā*), not as a name but as a descriptor. It conveys the hardships awaiting one who fails to meet religious obligations, particularly those involving offerings to Brahmins.

In the *Ṛg Veda Khila*

The name Durgā appears in the feminine form, clearly as a goddess, in a hymn of the *Ṛg Veda Khila* (RVKh), an appendix to the *Ṛg Veda* (RV).[3] This hymn, addressed to "night" (*rātrī*), is sometimes called the Rātrī Khila to distinguish it from the Rātrī Sūkta,[4] the only RV hymn to "night." Positioning RVKh 4.2 after the *Atharva Veda* (AV) in a chronological survey is debatable but plausible.[5] The composition of RVKh hymns might date as early as 1200 BCE or as late as 1000 BCE (Witzel 1997, 284–85), aligning with the tenth *maṇḍala* of the RV, which includes the Rātrī Sūkta. Determining the precise chronological order of the *durgā* references in the tenth *maṇḍala*, the AV, and the RVKh is challenging, as linguistic styles of the AV and RVKh suggest contemporaneity. However, the AV's non-personal reference to *durgā* as difficulty in traversing the earth (AV 12.4.23) conceptually resembles earlier RV passages. In contrast, RVKh 4.2 uses the feminine *durgā* explicitly for a goddess, echoing later interpretations, though the paths of influence remain unclear. Despite discussing the RVKh hymn here, I will argue for a much later composition date for the relevant verses.

The relevant verses in the Rātrī Khila of the RVKh 4.2 that mention or concern *durgā* are numbers 5 to 13. However, as one will notice, they look very much like insertions. A verse to Agni from the *Ṛg Veda*, placed here in bold font, is embedded within the inserted verses that refer to Durgā.

The Rātrī Khila[6]

ā rātri pārthivaṃ rajaḥ pitur aprāyi dhāmabhiḥ /
divas sadāṃsi bṛhatī vi tiṣṭhasa ā tveṣaṃ vartate tamaḥ /1
ye te rātri nṛcakṣaso yuktāso navatir nava /
asītis santv aṣṭā uto te sapta saptatiḥ /2
rātrīṃ pra padye jananīṃ sarvabhūtaniveśanīm /
bhadrāṃ bhagavatīṃ kṛṣṇāṃ vviśvasya jagato niśām /3
saṃvveśanīṃ saṃyamanīṃ grahanakṣatramālinīm /
prapannohaṃ śivāṃ rātrīṃ bhadre pāram aśīmahi /
mamāgne varco vihaveṣv astu //4//
stoṣyāmi prayato devīṃ śaranyām bahvṛcapriyām /
sahasrasaṃmitāṃ durgāṃ jātavedase sunavāma somam */5*
sāṃtyarthaṃ taddvijātīnām ṛṣibhiḥ samupāśritāḥ /
ṛgvede tvaṃ samutpann **ārātīyato ni dahāti vedaḥ** */6*
ye tvāṃ devi prapadyanti brāhmaṇā havyavāhanīm /
avidyā bahuvidyā vā **sa naḥ parṣad ati durgāṇi viśvā** */7*
ye agnivarṇāṃ śubhāṃ saumyāṃ kīrtayiṣyaṃti ye dvijāḥ /
tāṃ tārayati durgāṇi **naveva siṃdhuṃ duritāty agniḥ** */8*
durgeṣu viṣame ghore saṃgrāme ripusaṃkate /
agnicoranipāteṣu duṣṭagrahanivāraṇe duṣṭagrahanivāraṇy oṃ
     namaḥ /9
durgeṣu viṣameṣu tvaṃ saṃgrāmeṣu vaneṣu ca /
mohayitvā prapadyaṃte teṣāṃ me abhayaṃ kuru teṣāṃ me
     abhayaṃ kurv oṃ namaḥ /10
keśinīṃ sarvabhūtānāṃ paṃcamīti ca nāma ca /
sā māṃ samāṃ diśāṃ devī sarvataḥ parirakṣatu sarvataḥ
     parirakṣatu oṃ namaḥ /11
tām agnivarṇāṃ tapasā jvalaṃtīṃ vairocanīṃ karmaphaleṣu
     juṣṭām /
durgāṃ devīṃ śaraṇam ahaṃ pra padye sutarasi tarase
     namaḥ sutarasi tarase namaḥ /12
durgā durgeṣu sthāneṣu saṃ no devīr abhiṣṭaye /
ya imaṃ durgāstavaṃ puṇyaṃ rātrau rātrau sadā paṭhet /13
rātriḥ kuśikaḥ saubharo rātrir vā bhāradvājī rātristavaṃ
     gāyatram /
rātrīsūktaṃ japen nityaṃ tatkāla upapadyate //14//

Thomas B. Coburn (1984, 264–67) offers this translation:[7]

> 1. O night, the earthly space hath been filled with the father's orderings; great, thou spreadest thyself to the seats of the sky; bright darkness comes on.
> 2. The men-watching skillful ones that are thine, O night, ninety

(and) nine — eighty are they (and) eight, also seven (and) seventy of thine —

3. I take refuge in the night, the mother, the resting-place of all creatures,

(Who is) auspicious (*bhadrā*) blessed, black, the night of all the world,

4. Occasioning rest, drawing (things) in, garlanded with planets and constellations.

I take refuge in auspicious (*śivā*) night; O auspicious one, may we obtain what is best.

O Agni may your splendor abide in my invocations.

5. Reverently I will praise the goddess, (our) refuge, beloved of well-versed poets,

Durgā, (who is) equal to a thousand (others): **"To Jātavedas (Agni) we will press the Soma."**

6. For the sake of the tranquility of those who are twice-born, (they are your) followers, along with the seers,

You have your origin in the RV: **"may he burn up the possessions of the envious."**

7. The Brahmans who take refuge in you, the bearer of oblations, O goddess,

Whether ignorant or knowing a great deal **"he leads us over all difficulties."**

8. Those twice-born who praise the one who has the color of Agni, auspicious, beautiful,

She causes them to cross over difficulties: **"Agni (does this) as one (crosses over) the stormy sea with a boat."**

9. In difficulties, in battle that is painful or terrifying, in peril from enemies,

In attacks of fire and theft, in the warding off of seizers, O one who wards off wicked seizers, (you abide): Om hail!

10. In difficulties, in calamities, in battles, and in forests are you. Having deluded (human beings?), they take refuge (in you); make me unafraid of those (circumstances): make me unafraid to those: Om, hail!

11. May the one with (beautiful) hair among all creatures, Pañcamī by name,

The goddess, protect me from everything in every direction; may she protect from everything: Om hail!

12. In her who has the color of Agni, flaming with ascetic power, the offspring of Virocana, who delights in the fruits of one's actions,

In the goddess Durgā do I take refuge; O one of great speed, (well) do you cross: hail! O one of great speed, (well) do you cross: hail!

13. Durgā, in difficult places, "The goddess (es) is for our welfare."

He who always recites, night after night, this meritorious hymn to Durgā,

14. Kuśika Subharaḥ every night and Bhāradvājin every night,
(should recite) the Rātrī-praising Gāyatrī.
One should recite the hymn of Rātrī constantly. It is appropriate
for that time.

When discussing this hymn, Isidore Scheftelowitz regarded verses 5 to 14 secondary (Coburn 1984, 264). It certainly is unusual that the hymn, which begins in verses 1 to 4 with praises to "night," abruptly shifts praises to the goddess Durgā in verses 5 to 13, in a manner that appears to forge identifications between "night" and Durgā. The hymn ends with verse 14, which again mentions "*rātrī*," clumsily and ambiguously, both in its meaning and its grammatical form. There is no conflicting enumeration of verses in versions of this hymn (Coburn 1984, 264). Coburn observes that the phrase in verse 5 is a quotation from RV 1.99.1a, which is a single verse hymn to Agni, "with the other three *padas* being quoted seriatim in the following three verses" (Coburn 1984, 265n34).

What is evident from the foregoing information is that a Ṛg Vedic hymn (1.99.1) to Agni, who is invoked to help transport all through "severe hardships" (*ati durgāṇi*), "like a boat" (*nāveva*) on "extremely dangerous waters" (*sindhuṃ duritāty*), is interpolated piecemeal into the Rātrī Khila with verses invoking Durgā to do the same. Thus, some qualities first associated with Fire (Agni), such as dangerous yet capable of aiding one to navigate through difficult situations — one might imagine fire's vital role in helping one endure the night — are associated with Durgā as a goddess in the Rātrī Khila. Moreover, the hymn simultaneously describes Durgā as abiding within various perils (e.g., v. 10: difficulties, calamities, battles, and forests) and invokes her as leading worshippers safely through these dangers. In this regard, the hymn resembles the Rātrī Sūkta (see appendix I) of the RV, which it overtly references in verse 14. There, the goddess Night (Rātrī) is invoked to deliver the votary from the fear that Night herself induces. The polyvalent characters of Agni and Rātrī — dangerous, beautiful, and delivering — are incorporated, through association, into these early emerging presentations of the persona of Durgā.

A notable difference between the Rātrī Sūkta and the Rātrī Khila is that the former is simply a hymn addressed to Rātrī. By contrast, the Rātrī Khila's clumsy and discordant ending (RVKh 4.2.13.b–4.2.14b), which smacks of the insertion of the verses to Durgā (a sort of Durgā Stava, which it calls itself) within a hymn to Rātrī, ends as follows:

(4.2.13b) He who always recites, night after night, this meritorious hymn to Durgā,
(4.2.14a) Kuśika Subharaḥ every night, and Bhāradvājin
every night, (should recite) the Rātrī-praising Gāyatrī.
(4.2.14b) One should recite the hymn of Rātrī [*rātrī sūktam*]
constantly. It is appropriate for that time. (Coburn
1984, 264–67)

In contrast to the Rātrī Sūkta, the Rātrī Khila designates itself as a hymn to Durgā (*durgāstavam*) (4.2.13b). It also promotes as appropriate the regular recitation of the Rātrī Sūkta, probably nightly (4.2.14b). Despite its unclear grammatical form, line 4.2.14a seems to suggest that Vedic *ṛṣis* such as those named should or do recite a hymn to Rātrī every night. There are many variants on how this line is translated.[8] Regardless, the net intent of these concluding verses is to fuse an identification between Durgā and Rātrī, and to encourage the nightly recitation of this hymn, the Rātrī Khila, which it designates as a hymn to Durgā, as well as the Rātrī Sūkta, and frames these as common practices by Vedic sages. Another noteworthy feature in the Rātrī Khila is the exact occurrence in verse 12 of a passage in the *Taittirīya Āraṇyaka* (TA), to which we shall now turn.

In the *Taittirīya Āraṇyaka*

The Āraṇyakas are texts bridging the ritual concerns of the Brāhmaṇas, the textual genre that follows the Vedic Saṃhitās, and the speculative spirit of the Upaniṣads. The TA belongs to the Taittirīya recension (*śākhā*) of the *Black Yajur Veda*. In TA 10.1 we encounter variant versions of the renowned Ṛg Vedic Gāyatrī *mantra* (RV 3.62.10), which runs as follows:

> *tat savitur vareṇyam bhargo devasya dhīmahi /*
> *dhiyo yo naḥ pracodayāt //* (Coburn 1984, 118n110)
> Might we make our own that desirable effulgence of god Sav-
> itar, who will rouse forth our insights. (Jamison and
> Brereton 2014, 554)

In this Gāyatrī *mantra*, the main deity is Savitṛ. However, in the TA, variant forms replace Savitṛ with other deities, such as Viṣṇu, Garuḍa, Danti, and Rudra. They are not called Gāyatrīs but are simply dedicated to different deities. The following variant Gāyatrī, found within TA 10.1.7, is pertinent, because it does not just substitute another deity for Savitṛ:

> *kātyāyanāya vidmahe kanyākumāri dhīmahi /*
> *tan no durgīḥ pracodayāt //* (Coburn 1984, 118)
> We (let us) make Kātyāyanī the aim of our knowledge; let us
> contemplate Kanyākumārī; May Durgī impel us in
> that end.

Of note here is the grouping of three deities: Kātyāyanī, Kanyākumārī ("Virgin Girl"), and Durgī, with whom the other two are identified. Somewhat problematically, Durgī, Kātyāyanī, and Kanyākumārī appear as feminine only in the Ātharvaṇa recension.[9] Müller points out that in the text of the *Mahānārāyaṇa Upaniṣad* III.12 (derived from Jacob 1888, 4) the verse is "more correct," and reads: *kātyāyanyai vidmahe, kanyākumārīm dhīmahi, tan no durgā prakadayāt.*[10]

Let us tentatively call this short prayer within TA 10.1.7 — an adaptation of the Vedic Gāyatrī *mantra* and where the word Durgī appears — the Durgī-gāyatrī. Kātyāyanī, and Kanyākumārī continue to be associated with Durgā until the present day. It is not much of a stretch to link Durgī with Durgā. The 14th century Vedic commentator Sāyaṇa precisely made this modification.[11] Durgī may well have been an error introduced into TA at the time of insertion, or an alternate feminine epithet applied to the goddess in the early period derived from the masculine substantive *durga*. For instance, the masculine noun *caṇḍa* ("fierce, violent, or passionate"), gets transformed into the feminine forms *caṇḍī* and *caṇḍā*, both applied to the goddess Durgā.[12]

The enigmatic Durgī is not mentioned again in the TA, but about 50 lines later, TA 10.2.1 strings together seven verses (numbered here for convenience in the ensuing discussion) that use variants of the word *durga*, and mostly related to Agni.

jātavedase sunavāma somam arātīyato ni dahāti vedaḥ /
sa naḥ parṣad ati durgāṇi viśvā nāveva sindhuṃ duritāty
　　　　agniḥ // 1
tām agnivarṇāṃ tapasā jvalantīṃ vairocanīṃ karmaphaleṣu
　　　　juṣṭām /
durgāṃ devīṃ śaraṇam ahaṃ pra padye sutarasi tarase
　　　　namaḥ // 2
agne tvaṃ pārayā navyo asmānth svastibhir ati durgāṇi viśvā /
pūś ca pṛthvī bahulā na urvī bhavā tokāya tanayāya śaṃyoḥ
　　　　// 3
viśvāni no durgahā jātavedaḥ sindhuṃ na nāvā duritāti parṣi /
agne atrivan manasā gṛṇāno 'smākaṃ bodhy avitā tanūnām
　　　　// 4
pṛtanājitaṃ sahamānam ugram agniṃ huvema paramāt sad-
　　　　hasthāt /
sa naḥ parṣad ati durgāṇi viśvā kṣāmad devo ati duritāty
　　　　agniḥ // 5
pratno ṣi kam īḍyo adhvareṣu sanāc ca hotā navyaś ca satsi /
svāṃ cāgne tanuvaṃ piprayasvāsmabhyaṃ ca saubhagam ā
　　　　yajasva // 6
gobhir juṣṭam ayujo niṣiktaṃ tavendra viṣṇor anu saṃcarema
　　　　/
nākasya pṛṣṭham abhi saṃvasāno vaiṣṇavīṃ 6 loka iha
　　　　mādayantām // 7 //

Some variants on the word *durga* (i.e., *durgāṇi*, *durgahā*) appears five times in verses 1 to 5, but verse 2 explicitly refers to Durgā as a goddess (*durgāṃ devīṃ*). Verse 1 is simply RV 1.99.1 mentioned earlier, which beseeched Agni for help with difficult transits, and was inserted into the four verses (5–8) of the Rātrī Khila. The crucially important verse 2, which mentions the goddess Durgā, is found exactly so in the Rātrī Khila (v. 12), and may be translated thus:

> In her who has the color of Agni, flaming with ascetic power
> (*tapas*), the offspring of Virocana (*vairocanī*) who
> delights in the fruits of one's actions,
> In the goddess Durgā do I take refuge; O one of great speed,
> (well) do you navigate. Hail (to you)! (Coburn 1984,
> 119)

Timothy Lubin (2020, 38–39) notes that these seven verses in the TA that allude to Durgā are known as the Durgā Sūkta or the Pañca Durgāḥ. They are mentioned in the *Baudhāyana Gṛhyaśeṣasūtra* (BGŚS) 3.3, a supplement to the *Baudhāyana Gṛhyasūtra*, in the context of a constructed liturgy for monthly Durgā worship by Yajur Veda *brāhmaṇas*, and, known as the *durgākalpa* ritual. In that rite Durgā is addressed as Lady (*bhagavatī*), praised with the names Āryā, Raudrī, Mahākālī, Mahāyoginī, Suvarṇapuṣpī, Vedasaṃkīrtī, Mahāyajñī, Mahāvaiṣṇavī, Mahābhagavatī, Manogamī, and Śaṅkhadhāriṇī. The Śaiva and Vaiṣṇava associations are evident in these epithets. She is also explicitly called the consort of Rudra. Moreover, after offering adoration to each of these goddesses, the priest recites the Sāvitrī *mantra* and culminates that part of the litany of oblations with "To the adorable goddess Durgā I offer this oblation."[13] Lubin places the BGŚS in the first centuries CE (2020, 43). If his dating is correct, it would suggest that the TA 10.2.1 must predate it. Moreover, by the time of the Vedic ritual appropriation evinced by the BGŚS 3.3, Durgā had already been transformed into an orthodox goddess, associated with the sacrificial fire, Vedic (e.g., Āryā, Bhagavatī, Mahāyajñī), Śaiva (e.g., Raudrī, Mahāyoginī) and Vaiṣṇava (e.g., Mahāvaiṣṇavī, Śaṅkhadhāriṇī) associations, the Sāvitrī *mantra*, and verses culled from the TA. So, when should we place those verses to Durgā from the TA?

The *Taittirīya Upaniṣad*, which constitutes Chapters (*prapāṭhaka*) 7, 8, and 9 of the TA, may tentatively be dated at the 5th or 6th centuries BCE, and clearly appears to be pre-Buddhistic (Olivelle 1998, xxxvii). However, Chapter 10 of the TA, also known as the *Yājñikī Upaniṣad* (Macdonell 1900, 211) or the *Mahā-Nārāyaṇa Upaniṣad* (Olivelle 1998, 177) circulates independently, and is likely a later composition. In his survey of India's spiritual literature, J. N. Farquhar (1920, 49) dates this text as "probably not later than the third century B.C."[14] It is difficult to know how reliable Farquhar's date is, but if TA 10.2.1 is not a later insertion, it would suggest that the 3rd century BCE is a possible date for the first literary occurrence of Durgā as a goddess. But does the Rātrī Khila predate it?

Linguistic analysis suggests that the Āraṇyakas were composed between 1200 and 800 BCE, overlapping with the period attributed to the RVKh. Consequently, it cannot be definitively asserted that the TA predates the Rātrī Khila in the RVKh. Both texts refer to Durgā as a goddess, but the TA contains only a single mention of her name, embedded within verses that primarily celebrate Agni's salvific virtues. In contrast, the Rātrī Khila offers more elaborate descriptions of the goddess. Thus, the TA may represent the earliest occurrence of Durgā's name in Sanskrit literature, a view supported by scholars such as Coburn (1984, 115–21), Odile Divakaran (1984, 275), and Yuko Yokochi (2004, 16).

Scheftelowitz appropriately regarded the Durgā verses in the Rātrī Khila, which overtly depict Durgā as a goddess with descriptive attributes, as later additions. Lubin (2020, 42) reinforces this view, noting that the *Khilānukramaṇī* specifies RVKh 4.2 as containing only four stanzas (1–4), indicating that the expanded version, the so-called Rātrī Khila, postdates the original and includes interpolated verses. Additionally, the Rātrī Khila's use of terms such as *dvijāti* (verse 6) and *dvija* (verse 8) — technical terms linked to the development of the *āśrama* system in the Dharmasūtras — suggests a composition period no earlier than the mid-3rd century BCE, possibly extending a century or two later (Lubin 2005, 87–88 and 87n23; Olivelle 2012; Lubin 2020, 43). Lubin's proposal dates the Rātrī Khila, or what it calls the Durgā Stava, to around the mid-1st century BCE.

To avoid confusion with the *Mahābhārata* hymn ascribed to Yudhiṣṭhira, often called the Durgā Stava, I refer to this hymn as the Rātrī Khila. This distinction highlights the reality of various emerging hymns to Durgā competing for recognition and efficacy. Since the TA and Rātrī Khila verses on Durgā likely date no earlier than the mid-3rd century BCE, we must examine other potentially earlier textual sources to establish a firmer chronology for the goddess's development.

In the *Bṛhad Devatā*

A next likely candidate for early textual evidence of the goddess Durgā is the *Bṛhad Devatā* (BṛDe). The BṛDe, often assigned to c. 500/400 BCE, is a compendium of the divinities mentioned in the RV, and their myths. In BṛDe 2.77 we find this pertinent passage:

> *eṣaiva durgā bhūtvārcaṃ kṛtvā syātsūktabhāginī*
> *tannāmāni yamīndrāṇī saramā romaśorvaśī*
> *bhavatyagnyā sinīvālī rākā cānumatiḥ kuhūḥ* // 77
> She, having become Durgā, and having made a stanza, would
> own a [whole] *sūkta*.
> Her names are Yamī, Indrāṇī, Saramā, Romaśā, Urvaśī; she
> becomes Agnyā, Sinīvālī, Rākā, Anumati, and Kuhū.
> (L. Patton 1996, 167–68)

These verses refer to the goddess Vāc, who when mentioned in a particular couplet (*śloka*), stanza (*varga*), or hymn (*sūkta*) is major or minor, depending on the other entities with which she is identified and in accord with one of the three realms (earthly, middle, or celestial). Thus, if Vāc is in the earthly sphere and identified with rivers, the earth, plants, and so on, she owns the entire hymn.

The passage states that if Vāc (in the middle realm) were to be identified with Durgā, she would own the entire *sūkta*. The other goddesses with whom she is subsequently identified are minor. So here, Durgā is characterized as an important goddess, because through this identification Vāc owns the entire hymn.

Were the BṛDe composed in 500 to 400 BCE, and if that line referring to Durgā was not an insertion, it would affirm Durgā's presence in Sanskrit literature from that period onward. Unfortunately, according to Macdonell the first line in that passage is certainly an interpolation, since it "gives half a *śloka* ["couplet"] too much to the *varga*" (i.e., the formal size of the text's stanzas) (Macdonell 1904, 1.xxii). Macdonell (1904, 1.xxiii) notes that, except for Durgā, the names of all the other forms of the goddess Vāc mentioned in that selection are found in the *Naighaṇṭuka*. The *Naighaṇṭuka* is a collection of synonyms or thematically organized words that forms one of three sections (*kaṇḍa*) of the *Nirukta*, a glossary of obscure Vedic words.[15]

Macdonell (1904, 1.xi–xiii) suggests the line must have been an early interpolation since it occurs in manuscripts of both the long (B) and short (A) recensions of the BṛDe. He places the BṛDe no later than 400 BCE, because he sees it sandwiched between Yāska's *Nirukta* (dated by the translator L. Sarup at 500 BCE) and Kātyāyana's *Sarvānukramaṇī*, which predates the grammarian Pāṇini (Macdonell 1904, 1.xxi).[16] Coburn (1984, 118) uses this reference as evidence of the "Vedicization" of Durgā from the time of the BṛDe onward. However, Tokunaga (1979, 356–63) questions Macdonell's dates and through a compelling analysis dates the shorter A recension of the BṛDe between 100 CE and 600 CE, and the longer B recension (used by Macdonell) as between 600 CE and 1000 CE. Tokunaga (1981, 279–83) identifies two versions of the short A recension, one of which, likely the earlier, does not include Durgā in its list. These dates are substantially later than Macdonell's — there is a span of nearly a millennium and a half — and since both Tokunaga and Macdonell agree that the line mentioning Durgā is an insertion, it leaves us without much solid chronological evidence from the BṛDe. A reasonable set of dates for an earliest unknown version of the BṛDe is in the 400 BCE to 100 CE range, with the Durgā insertions likely occurring after that. In short, from the sources examined thus far, the emergence of Durgā as a goddess in Sanskrit literature could be as early as 1500 BCE, but a post 3rd century BCE date for the TA instances seems far more likely.

The Dharmasūtras and Dharmaśāstras

We next encounter something referred to as the Durgā-sāvitrī in the Dharmasūtras and the Dharmaśāstras. The distinction between these two genres is unclear, with the Dharmasūtras predating the Dharmaśāstras, which expanded upon the terse *sūtra* format in favor of the *śloka* verse format. Of the many Dharmasūtras mentioned in other sources, only the *Āpastamba*, *Gautama*, *Baudhāyana*, and

Vasiṣṭha survive (Olivelle 2000, 1–4). The *Vasiṣṭha Dharmasūtra* (VasDhS) 28.10 to 28.15 lists various purification texts and verses — said to be found in each Veda — the recitation of which leads one to be cleansed. Among these is listed the Durgā-sāvitrī (28.10.11), as if it is a well-known verse. It runs as follows:

> *sarvavedapavitrāṇi vakṣyāmyahamataḥ param /*
> *yeṣāṃ japaiśca homaiśca pūyante nātra saṃsayaḥ /10/*
> *aghamarṣaṇaṃ devakṛtaṃ śuddhavatyastaratsamāḥ /*
> *kūṣmāṇḍāni pāvamānyo durgāsāvitrireva ca /11/. . .*
> *etāni japtāni punanti jantūñ /*
> *jātismaratvaṃ labhate yadīcchet //15/* (Olivelle 2000, 458)
> Next, I will declare the purificatory text of all the Vedas by
> 　　who soft recitation or use in fire sacrifices people are
> 　　undoubtedly purified /10/
> They are: Aghamarṣaṇa, Devakṛta, Śuddhavatī, Taratsama,
> 　　Kūṣmāṇḍa, Pāvamānī, Durgāsāvitrī /11/. . .
> When these are recited softly, they purify creatures, and, if
> 　　someone so desires, he will aquire the memory of
> 　　past lives //15/ (Olivelle 2000, 459)

The *Baudhāyana Dharmasūtra* (BaudhDhS) 4.3.8.1–2 simply mentions *durgā* (i.e., the Durgā) in its list of efficacious verses to expiate sin, as if the verse or hymn to which it refers is well known.

> *athāpyudāharanti /*
> *aghamarṣaṇaṃ devakṛtaṃ śuddhavatyastaratsamāḥ /*
> *kūṣmāṇḍyaḥ pāvamānyaśca virājā mṛtyulāṅgalam /*
> *durgā vyāhṛtayo rudrā mahādoṣavināśanāḥ /*
> *mahādoṣavināśanā iti //8/* (Olivelle 2000, 334)

Then they also quote (in the following verse): "The Aghamarṣaṇa, the Devakṛta, the Śuddhavatis, the Taratsamās, the Kūṣmāṇḍīs, the Pāvamānīs, the Virājās, the Mṛtyulāṅgala, the Durgā (Sāvitrī), the Vyāhṛtis, and the Rudras (are texts) which are very efficacious for effacing sin" (Bühler 1882, 321).[17]

The *Viṣṇu Dharmaśāstra* (VDŚ) (aka *Viṣṇu-Smṛti* 56.9 and *Śaṅkhalikhita Dharma Sūtra* (ŚDS) 105 also mention the value of chanting purifying *mantras* and list the Durgā-sāvitrī among these (see Kane 1926, 101–2; Jolly 1880, 185; Jolly 1881, 130).[18] What is problematic is that it is not clear what is referred to by the Durgā-sāvitrī. Nandapaṇḍita, the 17th century commentator on the *Viṣṇu Dharmaśāstra* 56.9, simply explains *durgāsāvitrī* as: *jātavedase sunavāma somam ityeṣa ṛk.* In other words, the Durgā-savitrī is just RV 1.99.1, the shortest RV hymn, which was piecemeal inserted into the Rātrī Khila. It runs:

> *jātavedase sunavāma somam arātīyato ni dahāti vedaḥ /*
> *sa naḥ parṣad ati durgāṇi viśvā nāveva sindhuṃ duritāty*
> 　　*agniḥ //* (RV 1.99.1)

> For Jātavedas we will press soma. He will burn down the
>> property of the hostile.
> He will carry us across all difficult passages, across difficult
>> transits, as if with a boat across a river — Agni.
>> (Jamison and Brereton 2014, 237)

This would suggest that the Durgā-sāvitrī has nothing to do with a goddess, nor with the Vedic Sāvitrī/Gāyatrī verse, but is a salvific hymn that invokes Agni's help in navigating across difficult crossings.[19] It is difficult to know if the Durgā-sāvitrī or "the Durgā" referred to in these Dharma texts ever meant a variation on the Ṛg Vedic Gāyatrī, with Durgā's name substituted for Savitṛ, or if it meant the Gāyatrī variation that referred to Kanyākumarī and Kātyāyanī at the time of the composition of those texts. This may have been done on purpose, to allow ritualists to use what they deemed appropriate, such as lengthy hymns, short verses, or even shorter mantric syllables. In other words, "the Durgā" or even "the Durgā-sāvitrī" could point to an even longer hymnic recitation, such as the Rātrī Khila, whose inserted verses deem themselves a Durgā Stava.[20]

Dating the Dharmasūtras and Dharmaśāstras is fraught with uncertainty, though scholars agree on the sequence: BaudhDhS first, followed by VasDhS, and finally VDŚ much later. Patrick Olivelle (2000, 2009, 2010, 2012), who has conducted the most extensive recent work on these texts, concludes that all were composed in North India (2000, 5). He dates the composition of the BaudhDhS to the mid-1st century BCE to the early 1st century CE. While some scholars, such as P. V. Kane (1930–62, I), propose earlier dates, few convincingly argue for a much later period. However, Olivelle's dating of the BaudhDhS applies only to the Proto-Baudhāyana, comprising the first and most of the second books (*praśna*). The reference to "the Durgā" occurs in the fourth *praśna*, part of what Olivelle terms Deutero-Baudhāyana, which he dates to a later period, after the VasDhS (2000, 8). Olivelle (1999, xxxn10) speculates that Deutero-Baudhāyana was composed no earlier than the 3rd to 4th centuries CE. He places the VasDhS, which mentions the Durgā-sāvitrī, at the early to late 1st century CE (Olivelle 2000, 10; 2012, 131).

Thus, when Farquhar's dates for the occurrences of Durga in the TA (3rd century BCE) are placed in tandem with Olivelle's dates and in the various Dharmasūtras (VasDhS early to late 1st century CE; BaudhDhS, 4th *praśna* (later than the 3rd century CE)), respectively, one might reasonably infer the existence of some textual evidence of praise to Durgā, the goddess, by the 1st century CE. The compositional date of the VasDhS is one of the most reasonable for situating the certain mention of the goddess Durgā in Hindu Sanskrit literature, even if it was just a divinized verse uttered to Agni.[21] Based on his detailed study, Dominik Haas (2022, 82) notes that even the classic Gāyatrī *mantra* (i.e., RV 3.62.10) only became commonly referred to as such after circa 200 CE. The same went for the modified Gāyatrīs. So, arguably the term Durgā-sāvitrī could have evoked any hymn of praise to Durgā. Mieko Kajihara (2019,

25–26) is willing to assert that "at the time of the Dharma texts, some people worshiped Durgā and called their sacred formula by the name Sāvitrī."

Evidently, the name and attributes of the goddess Durgā have been incorporated into the Vedic corpus through various insertions, such as TA 10.1.7 (as Durgī) and 10.2.1, RVKh 4.2, and BṛDe 2.77. This reflects the evolving prominence of Durgā worship, significant enough to merit inclusion in the Vedic pantheon — a process Coburn terms "Vedicization" (1984, 118). These incorporations suggest that Durgā's origins were non-Vedic, although she was linguistically and conceptually aligned with the masculine and neuter forms of *durga*, as well as with Agni and Rātrī, both of whom share characteristics with her. Agni's salvific qualities, repelling dangers, parallel those of Durgā, while Rātrī offers protection and peace during the night. In TA 10.2.1, Durgā is portrayed with Agni-like attributes: flaming with ascetic power, the offspring of Virocana, a refuge for devotees, and one who swiftly navigates danger.

Since textual praises often follow established worship practices, it is plausible that a minor cult of Durgā existed before her name appeared in Sanskrit texts, possibly as early as the 3rd century BCE in the TA. The Rātrī Khila insertions (v. 5–14) likely date to the early centuries BCE, aligning with Lubin's (2020, 42–43) assessment. These verses describe Durgā more expansively than the terse mentions in the TA or the references to the Durgā-sāvitrī in the Dharmasūtras, the earliest of which is in the VasDhS (1st century CE).

The Rātrī Khila portrays Durgā as a goddess and a refuge. Its epithets attempt to situate her within the Vedic canon, not only through textual insertion but also by declaring her Vedic origins — claims unsupported by earlier Vedic texts. The hymn states that both learned and unlearned Brahmins who take refuge in Durgā can overcome difficulties, perhaps reflecting a contemporary reality or aspirational vision. It later expands this portrayal to include all twice-born (*dvija*) classes and asserts that Durgā provides tranquility for them and for *ṛṣi*s. The author of these verses, likely a Brahmin of *ṛṣi*-like status, appears to legitimize Durgā's worship within Vedic orthodoxy. The hymn further describes Durgā as present in difficulties, battles, calamities, fire, theft, and other perils, offering protection to those who take refuge in her. She deludes people, delights in karmic fruits, acts swiftly, removes fear, and protects universally. She is equated to a thousand, bears oblations, is auspicious, beautiful, long-haired, and named Pañcamī.

By the time of the BGŚS 3.3, composed in the first centuries CE (Lubin 2020, 43), Brahminic rituals had incorporated hymns to Durgā, drawing upon Vedic terminology loosely related to *durga* and Agni's salvific role. Durgā is linked to the Sāvitrī *mantra* and mantric praises of goddesses associated with her. In this context, Durgā emerges primarily as a boon-granting deity.

Durgā as a Refuge

The notion of Durgā as a refuge recurs frequently, as does her association with ascetic power. The latter connects her to the goddess Satī/Pārvatī, celebrated for her intense asceticism to win the ascetic god Śiva. However, Durgā's deep association with the concept of refuge has not been fully explored. Today, the idea of refuge is often linked to Buddhist practices, particularly the triple refuge in the Buddha, Dharma, and Sangha, known as the three jewels (*tri-ratna*). Early Buddhist texts, such as the *Dhammapada* (e.g., v. 188–92), emphasized the self or self-mastery as the most reliable refuge (Pérez-Remón 1980, 20–26), contrasting this with the traditional reliance on mountains, forests, and tree shrines for protection in times of fear (Carter and Palihawadana 2000, xxii, 35). These desolate places — described elsewhere as mountain clefts and caves — resemble the remote abodes of ascetics and renouncers, which were difficult to access (*dur-ga*) and therefore secure from external threats.

I have long grappled with finding a meaningful translation for Durgā, a term rendered in numerous unsatisfying ways, such as impassible, unassailable, hard to attain, invincible, fortress, and others. Previously, I proposed "formidable" as a possibility, as it conveys notions of honor, potency, protection, and the defensive qualities of a fortress — something difficult to breach, access, or traverse. However, it seems plausible that *durga* commonly referred to any safe refuge or abode where people sought shelter in times of fear and distress. Paradoxically, these refuges were often hard to reach, their inaccessibility deterring intruders. Such places included dense forest hermitages, mountain caves, and other remote locales.

The motif of escaping societal woes to remote refuges is a classic theme in Hindu and Buddhist mythology. The Buddha, in his legendary life story, undergoes intense austerities in forest groves and meditates under the Bodhi tree, which becomes sacralized in the process. This study will explore many examples of such remote refuges in the mythology and practice of Durgā worship. Buddhist ideas of refuge, centered on emancipatory self-realization, often stood in tension with traditional spiritual refuges, such as ascetic practices in mountain caves or the ritual worship of deities in forest groves. Shrines to deities, especially goddesses often identified as *yakṣīs*, remain in such remote locations today. Early Buddhist literature frequently characterized these as inadequate refuges.

Durgā may thus simply signify "She who is a Refuge," initially referring to a goddess linked to a sacred mantric verse. Over time, this concept evolved, and she became "She who is [the Supreme] Refuge," a Great Goddess and supreme deity with a richly constructed mythology and persona. A robust examination of the social, political, and religious history concurrent with the ascendency of Buddhism is crucial to understand the early development of Durgā worship.

We shall begin with textual references to Durgā from the Epic Period (c. 600 BCE–300 CE), before turning to other pertinent clues within the iconographic, epigraphic, and numismatic record.

Chapter 2

Durgā in Epic Literature

The major epics that we shall consider here are the *Rāmāyaṇa*, the *Mahābhārata*, and the *Harivaṃśa*. Durgā only appears in late versions of the *Rāmāyaṇa*, and not within the Epic Period heralded by the composition of the earliest extant Sanskrit version of that epic by Vālmīki. Thus, our focus will be on the *Mahābhārata*, where Durgā appears in two inserted hymns, and the *Harivaṃśa*, where Durgā appears in three (or arguably four) inserted hymns. In keeping with the forms in which Durgā appeared in the pre-Epic literature, where she was invoked in mantric verses, such as the Durgā-gāyatrī or Durgā-savitrī, and in Vedic hymns, such as the Rātrī Khila, she appears not in narrative episodes but in hymns of worship. One could regard these hymns as elaborations upon the shorter mantric formulae with which she was associated. They point to the emergence of her cult not through mythic narratives or related forms of religious literature, but from ritual contexts involving sacred utterances, prayers, and hymns associated with adoration for protection and empowerment.

Durgā in the *Rāmāyaṇa*

The oldest extant version of the *Rāmāyaṇa* (Rām), which was composed in Sanskrit, is attributed to the sage Vālmīki, who is also a character in the epic. Although there is a strong sense that much of the *Vālmīki Rāmāyaṇa* (VRām) was likely composed by a single person, there are evident insertions and additions. The editors of the critical edition place the VRām's date of composition at as early as 750 BCE but no later than 500 BCE, in part because even the Bāla Kāṇḍa of the VRām seems to know nothing of Buddhism and the great cities of the Magadhan kingdom, such as Pāṭaliputra, founded in approximately 460 BCE. Moreover, the VRām refers to Viśālā and Mithilā as separate kingdoms under separate rulers, although they had become the single city of Vaiśālī at the time of the Buddha (Goldman and Sutherland 1985, 22).

These VRām dates depend on those associated with the Buddha and early Buddhism, which are themselves disputed. Scholars often work backwards from the reign of the Mauryan emperor Aśoka (c. 269–232 BCE), attested to in inscriptions, and whose capital city of Pāṭaliputra was one of the world's grandest. Radiocarbon dating of an ancient tree shrine discovered beneath the brick layers of a temple built by Aśoka to mark the Buddha's birthplace at Lumbini, in present-day Nepal, dates it at 550 BCE (Fogelin 2015, 83). Although it may provide strong material evidence for the historical advent of Buddhism, the shrine could simply be evidence of ancient tree worship that predated Buddhism. The current temple at Lumbini is dedicated to Māyā Devī, who reputedly gave birth to the Buddha while holding onto a bending branch of a Śāl tree (*Shorea robusta*). In legend, Māyā Devī, the Buddha's mother, died not long after he was born. Embedded in this story there may be a not-so-tacit reference to Buddhism supplanting or absorbing renowned sites of *yakṣī* worship, such as at Lumbini, evincing tensions between Buddhism and goddess worship, which are significant in our study.

The preceding observations suggest that the earliest strata of the VRām predate the rise of the renowned Magadhan kingdom and the Mauryan dynasty under Candragupta (c. 340–298 BCE). Additions and accretions to the VRām may have continued well into the early centuries of the Common Era. There is no mention of Durgā in the VRām. Durgā makes an appearance much later in the Bengali version of the *Rāmāyaṇa*, composed by Kṛttivāsa in the 15th century CE. In VRām, Rāma worships the sun on the advice of the *ṛṣi* Agastya, prior to crossing over to the kingdom of Laṅka to do battle with the demon Rāvaṇa, but in the *Kṛttivāsa Rāmāyaṇa*, Rāma worships Durgā. Prior to the KRām, the episode of Rāma's worship of the Devī is found in the *Kālikā Purāṇa* (KālP 60.25–31), the *Mahābhāgavata Purāṇa* (36–38), and the *Bṛhad Dharma Purāṇa* (1.18–22), as well as in the *Devī Bhāgavata Purāṇa* (3.30) (Kinsley 1986, 109, 234; Chakravarti 1965, 150–57). We shall examine Durgā's presence in some of these Purāṇic sources in a later chapter and the second volume.

Much earlier than the KRām or these Purāṇas, the *Devī Māhātmya* (DM), an influential text that was inserted into the *Mārkaṇḍeya Purāṇa* (MārkP), tells of Durgā worship before battle with one's enemies. Although the DM refers to the autumnal festival of the Devī, some traditions had developed, particularly in Bengal, that Devī worship routinely occurred in the spring. But Rāma needed to worship in the autumn, the customary post-rainy season period for warfare. Since the gods rest in the autumn — more exactly, the rainy season or *caturmāsa*, which runs through the months of Āṣāḍha to Kārtika — the KRām frames Rāma's Devī worship as an unseasonable awakening (*akāla bodhana*), thereby offering an origin myth for Durgā's autumnal worship in the month of Āśvina (Östör 1980, 17–18; Kinsley 1986, 109; Somnath Mukhopadhyay 1984, 39). Many of the hymns we shall examine in this chapter present the motif of supplicating the goddess prior to a challenging ordeal, such as battle with one's enemies.

Durgā in the *Mahābhārata*

Durgā's first appearance of consequence in the Epic Period might be in two hymns within the *Mahābhārata* (Mbh), although these are often considered to be later insertions (and compositions). Some scholars date the Mbh between 400 BCE and 400 CE, and more typically between 200 BCE and 200 CE. Alf Hiltebeitel (2001, 14–15n56–57) evaluated and contested those traditional dating schemes of long duration, which acknowledge the encyclopedic synthesis in the Mbh's composition. Surprisingly, he proposed a much narrower composition period of between 150 BCE to 0 CE (3–31). More recently, by examining the concepts of *dharma* and *dharmaśāstra* as presented by the grammarian Patañjali (mid-2nd century BCE) versus the early Dharmaśāstras themselves, and some other conceptual notions (e.g., *dvija* (twice-born), *trivarga* (three goals: *dharma, kāma, artha*)) and practices (e.g., wearing the *yajñopavita*, sacred thread), Olivelle (2012) revised his dates for the earliest Dharmaśāstras (see previous chapter). He thus proposed the Mbh's final redaction during the first centuries of the Common Era (Olivelle 2012, 132). Let us thus tentatively place the date of the core of the Mbh in alignment with the currently typical view of between 200 BCE and 200 CE, with accretions and insertions continuing for several centuries thereafter.

It is difficult to pinpoint when the two hymns that mention Durgā were incorporated into the Mbh, but they have come to be named after her. In the language of the BṛDe on the goddess Vāc, examined in the previous chapter, who, when equated with Durgā, asserted her "ownership" of the hymns, it is now Durgā who, while identified with many other goddesses, comes to "own" these hymns. The Mbh hymns are commonly known as the Durgā Stava ("Praise [of] Durgā") (hereafter DStv) and the Durgā Stotra ("Eulogy [to] Durgā") (hereafter DSto). These hymns with their framing verses actualize their insertion into the Mbh, likely much later than the core text's conventional composition date of 200 BCE to 200 CE. I abbreviate the hymns with their framing verses as DStv+ and DSto+, with line numbering including the framing verses.[22] Durgā appears in lines 39 and 51 of the DStv, line 22 of the DSto, line 2 of the DStv+, and line 4 of the DSto+. The framing verses, which explicitly identify the goddess as Durgā, appear to have played a key role in elevating the name Durgā over the numerous others by which the goddess was addressed in the hymns. These hymns, both with and without their framing verses, are central to many of the arguments in this study and will therefore be analyzed in detail.

Verses Pertaining to Durgā in the Durgā Stava (DStv+)

The following verses derive from the most common version of the DStv+ as appears in the Vulgate.[23] In it, Yudhiṣṭhira, the eldest of the five Pāṇḍava brothers, heroes of the Mbh epic, recites a hymn to Durgā. We shall discuss the content of this hymn in greater detail later, and here present only the verses (numbered by line) in which Durgā's name appears. The first occurrence is in a portion of the framing narrative verses.

> 1 Going to the delightful city of Virāṭa, Yudhiṣṭhira
> 2 With his mind praised the goddess Durgā, queen of the
>   three worlds. (Coburn 1984, 268)

Within the actual hymn of praise, Yudhiṣṭhira uttered:

> 39 "O Durgā, you cause (people) to cross from difficulty
>   (*durgāt*) (to safety); therefore are you known to
>   the world as Durgā.
> 40 Of those who are lost in dreary forests, and of those
>   sunk in the great ocean,
> 41 Or of men held up by thieves, you are the supreme
>   refuge.
> 42 And in the crossing of waters, in dreary forests and
>   woods,
> 43 Those men who remember you, O great goddess,
>   they do not perish. (Coburn 1984, 270)
>
> . . .
>
> 51 Be a refuge for me, O Durgā, O refuge, O one who is
>   fond of her devotees." (Coburn 1984, 271).

The hymn proper ends with that mention of Durgā as a refuge, and the end portion of the framing verses commences with the goddess then appearing to Yudhiṣṭhira and promising him success. Among the things she tells him, she states:

> 62 And those who in going abroad, or in the city, in
>   battle, in danger from foes,
> 63 In a forest, in an impassable dreary wood, on the
>   ocean, in an abyss, upon a mountain,
> 64 Will remember me, as I have been remembered by
>   you,
> 65 For them nothing in this world will be hard to obtain.
>   (Coburn 1984, 271)

Although Durgā is associated with various other attributes in this hymn, including descriptions of her appearance and the other goddesses with whom she is identified, I focus here on lines emphasizing dangerous undertakings or situations linked to the term *durga*. Line 39 even explains that her name, Durgā, derives from her role in enabling safe passage through hardship (*durgāt*). The perilous scenarios extend beyond physical places such as impassable forests, oceans, and mountain paths to broader dangers such as general travel, city life, warfare, enemies, and robbery. Notably, Yudhiṣṭhira prays to Durgā for protection during the Pāṇḍavas' year of concealment in Virāṭa's kingdom, seeking both security in refuge and victory in battle. She eventually appears, promising him both.

Verses Pertaining to Durgā in the Durgā Stotra (DSto+)

The DSto is a more consistent hymn in its form and appearance in recensions of the Mbh.[24] It is often inserted (at Mbh 6.22.16) just six verses before Chapter 23, containing the *Bhagavad Gītā* (BG), which it seemingly attempts to overshadow. Here, as in the BG, the narrator Sañjaya explains the events on the battlefield to the blind king Dhṛtarāṣṭra. The first occurrence of Durgā is within the opening framing verses of what I designate the DSto+.

> 1 Having seen the army of the sons of Dhṛtarāṣṭra drawn
> up for battle,
> 2 Kṛṣṇa spoke (these) words for the sake of Arjuna's
> well being:
> 3 "Having become pure, O great-armed one, being
> about to engage in battle,
> 4 Recite the Durgā Stotra for the sake of conquering
> (your) enemies." (Coburn 1984, 272)

Among the many verses of praise that Arjuna speaks in the actual hymn, which I designate the DSto proper, he utters:

> 22 O blessed mother of Skanda, Durgā, who dwells in
> difficult places,
> 23 (You are) the syllable Svāhā and Svadhā, the smallest
> part, the utmost extremity, Sarasvatī.
>
> . . .
>
> 27 In dreary forests, fearful spots, and places of difficult
> access, and in the abodes of (your devotees),
> 28 Even in the nether regions do you constantly dwell;
> in battle you conquer demons. (Coburn 1984,
> 273–74)

Here, too, Durgā is associated with dangerous locales, not only ferrying devotees through hazards but also abiding within them, including the underworld. She is also described as dwelling in worshippers' homes. Her role as the mother of Skanda contrasts with the DStv, which portrays her as a chaste young virgin (l. 11). In the DSto+, Arjuna prays for victory in battle, and the goddess appears in the closing segments of the framing narrative, promising him success. Both the DStv+ and DSto+ will be analyzed in detail following a brief overview of the goddess hymns in the *Harivaṃśa*.

Durgā in the *Harivaṃśa*

Durgā also appears in hymns associated with the *Harivaṃśa* (HV). Sometimes called the *Harivaṃśa Purāṇa*, it is typically appended to the Mbh, bridging the Epic and Purāṇic genres, though here I treat it as part of the epic category. Its earliest strata may date to the 1st or 2nd centuries CE, with later insertions suggesting 11th-century court poetry (Hein 1986). Norvin Hein (1986, 296) supports P. L. Vaidya (1969, 1.xxxix), editor of the critical edition, who proposed 300 CE for most of the text. A. Couture (1991, 72–77), however, dates it to the 2nd or 3rd centuries CE, a view I find more convincing based on subsequent investigations. Three of the hymns in question are likely later insertions.

There are four panegyrics of interest in the HV. In HV Appendix I 8, line 2 of the critical edition, Durgā appears in the second stratum of a panegyric with two distinct layers, composed at different times. In the first stratum (HV 47.38–57), Viṣṇu addresses what seems to be a hymn of praise to the goddess Nidrā, within an elaboration on the Kṛṣṇa myth cycle. Coburn (1984, 113n89) observes that this first stratum is "the first — and only — time that a hymn employing numerous 'Goddess motifs' appears in the constituted text of the critical edition of the epic." This likely dates to the same period as the HV's core. Notably, Durgā's name does not appear in this stratum, which I hesitate to call a hymn since it is unlikely to have circulated independently, as hymns typically do. It is a series of predictions by Viṣṇu about how Nidrā will gain renown, likely modeled after existing hymns of praise. This reflects a trope of predicting already-existing realities, seen also in the *Devī Māhātmya* (DM). The trope involves predictions, framed as emanating from an ancient source, about a deity's mythic forms, names, deeds, worship regions, and renown — descriptions of a deity already known and venerated. More on this later.

In the HV critical edition's Appendix I 30, line 376, Durgā appears in Pradyumna's hymn of praise. In a few recensions of the HV critical edition's Appendix I 35 there appears a hymn by Aniruddha where Durgā is mentioned in line 35. We shall first examine Viṣṇu's Praise of Nidrā (First Stratum) and its relationship to the DStv+ and DSto+, since they appear closer in compositional characteristics, before turning to the Praise of Nidrā (Second Stratum) and Pradyumna's and Aniruddha's hymns in the HV.

Analysis of the Occurrences of Durgā in the Early Epic Hymns

The hymns under discussion that have been inserted into the epics often consist of two key components: the hymns themselves, which are paeans likely sung during rites of worship or empowerment, and the framing verses at their beginning and end, facilitating their insertion. Framing verses strategically situate the hymn within the narrative, possibly enhancing the paean's reputation, particularly if attributed to a hero or the gods. Once embedded, the hymn gains a new vehicle of transmission beyond its ritual context, with the potential for greater longevity within the narrative's lifespan. Both the framing verses and the narratives into which these hymns are embedded — in this case, the epics — offer insights into the intent behind their insertion.

Like most scholars, I initially examined the hymns and their frame verses as a unit, viewing the epics as the broader frame for their insertion. However, my work on Durgā worship in ritual contexts deepened my understanding of the role of hymnic memorization and recitation in oral traditions. Hymns are learned through listening or reciting and often circulate without frame verses. The Durgā Cālisa ("Forty [Verses] to Durgā"), for example, is a popular devotional hymn that begins directly with Durgā's names and epithets of praise, including mention of its recitational value. In liturgical settings, worshippers may repeat select verses from well-known hymns. For instance, the "*yā devī sarvabhūteṣu . . .*" stanza (*śloka*) from the DM (5.12) is commonly repeated by lay worshippers after prompts from priests during the Durgā Pūjā. Similarly, people often learn individual verses from overhearing hymns. The verse naming the Nine Durgās, beginning with Śailaputrī, is widely known across the Hindu world, wherever the DM is ritually recited. Interestingly, this verse is not part of the DM but originates from the Devī Kavaca ("Armor of the Goddess"), a hymnic appendage (*aṅga*) recited before the DM proper. We do not know when these limbs were composed and attached to the DM, which now rarely circulates without them.[25] For our purposes, it demonstrates that front and back framing verses are significant and warrant careful attention. Equally, the core hymn merits independent analysis, as it may have been composed and circulated well before its insertion into the MārkP, its vehicular text.

In the frame verses of the epic hymns under examination, the goddess eulogized is often called Durgā but is also referred to by other names, such as Pārvatī or Āryā, goddesses not mentioned within the hymns themselves. New connections appear to be drawn between the goddesses praised in the hymns and those in the framing verses. Additionally, the vehicular texts reveal broader agendas of the compilers. The DStv+, for example, continues to circulate widely and independently long after its composition, likely benefiting from its placement within the Mbh, as represented in some Mbh manuscript collections (see note 12 in this chapter). However, in my field experience, it now circulates with its frame verses, which diminish the goddess's status as articulated in the hymn itself.

Alternately, a hymn may be composed in tandem with its framing features, and at the same time as the text that will serve as its vehicle.[26] The first stratum of Viṣṇu's *Praise of Nidrā* suggests a hymnic-styled composition within the HV narrative. Often called a hymn, it is unlikely to have been recited ritually or independently before its later insertion into the HV, as it primarily consists of prophecies about Nidrā's future fame after her apparent destruction by Kaṃsa. Devotees do not typically recite predictive hymns celebrating their deity's already established renown. The second stratum, by contrast, is a distinct hymn of praise and clearly a later addition to the HV. Over the centuries, piecemeal additions or minor transformations may have altered the hymns.

Current versions often circulate with framing verses attached and are recited as if forming a unified composition.

The DSto technically refers only to the hymn sung by Arjuna but is often examined with its framing verses, collectively designated by me as DSto+. These frames begin with Kṛṣṇa advising Arjuna to recite what is called the Durgā Stotra when he sees the sons of Dhṛtarāṣṭra ready for battle (l. 1–6). After the hymn, the unnamed goddess, referred to as "she who is kindly disposed to people" (l. 33) and "who moves through the sky" (l. 34), appears and promises Arjuna victory (l. 35–37). Sañjaya elaborates further, describing the goddess as a granter of boons who vanishes after granting Arjuna confidence in his impending victory (l. 38–39). Sañjaya adds that reciting this hymn (i.e., the DSto) at dawn eliminates fear of demons (*yakṣa, rakṣa, piśāca*) and even the royal family (l. 41–45). It ensures freedom from bondage, victory in disputes and battles, good fortune, health, vigor, and a long life (l. 46–49). Arjuna's example of invoking the goddess to gain her grace is extended universally: any man who recites the hymn can secure her favor (l. 42–49). Sañjaya concludes with muddled verses recalling the BG, warning Dhṛtarāṣṭra that his sons are doomed and affirming that Arjuna and Kṛṣṇa, as the *ṛṣis* Nara and Nārāyaṇa, represent dharma and victory (l. 51–57).

The frame verses name the hymn the Durgā Stotra. However, within the hymn, the goddess is called Durgā only once, while other names such as Kālī, Bhadrakālī, Mahākālī, Caṇḍī, Kātyāyanī, Vijayā, Jayā, Kauśikī, Umā, Śākambharī, Sarasvatī, and Sāvitrī are also used. She is described as destroyer of Kaiṭabha and mother of Skanda. The DSto likely circulated independently before the name Durgā became firmly associated with the fierce, but benevolent, victory-assuring goddess. By the time the hymn was inserted into the Mbh as the DSto+, or through its designation as the DSto during insertion, the identification of the goddess as Durgā was evidently solidifying.

The DSto+'s greater consistency and presence in manuscript collections (see note 12 in this chapter) suggest it may have been inserted into the Mbh earlier than the DStv. Positioned just before the BG, the DSto+ uses framing language mimicking the BG, indicating awareness of the BG at the time of insertion. Even within the hymn, phrases such as "Of knowledges, you are the knowledge of Brahman" (l. 21) echo refrains extensively used in the BG (e.g., Chapter 10). This suggests the DSto was composed after the BG, likely attempting to mimic it.

Did the insertion aim to subordinate Viṣṇu/Kṛṣṇa's role in Arjuna's success to the goddess's grace? This seems unlikely, as the final verses reinforce Kṛṣṇa as the agent of victory. With the core Mbh tentatively dated between 200 BCE and 200 CE (per Hiltebeitel and Olivelle), the DSto's composition likely postdates the BG's composition, and its insertion as the DSto+ likely followed the BG's integration into the Mbh, perhaps significantly later, as it is absent from the critical edition's core text.

Yokochi (2004, 75) observes that most studies regard the composition of the DStv and DSto as quite late, even postdating the DM. This view largely stems from treating the hymns and their framing verses as a unit and examining their placement within versions of the Mbh. By separating the hymns from their frames, we will note in the next chapter stronger correlations with iconography, suggesting goddess worship, possibly under the name Durgā, at a much earlier period. This raises the possibility that the hymns were composed and circulated during a time consistent with the iconography and only later inserted into the Mbh with framing verses, even after the iconography had evolved to better align with Purāṇic narratives. The DSto+'s framing verses indicate the goddess was already being propitiated by kings before battle, prior to its insertion into the Mbh. However, the verses also subordinate her to Viṣṇu/Kṛṣṇa as the ultimate agent of Arjuna's success. This trope of subordination through elevation recurs throughout this study.

In the DStv+, the framing verses describe Yudhiṣṭhira praising Durgā, queen of the three worlds, with his mind, hoping she would appear to him and his brothers before they entered Virāṭa's city during their thirteenth year of exile. This was critical, as discovery would mean another thirteen years of exile. The hymn, never explicitly called the Durgā Stava, likely gained this title because the goddess is referred to as Durgā several times, with an etymology explaining her name: "You are known to the world as Durgā, because you cause (people) to cross from difficulty (*durgāt*) (to safety)" (v. 39). While the hymn includes a few Vaiṣṇava references (e.g., "you shine, like the wife of Nārāyaṇa" (l. 15) and "your face rivals Saṃkarṣaṇa's" (l. 17)), it does not explicitly situate the goddess within the Vaiṣṇava fold, by calling her Nārāyaṇa's wife, for instance. This suggests that the DStv may reflect a period when a burgeoning Nārāyaṇa/Saṃkarṣaṇa-centered Vaiṣṇavism competed with the cult of Durgā.

The opening framing verses, by contrast, are revealing, situating Durgā within a Vaiṣṇava context. They describe her as born from Yaśodā's womb (l. 3), Nārāyaṇa's most beloved (l. 3), a member of Nanda's cowherd family (l. 4), and responsible for Kaṃsa's destruction (l. 5). She was dashed on a precipice (l. 6), flew into the skies (l. 6), wears heavenly garments (l. 7–8), and is Vāsudeva's sister (l. 7). These details tacitly link her to the unnamed goddess Nidrā. This insertion suggests an effort to align Durgā with Vaiṣṇavism, though the hymn itself shows minimal explicit Vaiṣṇava connections.

I suggest that the DStv, or its precursor variants, with almost no explicit Vaiṣṇava associations, were likely composed for goddess-centered worship and rituals before the hymn's insertion into the Vaiṣṇava-oriented Mbh as the DStv+, accompanied by the framing verses replete with Vaiṣṇava references. This notion of precursor variants is not merely conjectural; the DStv+ explicitly describes itself as a hymn produced from "various versions" (*vividhaiḥ stotrasaṃbhavaiḥ*) (l. 9), confirming its earlier iterations. Hereafter, when referring not to the DStv as it currently exists, but to it or some unknown precursor version, I will use the abbreviation DStv*.

The closing frame recounts the goddess's appearance to Yudhiṣṭhira, where she promised victory, the defeat of the Kauravas, and the restoration of their kingdom to peace through her grace (l. 52–57). She assured him and his brothers happiness and health (l. 58–59) and pledged that if others remembered her as they did, she would grant rulership, long life, beauty, and offspring (l. 60–61). She vowed to protect supplicants during perilous travels through forests, mountains, oceans, battles, and cities or woodlands (l. 62–65). Reciting or listening to this hymn with devotion would ensure success in all endeavors (l. 66–67). Before vanishing, the goddess also guaranteed the Pāṇḍavas' concealment in Virāṭa's city would succeed (l. 68–71). These promises of power and boons are substantial, attributed entirely to her grace, but are moderated by the opening verses casting her as Vāsudeva's sister (l. 7). The closing verses inadvertently highlight the contexts and reasons why supplicants turned to Durgā during the period of the hymn's insertion, despite her apparent subordination to Viṣṇu/Kṛṣṇa in the opening frame. This reflects the trope of subordination through elevation.

The frame offers an implicit behavioral model in Yudhiṣṭhira's act of singing the hymn, and like the DSto+, explicitly states the benefits of its recitation. However, unlike the DSto+, the goddess Durgā herself extols its value. This motif parallels the BG, where Kṛṣṇa promotes the BG's teachings. Similarly, Durgā emphasizes the value of both recitation and listening to the DStv, a trope later seen in lengthier texts such as the DM. While recitation is an act of devotion to please the goddess, it also serves pragmatic purposes, marking the DStv as an early tract on *bhakti*, much like the BG. The BG advises caution, restricting its teachings to the disciplined and spiritually inclined (18.67), but the DStv+ is less prohibitive, requiring only devotion and purity without secrecy, prefiguring the public recitation of hymns in her honor, as seen with the DM today. While the DStv+ integrates Durgā into a Vaiṣṇava myth cycle, subordinating her to Viṣṇu/Kṛṣṇa, it also shows that goddess worship was independently popular at the time of its insertion. Durgā is portrayed as a protector from various dangers and as a boon-granter, with her broader capacities repeatedly emphasized in this hymn.

The Vaiṣṇava Context and Connection in These Hymns

In both the DSto+ and DStv+, Durgā is associated with Viṣṇu, particularly in their frame verses, likely composed during their insertion into the Mbh. However, while the DStv proper does not explicitly identify the goddess with Viṣṇu — beyond comparing her visage to Saṃkarṣaṇa's and her luster to Nārāyaṇa's wife — the DSto proper explicitly calls Durgā the "youngest sister of the lord of cowherds [Kṛṣṇa] . . . born in the family of the cowherd Nanda" (l. 14). This directly references the Kṛṣṇa Gopāla myth cycle, detailed in the HV, where the newborn Kṛṣṇa is exchanged for his "sister." Further examination of this myth reveals the intended connection between Kṛṣṇa and Durgā.

The HV primarily develops the Kṛṣṇa Gopāla myth cycle. In the section preceding Viṣṇu's Praise of Nidrā (HV 47.26–38), Viṣṇu seeks the aid of Nidrā ("[She who is] Sleep"), identified as the night of darkness (*kālarātri*, HV 40.26) and as Māyā ("[She who is the power of] Illusion," HV 40.26, 40.31). Viṣṇu enters the watery underworld and the bodies of the Six Fetuses, demons (*dānava*) who slept in Nidrā's womb as Kālarūpiṇī ("[She who has the] Form of Time"). He extracts their vital principles and gives them to Nidrā, instructing her to place them in the first six children born to Devakī, Kṛṣṇa's mother-to-be. The seventh child is transported to the womb of Rohiṇī, Vasudeva's other wife, in a nearby cowherd village. Viṣṇu explains he will incarnate as Devakī's seventh and eighth children, while Nidrā will be born to Yaśodā, wife of the cowherd Nanda, on the ninth day of the dark fortnight of Śrāvaṇa. Kṛṣṇa and Nidrā will then exchange mothers: Yaśodā will raise Kṛṣṇa, and Devakī's baby girl (Nidrā) will deceive Kaṃsa into believing she is his destroyer.

Viṣṇu instructs Nidrā to delude Kaṃsa, Devakī's brother and an incarnation of the *asura* Kālanemi, into killing the first six infants, who in fact are his own demon spawn. Kaṃsa must also be deceived into allowing the exchange of Kṛṣṇa and the baby girl and then roused to anger, so he kills the girl (HV 47.1–38). Nidrā, as Māyā, wields the power to delude and provoke anger, traits later linked to Durgā in her defeat of Mahiṣa. Nidrā is also associated with the Kālī-like goddesses Kālarātrī and Kālarūpiṇī, tied to blackness, night, and destructive Time. The hymnic portions of both the DSto and DStv refer to the goddess as Kālī. Kālī first appears descriptively in the Mbh (10.8.64–67), during Aśvatthāman's slaughter of the sleeping Pāṇḍava children, where she is linked to the delusive power of sleep (*kālarātrī*, see Coburn 1984, 112).[27] By contrast, the HV references Kālī explicitly only once, in Aniruddha's Hymn (1. 20), likely a later addition.

Viṣṇu's Praise of Nidrā (First Stratum) (PN-s1) occurs at HV 47.38–57, where Durgā is never explicitly mentioned. Viṣṇu begins the prophetic litany — I eschew the term hymn — by telling Nidrā that Kaṃsa will smash her against a rock, mistaking her for the child destined to kill him. "Being dashed, you will obtain an eternal place in the sky" (47.38, in Coburn 1984 and hereafter). She is described as black (*kṛṣṇa*) like Viṣṇu, with a face resembling Saṃkarṣaṇa's, and adorned with various ornaments and attributes. Viṣṇu declares, "Having taken a vow of celibacy, you will go to the heavens" (47.45), where Indra and the gods will consecrate her, and Indra will claim her as his sister — though she is not identified as Kṛṣṇa's sister here. The litany also grants her the Vindhya Mountain as an eternal abode, where she will illuminate the earth with a thousand shrines (47.48). The HV author was clearly aware of a widespread preexisting goddess cult with numerous dedicated shrines. I suggest that this hints at the existence of a Great Goddess cult, possibly as supreme deity, prior to the composition of the HV, which asserts itself unequivocally in the composition of the DM, a position I will develop throughout this study.

Viṣṇu then tells Nidrā that having "fixed your mind on me [i.e., Viṣṇu]" (47.49) she will destroy the demons Sumbha and Nisumbha, who are said to wander upon the Vindhya Mountain.[28] Unless this is a variant spelling or error, these are not (originally) the demons Śumbha and Niśumbha, whose killing by the Devī is later recounted in great detail in the DM.[29] Clearly, the litany seeks to subordinate the goddess Nidrā to Viṣṇu, who is both commanding her about her upcoming task and insinuating that her victories derive through veneration of him. By identifying Nidrā with various goddesses, whose myths, cults, and abodes appear to be already well known, the eulogy seeks to subsume all those highly popular and widely worshipped goddesses under the rubric of Nidrā, and simultaneously subordinate Nidrā to Viṣṇu. Alternately, it seeks to subsume the cult of a Great Goddess and possible contender for a supreme deity, known by various names, under the persona of Nidrā/Kālarātri. This is a trope of simultaneous elevation, subsumption, and subordination.

Nidrā is described as wandering the triple world (HV 47.50), granting boons, taking forms at will, followed by spirits, and delighted by offerings of flesh (47.50–51). Although unnamed, these traits overlap significantly with those of Durgā (and/or Kālī) in the DStv and DSto. The hymn states that Nidrā will be worshipped on the ninth lunar day with wild beast sacrifices (47.51), a practice still observed during Navarātra celebrations for Durgā. Worshippers are promised that "nothing will be hard to obtain" (47.52), including sons and wealth. The hymn then cites, verbatim, a verse from the DStv (l. 40–41) emphasizing refuge — a motif associated with Durgā (or Agni) in earlier litanies, although not explicitly here.

> 53 Of those who are lost in dreary forests, and of those
>   who are sunk in the great ocean,
> Or of men held up by thieves, you are the supreme ref-
>   uge. (Coburn 1984, 278)

The succeeding two lines (47.54–55) are:

> 54 You are success, fortune, support, fame, modesty,
>   knowledge, obeisance, intellect,
> Twilight, night, light, sleep, and also the night of
>   destruction.
> 55 Human bondage, terrible death, the destruction of
>   sons, the loss of wealth,
> Sickness, death, and fear do you, (when) worshipped put
>   to an end. (Coburn 1984, 278)

The adjectives in these verses parallel the descriptive adjectives for the goddess found in l. 44–47 of the DStv, cited below for comparison:

44 You are fame, fortune (*śrī*), steadiness, success, modesty, knowledge (*vidyā*), continuity, mind,
45 Twilight, night, light, sleep, moonlight, loveliness,
  patience, compassion.
46–47 (When) honored, you cause to perish the bondage
  of men, (their) delusion, death of sons, loss of
  wealth, sickness, death, and fear.

As the myth unfolds, the HV (Chapter 48) elaborates on the fate of Devakī's seventh child, Saṃkarṣana (HV 48.1–6). His name, meaning "extracted" (*karṣaṇa*), reflects his removal from Devakī's womb in a dream-like event orchestrated by Nidrā (Couture and Schmid 2001, 175). The fetus, believed miscarried, was placed by Nidrā into Rohiṇī, Vasudeva's second wife, making Saṃkarṣana Kṛṣṇa's elder brother. During Devakī's next pregnancy, in which Kṛṣṇa is born, Nidrā simultaneously manifests as Yaśodā's daughter in Mathurā. The boy and girl are exchanged.

To dispel doubts about the sources of Nidrā's power, the narrator Vaiśaṃpāyana clarifies that she emerges from Viṣṇu's body (*viṣṇoḥ śarīrajāṃ nidrām*) and follows his commands (*nirdeśakāriṇī*) (HV 48.10). While Saṃkarṣana and Kṛṣṇa survive, Nidrā, exchanged with Kṛṣṇa, faces Kaṃsa's wrath. Kaṃsa seizes her, twirls her in the air, and smashes her onto a stone, as with Devakī's other children. Yet, unscathed, Nidrā ascends into the sky. Transforming into a virgin girl (*kanyā*), adorned in black and yellow with unbound hair, she warns Kaṃsa of his fate: just as he dashed her onto the rock, he will be dragged and killed in an arena, and she will drink his warm blood (HV 48.34–35) (Couture and Schmid 2001, 175). After speaking, the goddess ascends to the heavens.

The HV vulgate (2.4.45–48; cr. ed. 612) adds that Nidrā, honored as a son in Mathurā, becomes known as Ekānaṃśā ("Indivisible One") and is worshipped by all the Yādavas (Couture and Schmid 2001, 175). Later, Kṛṣṇa grows up as a cowherd (*gopāla*) in Nanda and Yaśodā's household, ultimately fulfilling the prophecy by slaying Kaṃsa and reclaiming his princely inheritance. References to Nārāyaṇa, Vāsudeva, and Saṃkarṣana suggest an ongoing fusion of these deities into a unified Vaiṣṇava cult centered on Viṣṇu/Kṛṣṇa.

The narrative portions of HV Chapters 47 and 48 aim to link Kālarātrī, Nidrā, and Ekānaṃśā. Even if PN-s1 was an independent hymn later inserted into the HV, it explicitly identifies Nidrā/Kālarātrī/Ekānaṃśā with Kauśikī and aligns them with characteristics of a developing Durgā cult seen in the DStv (or a precursor variant, i.e., a DStv*). PN-s1 shares certain verses with the DStv almost verbatim. The framing verses of the DStv+, likely created to integrate Durgā into a Vaiṣṇava framework, explicitly name her as Vāsudeva's (Kṛṣṇa's) sister. The significant parallels between the hymnic portion of the DStv and Viṣṇu's PN-s1 suggest mutual awareness, raising the question: which influenced the other?

Although we cannot know with absolute certainty, the general assumption has been to place the DStv much later than the HV's PN-s1 (e.g., see Yokochi

2004, 75). This is reasonable if one has been looking primarily at the DStv+ rather than the DStv, which has been the norm.[30] I am inclined to place the DStv, or a DStv*, before the PN-s1. The DStv or DStv* may have circulated widely enough for verse 53 to be quoted verbatim and verses 54 to 55 paraphrased in the crafting of the HV's PN-s1. It seems unlikely that PN-s1, a prophetic litany, would ever have been recited independently as a hymn of praise to Nidrā, reflecting instead the trope of prophesying existing realities. It is even less likely that the composer of the DStv, centuries later, would adopt paraphrased verses from the PN-s1 for a hymn of pure praise to Durgā. If this suggestion is correct, this would date the DStv, or a simpler DStv* precursor, earlier than the HV's core.

Other circumstantial evidence for placing the DStv before the PN-s1 is that the DStv does not mention Nidrā as a distinct goddess, to which it might have been inclined if composed later, with full knowledge of the HV narrative context. It includes a reference to the goddess as "sleep," but almost exactly as does the PN-s1, namely in a list of descriptive nouns, together with "twilight," "night," and "light." Notably, when the PN-s1 presents that list of nouns describing Nidrā, it adds (with an emphatic *tathaiva ca*) "the night of destruction" (*kālarātrī*) immediately after the word, "night."[31] Kālarātrī is one of the names the HV uses to describe Nidrā earlier in the narrative, just before the litany. This suggests that PN-s1 consciously seeks to identify the Durgā/Kālī of the DStv, or a similar unknown DStv* variant, with Nidrā/Kālarātrī, rather than the reverse. Additionally, PN-s1 takes care to associate Nidrā/Kālarātrī with Kauśikī, linking her to the lineage of Kauśika, to which Indra belongs, and explains how Nidrā is regarded as Indra's sister. While the DSto identifies Durgā as Kauśikī, the DStv proper offers no connection between Durgā/Kālī and Kauśikī or Indra's lineage.

The DStv does not adopt many markers of the goddess's character found in PN-s1, nor does it explicitly link Durgā/Kālī to PN-s1 goddesses. Moreover, if the DStv+ was composed to subordinate Durgā/Kālī to Viṣṇu, it is notable that the DStv proper lacks Vaiṣṇava references. This strengthens the case that PN-s1 was influenced by the DStv or a related DStv* paean. Correlations with iconography, discussed in a later chapter, further support the possibility of the DStv's early composition.

Since the PN-s1 is found within the original constituted text of the HV, and not in the Appendix, we could place its composition no later than the end of the 3rd century CE, since scholarly consensus tends to favor a 300 CE date for the completion of the major portions of the HV.[32] Following Couture's (1991, 72–77) dating, the HV's composition would be no later than 300 CE, possibly a century earlier, as it developed alongside the Mbh rather than after it. This suggests an even earlier date, perhaps the late 2nd century CE, for the composition of the DStv hymn or a DStv* variant panegyric to Durgā. This, however, does not challenge the post-2nd century CE (or much later) date for the DStv's insertion into the Mbh as the DStv+.

The PN-s1 ends by Viṣṇu conveying a sort of mixed message to the goddess, although its intent clearly illustrates the trope of subordination through elevation.

> 56 Having deluded Kaṃsa, you alone will glory in the
>   world,
> For the sake of its enhancement, I (i.e., Viṣṇu) will
>   accomplish Kaṃsa's destruction.
> 57 Thus having instructed her, the lord disappeared.
> And she, having bowed to him and saying, "So be it,"
>   also vanished.

The goddess is portrayed as Viṣṇu's agent, executing his plans, with Kṛṣṇa's destruction of Kaṃsa framed as enhancing her glorification, although Viṣṇu remains the true architect behind her successes.

The DSto parallels the PN-s1 in subordinating the goddess to Viṣṇu while emphasizing her preeminence as stemming from his decree. Unlike the DStv+, the DSto incorporates the cowherd Kṛṣṇa mythos developed in the HV, identifying the goddess as Kṛṣṇa's sister (l. 14) and calling her Kauśikī (l. 15). This reflects familiarity with the Kṛṣṇa/Kaṃsa cycle and tacitly acknowledges Nidrā's Vaiṣṇava persona as *mahānidrā* ("great sleep"). Notably, the DSto situates the goddess on Mount Mandara (l. 7) rather than Vindhya, linking her to the Churning of the Ocean myth and Kṛṣṇa's later slaying of the demon Madhu in Purāṇic literature.

The PN-s1 identifies Nidrā with Kālarātrī, Māyā, and Kālarūpiṇī, aiming to align her with Kālī while subordinating this fierce goddess — associated with animal sacrifices on the ninth lunar day — to Viṣṇu. Unlike Durgā/Kālī in the DStv, who appears independent and powerful, the HV avoids these names, linking Nidrā to Indra as Kauśikī, his adopted sister. This indicates a deliberate Vaiṣṇava framing rather than a Śākta redefinition of a goddess developed solely within Vaiṣṇava contexts. The DStv+ frame verses describe the hymn as originating from "various versions" (*vividhaiḥ stotrasambhavaiḥ*, l. 9), indicating its widespread circulation. The hymn aligns with evidence of an independent Great Goddess cult in the early centuries CE, reflected in literary sources such as the mantric verses of the TA, the Durgā Sāvitrī in the Dharmasūtras, the ritual prescriptions of the BGŚS, and the Rātrī Khila. It is difficult to know if this cult vied to situate the Great Goddess as supreme deity, but these texts show a progressive elaboration of the goddess's characteristics, suggesting sectarian tensions in the post-Vedic period. The insertion of the DSto+ and DStv+ into portions of the Mbh manuscript collection, particularly in North India, whenever they may have occurred, is testament to the phenomenon of goddess worship by kings and warriors (in the examples of Yudhiṣṭhira and Arjuna).[33] Although the hymns are voiced by princes under duress, they reveal broader contexts within which the goddess was being worshipped, namely, in all dangerous situations, not just at the onset of martial challenges. This is noteworthy because most previous studies have been overly focused on Durgā's significant role in sovereignty and warfare.[34]

The hymns may date to 144 CE to 350 CE, a period Hein (1986, 296–97) calls "a dark age in Indian history," characterized by few inscriptions, sparse art, and limited literary evidence. This was the period between the decline of the Kuṣāna Empire after Kaniṣka's rule (now mostly accepted at 127 CE) and the rise of the long period of Gupta peace (c. 350–650 CE) (Lohuizen de-Leeuw 1949, 320). This was an era of religious transformation, including evidence of the Great Goddess tradition, the expansion of Durgā's cult, and the early growth of the Kṛṣṇa Gopāla cult. Vedic orthodoxy was reasserting itself, countering renunciant cultures and non-Vedic deities, while the foundations for *bhakti* literature were laid in the Purāṇas. These hymns illustrate a creative adaptation of religious traditions within Sanskrit texts, addressing evolving social and cultural realities. The DSto's composition likely postdates the HV's PN-s1, drawing on its motifs but developing independently. Regardless of precedence, the DStv and PN-s1 reflect dynamic interactions between emerging Śākta cults and Vaiṣṇava traditions, evident in references to Nārāyaṇa, Vāsudeva, and Saṃkarṣaṇa, as these deities were integrated into the Viṣṇu/Kṛṣṇa persona.

The DSto does refer to the goddess as the destroyer of Kaiṭabha (*kaiṭabhanāśini*) (l. 17). This tacit connection with the demon Madhu, through the Mount Mandara reference, and the explicit connection to the slaying of Kaiṭabha is significant, because the goddess is later famously linked in Episode One of the DM with aiding Viṣṇu in his destruction of the demons Madhu and Kaiṭabha. This reference to the destruction of Kaiṭabha contributes to why some scholars place the composition of the DSto after the DM, as noted by Yokochi (2004, 75). The longest of the seven extant versions of the DStv also includes the epithet *kaiṭabhamardini* (Crusher of Kaiṭabha).[35] The epithets "slayer" or "crusher of Kaiṭabha" pose challenges for assigning an early date to the DStv. If, as I and other scholars argue, the DM was composed in the mid-8th century CE, it would imply even later dates for the Mbh hymns, complicating efforts to align them with early iconography, as we will explore in later chapters. However, if the DStv and DSto predate the DM, as I suggest, the Kaiṭabha reference could simply be an insertion, or signify early competition between the goddess and Viṣṇu over credit for slaying Kaiṭabha — much like early texts attribute the slaying of Mahiṣa to both Durgā and Skanda.

The *Vāyu Purāṇa* (25.46–52) presents an account paralleling the DM's version but likely predating it (Yokochi 2004, 83). In this narrative, a maiden (*kanyā*) emerges from Viśvarūpa in response to Brahmā's prayer and aids Brahmā and Viṣṇu in slaying Madhu and Kaiṭabha, who threaten Brahmā. Identifying herself as Mohinī and "Māyā who executes Viṣṇu's commands" (25.48cd; Yokochi 2004, 83), she is later called Mahāvyāhṛti, Sāvitrī, and Ekānaṃśā by Brahmā (25.51cd). Here, the slaying is attributed to Viṣṇu, with the goddess merely assisting him. By the DM's composition, this portrayal had shifted. While the DM retains the goddess's role in deluding Madhu and Kaiṭabha, allowing

Viṣṇu to slay them, it refutes her subordination. She is named Mahāmāyā, and Brahmā's hymn (DM 1.65) declares her the origin of Viṣṇu, Śiva, and Brahmā, positioning her as supreme rather than Viṣṇu's agent.

In the DSto, the goddess is frequently called Kālī but is also named Śākambharī, Jayā, Vijayā, Sarasvatī, and Kātyāyanī. Śaiva/Skanda connections are evident, as she is called Umā and the mother of Skanda. Umā, linked to Pārvatī, Śiva's consort, aligns the goddess with Skanda, who in the Mbh is associated with dangerous female deities and credited with slaying Mahiṣa (Mann 2011, 18–21). The DSto is one of the earliest to name the goddess Caṇḍī (l. 10), suggesting a milieu influenced by both Śaiva/Skanda and Vaiṣṇava traditions. References to her as Śiva's consort, Skanda's mother, and Kṛṣṇa's sister subordinate her to male counterparts, raising doubts about its composition in a Śākta sectarian context, where the goddess would occupy the highest rank.

The insertion of the DSto+ into the Mbh may reflect a period wherein existed the widespread practice of invoking the goddess for victory in battle, which would otherwise seem conspicuously absent. Since Nidrā of the PN-s1, associated with boons of wealth, sons, and protection from travel dangers, lacks any connection to sovereignty or warfare, it would make her invocation by Arjuna before battle incongruous. Instead, Durgā/Kālī's veneration for military success is acknowledged through the DSto+'s placement before the great battle. However, its frame verses and position before the BG diminish the goddess's prominence, attributing ultimate agency to Kṛṣṇa. Similarly, the DStv+ aligns with a Vaiṣṇava agenda, subordinating Durgā to Viṣṇu. Despite its strategic placement amid Yudhiṣṭhira's plea for aid, it underscores Durgā/Kālī's widespread worship — not just for military victories but by kings, soldiers, and ordinary people in various forms of duress.

To recap the proposed chronology: the DStv, or an unknown DStv* variant, appears first, praising Durgā/Kālī as a goddess offering refuge and success in battle, independent of any other deity. This is followed by the PN-s1, which borrows lines from the DStv or its DStv* precursor but associates refuge and delusion — not sovereign success — with Nidrā/Kauśikī, subordinated to Viṣṇu. The PN-s1 likely dates to the core HV, around 200 CE to 300 CE, with the DStv or its DStv* precursor slightly earlier. The DSto comes next, incorporating features from earlier paeans while subordinating Durgā to Viṣṇu through references to the Nanda myth, casting her as Kṛṣṇa's younger sister. Composed after the BG, it may have been written contemporaneously with its insertion into the Mbh, as its lengthy closing frame verses emphasize familiar qualities of the goddess: refuge, victory, boon-granting, deliverance, and health. Finally, the DStv+ follows, less represented in manuscripts, with frame verses that subordinate the supreme Durgā of the DStv to Kṛṣṇa through the Yaśodā-Nanda myth cycle. These insertions likely occurred long after the original compositions or their precursor variants.

For instance, Kṣemendra Vyāsadāsa's *Bhāratamañjarī*, a sort of summary of the Mbh composed in the 11th century, omits any reference to these Durgā hymns (Yokochi 2004, 128n1), but such epitomes are known for omitting or altering episodes that did not serve their intent.[36] I suggest that the PN-s2, discussed next, and the two other hymns by Pradyumna and Aniruddha, respectively, followed in composition and their insertion into the HV.

As a caveat, we do not know for certain if the authors of these hymns were aware of the hymns that I have suggested preceded them. However, in the absence of contrary evidence, and the fact that these materials have endured until today, we are obliged to try to construct our vision of the past on what is available.

The Praise of Nidrā (Second Stratum)

I suggest that the insertion of the DStv+ into the Mbh would likely be followed by the appending of the Praise of Nidrā (Second Stratum) (PN-s2) to the HV. It is found in more than half the manuscripts available and is thus not regarded as intrinsic to the original composition and relegated to an appendix.[37] It very much has the sound and style of a proper paean, a hymn of praise. It is sometimes known as the Āryā Stava, and then placed in the beginning of the following chapter (*adhayaya* 48) in the voice of Vaiśampāyana, the *ṛṣi* narrator, rather than as an extension of Viṣṇu's paean to Nidrā. Upon examining it, we see that many of the names and epithets found in the DStv+, DSto+, and the PN-s1 are fully absorbed.

In it, regarding Durgā, Viṣṇu says:

> 1 "(You are) the virtuous Kātyāyanī, the goddess
>   Kauśikī, practicing celibacy,
> Mother of the one whose army is the Siddhas (Skanda),
>   the brave Durgā of great austerities. (Coburn
> 1984, 279)

The associations here appear to forge a connection between Durgā and the goddess Pārvatī, renowned for her ascetic practices performed to win the hand of Śiva. There are numerous other attributes associated with the goddess in this hymn, and not previously found in any of the earlier epic hymns, including identifications with many more fearsome goddesses. Evidently, by the time of its composition and attachment to the PN-s1, the development of the persona of a great goddess (*mahādevī*), explicitly called as such (l. 8) and named Durgā, was well underway.

The goddess is identified as Kātyāyanī and Kauśikī, celibate (l. 1), and the mother of the Siddhas' leader, called the brave Durgā of great austerities (l. 2). She is the eldest sister of Yama, wearing a blue silken garment (l. 4), and as in the DSto and DStv is named Jayā and Vijayā (l. 3). Described as "of many forms and deformed, of various sorts of forms" (l. 279), she has deformed and wide eyes (l. 6) and is venerated by savages, barbarians, and mountain folk (l.

9). Her abodes include mountain peaks, rivers, caves, forests, and groves (l. 6–7), the very refuges criticized as inadequate in the *Dhammapada* (e.g., v. 188–192) compared to Buddhist self-realization.

She is called the great goddess (l. 8), surrounded by cocks, goats, sheep, lions, and tigers (l. 11), and carries a peacock-feather banner as she conquers worlds (l. 10). Accompanied by bells (l. 12), she wields a trident, sharp spear, and the sun and moon as emblems (l. 13). Her favored days are the ninth of the dark fortnight and the eleventh of the bright fortnight (l. 14). She is identified as Vāsudeva's sister, Nanda's daughter (l. 15, 17), and, like Kṛṣṇa in the BG, the abode, basis, and supreme goal of all creatures (l. 16), bringing about the gods' victory (l. 17).

Clothed in bark and fine garments (l. 18), with disheveled hair, she is fond of flesh and boiled rice (l. 19). She is both Lakṣmī and Alakṣmī (l. 20), Sāvitrī among gods, mother of spirits (l. 21), and exists to slay demons (l. 20). Referencing the VRām and Mbh, she is the blessed words (*sarasvatī*) of Vālmīki, Sītā among plowmen, and Dvaipāyana's recollective power. She is Śakunī, Pūtanā, and Revatī (l. 39). Among Purāṇic women, she is Pārvatī (l. 42) and Arundhatī (l. 43), as well as Indrāṇī (l. 44), evoking Indra's consort rather than his sister. The hymn states she pervades the universe, all that moves and is stationary (l. 45), reiterating her Durgā-like associations with protection in battles, forests, and journeys (l. 46–49).

The growing litany of epithets and descriptions in this addition suggests a later composition date, reflecting the significant expansion of Durgā's cult. Many elements of the Great Goddess tradition, later crystallized in the influential DM, are already present. The PN-s2 does not introduce new demon-slaying exploits but elevates Nidrā/Durgā to a status nearly rivaling Viṣṇu/Kṛṣṇa, a shift inconsistent with the HV's agenda and the subordinating tone of PN-s1.

It is plausible that the PN-s2 initially circulated independently as a *paean* to Durgā, portraying her as a supreme Great Goddess (l. 2, 8) within a Śākta devotional context. However, when appended to PN-s1, its praises were subsumed under the persona of Nidrā, acting on Viṣṇu's commands. Even as a separate hymn, titled the Āryā Stava, it addresses Nārāyaṇī, a name that implicitly subordinates the goddess as Viṣṇu/Nārāyaṇa's consort.

The Goddesses in the Other *Harivaṃśa* Hymns

Pradyumna's Hymn

The next HV goddess eulogy after the two-parted Nidrā paean is known as Pradyumna's Hymn (hereafter PradH). It appears in the context of explaining how Pradyumna, the son of Kṛṣṇa and Rukmiṇī, prays to Durgā for aid to slay the demon Śambara.[38] The framing verses make a pronounced effort to identify the goddess with Pārvatī. Pradyumna reflects on his battle club, likening it to the staff of Death (l. 305), and recounts how Pārvatī appeared to him, stating she had slain the demons Śumbha and Niśumbha, wanderers upon the mountain (l. 311–12). He then initiates a mental prayer to Pārvatī, Śiva's beloved (l. 359).

Within the hymn, the goddess is called Kātyāyanī (l. 361, 362), mother of Guha (l. 361), Gārgī, queen of the mountains (l. 363), and slayer of Śumbha and Niśumbha (l. 364). She is Kālarātrī, the ever-chaste maiden (l. 365), the great goddess, and Jayā and Vijayā (l. 368). Holding a bell and adorned with a bell garland, she evokes the later Citraghaṇṭā or Candraghantā of the Nine Durgās. She wields a trident, slays the Asura Mahiṣa (l. 371), rides a lion, and has a lion emblem (l. 372). Identified as Ekānaṃśā, Gāyatrī (l. 373), and Sāvitrī (l. 374), the hymn reflects her integration with the HV's portrayal of Nidrā. The goddess is invoked for protection and victory in battle.

Notably, Durgā does not appear in the eulogy itself, but is identified in the concluding framing verses as the goddess that was praised by a host of other names within the hymn.

> 375 Protect me eternally, O goddess, give (me) victory
>   in battle."
> Having heard these words of desire, Durgā's mind was
>   well-pleased.

The frame explicitly identifies Durgā with Pārvatī, who is absent from the hymn proper. Durgā was explicitly linked to Pārvatī in the PN-s2 and only implicitly in earlier hymns through mountain associations and asceticism. By the time PradH was inserted into the HV, the narrative framing appears to have more firmly established the goddess as Durgā, while also identifying her as Pārvatī and Ekānaṃśā/Nidrā. These efforts, aiming to subordinate her to Śiva or Viṣṇu through relational ties, simultaneously shaped the persona of the Great Goddess, increasingly linked to the name Durgā.

The hymn explicitly mentions two key demon-slaying exploits of the goddess: the killing of the Asura Mahiṣa and of Śumbha and Niśumbha (not the earlier Sumbha and Nisumbha). However, tensions arise from the multitude of identifications. She is called the ever-chaste maiden (l. 365) yet also Pārvatī, Śiva's beloved. By this time, her distinctive peacock banner, prominent in earlier hymns, is no longer referenced. Coburn (1984, 282) observes the difficulty of determining the hymn's provenance, as the insertions are widely distributed in the manuscript tradition. The date of composition remains uncertain, and iconographic representations explored in a later chapter may provide further insights.

Aniruddha's Hymn

In the final goddess hymn (AniH) inserted into some versions of the HV, Pradyumna's son, Aniruddha, is said to have sung this hymn when he was imprisoned with Uṣā by her demon father Bāṇa, son of the demon Bali.[39] The framing material identifies the goddess as Kaumārī.

> 3 Then for the sake of protection, he took refuge in the
>   goddess Kaumārī.
> Hear this hymn to the goddess as it was sung by
>   Aniruddha.
> 5 Having bowed to the endless, indestructible, heavenly
>   primal god,
> The eternal Nārāyaṇa, the excellent, foremost lord,
> I will sing praises to Caṇḍī, Kātyāyanī, the virtuous god-
>   dess, revered by the world.

The opening verse situates Nārāyaṇa (Viṣṇu) as the supreme deity and the goddess as a significant celestial figure. The name Caṇḍī, first seen in the DSto, reappears, with the goddess described as a boon-grantress and sister of Indra and Viṣṇu (l. 11), as well as Indra's younger sister (l. 36). References to Kṛṣṇa Gopāla include her striking fear into Kaṃsa, delighting Yaśodā (l. 13), and being born in Gokula as Nanda's daughter (l. 14), reflecting absorptions from the Nidrā myth cycle..

The hymn's epithets are extensive. She is Kālī (l. 20), Kātyāyanī (l. 20, 21, 64), three-eyed, and as in PradH, identified with Śakunī and Revatī. She dwells on Vindhya and Kailāsa (l. 33), rides a lion, and has the bull as her emblem (l. 34), tying her to Pārvatī/Śiva (Kailāsa is Śiva's abode, and the bull his mount). Explicitly called Pārvatī, daughter of the mountain (l. 41), she is also Gaṅgā, Gāndhārī (l. 27), Sarasvatī (l. 28), Sāvitrī (l. 29), Gautamī (l. 13, 50), Kauberī (l. 31), Kuṣmāṇḍī (l. 32), and Ekānaṃśā (l. 30). She is explicitly called Durgā (l. 35), with the descriptive terms "inaccessible" and "hard to conquer," Importantly, at the eulogy's conclusion, the framing verses refer to her as Durgā, the great goddess (*mahādevī*) "whose valor is hard to surpass" (l. 67).

> 35 Inaccessible, hard to conquer, Durgā, seeing whom
>   terrified Niśumbha,
>
> . . .
>
> 67 Thus praised, the great goddess Durgā, whose valor
>   is hard to surpass,
> Came nigh unto Aniruddha in confinement. (Coburn
>   1984, 285–88)

The goddess is identified as Skanda's mother (l. 40, 41) and the slayer of Śumbha and Niśumbha, referred to as *niśumbhaśumbhamathanī* (l. 39). She appears to Aniruddha, frees him from his bonds, but instructs him to wait, as Kṛṣṇa will destroy the demon Bāṇa and rescue him. Aniruddha, delighted, praises her again, calling her Brahmāṇī, Indrāṇī, Rudrāṇī (l. 89), and twice Nārāyaṇī (l. 90, 93). The hymn concludes with the proclamation that anyone who recites it to Āryā will attain Viṣṇu's world (l. 95). Notably, as in the PN-s2, also called a hymn to Āryā, the goddess is never directly addressed as Āryā within the hymn. Although introduced as a hymn to Kaumārī, she is not mentioned, even as several other Vaiṣṇava-related goddesses appear.

In these passages, Durgā is prominently named both within the hymn and in the concluding framing verse, reinforcing her overarching identity. She is associated with perilous forests and mountains (notably the Vindhyas) and is linked to battle — described as fond of combat, invincible in warfare, and propitiated for victory. Ambivalently, she both instills and dispels fear. Identified as the *mahādevī* (great goddess), she is equated with Kātyāyanī, Kālarātrī, Kuṣmāṇḍī, and the mother of Skanda — epithets also tied to the Nine Durgās (*navadurgā*). While her lion mount is noted, she is also associated with the bull.

The hymn's Vaiṣṇava orientation is unmistakable. Despite eulogizing Durgā as the great goddess, it follows the subordinating-elevation trope, situating her within a Vaiṣṇava framework. Her growing persona is reflected in an expanding array of epithets and descriptions, contributing to the Great Goddess concept. She is twice called *mahādevī* (l. 65, 67), but her capacity for granting boons, such as freeing devotees from hardship and defeating enemies, overshadows her traditional ties to wild landscapes. Her alignment with feminine counterparts of male deities (e.g., Brahmānī, Indrāṇī, Rudrāṇī) prefigures her later association with the Mātṛkās in the DM and subsequent texts. Bhagawant Sahai (1975, 214) suggests Durgā eventually becomes one of the Mātṛkās, although Coburn (1984, 121n122) finds no evidence of this in the DM, associating the motif instead with the later *nava-durgā* tradition (Sahai 1975, 191–192).

The framing verses conclude with repeated "*namo 'stu te*" refrains (l. 82–93), including invocations of "O Nārāyaṇī, praise be to you" (*nārāyaṇī namo 'stu te*, l. 90, 93), prefiguring the Yā Devī and Nārāyaṇī Stuti hymns of the DM, if composed later than the AniH. Some manuscripts include the line "Hail to you, crusher of the enemy of the gods, Mahiṣa" (*mahiṣāsurāmardinī*, l. 85), indicating recognition of the omission of this feat in the hymn. This addition highlights the increasing prominence of the goddess as "Crusher" (*mardinī*) of Mahiṣa, although the epithet Mahiṣāsuramardinī had not yet emerged.

General Appraisal of the Epic Panegyrics

The examination of these Epic-era hymns reveals common themes in Durgā's evolving persona. The name Durgā is frequently linked to buffalo sacrifice (e.g., DSto) and the slaying of Mahiṣāsura (e.g., DStv, PradH). Her earlier character as a refuge and savior (e.g., DStv) continues but becomes centrally associated with victory and enemy defeat (e.g., DStv, DSto, PN-s2, PradH, AniH). She is repeatedly identified with goddesses personifying Victory, such as Jayā and Vijayā (e.g., DStv, DSto, PN-s2, PradH), and consistently portrayed as a boon-grantress across the hymns.

Her earlier association with peacock feather bracelets (e.g., DStv, PN-s1) and the peacock feather standard (e.g., DStv, PN-s1, DSto, PN-s2) disappears in later hymns, replaced by her identification with the lion as her mount (e.g., PradH, AniH). Durgā is explicitly identified with Kālī (e.g., DStv, DSto, AniH), but her connection to Nidrā is largely implicit, emerging through references to the Kṛṣṇa/Kaṃsa myth cycle, which aligns her ambivalently as Kṛṣṇa's sister or Viṣṇu's consort (Nārāyaṇī). She is credited with the slaying of demons such as Kaiṭabha (DSto), Mahiṣa (e.g., DStv), and Sumbha and Nisumbha (PN-s1), later named Śumbha and Niśumbha (PradH, AniH).

The name Kātyāyanī is absent in the DStv and PN-s1 but appears prominently in the DSto, PN-s2, PradH, and AniH. Similarly, Kauśikī is invoked in the DSto, PN-s1, and PN-s2 with varied depictions: in the DSto, she is clad in yellow and fond of Mahiṣa's blood; in PN-s1, she is identified with Nidrā, practicing celibacy, consecrated by Indra, and worshipped across a thousand sites; and in PN-s2, she merges with Kātyāyanī, maintaining associations with celibacy and austerities.

Durgā is a recurring figure, explicitly named in most hymns proper (e.g., DStv, DSto, PN-s2, AniH) and framing verses (DStv+, DSto+, and the framing verses of PradH, AniH). In the DStv, she is also called Jayā, Vijayā, and Kālī, with her identity solidified in the closing verse: "Be a refuge for me, O Durgā, O refuge, O one who is fond of her devotees" (l. 51) (Coburn 1984, 271). By contrast, the DSto features a profusion of names — Kātyāyanī, Kālī, Kauśikī, Bhadrakālī, Jayā, Vijayā, Caṇḍī, Umā, Śākambharī, Sarasvatī, and Sāvitrī, among others — but calls her Durgā only once (l. 22). While Durgā's ownership of the hymn is less apparent, her attributes as refuge, boon-grantress, and victor are central, reinforced in the framing verses that designate the hymn as the Durgā Stotra.

I believe it might be an error to conclude that Durgā worship arose out of the Vaiṣṇava sectarian tradition, and in this part ways with the conventional suggestion put forward by some scholars.[40] Rather, I suggest that from the insertions in the TA (arguably 3rd century BCE), the hymnic elaborations in the Rātrī Khila (possibly from the 1st century BCE), the references to the Durgā-sāvitrī in the Dharmasūtras (possibly 1st century CE), and the worship rites to Durgā in the BGŚS (early centuries CE) we see a continuity of efforts to incorporate the cult of an independent goddess, called along with other names Durgā, into both the Vedic sphere and within Vaiṣṇavism in the early period.[41]

The paeans, apart from their framing verses, point to widespread goddess worship during the early and late Epic Period, independent of Vaiṣṇava or Śaiva affiliations. Even the PN-s1, likely composed with the early stratum of the HV and aimed at subordinating the goddess within a Vaiṣṇava framework, reveals the amalgamation of multiple significant goddesses — possibly called Durgā, Kālī, Jayā, Vijayā, Kātyāyanī, and Kauśikī — into a singular independent deity.

Centered in the Vindhya region, these goddesses were boon-granters, saviors, and guardians in times of ordeal. Each had claims to being a great goddess. Increasingly, they were venerated by warriors and kings before battle, gaining prominence among the *kṣatriya* (ruler, warrior) classes. It is plausible that this widespread martial worship led to their incorporation into *kṣatriya*-oriented epics during the late Epic or early medieval period. By contrast, it is less convincing to argue that a goddess that developed as a subordinate within a Vaiṣṇava context could later emerge as a supreme deity, as articulated in the DM. While Vaiṣṇavism and Śaivism contributed to the amalgamation of these great goddesses, there likely existed independent goddess-centered sects where the goddesses were not defined as relatives of male deities.

The martial nature of the goddess in these hymns is evident in her attributes. The framing verses of the DStv+ depict her with a sword and shield (l. 8), while the hymn proper associates her with weapons such as a bell, noose, bow, and discus (l. 19, 20). In the DSto, she wields a spear, sword, and shield (l. 13). The PN-s1 describes her with an upraised three-pointed spear and gold-hilted sword (l. 40), and in the PN-s2, she carries a trident and sharp-edged spear (l. 13). In PradH, she holds a bell and trident (l. 370, 371). However, in AniH, she has eighteen arms but no weapons; instead, she tells Aniruddha that Kṛṣṇa, armed with the discus, will rescue him. This narrative highlights the ongoing tension between Śākta and Vaiṣṇava traditions regarding the best deity for protection, Durgā or Viṣṇu/Kṛṣṇa.

We now turn to the earliest extant goddess images that might represent Durgā, particularly from the central to eastern Gaṅgā river basin, with notable examples from Chandraketugarh.

Chapter 3

Proto-Durgās in the
Earliest Material Evidence

At this juncture, it is reasonable to turn to iconography to determine whether the earliest material artifacts align with the hypotheses derived from the textual tradition. In this chapter, we will examine a female figure depicted on numerous terracotta plaques, derived in quantity from Chandraketugarh, but with a wide north Indian provenance. These so-called *yakṣī* figures have distinctive hairpins, many of which resemble weapons, and other characteristics that correlate well with those describing the goddess praised in the early strata of epic hymns (i.e., DStv or DStv*, PN-S1, DSto). The correlations suggest that the female figure could arguably depict the Indian goddess Kauśikī, or Arədvī Sūrā Anāhitā, a goddess praised in the Zoroastrian Ābān Yašt, or some amalgam of these. Both these goddesses fuse riverine and warrior characteristics, and there are notable parallels between the Ābān Yašt's agenda to subordinate Anāhitā to Ahura Mazda, and the PN-s1's agenda regarding Kauśikī and Viṣṇu.

Many scholars thus far have pessimistically viewed the promise of iconographic examination of Durgā's cult. Based on a long and detailed study of the many early material artifacts, particularly Kuṣāṇa stone plaques and terracottas, D. Srinivasan observed that the rise of the Goddess was

> bereft of roots in Brahmanism as well as Buddhism and Jainism. In Mathurā, the region of her iconic concentration and probably artistic origin, no early folk myths or legends have left reference to a goddess battling a buffalo. . . . It does not help matters that the first full account of the battle between the Goddess and the Buffalo Demon fails to tally with the scene on Kuṣāṇa reliefs. It is well known that this account occurs in the *Devī-Māhātmya*, which is said to be added to the *Mārkaṇḍeya Purāṇa* by the sixth century A.D. (1997, 283)

Schmid (2002, 144) echoed this point, referencing the old *Skanda Purāṇa* (SP), which predates the *Devī Māhātmya* (DM) but still remains much later than the earliest images. Yokochi's studies (1999a, 2004, 2013) on the Vindhyavāsinī cycle and the goddess Kauśikī confirm that the older SP predates the DM. These findings will be revisited in a later chapter focusing on Durgā. Schmid (2011) incorporated Yokochi's revelations about the SP into her analyses of early images of a goddess slaying a buffalo, although these still reveal a gap of several centuries between the texts and the images. A detailed discussion of the SP will appear near the conclusion of this study.

We approach this examination with optimism, aiming to illuminate the enigma of the buffalo-slaying goddess by tracing connections to Durgā. Iconography may corroborate attributes described in the early epic hymns and reveal aspects of Durgā not apparent in the Purāṇic tradition, often unsuccessfully scoured for clues. Previous scholarship has largely overlooked connections between the epic hymns and early iconography, often dismissing the hymns as "late" compositions rather than acknowledging their possible earlier origins and "late" insertions. For instance, while Aniruddha's Hymn (AniH) may have been composed and inserted into the *Harivaṃśa* (HV) centuries after the first stratum of Viṣṇu's Praise of Nidrā (PN-s1), the PN-s1 likely dates to the composition of the HV core in the 2nd and 3rd centuries CE. Additionally, to me, similarities between PN-s1 and the Durgā Stava (DStv) suggest influences from the DStv or unknown DStv* variants on the PN-s1 rather than vice versa. This would imply that the DStv, or similar unknown compositions, circulated by the late 2nd century CE, even if the DStv was only later inserted into the *Mahābhārata* (Mbh) as the DStv+. If correct, these hymns are closer in date than the DM or early SP to the earliest extant artifacts, such as Kuṣāna plaques and Śuṅga terracottas, depicting goddesses that might represent Durgā.

The Mysterious Goddess with "Weapon" Hairpins

The most compelling earliest images that might represent Durgā are on terracottas that derive in quantity from Chandraketugarh in West Bengal. They depict female figures with bicornate hairstyles with stylized hairpins shaped as weapons. Such figures have been found along many sites in the Gaṅgā river valley, including Vaiśālī, Mathurā, Kauśāmbī, and Ahichchhatra, and even further through the Indo-Gangetic divide in Taxila, Sugh, and Bannu in the Northwest frontier provinces (Haque 2001, 85; Ahuja 2005, 345). The Chandraketugarh figures are found on numerous terracotta plaques said to derive from the Śuṅga period and territorial sphere.[42] It has been difficult to date these figures, many of which have not been obtained through systematic archaeological digs but from collections. And there are wide variations in dating stylistically similar images based on their region of production. So, the weapon-hairpin females from Tamluk are dated between the 3rd and 1st centuries BCE, while those from Chandraketugarh may range from as late as the 1st to the 3rd century CE (Chowdhury 2002, 20–21). Despite these variations, the tentative range from the 3rd century BCE to the 3rd century CE precisely overlaps with the Epic period, whose textual references concerning Durgā in the inserted hymns we examined in the last chapter, and so the examination of these female figures is appropriate. The most popular theme depicted on these terracotta plaques is a type of female figure designated a "Yakshi" (Yakṣī) by scholars such as Enamul Haque (2001). For convenience I shall refer to this distinct class of females as the Chandraketugarh goddess, rather than the lengthier "goddess with hairpins stylized as weapons," keeping fully in mind that their provenance is wide-ranging through much of North India, including sites such as Kauśāmbī, Mathurā, Ahicchatra, and Sonkh (Ahuja 2000, 112).

The "Yakṣī" is a common way of designating unidentified female figures that seem to be divine or semi-divine in nature, and there are examples of so-called *yakṣī* figures attributed to the earlier Mauryan period. The best known of these is the Dīdārgañj Yakṣī displayed in figure 3.1, and named after a suburb of Pāṭaliputra, the ancient Mauryan capital where it was found. There is no scholarly consensus whether this figure truly belongs to the Mauryan or later Kuṣāṇa period, and little consensus whether the figure even depicts a *yakṣī*.[43] D. Srinivasan (2005) argues that it depicts not a divine but a human female, namely, a *gaṇikā* or royal courtesan. In part, this is because the voluptuous figure holds a fly whisk or chowrie (*cāmara*), which is a characteristic attribute of a female attendant to a noble. Pratapaditya Pal (1988), however, has argued that a certain chowrie bearing female, as depicted on a Gupta coin, was likely a goddess. So, a chowrie-bearing female is not necessarily the figure of a human attendant and could represent a divinity. Whether she is a *gaṇikā* or a *devī*, the

Figure 3.1. The Dīdārgañj Yakṣī with fly whisk (c. 3rd century BCE to 1st century CE); 1.57 m, Chunar sandstone. *Source*: Bihar Museum, Patna. Photo by the author.

"Dīdārgañj Yakṣī" is a reminder that generic designations of such unclassifiable female figures as *yakṣīs* should be regarded with caution.

Male and female figures from the Buddhist *stūpas* at Bharhut, near Satna in Madhya Pradesh, dating to the Śuṅga period (2nd–1st century BCE), are explicitly labeled on inscriptions as *yakṣas* and *yakṣīs* (*yakho* and *yakhī*). One particularly intriguing figure, shown in figure 3.2, is named Cadā Yakhi. Its transliteration has varied due to differences in conventions, appearing as Chandra Yakṣī, Chhandā Yakṣī, or Candā Yakṣī in scholarly writings, partly because the non-aspirated palatal "c" is often rendered as "ch" for pronunciation. Alexander Cunningham (1879, 20, 138) rendered it as Chandā, arguing that if Chaṇḍā were intended, the inscription would use the cerebral "ḍ." Ramesh Chandra Sharma (1994, 38) interpreted it as Chhandā Yakhī, referring to the Yakṣinī Chhandā.

Buddhist and Jain traditions frequently labeled local gods and goddesses as Yakṣas or Yakṣīs to subordinate them to the Buddha or Jina within their respective pantheons. If one reads Cadā Yakhi as Caṇḍā Yakṣī, as Umakant Premanand Shah (1987, 221) does, it could represent an early instance of the goddess Caṇḍā (perhaps a variant of Caṇḍī) within the Buddhist pantheon. However, transliteration challenges often arise, particularly when artisans render Sanskrit names

Figure 3.2. Cadā Yakhi (Caṇḍā Yakṣī?) (c. 2nd century to 1st century BCE); near life-size, red sandstone. *Source*: Bharhut Gallery, Indian Museum, Kolkata. Photo by the author.

into Prakrit (Pālī), leading to potential errors. For instance, while Shah reads the Bharhut *yakṣinī* as Caḍā or Caṇḍā, the figure's graceful posture and form have also been interpreted as evoking the moon (e.g., Dehejia 2013, 79), rather than a fierce (*caṇḍā*) deity. However, Caḍā is written with a long "ā," while *candra* (moon) in Sanskrit generally uses a short "a," even in variant forms such as *canda*. This highlights the need for close scrutiny of explicitly labeled *yakṣīs* to determine their identities and symbolism accurately.

The Chandraketugarh "*yakṣīs*" are numerous, with distinguishing features that recur across many depictions. The most notable characteristic of these female figures, whether alone or with attendants, is their elaborate hairdos, often adorned with hairpins that resemble weapons, although the exact nature of these ornaments remains unclear. Notably, these figures are never shown holding weapons in their hands. The repeated occurrence of such features across numerous images suggests they represent a specific female divinity, rather than generic Yakṣīs. In museum exhibits (e.g., Musée Guimet in Paris and the Metropolitan Museum in New York), these figures are often labeled as proto-Durgās, possibly due to Durgā's association with weaponry. However, no systematic evidence or rationale has been provided for this identification. Given this study's focus on Durgā, these figures merit closer examination. We begin by analyzing the distinctive hairpins.

Today, one might associate the use of ornamental hairpins with Japanese *kanzashi*, which were worn since ancient times to avert evil, and often crafted as weapons. During the Han period in China (c. 2nd century BCE to 3rd century CE), the "hair-pinning" (*jili*) ceremony marked a girl's initiation into a marriageable age (c. fifteen to twenty years old). It was a key domestic rite, and upper-class girls decorated their hair with crowns trimmed with bells and gold hairpins (Sherrow 2006, 80). If we accept any measure of interaction between Han China's spheres of influence and the Gaṅgā river basin and Chandraketugarh culture, the hairpins could be symbols of a virginal female of marriageable age. Durgā/Kālī in the DStv (l. 11) is invoked as a chaste young virgin. Bronze hairpins, with three-pronged heads that terminate in an axe, thunderbolt (*vajra*), or the Nandipāda design, resembling the sorts of head pins depicted on the Chandraketugarh figures, have been excavated in India and belong to the 3rd or 2nd century BCE (R. G. Chandra 2014, 38).[44] Evidently, hairpins of the period may have possessed weapon motifs or simply assorted decorative features.

The connection between China and North India is plausible. The Yuezhi, originating in the grasslands of modern-day Gansu, migrated via the Ili Valley, Sogdia, and Bactria in the 2nd century BCE, eventually forming the Kuṣāṇa Empire, which ruled North India from the Tarim Basin to Pāṭaliputra. Their influence on South Asian Silk Road trade will be discussed later. Additionally, the ancient Southwest Silk Road, mentioned by the Han dynasty envoy Zhang Qian, connected Sichuan (Chengdu) to India via Myanmar and extended to Laos, Thailand, Cambodia, and Vietnam before the 3rd century BCE. Later called the Tea-Horse Road (Cha-Ma-Gudao), this route facilitated extensive interactions (Yang 2004).

Maritime trade also linked South Asia's east coast (e.g., Tāmralipti) with Southeast Asia by the 3rd century BCE. Brajadulal Chattopadhyaya notes that the lower Gaṅgā delta, with Tāmralipti and Chandraketugarh as key nodes, was a hub of interaction, connecting upper India, Central Asia, Egypt, the Mediterranean, Southeast Asia, and China (2003, 59). References to the Cīnas appear in the Mbh, while the *Arthaśāstra* (c. 2nd century CE) mentions Chinese silk (*cīnāṃśuka* and *cīnapaṭṭa*) (Basham 1959, 197). In Chandraketugarh and its vicinity, ornamental hairpins — possibly featuring weapon motifs — may have symbolized virgin girls of marriageable age, as seen in China and regions under its cultural influence.

Stella Kramrisch (1939, 89–110) proposed that the females depicted on those Chandraketugarh plaques might represent the Apsara Panchachuda (Pañcacūḍā), mentioned in the Mbh and some Purāṇas. In myth, Panchachuda, "[She who has] Five Crests," appears during the churning of the ocean and explains the nature of women to Nārada. However, this identification has limitations. Many depictions of these figures feature varying sets of hairpins — three, four, five, or six — on each of two hair buns, parted in the middle. Regional variations also appear: plaques from Chandraketugarh consistently show ten hairpins (five on either side, replicated), whereas examples from Tamluk, Champa, Kauśāmbī, and Mathurā show five hairpins on one side and five stalks of grain (possibly wheat or barley) on the other (Sengupta et al. 2007, 63). Occasionally, there are six hairpins, doubled to twelve.

E. H. Johnston (1942, 94–102) speculated that the goddess might represent Māyā from the *Saundarānanda Kāvya*, while G. R. Sharma (1960, 149) suggested an identification with the Vedic goddess Sinīvālī. Sinīvālī, invoked in *Ṛg Veda* hymns 2.32 and 10.184, is described as fair-fingered, broad-hipped, and presiding over childbirth, embodying fecundity (Kinsley 1986, 15; O'Flaherty 1981, 291). However, apart from comely arms and broad hips, little about the Chandraketugarh figures aligns with Sinīvālī's distinct attributes.

The Metropolitan Museum of Art in New York has an excellent example of the Chandraketugarh plaques in its collection, and I will discuss the one in figure 3.3 in detail, with comparisons to other similar images.[45]

This image (Haque 2001, 173, Pl. C137) portrays a large female in the center standing in a relaxed posture with one knee slightly bent and flanked by four or five smaller attendants. Since the plaque is broken, only the head of an attendant or devotee — possibly kneeling — is visible in the lower right. The central female's stature, large in comparison to the attending figures, suggests that she is a noblewoman or a goddess. It is far more likely that she is a goddess since there are numerous plaques with similar attributes — not just from Chandraketugarh — depicting her alone or with attendants.[46] Even if these plaques depicted a renowned human female, they likely point to her apotheosis, portraying her as or associating her with a goddess. More plausibly, such

Figure 3.3. Chandraketugarh goddess (c. 1st century BCE to 1st century CE); 26.7 × 20 cm, molded terracotta. Chandraketugarh, West Bengal. Accession Number 1990.281.
Source: Metropolitan Museum of Art. Public domain.

plaques served as votive tablets for a goddess, installed in homes and other spaces (Bautze 1995; Haque 2001). On the plaque under examination, a female attendant holds an honorific umbrella over the central figure, flanked by two others either fanning her with peacock feather fans or holding peacock feather standards, identifiable by their markings. The goddess and her attendants appear naked except for ornate belts at their hips. Their nudity, suggested by visible genitalia, is revealed upon closer examination to be a stylistic convention: they wear diaphanous garments through which their bodies are visible. This portrayal, typical for both male and female figures on these plaques, may symbolize divine attire, such as finely woven silk. The fabric could certainly be silk, which would affirm the Chinese connection and influence in this region. Much farther away, the Roman writer Seneca (54 BCE–39 CE) declared his dismay at the popularity of silk garments among the wealthy women of Rome, which when worn was veritably as if they were wearing nothing at all (Frankopan 2016, 19). The Roman historian Florus, who lived at the time of the emperor Trajan (r. 98–117 CE) speaks of Indian ambassadors in Rome, and that empire's trade in silk with India (Puri 1994, 255).

The goddess wears an elaborate necklace, armlet, and anklets. Virtually all the plaques depict her with such adornments. She also wears very prominent earrings and wrist bracelets, possibly made of peacock feathers. The design on the bracelets matches that on the peacock feather fans (or standards), strongly indicating that they are indeed made of peacock feathers. These are also evident on other plaques.[47] She wears another elaborate necklace that hangs down over and below her breasts. Her limbs are long, yet notably solid. Her left hand is on her hip, while the right arm extends downward, with its palm in the boon-granting gesture. In some plaques she has her hands over her head, in a gesture commonly used for heavenly damsels (*apsaras*) or other alluring females. A devotee (likely male) offers something large and round — perhaps a bowl or a fruit — to her (or receives something from her). In other plaques, the devotee holds (or receives) a brimming platter or bowl of offerings (or bounty).

The figure's hairdo is styled in an elaborate bicoronet fashion, parted in the middle, with a diadem featuring a prominent jewel and wide-ribboned ties hanging down on either side of her face. Her hair is adorned with ten hairpins, resembling various weapons or ornaments. Haque (2001, 96) notes that the typical array of weapons depicted on these hairpins includes swords, arrows,

Figure 3.4. Tamluk Yakṣī (c. 200 BCE to 100 BCE); 21.7 cm, molded terracotta. Accession Number EAX.201. *Source*: Ashmolean Museum, Oxford, UK. Photo by Michelle Hogue. Used with permission.

battle-axes, tridents, and elephant goads, although these identifications are not always clear or accurate. The concept of weaponized hairpins exists in East Asian traditions, such as the Japanese *shikomi kanzashi* and *shikomi kogai* or other concealed weapons (*kakushibuki*) (Mol 2003, 203). However, the Chandraketugarh hairpins appear to be decorative, featuring weapon motifs rather than functioning as actual weapons.

Another notable example is the Tamluk Yakṣī (figure 3.4), now housed at the Ashmolean Museum, University of Oxford. Discovered in 1883 at Tamluk, the ancient seaport of Tāmralipti on the Bay of Bengal, the finely crafted figure features a bicoronet hairstyle adorned with five hairpins on one side. The lowest pin resembles an elephant goad, the middle one a battle-axe, and the second from the top an arrowhead, while the nature of the remaining two is unclear.

Joachim Karl Bautze (1995, 13) observes that the lowest hairpin on most plaques is often an *aṅkuśa* (elephant goad), as seen on the Metropolitan Museum and Tamluk plaques. Other hairpins appear in various orders: one resembles a halberd-like axe, another a pointed spear or arrowhead, while others are more ambiguous. The topmost pin, for instance, might be interpreted as a club, trident, bell, lotus stalk, or comb-like object. Some pins evoke the *bira-bira kanzashi* style of Japanese hairpins, which feature tinkling elements such as bells or strips.

A key detail often overlooked is the frequent presence of dangling, beaded tassels on these hair ornaments. Such features point to a Chinese influence, akin to the *buyao* ("shake as you go") hairpins associated with Han noblewomen. The 1973 excavation of Mawangdui in Changsha, Hunan, revealed *buyao* hairpins among the possessions of Xin Zhui, the Marquise of Dai, who died around 163 BCE. Her funerary banner depicts her wearing such a hairpin (Avril and Ling-yün Shih 1997, 109). The prevalence of *buyao*-styled hairpins on the Chandraketugarh female figures may suggest their elevated or divine status.

In the Metropolitan Museum plaque, a *kinnara* (birdman) floats above the goddess, and an honorific banner upon a pole appears to be topped by a fish. The setting appears to be a temple or shrine because the images are flanked by pillars with lotus capitals bearing *yakṣa*-like figures that support a roof. On other plaques, the goddess may be depicted with peacocks, or other birds, such as an owl or a parrot, and with animals.[48]

Unravelling the Mystery of the Hairpin Goddess

The unusual juxtaposition of a goddess with weapons immediately leads us to think of Durgā or Nidrā, who are associated with various weapons in their hymns of praise. The Metropolitan Museum curators reasonably suggested that this might be an early form of Durgā, who, prior to the discovery of these images — this one dated at the 1st century CE — has no known representations until the 2nd century CE, the dates typically assigned to the earliest

Kuṣāṇa period imagery.[49] The curators suggest that the fans held by attendants in the plaques are made of peacock feathers and note that, in later examples, coins appear to flow from the goddess's hand, a gesture evocative of bestowing boons. This aligns with early hymns where Durgā is repeatedly described as a boon-granter. The flowing coins recall modern depictions of Lakṣmī, with whom Durgā is sometimes identified.

Bautze (1995, 14) marginalizes the interpretation that these plaques represent Durgā, because he notes that the images are also often associated with sheaves of grain and a string of pearls. He notes that images of Durgā do not typically appear until the 2nd century CE, and the martial nature of these figures is not evident because the weapons are ornaments. Moreover, although depicted as beautiful, Durgā is not typically erotic, although she is seductive to demons, he suggests, which seems to contradict his position. He points out that without the weapon ornaments the images may simply represent other attractive females, as found in earlier figurines, from sites such as at Mathurā.

Notable among Bautze's reasonable appraisals is that the goddess is "adorned" with what may be upraised weapons, rather than portrayed as wielding them. In the DStv of the Mbh and the PN-s1 of the HV, we find noteworthy correspondences with these images, and not exclusively because of their association with weapons. In the DStv, the goddess is described as having two upraised broad or long arms (*vipulau bāhū*) (l. 18) and swelling breasts and hips (*pīnaśroṇi-payodharā*) (l. 13), just like the figure in the Chandraketugarh plaques. In reference to the Tamluk goddess plaque, J. C. Harle and Andrew Topsfield (1987, 7) note that the arms are "plump and sensuously modelled" in contrast to her legs. Wide, long, or thick (*vipula*) arms is undoubtedly an unusual characteristic for a woman and is therefore certainly a non-trivial characteristic. *Vipula* also translates as abundant or numerous, meanings which have implications later in our discussion. However, in the DStv *vipula* is presented in the dual form (*vipulau*), clearly indicating that two of the broad arms are upraised. Significantly, the DStv verses on the goddess's weapons and ornaments do not explicitly say that she carries them in her hands, although Coburn (1984, 269) suggests "carrying" as a possible translation. That linguistic ambiguity in such hymns may well be why the ornaments alluded to eventually came to be represented as being "held" by the goddess. The two DStv verses describing these attributes run together, without any verb indicating "to carry in one's hands." Instead, she is described as being immaculate among women (*strīviśuddhā*) on earth (*bhuvi*) (l. 19), having a platter (or vessel) (*pātrī*), a lotus (*paṅkajī*) and a bell (*ghaṇṭī*) (l. 19), and a noose (*pāśam*), a bow (*dhanur*), a great discus (*mahācakram*), and assorted weapons (*vividhāny āyudhāni*) (l. 20) and adorned or decorated (*vibhūṣitā*) with large, earrings for her ears (*kuṇḍalābhyāṃ supūrṇābhyāṃ karṇābhyām*) (l. 21) . Let us cite these verses in Sanskrit for clarity.[50]

> *0011 namo 'stu varade kṛṣṇe kumāri brahmacāriṇi*
> *0012 bālārkasadṛśākāre pūrṇacandranibhānane*

> 0013 *caturbhuje caturvaktre* **pīnaśroṇipayodhare**
> 0014 **mayūrapicchavalaye keyūrāṅgadadhāriṇi**
> 0015 *bhāsi devi yathā padmā nārāyaṇaparigrahaḥ*
> 0016 *svarūpaṃ brahmacaryaṃ ca viśadaṃ tava khecari*
> 0017 *kṛṣṇacchavisamā kṛṣṇā saṃkarṣaṇasamānanā*
> 0018 *bibhratī* **vipulau bāhū** *śakradhvajasamucchrayau*
> 0019 **pātrī ca paṅkajī ghaṇṭī strīviśuddhā** *ca yā* **bhuvi**
> 0020 **pāśaṃ dhanur mahācakraṃ vividhāny āyudhāni** *ca*
> 0021 **kuṇḍalābhyāṃ supūrṇābhyāṃ karṇābhyāṃ** *ca*
>   **vibhūṣitā**
> 0022 *candravispardhinā devi mukhena tvaṃ virājase*
> 0023 **mukuṭena vicitreṇa keśabandhena śobhinā**
> 0024 **bhujaṃgābhogavāsena śroṇisūtreṇa rājatā**
> 0025 **vibhrājase cābaddhena bhogeneveha mandaraḥ**
> 0026 **dhvajena śikhipicchānām ucchritena virājase**
> 0027 *kaumāraṃ vratam āsthāya tridivaṃ pāvitaṃ tvayā*
> 0028 *tena tvaṃ stūyase devi tridaśaiḥ pūjyase 'pi ca*
> 0029 *trailokyarakṣaṇārthāya mahiṣāsuranāśini*
> 0030 *prasannā me suraśreṣṭhe dayāṃ kuru śivā bhava*
> 0031 *jayā tvaṃ vijayā caiva saṃgrāme ca jayapradā*
> 0032 *mamāpi vijayaṃ dehi varadā tvaṃ ca sāmpratam*
> 0033 *vindhye caiva nagaśreṣṭhe tava sthānaṃ hi śāśvatam*
> 0034 *kāli kāli mahākāli sīdhumāṃsapaśupriye*
> 0035 *kṛtānuyātrā bhūtais tvaṃ varadā kāmacāriṇi*

Importantly, she is said to have an upraised standard (*dhvajena*) of peacock tail feathers (*śikhipicchānām*) (l. 26) as well as wrist bracelets of peacock feathers (*mayūrapicchavalaye*) (l. 14), both of which are frequently depicted on the plaques. The relatively unusual and distinctive adornment of peacock tail feather bracelets, with designs that resemble the peacock tail feather standards, are unmistakable features of the depictions and offer solid evidence towards identifying this goddess with a *devī* of the sort praised in the DStv. But there is much more. Durgā in the DStv is described as having an armlet (*keyūrāṅga-dadhāriṇi*) (l. 14), also evident on the plaque. She has two ample earrings (*kuṇḍalābhyāṃ supūrṇābhyāṃ*) (l. 21), a diadem that is variegated (*mukuṭena vicitreṇa*) (l. 23), and a hair-band or braided hair (*keśabandhena*) (l. 23) (alternately, a hair-band that is a variegated diadem), all of which are evident on the terracotta image. The earrings on these goddesses are often pronounced in their size and decoration, frequently with one shown frontally and the other laterally, and align very well with the adjective *supūrṇa*, which means full or richly adorned. Also significantly, she is said have an opulent hip-belt (*śroṇisūtreṇa rājatā*) garment (*vāsa*) of (or "like") the coils (*ābhoga*) of serpents (*bhujaṃga*) (*bhujaṃgābhogavāsena*) (l. 24). This is exactly the appearance of the coiled belt around her hips on the dress that she is wearing. These verses have been differently translated by others, which is perhaps why the relationship has not been recognized.[51] Reinforcing this image, the next line describes her as radiant (*vibhrāja*) like Mount Mandara bound (*ābaddha*) with serpentine coils (*bhoga*) (line 25).[52]

Similarly, in the PN-s1 of the HV, the goddess is depicted as having ample arms (*vipulān bāhūn*) (47.39), having aloft (*udyamya*, which does not necessarily mean holding up with one's arms, but which could be construed that way) a three-pointed spear and gold-hilted sword (*triśikhaṃ śūlam udyamya khaḍgaṃ ca kanakatsarum*), an immaculate lotus and a vessel filled with honey (*pātrīṃ ca pūrṇāṃ madhunaḥ paṅkajaṃ ca sunirmalam*) (47.40), with a necklace shining like the rays of the moon on her breast (*śaśiraśmiprakāśena hāreṇorasi rājatā*) (47.41), with her two ears ornamented with heavenly earrings (*divyakuṇḍalapūrṇābhyāṃ*) (47.42), with a face that rivals the moon (*candrasāpatnyabhūtena tvaṃ mukhena virājitā*) (47.42), with a variegated diadem, braided hair (47.43), and arms like iron bars that sound like a coiled serpent (*bhujagābhoganirghoṣair bāhubhiḥ parighopamaiḥ*) (47.43). Alternate translations of *bhujagābhoganirghoṣaiḥ* could be "the screech/sound (*nirghoṣa*) of a snake (*bhujaga*) eater/enjoyer (*ābhoga*) (i.e., an owl or peacock) or "the sound (*nirghoṣa*) of an unfurling (*ābhoga*) snake (*bhujaga*)," or just the opposite "noiseless as an unfurling snake," since *nirghoṣa* can mean "soundless." It is worth noting that the reference to her arms here is ambiguous, because in the paean Viṣṇu simply states that she has broad or numerous arms (*vipulān bāhūn*), which resemble (*upamā*) his own arms on earth (*mama bāhūpamān bhuvi*) (47.39). Since this is not in the dual number (which would be *bāhau*), but a straight plural, it likely does not refer to the two-armed form as in the Kṛṣṇa *avatāra*, but the four-armed earthly form, in which Viṣṇu is typically depicted. Importantly, she has a standard of peacock feathers nearby (*dhvajena śikhibarhāṇām ucchritena samīpataḥ*) and is resplendent with a bracelet made from peacock tails (*aṅgajena mayūrāṇām aṅgadena ca bhāsvatā*) (47.44). She is called Kauśikī and is described as a boon-giver (*varadā*) (47.50). For the sake of convenience, the entire PN-s1 is cited in Sanskrit below, with the relevant verses and phrases mentioned above in bold print.[53]

> *tatas tvāṃ gṛhya caraṇe śilāyāṃ nirasiṣyati* /
> *nirasyamānā gagane sthānaṃ prāpsyasi śāśvatam* //
>   HV_47.38 //
> *macchavīsadṛśī kṛṣṇā saṃkarṣaṇasamānanā* /
> **bibhratī vipulān bāhūn mama bāhūpamān bhuvi** //
>   HV_47.39 //
> **triśikhaṃ śūlam udyamya khaḍgaṃ ca kanakatsarum** /
> **pātrīṃ ca pūrṇāṃ madhunaḥ paṅkajaṃ ca sunirmalam** //
>   HV_47.40 //
> *vasānā mecakaṃ kṣaumaṃ pītenottaravāsasā* /
> **śaśiraśmiprakāśena hāreṇorasi rājatā** // **HV_47.41** //
> **divyakuṇḍalapūrṇābhyāṃ śravaṇābhyāṃ vibhūṣitā** /
> **candrasāpatnyabhūtena tvaṃ mukhena virājitā** //
>   HV_47.42 //

mukuṭena tricakreṇa keśabandhena śobhitā /
bhujagābhoganirghoṣair bāhubhiḥ parighopamaiḥ //
HV_47.43 //
dhvajena śikhibarhāṇām ucchritena samīpataḥ /
aṅgajena mayūrāṇām aṅgadena ca bhāsvatā // HV_47.44 //
kīrṇā bhūtagaṇair ghorair mannideśānuvartinī /
kaumāraṃ vratam āsthāya atridivaṃ tvaṃ gamiṣyasi //
HV_47.45 //
tatra tvāṃ śatadṛk śakro matpradiṣṭena karmaṇā /
abhiṣekeṇa divyena daivataiḥ saha yokṣyate // HV_47.46 //
tatraiva tvāṃ bhaginyarthe grahiṣyati sa vāsavaḥ /
kuśikasya tu gotreṇa kauśikī tvaṃ bhaviṣyasi // HV_47.47 //
sa te vindhye nagaśreṣṭhe sthānaṃ dāsyati śāśvatam /
tataḥ sthānasahasrais tvaṃ pṛthivīṃ śobhayiṣyasi //
HV_47.48 //
tataḥ sumbhanisumbhau ca dānavau nagacāriṇau /
tau ca kṛtvā manasi māṃ sānugau nāśayiṣyasi // HV_47.49 //
trailokyacāriṇī sā tvaṃ bhuvi satyopayācitā /
bhaviṣyasi mahābhāge varadā kāmarūpiṇī // HV_47.50 //
kṛtānuyātrā bhūtais tvaṃ nityaṃ māṃsabalipriyā /
tithau navamyāṃ pūjāṃ ca prāpsyase sapaśukriyām //
HV_47.51 //
ye ca tvāṃ matprabhāvajñāḥ praṇamiṣyanti mānavāḥ /
na teṣāṃ durlabhaṃ kiṃcit putrato dhanato 'pi vā //
HV_47.52 //
kāntāreṣv avasannānāṃ magnānāṃ ca mahārṇave /
dasyubhir vā niruddhānāṃ tvaṃ gatiḥ paramā nṛṇām //
HV_47.53 //
tvaṃ siddhiḥ śrīr dhṛtiḥ kīrtir hrīr vidyā saṃnatir matiḥ /
saṃdhyā rātriḥ prabhā nidrā kālarātris tathaiva ca //
HV_47.54 //

Clearly, the PN-s1, like the DStv, also provides notable resemblances to the Devī depicted on the Chandraketugarh plaques. She has broad and strong arms, distinctive earrings, necklace, and hairstyle, is associated with upraised weapons (a three-pointed spear and sword hilt) and objects (such as a lotus and a platter (*patrim*)). Could one or all the items in the goddess's hair on the Chandraketugarh plaques be the hilt of a sword? In certain plaques they could be construed that way. If the hairpins are like swords or spears, perhaps the protruding portions of the hairpins could be construed as decorative grips on a hilt together with weapon-like pommels, although this strikes me as somewhat far-fetched.

Notably, this hymn also describes the goddess as having a hair-band or bound/braided hair (*keśabandhena*). The goddesses on the Chandraketugarh plaques similarly feature braids across their foreheads, although some scholars interpret these as bead strings (Haque 2001, 130; Sengupta et al. 2007, 61). Most strikingly, the goddess is associated with a raised standard of peacock feathers and a peacock feather bracelet. The Metropolitan Museum plaque (figure 3.3) depicts attendants holding large peacock feather fans or flags, while the bracelets worn by the goddess bear markings suggestive of peacock feathers. Although ornate bracelets with peacock feather motifs are common in these plaques, definitive identification of the material remains challenging.

Typically, most of the hairpin goddess plaques that have been found only depict the goddess. However, another noteworthy, large, detailed plaque providing more context, such as the one at the Metropolitan Museum, depicts next to the goddess a tall, highly decorated column, which appears to be topped with a peacock (Haque 2001, 143, Pl. C89). Haque writes that the column "shows the *ghata*-base on a stepped pedestal, octagonal shaft and the bell-shaped fluted capital with winged addorsed lions above the abacus. On the top of it is a squatting dwarf caryatid with a pedestal on its head supported at two ends by his two hands, probably for the peacock" (2001, 130). Although the peacock may simply be one of several birds that decorate the top of the plaque, its position on another plaque fragment (Haque 2001, 144, Pl. C97), clearly illustrates that the peacock is perched atop the column. This leads Haque (2001, 131) to have designated it a *māyūrastambha* (peacock post or column). Another example of the peacock topping the freestanding column includes one reproduced in Sengupta et al (2007, 82, Accession Number 01.08). This peacock column is a rather distinctive feature to depict beside the goddess, in the few examples that we have available.

I have proposed that the DStv or DStv* likely influenced the PN-s1. More importantly, both hymns reference a goddess whose features bear striking similarities to the goddess depicted on the Chandraketugarh plaques. While the PN-s1 does not explicitly mention Durgā, it addresses the goddess Nidrā, who is said to be renowned as Kauśikī. However, verse 47.53 of the PN-s1, identical to DStv (l. 40–41), states:

> Of those who are lost in dreary forests, and of those who are
> sunk in the great ocean,
> Or of men held up by thieves, you are the supreme refuge.

These qualities of providing refuge are quintessentially associated with Durgā, as seen in her earliest descriptions, even preceding the DStv. Although the PN-s1 does not name Durgā as the goddess with the peacock standard, feather bracelets, weapons, lotus, jar, necklace, and other attributes, it vividly describes a goddess closely aligned with Durgā as explicitly named in the DStv.

The Chandraketugarh plaques, depicting a goddess with distinctive features described in the DStv and PN-s1, suggest these hymns could have been composed close to the plaques' time of production, typically dated no later than the 3rd century CE, and often earlier. This assertion is bolstered by the scarcity of similar goddess depictions (e.g., with peacock standards and bracelets) beyond the 6th century CE, particularly outside North India, the likely region of the Mbh and HV composition. Ancient hymns, such as the DStv, may endure even as their iconographic references fade. However, it is unlikely that such hymns would have been composed centuries after the decline of such distinctive iconographic attributes. Therefore, based on archeological evidence from the Chandraketugarh terracottas and the likely composition periods of the epics, it is plausible that the DStv or a similar paean to a Durgā-like goddess was composed as early as the 2nd century BCE and not much later than the 2nd or 3rd centuries CE.

Naming the Chandraketugarh Goddess

It is plausible that the peacock feather goddess with upraised weapons depicted on the Chandraketugarh plaques was a precursor to the Durgā/Kālī or Nidrā/Kauśikī eulogized in the early epic hymns. Worshippers at the time of the DStv and PN-s1 composition may well have identified the goddess depicted on these plaques with Durgā/Kālī/Nidrā/Kauśikī, given the overlap in their attributes. Could such a widely revered goddess, represented across a vast region, simply vanish from memory or be intentionally disregarded? Perhaps. Yet, it is more likely that her name and characteristics endured within the early hymns, even as she was assimilated into the personas of other goddesses (or gods). This invites the question: What might the name of the peacock-braceleted goddess with the peacock standard have been? Exploring this hypothesis, as others have done, remains critical.

Although the DStv and PN-s1 share similarities, the PN-s1 does not mention Durgā/Kālī, instead presenting Nidrā as attaining fame under the name Kauśikī, linked to Indra. The PN-s1 associates Kauśikī with the Vindhyas and notes her widespread cult (l. 48). While the name Kauśikī is absent from the DStv, it appears in the Durgā Stotra (DSto) (l. 15) and the second stratum of the PN (PN-s2) (l. 1). Over time, the myths of Durgā/Kālī and Kauśikī/Nidrā fused, particularly through their association with the Vaiṣṇava Kṛṣṇa/Kaṃsa myth cycle. Both the DStv and DSto connect the goddess with the buffalo. The DStv calls her Durgā and Kālī (l. 35), eulogizing her as the "Destroyer of the Demon Mahiṣa" (l. 29) and describing her as four-armed and four-faced (l. 13). Early terracottas from Mathurā during the Kuṣāṇa period depict a likely Durgā or proto-Durgā as a four-armed goddess subduing a buffalo, which we will examine in the next chapter. By contrast, the Chandraketugarh plaques consistently depict a two-armed goddess, unconnected to a buffalo demon, suggesting she may have been Kauśikī. Through the PN-s1 and PN-s2 of the HV, Kauśikī appears to have been absorbed into the Vaiṣṇava fold.

Interestingly, the PN-s1 likens Kauśikī's arms to Viṣṇu's four-armed form (HV 47.38), which could indicate a broader association with multiple arms. It is plausible that the DStv reflects a goddess cult closer to Mathurā and western regions, while the PN-s1 reflects one centered in the Vindhyas. The replication of themes and verbatim verses between the hymns suggests interaction and eventual fusion of these two goddess traditions.

Bihani Sarkar (2017, 61–65) does not refer to these images at all, seeing the first instances of images aligned with Nidrā as evolved from the Mbh and HV hymns in the Viṣṇu-Durgās of the Pallava period in the 7th century as found in Mahābalipuram. She does propose (albeit cautiously) that the buffalo-slaying images from Mathurā, discussed in the next chapter, are Nidrā-Kauśikī, in part because the goddess carries the trident and sword, as mentioned in the HV. She acknowledges that "a link can be established between the *Harivaṃśa*'s description of Nidrā-Kālarātri and the image of the Kuṣāṇa warrior goddess" (2017, 65). I believe an early composition date for the DStv or DStv* provides possible evidence for such a link closer to the time when it was occurring and will discuss this further in the next chapter.

Yokochi (2004, 8n14) also does not discuss the hairpin goddesses. She distinguishes among Durgā in the Vedas (e.g., *Taittirīya Āraṇyaka*, Rātrī Khila), the origin of the buffalo-slaying goddess (e.g., the Mathurā plaques discussed in the next chapter), and the "warrior goddess," which is the focus of her work on Kauśikī-Vindhyavāsinī.[54] Roughly, she proposes (2004, 13–16) that the Warrior Goddess was a fusion of the buffalo slaying goddess with Vindhyavāsinī. This Warrior Goddess was absorbed into the Śaiva fold, as a Consort Goddess, Pārvatī. This Consort Goddess, she proposes, ultimately evolved into the Supreme Goddess as expressed in the DM. I am partly aligned with this perspective, but do not discount the existence of a Great Goddess or even a "Supreme Deity as Goddess" cult from an earlier period prior to the PN-s1 of the HV, a point that she rejects (2004, 10), but which was proposed by Coburn (1984, 241) and Charlotte Vaudeville (1975). More on this later, as I propose that goddesses such as Anāhitā, Nanā, and others provided an early nucleus of Supreme Deity as Goddess worship around which goddesses such as Kauśikī, Kālī, Jayā, Vijayā, Pārvatī, and Durgā could develop, allowing Caṇḍī/Caṇḍikā/ Durgā to emerge as the Supreme Deity as Goddess of the DM.[55]

Of the various viable names for the hairpin goddess, Kauśikī is compelling because of her association with the peacock, which is depicted on her standard and on her bracelets (HV 47.44). Even today, Vindhyavāsinī, the main goddess of the Vindhyas, is associated with birds, and her black stone image in the famed temple at Vindhyachal portrays her as bird-faced.[56] Pertinently, the local temple authorities plainly identify the image as Kauśikī. They, and most devotees, now also routinely identify her directly with the Kṛṣṇa-Kaṃsa myth cycle (Humes 1996, 75n3). Nidrā, when connected with Kauśikī in the PN-s1, is depicted as flying to the Vindhyas after her episode with Kaṃsa. With the Kaṃsa myth centered in Mathurā, we have almost an explicit link between the goddess of the Mathurā region (the buffalo slayer, or Durgā?) and the goddess of Vindhyachal (Kauśikī?). Humes (1996, 75n3) notes that Kauśikī is the feminine form of Kauśika, which typically means an owl. Even so, the term *kauśika* may be used for any bird that is an eater of snakes. This includes the peacock, which is equally associated with this habit, as well as the owl and the parrot, birds that are also depicted on the Chandraketugarh plaques with the goddess.

There are images on the Chandraketugarh plaques that depict a goddess with wings, but these do not appear to have weapon hairpins.[57] Kauśikī's image at Vindhyachal temple is likely of much later provenance than the time when the HV's PN-s1 was composed. It has distinctly Vaiṣṇava characteristics, because like Viṣṇu images she is portrayed with four arms and holds similar items. The four arms align with what might be inferred by HV.47.39. One hand is in the *abhayā mudrā* ("fear-not gesture"), while she holds a conch shell, discus, and mace in the others. In a Durgā-like feature, however, she is portrayed atop a lion mount.

The PN-s1 portrays Kauśikī as dark-complexioned (l. 39) and surrounded by throngs of spirits (*kīrṇā bhūtagaṇair*, l. 45; *kṛtānuyātrā bhūtais*, l. 51). Notably, the image of Vindhyavāsinī, identified as Kauśikī, is crafted from black stone rather than adorned with a golden mask. The terracotta plaques from Chandraketugarh further align with this depiction, frequently featuring squat, pot-bellied, or deformed *yakṣa*-like figures near the goddess. The Tamluk plaque in the Ashmolean Museum vividly illustrates this connection, showing finely crafted *bhūtas* (or *yakṣas?*) on the goddess's skirt below her hip belt, reinforcing the hymn's description of her being surrounded by spirits. Kauśikī in the PN-s1 is linked to offerings of flesh and the sacrifice of wild beasts on the ninth lunar day (l. 51), practices still observed at the Vindhyavāsinī temple. The PN-s2 identifies both the ninth day of the dark lunar fortnight and the eleventh day of the bright lunar fortnight as particularly beloved to her. By then, Kauśikī had been merged with figures such as Kātyāyanī, Durgā, Jayā, and Vijayā. This association persists, as confirmed by my field studies in Banāras, where the eleventh day of the waxing fortnight during the spring and autumn Navarātras remains a significant occasion for worshippers at Vindhyavāsinī.

In the earliest hymns, Kauśikī is associated with slaying the demons Sumbha and Nisumbha in the Vindhya mountains (PN-s1, l. 48–49). Centuries later, the DM and other Purāṇic texts reinterpret her name as derived from *kośa* (sheath), linked to her emergence from Pārvatī. Earlier, in *Vālmīki's Rāmāyaṇa*, Kauśikī is portrayed as a river goddess, also known as Satyavatī and the elder sister of the sage Kauśika (Viśvāmitra), son of Gādhi. The Mbh (1.65.30–32; 3.82.124; 3.85.9) also connects Viśvāmitra to the creation of the Kauśikī river, where he performed austerities and gave it another name, Pārā (Goldman and Sutherland 1985, 349n8). The transformation of river goddesses into broader divine personas has precedent in Hinduism, as seen with Sarasvatī (Rohlman 2018). The Chandraketugarh goddess, if identified as Kauśikī, retains possible riverine associations. Notable motifs include the fish-topped standard on the Metropolitan Museum plaque and the *makara* (sea monster) buckle on the sash across the goddess's torso on the Tamluk plaque.

The ancient Kauśikī mentioned in the epics is likely the river currently known as the Kośī, whose headwaters flow from some of the world's highest peaks, namely Mount Everest (first highest), Kangchenjunga (third highest) and Lhotse (fourth highest). The Kośī is routinely identified as such in most contemporary studies.[58] The Kośī flows through Nepal into Bihar and eventually joins the Gaṅgā. Its tempestuous tendency to flash flood has earned it the epithet the "Sorrow of Bihar." The Gaṅgā is regarded as Kauśikī's elder sister. But while in mythic accounts the Gaṅgā's descent to earth is relatively gentle, broken by her entanglement in Śiva's matted locks — a point of great significance that stands in contrast to other rivers — Kauśikī's nature is unpredictable and tempestuous. The river can rise as much as thirty feet in a day (Hill 2008, 225).

An indigo planter described a flood in 1875 CE, saying: "Miles of rich land, once clothed in luxuriant crops of rice, indigo, and waving grain, are now barren reaches of burning sand . . . . It was a scene of utter waste and desolation" (Inglis 1878, 340–432). This account underscores the dual nature of the Kośī river — its fertile floodplain contrasts sharply with its destructive potential. Annual flooding, with severe episodes in the past, likely contributed to the ambivalent persona of a riverine goddess, embodying both beneficence and destructiveness. Some of the goddess's unusual attributes, such as broad or numerous arms (*vipulān bāhūn* can mean both full or multiple arms), or those described as noisy or quiet (*nirghoṣa* has an ambivalent meaning), akin to a coiled serpent, may stem from riverine symbolism — perhaps reflecting rushing tributaries or the river's multiplicity.

D. Srinivasan (1997) explored the origins of multiple arms in Hindu iconography, analyzing early goddess imagery, albeit inconclusively. This symbolism could link the multiplicity of arms (or heads) in Hindu deities to their riverine origins. River goddesses in Hinduism often embody ambivalence — fertile providers essential for agriculture but also agents of destruction. Their flood zones, crucial for sediment deposits, their multiple tributaries resembling appendages, and their headwaters emerging from cloud-covered peaks all reinforce this connection. While tangential to this study, such patterns suggest a fertile avenue for further exploration.

Extrapolating this riverine interpretation, we are led to wonder about Kauśikī's association with the destruction of the demons Sumbha and Nisumbha. Might these demon kings and their subjects refer to groups of marginalized peoples that were destroyed in a particularly consequential deluge? The term Śumbhadeśa occurs in Kalidāsa's *Raghuvaṃśa* and other writings, such as the Buddhist Jātakas, and refers to a prosperous, populous country.[59] True, in the PN-s1 (l. 48) these demons' abode is said to be the Vindhya mountains, Kauśikī's abode, and not some lowland region prone to devastation through flood waters. Even so, the locale of the Vindhyas was very ambiguous nearly two millennia ago, as was the location of ancient Śumbhadeśa. Some place the latter within the floodplains of the Hoogly (Bhāgīrathī) river, where the towns of Paṇḍua, Saptagram, and Tribeni are now situated.[60] The Kauśikī (Kośī) does feed almost directly into the same floodplain. When the PN-s1 speaks of Kauśikī causing the earth to shine with a thousand places (*tataḥ sthānasahasrais tvaṃ pṛthivīṃ śobhay- iṣyasi*) (l. 48), might this simply refer to her widely dispersed flood waters? One could also infer the river's flowing waters, flood pools, irrigation channels, and other such sites serving as loci for places of worship, around which shrines and temples developed.

One of the sources of the Kauśikī River is Mt. Kangchenjunga (8,586 m), once regarded as the world's highest mountain until 1852 CE.[61] The mountain's name derives from the Tibetan *gangs chen mdzod lnga* ("Five Treasures of the Great Snow"), referencing its five peaks. Sikkimese traditions identify these treasures as salt, gold and turquoise, religious books and wealth-increasing jewels, weapons and armor, and grains and medicines (Nebesky-Wojkowitz 1976, 20). The enigmatic hair ornaments on the Chandraketugarh goddess, if she represents the divinized river Kauśikī, may symbolize these five treasures, some of which are weapons — perhaps an allusion to her headwaters emanating from Kangchenjunga. Notably, some Chandraketugarh plaques replace the hairpins with floral herbs or grain stalks, further associating the goddess with fertility and abundance. However, such interpretations must remain speculative.

When the Kośī floods, even today, it can change its course, pick up on old channels, and, if conjoined with flooding from the Gaṅgā river basin, submerge regions from as far west as Vindhyachal and east to Tamluk.[62] The Kauśikī River, the third largest tributary of the Gaṅgā after the Yamuna and Ghaghara (Jain et al. 2007), would have been well-known in ancient Magadha and neighboring kingdoms such as Kāśī and Aṅga. Its dual nature — beneficent yet unpredictably destructive — likely necessitated regular sacrificial and placatory offerings. This aligns with the provenance of the Chandraketugarh goddess plaques, which originate from a wide region extending from Tāmralipti to Mathurā. The prominence of Devī worship in this area is attested by Daṇḍin (7th–8th century CE), who, in the *Daśakumāracarita*, mentions a goddess celebration at Dāmalipta (Tāmralipti or Tamluk) in honor of Vindhyavāsinī, the goddess of the Vindhya mountains (Kale 1986, 104, 148).

Rival names proposed for the goddess depicted on the Chandraketugarh plaques include Kātyāyanī, Jayā, Vijayā, and others from the PN-s2, the DSto, and the later HV hymns. However, these names are less prominent as primary epithets in the hymns and bear fewer direct correlations to the plaques' features. Kauśikī emerges as a strong contender for the goddess's name, as her attributes in early epic hymns align with those on the plaques, and with her characteristics later assimilated into Nidrā, Durgā, Kālī, and related deities. However, a significant challenge to this identification is her consistent depiction with two arms, whereas the PN-s1 and the DStv describe goddesses with multiple arms.

Connection to Another Important River Goddess

Another viable contender for the name of the Chandraketugarh plaque goddess is Āryā. This is because in some circulating versions the PN-s2 begins when the PN-s1 ends and the narration is passed back from Viṣṇu to Vaiśampāyana, the narrator of the HV, who recites what he calls the Āryā Stava. He also calls the goddess Nārāyaṇī, queen of the three worlds (see Sanskrit verses from HV 47.54 cited above). The PN-s2 hymn proper begins with the verse:

> *āryā kātyāyanī devī kauśikī brahmacāriṇī* / HV_App.I, 8.1 /
> *jananī siddhasenasya durgā vīrā mahātapāḥ* // HV_App.I, 8.2
> //
> (You are) Āryā, Kātyāyanī, goddess Kauśikī, celibate one /
> Mother of the divine army, brave Durgā, great ascetic.

The term *āryā* could simply be rendered as "respectable" or "noble," but it is evidently picked by those who refer to this insertion as the Āryā Stava to evoke a connection to the goddess Āryā. Was the PN-s2, and its naming of the goddess as Āryā, inserted in recognition that the PN-s1 was in fact dedicated to Āryā, or a goddess derived from or related to Āryā? If so, who might this goddess Āryā be?

The *Aṅgavijjā*, a Jain text dated at the 4th century CE, refers to Ajja-mahā (the great Āryā), and the *Mānava Gṛhya Sūtra* 2.13 to 2.15, dated between the 5th and 3rd century BCE, refers to a festival to Great Āryā, the mother of Skanda (White 2003, 39–40n83, 84).[63] In the above verse, *siddhasena* could be translated as Skanda, who heads an army, making the phrase *jananī siddhasenasya* mean "Mother of Skanda." Thus, labeling the PN-s2 as the Āryā Stava might have been an attempt to assimilate Skanda's cult more firmly into that of the goddess, who is progressively identified as his mother, Skandamātā. That identification is also explicit by the time the DSto+ was inserted into the Mbh. As Skandamātā ("The Mother of Skanda") (DSto, l. 22), Durgā continues her associations with the peacock, which is linked to both those deities.

A more intriguing and compelling connection, however, is to the goddess Anāhitā, who appears in the Zoroastrian tradition. In writings from the *Avesta*, she originally appears as Arədvī Sūrā Anāhitā (also known as Ardwīsūr Anāhīd). While Sūrā and Anāhitā can be generic terms meaning "mighty" and "pure/ undefiled" respectively, and also applied to other deities, it is Arədvī, which perhaps originally meant "the moist," that better indicates the distinctive feature of the goddess (Ustinova 1999, 85n39). Although Arədvī has homophonic resonances with Arya devī ("Goddess of the Aryas"), where Arya (*airiia*) in the *Avesta* refers to the ethnic group distinguished from the non-Arya (*anairiia*), there is no other linguistic support for this derivation. Arədvī has also been interpreted as meaning "to flow," and may well be the Vedic Sarasvatī.[64] The goddess Arədvī Sūrā Anāhitā is primarily praised in Yašt 5, one of the *Avesta's* longest hymns.[65]

Yašts are hymns composed in the Younger Avestan language but include potentially ancient verses. Although Yašt 5 is entitled the Ābān Yašt or Hymn to the Waters, it primarily honors the goddess Arədvī Sūrā Anāhitā, closely linked to water. The hymn portrays the goddess (*yazatā*) as a beautiful, strong maiden associated with prosperity, fertility, and as a river. She flows from Mount Hukairya into the Vourukasha Sea (v. 3), the mythic source of all rivers. Mount Hukairya, the pinnacle of High Harā, is an *axis mundi* at the universe's center and the origin of the world's mountains (Eastburn 2011, 45). Arədvī Sūrā Anāhitā is described with thick arms adorned with beautiful armlets, and her numerous long bays and channels/outlets (v. 4–7). Each of her thousand outlets houses a palace with a hundred windows and a thousand columns (v. 101). Notably, she is clad in beaver skins (v. 129), rides a chariot pulled by clouds, wind, rain, and sleet (v. 120), and grants victory in battle while destroying enemies. She accepts sacrificial offerings, often of a hundred horses, a thousand oxen, and ten thousand lambs (e.g., v. 68, 72), acting as a boon-granting figure.

Yašt 5 is framed as an invitation from the Zoroastrian high god Ahura Mazdā to the prophet Zoroaster (Zarathustra, Zaraθuštra). Ahura Mazdā praises Anāhitā, stating she emanated from him (v. 7), and urges Zoroaster to sacrifice to her on his behalf (v. 1). However, Ahura Mazdā also claims to have made offerings to the goddess, asking for the boon that Zoroaster would accept his teachings, obey, and proselytize them. She granted this boon (v. 17–19). Thus, Arədvī Sūrā Anāhitā emerges as both a boon-granter to the highest Zoroastrian god and a being said to originate from him.

Before addressing the similarities between this Yašt and PN-s1, it is important to note that the *Avesta* and the *Ṛg Veda* were composed in closely related ancient languages. The *Avesta* includes material from various periods, with its earliest portions, the *Gāthās*, composed in Old Avestan. These are attributed to the prophet Zoroaster but are believed by followers of the Mazdean religion to have been created by the high god Ahura Mazdā and given to Zoroaster. Variants of Zoroastrianism dominated ancient Iran and its empires until the advent of Islam. The precise timing of Zoroaster's life remains uncertain. Most sources place him around 1000 BCE (Kellens 1987), although academic estimates range from 1750 BCE to 258 years before Alexander the Great (Shahbazi 1977). The latter date, from the Pahlavi tradition, places him just before the Achaemenid dynasty's rise under Cyrus the Great (r. 549–530 BCE) (Malandra 2009).

Yašt 5 in its current form appears to have been composed over a long period of time.[66] The oldest strata of the hymn (verses 3–5, 96, 132), likely pre-Zoroastrian in origin, celebrate the river goddess Arədvī Sūrā. Other verses (e.g., v. 1, 6–7, 94–95, 104–18) align more closely with Zoroastrian teachings, depicting Ahura Mazdā as the deity who created her and all other gods (*yazatas*) to aid in the cosmic battle between good and evil. This integration likely predates the Achaemenian period, during which Zoroastrianism and Ahura Mazdā's prominence were particularly strong (Boyce 1979, 61–62). Verses such as 123 to 128 suggest a priest describing a cultic statue of the goddess. Mary Boyce (1979) attributes these additions to the reign of Artaxerxes II (r. 404–359 BCE), when the Semitic goddess Anaïtis was syncretized with Arədvī Sūrā, and image worship was introduced. Anaïtis, potentially the goddess of Venus, was worshipped in Persia before Zoroastrianism and associated with the powerful Mesopotamian goddess Ištar (Ishtar), known as "the Lady." Ištar herself was a syncretic blend of figures such as the Sumerian Inanna and goddesses linked to love and war. The Greeks referred to her as Aphrodite Anaïtis (Boyce 1979, 61). Traits of Anaïtis and Inanna-Ištar seem to have fused with those of Arədvī Sūrā.

The most recent strata of Yašt 5 verses likely originate in the Sasanian period (224–651 CE), when the hymn transitioned from oral tradition to written text (Boyce 1982, 61). Boyce (1982, 61–62) suggests this occurred in the 4th century CE under Šāpūr II (r. 309–379 CE). These later verses include repetitions and borrowings from other hymns, amplifying the hymn and the goddess's stature (Boyce 1982, 61). Qaderi (2017) recently proposed that Anāhitā was the Mesopotamian goddess Antu/Annunit(um) ("skirmisher" or "martial one"), representing the war-like aspect of Akkadian Ištar and Sumerian Inanna. This goddess was incorporated into the Achaemenid pantheon and eventually merged with Arədvī Sūrā, an Iranian river goddess celebrated in the *Avesta's* Yašt 5. If Qaderi is correct, it underscores a dynamic fusion of a river goddess with a war goddess, paralleling the evolution of Kauśikī/Nidrā/Kālī in the HV's PN-s1.

Drawing comparisons between an Indo-Iranian *Avesta* hymn such as Yašt 5 with hymns from the Indian epics is not at all unreasonable. Significant portions of Yašt 5 were likely composed from the pre-Achaemenian up to the middle of the Sasanian period. Yašt 5 is one of the longest and certainly one of the most important *Avesta* hymns, since it was evidently utilized, added to, and edited for centuries. It continues to be used today in Mazdean worship.[67] This is similarly true of the Indian epic hymns — such as the DStv, which is still recited today. While their origins may not be as early as Yašt 5, they clearly demonstrate compositional layering over time. Additionally, the goddess Anāhitā was revered with a status comparable to that of Ahura Mazdā, the highest god in the Zoroastrian pantheon. Notably, Yašt 5 is a hymn dedicated to a goddess, used ritually during the same period that Indian epic goddess hymns under examination were being composed. The imperial conquests of the Achaemenians (550–330 BCE), Macedonians under Alexander (323 BCE), Mauryas (322–185 BCE), Seleucids (312–63 BCE), Śuṅgas (185–75 BCE), Kanvas (75–30 BCE), Parthians (247 BCE–224 CE), Kuṣāṇas (30–375 CE), Sasanians (224–651 CE), and Guptas (320–550 CE) created extensive cultural and regional overlaps. To dismiss the potential for mutual influences, cultural synergies, and transcultural interactions regarding their key divinities would be an oversight. Later, we will explore "out of India" influences in depictions of deities with multiple arms, a motif that appears distinctly South Asian in origin. Anāhitā was undoubtedly integrated into the Kuṣāṇa pantheon as the goddess Ardoxšo (Ardoxsho), evidenced by her appearance on their coinage. On these coins, she is portrayed with a cornucopia, reminiscent of the Greco-Roman goddess of fortune Tyche, who is often shown with a turreted crown symbolizing her role as a protector of cities (Pal 1986, 79).

When examining PN-s1, we observe that Viṣṇu adopts some features of Ahura Mazdā's persona in Yašt 5 by associating the goddess Nidrā/Kauśikī with himself and praising her in a manner that subordinates her to him. The many sacrifices offered to Anāhitā in Yašt 5 parallel the references in PN-s1, where Nidrā/Kauśikī delights in offerings of flesh and receives sacrifices of wild beasts (l. 51). Both hymns praise the goddesses' appearances, describing them adorned with earrings, radiant necklaces, and distinctive crowns. Both also function as boon-givers. In Yašt 5:132, Anāhitā is invoked to descend from the stars, echoing PN-s1, where Nidrā/Kauśikī ascends to the heavens for Indra's consecration. Heaven thus serves as an abode for both goddesses.

Notable similarities exist between Kauśikī's obscure riverine symbolism and that of Anāhitā. PN-s1 describes Nidrā/Kauśikī's arms as broad (l. 39) or resembling iron bars that rustle like snake coils (l. 43), while Yašt 5 portrays Arədvī Sūrā's arms as beautiful but thick as a horse's shoulder (5.7). Such imagery suggests a shared association with riverine goddesses. Kauśikī is said to reside on the Vindhyas, the best of mountains (l. 48), just as Arədvī Sūrā resides on Mount Hukairya (5.3). A PN-s1 verse states that Kauśikī will "cause the earth to shine with a thousand places," resonating with Yašt 5's description of Arədvī Sūrā's thousand bays and channels (5.4). Further, Yašt 5 elaborates that each channel contains a palace with a hundred windows, a thousand columns, and ten thousand balconies (5.101). These palaces, adorned with scented beds and pillows, lie along the goddess's flow as she descends from great heights (5.102). While it is unclear whether this refers to her presence in homes, shrines, or palaces near water, the imagery of a thousand resplendent places clearly ties her to her riverine nature.

Water remains central to goddess worship, with ponds, wells, springs, and rivers integral to shrines and temples, especially those sacred to goddesses. Kauśikī may also represent a riverine goddess whose features blended with those of Arədvī Sūrā Anāhitā as the latter's cult spread into the Indian subcontinent. Scholars have drawn parallels between Arədvī Sūrā Anāhitā and the Vedic goddess Sarasvatī (W. Malandra 1983, 119). Sarasvatī's attributes extended to other river goddesses, such as Gaṅgā and Yamuṇa, while all maintained their distinct identities. Similarly, aspects of Anāhitā's persona may have merged with conceptions of Kauśikī, who herself embodied traits of other goddesses tied to fortune, sovereignty, victory, and knowledge — qualities also inherent in Arədvī Sūrā Anāhitā. It is important to note that this riverine goddess trope may reflect a broadly shared tradition influenced across regions, rather than simply via an eastward vector of ideas.

Since Yokochi (2004) did not examine the hairpin goddess plaques, which likely date to before 300 CE and possibly as early as 300 BCE, she lacked evidence to support the existence of a Great Goddess or a Goddess as Supreme Deity cult in India (2004, 10). However, it is evident that fusions of Great Goddess traditions have long existed, encompassing figures such as Inanna-Ištar and other war goddesses, Anaïtis, Arədvī Sūrā, and the Kuṣāṇa Ardoxšo.

I propose the potential inclusion of the hairpin goddess, who might represent Kauśikī. Inanna, associated with the lion and sometimes depicted with wings and projecting weapons, offers a close, although distinct, iconographic parallel to the weapon-like hairpins on the Chandraketugarh plaques. These similarities, despite differences, suggest a shared visual language of power and martial prowess. The fusion of such goddesses' attributes, combined with those from the Indian subcontinent — discussed in subsequent chapters — may have contributed to the kernel of Great Goddess traditions, culminating in the Goddess as Supreme Deity of the DM. This hypothesis will be elaborated in the chapters that follow.

Although the origins of Anāhitā and Zoroastrianism remain somewhat obscure, both were embraced by the Persian Achaemenids. Zoroastrianism positioned Ahura Mazdā as the supreme deity, but Anāhitā was likely the most prominent goddess in its pantheon (Saadi-nejad 2021, 3). While Cyrus, Darius, Xerxes, and other Achaemenian rulers zealously promoted Ahura Mazdā's supremacy, inscriptions from the reign of Artaxerxes II (404–359 BCE) mention Anāhitā alongside Mithra and Ahura Mazdā as sources of his kingship (de Jong 1997, 271; Lecoq 1997, 269). This suggests that her worship persisted and eventually regained prominence. By the 3rd century CE, Anāhitā's headgear had become a symbol of nobility, worn by monarchs — a significant development for understanding later goddess iconography (Mosig-Walburg 1982, 31–37). More notably, Artaxerxes II is credited with establishing images of Anāhitā throughout his empire, a dramatic departure from traditional Persian practices. This was remarked upon by the Greek historian Herodotus (mid-5th century BCE) and the Babylonian writer Berosus, who lived during Alexander the Great's era (de Jong 1997, 92, 268, 270–74). Such actions underscore her enduring influence and the evolution of her role within the Zoroastrian religious framework.

Despite this evident proliferation of images of Arədvī Sūrā Anāhitā at the time of Artaxerxes II, none that can be unequivocally identified as her are to be found in Persia in the Achaemenian period, nor in the subsequent Hellenistic or Parthian period. She only emerges on the coins of the Kuṣāṇo-Sasanian (or Indo-Sasanian) kings Ardašīr I (180–242 CE) and Ardašīr II (r. 379-383 CE), and thereafter (e.g., Šāpūr (Shapur) I, Bahram II, Narseh, Hormozd II, Šāpūr (Shapur) III).[68] In one specimen of Ardašīr I, she holds a circular diadem with ribbons, and wears a distinctive crown with three large projections (Shenkar 2014, 253, fig. 26). Her role in conferring sovereignty is also attested to by Plutarch (*Lives, Artaxerxes*), whose biography of Artaxerxes II indicates that the monarch was initiated at a warrior goddess's temple. This goddess was most likely Anāhitā, although Athena and Ištar are other conjectures.[69] Ardašīr I's fierce devotion to Anāhitā is evident in his practice of beheading enemies and displaying their heads at her temple. Similarly, the Sasanian king Šāpūr II (309–379 CE) executed Christians in Pārs (Persia) and sent their heads to an Anāhitā temple for display — an honor she alone received among deities (Chaumont

1958, 159–60). A notable monumental relief at Naqš-e Rostam likely depicts Narseh (r. 293–302 CE) receiving kingship from Anāhitā, to whom he was personally devoted. In contrast, a later relief at Tāq-i Bustān portrays her (holding a water jug) in a secondary role to Ahura Mazdā, who bestows kingship on either Pērōz (459–484 CE) or Khosrow II (591–628 CE) (Boyce, Chaumont, et al. 1989, 1003–1011). The shifting status of Arədvī Sūrā Anāhitā relative to Ahura Mazdā, as well as the tension between iconic and aniconic worship, has been a recurring theme certainly since the time of Zoroaster. These dynamics will later be revisited in the context of Durgā and the Hindu pantheon in our study.

The paramount place of Anāhitā in the Zoroastrian pantheon, which continued through to Sasanian royalty — she is the only goddess mentioned in their inscriptions — suggests that she would probably have been depicted in more than their coinage and monumental reliefs, even if aniconic preferences periodically arose. This has led scholars to identify various figures depicted on Sasanian bronzes or silverware (such as pitchers and vases) as Anāhitā.[70] Although such identifications are plausible, definitive evidence linking these figures to Anāhitā is lacking. However, many of these representations feature haloes and portray the figures either nude or clothed in transparent garments. They are frequently depicted with birds such as doves and peacocks, and occasionally with birds of prey such as hawks (Hanaway 1982, 292). William Hanaway Jr. (1982, 293) highlights a Sasanian bronze tray (housed in the Staatliche Museen, Berlin) adorned with pairs of peacocks alternating with four water pitchers, encircled by a watercourse filled with fish — symbols associated with Anāhitā in her roles as a fertility and water goddess.

When comparing these symbols with those on the Chandraketugarh goddess plaques, notable similarities emerge. The Chandraketugarh goddess, like Arədvī Sūrā Anāhitā, is two-armed and associated with aquatic creatures such as fish or the *makara*. She is linked to the peacock or the owl, a bird of prey, sometimes holding an unidentified object that could be a water vessel and is dressed in diaphanous clothing. While neither the Sasanian figures nor the Chandraketugarh goddesses can be definitively identified, there are compelling symbolic affinities with Arədvī Sūrā Anāhitā. Despite her associations with warfare, blood sacrifice, and sovereignty, Anāhitā is generally depicted as two-armed and benign, emphasizing her riverine origins and boon-granting functions.

Nevertheless, there are significant differences between the descriptions of Arədvī Sūrā Anāhitā and the goddess in early Indian epic hymns. Arədvī Sūrā is described wearing a garment made of fine beaver (*baβra*) skins, shining like silver and gold (Yašt 5, v. 129), whereas Nidrā/Kauśikī in PN-s1 is clothed in a dark-blue linen garment with a white upper garment (l. 41). In PN-s2, she is said to wear bark yet is described as well-dressed (l. 18). While beavers were unknown in India, the word *baβra* is cognate with Sanskrit *babhru* ("reddish-brown, tawny"). In the DSto (l. 8), the goddess is referred to as *kṛṣṇapiṅgale* ("O black and reddish-brown/tawny one") and *kapile*, which may mean brown or tawny, or reference animals such as mice, dogs, or monkeys of that coloration. These descriptors might echo Arədvī Sūrā's beaver-pelt garment, although they lost relevance in the Indian context.

In the DStv (l. 24), the goddess wears a garment of snakes' hoods (Coburn 1984, 269), which could symbolically replace the beaver with the snake — an animal more familiar in India and associated with water. In the DSto (l. 15), the goddess is dressed in yellow, possibly evoking the silver and gold gleam of the beaver-pelt garment. Another striking difference lies in complexion. Arədvī Sūrā Anāhitā is described as white-skinned or having white arms (v. 7), while in the DStv (l. 11, 17) and PN-s1 (l. 39), Nidrā/Kauśikī is black. In the DSto, she is ambiguously "white one, black one" (*śvete kṛṣṇe*) (l. 17) or reddish-brown. The PN-s2 and texts such as PradH and AniH do not specify complexion, although by naming her Kālarātrī or Kālī, they imply dark skin. The tension in assigning her complexion — white in some contexts, dark or ruddy in others — may reflect symbolic variations tied to a river's changing state. A river can appear clear or white during the dry season and turn silty, dark, or reddish-brown during rainy season floods. This natural phenomenon might underlie the differing color attributes, connecting the goddess's imagery to the dynamic qualities of water.

In sum, our analysis of the so-called *yakṣī* plaques, which depict a female figure with hairpins resembling weapons, suggests they may represent a goddess of considerable renown. When correlated with the DStv (or DStv*) and PN-s1, which we have dated to roughly the same period (before 300 CE), notable symbolic parallels emerge, such as a peacock flag or standard, peacock bracelets, thick arms, a distinctive headdress, and uplifted weapons. These observations support the hypothesis that the hairpin goddess might be identified as Kauśikī, based on textual correlations. This goddess appears to represent a fusion of riverine and warrior attributes. Intriguingly, PN-s1 shares distinctive parallels with the Ābān Yašt, a Zoroastrian hymn to Arədvī Sūrā Anāhitā, herself a composite of river and war goddesses. Whether the hairpin goddess aligns more closely with Anāhitā (notably two-armed) or Kauśikī (notable for her peacock standard and earrings) remains an open question. In the Ābān Yašt, Ahura Mazdā appropriates the goddess's renown, a dynamic paralleled in PN-s1, where Viṣṇu assumes a similar role toward Nidrā/Kauśikī. More broadly, these correspondences suggest the potential existence of a Great Goddess tradition — even vying for a Goddess as Supreme Deity tradition — in northern India, particularly along the Gaṅgā river valley, in tension with other sectarian traditions such as Vaiṣṇavism. The interplay between goddess traditions in Central Asia and the Indian subcontinent remains central to this study. In the next section, we turn to early South Asian iconography of the buffalo-subduing goddess from Mathurā and its environs, a figure also hinted at in the DStv, DSto, and PN-s1.

Chapter 4

The Earliest Buffalo-Subduing Goddess Images

The next set of early images that we need to examine are of the type that become most firmly identified with and as Durgā. These are images of a deity subduing or slaying a buffalo, which I shall refer to as buffalo-subduing goddess images. These images are loosely referred to as Kuṣāṇa plaques since they have been generally dated to the Kuṣāṇa period and derive from regions of Kuṣāṇa influence. In this chapter, we shall look for correlations between these early buffalo-subduing goddess images and the early epic hymns (i.e., the DStv or DStv*, PN-s1, and DSto, in particular). Such correlations have been overlooked mostly because the Durgā Stava (DStv) and Durgā Stotra (DSto) have been allocated in composition to a later period, better aligned with the period of their possible insertion into the *Mahābhārata* (Mbh). By separating them from their frame verses and suggesting that they may have been composed much earlier, we are able to discern noteworthy correspondences between the goddess on the Kuṣāṇa plaques and the one described in the hymns.

An Indus Valley Precursor

Before proceeding with the Kuṣāṇa materials, it is worth noting at the outset that the earliest related image on the Indian subcontinent of a figure subduing a buffalo comes from an Indus Valley planoconvex tablet illustrated in figure 4.1a. It derives from the Mature Harappa 3C period (c. 2200–1900 BCE).

It shows a figure with a foot on the head of a water buffalo, and with one hand grasping one of its horns while the other plunges a spear into its back. A gharial — a type of Indian crocodile — is also portrayed in the scene as if part of a series of killings. A figure in a seated posture, with the soles of its feet pressed together, looks on. The figure resembles ones found on a few other key seals, since its arms reach down to its knees, and three prongs or branches appear to emerge from its head or headdress.

Figure 4.1b, which shows the reverse of this tablet, depicts a female figure standing above an elephant and throttling two large felines (tigers?), one in each hand. The wheel symbol in the Indus Valley script is shown above her head.

Figure 4.1a. Figure spearing buffalo, Indus Valley planoconvex tablet (c. 2200–1900 BCE); 3.91 × 1.62 cm. Harappa, Lot 4651-01, Harappa Museum, H95-2486. *Source*: Copyright J. M. Kenoyer/ Harappa.com. Courtesy Department of Archaeology and Museums, Government of Pakistan. Used with permission.

Figure 4.1b. Figure choking felines, reverse of Indus Valley planoconvex tablet (c. 2200–1900 BCE); 3.91 × 1.5–1.62 cm. Harappa, Lot 4651-01, Harappa Museum, H95-2486. *Source*: Copyright J. M. Kenoyer/Harappa.com. Courtesy Department of Archaeology and Museums, Government of Pakistan. Used with permission.

The tablet is intriguing for several reasons. For one, it is a clear depiction of a person spearing a buffalo in a manner strongly resembling buffalo-subduing goddess imagery from a much later period; however, in the seal one cannot ascertain the gender of the buffalo spearer with certainty. The adjacent figure with its "soles pressed together posture" is akin to the various seals that some early Indologists speculated to be early representations of the god Śiva. While there is inadequate evidence to accept such an identification, we have a figure of some importance in an unusual posture, with a significant headdress suggestive of a god or king, who is replicated in several seals. The person spearing a buffalo, together with the presence of the crocodile nearby, evokes the scene of a sacrificial rite in which a buffalo and crocodile are killed.

There is not too much that we can derive from such evidence as the Indus plaques regarding such possible animal sacrifice in the post-Indus period until the Mauryan period. From Mauryan rock edicts we know that animal sacrifice was commonplace — daily in the royal kitchens, and in hundreds of thousands in ritual worship — during that time (Edict I) and for hundreds of previous years (Edict IV). It was a practice that Aśoka (c. 269–232 BCE) prohibited.[71] The early inscriptions provide the earliest written records of religious practices on the subcontinent in the Mauryan period.[72] The DStv refers to the goddess Durgā as Kālī being fond of flesh, liquor, and beasts (l. 34), and the DSto refers to Durgā being fond of Mahiṣa (buffalo) blood (l. 15). The Praise of Nidrā (First Stratum) (PN-s1 l. 51) speaks of the goddess Kauśikī constantly delighting in offerings of flesh and receiving worship sacrifices of wild beasts. Aśoka's capital of Pāṭaliputra (modern Patna in the state of Bihar), and a few neighboring cities, such as Rājagṛha, were at the center of the Magadha kingdom, which was ruled by a succession of dynasties such as the Barhadratha, Haryaṅka, Śiśunāga, and Nanda, prior to Aśoka's own Mauryan dynasty. We know that the Buddha and the Jina emerged to teach their philosophies in this region, and both traditions obtained some measure of royal patronage during and after their lifetimes. Chandragupta Maurya reputedly embraced Jainism in his old age, and Aśoka converted to Buddhism. Both Buddhism and Jainism denounced animal sacrifice.

Although animal offerings were integral to Vedic sacrificial rites (e.g., the *aśvamedha*), a significant portion of such offerings likely went to goddesses, especially in the region around 500 BCE and possibly earlier — potentially as far back as the Indus Valley Civilization. However, a gap of nearly a millennium exists, spanning from the Indus Valley imagery to the pre-Mauryan period, during which evidence of animal sacrifice traditions is absent. Despite this, goddess-directed sacrificial worship in the Magadhan kingdoms likely stood in tension with Buddhist and Jain principles of non-harming, especially when these traditions were endorsed by ruling elites.

From approximately 500 BCE onward, it is plausible that goddesses began to undergo transformations. Fierce deities demanding blood sacrifices likely evolved into more benign forms to align with the Buddhist and Jain values of *ahiṃsā* (non-harming), while coexisting with those retaining their sacrificial demands. These transformed goddesses shared certain attributes with their fiercer counterparts, but their violent traits were subdued or reinterpreted to fit nonviolent paradigms. A prominent example is the Buddhist goddess Hārītī, originally a child-devouring *yakṣī*, who was converted by Śakyamuni Buddha into a protector of children and a symbol of maternal care (Shaw 2006, 110–42). At the same time, Central Asian goddesses such as Anāhitā, who accepted blood sacrifices, retained their comely and attractive depictions, illustrating a complex interplay between fierce and benign goddess archetypes. This duality underscores the adaptability of goddess traditions across regions and belief systems, accommodating both sacrificial and nonviolent paradigms depending on the cultural and religious context.

While the spread of Jainism and Buddhism throughout the Mauryan Empire is often attributed to the rulers' sympathies toward these traditions, it is reasonable to infer that other religious practices, such as goddess cults involving blood sacrifices, also had the opportunity to expand within the empire, even without direct patronage. This does not necessarily suggest that goddess worship with blood sacrifice originated exclusively in the Magadha region, as such practices likely existed elsewhere on the Indian subcontinent. However, the Mauryan Edicts provide the most concrete evidence of its presence within their empire.

Later texts, such as the Purāṇas, further illuminate these traditions. For instance, the *Kālikā Purāṇa* (KālP) explicitly mentions various animals offered to the goddess in sacrificial rites, including buffaloes, crocodiles, male birds, tortoises, fish, deer, rhinoceros, lions, and tigers (Kane 1958, 5.165–67). These references suggest that animal sacrifice to goddesses was a well-established ritual practice by the time of the Purāṇas, reflecting a continuity of goddess worship traditions that coexisted alongside the nonviolent ideologies of Jainism and Buddhism in the region. The Praise of Nidrā (Second Stratum) (PN-s2) speaks of the goddess Durgā/Kauśikī as surrounded by cocks, goats, sheep, lions, and tigers (l. 11), perhaps evocatively describing her forest abode, but also likely referring to the many animals brought to her sacred shrines for sacrifice.[73]

The Indus Valley planoconvex image is even more interesting when viewed in tandem with the image on the reverse. There we have a clear depiction of what is most likely a female (identifiable by her breast) who is probably a queen or goddess, since she is choking two large felines, which resemble tigers or lionesses. We know that Devī, and Durgā in particular, is associated with the lion, but this is her mount (*vāhana*) and she is not typically depicted as subduing or defeating it.[74] Nevertheless, the image evokes plaques or reliefs from the ancient Middle East in which a powerful figure is shown subduing felines or bulls. For instance, the Gebel el-Arak knife handle (Musée du Louvre, E 11517)[75] from Abydos, Egypt, dated at about 3450 BCE, shows a man grasping two rampant lions by the neck. The Indus Valley image evince the proclivity to produce reliefs with deities or heroic figures subduing animals in the northwest of the Indian subcontinent at Indus Valley sites from well before 1000 BCE.

There is a hiatus of nearly a thousand years before the next set of goddess images appears — depictions that are unmistakable due to the goddess having more than two arms, distinguishing her from royal human figures, and subduing a buffalo. From that time to the present, distinct types of these images have emerged. To classify them, I have adapted M. Seshadri's (1963) scheme, which identifies four major types:

> Theriomorphic (T): The *devī* subdues a buffalo.
> Victorious Goddess (V): The *devī* stands atop the severed head of a buffalo.
> Anthropomorphic (A): The demon is primarily human but retains buffalo features, such as a head, horns, or snout.
> Emergent Demon (E): The demon emerges from the severed neck of the buffalo.

Stietencron (2005, 115–72) expands upon Seshadri's first category, dividing it into two subtypes:

> 1a. The goddess wrestling with a rearing buffalo.
> 1b. The goddess lifting the buffalo from behind.

These classifications underscore the evolving iconography of the buffalo-subduing goddess, reflecting shifts in artistic representation and mythological emphasis across time and regions. Yokochi (2004) divides the buffalo-subduing images into three categories: the Kuṣāṇa, the Gupta, and the Medieval, with four subdivisions for the Gupta.[76] Since the focus in this chapter is on the earliest iconography, I will primarily discuss Seshadri's group 1, the Theriomorphic (T) forms, and the 1a type in Stietencron's scheme. The other types will be discussed in a later chapter. This (T) or (1a) form is the type in which the goddess subdues a rearing up buffalo with her bare hands, without the aid of any weapon whatsoever.

Theriomorphic (T) Depictions of Mahiṣa

In all the Theriomorphic images, a goddess confronts a buffalo (*mahiṣa*), typically controlling or subduing him with her arms or feet. The origins of the myth of the goddess's destruction of a buffalo are obscure. It is potentially problematic to assume that the buffalo depicted on early imagery is a demon (*asura*), without some textual substantiation. Of course, it is fairly evident that in many of the late medieval cases, the buffalo in question is the demon, Mahiṣa. The purely Theriomorphic Mahiṣa appears to have lingered in paintings until the 18th century (Seshadri 1963, 14). For now, we shall simply refer to the buffalo as a buffalo, rather than as the demon buffalo, Mahiṣa, until our examination allows us to think differently.

Kuṣāṇa Plaques

V. S. Agrawala (1947–48) noted that some of the earliest depictions of a goddess subduing a buffalo, such as the ones shown in figures 4.2 and 4.3, are housed in the Government Museum of Archaeology in Mathurā, several of which I examined in 2007 and again in 2017 (see figure 4.3). Mathurā was a significant hub within the vast Kuṣāṇa Empire, which controlled northern India during the first few centuries of the Common Era. Schmid (2002, 144), citing H. Härtel (1992, 81), highlights that these earliest known representations originate from the Mathurā region and likely date to the 1st century CE. Renowned for its craftsmanship, Mathurā was a major center for image production.

To date, at least thirty-four images of a goddess subduing a buffalo from the Kuṣāṇa period, many from the Mathurā region, have been identified (D. Srinivasan 1997, 16). This suggests that the Kuṣāṇas may have been the source of the buffalo-subduing goddess cult in India or were the first to immortalize it in durable material forms. While Durgā is traditionally associated with the slaying of the Buffalo Demon, Mahiṣa, and is often referred to as Mahiṣamardinī, it is prudent to approach these early images cautiously, refraining from assumptions about the name of the goddess or the nature of the buffalo she subdues.

On examining six statuettes of these buffalo-subduing goddess plaques at the Mathurā museum, R. C. Agrawala (1958, 123) noted the absence of the lion mount of the goddess on the reliefs that derive from Palkhera, well II. Five of the reliefs had six-armed goddesses and one was a four-armed specimen.[77] In one of the six-armed images the goddess stands in the *samapāda sthānaka* ("even-footed bodily position") pose and with a relaxed mood presses down on the buffalo with her one of her lower hands. On this collection, see Odette Viennot (1956, 368–73, esp. the plaque on p. 369 as seen in figure 4.2). Made of red sandstone and rather eroded — they were discovered at the bottom of a well — the plaques are 20 cm or smaller. The goddess is sometimes depicted with a spear and a trident, and on occasion, with a sword. She holds some obscure object in two upraised hands, variously ascertained as a drum (Viennot 1956, 372), a serpent (Vogel 1910, 97), and by V. S. Agrawala as a piece of intestine ("bowel") (1958, 123). R. C. Agrawala (1958) thought it to be an iguana (*godhā*). He recognized resemblances with similar depictions of a multi-armed goddess in a Gupta relief on the exterior of Chandragupta II Cave No. 6 at Udayagiri near Bhilsa (see figure 5.4).[78] In a following chapter, under the section on Gupta Theriomorphic images, I offer what I hope is a persuasive explanation for what this object is, hitherto unmentioned or inadequately identified in earlier studies.

R. C. Agrawala noted that images in the Mathurā museum from Palkhera, well II, portray the goddess with dress and ornamentation that is distinctly Kuṣāṇa in style (1958, 123). Rather unusually, this same style of depiction, but belonging to a much later period, is found at Ahichchhatrā, in the Bareilly district of Uttar Pradesh, part of the ancient Pañcāla kingdom. Terracotta figures

Figure 4.2. Buffalo-subduing goddess (dated 200–299 CE); 23 × 10 cm, Mathurā sandstone. Palkhera site (Mathurā District). Mathurā Museum No: 15.875. Accession Number 52752. *Source*: Courtesy of American Institute of Indian Studies. Used with permission.

were unearthed in stratum II (750 –850 CE) and stratum III (350–750 CE). Number 120 shows the Devī squeezing the buffalo by the throat with her left hand.[79] However, R. C. Agrawala disputes V. S. Agrawala's assigning of a similar terracotta plaque of a four-armed goddess to the Gupta period (1958, 124). He argues that the crude rendition is atypical of Gupta artists, and that the goddess's pose (effortless) and her ornamentation suggest a date as early as the 2nd century CE (i.e., approximately the same time as the Kuṣāṇa period).

The plaque resembles statuette no. 881 at the Mathurā Museum, where the goddess wears a classical Kuṣāṇa girdle and *dhoti*.[80] Based on features such as the unemotional facial expression, non-dynamic posture, characteristic clothing and ornamentation (girdle, lower garment, ear ornaments, and anklets), and crude style, R. C. Agrawala (1958, 124) identified this and similar four-armed figures as Kuṣāṇa. This contradicts J. N. Banerjea's claim that buffalo-subduing goddess images "can hardly be dated before the Gupta period," with the

Figure 4.3. Buffalo-subduing goddess (labelled 1st–3rd century CE); 20 × 10 cm, terracotta plaque. *Source*: Mathurā Museum. Photo by the author.

miniature stone figures from Bhīṭā cited as among the earliest representations (R. C. Agrawala 1958, 124, quoting J. N. Banerjea). Other plaques in museum collections also support a Kuṣāṇa attribution. For example, two plaques at the Museum Fünf Kontinente (Five Continents Museum), formerly the State Museum of Ethnology (Staatliches Museum für Völkerkunde) in Munich (MU 199, MU 200) depict the goddess subduing the buffalo similarly to the Palkhera images, notably without the lion (Mitterwallner 1976, 205–6, figs. 1 and 2). These plaques, from Rajakhera, 40 km southeast of Agra, reinforce a Kuṣāṇa-period origin (Mitterwallner 1976, 196–97). The earliest extant images likely show the goddess subduing the buffalo with two bare hands, while additional hands (four, six, or more) wield objects.

R. C. Agrawala not only assigns the cluster of Palkhera images to the Kuṣāṇa period but asserts that other material evidence from Rajasthan shifts the antiquity of the buffalo-subduing goddess cult to pre-Kuṣāṇa times. In particular, he

Figure 4.4. Buffalo-subduing goddess from excavations at Nagar
(Late Kuṣāṇa period, c. 3rd century CE); approx. 7.7 × 22.9 cm,
white terracotta. *Source*: Hawa Mahal Collection, Rajasthan.
Photo by the author.

refers to images on display at the museum at Āmber (near Jaipur) and unearthed at Nagar (also known as Karkoṭanagar), a major center of the Mālava republic. Fashioned of white clay, one terracotta plaque depicts the goddess lifting the buffalo up to her knees, just as in the iconography of the earliest images from Palkhera mentioned above (see R. C. Agrawala 1958, 125, fig. 1). It is displayed in figure 4.4.[81]

In the Palkhera images, the goddess subdues the buffalo with one lower arm while holding a trident and rectangular "shield" in the upper two of her four arms. Notably, the goddess's lion, absent from the Palkhera examples, sits docilely below. Other plaques, such as Mathurā Museum No. 2317, show the lion in a similar posture to the lower right. A plaque fragment from Nagar, also in white clay, depicts the goddess dynamically straddling the buffalo and gripping its horn (R. C. Agrawala 1958, 126, fig. 2). Viennot (1956, 372) dated the first Nagar image to the late Kuṣāṇa or early Gupta period, but R. C. Agrawala disagrees. Based on facial features, dress, and ornaments resembling contemporary styles from Karle and other sites, he places them in the pre-Kuṣāṇa period, around the 1st century BCE to the mid-1st century CE (1958, 127). However, broader consensus attributes the Nagar images, particularly for their refinement and dynamism, to the late Kuṣāṇa period (c. 3rd century CE).

A notable plaque in the Museum für Asiatische Kunst, Berlin (figure 4.5), is described as belonging to the Kuṣāṇa period. It depicts an eight-armed goddess subduing a buffalo in a manner similar to the Palkhera and Nagar images. One of her right arms presses the buffalo's lower back, while a left arm grips its neck, forcing the head upward and backward. Two other arms hold the sun and moon, symbols linked to the goddess Nanā, along with the lion. This celestial motif persists in literature and imagery, such as in the *Haravijaya* (47.23), a 9th-century Kashmiri epic, where Kālarātri, a dark aspect of Durgā, plays with the sun and moon as jeweled balls at the cosmic endtime (Sarkar 2017, 27). Pal (1975, 230–31) also notes a later Kashmiri image of a goddess seated on a lion throne, holding the sun and moon in her upper hands.

In the Berlin image, the other arms hold various objects, while two arms above her head hold a decorated, elongated item, a recurring motif in early depictions. The goddess stands atop two couchant lions, one foot on each, suggesting they serve as her emblem or mount. It appears the buffalo-subduing goddess, initially depicted without a lion, was increasingly associated with it during the Kuṣāṇa period. This plaque likely dates to the late Kuṣāṇa period (c. 3rd to early 4th century CE).

In sum, evidence suggests that the earliest depictions of a goddess subduing a buffalo originate in northern India (Nagar, Mathurā, Agra, etc.), where she subdues the animal with her bare hands. While the Palkhera Mathurā images were found in a well, complicating stratigraphic dating, the materials used (e.g., red sandstone) and ornamentation styles support a conservative attribution to the Kuṣāṇa period. Scholars debate the precise dates of the Kuṣāṇa period, although its high point during the Kaniṣka Era (127 CE) is widely recognized

Figure 4.5. Buffalo-subduing goddess (circa 300 CE); 46 × 25
× 9 cm, half-relief, reddish, light spotted sandstone. Mathurā
Identification Number: I 5817. *Source*: Museum für Asiatische Kunst,
Berlin. Photo: Iris Papdopolous. CC-BY-SA-4.0.

(DeCaroli 2015, 24). Unlike the Chandraketugarh goddesses, these figures generally have more than two arms. The earliest buffalo-subduing goddess images show her with four, six, or eight arms. While she carries weapons such as a trident and other objects, she subdues the buffalo using two bare hands. In many images, two of her other arms hold an object above her head, which scholars have speculated to be a drum, iguana, intestine, garland, or wreath. The lion does not appear in the earliest imagery but is seen in later depictions, typically sitting docilely to the side, below, or even serving as her footrest. In some images, she stands atop one or two lions. Most of these representations are dated to the Kuṣāṇa period and originate from the eastern Kuṣāṇa territories, particularly Mathurā. Similar images appear in post-Kuṣāṇa (Gupta) strata, and a few scholars propose earlier origins. However, it is reasonable to assert that a buffalo-subduing goddess was worshipped in north-central and Northwest India during the Kuṣāṇa period. By this time, the goddess became associated with a lion, likely as her symbolic mount. We now turn to hypotheses about her emergence based on material and literary evidence.

The Identity of the Bare-Handed, Buffalo-Subduing Goddess

Although the exact dates of the Kuṣāṇa empire's rise and peak remain uncertain, the Rabatak inscription, discovered in 1993 CE, provides clear information about the succession of certain rulers (Sims-Williams and Cribb 1996; Sims-Williams 2004, 53). Most scholars place the Kuṣāṇa empire's highpoint, under rulers such as Kujula Kadphises, Vima Taktu, Vima Kadphises, and Kaniṣka I, between the mid-1st and 2nd centuries CE. For example, Robert DeCaroli (2015), in agreement with Harry Falk (2001, 121–36), dates the start of the Kaniṣka Era to 127 CE. This timeframe aligns with the suggested dates for the early epic hymns such as the DStv or its DStv* precursors and the approximate period of PN-s1, warranting a comparative examination of these texts and material finds.

The DStv (l. 13) describes the goddess as possessing four arms and four faces (*caturbhuje caturvaktre*). While the Kuṣāṇa goddesses lack four faces, they often have four or more arms, creating a compelling partial correlation. The next hymnic reference to a multi-armed goddess does not appear until Aniruddha's Hymn (AniH), a later insertion into the *Harivaṃśa* (HV), which describes the goddess with eighteen arms (l. 62), or the *Devī Māhātmya* (DM), also of later provenance. The mention of four faces (*caturvaktre*) in the DStv may be an error introduced during a period when multifaced Tantric goddesses were common. The HV (48.30) uses *candravaktrā caturbhujā* ("moon-faced, four-armed") to describe the goddess, suggesting *candra* could have been mistakenly replaced by *catur*.

The DStv (l. 18) describes the goddess with two broad, upraised arms, likened to Indra's standard, a feature often seen in Kuṣāṇa plaques where two arms hold the ambiguously identified object above her head. The DStv (l. 19, 20) also describes the goddess with upraised items such as a bell, noose, bow, discus, and assorted weapons, paralleling the Kuṣāṇa representations where the goddess holds various objects, including weapons.

Identifying most items carried by the goddess on the Kuṣāṇa plaques is difficult due to their poor condition. However, the DStv (l. 29) refers to the goddess as "Destroyer of the Asura Mahiṣa," which is likely the earliest literary reference to a goddess defeating a buffalo (*mahiṣa*), explicitly identifying it as a demon. The DStv also names her Durgā (l. 39, 51) as a refuge ferrying people through perils (l. 36–43). She is called Jayā and Vijayā (l. 31) for granting victory (l. 32) and Kālī (l. 34) as one fond of liquor, flesh, and beasts. While the DStv's Durgā/Jayā/Vijayā/Kālī does not perfectly align with the Kuṣāṇa goddess, there are notable parallels, especially her role as the destroyer of a buffalo demon.

Interestingly, the DStv makes no mention of a lion, nor does PN-s1, which appears influenced by the DStv or a DStv* variant, and references neither buffalo nor lion. However, the DSto (l. 15) mentions the goddess as fond of *mahiṣa*'s blood, leaving it unclear whether this refers to a buffalo or the Buffalo Demon, Mahiṣa. The DSto also expands the goddess's epithets, including Durgā, Kālī, Caṇḍī (possibly the first mention), Kātyāyanī, Jayā, Vijayā, Kauśikī, Umā, Śākambharī, Sarasvatī, and others. This suggests an effort to unify a broader array of goddesses under one persona. Like the DStv, the DSto lacks any reference to a lion, implying that during their composition — likely the early Kuṣāṇa period in the Mathurā region — the buffalo-slaying goddess cult existed but was not yet associated with a lion.

The PN-s2, like the PN-s1, mentions neither buffalo nor buffalo demon. However, the goddess is said to favor flesh and boiled rice (l. 19) and is surrounded by cocks, goats, sheep, lions, and tigers (l. 11). It is unclear whether these animals are sacrificial offerings (e.g., cocks, goats, sheep) or whether lions and tigers symbolize mounts or familiars. In the PN-s2, the goddess appears as Durgā, Jayā, Vijayā, Kātyāyanī, Kauśikī, and others. The full amalgamation of goddess personas, incorporating the lion mount and the buffalo demon slaying, emerges by the composition of Pradyumna's Hymn (PradH), later added to the HV. In PradH (l. 371, 372), the goddess is explicitly "slayer of the Asura Mahiṣa," "mounted on a lion," and possessing a lion emblem. She is named Durgā, Jayā, Vijayā, Ekānaṃśā, Gāyatrī, Kālarātri, Kātyāyanī, and more, with special emphasis on her trident (l. 371).

This is noteworthy, because while the earliest images from the Kuṣāṇa period have a goddess subduing a buffalo with her bare hands, the images that emerge from the Gupta period that follows depict her piercing the buffalo with a spear or trident.[82] This again suggests that the earlier set of hymns may well be closer to the period of provenance of the bare-handed buffalo-subduing goddess. And the PradH belongs to the late Kuṣāṇa period at the earliest, and more likely to the Gupta period, when the trident, the lion mount, and the slaying of the buffalo-demon Mahiṣa were firmer symbolic features of a great goddess, progressively and repeatedly known as Durgā, Jayā, and Vijayā.

Buffalo Sacrifice

Before delving into the trident-wielding Gupta goddess images in the next chapter, it is worth considering the origins of the concept of a goddess subduing a buffalo with her bare hands and her association with a lion. Goddesses linked to lions have a long history, which we will explore later, but a goddess subduing a buffalo has no known precedent in the Indian subcontinent — or elsewhere — before the Kuṣāṇa images. The buffalo is traditionally regarded as the mount of Yama, the god of death, leading to interpretations that the goddess subduing the buffalo symbolizes a conquest over death. This notion is occasionally expressed by contemporary Durgā worshippers, but there is no ancient textual evidence to support it. Interestingly, in the PN-s2 (l. 4), a hymn composed much closer to the time of the buffalo-subduing imagery, the goddess is referred to as Yama's eldest sister, which contradicts the idea that she would be subjugating his mount.

The earliest mentions of buffaloes in textual sources can be traced back to the *Ṛg Veda* (RV). RV 5.29.7–8 describes the sacrifice and consumption of the flesh of three hundred buffaloes by Agni, while RV 6.17.11 refers to a sacrifice of a hundred buffaloes, both seemingly in honor of Indra. It is speculative but intriguing to consider whether the goddess supplants Indra as "king of the gods" in later imagery. Other RV verses (e.g., 8.58.15, 8.66.10) suggest buffalo sacrifice, but such references are sparse. In later Vedic literature, the buffalo is among the animals sacrificed to Varuṇa, although animal sacrifice appears to have declined from the Brāhmaṇa period onwards within Āryan, Vedic circles. While Vedic references to buffalo sacrifice are limited, modern buffalo sacrifice remains widespread in South and Southeast Asia. This practice, rooted in both the Indus Valley Civilization and tribal traditions, now involves the common water buffalo (*Bubalus bubalis*), although it may originally have been the wild water buffalo.

The wild water buffalo (*Bubalus arnee*) likely ranged from Mesopotamia to Indochina, while the common water buffalo (*Bubalus bubalis*) resulted from its breeding with domesticated livestock (Hedges et al. 2018). The wild water buffalo is now confined to parts of South and Southeast Asia and was likely hunted to extinction in much of its former range. Some specialists even question whether pure-bred animals remain (Hedges et al. 2018). Speculatively, the wild water buffalo's habitat — rivers, lakes, and ponds — frequently identified as abodes of the Devī, may have contributed to its symbolic association with the Goddess. Older male wild water buffaloes, often solitary and territorial, likely posed threats to humans sharing these water sources (Hedges et al. 2018), further reinforcing their mythic and symbolic significance.

The wild buffalo is depicted on some Indus Valley Civilization seals. The planoconvex tablet illustrated above depicts the spearing of a buffalo in a sort of sacrificial rite. The figure in the unusual sitting posture alongside that scene also appears on other seals.[83] The seated figure again appears flanked by fish and beside a crocodile in a depiction on a triangular prism from Mohenjo-daro (M-2033B) (Parpola 2015, 181). Were all these creatures typical sacrificial offerings made to a particular deity? Were the buffalo horns then used as a headdress signifying divinity? Several scholars arrive at this conclusion (e.g., Possehl 2002, 143), but answers to these questions, whether affirmative or negative, must remain speculative.

Iconographic Parallels

The imagery of the goddess subduing or killing the buffalo on the Kuṣāṇa plaques has its closest parallels in those depicting the winged goddess of victory, Nike, or those of the deity Mithras, engaged in a tauroctony, the sacrifice of a bull.[84] In tauroctonies featuring Nike and Mithras, the deity is depicted half-straddling a bull, holding it down with a bent knee. The beast's head is pulled back by the nostrils or muzzle and slain with a short sword or dagger. Nike tauroctony images predate those of Mithras by several centuries, with the earliest Mithraic depictions dating to around the third quarter of the 1st century CE (R. Beck 1998, 118). Nike's representations, which likely influenced the Mithraic ones, show her looking directly at the bull she is about to sacrifice (Ulansey 1991, 30). By contrast, Mithras is almost always depicted looking away from the bull, drawing comparisons to the Greek hero Perseus, who avoids Medusa's petrifying gaze (Ulansey 1991, citing Saxl 1931, 14). The Kuṣāṇa plaques of the buffalo-subduing goddess occupy a middle ground between these two styles. The goddess neither looks directly at the buffalo nor averts her gaze entirely. Instead, her calm gaze is typically directed forward, occasionally hinting towards the buffalo. This tradition of a neutral gaze continues in later depictions of the goddess in both sculpture and clay imagery.

The consensus among scholars today is that there are astral connotations in the symbols of the Mithraic tauroctony, particularly because the sun and moon are frequently depicted, although their opinions vary as to what the astral symbols represent.[85] The scorpion, snake, and dog depicted in the tauroctony may symbolize the constellations Scorpio, Draco/Hydra, and Canis, respectively. While the bull is commonly associated with Taurus, Mithras may represent the Sun, the Sun in Leo, or even the constellation Perseus. Although there is no scholarly consensus on the exact meanings of these symbols, Porphyry, a 3rd century CE Platonic author, suggested in *De antro nympharum* (6) that the Mithraic temple, often cave-like, symbolized "the cosmos, whose furnishings, by their proportionate arrangement, symbolize the cosmic elements and climes" (R. Beck 1998, 124–25; T. Taylor 1917, 18–20). This implies that the tauroctony scene had astral associations, making it plausible that the Kuṣāṇa plaques of the buffalo-subduing goddess also carry implicit cosmic symbolism. Some scholars (e.g., Ghosha 1871, v–vi) have observed that the constellations Virgo, Leo, and the Centaur appear together in the autumnal night sky. This alignment may have influenced ancient myths, fostering widespread narratives linking a lion-riding virgin goddess with a half-man, half-beast figure.

While the parallels with Mithras have been noted by other scholars, the Nike tauroctonies offer us more compelling similarities than those of Mithras, for one because we have a female deity sacrificing a bull.[86] Nike (Roman equivalent: Victoria), the personification of victory, is often depicted as winged. Similarly, the Hindu goddess of the epic hymns is frequently called Jayā and Vijayā (both meaning "victory") and, in her association with Nidrā, is described as flying through the skies, evoking a winged persona. Both the DStv and DSto center on themes of victory in battle. Although Nike was a goddess in her own right, with her own priestesses and cult sacrifices, she was often linked with Athena as Athena Nike. Similarly, Jayā and Vijayā are closely associated with Durgā. It is plausible that the bull symbolizes an enemy, its king, or his power, and Nike's act of vanquishing the bull could commemorate a military victory over a formidable foe or serve as a hopeful omen of success in an upcoming battle or competition.

At sites such as Khalchayan (southern Uzbekistan), under early Kuṣāṇa rule, Nike is depicted alongside an enthroned ruler and his wife (Harmatta et al. 1994, 309). She also appears with Mithra(s) — wearing a Phrygian cap, suggesting the Greco-Roman Mithras rather than the Iranian Mithra — and a bearded god with a radiate halo, likely Zeus, who was perhaps conflated with the pre-Zoro-astrian solar deity Ahura Mazdā (Harmatta et al. 1994, 309). Nike features on the coinage of Sanab, a Kuṣāṇa viceroy, preceding Kujula Kadphises, and was used by Kujula Kadphises on coins commemorating his victories, where he adopted the title *mahārāja rājātirāja* ("Great King, King of Kings") (Harmatta et al. 1994, 318). Nike, often shown with a wreath crowning victors, appears in Hellenic coinage, such as that of Lysimachus (360–281 BCE), and in Bactrian coins of Seleucid ruler Antiochus I Soter (r. 281–261 BCE). This motif con-tinued in coins of Eucratides I (170–145 BCE), Menander I Soter (165–130 BCE), and Archebius (85 BCE) (Stančo 2012, 176). Nike is also seen crowning Kuṣāṇa leaders such as Heraios (1–30 CE) and Ubouzanes (c. 77 CE) (Stančo 2012, 177). A distinctive feature of the wreath is its two ribbon-like extensions, resembling a diadem with ties to secure the crown of victory.

The religious life of Central and South-central Asia, west of the Indian sub-continent, was undoubtedly highly syncretic. From the Persian Achaemenid Empire's (550–330 BCE) expansion into the Indus Valley under Darius I to Alexander the Great's (356–323 BCE) conquests beyond the Indus, this region experienced prolonged interactions with large western empires. During the Mauryan period (322–185 BCE), the Indian subcontinent was largely unified, and the Mauryan Empire extended beyond the Indus into areas influenced by Persian and Hellenic cultures. This created a region of cultural overlap where South Asian religious traditions, particularly Buddhism, spread westward, while Achaemenid and Hellenic religious influences moved eastward.

Later, the Greco-Bactrian Kingdom (250–125 BCE), with ties to the Chinese Han Empire, gave way to the Indo-Greek kingdoms (180 BCE–10 CE). Indo-Greek rulers such as Menander (Milinda) likely reached as far east as the Śuṅga capital of Pāṭaliputra. The Kuṣāṇa Empire (30–375 CE) then rose to prominence, and under Kaniṣka, extended from Turfan in China to Pāṭaliputra, as recorded in the Rabatak inscription. This period coincides with the earliest known imagery of goddesses that may represent Durgā or proto-Durgās, from the Chandraketugarh weapon-hairpin goddesses to the buffalo-subduing goddess of the Mathurā plaques. It is plausible that these goddesses were amalgams of divine figures from both South Asia and the west. The similarities between Nike's tauroctony imagery and the buffalo-subduing goddess cannot be ignored. While Nike's bull sacrifice imagery influenced the Hellenized cult of Mithras (Clauss 2000, 79), it is likely that both traditions were familiar to the artists creating Kuṣāṇa depictions of the buffalo-subduing goddess. To trace the conceptual and iconographic origins of this imagery, it is essential to consider influences from both the east and west.

A key difference between the Nike and Mithras tauroctony images and the earliest buffalo-subduing goddess depictions is that the Hellenic deities slay a bull, not a buffalo. This distinction may reflect the cultural context of the Indian subcontinent, where bulls and cows were symbols of sacrality and veneration. Śiva, for example, was closely associated with the bull, and the cow would not have been seen as an appropriate symbol of a dissonant power to be vanquished. Instead, the wild water buffalo may have served as its symbolic equivalent. Another notable difference lies in the method of subjugation. In the earliest representations of the buffalo-subduing goddess, she defeats the buffalo with her bare hands rather than with a weapon such as a knife, sword, or spear, as seen in Nike and Mithras imagery. This distinction may find a rationale in ancient Zoroastrian concepts of the primordial battle between Ahura Mazdā and Ahriman, representing light and darkness, as explored in the following discussion.

An early significant mention of Ahura Mazdā is found in the Behistun (Bisitun) Inscription from western Iran, attributed to Darius the Great and dated between 521 and 519 BCE, before his death in 486 BCE (Gershevitch 1985, 828). In this inscription, Darius credits his military successes to the grace of Ahura Mazdā, portraying kingship as conferred by this supreme deity, under whose protection he rules. This theme persists through successive Achaemenid emperors until Artaxerxes II (405–359 BCE). In the Susa A inscription, Artaxerxes II names a triad of deities — Ahura Mazdā, Anāhitā, and Mithra — as divine agents of his rule and protectors (Gershevitch 1985, 694). Significantly, the inclusion of Anāhitā on par with Ahura Mazdā signals a shift in the Achaemenid pantheon, where other deities, such as Mithra and Anāhitā, rose — or were restored — to prominence, despite earlier suppression efforts. Additionally, there is evidence that Ahura Mazdā was viewed pejoratively in other cultures. For instance, in the Babylonian Talmud (*Bavli*), edited in Sasanian Babylonia and completed around the 6th to 7th century CE, Ahura Mazdā is implied to be a demon (Kiperwasser 2015, in Shenkar 2014, 29). This exploration of Zoroastrian thought during the Achaemenid period is relevant not only for tracing iconographic connections but also for uncovering possible metaphysical similarities and shared cultural notions.

Why Bare Hands?

In Zoroastrian thought, killing evil spirits, known as *khrafstra* (Avestan: *xrafstra*; Zoroastrian Persian: *khrafstar*), was considered a virtuous act as it diminished the domain of evil. Originally, *khrafstra* referred to wild beasts or predators but later came to include harmful insects, birds of prey, and reptiles such as snakes (de Jong 1997, 338). Felines, including lions and tigers, as well as any creature harmful to humans, livestock, or crops, were also classified as *khrafstra*. The wild water buffalo, one of India's most aggressive bovids, fits this category. Known to attack and kill humans unprovoked, its only natural enemies are tigers (and lions, when they coexisted), although even these predators may die in such confrontations. Wild buffaloes damage crops, kill domestic bulls, and breed with domestic cows, often producing calves too aggressive for domestication, with the potential to harm the mother during birth (van der Geer 2008, 120).

The wild buffalo, like lions and tigers, would have been seen as a scourge to human populations. The term *khrafstra* may derive from the verbal root *skrep-* ("bite, sting, pierce") (Boyce 1975, 90n38), making the buffalo's horns emblematic of this danger and marking it as worthy of killing. Beasts of prey were considered Ahrimanic, associated with Ahriman (Angra Mainyu), the principle of evil in Zoroastrianism. Ahriman embodied the Lie (*druj*), contrasted with Truth (*aša*), and symbolized falsehood, disorder, and death (Ahmadi 2015, 159). This mirrors later Indic conceptions of demons (*asura*), who are linked with illusion (*māyā*) and unrighteousness (*adharma*), both of which disrupt cosmic order. Notably, the term *asura*, originally linked to the supreme deity Ahura Mazdā, shifted to denote demons, such as Asura Mahiṣa. The goddess who defeats this demon is herself associated with illusion in her aspect as Mahāmāyā.

In Zoroastrian ideology, there were also mythic *khrafstra*, such as dragons (e.g., the three-headed, human-devouring Aži Dahāka and the semi-human Snāvikhka) and the evil bird Kamak (Boyce 1996, 91). Killing a *khrafstra* was considered a meritorious act that could atone for both involuntary and deliberate sins, with quantity enhancing its value (Boyce 1996, 298–300). This ideology may have influenced sacrificial practices involving large numbers of animals, including unconventional offerings such as crocodiles, rhinoceroses, lions, or tigers — if these sacrifices were enacted and not simply included in theoretical lists of acceptable offerings.

Herodotus (*Histories* 1.122, 1.142) notes that the Magi, the Zoroastrian priesthood, customarily killed evil animals "of all kinds" with their bare hands (K. Patton 2009, 417n30). While it is unlikely that the Magi subdued large and powerful *khrafstra* bare-handed, limiting themselves to snakes, birds, and insects, divine figures in myth, such as a goddess, might be imagined defeating a demonic *khrafstra* of immense power bare-handed. Such imagery may have influenced the conception of the goddess as a "crusher" rather than merely a "killer" of the buffalo demon, aligning her portrayal with the symbolic destruction of chaos and evil embodied by *khrafstra* in Zoroastrian thought.

Once dead, a *khrafstra* was regarded as more polluting than a live one, and orthodox Zoroastrians would not willingly touch them with bare hands (Boyce 1979, 44). Is this perhaps why the goddess is shown in later depictions, not killing the buffalo with her hands, but merely crushing it beneath her feet? In Zoroastrian thought, merit did not derive only from killing *khrafstras*, but also from blood sacrifice. The sacrificial flesh of beneficial animals was clean, and just as killing *khrafstras* could compensate for transgressions, so could sacrifices of the flesh of *gōspand* and other beneficent animals (Boyce 1975, 302). The *gōspand* (from *gav spenta*, literally "beneficent bull") referred to all animals sprung in a creation myth from a divine Bull, and thus were primarily cattle, but came to include sheep and goats (Boyce 1975, 302n43).[87] In the Zoroastrian hymn of praise to the goddess Anāhitā, the Ābān Yašt 5 (Yašt 5.21, 25, 29, 33, etc.), she is known to accept a hundred stallions, a thousand steers, and ten thousand sheep, which appears to be a sort of standard allotment of offerings to her (Gershevitch 1985, 659).

In summary, deities such as Nike and Anāhitā, well documented in Central Asia and the Iranian plateau, provide evidence of goddesses associated with animal sacrifice, including bovines. These figures embody conceptual notions that crushing evil creatures is meritorious and that the wild water buffalo could symbolize such evil power. Anāhitā, equated with Ahura Mazdā, the supreme deity of the Zoroastrian pantheon, and Nike, associated with granting rulership and victory, share qualities attributed to Durgā/Jayā/Vijayā in the DStv and DSto.

There are strong conceptual reasons for depicting the goddess crushing a buffalo with her bare hands or trampling it underfoot. The Sanskrit word *mahiṣa* means both "powerful, great" and "buffalo," making the wild water buffalo an ideal symbol of malevolent power for a culture that viewed bulls and cows as sacred and benevolent. This symbolism is reinforced if other beasts, such as lions, were aligned benignly with the goddess. The demonic buffalo thus represents deceptive power and a threat to cosmic order — a formidable adversary, yet no match for the victorious sovereign goddess. Although no direct textual evidence links the early buffalo-subduing goddess on Kuṣāṇa plaques to Durgā, Jayā, or Vijayā, it is plausible that this goddess was already associated with these names. Sarkar (2017, 65) cautiously suggests that the goddess on the plaques might represent Nidrā-Kālarātri, known as Kṛṣṇa's sister, although this connection may have arisen only with the composition of the HV's PN-s1. Later, the buffalo-subduing goddess from the Kuṣāṇa plaques may have fused with the Chandraketugarh goddess, whom I propose could be identified as Nidrā-Kauśikī or even Anāhitā. However, no mixed iconographic representations of such a fusion have yet been identified.

Sources of the Goddess's Lion

Although the DStv and DSto refer to the goddess Durgā/Jayā/Vijayā/Kālī defeating the buffalo, and very likely the Buffalo Demon, Mahiṣa, there is no mention of the goddess's emblematic lion. Reference to her surrounded by animals, including tigers and lions, appears in the PN-s2, but it is only in PradH (l. 371, 372) that she is described as destroying the Asura Mahiṣa, holding a trident, being mounted on a lion, and having the best of lions as her emblem. The author of PradH seems to be utterly familiar with imagery that portrays her with these attributes. Such imagery seems to appear on the subcontinent in the late Kuṣāṇa and early Gupta periods. In the late Kuṣāṇa imagery, the goddess may hold a trident and stand atop a lion or lions, or have a lion emblematically sitting nearby, while in the Gupta images, she spears the buffalo with her trident.[88] We shall examine the Gupta imagery later, but first we need to examine the sources of the goddess's association with the lion.

Although lions ranged from India to Greece — Herodotus mentions their abundant presence — they were progressively destroyed in many parts of the world. There is still a small population of about 500 Asiatic lions (*Panthera leo persica*) that survive in the Gir Forest National Park in Gujarat, India today. So, it would not be unreasonable to look for the origins of symbolic association between a goddess and lion on the Indian subcontinent.[89] The planoconvex tablet from the Indus Valley Civilization mentioned earlier depicts a powerful figure throttling two large felines, possibly lions or tigers. This motif recurs on other seals, where the felines are more likely tigers, given their stripes.

The earliest definitive South Asian sculptural depictions of lions appear on the capitals of columns attributed to the Mauryan emperor Aśoka, located at Sārnāth, Sanchi, Vaiśālī, Rāmpurvā, and Lauriyā-Nandangarḍ. The best known is the quadruple addorsed lion capital from Sārnāth, now India's National Emblem. Alongside the bull, the lion served as a potent symbol of royalty in the centuries before the Kuṣāṇa terracottas of the buffalo-subduing goddess. Stylistically, the Aśokan lions show Achaemenid influence, while other elements, such as the portrayal of the bull, exhibit affinities with animal sculptures on Indus Valley seals (Harle 1994, 24). As free-standing pillars have no known precedents on the Iranian plateau, they may represent an Indian elaboration on earlier wooden pillars, likely topped by copper animal figures. However, without further material evidence of figures associated with lions on the Indian subcontinent, we must explore other potential sources of this symbolism. While tracing the ancient and widespread connections between goddesses and lions is beyond the scope of this study, I will highlight key features likely tied to the emergence of lion imagery on the earliest Kuṣāṇa plaques depicting Durgā/Jayā/Vijayā/Kālī.

Kybele (Cybele)

One of the earliest images linking a "goddess" with a "lion" is the statuette displayed in figure 4.6 found in a grain bin at Çatalhöyük, an ancient settlement in southern Anatolia, to the southeast of modern Konya in Turkey.

Çatalhöyük was occupied between 7500 and 5700 BCE. The statue depicts a rotund woman, reminiscent of the far more ancient "Venus" or "mother goddess" image from Dolní Věstonice, in the modern Czech Republic, which is one

Figure 4.6. Seated woman "goddess?" of Çatalhöyük on feline throne; 11 × 12 cm, baked clay. CC-BY-SA-4.0. *Source*: Ankara Museum. Photo: Sefer Azeri.

of the world's earliest ceramics, dated to 25000 BCE or earlier. The Çatalhöyük "goddess" has pendulous breasts and sits upon a throne. She is either flanked by two felines upon whom her arms rest, or the feline heads (not definitively lions, and perhaps leopards) are a decorative feature of the arms of her throne. This image is sometimes cited as a precursor of images of Kybele (Cybele), who emerges as a mother goddess and perhaps the most important cult figure in ancient Phrygia (modern western Turkey), from as early as the 8th century BCE (Roller 1999, 38–39).[90]

Inscriptions identify Kybele as Matar (mother) and *kubileya* (linked to her mountain domain) (Roller 1999, 108). She is often associated with a drinking vessel and accompanied by lions, birds of prey, and imaginary creatures (Roller 1999, 109). Under Attalus I (269–197 BCE), ruler of Pergamon (modern western Turkey), Kybele's cult was adopted by the Romans in 204 BCE. Known as Magna Mater ("Great Mother"), she was a city protector, initially housed with the goddess of Victory on the Palatine Hill until her own temple was completed as a symbolic statement of triumph, such as over Hannibal and the Carthaginians (Takács 1996, 374). Her worship involved ecstatic dances by self-castrated priests (*galli*) and festivals featuring *tauroboliums* (bull sacrifice) and *crioboliums* (ram sacrifice), where sacrificial blood flowed over and purified participants. These rites likely originated in Phrygia and were imported to Rome (Özkaya 1997, 97–103).

As Kybele's cult migrated westward, blending with Greek and Roman goddess traditions, it is plausible that it also moved eastward, merging with local goddess traditions. Parallels between Kybele's features and those of Durgā — such as motherhood, a drinking vessel, lions, mountains, association with Victory, and animal sacrifice — are too numerous to dismiss as coincidental. M. C. Joshi (1994, 203–209) cites a 491 CE inscription from Chhoti Sadri, Rajasthan, describing a goddess riding a chariot pulled by lions, which may reflect Kybele's influence, as Durgā is rarely portrayed this way. Additionally, Nanā's side-saddle depiction, invented by Greek artists in the 5th to 4th centuries BCE, is believed to syncretize features of Artemis (a virgin associated with nature and the hunt) and Phrygian Kybele (Westenholz 2014, 190).

Sekhmet

An ancient and close association between a goddess and a lion is found in the Egyptian deity Sekhmet, often depicted with a woman's body and the head of a lion or lioness. Unlike goddesses accompanied by lions, Sekhmet *is* the lion. Her name, meaning "Power" or "[She who is] the Powerful One," reflects her destructive and fierce nature. Sekhmet was linked to the blazing sun god Ra (Re) and the heat of the desert wind. Pharaoh Amenhotep III (r. 1391–1353 BCE or 1388–1351 BCE) commissioned hundreds of statues of Sekhmet, likely for his mortuary temple, underscoring her association with death (Scott 2008, 223). Nearly 600 of these two-meter-high statues have been discovered. Sekhmet was a war goddess, and the king's destruction of his enemies was compared to her wrath. She was also connected to pestilence and disease, yet her priests were skilled in combating the demonic spirits believed to cause illness.

In Egyptian myth, Sekhmet introduces death to the world as the Eye of Ra, punishing humanity for neglecting him. Known as "She who dances on blood," she nearly annihilates humanity before being tricked by the gods, who dye beer to resemble blood. Sekhmet drinks it, falls into a stupor, and awakens as the benign goddess of love, Hathor (Pinch 2004, 187–89). This myth resonates with Durgā/Kālī's destruction of demon armies and Kālī's rampage threatening world annihilation. Sekhmet's duality as both a destructive force and a healer draws parallels to Hindu goddesses such as Śītalā and Mariyāmman, who are similarly associated with disease and its cure.

At the ancient city of Leontopolis in the Nile Delta of Lower Egypt, temples were dedicated to Sekhmet and her son Maahes, the lion prince. Maahes, also lion-headed, was regarded as a god of war. The city, named Leontopolis ("city of lions") by the Greeks, housed live lions within the temples of Sekhmet and Maahes — a motif echoed in descriptions of Indian goddess temples, such as in Bāṇa's *Kādambarī*. The female pharaoh Hatshepsut (c. 1507–1458 BCE) associated herself with Sekhmet and Mut, a mother goddess with whom Sekhmet was being assimilated. Celebrations in honor of Mut included great sacrifices alongside drunken and sexual revelry, often aimed at appeasing lion deities such as Sekhmet (Bryan 2005, 182).

Herodotus (*The Histories*, Book II.60) writes of similar festivals in 440 BCE at Bubastis in the Nile Delta, where the goddess, identified as Artemis by the Greeks, attracted as many as 700,000 celebrants. These festivals involved heavy wine consumption, surpassing that of the entire year, and included drunken women exposing themselves. Such orgiastic rites parallel the celebrations of Kybele, noted above, and evoke comparisons with the Śabarotsava, related to Durgā festivities in India, as described in texts such as the *Kālikā Purāṇa*.

But how likely is it that the cults of Egyptian, Anatolian, and Greco-Roman deities such as Sekhmet, Mut, Kybele, and Artemis intermingled with those of Indian deities such as Durgā and Kālī? Evidence suggests that interactions between India and the Greco-Roman world in the 1st century CE were far more extensive than previously assumed. Strabo (*Geographica* 2.5.12), writing around the time of Jesus of Nazareth, noted that approximately 120 ships sailed annually from Egypt's Red Sea ports to India. The *Periplus Maris Erythraei*, a mariner's manual written by an Egyptian Greek in 60 CE, describes the discovery in 40 CE of monsoon winds enabling large vessels to cross the Arabian Sea. Half the text is dedicated to Roman Egypt's trade with India, detailing numerous ports along the Malabar Coast (the primary trading area) and, to a lesser extent, the Coromandel Coast. It also hints at voyages reaching Tāmralipti, near the mouth of the Gaṅgā (Casson 2012, 26–27).

Contemporary accounts reveal that India exported lions (both black-maned and maneless), tigers, rhinoceroses, elephants, serpents, parrots, peacocks, ivory, tortoiseshell, spices (e.g., *malabathrum* for flavoring wine), and precious stones, among other goods (Warmington 2014, 40–41, 148, 156). Meanwhile, wine, glass, tin, and even slave girls were imported from Greco-Roman ports (Warmington 2014, 60, 262, 269, 365). These records confirm the lion's presence and prominence in India by the 1st century CE and demonstrate substantial trade links between Egypt, the Greco-Roman world, and eastern India, including likely interactions with regions such as Chandraketugarh, even if not explicitly mentioned.

Herodotus's conflation of Sekhmet/Mut with the Greek Artemis exemplifies *interpretatio graeca*, the practice of explaining foreign religions through parallels in Greek myths, deities, and rituals. Similarly, by drawing comparisons between these ancient goddesses and aspects of Durgā's myths and rituals, I am engaging in a form of *interpretatio indica*. While direct connections between the lion-goddess Sekhmet and Durgā cannot be firmly established, Sekhmet's persona and festivals resonate with those of Artemis, who was still worshipped in Ephesus in the 2nd century CE. Scholars have also noted parallels between Artemis and the Phrygian goddess Kybele, discussed earlier.

Nanā

While Sekhmet was a lion goddess and Kybele was associated with a lion throne or chariot, one of the most integrative and relevant parallels to Durgā and her lion is the Kuṣāṇa goddess Nanā. Nanā's roots trace back to the ancient Sumero-Babylonian goddesses Inanna-Ištar (Ishtar), all of whom are depicted as lion-riding. Inanna, whose name first appears in the mid-4th millennium BCE, was the patron deity of Uruk, where her main sanctuary stood, and she was preeminent among Sumerian goddesses. She was patronized by Akkadian king Sargon (c. 2334–2284 BCE) as a goddess of sovereignty and martial support, likely influenced by her fusion with the Semitic goddess Ištar during his reign (Leick 2009, 89).

By the Third Dynasty of Ur (UR III, c. 22nd–21st century BCE), Inanna embodied erotic appeal, and the kings of Ur identified with her mythic lover Dumuzi ("shepherd") through ritualized marriage. She represented sexuality and fertility, essential to life and reproduction, and was the patron of prostitutes. Her devotees included individuals of ambiguous gender and sexual orientation, such as transsexuals and transvestites (Leick 2009, 89). Like Ištar, Inanna was associated with trickery, destruction (akin to her sister, the goddess Ereshkigal), and the planet Venus.

In the so-called Anubanini petroglyph, located in Kermanshah Province, Iran, and perhaps deriving from the Akkadian empire period (c. 2300 BCE), the goddess Inanna-Ištar (as her Lullubian counterpart, Ninni) presents two captives to the Lullubian king Anubanini. He stands with a foot upon a supine captive, over a lower row of six captives. The iconographic form of this relief will later be mimicked in the Achaemenid Behistun reliefs from the 5th century (Brosius 2021, 94–95). Ninni (Inanna-Ištar) is depicted with characteristic horns on her headdress and weapons that extend from beyond her shoulders, like arrows from a quiver. An Akkadian cylinder seal (c. 2334–2154 BCE) in the Oriental Institute of the University of Chicago depicts Inanna-Ištar much more clearly, with similar characteristics.[91] She is winged and wears a horned headdress. She has a foot atop a lion, which she controls with a rein, and has six weapons extending from behind her shoulders. She holds a weapon in her other hand. An eight-pointed star is visible, a likely symbol of Venus (Black and Green 1992, 170).

Parallels between Inanna-Ištar and Durgā-Nidrā-Kauśikī are immediately evident, most notably in their lion mounts. Inanna-Ištar's weapons also evoke comparisons with the Chandraketugarh hairpin goddess, who is occasionally depicted as winged. The fusion of erotic appeal with martial prowess and kingly empowerment is a striking blend, mirrored in Durgā-Nidrā-Kauśikī. While many other similarities could be drawn, it is expedient to focus on the goddess Nanā, who absorbed Inanna-Ištar's characteristics and was worshipped closer in time and region to Durgā-Nidrā-Kauśikī's emergence in written and material records.

The name Nanā (Nanaia, Nanaya) may derive from the Elamite language, suggesting her origins in Elam, an ancient civilization in southwestern modern-day Iran. She appears in a Sumerian pantheon list from the Ur III period (2112–2004 BCE) (Westenholz 1997, 58–60). While ancient Babylonian texts equate her with Ištar, she was also worshipped independently (Ambos 2003, 233). Cuneiform sources portray her as distinct from Inanna-Ištar (Westenholz 1997, 80). Nanā, considered a daughter of Sin, the Moon god, shared Ištar's dual role as a goddess of love, sexuality, and war (Ambos 2003, 234). Her earliest known depiction is on a stone land-grant document (*kudduru*) of Babylonian king Melišpak II (1186–1172 BCE). In this depiction, Nanā, wearing a tall hat, sits on a throne with legs carved like lion paws. Above her are three symbols: the star of Ištar, the crescent moon of Sin, and the sun disk of Šamaš (Shamash), signifying her connection to this divine triad (Shenkar 2014, 117).

The enduring significance of Nanā among her devotees is vividly demonstrated in the *Inscription from the Temple of Ishtar*, which recounts the deeds of the Assyrian emperor Ashurbanipal (668–c. 627 BCE), ruler of what was then the largest empire in history. The inscription details his conquest of Elam, including the sack of Susa in 646 BCE, the destruction of numerous cities, the submission of three Elamite kings, and most notably, the return of the goddess Nanā (Nanaya) to Assyria. Ashurbanipal claimed that Nanaya had been angry for 1,635 years since her removal from Uruk to Elam. According to him, she had preordained his rise to power to restore her and other gods to their sanctuaries. On her command, Ashurbanipal invaded Elam, carrying Nanaya back in a grand procession to her sanctuary at Ehilianna in Uruk (Gertoux 2015, 25–26; van Koppen 2013, 380).

Ashurbanipal framed his invasion as a mission to reclaim Assyrian gods taken by Elamite kings over the previous 1,500 years (Dubovský 2013, 453). This underscores the centrality of tutelary deities in ancient political and religious life. Nanā's connection to sovereignty, her role as a protector of kingdoms, and the ruler's duty to act on her behalf resonate strongly in this historical narrative. These themes are also central to Durgā, suggesting that Nanā's influence on Durgā's persona may have extended beyond their shared lion mount. It is also significant that Ashurbanipal restored other deities to their "rightful" places of worship, a motif echoed in Durgā's later myths, as in the DM. Durgā's narratives do not merely establish her supremacy but emphasize her role in restoring lesser gods and goddesses to their celestial domains, paralleling Ashurbanipal's restoration of the divine order. This is a feature germane to the thesis presented in the last chapter of this volume.

Nanā's cult is well documented in Western Iran during the Parthian period (247 BCE–224 CE), where the Greeks in Palmyra identified her with Artemis (Kaizer 2002, 94–96, 106). However, the eastward spread of her cult from Mesopotamia is less clear. She emerges in Central Asia on coins minted by Indo-Scythian (Śaka) rulers at the end of the 1st century BCE. On the reverse of coins from Sapalbizes (Sapadbizes), a ruler of western Bactria known only through his coinage, Nanā is depicted in zoomorphic form as a lion. The inscriptions flanking the lion read "NANAIA," and above it is a *tamga* (tribal emblem) of a mountain and crescent moon. Similar imagery appears on the coins of Arseiles (Agesiles), a contemporary of Sapalbizes and precursor to the Kuṣāṇa rulers.

Under the Kuṣāṇa king Vima Kadphises, Nanā (spelled NANA, NANAIA, and NANAÞAO) transitions into human form on coinage. During the reign of Kaniṣka I (c. 127–150 CE), she become the most prominent, and likely the highest deity in the Kuṣāṇa pantheon (Shenkar 2014, 120). The Rabatak Inscription, discovered in 1993 and deciphered in 2000, confirms Kaniṣka's kingship as granted by Nanā and other gods. It lists the pantheon's leading deities, including Nanā, Umma, and Aurmuzd, and describes Kaniṣka's empire as extending to Saketa, Kauśambī, Pāṭaliputra, and Campa (modern Bengal).

Nanā appears frequently on Kuṣāṇa coinage, often depicted standing with a halo, wearing a crescent-topped diadem, and holding a bowl and staff. On many coins, she is seated sideways on a lion (Shenkar 2014, 120). Falk (2015) suggests this motif reflects the astrological confluence of Venus (symbolized by the crescent) and the constellation Leo. A unique depiction on a coin of Kaniṣka III shows Nanā holding a diadem, a symbol of investiture (Mukherjee 1969, figs. 1 and 1A), although she is more commonly shown wearing one herself. The diadem is significant to arguments presented in the final chapter and underscores its importance throughout this study.

Nanā provides compelling evidence of an ancient, enduring goddess associated with a lion. As the supreme deity of the Kuṣāṇa pantheon, particularly under its most powerful ruler, Kaniṣka, she symbolized sovereignty and conferred it upon kings and emperors. Nanā herself was regarded as sovereign among deities, signified by her wearing the diadem of kingship. As DeCaroli (2015, 95) observes, the diadem is the most common symbol of kingship on Kuṣāṇa coinage. Mathurā, a major Kuṣāṇa capital, is also the source of the earliest imagery of the buffalo-subduing goddess with a lion, dating to their rule in the region. In the absence of alternative evidence, Nanā must be considered a primary influence on the buffalo-subduing goddess's association with the lion. She is arguably a Goddess as Supreme Deity, who might have served as a model for the subsequent Indic developments of such a figure as evinced in the DM.

However, notable differences remain. Nanā is typically portrayed seated on her lion, while the buffalo-subduing goddess is shown with the lion at her side or beneath her feet, often standing atop one or two lions. Today, lion-riding forms of the Great Goddess, Durgā, known as Siṃhavāhinī ("[She who is] the Lion Rider") or Śerāṅvālī ("She of the Lion"), are widespread in statuary, paintings, and lithographs, particularly in northern India. Coins from the Gupta period suggest a fusion of symbolism, merging Ardoxšo, a Central Asian cornucopia-bearing goddess, with Lakṣmī, who holds a lotus and rides Nanā/Durgā's lion. This reflects the Vaiṣṇava absorption of the Great Goddess as Viṣṇu's consort (Pal 1986, 79). Nonetheless, lion-riding depictions do not appear in the earliest imagery of the buffalo-subduing goddess. Additionally, Nanā is consistently depicted with only two arms in Kuṣāṇa coinage, prompting further inquiry into the origins of the buffalo-subduing goddess's multiple arms.

The Buffalo-Subduing Goddess's Many Arms

One of the most striking features of Indian deities is their multiple arms, often interpreted as symbols of their numerous attributes and powers. The buffalo-subduing goddess plaques are among the earliest examples of this motif, making it worthwhile to explore its origins. In her comprehensive study of the "multiplicity convention," D. Srinivasan (1997) examines why Indian deities are portrayed with multiple limbs, particularly many eyes, arms, and heads. She observes that this convention emerged and became normative between the 2nd century BCE and the 3rd century CE (1997, 3). Srinivasan further notes that the multiplicity tradition remained largely confined to Hindu deities for over 500 years, only appearing in Buddhist and Jain iconography after the 5th century CE (1997, 15). This timeline aligns closely with the early depictions of the buffalo-subduing goddess, suggesting that the motif of multiple arms was initially a distinctively Hindu innovation, and perhaps aligned in some manner with goddess symbolism.

When examining the relationship between literary references and iconography, Srinivasan notes,

> a serious gap in information surrounds the figure of the warrior goddess, Mahiṣāsuramardiṇī [*sic*], who kills the buffalo demon. She is a very popular deity in Mathurā where about thirty-four images of the goddess are found that date to the Kuṣāṇa period. . .. The reliefs nearly always depict the goddess with multiple arms holding weapons and attributes of victory. Her fight with the demon would seem to be an important element in her cult icons of this period. Yet, there are no satisfactory reference in the Vedas or the Mahābhārata to explain this goddess, her feat, her multiple arms and her attributes. . . . Must we then begin the interpretation of the Kuṣāṇa images with the first account of the goddess's combat in the Devīmāhātmya? The main obstacle however is the apparent incongruity between the text and the Kuṣāṇa images; the former is much more elaborate than the latter. Therefore, it is difficult to apply the evidence from the Devīmāhātmya directly to the images. As such, the significance of the early images of the warrior goddess and her multiple arms cannot be satisfactorily explained. Currently, it is not possible to go beyond a description of the type, its variations and a possible hypothesis for the advent and meaning of the multiple arms. (1997, 16)

I have presented this quote at length as it summarized the state of scholarship on this issue at the time. Subsequently, Sarkar (2017, 64–65) identified a connection between the descriptions of Nidrā-Kālarātrī in the HV and the so-called Kuṣāṇa warrior goddess. While Sarkar refrains from dating the composition of the HV, she cites J. Brockington's estimation of "between the 1st to the 3rd centuries and even into the 4th" (2017, 111n30).

I propose that closer examination of the goddess hymns inserted into the Mbh and the HV can shed further light on this issue. The oversight of these hymns has diverted scholarly attention to texts such as the DM and, more recently, the earlier *Skanda Purāṇa* (SP). While these texts are significant in the development of the Great Goddess as Supreme Deity, they offer less insight into the early strata of iconography. The epic hymns, by contrast, provide more compelling links to the buffalo-subduing goddess's early iconographic depictions. For instance, the HV's PN-s1 does not explicitly mention Durgā but exhibits parallels with the DStv or an unknown DStv* variant that does. This is a crucial point, as it points toward the amalgamation of Nidrā-Kauśikī-Kālarātrī with Durgā.

Earlier, I tentatively proposed that the so-called multiplicity convention may have originated with riverine goddesses such as Kauśikī (and Anāhitā). Their tributary sources may have been imagined as broad, noisy, or quiet "arms," a multiplicity motif later extrapolated to other deities such as Viṣṇu and Śiva.

While riverine deities such as Anāhitā (and possibly Kauśikī/Nidrā) were initially depicted with two arms, their personas may have intersected with concepts unique to the Indian subcontinent, fostering the development of multiple limbs in divine iconography. The idea of a deity with multiple body parts connected to cosmic creation is well-established in the Vedas. For example, the cosmic being Puruṣa is described as thousand-eyed, thousand-footed, and thousand-headed in the RV 10.90. Closer in date to the relevant iconographic representations, the *Bhagavad Gītā* (BG) provides a notable example in Kṛṣṇa's revelation to Arjuna of his cosmic sovereignty and universal form (*viśvarūpa*).

Arjuna exclaims:

> I see all gods in your body, O God,
> And all creatures in all their varieties (BG 11.15)
> . . . . . .
> Many arms, eyes, bellies and mouths do I see.
> No end do I see, no beginning, no middle,
> In you, universal in power and form (*viśveśvara viśvarūpa*).
> (BG 11.16) (Van Buitenen 1981, 113)

Evidently, at the time that the BG was composed the multiplicity convention akin to the RV's Puruṣa was still present and vibrant in conceptions of a supreme being.[92]

Significantly, the BG (11.18) explicitly connects Kṛṣṇa to the Vedic tradition when Arjuna identifies him as the supreme being (*tvaṃ puruṣa*) and highlights his innumerable arms (*ananta bāhun*) (BG 11.19). The motif of a multitude of mouths, eyes, arms, legs, feet, bellies, and teeth (*bahuvaktrane-traṃ bahubāhūrupādam bahūdaraṃ bahudaṃṣṭrā*) is reiterated in BG 11.23, with subsequent verses describing the destruction of armies and worlds within Viṣṇu's many mouths. Terrified by this vision, Arjuna requests that the thousand-armed (*sahasrabāho*) universal form (*viśvamūrte*) be replaced by the more comprehensible four-armed form (*rūpena caturbhujena*), holding a discus, club, and adorned with a crown/diadem (*kirīṭinaṃ gadinaṃ cakrahastam*) (BG 11.46).

This passage clearly establishes Viṣṇu/Kṛṣṇa's four-armed form as a visually manageable representation of the primeval, infinite cosmic form (*viśvam-anan-tam-adyaṃ*) (BG 11.47). Vāsudeva then assumes the requested four-armed form before returning to his two-armed human form (BG 11.50). Notably, the standard four-armed form does not include a conch (*śaṅkha*); its defining attributes are the club (*gadā*), discus (*cakra*), and diadem/crest/crown (*kirīṭa*). D. Srinivasan (1997, 21) observes that this iconography precisely corresponds to depictions of Vāsudeva-Kṛṣṇa in Mathurā art during the Kuṣāṇa period.

The BG verses imply that four-armed depictions of Viṣṇu were already commonplace at the time of the BG's composition. Arjuna is convinced of Kṛṣṇa's supreme divinity through a vision of the terrifying cosmic form. Once convinced that his seemingly human friend is indeed Viṣṇu, called by many other names,

Arjuna apologizes profusely for his earlier ignorance. He then requests that Kṛṣṇa not return to his two-armed human form but instead assume the familiar four-armed divine form, through which Viṣṇu was evidently well-known. This suggests that four-armed representations of Viṣṇu must have existed during and prior to the BG's composition, providing a valuable clue for dating the text.

The earliest known image of Viṣṇu, or a Vaiṣṇava-related deity, was discovered at Burhikhār, near Malhār (Bilaspur District, Madhya Pradesh), shown in figure 4.7. It is reasonably well-dated by a Prakrit inscription in Early Brāhmī script, which records that the image was installed by a lady named Bharadvājā (Bajpai 1981, 146) or Bhāradvājī (Sircar 1971, 85). While scholars debate whether the figure represents Viṣṇu or a related deity (a Vṛṣṇi), it features a tall headdress and holds a large club and a discus in two of its four arms — attributes described in the BG as characteristic of Viṣṇu's divine, earthly form. It is

Figure 4.7. Earliest statue of four-armed Viṣṇu or Vaiṣṇava-related deity (Vṛṣṇi) (c. 1st century CE); approx. height 0.76 m, sandstone. Burhikhār, near Malhār. *Source*: Courtesy of Vinay Gupta (ASI). Used with permission.

unclear if the figure's remaining two hands hold a conch or pitcher, or if they are pressed together in an *añjali* gesture.

K. D. Bajpai (1981, 146) dates the Burhikhār image to the 2nd century BCE, while D. C. Sircar (1971, 85) places it closer to the 1st century BCE or early 1st century CE. The figure's pleated skirt, position of the conch or pitcher, and distinctive earrings evoke comparisons to images identified as Vāsudeva-Kṛṣṇa on rare square silver coins of Agathocles of Bactria (r. c. 190–180 BCE), found at Ai-Khanoum (modern Afghanistan). On the reverse, these coins depict a figure holding a plough and pestle, identified as Saṅkarṣaṇa (Balarāma) (MacDowall 2007, 244). These coins demonstrate Hindu deities portrayed with Greek stylistic elements, particularly those associated with the Bhāgavata-Vāsudeva cult. However, it is notable that the deities depicted on Agathocles' coins are two-armed, contrasting with the four-armed representation of the Burhikhār image.

The multi-limbed portrayal of deities appears to be a distinctly Indian characteristic. For instance, the god Śiva appears with four arms on certain coins of Kaniṣka, whose rule is estimated to have begun in 127 CE. The deity holds the trident, thunderbolt, water-pot (and elephant goad), and an animal (perhaps an antelope or goat). These coins may be among the earliest depictions of a deity with multiple arms (Pal 1986, 77). However, if Kaniṣka's dates are correct, and even if we postulate a late date of the early 1st century CE, rather than the 2nd century BCE for the Malhār image, it suggests that the Vaiṣṇava-Bhāgavata-Vāsudeva-Kṛṣṇa (or related) multi-armed image is of earlier provenance than the Śivas on the Kuṣāṇa coinage. By the time of the composition of the BG, four-armed images of Bhagavata-Viṣṇu were evidently well-known and seemingly routinely regarded as a sort of earthly form of a supreme, cosmic deity. Moreover, for such images to be produced in quantity, they would likely emanate from a later period than the Malhar image.

I have turned to the BG not solely because it provides an early textual reference to a cosmic being with multiple arms, particularly Viṣṇu-Kṛṣṇa with four arms. D. Srinivasan (1997, 9) observed that Vaiṣṇava images, along with those of Devī and Śiva, are among the earliest depictions featuring multiple arms. The BG could only have been composed after four-armed images were commonplace, as it references a "well-known" four-armed form, which likely reflects the prior existence of such imagery. More relevant to our focus is the close link between the cult of Durgā/Kālī/Jayā/Vijayā and Vaiṣṇava mythology, particularly in the persona of Nidrā/Kauśikī and the Kṛṣṇa-Kaṃsa myth cycle. The PN-s1 was composed alongside the core of the HV, which is dated later than the BG. We estimate the HV's core to the late 2nd or early 3rd century CE, implying that the BG, with its references to the four-armed Viṣṇu, predates this period. This provides a possible terminal date of approximately the late 2nd century CE for the BG, aligning with iconographic evidence such as Kuṣāṇa coinage and the four-armed Malhār figure. Conversely, based on the material evidence of four-armed Viṣṇu images, it is improbable that the BG predates the 2nd century BCE, which marks the earliest likely date for the Malhār figure.

Based primarily on the BG's assumption that four-armed Viṣṇu images were commonplace, and since there is scant evidence of these until the Kuṣāṇa period, it is reasonable to suggest placing the completed composition of the BG at between the 1st and mid-2nd century CE, or even a bit later.[93] We are, of course, basing this suggestion purely on material evidence at our disposal, and not the hypothetical existence of earlier images made from nondurable materials.

The DStv (hymn proper) (l. 11) explicitly refers to the goddess as "black one" (*kṛṣṇā*), the feminine equivalent of Kṛṣṇa, and two lines later describes her as having four arms (*caturbhuja*) and four faces (*caturvaktra*). Subsequent verses draw numerous comparisons to Vaiṣṇava deities without directly identifying her with them. She is described as "like the wife of Nārāyaṇa" (l. 15), and her face, as black as dark clouds, is said to rival Saṃkarṣaṇa's (l. 16). Notably, her hymnic description suggests she could have more than two arms. As previously noted when discussing the Chandraketugarh hairpin goddess, the language of the hymn implies she holds a platter or vessel (*pātrī*), a lotus (*paṅkajī*), a bell (*ghaṇṭī*) (l. 19), a noose (*pāśam*), a bow (*dhanur*), a great discus (*mahācakram*), and assorted weapons (*vividhāny āyudhānī*) (l. 20). Additionally, she is described with two upraised arms (l. 18). A devotee or artist reciting or hearing this hymn could easily imagine the goddess with far more than four arms — at least six to hold the mentioned items, with two additional arms raised. The reference to "assorted weapons" invites the imagination to conceive of an unlimited number of arms. In the hymn proper, the DStv goddess is not yet bound by Vaiṣṇava prescriptions and can be envisioned as a supreme cosmic deity with multiple arms and heads. However, by the time of the DStv+'s insertion into the Mbh, its framing verses firmly associate her with the Kṛṣṇa-Kaṃsa myth cycle.

Interestingly, the PN-s1 also describes her explicitly as black, like Viṣṇu in color, with a face resembling Saṃkarṣaṇa's (l. 39). A crucial verse further elaborates: *bibhratī vipulān bāhūn mama bāhūpamān bhuvi* (HV 47.39). The first part (*bibhratī vipulān bāhūn*) has often been translated as "having broad arms" (Coburn 1984, 276) but could also mean "bearing numerous (*vipulān*) arms." As noted earlier regarding the Chandraketugarh hairpin goddess, *vipula* carries diverse meanings, including large, long, great, abundant, and even noisy. The second part (*mama bāhūpamān bhuvi*) is frequently rendered ambiguously as "like my arms on earth" (Coburn 1984, 276). However, a more precise translation might be "resembling my arms [when manifesting/dwelling] on earth." The term *bhuvi* contrasts with dwelling in the heavenly realm, emphasizing the earthly manifestation, while *upamā* signifies resemblance, often implying a strong correspondence or likeness.

This interpretation is supported by the next verse, which describes the goddess as holding an upraised three-pointed spear, a gold-hilted sword, a vessel filled with honey, and an utterly spotless lotus (l. 40). While *udyamya* ("having upraised") does not unequivocally mean holding in one's hands, it is reasonable to envision the goddess with four arms, each holding one of these four items. The PN-s1 acknowledges the cosmic nature of the goddess, consistent with her multi-faced and multi-armed depiction in the DStv. However, it appears to constrain her portrayal to align with the Vaiṣṇava earthly form — likely as four-armed and possibly single-faced — adapting her cosmic identity to a Vaiṣṇava framework. While one does later encounter Vaiṣṇava imagery with multiple faces, notably that of a lion and boar, which represent divine emanations, the early buffalo-subduing goddess imagery is only single faced and multi-armed.[94]

The DSto also evokes the image of the goddess with at least four arms. The hymn proper (l. 12) describes her as bearing a standard of peacock tails (*sikhipicchadhvaja*) and adorned with various ornaments (*nānābharaṇabhūṣita*). Additionally, she wields a lofty spear (*aṭṭaśūlapraharaṇa*) and carries a sword and shield (*khaḍgakheṭakadhāriṇī*) (l. 13). While she does not necessarily require four arms for all these items, a depiction with a sword and shield would likely necessitate two arms, with the spear and standard requiring two more. The PN-s1 (l. 44) describes the upraised standard (*dhvaja*) of peacock tail feathers (*sikhibarha*) positioned nearby (*samīpataḥ*) rather than in her hand, focusing instead (l. 40) on the items she holds in her four hands: a three-pointed spear, a gold-hilted sword, a vessel filled with honey, and an utterly spotless lotus. Pradyumna's Hymn (PradH), likely a later insertion into the HV, portrays the goddess (l. 372) mounted on a lion and bearing a lion emblem, reminiscent of Nanā, the lion-riding goddess. Here, she holds a bell and a trident, items requiring only two hands. However, Aniruddha's Hymn (AniH), another late addition to the HV, describes her as three-eyed (l. 21), with a lion as her vehicle and a bull as her emblem (l. 34), hinting at Śaiva connections. The multi-armed vision is explicit in AniH, where she is said to have eighteen arms (l. 62), with all her limbs shining from a necklace adorned with flames from her diadem (l. 63).

In sum, the evidence from these epic hymns offers the clearest and earliest scriptural parallels to the iconography of the goddess. Their content strongly suggests that the composition of these hymns, or earlier variants, likely coincided with the earliest strata of goddess representations. Viewed collectively, they indicate that multi-limbed portrayals of deities were a distinctly Indian innovation, often used to evoke cosmic or universal forms of a supreme deity. This imagery has its roots in the Vedas and finds expression in the BG.

The BG appears contemporaneous with the PN-s1 in the HV, while the DStv or a DStv* variant may have been composed slightly before or after the BG. The DStv explicitly mentions a four-armed great goddess, named Durgā/Kālī/Kṛṣṇā/Jayā/Vijayā, as the slayer of the Asura Mahiṣa. It also evokes a goddess with many more arms wielding an assortment of weapons, allowing for an imaginative portrayal beyond four arms. The PN-s1, which may have been composed after the BG, is part of the early HV stratum and seems familiar with the DStv or a DStv* variant. However, it avoids naming the goddess Durgā/Kālī/Jayā/Vijayā, instead equating Nidrā/Kauśikī with Viṣṇu. In this hymn, the goddess is portrayed with four arms resembling Viṣṇu's earthly divine form but holding a trident, sword, honey-filled vessel, and lotus — distinct from Viṣṇu's discus and club. Notably, the PN-s1 makes no reference to buffalo-subduing, precluding a direct link to early buffalo-subduing goddess imagery. The DSto appears aware of both the DStv and the PN-s1, naming the goddess Durgā/Kālī/Jayā/Vijayā and Kauśikī while situating her within the Kṛṣṇa-Kaṃsa myth cycle. It portrays her fondness for Mahiṣa's blood and associates her with names such as Caṇḍī, Kātyāyanī, and Sarasvatī. Likely composed after the BG, the DSto integrates Vaiṣṇava elements, presenting the goddess with weapons but maintaining the four-armed form consistent with Vaiṣṇava iconography.

The PN-s2 (Āryā Stava) follows the DSto in its naming conventions but does not mention buffalo-subduing. Both the PN-s1 and PN-s2 describe the goddess as favoring flesh sacrifice, consistent with earlier depictions. By the time of the PradH, the buffalo-subduing motif becomes normative, although the goddess is possibly described with only two arms. The AniH makes no reference to Mahiṣa but describes the goddess with eighteen arms and as defeating Śumbha and Niśumbha. This suggests that earlier Vaiṣṇava milieus of the HV promoted two- or four-armed depictions of the goddess while avoiding the buffalo-subduing mythology. Meanwhile, multi-armed depictions tied to the Mahiṣa myth likely developed in non-Mbh hymns, flourishing alongside Vaiṣṇava traditions.

The gradual ascendance of the goddess as Durgā, Jayā, and Vijayā eventually necessitated the incorporation of the Mahiṣa-subduing mythology and multi-armed imagery. This evolution marked her acceptance as a Great Goddess — associated with sovereignty, victory in battle, and demon-slaying. The initial reluctance to accept these features in Vaiṣṇava traditions may reflect sectarian tendencies to ascribe supremacy and demon-slaying roles exclusively to Viṣṇu or Śiva.

The goddess Nanā, who likely contributed the lion to the imagery of the buffalo-subduing goddess, appears to have adopted the four-armed representation through her interaction with Indian iconography. Four-armed depictions of Nanā subsequently feature on coins minted during the reign of the Sasanian king Pērōz I (r. 459–484 CE) (Shenkar 2014, 123). The Sasanian Empire (224–651 CE), which succeeded the Parthian Empire, controlled a vast territory spanning from modern-day Pakistan in the east to Egypt, Turkey, and Armenia in the west and northwest, serving as the last Iranian empire before the advent of Islam. This suggests the westward expansion of the multi-limbed motif from India.

In Sogdiana, north of Bactria with its center at Samarkand, late Sogdian art frequently depicts Nanā as four-armed. She is often seated on a lion, either marching or prone, holding personifications of the Sun and Moon in her hands (Shenkar 2014, 124). Nanā, likely the most significant deity in the Sogdian pantheon, is commonly portrayed in paintings at Panjikent (modern Tajikistan) wearing blue garments (Shenkar 2014, 124–25). This evokes a parallel with Nidrā/Kauśikī, who is described in the PN-s1 as wearing a dark-blue linen garment. In Ustrushana, another Sogdian principality, Nanā is shown battling demons (Shenkar 2014, 124), a depiction that resonates with the warrior-like qualities of Durgā in India.

In Chorasmia, Nanā is portrayed on silver bowls. One such bowl, dated by inscription to 658 CE and displayed at the British Museum, shows her as four-armed, holding a scepter and a bowl in two hands, while her upraised hands hold the Sun and crescent Moon. She wears a crenellated crown adorned with a crescent moon motif, and similar depictions appear on bowls from the 6th and 7th centuries (Shenkar 2014, 125).

An image of a multi-armed Durgā, astride two lions and subduing the Buffalo Demon Mahiṣa with her bare hands, is housed in Berlin's Museum für Asiatische Kunst (No. I 5817) and shown in figure 4.5. This image, with two upraised arms holding the Sun and crescent Moon, is attributed to the Kuṣāna period. If accurate, it reflects a clear fusion of Nanā's lion-riding attributes with Durgā's buffalo-slaying iconography, likely emerging in the Mathurā region of the Indian subcontinent.

A speculative connection between Nanā and Durgā in the present day arises in the shrine of Hiṅglāj (Hiṇgulā, referring to cinnabar or mercury sulfide) Devī, situated by a tributary of the Hingol River in southern Balochistan (Schaflechner 2018, 90n55). This temple is considered one of the *śakti pīṭhas*, sacred seats of the Goddess where, according to myth, parts of Satī's body fell after her self-immolation. Hiṅglāj Devī is the most visited pilgrimage site in Balochistan and is believed by Hindus to mark the location where Satī's *brahmarandhra* (or alternatively, her navel or womb) fell (Schaflechner 2018, 44–45, 217, 246). The *brahmarandhra* ("Brahmā's crevice") refers to the psychic opening at the crown of the head, associated with the release of the soul at death, and in *kuṇḍalinī yoga*, it aligns with the *sahasrāra*, the thousand-petaled lotus node.

Just as Satī's *yoni* (vagina) is believed to have fallen at Kāmākhyā in Assam, the site of the *brahmarandhra* holds profound significance, particularly for Tantric practitioners and certain yogic sects. However, due to its location in modern-day Pakistan, access for Hindu pilgrims has become more challenging. Interestingly, the site also attracts Muslim devotees, who associate the goddess with the tomb of a Muslim saint, calling her Bībī Nānī ("Venerable Old Lady").

En route to Hiṅglāj, pilgrims often stop at a mud volcano called Candrakupa ("Moon Cave"), which symbolizes the solar (heat) and lunar elements connected with Nanā. Francesco Brighenti (2016) explores the speculative hypothesis proposed by 19th-century scholars that Hiṅglāj may have originally been a shrine to Nanā. Astral symbols, such as the sun and crescent moon, found at or near the site may have inspired Parthian or Śaka invaders of Balochistan to dedicate it to Nanā. Over time, this association may have been Islamicized as Bībī Nānī, linked to the wife of the Prophet Muhammad's son-in-law, Alī (Brighenti 2016, 44).

Although this provides no firm identification of Hiṅglāj Devī with Durgā, the shrine's possible transformation into a Nanā site — and Nanā's lion-riding and astral symbolism — may have connected it to Durgā's imagery. Moreover, modern interpretations, including online representations, often conflate the myths of Satī's dismemberment with Durgā, especially when Satī is viewed as Śiva's spouse, reflecting the ongoing assimilation of local goddesses into the broader rubric of Durgā.

Chapter 5

The Wondrous Diadem

In the previous chapter, we focused on buffalo-subduing goddess images classified as Seshadri's type I or Stietencron's type 1a, representing the demon in Theriomorphic form (T). Unlike Seshadri and Stietencron, I have refrained from referring to these images as Mahiṣamardinī, as the term does not appear in early literary records from the period when these images were produced. While it became evident that the goddess in these images was likely known as Durgā, she may also have been identified by other popular names.

This raises terminological challenges concerning what the creators and worshippers of these images actually called them. Scholars of iconography across centuries have offered differing classifications and labels for such images, revealing a lack of consistency. Seshadri (1963, 27–29) cataloged some of these variations, and I will not replicate them in detail here. For example, some descriptions specify that in images of Caṇḍī, the demon should be bound by a noose, the goddess's right foot placed on the lion's back, and her left foot on the demon's body. Kātyāyanī should be depicted as ten-armed, with a crescent moon adorning her hair, and the demon emerging from the buffalo pierced in the chest with a trident. She must also be posed in the *tribhaṅga* stance. Interestingly, the same description is sometimes applied to Caṇḍī. Durgā-Lakṣmī is said to stand on a lotus pedestal or a buffalo head, and so on. Despite these varied and often contradictory prescriptions, most buffalo-destroying images, regardless of subcategory, are routinely identified as Durgā.

This chapter continues the iconographic exploration, shifting to Gupta-era depictions of the buffalo-subduing goddess. A Rājghāṭ seal and a panel from the Bhumarā Śiva temple depict the goddess pressing the buffalo's head with her foot while spearing it. Several images from Madhya Pradesh's Udayagiri caves show the goddess with multiple arms, wielding various weapons, and spearing the buffalo. A striking object held aloft by the goddess in these depictions, previously interpreted as a serpent, drum, or garland, is argued here to represent her self-coronation with a wondrous diadem (*vicitra-mukuṭa*), a symbol of divine supremacy referenced in the Durgā Stava (DStv) and alluded to in other texts. The extensive attention given in this chapter to the diadem, and to the peacock standard in the following chapter, as symbols of supreme divinity relates to a key argument developed in this volume's final chapter.

Durgā as Slayer of the Buffalo Demon
(Mahiṣāsura-nāśinī)

Early Gupta Images

Having established a reasonably clear correlation between the earliest buffalo-subduing goddess imagery (e.g., Kuṣāṇa plaques) and Durgā or proto-Durgā (B. Sarkar 2017, 25), I now turn to correlating additional early iconographic depictions with textual evidence to further substantiate this connection. Importantly, this analysis seeks to provide plausible interpretations for several symbolic elements, such as the upheld "wreath" and the "peacock banner," which have not been satisfactorily addressed in previous studies. To do so, we examine the next stratum of buffalo-subduing goddess imagery, originating in the early Gupta period. Yokochi (1999a, 2004, 133–41) has extensively analyzed these so-called Gupta iconic types, and I will draw on some of her typologies in the discussion that follows.

A defining feature of these images is the depiction of the goddess using a weapon — typically a trident — to defeat Mahiṣa. Gupta representations are distinguished by their exceptional craftsmanship and artistic finesse. The Guptas ruled northern India from approximately 320 to 550 CE, a period often described as a golden age of Hinduism. However, more recent scholarship, such as that of D. N. Jha (2023), has questioned this characterization, emphasizing the social inequalities of the era.

Bhumarā, Rājghāṭ, and Bhīṭā

Among early representative images from the Gupta period are some that derive from Bhumarā, Rājghāṭ, and Bhīṭā, each of which we shall examine in turn. A beautiful buffalo-subduing image displayed in figure 5.1 is found on a small round panel from a Gupta temple dedicated to Śiva from Bhumarā, Madhya Pradesh. Yokochi (2004, 135) categorizes it as the Northern subtype, noting it is preserved in the Allahabad Museum (AM-SCL-152).[1] It depicts a four-armed goddess trampling the head of the buffalo with her right foot. She holds the animal's hind leg with her lower left hand and pierces the beast with a trident held in her upper right hand. Her upper left and lower right hands respectively hold a circular shield and sword.[2] The shield has distinctive decorative features on its underside. Alternately, it may not be a shield, but some other object that is held like a shield. This motif, in which the *devī* pulls on the buffalo's hind leg, is recurrent in Gupta images, while other regions (e.g., Cāḷukya) have the animal lifted by its tail. The goddess has long curly hair that falls to her

Figure 5.1. Buffalo-subduing goddess in *candraśālā* (c. 451–499 CE); 55 × 74 cm, dark pink stone. Gupta Period Bhumarā, Satna, Madhya Pradesh. Accession No: 21888. *Source*: Courtesy of American Institute of Indian Studies. Used with permission.

Figure 5.2. Buffalo-subduing goddess on medallion; 2 cm diameter, slate colored. Found at Rājghāṭ, near Banāras. *Source*: Iyer (1969), Artibus Asiae 31, no. 2/3. Used with permission.

shoulders, wears a necklace, and has a bracelet on each wrist. An attendant with something, identified by some as a fly whisk (*cāmara*), stands to her right. Sir John Marshall dated this temple to the 6th century CE, but R. D. Banerji (1924), seeing affinities with the Pārvatī temple at Nachnakuthara, placed it in the 5th century CE (R. C. Agrawala 1958, 128; Seshadri 1963, 7). The image's source (from a Śiva temple) and the goddess's trident weapon immediately indicate trends in the Gupta period to connect the goddess with Śaiva traditions.

A small seal (2 cm in diameter) excavated at Rājghāṭ, depicted in figure 5.2, shows a four-armed *devī* thrusting a spear into the upper back of a buffalo while grasping its rear leg or tail (Iyer 1969, 179–84). It is unclear whether the spear is a trident. The goddess's right foot rests on the buffalo's head. The general characteristics of the seal resemble those of the Bhumarā temple medallion, although the latter includes an additional *gaṇa*. Yokochi (2004, 135) identifies this seal as an exemplar of the Northern subtype.

In her upper left hand, the goddess holds an object identified by K. Bharata Iyer (1969, 183) as a flaming *cakra* (wheel), although its positioning suggests it may be more akin to a shield. A flaming shield or *cakra* is unusual, however, and the object may instead represent something like a fan or whisk. It recalls the aegis of the goddess Athena, which is often depicted as a shield with tassels that resemble flames, as seen in figure 5.3b. Such depictions are common on the coins of King Menander I (depicted with a diadem in figure 5.3a), who ruled

Figure 5.3a. Silver drachma of King Menander I of Bactria (155 BCE to 130 BCE) depicting diademed and draped bust of Menander I. Identifier: 1993.30.4. *Source*: Courtesy of American Numismatic Society. Public domain.

Figure 5.3b. Silver drachma of Menander I (reverse) depicting
Athena Alkidemos advancing holding shield and a thunderbolt, with
Kharoṣṭhi script. Identifier: 1993.30.4. *Source*: Courtesy of American
Numismatic Society. Public domain.

the Indo-Greek kingdom (c. 165–130 BCE) from his capital at Sagala (possibly modern Sialkot, Pakistan). The aegis is a mysterious item associated with Athena and Zeus, resembling a shield in its defensive capabilities and considered impervious even to Zeus's thunderbolt (Yasumura 2013, 74–93).

The object in the upper right hand is indistinct. The goddess is portrayed with prominent earrings. This image is far more dynamic in its representation than the one at Bhumarā. The reverse of the seal has damaged depictions, perhaps of a Brahmā figure, a horse sacrifice, and possibly the word "Chandoga" in Gupta Brāhmī characters from the 4th or 5th centuries CE. The vowel formation on the seal is difficult to discern. Apparently, the word "Chandoga" ("a chanter of Vedic hymns") appears on other items found at Rājghāṭ (Iyer 1969, 184). Iyer (1969, 184) dates the seal to the early Gupta period (4th to 5th century CE) and earlier than the Bhumarā relief.

Between 1909 and 1911, Sir John Marshall excavated stone reliefs at Bhīṭā, located 12 miles southwest of Allahabad (modern Prayagraj) and 35 miles east of ancient Kauśāmbī in Uttar Pradesh. These reliefs depict a two-armed goddess battling the buffalo demon with her bare hands, notably without the presence of a lion. The discovery of over a hundred Kuṣāṇa coins and several stone sculptures with Gupta stylistic elements, some bearing inscriptions, supports the view that Bhīṭā flourished during both the Kuṣāṇa and Gupta periods (Samir K. Mukhopadhyay 1972, 71).

The simple iconographic style of the images, coupled with the portrayal of the goddess, suggests they belong to the Kuṣāṇa period (c. 1st to 2nd century CE). The Bhītā imagery indicates that the buffalo-slaying goddess may initially have been depicted with two arms — similar to the two-armed Chandraketugarh hairpin goddess — during the early Kuṣāṇa period. By the later Kuṣāṇa period, portrayals of the goddess had evolved to include four, six, or more arms, reflecting her growing divine stature. Hypothetically, one could trace a progression from the two-armed Chandraketugarh goddess (possibly Kauśikī, assimilating Anāhitā) to the two-armed buffalo-subduing goddesses of Bhītā, culminating in the multi-armed buffalo-subduing goddesses of the later Kuṣāṇa period, likely identified as Durgā. As a speculative aside, the wings depicted on the two-armed Chandraketugarh figures (both male and female) might have inspired the development of four-armed divine forms in iconography. This creative adaptation could have paved the way for the multi-armed portrayals that became characteristic of later depictions.

Udayagiri

Several images at Udayagiri are crucial in furthering our investigation of the rise of Durgā as the buffalo-subduing goddess. Udayagiri is a mile and a half long ridge of white sandstone a few miles from Besnagar and five miles from Sanchi, in the state of Madhya Pradesh.[3] In the late 19th century, Cunningham (1880, 50) noted and described a twelve-armed buffalo-subduing goddess image at a rock-cut shrine located there. He also noted the presence of the inscription above it and offered a translation (see also Patil 1948, Pl. 9, 14). It is the image carved on the far right of a triad of images to the right of the cave entrance.[4] The generally accepted numbering system introduced by the state of Gwalior's department of archaeology identifies it as Cave 6. I shall call this the Cave 6A image to distinguish it from a second very worn one that I designate as the Cave 6B image, and which I shall discuss in a later section.

The Cave 6A image has garnered the most attention. Kenneth de Burgh Codrington considered the 6A image to be medieval, but there is an inscription of Candragupta II, dated 82 of the Gupta calendar (c. 401/402 CE) directly above the images (Seshadri (1963, 7) citing Codrington (1926, 60)). Yokochi (2004, 139) accepts this inscriptional date, and regards this as the earliest image of the Gupta subtype. A few subsequent studies date the reliefs later than the date of Candragupta II's inscription, placing them in the 7th century (see Barrett (1975–76, 64–67), and Viennot (1971–1972, 72)). Seshadri (1963, 7), citing Cunningham, notes that the goddess wields a shield, bow and arrow, club, discus, and thunderbolt. Damage to the image, as seen in figure 5.4, makes some identifications difficult, but it is clear to me that the goddess wields a shield, sword, thunderbolt, and an arrow.

Figure 5.4. Cave 6A image, approx. 1 × 1 m, white sandstone.
Udayagiri, Madhya Pradesh. *Source*: Photo by the author.

The goddess's lowest right hand holds an unidentifiable object, while one of her left hands raises the buffalo's rear by gripping its leg. Her right foot tramples the buffalo's head as she plunges a long trident (*triśūla*) into its back. Another left hand holds what appears to be a bow, accompanied by an unusual inverted cone-shaped object situated behind it. This object has been variously interpreted as a large drinking goblet, a quiver for arrows, a gigantic upraised bell, or a flag or standard. Its surface is marked with a distinctive pattern of rectangular decorations. The nature of this object remains unclear, but I shall revisit and attempt to decipher its significance later.

R. C. Agrawala proposed that the upper two hands hold an iguana (*godhā*), a suggestion echoed by Banerjea (1956, 498), who associated it with depictions of *godhā* (alligator or lizard) seen on pedestals of Pārvatī images in Bengal and in Hoysala figures of Pārvatī. Seshadri (1963, 8n27) speculated that it might be a snake, as some buffalo-subduing goddess images include this motif. The posture, reminiscent of Śiva holding a snake horizontally above his head, suggests the goddess may be performing an honorific gesture, such as crowning herself or removing an elongated head or hair ornament.

Notably, the three-jeweled decoration associated with the elongated object might align it with her headdress. However, the elongated item appears to bear the jeweled adornments directly, casting doubt on earlier interpretations that it represents a serpent, iguana, or drum. The continuity between her hair, which flows into ornamental strands, and the elongated item suggests she is either

Figure 5.5. Cave 17 image, approx. 1 × 1 m, white sandstone. Udayagiri, Madhya Pradesh. *Source*: Photo by the author.

attaching it to or removing it from her head, emphasizing its significance as a headdress-related element rather than a separate symbolic object.

Deciphering the Upraised "Wreath"

In figure 5.5 we see another rock cut representation of a multi-armed buffalo-subduing goddess at Udayagiri, on the exterior of Cave 17. In three of her right hands, the goddess holds an arrow, trident, and an unidentifiable item, with a long, thick shaft descending downward. In four of her left hands, she holds a bow, a shield, an unidentified object (it could possibly be a cup, an inverted bell, a fan, or a flag), and something else, resting on her lap. Given its position, which looks like it might be thrust into the buffalo's neck, J. C. Harle (1971–72, 46) reasonably speculates that the item on her lap might be a sword, which was used in combat with the buffalo. Unlike the Cave 6A image, which is similar to the Bhumarā and Rājghāṭ images, in this relief one of her left hands holds the buffalo by the mouth and bends its head upwards, while one of the right hands firmly grasps its tail. She pierces the buffalo in the back with a trident-headed spear held in one of her right hands (R. C. Agrawala 1958, 129; see also Stietencron 2005, 147).[5] Here, too, she holds the decorated elongated item above her head in her two uppermost hands, as if ready to bind it to or remove it from her hair or headdress. In the center of the elongated item and positioned directly above her head, somewhat eroded but clearly visible, there appears to be a circular decoration. The relatively narrow elongated shape of the item in this relief, in comparison to its counterpart on the Cave 6A relief, makes the interpretation that it is a drum or a lizard even more unlikely.

Instead, these two arms and what they hold evoke references to Durgā with strong upraised arms, tying her hair with a variegated diadem. Consider the phrasing in the DStv, in which the goddess is described as *bibhratī vipulau bāhu śakradhvajasamucchrayau* ("possessing two expansive/broad (*vipula*) arms like Indra's banner ahoist (*samucchraya*)"). Here we have an explicit reference to her upraised arms and even a tacit comparison to an honorific symbol (Indra's banner).[6] And later in that same hymn, Durgā is described as *mukuṭena vicitreṇa keśabandhena śobhinā* ("adorned with a multicolored, hair-band diadem, or adorned with a variegated diadem [and] with braided hair"). Even if we were to read *keśabandha* as braided hair, rather than as a hair-band, we note on both the Udayagiri Cave 6A image and Cave 17 images that the Devī has braided hair. A diadem (*mukuṭa*) may also be a hair-band. In the *Abhinaya Darpaṇa*, a short treatise on gestures in dance, attributed to the sage Nandikeśvara, the term *keśa-bandha* refers to tying the hair and has Durgā as its patron deity. It claims to be an abridged treatment of the expansive *Bharatārṇava*, an exposition on dance in 4,000 *ślokas* (Coomaraswamy and Duggirala 1917, 43).

Phyllis Granoff comes very close to the correct identification when, speaking of the item in the Cave 6A image, she notes,

> it has exactly the same texture and appearance as the hair so carefully represented below it. It is braided and bejewelled; the main ornament composed of three circular forms is in fact partly attached to the hair below. The goddess is thus holding a piece of her hair and seems about to bind it in an elaborate chignon. The result would probably look something like the hair of . . . a Mahiṣāsuramardinī from an 8th century temple at Osiāñ in Rajasthan. At Osiāñ the goddess displays an elaborate hairdo, with a large crest-jewel very much like the one we see in the unbound hair of the goddess at Udayagiri. (1979, 142)

By focusing quite thoroughly on the related Purāṇic literature, particularly the *Vāmana Purāṇa*'s account of the goddess Kauśikā's battle with the demon Ruru, Granoff goes on to the interesting speculation that this is a demonic intestine with which the goddess ties up her hair. She then develops the argument that the Udayagiri reliefs fuse the myths of the goddess Śumbhaniśumbhahananī with Mahiṣāsuramardinī. However, it is unlikely that the intestine would be ornamented.[7]

Within the Purāṇic corpus, Chapter 68.10 to 68.23 of the old *Skanda Purāṇa* (SP) describes the goddess Kauśikī's defeat of Mahiṣa (see Yokochi 2004, 191–192 for a synoptic translation). In this narrative, the goddess is invited to a sacrifice conducted by Śaradvat Gautama in Svarṇākṣa. Hearing of her presence, the demon Mahiṣa — described as the son of Sumbha (*sūnuḥ sumbhasya* (68.12)) but distinct from the demon Śumbha — hurries to confront her. While "Mahiṣa" may simply be his name, the text confirms his buffalo form, describing his curved horns, broad hooves, large head, and fine tail. Mahiṣa, characterized as vengeful, cruel, and proud of his power, roars loudly as he seeks to challenge the goddess.

The goddess, referred to as Vindhyavāsinī, responds swiftly. Mahiṣa, depicted as the son of the demon king and an enemy of Indra, charges at Kauśikī. She, described only as wearing a pearl necklace on her bosom, resists his attack, seizes his horn, and hurls him to the ground. She then presses his head to the earth with her foot, lifts him by the tail, and kills him with her trident. After completing this act, Kauśikī returns to her abode on Mount Vindhya.

While early buffalo-subduing goddess imagery rarely aligns perfectly with Purāṇic descriptions, this account corresponds closely with Gupta-period depictions, such as those from Bhumarā, the Rājghāṭ seal, and Udayagiri Cave 6A. In these, the goddess steps on the buffalo's head and pierces him with her trident. However, these images often show her holding one of his rear legs rather than his tail. Notably, in Udayagiri Cave 17, she holds the buffalo's tail but does not step on his head. Later depictions, such as those in the hall of Cave 1 at Badami and at Alampur, better reflect this SP description. Stietencron (2005, 141) dates the Badami and Alampur images to the last quarter of the 6th century CE and the 9th century CE, respectively.

Chapter 68 of the SP, although brief, appears to be a later insertion, as Mahiṣa is previously shown advising the demons Sunda and Nisunda against warring with the gods (see Yokochi 2004, 128). This retelling of the Mahiṣa myth seems to assimilate the buffalo-subduing goddess into the persona of Kauśikī/Vindhyavāsinī, a process likely solidified in the Gupta iconic representations between the 4th and 6th centuries CE (Yokochi 2004, 150). However, except for her trident and pearl necklace, the text does not describe her other weapons or ornaments, necessitating a shift away from early Purāṇas to identify the enigmatic object she holds.

To seek further clues about the unidentified objects and symbolic elements in the Udayagiri buffalo-subduing goddess reliefs, we must revisit the DStv. The hymn vividly describes features such as the goddess's variegated diadem, braided hair, and uplifted broad arms, all of which appear prominently in the Udayagiri sculptures. The introductory frame verses of the extended DStv+ describe her wielding a sword and shield — attributes clearly seen in Udayagiri Cave 6A and the shield also in Cave 17. Her face is likened to the full moon (*pūrṇacandranibhānana*), and indeed, her visage appears rounded, if not radiant, in both reliefs. The DStv also attributes to her items such as a goblet (*pātrī*), bell (*ghaṇṭī*), noose (*pāśa*), bow (*dhanus*), a great discus (*mahācakra*), and a variety of weapons (*vividhāny āyudhāni*). Both reliefs depict her carrying a bow and possibly a drinking vessel, although the object is unusual and warrants closer scrutiny.

Some items, such as the noose, bell, and discus, are not visible in the reliefs, possibly due to damage. In the Cave 17 relief, the unidentified object in her upper left hand could be an inverted bell rather than a cup, but its damaged state makes precise identification difficult. The goddess's association with "diverse weapons" (*vividha āyudhāni*) suggests that consistency in their depiction was not essential — she could be recognized through any combination of these attributes. The hymn describes her as the "Destroyer of the demon Mahiṣa" (*mahiṣāsura-nāśinī*), but it does not specify how the slaying is carried out, leaving artistic interpretations open.

Additional details in the DStv+ include her armlets (*keyūrāṅgadadadhāriṇi*) and earrings (*kuṇḍalābhyāṃ supūrṇābhyāṃ karṇābhyāṃ ca vibhūṣitā*). Both are visible in the Udayagiri reliefs, with the earrings especially pronounced in Cave 17. The hymn also mentions bracelets made of peacock tail feathers (*mayūrapicchavalaya*) and an upraised flag of peacock tails (*dhvajena śikhipicchānām ucchritena virājase*). Although the reliefs depict her with bracelets, it is unclear if they are made of or decorated with peacock feathers. The object resembling an inverted cone with rectangular patterns in Cave 6A could be a drinking goblet, quiver, large bell, or even a flag or standard. If it is the *dhvaja* of peacock tails mentioned in the DStv, it aligns symbolically with her supreme divine status. Similarly, the inverted bell-like object in Cave 17 could represent a peacock feather fan or flag, linking both images to the hymn's descriptions.

From these observations, we can infer that the sculptors of the Udayagiri images may have been familiar with the goddess's attributes as described in the DStv or similar such hymns. While no other textual sources, including the Purāṇas, match the details of the Udayagiri sculptures as closely, the temporal proximity of the DStv or unknown DStv* variants to the production of these reliefs suggests a shared conceptual framework. Ritual hymns, constantly repeated in devotional contexts, would have been instrumental in transmitting the goddess's attributes. Specialists and votaries would have recognized these traits, ensuring consistency between verbal descriptions and visual representations.

Given the enduring recitation of the DStv+ — even in contemporary Bengali Durgā Pūjā rituals — it is plausible that the hymn, or a variant, was already in circulation during the Gupta era, influencing the imagery at Udayagiri. While this does not imply that the DStv directly dictated the reliefs' design, there was likely a reciprocal relationship between verbal and visual portrayals, ensuring the goddess was identifiable across mediums. Based on parallels with the Praise of Nidrā (First Stratum) (PN-s1) in the *Harivaṃśa* (HV), which echoes some of the DStv's content, and the hymn's probable 3rd century CE or earlier origin, its influence during the Gupta period seems reasonable.

If we accept the date of 401/402 CE for the Udayagiri relief, based on the nearby Candragupta II inscription, it offers a tentative but compelling indication through material evidence that the DStv or similar hymns were composed and circulating by this time. Furthermore, since the goddess is depicted with both a sword and shield — attributes mentioned in the DStv's framing verses — it raises the possibility that the DStv was already circulating with its framing material (DStv+) and might have been embedded within the *Mahābhārata* (Mbh) by then. However, in the absence of more conclusive evidence, this remains speculative.

Line 20 of the DStv describes the goddess as shining with a face rivaling the moon. Upon close inspection, one can discern a crescent moon and other celestial orbs on the back of the shield depicted in the relief, positioned near her face. Such correlations suggest that contemporaries may have identified this image as Durgā, Destroyer of the Buffalo Demon Mahiṣa (Durgā Mahiṣāsura-nāśinī), explicitly named in DStv lines 29, 39, and 51.

The enigmatic object held above the goddess's head in the Udayagiri Cave 6A and Cave 17 images, if identified as the variegated diadem bound to braided hair — as is likely — merits further exploration. This interpretation aligns more plausibly than earlier hypotheses suggesting the object is a drum, iguana, bowl, intestine, or basket. The diadem motif invites comparisons with various Kuṣāṇa plaques, carved from the region's distinctive mottled red sandstone, many of which are now housed in the Government Museum at Mathurā. These plaques, often considered the earliest depictions of the buffalo-subduing goddess, also feature the goddess holding an overhead object.

In his study of these images, Harle (1969, 151), comparing them to the Udayagiri Cave 6A image, suggested that the overhead object represents a lotus garland for the head. He drew upon the *Devī Māhātmya* (DM), which describes the gods investing the goddess with various weapons and adornments. In the DM, the Ocean (*jaladhi*) presents her with a lovely lotus for her hand, a lotus garland for her chest, and unusually, a garland of unfading lotuses for her head (*paṅkajāṃ mālāṃ śirasi*). A head garland is indeed rare in iconography.

However, Harle himself acknowledged inconsistencies in this interpretation. Traditional garlands are typically uniform in thickness and adorned with floral designs, while the object in question is thickest in the middle and lacks clear floral motifs. Harle (1971–72, 44) later reiterated his position, suggesting that the "garland" might represent a long garland folded several times upon itself, explaining its unusual appearance. This interpretation has persisted in contemporary discussions (e.g., Schmid 2011, 121–22). A more recent interpretation by D. Srinivasan (2022) partially revises this view, suggesting that the object represents an honorific garland, but proposes that it symbolizes an act of self-coronation by the goddess. I concur with this interpretation to an extent and will revisit Srinivasan's argument in conjunction with my own analysis later in this study.

There is, in fact, a third image at Udayagiri of the goddess wrestling with a buffalo, on the side wall extending to the left of the entrance to Cave 6 and shown in figure 5.6. I am designating this image Cave 6B.

The very worn relief in Cave 6B at Udayagiri depicts what is likely a twelve-armed representation of the buffalo-subduing goddess. This relief resembles the

Figure 5.6. Cave 6B image, approx. 1 × 1 m, white sandstone.
Udayagiri, Madhya Pradesh. *Source*: Photo by the author.

image in Cave 17, as the buffalo rears upward against the goddess's body, its head positioned near her left shoulder. One of her right arms presses stiffly on the buffalo's haunch, echoing depictions found in Kuṣāṇa sandstone plaques, which are widely regarded as some of the earliest representations of the buffalo-subduing goddess. It is plausible that this worn Cave 6B image and the less worn Cave 17 image represent an earlier phase of sculptural development compared to the more refined Cave 6A image, which is located below a dated inscription from 401/402 CE.

Mitterwallner (1976, 200–1) suggests a developmental sequence: the Cave 6B image as the prototype for Cave 17, followed by the more polished Cave 6A. This sequencing aligns with stylistic details, such as the goddess's multiple thin bangles in the Cave 6B and Cave 17 reliefs, contrasting with the single bangles seen in the Cave 6A image, a Gupta-era stylistic hallmark (Harle 1971–72, 47–48). In the worn Cave 6B image, the object held aloft by the goddess is clearly visible, although its decorations are no longer discernible. Harle notes its "pouchier and more drooping" appearance compared to traditional garlands, while its ends project beyond the goddess's grasp, similarly to other depictions in this posture (1971–72, 44–48).

While the DM describes a lotus garland for the goddess's head, this identification seems less compelling than the ornate variegated diadem mentioned in the PN-s1. In the PN-s1, the goddess — who is neither explicitly identified as Durgā nor linked to the slaying of Mahiṣa — is described with features

mirroring those in the DStv, including broad arms, a resplendent face rivaling the moon, and ornamented ears. Notably, she is adorned with a diadem
described as *"tricakreṇa keśabandhena śobhitā,"* or "a hair-band diadem with
three discs." This description is strikingly similar to the DStv's depiction of a
goddess "adorned with a variegated diadem and hair-band" (*mukuṭena vicitreṇa
keśabandhena śobhinā*).

The term *vicitra*, often translated as "variegated" or "multicolored," carries
a deeper connotation of something extraordinary, surprising, or awe-inspiring.
Such a diadem, far more striking than a garland or simple hair ornament, would
have captured the imaginations of both audiences and sculptors. Moreover,
mukuṭa, typically translated as "tiara" or "crown," is best understood here as
a diadem, a type of crown bound around the head, in keeping with its Greek
etymological root.

The diadem depicted in the Cave 6A image appears to align with this description. It features three decorative discs with floral motifs and suspended tassels,
potentially corresponding to the *tricakreṇa* (three-disc) attribute in the PN-s1.
Although the PN-s1 does not use the term *vicitra*, the diadem's exceptional
design and ornamental complexity underscore its significance as a head-binding
symbol of divinity and supremacy.

Let us consider one more example to see if it complies with our proposal that
the upraised "wreath" is an honorific diadem. Item 1987.142.289 in the Samuel

Figure 5.7a. Śuṅga hairpin goddess (2nd century BCE); 7.1
cm, copper alloy. Possibly from Kauśāmbī. Object Number:
1987.142.289. *Source*: Samuel Eilenberg Collection, Gift of Samuel
Eilenberg, in honor of Steven Kossak, 1987; Metropolitan Museum
of Art. Public domain.

Figure 5.7b. Śuṅga hairpin goddess (reverse) (2nd century BCE); 7.1 cm, copper alloy. Possibly from Kauśāmbī. Object Number: 1987.142.289. *Source*: Samuel Eilenberg Collection, Gift of Samuel Eilenberg, in honor of Steven Kossak, 1987; Metropolitan Museum of Art. Public domain.

Eilenberg Collection at the Metropolitan Museum of Art is unusual because it is an image of the goddess with hairpin weapons that is fashioned from bronze, as shown in figures 5.7a and 5.7b (Lerner and Kossak 1991, 53–55).[8]

This image likely dates to the Śuṅga period (2nd century BCE to 1st century CE). While most representations of this goddess are terracotta reliefs, this bronze sculpture is modeled in the round, offering insights into the intentions of the relief makers that two-dimensional plaques cannot adequately convey. As is common in the terracotta plaques, the goddess faces forward, with her left hand resting on her hip and her right arm bent, the forearm extending outward perpendicular to her body. Unfortunately, the right hand and both feet (severed just above the ankles) are missing, leaving it unclear whether she held an object or made a specific gesture (*mudrā*). In the plaques, the goddess is often depicted in the boon-granting gesture (*varadā mudrā*).

The bronze figure wears a skirt with a prominent belt, partially concealed by an upper bodice covering her hips. She has a long necklace, a tubular earring in her left ear, a hoop earring in her right, and large, prominent bangles on her wrists. Her hair is parted at the center and styled into two buns, with three hairpin-like weapons protruding from each side. On the left, the hairpins unmistakably resemble a battle axe, an arrow, and a goad. On the right, the hairpins are identical to one another but do not definitively resemble weapons. They may represent spears, sword hilts, or incomplete weapon forms. Atop her head is a sort of crown, with a floral-decorated band extending above her ears. This hair-band features undecorated, swag-like ends that trail behind her head, a detail crucially visible in the bronze but not apparent in the terracotta plaques (see figure 5.7b). This decorative feature may resolve a recurring interpretative issue. As described by Lerner and Kossak (1991, 54), "the long, ropelike terminals of the lotus garland that appear on the back of the bronze but are not depicted on the terracotta plaques explain the looped ends of the wreaths held by the Durgas (*sic*) in the Kushan — and early Gupta — period portrayals." Notably, the illustrative plaque from the Metropolitan Museum (referenced earlier) appears to also depict the goddess with this hair-band feature, with its ends trailing over her shoulders. This correspondence reinforces the connection between these representations and their broader iconographic evolution.

In the quoted passage, we observe that recent interpretations of the upheld item regard it as a floral "garland" (following Harle) or "wreath," either bound to the goddess's head or held above it. To support the latter interpretation, we can turn to D. Srinivasan's detailed explanation (1997, 294–95), which highlights that the goddess Nanā is depicted on Kuṣāṇa coinage either wearing a wreath or holding one in her hand. The act of self-coronation by deities is also common in Indo-Greek and Śaka coinage. For example, Heracles crowns himself on a round tetradrachm of Demetrius I and a bronze square coin of Azes.

Numerous examples also depict the goddess Nike (Victory) holding a wreath or crowning a king (e.g., the Kuṣāṇa ruler Heraios) or even a deity (e.g., Dionysus), as seen in the art and coinage of the Bactrians, Kuṣāṇas, Indo-Parthians, and Indo-Greeks such as Menander (Stančo 2012, 176–77). Nike is frequently shown flying, and her iconic winged figure, such as the *Nike of Samothrace* on display at the Louvre, remains widely recognized. These symbolic portrayals resonate strongly with Nidrā's flight from Mathurā to Vindhya, Nidrā/Kauśikī's winged persona in Vindhyachal, and the names Jayā (Conquest) and Vijayā (Victory) applied to Durgā/Kālī in the DStv and Durgā Stotra (DSto), as well as to Durgā/Kauśikī in Praise of Nidrā (Second Stratum) (PN-s2).

In the *Taittirīya Brāhmaṇa* (TB) (1.6.4.1–3), Prajāpati, the creator of all beings, fashioned a wreath from the essence of all creatures and the four quarters of the world. When he placed it upon himself, all creatures finally acknowledged his superiority. He later placed this wreath on Indra, symbolically transferring his sovereignty to the god. Similarly, in TB 1.8.9.6, Hopkins (1909, 43–44) notes that a lotus-wreath is worn by the sacrificer in Vedic ritual, symbolizing the power of Vṛtra, the primordial demon slain by Indra. In the previous chapter, we traced the robust symbolic affinities between deities such as Nanā and the buffalo-subduing goddess depicted on Kuṣāṇa plaques. The motif of the wreath, signifying sovereignty and superiority, has clear Vedic antecedents. Notably, in the TB, we encounter the motif of self-coronation by Prajāpati, along with the symbolic transference of sovereignty when Prajāpati bequeaths the wreath to Indra. Furthermore, the Vedic tradition associates wearing the wreath with the acquisition of sovereign power, signifying the defeat of chaos and evil (Vṛtra) by the supreme deity (Indra).

Although there is no unequivocal textual evidence stating that the "wreath" worn by the buffalo-subduing goddess carries these precise connotations, the circumstantial evidence is compelling, particularly when viewed alongside the Kuṣāṇa plaques. In these depictions, the goddess holds the "wreath" above her head in an act of self-coronation. Most recently, D. Srinivasan (2022) has convincingly argued that this item represents self-coronation. She refutes earlier suggestions, such as Granoff's (1979) proposal that the object is a piece of intestine, and Schmid's (2011) repetition of this interpretation. Instead, she identifies it as an honorific floral garland or wreath, a motif traceable from ancient Greece to Mathurā. She concludes that "the gesture can be followed as it traveled into the early art of Mathurā; in Mathurā it ought to have denoted the successful accomplishment of a suprahuman feat. In response to such an achievement, these gods [Śiva is also depicted with such a gesture] crown themselves with a floral garland, the traditional Mathurā emblem for bestowing honor" (D. Srinivasan 2022, 71). However, I suggest that this item is not merely a generic, textually unidentified honorific "wreath," as Srinivasan and O. Divakaran (1984, 286) propose. Rather, it corresponds to the wondrous or variegated diadem (*vicitra-mukuṭa*), a symbol of divine sovereignty frequently referenced in early epic hymns. If this diadem is not represented by the item held aloft by the goddess, then we are left to ask: Where is this significant attribute depicted in her imagery?

Let us reconsider the bronze image alongside the descriptions of the goddess from the PN-s1 and the DStv. In the PN-s1, the goddess is described as wearing a dark-blue linen garment and a white upper garment (47.41), features that align with the attire depicted on the bronze (although the color cannot be discerned). On her breast, she is adorned with a necklace that shines like the moon's rays (47.41), and a similar necklace is present on the bronze. Her ears are embellished with heavenly earrings (47.42), which are also visible on the bronze. The hymn describes her as beautified by braided hair or a hair-band and a wondrous or variegated diadem (*mukuṭena vicitreṇa keśabandhena śobhinā*) (47.43). While the term *keśabandha* may refer to hair tied up into a bun rather than braided or adorned with a hair-band, the plaques and bronze goddess appear to feature both elements.

The bracelets described in the hymn are decorated with peacock feathers (47.44), and while bracelets are prominent on the bronze image, the details of their decorative motifs are unclear due to wear. Notably, this bronze goddess has three sets of hairpin weapons on each side, fewer than the more typical five found in similar depictions. Despite this difference, the numerous correspondences between the bronze figure (and the related terracottas from Chandraketugarh) and the PN-s1 description are striking. These parallels strongly suggest that the goddess represented in the bronze image may be

Kauśikī, the only specific name given to Nidrā in the hymn. This identification provides additional evidence linking the Chandraketugarh goddesses with the textual tradition of PN-s1 and reinforces their connection to the proto-Durgā archetype.

The goddess depicted in the bronze image also shares notable similarities with the goddess described in the DStv, who is adorned with bracelets of peacock feathers and the variegated diadem. Additionally, the DStv describes the goddess as wearing a hip-belt (*śronisūtra*) and a garment (*vāsa*) resembling the coils (*ābhoga*) of serpents (*bhujaṅga*), which make her radiant (*vibhrāja*), like Mount Mandara bound (*ābaddha*) with serpentine coils (*bhoga*). This description aligns with the belt visible around the hips of the bronze goddess's skirt, partially concealed by her bodice. Such belts are more prominent on the related goddesses depicted in the Chandraketugarh terracotta plaques.

The DStv is addressed to Durgā, also known as Jayā and Vijayā, indicating a close connection between Kauśikī and Durgā, more through shared attributes than explicit identification. The explicit identification of Durgā as Kauśikī, however, emerges only later, in the PN-s2 (also called the Āryā Stava). As concluded in the previous chapter, it is reasonable to infer that the Chandraketugarh images may represent Kauśikī or proto-Durgās (assimilating Anāhitā) at this juncture. This is significant when we consider the Kuṣāṇa red sandstone images depicting the goddess overpowering the buffalo and holding what may well be the *vicitra-mukuṭa*. If this wondrous headband diadem is indeed what is portrayed on many of these images, it identifies the goddess as Durgā, described in the DStv as the queen of the triple world (v. 2). Whether the DStv (or DStv* hymns) influenced the makers of these Kuṣāṇa Mahiṣāsuranāśinī plaques or whether these hymns were inspired by such depictions, they are likely roughly contemporaneous — a point that inclines me to favor the former hypothesis.

This portrayal of Durgā holding aloft what is arguably the "wondrous diadem" is evident in the earliest Mahiṣāsuranāśinī images of the Kuṣāṇa period and carries forward into Gupta depictions, such as those at Udayagiri (c. 400 CE). However, by the mid-Gupta period, the "wondrous diadem" ceases to appear in Mahiṣāsuranāśinī images. For instance, a late Gupta representation (MM 842) depicts the goddess wielding a sword, dagger, and noose while subduing the buffalo demon (R. C. Agrawala 1958, 128). This disappearance of the diadem may correlate with the rise of Purāṇic versions of Durgā's victory over the buffalo demon, such as in the SP and the DM, where this attribute is no longer mentioned. In its place, the DM describes a lotus garland given to the goddess by the Ocean (DM 2.27–28) and a crest jewel bestowed by the Sea of Milk (DM 2.24). These elements may reflect a transformation of the diadem's significance, shifting from an overt symbol of divine supremacy to a subtler expression of the goddess's exalted status — a theme to which I will return in the last chapter of this volume.

More pertinently, the presence of descriptive motifs such as the wondrous diadem, peacock feather bracelets, and banner in the DStv or related hymns reinforces the likelihood of their earlier composition, likely during the Kuṣāṇa to mid-Gupta period. It seems improbable that hymns would be composed in later periods describing attributes of the goddess that were no longer recognizable or depicted.

Chapter 6

The Peacock Standard

The interweaving of iconography and textual traditions serves as a compelling lens to understand the evolution of Durgā's status and the broader theological developments within Hinduism. This chapter seeks to reinterpret certain mischaracterized iconographic elements, such as shields and quivers in Kuṣāṇa and Gupta art, by linking them with early epic hymn descriptions. These elements are re-examined as peacock feather standards — a symbol of sovereignty central to Durgā's depiction. This reinterpretation not only clarifies their iconographic significance but also highlights their potential influence on the development of the Peacock Goddess (Mahāmāyūrī) in Buddhism and offers intriguing parallels with the Chinese goddess Xi Wangmu, the Sovereign Mother of the West.

These explorations underscore the rich interregional cultural exchanges that shaped religious iconography and ideology, connecting South Asia with Egypt, Mesopotamia, Central Asia, and China. Such exchanges challenge the tendency to view South Asian religious culture in isolation, an approach that has often hindered broader scholarly insights. By examining symbols of sovereignty, such as self-coronation with the diadem and the association with the peacock banner, we note more compelling evidence for Durgā's assertion of supremacy within the Hindu pantheon. These elements are critical to the argument advanced in the final chapter of this volume, which explores how the *Devī Māhātmya* (DM) (discussed in chapter 9) skillfully recast the theology of the Great Goddess as the Supreme Deity.

Deciphering the Peacock Standard

We now turn to another enigmatic item frequently depicted on the Kuṣāṇa sandstone plaques, the Nagar terracotta plaque, and the Udayagiri cave reliefs. This checkered object is typically portrayed to the upper left of the goddess (or upper right in the plaques). In Udayagiri Cave 17, it was initially thought to resemble an inverted bell or drinking cup. However, in the Udayagiri Cave 6A image, the object takes on a large, inverted cone shape with distinctive rectangular patterning, leading some scholars to postulate that it is a quiver. While plausible for the item in Cave 17, this interpretation seems less likely for the Cave 6A depiction due to its extreme width at the top and lack of features typically associated with quivers.

A closer examination of the Kuṣāṇa sandstone plaques, which share iconographic elements such as what is possibly the *vicitra-mukuṭa*, reveals similar checkered items. However, these plaques lack depictions of bows, making it unlikely that the goddess would be equipped with a quiver. Instead, the object on these plaques appears ovoid or fan shaped. The terracotta plaque from Nagar, Rajasthan (figure 4.4), now in the Hawa Mahal collection in Jaipur, offers a clearer portrayal. Here, the item resembles a large rectangle with a fringe-like feature along its lower third — typical of banners — while the upper two-thirds display a characteristic crosshatch design. The crosshatch pattern led Barrett (1975, 64) to interpret the object as a wickerwork shield. Similarly, R. C. Agrawala (1958, 125) described it as a "typical rectangular shield." This interpretation is plausible, especially since the four-armed goddess often uses two arms to subdue the buffalo, while another wields a weapon resembling a double-pronged trident. This dual-pronged weapon is likely a thunderbolt (*vajra*), also visible in the Udayagiri Cave 6A relief.

Coins of the Indo-Greek king Menander I depict the goddess Athena holding a thunderbolt alongside what is often mischaracterized as a "shield." Closer examination reveals that this "shield" is more accurately identified as Athena's aegis, a protective emblem often associated with her. Notably, the shields found on the Udayagiri images are typically circular, which contrasts with the rectangular or fan-shaped checkered object depicted in Cave 6A and the Nagar terracotta plaque. Instead, I propose that this object is a depiction of the goddess's upraised standard of peacock tail feathers (*dhvajena śikhipicchānām ucchritena virājase*), an attribute explicitly mentioned in the Durgā Stava (DStv 1 26), and the Praise of Nidrā (First Stratum) hymn (PN-s1 1 44: *dhvajena śikhibarhāṇām ucchritena samīpataḥ*). This peacock standard, referenced as an emblem of the goddess, could function similarly to Athena's aegis as a symbol of divine authority and protection.

The peacock standard also appears in the Praise of Nidrā (Second Stratum) (PN-s2) and the Durgā Stotra (DSto), highlighting its consistent significance in textual traditions. These affinities between the DStv and the buffalo-subduing goddess imagery — designated as Mahiṣāsuranāśinī — reinforce the connection between early iconographic and textual representations. Furthermore, the PN-s1 links Nidrā/Kauśikī to the terracotta plaques from Chandraketugarh. On those plaques, peacock-themed elements are evident, such as the *māyūrastambha* (peacock pillar) or a peacock flag often depicted beside the goddess, possibly held by an attendant or independently standing nearby. In contrast, the Mahiṣāsuranāśinī plaques feature the goddess herself holding the peacock-tail feather standard, signifying her direct association with this symbol of sovereignty. If we revisit the depiction in Cave 6A at Udayagiri, the inverted conical object closely resembles folded peacock tail feathers, with its segmented design evocative of the distinctive "eye" motifs of peacock plumage. Similarly, older photographs of the Cave 17 relief reveal faint decorative details on the upper portion of this item, resembling feathers (Stietencron 2005, 134). This alignment of textual and visual evidence supports the identification of the enigmatic checkered item as the *dhvaja śikhipicchānām*, a vital iconographic symbol of the goddess's supremacy. Its presence in Kuṣāṇa and Gupta art underscores its continuity as a symbol of sovereignty and divine power throughout early Indian religious traditions.

In his analysis of this item — suggested here as the *śikhipiccha-dhvaja* (peacock-tail standard) — Harle (1971–72, 45) expressed puzzlement over the Cave 6A image. Referring to an element visible in old photographs but now missing, he observed it "appears to be the butt of what may have been a *gadā* down by the goddess's left foot, but that is all, unless the large funnel-shaped object apparently covered with scales or petals is part, or rather the top, of an object held by one of the missing left hands of the goddess." He added, "I had previously dismissed this object as a part, although a mysterious one, on the ground, perhaps an unusual representation of clouds or rocks, but a certain similarity in shape and position to one of the unidentified objects held by the Cave No 17 goddess suggests that it may be part of one of the attributes of the goddess."

I find Harle's conjecture that this element is the bottom of something — and not the butt of a *gadā*, as Cunningham (1880, 50) suggested — compelling. It is likely the base of the peacock banner, which in Cave 6A extends from one of the goddess's left hands to the floor. The upper portion, resembling an inverted cone, matches Harle's description of the "funnel-shaped object," while the "scales or petals" correspond to peacock tail feather markings. Examining the items gifted to the Devī in the DM, Harle (1971–1972, 46) noted she did not receive a *gadā* (club). Regarding the Cave 17 object, he speculated, "it has a fairly narrow shaft or stem, which appears slightly curved and is surmounted by something of considerable bulk, almost certainly not the blade of an axe."

Seeking correspondences with the gifts to the Devī in the DM, Harle concludes, "this would eliminate all the possibilities except the lotus. Here the suspicion arises that this is the same object with its scales and petals on the far left of the Cave No. 6 Durgā-mahiṣāsuramardinī" (1971–72, 47). I agree that the object in Cave 6A aligns with this conjecture, but Harle reached an impasse. Regarding the Cave 17 object, he remarked, "it appears to be funnel-shaped . . . its position being between shield and bow is very similar. The object in Cave No. 6 is not a lotus but the fact remains that it appears to consist of lotus petals. No solution to this problem appears possible at present" (1971–72, 47).

I propose that both objects are likely representations of the *śikhipiccha-dhvaja* (peacock-tail standard). In a note, Harle (1971–72, 48n9) emphasizes that if the Cave 6A object is indeed one of the goddess's emblems, it should correspond to a known symbol and be consistent with the time and place of its depiction. I concur, and the *śikhipiccha-dhvaja*, like the *vicitra-mukuṭa*, fits these criteria. Both are emblematic attributes referenced in early hymns and closely align with iconographic features across distinct periods and regions. The inability of scholars to locate these items within the later Purāṇic corpus underscores their earlier origins, as the Purāṇic material postdates this imagery.

Figure 6.1. Kuṣāṇa goddess on a lion holding what is likely the peacock tailfeather flag (2nd century CE); 26 × 6 × 11 cm, sandstone. Uttar Pradesh. I 5894, "Durga auf dem Löwen." *Source*: Museum für Asiatische Kunst, Berlin. CC-BY-SA-4.0.

A final example supporting the identification of the peacock banner is a Kuṣāṇa plaque displayed at the Berlin Museum für Asiatische Kunst (figure 6.1). The goddess is shown standing on a lion, with one right hand raised in a fear-not gesture. Another right hand, positioned behind her, may hold a short sword or *vajra*, although this is unclear. Most notably, her left hand grasps a rectangular banner attached to a pole. While some scholars have interpreted this as a trident, the pole's curving lines differ from the typically straight shafts of tridents. The checkered design on the banner recalls patterns seen on similar plaques. This item is most plausibly the peacock-tailfeather banner (*śikhipic-cha-dhvaja*), an emblem repeatedly associated with the goddess in early hymns and consistently depicted in her earliest iconography.

Let us reconsider the dates of the *Harivaṃśa* (HV) and the DStv or its unknown DStv* variants, both of which describe the goddess with attributes consistent with pre-Purāṇic imagery. The red mottled sandstone plaques from Mathurā, likely from the Kuṣāṇa period, suggest that the DStv or a variant (DStv*) either influenced or was influenced by these representations. Since the Kuṣāṇas expanded into Mathurā by the 1st and early 2nd centuries CE, the DStv or DStv* is reasonably placed within this timeframe. Meanwhile, the earliest portions of the HV, containing the PN-s1, would date to the late 2nd century

CE, aligning with scholarly proposals (e.g., Couture) for an early composition of this appendix to the *Mahābhārata* (Mbh).

The HV must have been composed after the core Mbh, and the *Bhagavad Gītā* (BG), which we have situated around the early 2nd century CE or perhaps somewhat earlier. Supporting this chronology, Aśvaghoṣa, the Buddhist poet of the 1st to 2nd centuries CE, quotes verses he attributes to the Mbh but that appear only in the HV. This suggests that the earliest portions of the HV were composed during the Kuṣāṇa expansion into Mathurā and adjacent regions. This timeline would also accommodate the composition of the DStv or its variants.

This proposed timeline situates the DStv or DStv* as early as the 1st or 2nd century CE, significantly earlier than commonly suggested by scholars who conflate its composition with its eventual insertion into the Mbh. This earlier dating implies that the cult of Nidrā/Kauśikī might have flourished as early as the Śuṅga dynasty, which succeeded the Mauryan Empire, and certainly during the later Hindu dynasties leading up to the Kuṣāṇas. Notably, the Mauryas, among the most powerful dynasties in the subcontinent's history, used the peacock as their imperial emblem, with the term "Maurya" often linked to *mayūra* (peacock). Aśoka, the greatest Mauryan emperor, is reputed to have subsisted on a diet that included antelopes and peacocks (Mookerji 1986, 62).

Additionally, a Mauryan pillar, namely the one at Lauriya-Nandangarh, features a 4-inch peacock symbol on the buried portions of its shaft (A. C. Carlleyle 1885, 46–47). While this marking has been interpreted simply as an imperial symbol, it might also be linked to the peacock standard (*śikhipiccha-dhvaja*) associated with Kauśikī. The name Kauśikī itself, meaning "She who catches Snakes," typically refers to the owl but could also relate to the peacock. This connection raises the possibility that peacock motifs and symbols, including tail feathers, played a role in Mauryan imperial iconography and were associated with sovereign power. It is conceivable that the cult of Kauśikī, centered in Magadha and the Vindhyachal region, thrived during the Mauryan era. However, its spread across the empire may have been constrained, particularly following Aśoka's conversion to Buddhism and the subsequent prohibition of animal sacrifices. Given that blood sacrifice of wild animals was a significant aspect of Kauśikī's worship (PN-s1 47.51), such practices might have faced suppression under the Mauryan regime until the Śuṅgas rose to power.

While the Mauryas supported Buddhism, the Śuṅgas, succeeded by the Kāṇvas and Sātavāhanas, were proponents of Hinduism. By the 2nd century BCE, the Śuṅga empire stretched from Mathurā in the West to Chandraketugarh in the East, encompassing Vindhyachal at its center. This region likely saw the flourishing of goddess worship, particularly centered on Vindhyachal, during the Śuṅga reign (2nd century BCE to 1st century CE). Evidence for such worship is vibrant in the Chandraketugarh Yakṣī images, which could represent Nidrā/Kauśikī, given their distinct features like peacock bracelets, occasional associations with a peacock standard or pillar (*mayūrastambha*), and "weapon" hair ornaments. These images span from the 2nd or 1st century BCE to the 1st century CE or slightly later.

By the 1st century CE, depictions of Durgā Mahiṣāsuranāśinī, the buffalo slayer, emerge. These portray the goddess wielding weapons, incorporating traits of the Vindhyan goddess, known for slaying Sumbha and Nisumbha (not Śumbha and Niśumbha). Nidrā/Kauśikī appears to have fused with the cult of Mahiṣāsuranāśinī during this period. Yokochi (2004, ch. 5.1) places this amalgamation around the old *Skanda Purāṇa* (SP) (c. 6th century CE) due to insufficient earlier textual evidence. However, the Kuṣāṇas, ruling northern India from the 1st to 4th centuries CE, supported and depicted the buffalo-subduing goddess, explicitly identifying her as Durgā in the DStv or its variants. This suggests the fusion of Nidrā/Kauśikī with Durgā Mahiṣāsuranāśinī could have occurred during the Kuṣāṇa period.

According to the PN-s1, the Vindhyan goddess Nidrā/Kauśikī was already viewed as a demon-slayer. She is described as black-skinned (47.39), virginal (47.45), fond of animal sacrifices (especially on her ninth lunar day festival) (47.51), and surrounded by fearsome elemental spirits (47.45, 51). Thus, it was not solely her identification as the killer of Mahiṣa, as depicted in the DStv, that defined Durgā's broader mythic persona. Instead, the later DStv+ reflects a fusion of Nidrā/Kauśikī's attributes with those of the buffalo-slaying, boon-granting, and salvific Durgā (v. 39, 52). The DStv+ also integrates her with Kālī (v. 34), embodying Nidrā/Kauśikī's virginal chastity, dark skin (v. 11), fondness for blood sacrifices (v. 34), and association with spirits (v. 35).

The DStv+ introduces a pivotal shift by associating the worship of Durgā with victory in battle, marking a significant transformation of the goddess Nidrā/Kauśikī/Kālī's persona. This motif of sovereignty likely reflects influences from the northwest and north-central regions of India during the Kuṣāṇa period, even if the hymn's insertion into the Mbh occurred later. Yudhiṣṭhira addresses Durgā with epithets such as Jayā (Conquest) and Vijayā (Victory) (v. 31–32), seeking her aid in reclaiming his kingdom (v. 48). When the goddess appears, she offers repeated assurances of success in battle (v. 55–57, 61). Thus, the DStv+ underscores the goddess's evolving role as a patroness of royalty, warfare, and kingly endeavors. This motif, wherein a king or prince prays to the goddess for assistance in dire circumstances, recurs across centuries. In the DStv+, it is Yudhiṣṭhira; in the DSto+, it is Arjuna. Later narratives feature similar scenarios: Pradyumna sings a hymn for protection, King Suratha turns to Durgā in the DM to regain his kingdom, King Naravāhanadatta seeks Caṇḍikā/Kālarātrī's favor in the *Kathāsaritsāgara* (15.1.99–102), and Prince Sudarśana prays to Durgā in the *Devī Bhāgavata Purāṇa* (discussed in the second volume of this study).

As the Kuṣāṇa Empire gave way to the Gupta dynasty, the rise of Purāṇic Hinduism fostered a detailed narrative elaboration of the goddess's myths. While the PN-s1, DStv, and DSto merely allude to the goddess's slaying of Mahiṣa, the *Varāha Purāṇa* recounts the myth without naming Durgā. Over time, Durgā became increasingly recognized as the slayer of the Buffalo Demon in texts such as the SP. By the time of the composition of the DM, and its placement within the *Markaṇḍeya Purāṇa*, itself framed as a supplement-like text to the Mbh, the tradition of the Great Goddess had crystallized. Moreover, the DM articulated a theologically nuanced notion of the Great Goddess as the Supreme Deity. The remainder of our study traces these and ancillary developments.

The Peacock Goddess

The epic hymns reveal that in subsequent centuries Kauśikī/Durgā's distinctive peacock feather bracelets were the first to vanish, as was her association with the peacock standard, which lingered for a somewhat longer period. Her buffalo-slaying mythology grew, as did the link with the lion as her mount. Nevertheless, the Devī's association with the peacock standard was evident in the DStv (l. 26) as well as the DSto (l. 12) and PN-s2 (aka the Āryā Stava) (l. 10). In the latter two hymns she is unequivocally identified as Durgā, along with other epithets, such as Kālī, Bhadrakālī, Vijayā and Jayā, Kātyāyanī, and, of course Kauśikī. Interestingly, a version of the Āryā Stava was translated into Chinese, where it forms part of Yijing's translation of the *Suvarṇabhāsa Sūtra* (*Sūtra of Golden Light*). The *sūtra*, perhaps in existence from about the 1st century CE, according to Ludvik (but this is questionable), was influential in Buddhist Asia, and various versions circulated in Tibetan, Khotanese, Sogdian, Tangut, Mongolian, and Old Uighur, as well as Chinese (Ludvik 2006, 4–5). Although other Chinese translations of this *sūtra* exist, dating from about 436 CE, only Yijing's version, called the *Jinguanming zuishengwang jing*, and completed in 703 CE, contains the Āryā Stava. The extant Sanskrit version does not contain it. In Yijing's Chinese Buddhist version of the *sūtra*, the hymn is dedicated to the goddess Sarasvatī (Biancai tiannü). The riverine connection of Sarasvatī with the Āryā Stava is interesting, because we have already drawn a connection between the hymn and the river goddess Kauśikī, as well as with the riverine Middle Eastern goddess Arədvī Sūrā Anāhitā. Moreover, the only occurrence of the word *durgā* in the HV's version of the Āryā Stava is found in a line that reads:

> *āryā kātyāyanī devī kauśikī brahmacāriṇī /*
> *jananī siddhasenasya durgā vīrā mahātapāḥ /*
> (You are) the virtuous Kātyāyanī, the goddess Kauśikī, prac-
>   ticing celibacy,
> Mother of the one whose army is the Siddhas (Skanda), the
>   brave Durgā, of great austerities. (Coburn 1984, 279)

Catherine Ludvik (2006, 20n8), feeling that Coburn's translation of *āryā* as "virtuous" does not capture the intended meaning, renders it as:

> Noble goddess Kātyāyanī, Brahman-practising (celibate)
> Kauśikī
> Mother of him whose army consists of accomplished [war-
> riors] [Skanda]
> Durgā the brave, of great *tapas*.

Ludvik (2004, 716) notes that many manuscripts read *ugracārī* ("fierce going") instead of *durgā vīrā* ("Durgā, the brave"). Yijing's Chinese translation seems to derive from a blend of the two, reading *yong* (*vīrā*) and *meng* (*ugrā*) rather than having something closer to the meaning of *durgā* ("difficult to access"). She does note that *ugracāriṇī* is an epithet of Durgā. The name Durgā, however, is generally difficult to find in the Buddhist canon, although it is unlikely that the Buddhists were unaware of Durgā. In fact, we have already seen a number of parallels between aspects of Durgā's persona and that of the Buddha, or certainly of bodhisattvas in the Mahāyāna tradition. Durgā is constantly referred to as a raft to enable persons to traverse difficult waters, and a refuge from all sorts of dangers. This resonates with notions of the Buddha, his teachings, and community as the ultimate refuge, and that Buddhism itself is a raft to carry beings beyond the turbulent waters of saṃsāric existence to the far shore of freedom from sorrow and illusion.[1]

Iconographic evidence of the Buddhist goddess Mahāmāyūrī ("The Great Peacock" or "The Great Peahen") first appears in Cave 6 at Ellora, site of a renowned complex of Hindu, Buddhist, and Jain rock-cut caves located in Aurangabad, Maharashtra. There, she holds a peacock feather in her right hand and a spherical object, possibly a jewel or fruit, in her left. A peacock is depicted to her immediate right, accompanied by small female attendants and framed by *makara* (sea-monster) arches, under which fly chubby figures. To her right is a figure at a desk, often identified as a scribe reading or writing a text. Chinese translations of the Sanskrit *Mahāmāyūrīvidyā-rājñī* from as early as 516 CE indicate the goddess was invoked for rain, protection against various dangers, and immunity from snake poison, suggesting her worship in India during or before this time. Later texts and depictions show Mahāmāyūrī with a peacock as her *vāhana* (G. Malandra 1993, 96–97).

It is plausible that the Hindu goddess Nidrā/Kauśikī, associated with the peacock, evolved into or influenced the Buddhist Mahāmāyūrī, although they may have developed independently. As Nidrā/Kauśikī faded from the Hindu pantheon, she became identified with Āryā, Durgā, Jayā, Vijayā, Kumārī, and Skandamātā (the last two retaining her peacock association), as well as with Kālī and Kātyāyanī. Meanwhile, the symbolic importance of the peacock was absorbed by deities such as Kumāra (Skanda), whose mount is the peacock, and Kṛṣṇa, frequently adorned with peacock feathers.

Related Buddhist Goddesses

The case of Mahāmāyūrī provides an entry point to examine Buddhist interactions with the cult of the Goddess, an area requiring greater attention. The earliest Buddhist association with a goddess is Prajñāpāramitā, the deified embodiment of wisdom (*prajñā*), emerging with the *Prajñāpāramitā* literature as early as the 2nd century BCE. Effigies of Prajñāpāramitā, however, do not appear until the 7th century, notably at Ellora (Shaw 2006, 172).

Devotional aspects of Buddhism facilitated the incorporation of local goddesses into its pantheon, often through textual rather than iconographic means. A significant example is the *Pañcarakṣā*, a glorification (*māhātmya*) of five goddesses, often accompanied by paintings (*citrarūpa*) in manuscript copies. This text holds a role in Mahāyāna Buddhist households similar to the DM among Hindus. Widely venerated in Nepal, the Himalayan regions, Central Asia, China, Korea, and Japan, the *Pañcarakṣā* reflects intersections of goddess worship within Buddhist and non-Buddhist traditions. Conceptual and terminological parallels with Durgā's cult highlight these interactions, warranting deeper exploration.

Verses from the *Pañcarakṣā* are read regularly or at festival times, just as is the DM, with which it has been compared, and some are held in such high repute that they were even used for oath takings by Buddhist witnesses in legal proceedings (D. C. Bhattacharyya 1972, 85–92).[2] Although this may no longer be the case, it is likely that upper-class Newari homes in Nepal still possess a copy of the *Pañcarakṣā* (Kim 2010, 260). The five goddesses are: Mahāpratisarā, Mahāmāyūrī, Mahāsāhasrapramardinī (or -marddinī, -marddanī, -mardanī), Mahāsītavatī (or -sitavatī, -śitavatī), and Mahāmantrānusāriṇī (or -mantrānudhāriṇī), and they are renowned for their powers of protection. These five goddesses are actually deified mantric verses (*vidyā*), reputedly uttered by the Buddha himself (*buddhavacana*), and typically any one *mantra* could be chosen as the ruler (*rājñī*) over the others.[3] The verses would typically be inscribed on some medium, transformed into and worn as amulets for protection against worldly ailments. In time, these mantric verses were transformed into divine forms. Texts such as the *Sādhanamālā* and *Niṣpannayogāvalī* prescribe how these goddesses should be portrayed in artistic depictions. We do not know when the *Pañcarakṣā* goddesses were developed as a group, but the Mahāmāyūrī-*mantra* was popular between the 4th and 8th centuries CE. According to D. C. Bhattacharyya (1972, 90, n. 46), citing J. N. Banerjea (1966, 71) and others, the spell is mentioned in Bāṇabhaṭṭa's *Harṣacarita* (first half of the 7th century CE), and the *Āryamañjuśrīmūlakalpa* (8th or 9th century CE), and was translated into Chinese four times during this period. The sculpture of the goddess Mahāmāyūrī depicted at Ellora by about the 8th century CE is the earliest representation of these five goddesses known thus far.[4] Manuscripts of all five goddesses derive from the 11th century CE (D. C. Bhattacharyya 1972, 91).

The worship of the *Pañcarakṣā* goddesses was closely tied to averting drought, ensuring rainfall, and securing abundant harvests, drawing parallels with the Devī as Śākambharī in the DM. In the DM, Śākambharī's tears bring forth edible plants, sustaining humanity, a motif echoed in her earlier mention in the DSto (l. 17). Each *Pañcarakṣā* goddess had specific protective associations: Mahāpratisara safeguarded pregnancy and childbirth; Mahāmāyūrī protected against snakebite and poisons; Mahāsāhasrapramardinī shielded devotees from demons (*rākṣasa*), *bhūta*, and *yakṣas*; and Mahāśītavatī offered protection from illness, particularly smallpox.

D. C. Bhattacharyya (1972, 87) observes parallels between these goddesses and the Buddhist Tārā, as both are portrayed as mothers of the triple world, deliverers from dangers such as thieves, wild beasts, and shipwrecks, and revered by gods (including Brahmā, Viṣṇu, Maheśvara, and Indra), Tathāgatas, and human devotees. Often referred to as Tāraṇī, a raft ferrying one to safety, they evoke striking similarities to Durgā, whose name signifies a raft over life's troubled waters. Durgā's role as sovereign of the triple world and her veneration by gods and humans further aligns her with these Buddhist goddesses. Simply hearing the names of these deities is said to dispel sins and misfortunes, emphasizing their salvific power. This resonates with attitudes towards the benefits of the recitation and hearing of the DM, which we shall examine in detail in a later chapter.[5]

D. C. Bhattacharyya (1972, 88) observes that Tārā and the *Pañcarakṣā* goddesses are often called Skandamātā, reflecting their connection to the Matṛkās, who are sometimes depicted nursing Skanda/Kārttikeya in his youth, thereby linking them directly to Durgā. Tārā's iconographic and conceptual parallels with Durgā are strikingly close (D. C. Bhattacharyya 1972, 89). The earliest known sculptural representation of Tārā may be in Ellora's Cave 6, positioned opposite Mahāmāyūrī, with whom connections have already been noted.

Among the *Pañcarakṣā* goddesses, Mahāpratisara's association with Vasumatī, the Earth Goddess, ties her to fertility and agricultural prosperity. Mahāmāyūrī, as previously discussed, appears to derive from or develop in tandem with Nidrā/Kauśikī and Skandamātā, due to her peacock association, aligning her with Manasā, the goddess protecting against snakebites (D. C. Bhattacharyya 1972, 89). The Mahāmāyūrī-*mantra* shares features with the Mahāgāruḍi-*mantra* of the Purāṇas, which also offers protection from venomous snakes. The peacock (*mayūra*) itself is said to have originated from Garuḍa.

Mahāśītavatī evokes Śītalā, the goddess associated with smallpox, while Mahāmantrānusāriṇī ("[She who is] Aligned with the Great Sacred Utterances") corresponds to the Devī as the embodiment of the Gāyatrī-*mantra*, considered the *mahāmantra* encompassing all *mantras*. D. C. Bhattacharyya (1979, 89) notes that in the later *Skanda Purāṇa* (SkP 47.63), Durgā is identified as Harasiddhi, bearing the epithet Mahāmantraviśāradā ("[She who is] Proficient in Great Sacred Utterance[s]"), which is nearly synonymous. Similarly, Mahāsāhasrapramardinī ("[She who is] the Great Crusher of a Thousand [demons]") evokes Durgā as Mahiṣāsuramardinī, the Slayer of the Buffalo Demon. These connections demonstrate that alongside the Śākta, Śaiva, Vaiṣṇava, and other Hindu sects, Buddhist scholar-monks and other groups, including Jains, actively assimilated local goddess cults into their religious systems. This theme will be revisited in the concluding chapter.

A Noteworthy Chinese Parallel

As far as cultural interactions between India and China are concerned, we have already discussed how trade along the southern branch of the Silk Road, as well as the Southwest Silk Road, was extensive during the Han dynasty (206 BCE–220 CE). We are aware of Indian scholars in China translating Buddhist texts into Chinese in the 1st century of the Common Era. Prabodh Chandra Bagchi (2011, 13) refers to the Indian scholars Kāśyapa Mātaṅga and Dharmarakṣa who visited China in 68 CE, and for whom the first Buddhist monastery (Po mas sse, White Horse Monastery) in Luoyang was built.[6] It was during this period that we find a striking presence of the cult of the goddess Xi Wangmu, Sovereign (Venerable, Great, Queen) Mother of the West.[7] Xi Wangmu, believed to reside in a western paradise and preside over immortality, was frequently depicted in frescoes, stone reliefs, and bronze mirrors found in tombs across China. Her worship may trace back to the Shang dynasty (1766–1122 BCE), with oracle bones referencing offerings to the Western Mother (*xi mu*) and Eastern Mother (*dong mu*) for divine favor (Cahill 1993, 12). During the Shang period, the western direction was linked to the tiger, a symbol of death and passage to the spirit world, although it remains unclear if Xi Wangmu's tiger association directly derives from these early symbols.

By the Warring States period (403–221 BCE), texts from Daoist, Confucian, and Legalist traditions described numerous goddesses collectively called Xi Wangmu. These figures were associated with stars, sacred mountains, and sages, likely originating from diverse regional cults. Over time, these goddesses coalesced into the singular figure of Xi Wangmu. This process mirrors the South Asian evolution of goddess traditions, where Durgā emerged as the Great Goddess, unifying various regional and sectarian forms into a singular, overarching deity.

The earliest explicit reference to Xi Wangmu appears in the *Zhuangzi* (late 4th century BCE), a foundational Daoist text. In the "Great Teachers" chapter, the *Zhuangzi* lists those who have attained the Dao — an invisible, immanent principle that precedes and transcends creation — such as the sun, the moon, the Yellow Emperor, and Xi Wangmu. It states: "The Queen Mother of the West obtained it and took up her seat at Shao kuang. No one knows her beginning; no one knows her end" (Cahill 1993, 14). Xi Wangmu's connection to the mythical Shao Kuang, a holy mountain in the west, and her transcendent, timeless nature resonate with aspects of Durgā.

In the *Xunzi*, attributed to the Confucian philosopher Xun Kuang, Xi Wangmu appears as the teacher of the mythical Emperor Yu, credited with saving the world from a deluge. In the Tian Lun (Heavenly Discourses) chapter of the *Xunzi*, Xi Wangmu not only imparts wisdom to Yu, empowering him to rule and granting him sovereignty, but also aids him in overcoming the chaos of the flood. This link between the goddess and imperial authority, as well as her role in providing salvific guidance, strongly parallels Durgā's association with sovereignty and protection. While direct evidence of cultural exchange in these parallels remains limited, the similarities suggest deeper interconnections rather than independent, unrelated developments or purely psychological archetype explanations.

In the *Classic of Mountains and Seas*, Xi Wangmu is linked to the Jade Mountain and described as human-like but with a leopard's tail and tiger's teeth. She emits whistles, roars, or screams (*xiao*) and wears a distinct *sheng* headdress in her disheveled hair. The *sheng* (literally "victory") headdress, often depicted as circles in groups of two or three connected by straight lines, is interpreted by Anne Birrell (1999, 24) as a victory crown and one of Xi Wangmu's most enduring symbols, although its exact appearance remains debated. Some suggest it represents a stellar crown, while others associate it with weaving, a craft linked to the Sovereign Mother in certain contexts. The feline traits of Xi Wangmu, eventually externalized as her familiar, the tiger, along with her disheveled hair and howling or roaring sounds, connect her to shamanistic traditions. Southern Chinese shamans often wore animal skins and produced unusual vocalizations during rituals.

Parallels with Durgā emerge from these descriptions. Early Indic hymns portray Durgā/Kālī with fierce, harsh laughter and, in the DSto (l. 15), a wolf-like face. Similarly, the PN-s2 (l. 19) describes her disheveled hair. The *sheng* headdress evokes Durgā's *vicitra-mukuṭa*, the wondrous or three-disced diadem symbolizing sovereignty. Both crowns signify victory and divine supremacy, emphasizing the shared motif of a powerful goddess crowning herself or being crowned.

During the Han dynasty, a period marked by extensive Silk Road trade between China and India, there is a notable rise in sources documenting Xi Wangmu's cult. This era saw the amalgamation of attributes from various local goddesses into a singular, unified persona of Xi Wangmu as a great goddess. In the *Classic of Mountains and Seas* (Birrell 1999), dating to the Former (Western) Han dynasty (206 BCE–8 CE), she is depicted on Tortoise Mountain (associated with serpent shamans), leaning on a stool, adorned with a *sheng* headdress, and holding a staff (Cahill 1993, 19). Three azure birds are shown bringing her fruits. Although closely linked with the northwest mountains of Kunlun and Tortoise Mountain, regarded as cosmogonic world centers, her abode is described as any mountain, as she is believed to traverse freely through skies and space. This portrayal resonates with Durgā/Kauśikī as depicted in early Indic epic hymns. The goddess's celestial mobility, her connection to mountains, and the symbolism of azure birds evoke parallels with the Indic tradition, where Durgā is often associated with elevated realms, animal symbols, and cosmic sovereignty.

By 3 BCE, a brief apocalyptic peasant cult devoted to Xi Wangmu emerged across China during a period of significant civil unrest and drought ravaging the Western Han dynasty. These conditions, compounded by rebellions and the astrological phenomenon known as the Hound of Heaven — believed to signify famine and revolt — created fertile ground for the cult's rise (Seiwert 2003, 31–32). Some attributed the unrest to an excessive rise in the feminine principle (*yin*), possibly reflecting the growing prominence of goddess worship. Followers of this cult, identifying as envoys or servants of Xi Wangmu, engaged in rituals where they passed stalks of grain or hemp and exchanged goddess-emblems or tokens. With disheveled hair, they marched barefoot in large processions, shouting, dancing, and singing in veneration of the Sovereign Mother. They also circulated talismans bearing the inscription: "The Mother informs all people that those who carry this writing will not die" (Seiwert 2003, 32).

We also note that the Sovereign Mother was worshipped by the elite in Han China, such as the imperial family, wealthy nobles, and the military (see Cahill 1993, 23–24). The *Wuyue Chunqiu* (*Springs and autumns of Wu and Yüeh*), a history from the 1st century CE, recounts how the king of Yue set up an altar in the west and east of his capital. The western altar was for the worship of *yin*, under the name of Xi Wangmu, and the one in the east was for her male counterpart, the *yang* principle, Tung Wang Kung. Xi Wangmu is often depicted as accompanied by the Jade Maidens (Yu Nü), who sing and dance and are messengers of the goddess. They impart wisdom to sages, but seekers of transcendental knowledge are warned against making love to them.

In the centuries following the late Han dynasty, Xi Wangmu's persona underwent significant transformations, shifting from a wild, shamanic figure to a courtlier one, as reflected in her depictions wearing royal robes and jeweled headdresses (Cahill 1993). Efforts were made to associate her with and subordinate her to prominent male figures, such as Emperor Yu. Nonetheless, her worship persisted and saw revivals during various periods, including the rise of Shang Qing Daoism in the Tang dynasty. In Daoist texts, she is closely linked with the number nine, symbolizing nine-leveled mountains, pillars, or jade palaces, and the nine primordial supreme powers (*jiuling*). She is also referred to as Nine Radiance and Sovereign Mother of the Nine Heavens and worshipped with lamps bearing nine flames (Cahill 1993, 68–69, 126).

Xi Wangmu's role as a teacher of sages and emperors and as the ultimate source of esoteric teachings on self-transformation and Daoist alchemy positions her as the mistress of all Daoist scriptures. These attributes parallel Durgā's portrayal as the mother of the Vedas (DSto, 1. 16, 24), the goddess of ascetics (PN-s2, 1. 34), and the embodiment of the knowledge of Brahman (PN-s2, 1. 41). Durgā's association with the number nine is similarly well-established in Indian traditions. Suzanne Cahill (1993, 77) also notes Xi Wangmu's later connections with seedy melons and fruits, evoking Durgā's ties to goddesses such as Śākambharī and Kūṣmāṇḍā, the melon deity. The apocalyptic cult of Xi Wangmu in 3 BCE, thought to have arisen in response to a devastating drought (Seiwert 2003), resonates with the DM's reference (11.42–46) to Śākambharī, a form of the Devī who rescues the world from drought.

There are some intriguing connections between Xi Wangmu, in her persona as cosmic Weaver (creator), and the Chinese myths of Weaver Girl. Weaver Girl fell in love with Cowherd Boy (also known as Buffalo Boy) and began to neglect her loom. She was forced to return to the heavens, and Xi Wangmu drew her hairpin across the sky separating the lovers with the creation of a celestial river (the Milky Way). Only once a year are they allowed to reunite during the autumn festival of Double Seven (the seventh day of the seventh month). One cannot help but see resonances between Kṛṣṇa and Cowherd Boy, who in another version of the myth steals the clothes of Weaver Girl (and her six sisters) while they are swimming in a lake. This myth evokes the myth of Kṛṣṇa's dalliance with the cowgirls (*gopī*). It is also intriguing that Xi Wangmu is portrayed as possessing a hairpin weapon that is used with such power as to divide the heavens. Xi Wangmu used ten thousand magpies to create a bridge for the lovers to meet once a year, again accentuating her association with birds (Monaghan 2011, 153). During the Han dynasty, the Double Seven Festival (also called the Magpie Festival or the Qixi Festival and still celebrated) was particularly popular with unmarried girls in certain regions of China, evoking features of Durgā's virginal persona (Cahill 1993, 98, 168–69, 254).

Chapter 7

The Rise of Durgā Mahiṣāsuramardinī

This chapter explores the evolving representation of the goddess trampling the buffalo demon and the development of the term Mahiṣamardinī, with particular emphasis on the concept of *mardana* (crushing). Notably absent in early texts, the term appears to have originated within Śaiva sectarian literature around the 7th or 8th century CE. I suggest restricting the application of Mahiṣamardinī to post-7th century depictions where the goddess is shown with her foot on the buffalo demon. The motif is celebrated in the *Caṇḍīśataka* by Bāṇabhaṭṭa (also known as Bāṇa) from the 7th century, which also identifies Caṇḍī as an alternate name for Durgā. This chapter also investigates mentions of human sacrifice in Xuanzang's accounts and fictional works such as Bāṇa's *Kādambarī*, the *Mālatī-mādhava*, and *Gauḍavaho*, associating these rituals with Durgā, Kālī, and Cāmuṇḍā. The *Mahābhārata* (Mbh) attributes Mahiṣa's defeat to Skanda, providing minimal details about the buffalo demon. We further examine Skanda's worship and its eventual decline in favor of Durgā, a theme revisited in the final chapter of this volume, which addresses theological conflicts and the *Devī Māhātmya*'s (DM) integrative portrayal of the Divine Feminine.

Mahiṣāsuranāśinī, Mahiṣāsuraghātinī, and Mahiṣamardinī/Mahiṣāsuramardinī

Before proceeding to a more thorough, albeit far from exhaustive, study of various types of so-called Mahiṣamardinī images in a later chapter, it must be pointed out that this epithet has been used rather loosely in prior scholarly studies.

The Slayer of the Buffalo Demon

The epithet Mahiṣāsuramardinī (Crusher/Slayer of the Buffalo Demon Mahiṣa) is now firmly associated with Durgā, but its precise origins in the literary record remain unclear. The earliest reference to Durgā as the Slayer of the Buffalo Demon occurs in the Durgā Stava (DStv) or a related DStv* variant, where she is described as Mahiṣāsuranāśinī (Slayer of the Demon Mahiṣa, l. 29). I have argued that the core of the DStv, or a variation of it, likely circulated in Śākta devotional circles as early as the composition of the Mbh and possibly contemporaneously with the *Harivaṃśa* (HV). This timeline aligns with the Kuṣāṇa-period imagery from Mathurā, although the term Mahiṣāsuramardinī does not appear in the DStv. Instead, the DStv and its extant versions employ epithets such as Mahiṣāsuradarpaghnī (Destroyer of the Demon Mahiṣa's Pride) and Mahiṣāsuraghātinī (Injurer of the Demon Mahiṣa). Where *mardinī* does appear in these versions, it is applied to the demon Kaiṭabha, as in Kaiṭabhamardinī.

The next textual mention of the goddess defeating Mahiṣa is found in Pradyumna's hymn (PradH) to Kātyāyanī, an appendix to the HV. Here, the goddess is called Mahiṣāsuraghātinī (Killer of the Demon Mahiṣa, HV App. I.30.371). She is also referred to as Pārvatī, Gārgī, Kālarātri, Kātyāyanī, Jayā, Vijayā, and Ekānaṃśā, and linked to Śaivism through her trident and identification as Śiva's beloved (*śaṅkarapriya*, I.30.359). Additionally, she is described as riding a lion (*siṃhavāha*) and bearing a lion as her ensign (*siṃhapravaraketana*, I.30.372), with bell imagery tying her to goddesses such as Candraghaṇṭā. Notably, three of her names — Kālarātri, Kātyāyanī, and Candraghaṇṭā — are found in the Navadurgā cluster of the Devī Kavaca, an appendix to the DM.

While the composition date of PradH is uncertain, its inclusion of a wider assortment of goddesses suggests a later date than the Praise of Nidrā (First Stratum) (PN-s1) from the HV core and definitely postdates the DStv. In PradH, Kauśikī is notably absent, although the goddess is still associated with defeating Śumbha and Niśumbha, evoking Kauśikī's role in the PN-s1. However, PradH explicitly connects the goddess with Mahiṣa's defeat, marking an important development in her mythic persona. Even so, the specific term Mahiṣāsuramardinī remains absent.

In the hymn attributed to Aniruddha (AniH), found as an insertion in some manuscripts of the HV, we encounter a notable line at HV App I.35.85 or 86: "Hail to you, Crusher of the Enemy (*ari*) of the Gods (*sura*), Mahiṣa (*mahiṣa-surāri-mardini*)." Although this phrase introduces the term *mardinī* (with the short i vocative ending), it does not constitute the now-familiar epithet Mahiṣāsuramardinī. This insertion likely reflects a later period. In AniH, the goddess is explicitly identified as Durgā and a host of other goddesses, including Caṇḍī, Kātyāyanī, Gautamī, Nidrā (as Nanda's daughter), Kālī, Śakunī, Revatī, Gaṅgā, Gāndhārī, Sarasvatī, Sāvitrī, Ekānaṃśā, Kauberī, Kuṣmāṇḍī, Brahmāṇī, Indrāṇī, Rudrāṇī, and Nārāyaṇī. She is described as dwelling on both the Vindhya and Kailāsa mountains.

The hymn establishes connections between Kauśikī — who slays Sumbha/Śumbha and Nisumbha/Niśumbha — and Durgā, the slayer of the Buffalo Demon, along with other deities. The inclusion of Skandamātā and Kuṣmāṇḍī further links the hymn to the Navadurgā of the Devī Kavaca. Additionally, the goddess is identified with figures resembling the Mothers (Mātṛkās), illustrating conceptual continuity with the DM in constructing the Great Goddess (Devī), also known as Durgā. The lack of references to distinct elements of the DM suggests that the AniH predates or is contemporaneous with the DM, yet later than the DStv or its variants, as well as PradH. The introduction of the term *mardinī* in the inserted line indicates a developing emphasis on "crushing" as the method of Mahiṣa's defeat, reflecting evolving interpretations of Durgā's mythological role.

The Crusher of the Buffalo Demon

D. Srinivasan (1997, 282) and C. Schmid (2011, 115) note the premature application of the term Mahiṣamardinī by scholars, but they do not trace its historical usage. In fact, the term Mahiṣāsuramardinī is absent from Sanskrit literature for nearly half a millennium into the Common Era and was likely not in common use even at the time of the DM, where it does not appear. This raises questions about the routine scholarly application of Mahiṣamardinī or Mahiṣāsuramardinī to earlier images, particularly those predating any textual evidence of the epithet. The issue mirrors the tendency to retroactively apply the name Durgā to goddesses not explicitly identified with her (e.g., Rātrī or Vāc) before clear textual corroboration. Although *mardinī* (meaning "crusher") is occasionally used for other demons (e.g., Kaiṭabha), it is not combined with Mahiṣa or Mahiṣāsura in early literary sources. In contrast, the masculine equivalent *mardana* appears approximately one hundred times in the Mbh, typically describing the crushing of enemies (*arimardana*) or warriors (*kṣatriyamardana*). The phrase *daityadānavamardana* ("Crusher of Daityas and Dānavas," demon classes hostile to the gods) is applied to Indra (Monier-Williams 1986), possibly prefiguring the later usage of *asuramardinī*.

The phrase Mahiṣāsuramardinī eventually appears in the Purāṇas, although pinpointing its first occurrence is challenging due to the layered composition and interpolations within these texts. The *Mārkaṇḍeya Purāṇa* (MārkP), widely regarded as one of the earliest Purāṇas (Rocher 1986, 191–92), contains the DM, a seminal text on the Great Goddess. However, the DM itself does not use the terms Mahiṣamardinī or Mahiṣāsuramardinī, whether it is considered a later insertion into the MārkP or part of its earliest stratum. This absence suggests that even if these epithets were in nascent use during the composition of the earliest Purāṇic material, they were not yet widespread or significant enough to feature in the DM.

Without attempting to be exhaustive or provide a comprehensive chronology of occurrences, here are illustrative instances of the epithet Mahiṣāsuramardinī. One of its earliest known uses appears in a text dedicated to Śiva, the *Śivadharma* or *Śivadharmaśāstra*. The classification and dating of this text are ambiguous. While the title suggests it belongs to the Dharmaśāstra tradition, R. C. Hazra notes that it frequently appears in Purāṇic lists as an Upapurāṇa ("Minor Purāṇa") and proposes a composition date between 200 and 500 CE

(Bonazzoli 1993, 342). If accurate, this would indicate an early occurrence of the term Mahiṣāsuramardinī.

However, the earliest extant manuscripts of the *Śivadharma*, found in Nepal, date no earlier than the 9th century CE. These manuscripts likely migrated from northern India, similar to the early *Skanda Purāṇa* (SP). Hans Bakker (2014, 137–39) suggests that such transmissions most likely occurred in the late 7th century CE, during the late Gupta period, or in the early 8th century under the Pāla king Dharmapāla (De Simini 2016, 65–66). The lack of early manuscripts does not necessarily reflect the composition date, as even foundational texts such as the Mbh and HV are not preserved in their earliest manuscript forms. The *Śivadharma* was composed for uninitiated lay devotees, emphasizing enjoyment (*bhukti*) of the world and auspicious rebirths, such as that of a pious king or Brahmin, while reserving liberation (*mukti*) for those who underwent proper Śaiva initiation (De Simini 2016, 50). Its social context situates the text in the 6th or 7th century CE (Bisschop 2010b, 483n35). Chapter 6, the Śāntyadhyāya, contains verses for propitiating various divinities, including Maheśvara, Umā, Kārttikeya, Ambikā Mātṛ, and Mahāmahiṣamardanī (Bisschop 2010a, 40; 2018, 150). In this chapter, Mahāmahiṣamardanī is described as the mother of all auspiciousness (*sarvamaṅgalamātā*) and the destroyer of all misfortunes (*sarvopadravanaśinī*). She wields a bow, discus, sword, and spear, with one hand raised in a threatening gesture (*ātarjanodyatakarā*). Her complexion is a glossy black (*snigdhaśyāmena varṇena*), and she crushes a great buffalo (*mahāmahiṣamardanī*) (Bisschop 2018, 71; Sarkar 2017, 73). Notably the term used for crushing in this text is *mardanī*, rather than the now commonplace *mardinī*.[8]

We find the phrase Durgā Mahiṣamardinī in the *Agni Purāṇa*:

> *kramānmadhye cogracaṇḍā durgā mahiṣamardinī* /185.006ab/
> *oṃ durge durge rakṣaṇi svāhā daśākṣāro mantraḥ*
> //185.006cd/[9]

There, we also find instances of the term Crusher of the Great Buffalo (*mahāmahiṣamardinī*) — which arguably first occurs in the *Śivadharma*, albeit as *mahāmahiṣamardanī* — in Tantric root-mantric verses, such as:

> *viṣaṃ mahiṣakāntāgnirudrijyotirvakadvayam* /307.017ab/
> *oṃ hrīṃ mahāmahiṣamardini ṭha ṭha mūlamantraṃ mahiṣa-*
>   *hiṃsake namaḥ* /
> *mahiṣaśatruṃ bhrāmaya hūṃ phaṭ ṭha ṭha mahiṣaṃ heṣaya*
>   *hūṃ mahiṣaṃ hana devi hūṃ mahiṣanisūdani phaṭ*
>   *durgāhṛdayamityuktaṃ sāṅgaṃ sarvārthasādhakam*
>   //307.017cd/[10]

This term, *mahāmahiṣamardinī*, also occurs in the *Śiva Purāṇa*[11] and the *Liṅga Purāṇa*[12] The *Garuḍa Purāṇa* contains the phrase *devī mahiṣamardinī*,[13] and the Revakhaṇḍa of the *Vāyu Purāṇa* contains *mahiṣavimardinī* (*vimardinī* intensifies the meaning of *mardinī*).[14] We do find the full epithet, *mahiṣāsuramardinī*, in the *Liṅga Purāṇa*.[15] It is somewhat surprising that the epithet for the buffalo-slaying goddess is relatively rare even in this literature. And when we note the many synonyms encountered in the aforementioned examples for "[She who is] the Destroyer" of Mahiṣa, such as *vimardinī*, *ghātinī*, and *nāśinī*, we are led to wonder about how and why the term *mardinī* ultimately gained prominence. The answer may lie in the observation that in almost all contexts, the epithets *mahiṣamardinī* or *mahiṣāsuramardinī* appear in hymns of praise, where the goddess's many epithets are lauded. Or they appear in Tantric mantric verses, which are evidently used in ritual contexts. Such repeated recitations of the verses and hymns, widespread among devotees (*bhākta*) and adepts (*sādhaka*), could have led to the ascendency of the term Mahiṣāsuramardinī, with whom Durgā is explicitly identified, initially particularly in Śaiva sectarian literature.

The Symbolic Significance of "Crushing"

Why did the term *mardinī* achieve pre-eminence over other epithets associated with the Goddess? Although commonly translated as "destroyer," *mardinī* is more accurately rendered as "crusher." Other terms, such as *ghātinī* or *nāśinī*, more directly convey the sense of slaying or annihilation. However, *mardinī* carries a particular resonance, not only for its vivid imagery of trampling and crushing but also for its subtle alignment with the name Durgā. The name Durgā signifies an arduous (*dur*) passage (*ga*), echoing the immense devastation she unleashes in the prelude to her battle with Mahiṣa in the DM. There, the destruction is so overwhelming that the demon army cries out for her to stop, as the earth becomes impassable with the corpses of demons, elephants, and battle debris (DM 2.63–64). This "difficult path" of carnage metaphorically aligns with her name and the notion of her trampling over slain enemies.

In the final confrontation with Mahiṣa, the demon undergoes multiple shape-shifts before his ultimate demise. Initially, caught in the Devī's noose, he transforms from a buffalo into a lion, whom she beheads. He then takes the form of a sword-wielding man, whom she dismembers with her arrows, before turning into an elephant that attacks the Devī's lion. She severs the elephant's trunk with her sword, forcing him to revert to his original buffalo form. At this point, the Devī leaps upon him, pressing her foot onto his neck (*pādenākramya kaṇṭhe*), while piercing him with her spear (*śūlenainam atāḍayat*) (DM 3.37). This sequence of events suggests that the author of the DM was aware of various preexisting modes of envisioning the Devī's battle with Mahiṣa. These depictions include snaring him with a noose, beheading a lion-form demon, shooting him with arrows, severing an elephant trunk with a sword, quaffing from her cup, and finally piercing him with a spear. The multifaceted nature of these descriptions likely contributed to *mardinī*'s prominence, as it encapsulates the visceral and dynamic act of crushing, trampling, and utterly overpowering the demon — making it an apt and evocative epithet for the Goddess.

It is not the spear that causes him to appear in his true demonic form. The next line of the text states that, pinned down by her foot (*padākrānta*) and thus restrained by the strength of the Devī, he emerged halfway (*ardhaniṣkrānta*) out of his own [i.e., buffalo] mouth or neck (*nijamukhāt*) (DM 3.38). It is interesting to note that in the DM account we are not explicitly told in what form he emerges, given his many previous transformations. There is a general assumption that he emerges in an anthropomorphic form, but this is derived from iconographic depictions. Portraying him as a human is the norm in the so-called Emergent Demon (E) iconographic depictions. This notion is found in the *Skanda Purāṇa* (SkP 1.3.1.10.1–11.46 and 6.119.1.121.86) (i.e., not the oldest version), in which Mahiṣa is a cursed human (Granoff 1979, 148n19). The DM continues to tell us that the great (buffalo) demon (*mahāsura*), the same one who had emerged halfway (as a human?), still fighting, was felled by the Goddess, who had severed his head (*śiraś chittvā*) with her great sword (*mahāsinā*) (DM 3.39).

It is merely the power of the Goddess's foot that utterly subjugates this lord of demons, who had even scattered the gods from the heavens. Her power is overwhelming. The foot subordinates, subdues, and ultimately vanquishes Mahiṣa. He is utterly crushed by Durgā. Thus, we can see, from the DM's version of the myth, why the Devī's foot and the symbolism of "crushing" is so much more fitting than having her merely slay the great demon with her spear or sword, even though the DM does not use the term *mardinī*. The severing of his buffalo head and slaying of his emergent form is but the denouement to Mahiṣāsura's thoroughly humiliating and inescapable defeat. But does this trope of the Devī "crushing" Mahiṣa emerge through the DM or does the DM pick up upon it from existing iconographic representations?

We recognize the preexisting trope of the power of the divine foot in Rāvaṇa's attempt to topple Mount Kailāsa. The myth is recounted in Vālmīki's *Rāmāyaṇa* and often depicted — such as in a large relief at Kailāsanātha temple at Ellora, which shows the demon in his feeble attempt, about to be pinned under the mountain by the power of Śiva's foot. An explicit reference to the goddess's foot is found in a dedicatory inscription at Gopikā cave at the Lomaśa Ṛṣi cave complex in the Nāgārjunī hills. It was carved to mark the installation of a Kātyāyanī *mūrti* by the Maukhari ruler, Anantavarman (c. 6th century CE), who considered the area to be part of the Vindhya Mountains, Kātyāyanī's abode. There, we read the phrase, "having put to shame (*ākṣipya*) the diverse splendours of a blossoming lotus, the Devī's foot, with jingling anklet, was placed (*nyasta*) disdainfully (*sāvajñāṃ*) on the head (*śirasi*) of Mahiṣāsura. . . ."[16] The eloquence of this phrasing, even in the abbreviated portion I present here, is testament to the growing focus on the Goddess Kātyāyanī's (i.e., Durgā's) foot, both as a symbol of beauty and devastating majesty. It perhaps also prefigures the popularity of the Victorious Goddess (V) images that emerge in quantity during the Pallava period. In those Victorious Goddess images, the

Devī is simply shown standing with her feet together (*samapāda mudrā*) upon a severed buffalo head.

The *Caṇḍīśataka*

The foot of the goddess firmly planted on Mahiṣa's head is most evident in verses such as this one from the *Caṇḍīśataka*, composed in the first half of the 7th century in the reign of King Harṣa.[17] Harṣa ruled a large empire from his capital in Kanauj, after the fall of the Gupta Empire. The verse reads,

> May [the goddess] Śivā, who pulled out the trident [*śūla*]
> from the body of the buffalo once it had performed
> its task, protect you; Śivā, who smiled gently when
> Jayā said in jest, "Lord [i.e., Siva] just as you bear the
> bull as your emblem [*vṛṣadhvaja*], so now does our
> mistress bear the buffalo as her emblem [*mahiṣadh-
> vaja*], for the enemy of the gods, who assumed the
> form of a buffalo, lies clinging to the edge of her foot
> [*pādaprāntaviṣakta*]." (v. 32, trans. Granoff (1979,
> 150))[18]

The *Caṇḍīśataka* (*Hundred [Verses] to Caṇḍī*), Bāṇa's lyric hymn of praise to the goddess Caṇḍī ("[She who is] Fierce") dedicates all but four of its 102 verses (*āśis*) to the goddess's battle with Mahiṣa. Moreover, they are mostly focused on his destruction by the blow from her left foot and one thrust of her spear. Paralleling the image of Mount Kailāsa crushing Rāvaṇa, in one verse we read,

> The goddess mistook the back of the black buffalo for the
> Vindhya mountain, her own abode; the buffalo's roar
> which scorns the rumble of the ocean was drowned
> by the tinkling of her anklets as they hit the buffalo's
> back. The streams of blood which flowed from the
> wound she mistook for the red smear [i.e., decorative
> lac] on her foot. Thus, she killed the demon without
> ever realizing that she did so. May that foot protect
> you! (Bhattacharji 1980, 13, stanza 2)[19]

The recurring image of the jingling anklet on the Devī's foot may have absorbed the symbol of the bell (*ghaṇṭā*) with which the Goddess is associated as early as the DStv and PradH, but which is a less depicted attribute in her later iconography. Bāṇa's repeated focus on the foot of the Devī atop Mahiṣa suggests that he is influenced less by narrative accounts and more by visual representations of this act, which he transforms into verbal visions through his poetry. George Quackenbos (1965, 247) notes that in more than sixty of the verses "the killing of Mahiṣa is attributed to the power of the goddess's kick," and that most of the verses praise the kick even more than the goddess as that which conquers the buffalo demon (251). Although the tableaus poetically painted by each of his verses do further the development of a story, Bāṇa is evidently not really recounting details from a mythic account but insinuating emotions and often asking the sorts of questions that beg for a narrative explanation. Consider, for instance, the first stanza:[20]

> "Spoil not thy coquetry, O brow; O lower lip, why this dis-
>   tress? O face, banish thy flushing;
> O hand, this (Mahiṣa) is not indeed living; why dost thou
>   brandish a trident, with desire for combat?"
> While Devī (Caṇḍī) caused by these words, as it were, the part
>   of her body that displayed signs of rising anger to
>   resume their normal state,
> Her foot, which took away the life of (Mahiṣa), Foe of the
>   Gods, was set down upon his head.
> May that foot of the Devī (Caṇḍī) destroy your sin!" (trans.
>   Quackenbos 1965, 267).

Nearly one-fifth of the *Caṇḍīśataka*'s verses emphasize Caṇḍī's superiority over male gods, with several stanzas (75–77) tacitly aligning Śiva, her spouse, with Mahiṣa, highlighting their shared traits. This reflects a context in which the goddess Caṇḍī has ascended to near supremacy within the Hindu pantheon, apart from her connection to Śiva, as she is often identified as his wife in Bāṇa's poem. Scholars note the juxtaposition of the erotic (*śṛṅgāra rasa*) with the devotional (*bhakti rasa*), as the youthful beauty of the goddess is vividly described (e.g., stanzas 71, 72, 74, 77, 81, and 85). This tension likely arises from efforts to reconcile the goddess's original virginal nature — seen in Nidrā/Kauśikī and Durgā as depicted in the PN-s1 and DStv, respectively — with her portrayal as Pārvatī, Śiva's consort. The *Caṇḍīśataka* was evidently composed during a period of dynamic interactions between Śāktism and Śaivism. Interestingly, of the four verses that do not reference the Mahiṣa episode, three recount Kaṃsa's failure to kill the goddess, directly linking the poem to the Nidrā myth cycle and its associations with Vaiṣṇavism.

The epithet Caṇḍī was evidently ascendant in Bāṇa's period, more so than Durgā.[21] Despite its title, the *Caṇḍīśataka* uses the epithet Caṇḍī or Caṇḍikā in only five verses (Quackenbos 1965, 258). However, Bāṇa also references Caṇḍikā in his other works. In his *Kādambarī*, often considered one of the first Sanskrit novels, Bāṇa describes a fierce tribal Śabara leader, Mātaṅga, whose arms bore scars from repeated blood offerings to the goddess Caṇḍikā (Layne 1991, 31). Earlier studies frequently mistranslated Caṇḍikā as Kālī, as seen in C. M. Ridding's 1896 translation (28), leading some scholars to overlook the occurrence entirely.

In the *Harṣacarita*, Caṇḍikā (or Caṇḍika in its masculine form) is mentioned as a deity to whom Harṣa's desperate subjects offered sacrifices, including their own flesh, to cure his father's illness. Coburn (1988, 98n25), consulting Sanskrit editions by S. Kuñjan Pillai (1958, 226) and Kane (1973, 21), notes the use of the masculine form *caṇḍikam*. However, the same rites included devotees burning themselves in propitiation of the Mothers, linking such practices to goddess worship. Caṇḍikā is described as flirtatious (*vibhraman*), akin to a lover's meeting (*abhisārikā*) with Mahākāla (Kāle 1928, 337), which may explain why the DM associates this name with the Devī's form that captivates Śumbha and Niśumbha. These references establish Caṇḍī/Caṇḍikā as a goddess venerated by fierce tribals (Śabaras), involving rituals of blood and, possibly, flesh offerings. This aligns with her depiction as a deity of intense and austere devotion.

Notably, the *Caṇḍīśataka* and Bāṇa's other works lack any reference to the slaying of Śumbha and Niśumbha, a myth central to the DM, where the Goddess is frequently called Caṇḍikā. This absence suggests, contrary to F. E. Pargiter (1904, xii) and Coburn (1984, 98), that the DM was likely composed after the *Caṇḍīśataka*. The DM seems to have integrated the increasingly prominent iconographic motif of the Devī's foot atop Mahiṣa into its narrative, while also appending a broader storyline about the defeat of Śumbha and Niśumbha to advance its theological aims. Interestingly, while the DM popularized the name Caṇḍikā, known from Bāṇa's works, and mythologized the goddess's triumph over Śumbha and Niśumbha, neither the name nor the narrative appears to have resonated deeply with the public imagination or gained significant iconographic traction in the period following the text's composition.

In examining the epithet Caṇḍikā, Coburn primarily identified its occurrence in Bāṇa's writings, although it appears earlier as a name for Pārvatī, alongside Kālī and Durgā, in the *Amarakośa*, typically dated to the 5th century CE. Additionally, Caṇḍikā features in Tantricized ritual texts of Atharvaveda Brahmins in Odisha during the centuries following the DM. Alexis Sanderson (2007, 207, 215, 219) highlights rites such as the Ciṭimantra for subjugating enemies, and a long *mantra* invoking the goddess Pratyaṅgirā for both protective and hostile purposes, where Caṇḍikā is listed as one of her *śakti*s, alongside Vārāhī, Indrāṇī, Cāmuṇḍā, and others. Beyond Caṇḍikā, this corpus features goddesses such as Āsurī, Kālī, Durgā, Pratyaṅgirā, Kṛtyā, Bhadrakālī, Parā, Tripurabhairavī, Maṅgalacaṇḍī, Gharmaṭikā (also Gharmaṭī or Gharmuṭikā), and Dhūmāvatī. Sarkar (2017, 84–85, esp. n17) notes Caṇḍikā's invocation in the earliest strata of Tantric Vidyāpīṭha texts, such as the *Niśvāsaguhya* and *Tantrasadbhāva*, likely contemporaneous with, but possibly later than, the DM. These sources generally align in identifying Caṇḍikā with Durgā.

Xuanzang's Deadly Encounter

It is pertinent to return to our discussion of the oscillation of royal patronage between Buddhism and Hinduism in northern India. Aśoka's conversion to Buddhism likely tempered the blood sacrifices to the *yakṣinī* cults of the goddess in the Vindhyas, typified by Nidrā/Kauśikī. Nevertheless, these likely revived during the subsequent periods of Śuṅga and Gupta rule, with the ascendency of Durgā/Kālī/Kātyāyanī. Harṣa's conversion to Buddhism would again renew a moderation of the fiercely sanguine styles of worship of Durgā/Caṇḍī throughout his empire. From the account of Xuanzang's life, we know that the renowned, well-travelled Chinese Buddhist pilgrim received a warm reception in Harṣa's court. This is precisely the period of the composition of the *Caṇḍīśataka*.

Yet, in 636 CE, Xuanzang tells of a traumatic incident on his travels with eighty others from Ayodhyā (ancient Sāketa) on a boat on the Gaṅgā River en route to Hayamukha. They were suddenly attacked by ten pirate boats, taken ashore, undressed, and searched for their jewelry. The pirates appraised Xuanzang's demeanor and appearance as an ideal human sacrifice to their deity (likely Durgā/Caṇḍī/Kālī), something they sought every autumn to secure good fortune. Until then, they had feared that the sacrificial period for that year had almost passed. Xuanzang explained that his mission was to study Buddhist doctrine and revere the Buddha and Gṛdhrakūṭa Mountain (i.e., Vulture Peak, near Rājagṛha, modern Rajgir, Bihar), and although they might deem his defiled body suitable for sacrifice, killing him would cause them calamity. Unpersuaded by his warning, and refusing the pleas of the other travelers, some of whom were willing to offer up their own lives in his stead, the brigands carried and bound him to their altar, smeared with wet mud, and located in the middle of a forest grove. Here we again clearly see the association of blood sacrifices and a forest grove with a site of goddess worship to which the pirates had turned for refuge. Worship takes place not far from the river, and the altar is smeared with mud, both of which are characteristics found in the DM's description of the worship conducted by king Suratha and the merchant Samādhi.

To the bandits' astonishment, while they stood there with knives drawn, Xuanzang calmly asked for some space and a moment to compose his mind. Then, with singular focus he meditated upon the Bodhisattva Maitreya, asking for rebirth in the Tuṣita Heaven, where he might receive the teachings of the *Yogācārabhūmi-śāstra*, and then be reborn in this very place to instruct and convert his tormentors to a life free from such evil doing. Amid this deep and rapturous absorption, a dark typhoon suddenly blew up, levelling trees, and terrifying his captors. The brigands repented of their acts, inquired into who he was, and only when accidentally brushing up against him, drew Xuanzang out of his meditative trance. They received his pardon, and after he preached to them about the sufferings in the Avīci hell awaiting practitioners of such deeds, they made amends and converted into lay followers of Buddhism (Beal 1911, 86–90; Li Rongxi 1995, 76; Wriggins 2004, 91–92).

If we take Xuanzang's narrative at face value rather than assuming any embellishment, much less total fabrication, on his part, the episode reveals the co-existence of forms of worship of the goddess, involving blood — even human — sacrifice, in rivalry and tension with the pacific approach of

Buddhism. Such tensions may also have played a role in shaping the ambivalent character of Durgā as both fierce and benign, which is evident in her portrayal in the *Caṇḍīśataka*. Notably, in Bāṇa's texts, the goddess Caṇḍī or Caṇḍikā slays the buffalo demon Mahiṣa and is worshipped with blood or flesh offerings culled from devotees themselves. In the *Kādambarī* and Xuanzang's account the goddess is amenable to human sacrifice of others.

Which Came First: *Caṇḍīśataka* or *Devī Māhātmya*?

One of the earliest mentions of the name Caṇḍī for the goddess appears in the Durgā Stotra (DSto) (l. 10), and in the AniH, inserted into the HV (Appendix I.35, lines 7 and 31). Pargiter (1904, xii), in his introduction to the MārkP, cautiously speculated that Caṇḍikā may have first appeared in the DM, likely because he believed the DM predates the *Caṇḍīśataka*. However, while the *Caṇḍīśataka* employs both Caṇḍī and Caṇḍikā, their use is less frequent than the title might suggest, with the names appearing in only five of the poem's 102 stanzas (Quackenbos 1965, 258). In contrast, Bāṇa prominently uses Caṇḍī in the title of his poem. The DM notably avoids the epithet Caṇḍī, instead using Caṇḍikā twenty-nine times. The name Caṇḍikā is absent in the first episode involving Madhu and Kaitabha, appears six times during Mahiṣa's destruction, and is used twenty-three times in the final episode dealing with Śumbha and Niśumbha (Coburn 1984, 94–98). These patterns suggest that the DM was composed after the *Caṇḍīśataka*, weaving together the three key mythic exploits of goddesses progressively amalgamated into the persona of the Great Goddess. The DM's preference for Caṇḍikā over Caṇḍī — Caṇḍikā is still relatively obscure — may reflect a transitional phase in the prominence of these epithets, as seen in the *Caṇḍīśataka*, *Kādambarī*, and possibly the *Harṣacarita*. Yokochi (2004, 141) identifies four early textual sources on the buffalo-slaying goddess's myths from the 6th to mid-8th centuries: the *Caṇḍīśataka*, Anantavarman's inscriptions, the SP, and Vākpatirāja's *Gauḍavaho*, the latter two to be examined further. The *Kādambarī* is also pertinent to this study and should be included in this context.

The *Kādambarī*

In the *Kādambarī's* florid description of the Śabara tribals and their forest environment in the Vindhyas, we notice many of the symbolic tropes associated with the goddess, ones that later appear in the DM. There are forest goddesses, herds of wild buffaloes, with dagger-pointed horns, flocks of peacocks, and elephants attacked by lions (Layne 1991, 27–29). Peacock tail feathers are borne by some of the Śabaras, and their leader's bow is decorated with peacock tail feathers. The impressive Śabara leader's appearance is described in detail, with references to the goddesses Caṇḍikā, Kātyāyanī, and Ambikā, whose trident is described as moistened by buffalo blood. Durgā is described as his only refuge (Layne 1991, 33). The Śabaras are described as fulfilling their duty through human sacrifice, and their worship is made with animal blood and flesh (Layne 1991, 33). In other instances where Durgā appears in the *Kādambarī*, she is paired with the Trident-Wielder (i.e., Śiva) (Layne 1991, 57) and is associated with fortresses (Layne 1991, 58). Her image is described as carved into the roots of giant trees (Layne 1991, 222), and she is a goddess who accepted human sacrifices as offerings (Layne 1991, 223).

Caṇḍikā's image in her temple is described as atop a pedestal of black stone before which stood an iron buffalo, identified as the demon Mahiṣa, which brushed up against her pedestal and caused her trident to shake (Layne 1991, 223–25). The offerings made to her were primarily vegetative, but resembled offerings of flesh and blood. So, the red lotuses looked like the eyes of slain buffaloes, the buds of the *agasti* and *kiṃśuka* flowers like the claws of lions and tigers, and the fruit evoked the appearance of severed heads and skulls (Layne 1991, 224). Lion cubs, the favored pets of Ambikā, played in the temple grounds, and roosters pecked out the rice from offerings mixed with blood. Evidently, actual blood offerings and their symbolic equivalents were commonplace. The door of Caṇḍikā's shrine was decorated with bracelets made of peacock necks, and her image was surrounded by weapons including axes and spears that had been used for the beheading of animal offerings. She was slim, dressed sensuously, with a gold head band and a pomegranate flower earring, and her lips were reddened by betel, resembling blood (Layne 1991, 224–25).

An old Draviḍa ascetic, who worships Durgā, Caṇḍikā, and Ambikā, who are all identified with each other, offers some comic relief from the powerful fascination with fear, revulsion, and sanguinary violence conjured up by the preceding descriptions in the *Kādambarī*. The ascetic, who is portrayed as a crackpot, is described as constantly bothering Durgā through prayers in the hopes of attaining rulership of the south. He seeks after various supernormal powers (such as making love to a *yakṣī*), believes he has other powers (such as awakening sexual arousal in old female ascetics by throwing powder on them), and had collected all sorts of charms, prayers, and stories. He had even composed a paean to Durgā (Layne 1991, 225–26). His body was ravaged by a litany of injuries, some self-inflicted by his foolishness, so that his features were even more distorted than Caṇḍikā's, whose frown contracted her crooked eyebrows.

Bāṇa's depiction of Caṇḍikā/Durgā/Ambika aligns closely with the traits found in early iconography and epic hymns. The buffalo demon Mahiṣa is shown pressed against her base, and offerings include peacock-neck bracelets, blood sacrifices, symbolic equivalents, and various weapons. The ascetic priest of her temple exhibits Tantric tendencies, focusing on powers, spells, and sexuality. He composes a panegyric to Durgā, suggesting that hymnic tributes were a regular feature of her shrines. Both the shrines and the goddess are described as refuges, contrasting with the Buddhist notion of refuge. Notably, the ascetic worships Durgā with the aim of attaining sovereignty, a defining element of her evolving persona. At the same time, Bāṇa depicts Durgā/Caṇḍikā/Ambikā as Śiva's spouse, a portrayal that differs significantly from the DM, which emphasizes her independent and supreme character. Furthermore, the DM integrates the Great Goddess into a framework more compatible with orthodox values. In the *Kādambarī*, Kātyāyanī is equated with Durgā, depicted as a lion-riding, trident-wielding goddess trampling the demon Mahiṣa (Layne 1991, 13, 31, 128). The imagery of lion cubs playing in the temple grounds evokes parallels to the temples of the lion goddess Sekhmet and her son Maahes at Leontopolis in Egypt, hinting at broader cultural resonances.

In its masterful retelling of three central myths — the slayings of 1) Madhu and Kaiṭabha, 2) Mahiṣa, and 3) Śumbha and Niśumbha — the DM skillfully merges the narrative and poetic elements of the *kāvya* tradition (as seen in the *Caṇḍīśataka* and *Kādambarī*), the devotional *bhakti* ethos of the Purāṇas, and the empowering Tantric practices of ritual, *mantra* recitation, and asceticism. While the DM provides the most famous account of Mahiṣa's defeat, its theological core lies in the Śumbha-Niśumbha episode, where the Devī absorbs all her manifestations into herself (DM 10.4), unifying her persona as the Great Goddess as Supreme Deity. The Śumbha-Niśumbha myth, however, is weakly attested in earlier literature, appearing most prominently in the SP, where the demons are named Sumbha and Nisumbha. Even so, their defeat remains sparsely represented in iconography, both historically and in contemporary depictions. If the DM had been in wide circulation before the *Caṇḍīśataka* or *Kādambarī*, it is reasonable to assume that Bāṇa would have referenced the Śumbha-Niśumbha episode, especially given his mentions of Caṇḍikā. Instead, the concise and dramatic Mahiṣa slaying, with its vivid visual appeal, ultimately resonated more deeply with public sentiment than the DM's expansive portrayal of Śumbha-Niśumbha's demise. Over time, the name Caṇḍikā diminished in prominence, while Caṇḍī — bolstered by the *Caṇḍīśataka* and its strong association with Mahiṣa's slaying — endures alongside Durgā as one of the Goddess's enduring names.

The *Mālatī-mādhava*

Xuanzang's account of a deadly encounter with brigands intent on human sacrifice raises questions about the goddess to whom such offerings might have been dedicated — if his account was not a product of imaginative storytelling. The early iconography examined so far portrays the goddess adorned with weapon-like hairpin ornaments or slaying the buffalo demon Mahiṣa. Similarly, the epic hymns only mention the goddess's preference for animal sacrifices, with no explicit reference to human sacrifice. Bāṇa's *Kādambarī* describes a Śabara chieftain whose scarred arms result from blood offerings to Caṇḍikā, and his *Harṣacarita* recounts devotees offering their own flesh. While the *Kādambarī* notes the Śabaras practiced human sacrifice (Layne 1991, 33), it remains unclear to which deity these offerings were directed — or whether these accounts reflect literary tropes and fanciful stereotypes, as perpetuated even in contemporary film depictions such as *Indiana Jones and the Temple of Doom.*

Descriptions of Caṇḍikā temples in literature evoke imagery suggestive of human sacrifice but ultimately indicate animal offerings, with symbolic items resembling human heads, skulls, tongues, and eyes. The subject of human sacrifice in India remains contentious among scholars. Some, such as Bakker (2019), argue it was practiced, albeit not widely, while others, such as G. U. Thite (1996), suggest it was a textual construct meant to complete sacrificial possibilities (Lincoln 1986, 183). References to human sacrifice (*puruṣamedha*) appear in the *Śatapatha Brāhmaṇa* (13.6.1–2), *Taittirīya Brāhmaṇa* (3.4.1.1ff.), and *Vājasaneyi Saṃhitā* (30.1–22), and archaeological evidence of human remains at fire altar sites lends credence to its historical occurrence (Smith and Doniger 1989, 220n31). Over time, however, human sacrifice was largely replaced in mainstream Hinduism by animal and vegetable substitutes for the human victim (Heesterman 1993, 31ff.).

A clue to instances of human sacrifice in literary accounts is found in the playwright Bhavabhūti's *Mālatī-mādhava*, a drama in ten acts. Scholars typically date this text to the early 8th century (Mirashi 1974, 4). Although the play is fundamentally a love story, a dramatic, visually graphic, and emotionally terrifying scene centers on the temple of a goddess called Cāmuṇḍā, who is also known as Karālā. In it, Kapālakuṇḍalā, a female devotee of Cāmuṇḍā, and her priestly *guru*, Aghoraghaṇṭa, capture the heroine, Mālatī, intending to offer her as a sacrifice to the goddess. Meanwhile the forlorn Mādhava, Mālatī's true love, has been wandering the grisly charnel grounds near Cāmuṇḍā's temple, unsuccessfully trying to sell dripping human flesh to the unwholesome denizens for their offerings. Mādhava hears Mālatī's cries, and rushes to her aid. The temple's horrific surroundings are described in detail and include imagery of dreadful spirits with long gaunt bodies, gaping mouths, and lolling tongues; one casually gnaws off the flesh from deep in the interstices of a skeletal frame resting on its lap. The female spirits adorn themselves with entrails, anoint themselves with blood paste, and quaff wine made from marrow in cups fashioned from human skulls. The river beside the cemetery is formidable and foreboding, since the howl of jackals and the hooting of owls from its banks blend with the chilling slosh of its waters, whose smooth flow is disrupted as it moves over the rotting skulls in its bed (Kale 1928, 45–46).

Mādhava enters upon the scene and sees Kapālakuṇḍalā and Aghoraghaṇṭa worshipping the goddess, and Mālatī dressed in clothes and garlands dyed in red lacquer, the garb of the sacrificial victim. The goddess worshippers praise Cāmuṇḍā by singing a hymn which is a paean to her deadly *tāṇḍava* dance, which delights Śiva. It describes how Cāmuṇḍā's foot planted on the earth burdens the entire quarter of the cosmos; her gaping mouth is as vast as Pātāla, the underworld, and can swallow the seven oceans. She has matted hair, wears a skirt of elephant hide, has hissing black snakes as armlets, and exudes a blazing fire. The swirling banner at the top of her lofty skull-staff disrupts the constellations. Her whirling dance causes the hooves on the flailing elephant hide to pierce the moon, which drips an ambrosia enlivening every skull on her necklace, each of which shriek in laughter (Kale 1928, 47; Coburn 1984, 136). Just as they are about to sacrifice Mālatī, Mādhava rushes up and wrests her away. Kapālakuṇḍalā urges Aghoraghaṇṭa to kill the intruder, and he moves to behead Mādhava as punishment for thwarting their human sacrifice. The two battle and the heroic Mādhava slays the evil Aghoraghaṇṭa.

The *Mālatī-mādhava* provides critical insights into perceptions of goddess cults during its period of composition (c. early 700s CE). It reveals that blood sacrifice — and even human sacrifice — was associated with certain goddess worship practices, at least by reputation. While Bhavabhūti may have heightened these elements for dramatic effect, such tropes were evidently familiar enough to his audience to resonate. The portrayal of human sacrifice and the ominous atmosphere of goddess temples suggests these ideas were already entrenched stereotypes. These depictions likely appealed to audiences aligned with *ahiṃsā* (non-harming) traditions, such as Jains and Buddhists, who would have viewed such practices as abhorrent. The *Mālatī-mādhava* critiques zealous, disreputable followers of goddess cults, reflecting societal discomfort with the reputed darker aspects of these traditions. First performed at a Śaiva festival (Warder 1983, 273), the play underscores the interplay between Śaiva and Śākta traditions of the period. The goddess Cāmuṇḍā, also called Karālā, is portrayed as the recipient of macabre offerings, aligning her with fierce and fearsome aspects of goddess worship. This depiction added dramatic tension to the play and highlights the contentious role such beliefs occupied in the religious and cultural discourse of the time.

The Goddess Kālī

The terrifying character of the goddess Cāmuṇḍā/Karālā evokes imagery reminiscent of Kṛṣṇa's revelation to Arjuna as Time (Kāla), the destroyer of worlds (*kālo 'smi lokakṣaya*), in the *Bhagavad Gītā* (BG 11.32). The description of Cāmuṇḍā/Karālā aligns with depictions of fearful Tantric goddesses, particularly Kālī. Kālī warrants further consideration, as her name appears alongside Durgā, Jayā, and Vijayā in the inserted Mbh hymns, the DStv, and DSto. These hymns provide limited details of her persona, emphasizing shared traits with the aforementioned goddesses. In the DStv (1. 34–39), she is called great Kālī (*mahākālī*), fond of liquor, flesh, and beasts, and wanders freely with a retinue of spirits. These traits align with Cāmuṇḍā/Karālā's characteristics. She is described as a boon-giver and burden-remover. In the DSto (lines 8–9), she is a young virgin, called Mahākālī and Bhadrakālī, and portrayed as reddish, black, or tawny, adorned with skulls. She is also associated with the destruction of Kaiṭabha (l. 15). Many of these attributes parallel Bhavabhūti's description of Cāmuṇḍā/Karālā in the *Mālatī-mādhava*.

An early literary occurrence of Kālī's name is in the *Muṇḍaka Upaniṣad* 1.2.4, where she is listed among the seven tongues of Agni, alongside Karālī. The term Karālī, a feminine form of Karālā, means terrifying or gaping wide with protruding teeth. This gaping-mouth feature is not attributed to Kālī or other goddesses in the epic hymns but is central in Bhavabhūti's portrayal of Karālā and Cāmuṇḍā.

Kālī, also called Kālarātri, appears in the Mbh (10.8.64–69) proper, as the dreadful persona of Aśvatthāman.[22] The Mbh's depiction of Kālī could well be contemporaneous with the DStv or a variant, which perhaps circulated independently during the composition of the Mbh or shortly thereafter, long before its incorporation into the epic. In the Mbh, Kālī is described with bloody mouth and eyes, garbed in blood-soaked garments and garlands, wielding a noose with which she ensnares men, elephants, and horses. Her destructive visions haunt the Pāṇḍavas, reflecting the horrors they witness on the battlefield. This imagery foreshadows their anguish when Aśvatthāman slaughters their children and parallels a form of post-traumatic stress, as the Pāṇḍavas repeatedly relive the nightmares of war. Night becomes a time not of peace but one of terror and violence.

Kālī embodies the shadow side of battle, representing not only conquest and glory but also its devastating cost. Her role parallels that of Durgā, emphasizing the duality of victory and destruction. While Kālī does not appear in the HV except in AniH (l. 20), likely a late insertion, she is identified there as Kātyāyanī, both the creator and remover of fear. The name of the celebrated playwright Kālidāsa ("Servant of Kālī") reflects the rise of Kālī's cult during the Gupta era (4th–5th century CE). In the *Kumārasambhava* (7.38–39), Kālidāsa includes Kālī in Śiva's wedding procession, following the Mātṛkās (Mothers), who present gifts to the groom. She is portrayed adorned with a necklace of skulls.

The *Gauḍavaho*

In the *Gauḍavaho*[23] (c. mid-8th century), composed by Vākpatirāja, court poet to Yaśovarman (725–752 CE), ruler of Kanauj, the poet glorifies his patron's military campaign that culminates in the defeat of the king of Gauḍa. As Yaśovarman's army passes through the Vindhyas, he halts to worship the Mahiṣa-slaying goddess in a temple vividly described with ghastly imagery. The temple's door is smeared with blood (*Gauḍavaho*, v. 294), and severed heads pile high, their hair darkening the shrine, which even lamps cannot adequately illuminate (v. 318). Knives offered by heroes fill the temple (v. 306), and owls haunt the sanctum (v. 306). Tantric Kaula women scramble to glimpse a human sacrificial victim (v. 319). The pervasive sanguinary imagery — real blood, red banners, and red lacquer — heightens the temple's horrifying atmosphere (e.g., v. 285, 305, 310, 311, 322, 326, 327). Yet, despite the gore, the goddess is described as compassionate, her heart "soft with the ambrosia of compassion" (v. 337).

This goddess, associated with slaying Mahiṣa, is frequently linked to buffalo imagery (e.g., v. 285, 286, 305, 316). She is named Kālī (v. 297), Night (v. 334), and Kālarātri (v. 337). The text references her encounter with Kaṃsa, when she flew into the sky after being dashed against rocks by him (v. 326). Her temple is surrounded by peacocks, a connection to her son Kumāra's peacock mount (v. 299), and her worship is associated with tribal groups such as the Śabaras and Kols. The presence of owls and peacocks aligns her with Nidrā/Kauśikī, who shares such avian associations. Intriguingly, trees are said to worship her, their red sap flowing as a substitute for sacrificial blood (v. 330), adding a symbolic layer to her rites.

Although the goddess Cāmuṇḍā/Karālā described in the *Mālatī-mādhava* is not explicitly named Kālī, her Kālī-like traits, as elaborated in the *Gauḍavaho*, are unmistakable. However, the *Mālatī-mādhava* likely predates the *Gauḍavaho*. The goddess Cāmuṇḍā is mentioned in the DM, which many scholars place earlier than the *Mālatī-mādhava*, but this assumption is difficult to substantiate. Coburn (1984, 135–36) found no instance of the epithet Cāmuṇḍā in earlier Vedic or epic literature and agreed with Pargiter's assertion that the DM marks the first occurrence of the name. Yet this seems unlikely, as the DM explicitly provides an etymology for the name, linking it to her beheading of the demons Caṇḍa and Muṇḍa, while identifying her with Kālī.

Similarly, the *Varāha Purāṇa* (VarP, Chapter 96) derives Cāmuṇḍā's name from her slaying of the demon-king Ruru by separating his body (*carma*) from his head (*muṇḍa*). Both derivations capitalize on the term *muṇḍa*, which can mean skull, head, or shaved head. These texts have agendas distinct from the *Mālatī-mādhava*. The *Mālatī-mādhava*, a love play, uses the danger posed by sinister forces as a dramatic device and trenchantly critiques such forms of worship. In contrast, the DM and VarP aim to incorporate deities such as Cāmuṇḍā into a cohesive theological framework that exalts the Great Goddess.

Cāmuṇḍā was a fearsome goddess worshipped in the 6th century CE, and therefore already known to the authors of the DM and VarP in her own right through the notoriety of her temple(s), methods, and ends of worship. The philosopher Bhāvaviveka, founder of the Svātantrika branch of Madhyamaka Buddhism, who is thought to have lived between 490 and 580 CE, disparaged comparison between the fierce Cāmuṇḍā and the benign Buddhist savior figure, Tārā. He wrote: "[H]ow can there be any similarity between the [ritual] knowledge of, for instance, Cāmuṇḍā which is replete with coarse and unbearable affliction, teaching a mundane purpose, and that for instance, [the gentle] Tārā which is knowledge of absolute significance" (Sarkar 2013, 419, cited in Kapstein 2001, 249).

Bhavabhūti may have taken creative liberties with the construction of the names of Cāmuṇḍā's worshippers, which tacitly resonate with features that we associate with the fierce goddess, such as her skull-necklace and a fearsome bell. Kapālakuṇḍalā means "She who has Skulls as Earrings," and Aghoraghaṇṭa means "Disgusting Bell." Nevertheless, it seems that Cāmuṇḍā and Karālā were goddesses resorted to by many worshippers and problematized in the light of Buddhist values. Cāmuṇḍā's notoriety was certainly enhanced through compositions such as the *Mālatī-mādhava*. As later compositions, the DM and the VarP would be compelled to work Cāmuṇḍā into their amalgamating schemes. Were it the contrary and the *Mālatī-mādhava*'s reference to Cāmuṇḍā were influenced by the DM, one might expect some tacit reference to Cāmuṇḍā/Kālī's deeds portrayed there. But there are none. With the advancing success of the DM, the equation of Kālī with Cāmuṇḍā became normative, and Kālī was mostly transformed from a fearsome although arguably comely goddess to one with Cāmuṇḍā's gaunt and hideous appearance. Her dark but attractive depictions persist in lithography, particularly in Bengal, for instance, and may simply be a persistence of this benign vision of Kālī, rather than the transformation of her appearance from what was originally hideous to beautiful, as has been suggested in some recent scholarship.[24]

Cāmuṇḍā/Karālā in the *Mālatī-mādhava* is notable for her gaping mouth, capable of consuming the world's oceans — a motif later echoed in the DM with Kālī/Cāmuṇḍā drinking the blood of the replicating demon Raktabīja to prevent his regeneration. Another defining characteristic of Cāmuṇḍā/Karālā is her destructive dance, where her powerful foot crushes creation itself. This imagery foreshadows myths as in the *Liṅga Purāṇa* (2.106), where Kālī, after a bloody rampage destroying the demon Dāruka, threatens the cosmos until Śiva intervenes. Disguised as a crying baby, Śiva lies on the battlefield, stopping her rage when she picks him up to suckle him, allowing him to absorb her anger through her breast milk. Similarly, in another myth, Śiva as Naṭarāja defeats Kālī in a dance competition. These narratives mark a shift in the role of cosmic destruction from the great goddess's crushing foot to Śiva's *tāṇḍava* dance, where his own foot becomes the symbol of creation's annihilation. This transition underscores Śiva's ascendency in cosmic mythology through incorporating aspects of the goddess's earlier destructive persona.

Mahiṣāsuramardinī

Returning to our pursuit of the motif of "crushing," with which the *Caṇḍīśataka* abounds so thoroughly, we note that the imagery persists to the 10th century CE, in a verse from the Rāṣṭrakūṭa charter (926 CE) from Chinchani village. There, in a verse that evokes *Caṇḍīśataka*, v. 2 (quoted above) we read:

śulabhinnasya vinyasto mahiṣasya balād gale /
durgāyāḥ pātu vaḥ pādas tadraktālaktakāṅkitaḥ //
Besmeared by the scarlet lac of his blood (*raktālaktakāṅkitaḥ*),
    may the foot of Durgā (*durgāyāḥ . . . pādas*) clamped
    on Mahiṣa's throat (*mahiṣasya . . . gale*) protect,
    while trident-pierced (*śūlabhinnasya*) the Asura.
(Sarkar 2013, 428)

The *Caṇḍīśataka* (v. 6, 8) prefigures the motif of the demon's salvation through his destruction under the goddess's foot, a theme later expanded in the Purāṇic corpus. This symbolism of Durgā's foot crushing enemies resonated with sovereigns seeking victory and non-martial devotees seeking protection from external dangers. The *Kālikā Purāṇa* (Chapters 60.81–135) elaborates on this by recounting Mahiṣa's death across three eons. First, he was slain by Ugracaṇḍā, an eighteen-armed fierce form of the goddess; then by Bhadrakālī, a sixteen-armed manifestation; and finally, by Durgā, who crushed him to death, now and hereafter. Mahiṣa, as conqueror of the triple world, desired only a liberating death at Durgā's feet. She granted his wish, decreeing that he would always be depicted beneath her feet and venerated alongside her. By this point, the identification of Durgā as Mahiṣāsuramardinī — with the buffalo demon eternally portrayed beneath her feet — was firmly established, consolidating her role as both savior and sovereign.

In Tantric Metaphysical Symbols

Moreover, as evidenced in the boon requested by the merchant Samādhi in the frame tale of the DM, the Devī's persona as a force for spiritual liberation or empowerment continues to develop in texts of much later provenance. In various Tantric texts, such as Kṛṣṇānanda Bhaṭṭācārya's *Bṛhad Tantrasāra* and the *Kulacūḍāmaṇi Tantra* (Chapter VII in particular), as well as the rather Tantricized *Kālikā Purāṇa*, ritual procedures for the worship of Mahiṣamardinī are described. East Indian recensions of the *Kulacūḍāmaṇi Tantra* 7.22–35 (e.g., Vedāntatīrtha 1915, 42–46) contain a hymn to Mahiṣāsuramardinī, which is also found in the Bengali *Tantrasāra*.[25]
Within these texts one discerns features of the sophisticated metaphysical systems and procedures entailed in the attainment of self-realization that we associate with the Kaula traditions of Kashmir, which will be discussed in more detail in the second volume. One's own inner failings and one's consciousness in spiritual bondage are likened to demons, which the Goddess Durgā, explicitly identified as Mahiṣamardinī, is asked to crush, thereby granting the aspirant liberation. Her worship can grant not just spiritual liberation (*mokṣa*), but fortune (*śrī*) and sensual delight (*kāma*). Thus, the iconographic image of Mahiṣāsuramardinī, Crusher — more so than Killer — of the Demon Mahiṣa continues to live on, because the conceptual image of the crusher (*mardinī*)

most effectively conveys an array of potent meanings to a wide assortment of her worshippers. While the demon Mahiṣa may have symbolized rival supreme deities or even earthly rulers in the earliest centuries, Mahiṣa soon grew to also represent all manner of worldly dangers, and then metaphysical notions of delusion and spiritual bondage. This broadened the meaning and appeal of the Devī, promoted through texts such as the DM, into a powerful ally beyond the immediate concerns of sovereignty, or a refuge from the host of perils within the world, to a source of empowerment or a salvific force from the existential angst of rebirth and saṃsāric existence.

From this survey we can reasonably assert that it is prudent to designate the earliest known imagery of the buffalo-subduing goddess as Mahiṣāsuranāśinī, that is, "Slayer of the Demon (Buffalo) Mahiṣa." One could also reasonably assert that the more prudent term Mahiṣanāśinī is not necessary, because the buffalo is identified as a demon in almost all instances encountered in the earliest relevant literary record. Despite that, it would seem judicious to restrict the term Mahiṣāsuramardinī only to images in which the goddess's foot is in some manner planted upon Mahiṣa, while utilizing Mahiṣāsuranāśinī (or its killing variants, such as Mahiṣāsuraghatinī, rather than crushing ones) for any other types of buffalo slaying images. Of course, it would be most sensible to restrict usage of the term Mahiṣāsuramardinī to images in which the goddess's foot is planted upon Mahiṣa and which were produced after the period of the early Purāṇas, the *Śivadharma*, the *Caṇḍīśataka*, and the DM — although the term itself does not appear in the latter two — because it is only then that term and the conceptual framework were gaining in prominence.[26] All these images could also reasonably be called Durgā because this name appears and is used in the earliest corresponding textual material for the many-armed goddess who subdues the buffalo demon Mahiṣa.

In the hope that epigraphic material might offer some firmer dating for the use of the epithet Mahiṣamardinī, I noted that Sarkar (2017, 22, 121) citing Vogel (1911, 150–52) refers to an inscribed image of Mahiṣāsuramardinī commissioned by a king named Bhogaṭa of Kiṣkindha. Unfortunately, my inspection of that source revealed that the goddess is mostly known as Devī Aṣṭabhujī, because she is depicted with eight arms. This so-called Svāim image inscription, named after a hamlet of the Himgir *pargaṇā*, and which Vogel (1911, 113) tentatively dates at the 8th or 9th century CE, refers to the goddess as Bhagabatī (i.e., Bhagavatī). She is depicted as slaying two demons, arguably Śumbha and Niśumbha. As previously noted, such images of the Devī slaying two demons are uncommon, because the myth of the Devī's destruction of Śumbha and Niśumbha did not capture the public or the iconographer's imagination anywhere as robustly as the slaying of Mahiṣa. Since the pedestal depicts two lions devouring a buffalo, the goddess Bhagavatī has again loosely been labeled as Mahiṣāsuramardinī. This is problematic because it conflates what might be the Śumbha/Niśumbha slaying goddess with what might be the one who crushes the buffalo demon. Both may be properly called Durgā, or Devī, but in myth the manifestations of the Devī to slay the demon Mahiṣa and the demons Śumbha and Niśumbha occur in different eons.

Appraising the Myth of Skanda[27]

No analysis of the slaying of Mahiṣa can ignore the fact that in the earliest literary account it is Skanda that is credited with this deed.[28] This occurs in the Mbh (3.221.52–69), when a demonic horde attacks the gods in heaven. In van Buitenen's translation of the respective passages, we read:

> . . . From the dread army of the Daityas there emerged a power-ful Dānava, Mahiṣa by name, who had grabbed a great moun-tain; and the celestials seeing him hold high a mountain - like the sun that is completely decked with clouds — ran, king, ran. Mahiṣa fell on the Gods and hurled his mountain; and the grim-looking stone mass in its fall felled a myriad God soldiers and crushed them on the earth, O lord. Along with the other Dānavas this Mahiṣa, panicking the Gods, stormed nimbly into the mêlée as a lion pounces on small game. Indra and the celes-tials saw Mahiṣa fall upon them and fearfully fled from the bat-tlefield, arms broken, and crests fallen.

> Angrily Mahiṣa then at once attacked Rudra's chariot, and he ran to and grabbed hold of Rudra's chariot pole; and when the furious Mahiṣa vehemently made for the chariot of Rudra, heaven and earth groaned deeply and the great seers fainted. The big-bodied Daityas, the likes of rain clouds, roared and they were sure that victory was theirs. But even in this pass the blessed lord declined to kill off Mahiṣa in battle, for he remem-bered that Skanda was to be the death of the miscreant. But Mahiṣa, recognizing Rudra's chariot, bellowed evilly, striking fear in the Gods and delighting the Dānavas.

> And when this grisly danger beset the Gods, out came Mahāsena, furiously blazing sun, girt in his blood-red robe, sporting blood-red garlands and jewelry, blood-mouthed, the strong-armed, gold-armored lord riding his sun-like, gold-spar-kling chariot; and on seeing him the Daitya army suddenly van-ished from the field. And, great king, puissant Mahāsena threw his blazing, shattering spear at Mahiṣa, and once, thrown, the spear hit the big head of Mahiṣa; and Mahiṣa's head was split, and he fell down relinquishing his life. Throw after throw the spear smote the foes in their thousands and then, as witnessed the God and the Dānavas, it returned again to Skanda's hand. Mostly killed off by the cunning Mahāsena with his missiles, the remnant of the gory Daitya troops, frightened and panicked by Skanda's unstoppable Companions, fell and were eaten by the hundreds. They feasted on the Dānavas and gulped their

> blood; and in no time they cleaned the world of Dānavas and
> made very merry. (van Buitenen 1975, 663–64)

The richly detailed narrative in this account contrasts sharply with the simpler epithets and mantric verses previously encountered concerning Mahiṣa's destruction. The motif centers on the gods, led by Indra, being displaced by demons (*daityas*), empowered by their leader, Mahiṣa. Although Mahiṣa can mean buffalo, in this account, he is not explicitly described as one; the term may simply connote "powerful" or "great." Rudra (Śiva), capable of defeating Mahiṣa, defers to Skanda (Mahāsena) to perform the task.

Skanda is depicted as both resplendent in golden armor and chariot yet simultaneously clad in blood-red regalia. His boomeranging spear is a formidable weapon, capable of repeated devastating strikes. His army's companions (*pārṣadāḥ*) revel in gruesome acts, devouring demons and drinking their blood, wiping out the horde entirely. This imagery evokes parallels with Kālī's annihilation of Raktabīja in the later DM and the drunken revelry of the Devī's companion goddesses.

The account concludes with Maheśvara (Śiva) offering praise, declaring this Skanda's first great feat. The chapter ends by proclaiming that those who recite this section on Skanda's birth will attain his realm in the afterlife and prosperity in this life. This structural pattern resembles the DM, where the gods sing hymns of praise following the Devī's victory, and the text closes with verses extolling the benefits of its recitation.

Who Is Skanda?

It is beyond the scope of this study to examine the origins of Skanda exhaustively, but the Mbh is one of the earliest literary sources of his appearance. Based on a close study of his cult in the period of its development Richard Mann (2007, 449) found that Skanda began as a fearsome deity, who needed to be propitiated to prevent his destructive actions. He was associated with dangerous groups of beings such as the Mātṛs (Mothers) and the Grahas (Graspers). In Ayurvedic traditions (e.g., *Suśrutasaṃhitā*), he himself was a Graha and their leader. Nevertheless, in the Mbh, particularly its Forest Book (*Āraṇyakaparvan*), he is characterized as the son of Śiva and general of the army of the gods.

The Mbh's account of Skanda's defeat of Mahiṣa recalls the planoconvex tablet from the Indus Valley Civilization, which depicted a figure, ostensibly male, spearing a wild water buffalo (see figure 4.1a). Although Mahiṣa is not identified as a buffalo in the Mbh telling, the term Mahiṣa does hold that meaning. And the squatting figure nearby on the tablet, who appears to oversee the act, was labeled a "proto-Śiva" by early Indologists. Thus, we have the image of a male figure killing a buffalo while a Śiva-like figure looks on. Were this an early depiction of Skanda, his cult would extend back to Indus Valley times.

Asko Parpola (1990, 265, 270, 272–77) makes that assertion based on other suggestive evidence but recognizes that it must remain highly speculative.

N. Gopala Pillai (1937) proposed a fascinating theory regarding Skanda's origins, suggesting a potential link to Alexander of Macedonia. While scholars such as Mann (2007) and Fred Clothey (2005) have given this theory scant attention, certain aspects merit closer examination. Pillai notes that Alexander, known as Iskandar Dhu' Iquarnein ("Two-Horned Alexander") among the Arabs, was venerated as a god up to the Islamic period and regarded as a prophet by some Muslim groups. Historically, Alexander declared himself or was proclaimed a son of Zeus-Ammon/Amun at the Oracle of Siwa in Libya. His enduring fame is reflected in the *Alexander Romance* traditions, which date back to the 3rd century CE and celebrated his exploits across the Hellenic kingdoms.

Despite Alexander's prominence, he is conspicuously absent from Hindu, Jain, or Buddhist literature, a silence Pillai finds striking. To address this absence, he seeks possible allusions to Alexander within the Indic tradition. He suggests, for instance, that Alexander's Persian name, Iskander, might have evolved into Iskanda, and subsequently, Skanda. This parallels the adaptation of the Graeco-Bactrian king Menander's name into Milinda in the Buddhist *Milindapañha*. Pillai's broader arguments on Skanda's potential derivation from Alexander — or influence on his traits — are extensive and debated. However, a key aspect of his theory relates to Skanda's defeat of Mahiṣa, an association that warrants further consideration.

Alexander's pivotal conquest of Darius III (aka Artashata or Codomannus) and the Achaemenid Empire — then the world's most powerful empire — forms the basis of Pillai's theory (1937, 956–57). Pillai argues this victory precipitated the decline of the Achaemenid high god Ahura Mazdā, and he identifies echoes of this event in the myth of Skanda's defeat of Mahiṣa Asura. For Pillai, the Sanskritized remnants of Alexander's overthrow of Ahura Mazdā's supremacy are embedded in the Skanda-Mahiṣa narrative.

While compelling, Pillai's argument has limitations. For instance, while *asura* (demon) is clearly linked to the Avestan *ahura* (divine being), Mazdā is generally seen as cognate with the Sanskrit *medhā* (wisdom), not *mahiṣa* (buffalo or powerful). However, Pillai suggests Mazdā could have been reinterpreted as *mahiṣa* due to phonetic similarities or even as *medha* (short *a*), a term for sacrificial animals in Sanskrit (e.g., *aśvamedha,* the horse sacrifice). With the buffalo holding prominence as a sacrificial animal in South Asia, Mahiṣa became the archetypal foe of the gods. This speculation highlights how myths might evolve through cultural exchanges, adapting to regional contexts while retaining core elements. If correct, Pillai's theory underscores the possible interconnectedness of West and South Asian religious traditions during the post-Achaemenid period.

Why Does the Goddess Supplant Skanda as Slayer of the Buffalo?

It is beyond the scope of this study to fully assess Pillai's arguments, which ultimately remain speculative. Nonetheless, they highlight a direction worth exploring and will inform theoretical arguments presented in the final chapter of this volume. While Skanda's defeat of Mahiṣa marks the first literary reference to this deed, even in the Mbh, two hymns (the DStv and DSto), albeit inserted at a later time, implicitly attribute this achievement to the goddess. Over time, the goddess's triumph over Mahiṣa supersedes Skanda's claim, despite Śiva's praise in the Mbh, declaring that this act would be Skanda's first great feat and secure his eternal glory in the three worlds (Mbh 3.221.76). Skanda's enduring fame is tied primarily to his role in the destruction of the demon Tāraka, not Mahiṣa. Why? The early composition and circulation of the DStv or its hymnic variant during the Mbh period would suggest a competing narrative was already in circulation. Did the goddess embody or accomplish something more compelling than Skanda?

To address these questions, we must turn to the DM, the most influential account of the goddess's defeat of Mahiṣa, referenced extensively and examined in detail in the next two chapters. This remarkable text provides critical insights into the ascendency of the Great Goddess, both as Durgā and into a specific configuration of a supreme deity, and her decisive triumph over the buffalo demon Mahiṣa. While this sequence deviates from a strictly chronological approach, the DM's pivotal role in the evolution of Durgā's cult warrants immediate attention. This textual analysis is correlated with iconographic depictions of the Anthropomorphic (A) and Emerging (E) depictions of the buffalo-slaying goddess in two subsequent chapters. The SP and related myths in the VarP only follow thereafter, offering a comparative analysis to illustrate their foundational contributions to the Devī's mythos and how they serve as precursors to the elaboration found in the DM.

Chapter 8

Durgā in the *Devī Māhātmya*

The *Devī Māhātmya* (DM, also known as *Devīmāhātmyam*) holds pivotal importance in Hindu Śākta traditions, presenting a vision of the goddess (*devī*) as Supreme Reality. She is the Great Goddess (Mahādevī), with all other goddesses as her aspects or manifestations. Combining the powers of all male gods, she surpasses them, embodying both transcendence and immanence. Unlike God, she is Goddess — Absolute Reality envisioned as an irresistibly beautiful, formidable, and supremely powerful woman. The DM conveys this through a compelling narrative recounting the Devī's manifestations and key mythic deeds. It is embedded within the *Mārkaṇḍeya Purāṇa* (MārkP), often dated to the 5th or 6th century CE (Mirashi 1964, 181–84). However, Pargiter (1904, viii–xiii), in his translation of the MārkP, argued that the DM was a later addition. A new critical edition of the Sanskrit text, edited by M. L. Wadekar and published by the Oriental Institute in 2011, treats it as an integral part of the MārkP.[29] Even so, the DM (certainly the myths that it recounts, and some of the hymns of praise to the Goddess within it) may well have circulated independently prior to its insertion into the MārkP. From a variant found in a discovered manuscript of the DM, J. N. Tiwari (1983) speculates that it might have circulated in a shorter version than what we encounter today. We will examine and argue for approximately a mid-8th century date for the DM's composition later in this study. Like the *Bhagavad Gītā* (BG), which circulates independently from the *Mahābhārata* (Mbh), the DM currently still circulates as an independent ritual text, sandwiched between shorter tracts, known as limbs (*aṅga*).

The DM, also known as the *Caṇḍī*, appears to mimic the BG in that the latter is supposed to consist of 700 verses (see Coburn 1991, 27). There are early versions of the BG with as many as 745 verses, but the BG is attributed with 700 verses according to a recension commented upon by the influential non-dualist Vedānta philosopher Śaṅkara in about the 8th century. Of course, just as there are variations in the number of verses of the BG, many of the seventy or so commentaries on the DM share a concern in dividing up the text to arrive at the figure of 700 verses. This is because the text has for long also been known as the *Durgā Saptaśatī (Seven Hundred [Verses] to Durgā)* (DS), or even just the *Saptaśatī*, to some extent inhibiting efforts to tamper with it through the insertion of additional verses. Coburn (1984, 51n155) notes that the shortest version has 573 verses, but this is expanded to 700 by considering phrases such as "the sage said (*ṛṣir uvāca*)" as a full verse.[30] The 13th century Marathi saint Jñāneśvara (also known as Dnyaneshwar) referred to the BG as the *Saptaśatī*, comparing it to the DM, which also has 700 verses. This offers evidence that it was known as the *Durgā Saptaśatī* during his time (i.e., 1275–1296 CE).[31] The widespread recognition of the DM as the *Durgā Saptaśatī* underscores the identification of Durgā as the Great Goddess (Devī). Another enduring name is the *Caṇḍī*, and the text is sometimes referred to as the *Caṇḍī Pāṭha* (*Recitation of the Caṇḍī*). In my fieldwork in Nepal and India, particularly in Banāras, I find that most people refer to the text as the DS, with the *Caṇḍī* being the more common alternative to the DM, which is far less encountered. Despite this, I use DM, the term more prevalent in academic discourse, although the DS strongly affirms the focus of my study on the identity of Devī as Durgā.

The DM is often cited as the third most widely known and recited Hindu scripture, following the BG and Tulsidāsa's *Rāmacaritamānas*. Whether or not this claim is entirely accurate, it attests to the text's renown across the Hindu world. Its popularity owes much to the compelling mythic narratives, which are recited aloud during the spring and autumn Navarātra festivals. The DM, divided into thirteen chapters, consists of a frame story encompassing three myths detailing the Goddess's exploits. Among recent academic studies of the DM, Raj Balkaran (2018) offers one of the most detailed and intriguing interpretations for the structure of the scripture.[32]

No study of Durgā should ignore the significance of the DM in delineating the persona of the Devī, her subsequent iconographic representations, textual retellings of her myths, and the ritual life that it influences. I shall thus recount the DM in some detail, providing an accurate summary of the content of the scripture.[33] My focus will be on extracting elements that reveal something about the nature of the Devī, rather than on the full detail of the narratives themselves. Although I paraphrase the DM, my language and discussion is based on my close reading of the Sanskrit and at times a virtual translation of verses of the text. Because Coburn (1991) presents one of the most respected contemporary translations, I generally defer to his translations, unless I opt to present my own.

The Frame Tale (Opening)

As an insertion into the MārkP, the DM begins with the sage Mārkaṇḍeya teaching his disciple Krauṣṭuki about the various Manus, divine beings that preside over long periods of cosmic time known as *manvantaras*. Fourteen *manvantaras* form an even longer period known as a *kalpa*. According to the MārkP, when approached for instructions by a disciple of Vyāsa named Jaimini, Mārkaṇḍeya directed him to four learned birds. Thus, the larger frame story in the MārkP is of the birds, learned Brahmins who were under a curse, instructing Jaimini in Mārkaṇḍeya's teachings to Krauṣṭuki. As with the Mbh, the story that we are receiving is not a "first-hand" account. It is a retelling of a retelling, of stories nested one within the other, remembered and passed on from teacher to disciple. In this sense it is exemplary of *smṛti* literature, "that which is remembered." As Mārkaṇḍeya begins his narrative about the eighth Manu, Sāvarṇi, who presides over the eighth *manvantara*, he seemingly digresses with what is the DM, which, to some extent, is really an origin myth of Sāvarṇi, a son of Sūrya, the Sun God. Balkaran (2020) analyzes the *Sūrya Māhātmya* also embedded within the MārkP, arguing that its placement along with the DM within the MārkP illustrates a symbiosis between Sun and Goddess worshipping traditions, in which "this-worldly" goals that preserve the cosmic and social orders are valued and upheld. Since it is through the power of the Devī that this royal empowerment occurs, the DM is pivotally a text about how an earthly king may attain cosmic sovereignty.[34] Thus, the DM begins with Mārkaṇḍeya telling Krauṣṭuki about a certain great king named Suratha, of the Caitra lineage (*vaṃśa*) who ruled the whole earth during the Svārociṣa interval, the second of the fourteen *manvantara* periods. Suratha was eventually reborn as Sāvarṇi, the eighth Manu and the son of Sūrya, the Sun. Since a *manvantara* is 306,720,000 years in duration, and we are believed to be in the Vaivasvata, the seventh *manvantara*, Sāvarṇi's rule in the eighth *manvantara*, spoken of in the past tense (*manvantarādhipaḥ babhūva)* (DM 1.2), suggests that the events of the DM's frame story took place a rather long time ago, in a time cycle or *kalpa* prior to our current one. In the cyclical time frame of this worldview, however, the rule of the eighth Manu is again approaching.

Mārkaṇḍeya recounts how the caring king Suratha, once ruler of a vast empire, was defeated in battle by his inferior enemies, the Kolāvidhvaṃsins, and, weakened, was forced to retreat to the rule of his own country. Unfortunately, his corrupt ministers seized his army and treasury, robbing him of his capacity to rule. Claiming he was off hunting, Suratha rode away alone into the dense forest. There he encountered the sage Medhas's hermitage, surrounded by docile wild beasts and teeming with disciples. This part of the frame narrative evokes the classic motif of the *kṣatriya* hero (e.g., Rāma of the *Rāmāyaṇa*; the Pāṇḍava princes of the Mbh), disenfranchised from power and being sheltered by a forest-dwelling sage (typically a Brahmin), who recounts mythic tales and imparts valuable teachings. Medhas took him in graciously, and Suratha dwelt there for some time, somewhat at a loss, his mind tormented with selfish thoughts. He lamented the loss of his city that his fathers had protected for so long, and worried about the welfare of his subjects, and even his favorite elephant. He suspected that his sycophantic hangers-on were now serving other rulers, and that his painstakingly enriched treasury was being depleted by profligate spending. It was then that he met and struck up a conversation with Samādhi, a once wealthy merchant (*vaiśya*), who looked despondent (DM 1.3–17).

Samādhi explained that his own greedy wife and sons, coveting his wealth, deprived him of it and banished him. He retreated to the forest to mourn his misfortune, but still wondered about the well-being of his kinfolk. Suratha was puzzled and asked why Samādhi would be concerned about persons who treated him so badly. The merchant replied that he himself was puzzled about his soft-hearted feelings of affection for such disreputable and hard-hearted characters. Sensing a similarity in their plight, the two approached Medhas and asked his advice. Suratha explained how, even though they both could intellectually understand the folly of their feelings — he for his kingdom and aspects connected with it, and the merchant for his family, servants, and so on who treated him so badly — they were unable to overcome the turn of their thoughts and feelings and were miserable on account of it (DM 1.18–33). How is it, they wondered, that even those who do know better, like themselves, are nevertheless firmly within the grip of delusion, utterly blind to the necessary discriminating insight? Why did they act as if they were ignorant? These questions, which are of crucial significance in comprehending the persona of the Goddess (Devī), allow Medhas to launch into his answer, which is an explanation of the Devī's unvanquishable power to delude. Medhas's answer is the glorification (*māhātmya*) of the Goddess.

Medhas begins his explanation by pointing out that all creatures, including human beings, are in the grip of delusion and egoism, being bound to mundane life since they misunderstand the nature of reality due to the power of Mahāmāyā ("[She who is the] Great (*mahā*) [Matrix of] Illusion/Phantasmal Reality (*māyā*)"). He explains that Mahāmāyā is Yoganidrā, the yogic sleep of Viṣṇu; she forcibly takes hold of the minds of all in the world, even men of knowledge, deluding them. Not only is she the creator of the entire universe, unanimated and animated, but ultimately grants boons that liberate beings. In fact, she is the supreme knowledge (*paramā vidyā*) that is the very cause of release from her power of delusion. She is the lady who is the overlord of all lords (*sarveśvareśvarī*) (DM 1.33–44).

This prelude is of crucial significance, because it contextualizes much of the rationales behind the Devī's mythic exploits that are to follow. In broad but vivid brushstrokes, it paints the key features of her persona as Absolute Divinity. At the very outset, the DM also forges a connection between the Devī and the goddess Nidrā (here she is Yoganidrā). Even more broadly and potently, the Devī is introduced as Mahāmāyā, an epithet that connects her with an array of metaphysical systems such as Buddhism and Vedānta. The mother of the historical Buddha, Siddhārtha Gautama, is generally known as Māyādevī or Mahāmāyā. Māyā is the power that keeps beings in the grip of spiritual ignorance or bondage, and in many philosophies of liberation, the highest goal of life is to gain liberation (*mokṣa, nirvāṇa*) from this power. In Tantric systems, Māyā is a factor that separates a pure realm (*śuddhādhvan*) of consciousness from the lower, impure domain (*aśuddhādhvan*) of manifestation (Davis 1991, 44–46). The Devī is framed not merely as Māyā, but Mahāmāyā, a deluding power that is supreme, and arguably, beyond defeat. It is vital to recognize that by so doing the DM is providing a metaphysics, and not merely a series of myths about a deity to whom one may turn devotionally. It is saying something about the human condition, the driving principles within living things and the creation, and their place within an overarching depiction of reality.[35]

Suratha asks a leading question about the origins of the goddess Mahāmāyā, and her true form (*svarūpā*) and activities. The *ṛṣi* replies that Mahāmāyā is eternal, and that in actuality she is everything since the world itself is her very form (*mūrti*). Although eternal, she manifests in various ways to effectuate the work of the gods and is thus said to have "arisen" or "appeared" (*utpanna*) frequently (DM 1.45–48). The preceding passages are enormously significant, because they unequivocally assert that the Devī is not "created" or "born," as is sometimes erroneously conveyed in some scholarly analyses, particularly when discussing her emergence in the Mahiṣa myth. Although the term *utpanna*, which is frequently used to refer to the Devī's manifestations, may be interpreted as "created" or "born," its meaning is explicitly clarified here at the outset of the DM. She is eternal, but manifests, arises, comes forth, appears, emerges, and so on, and may only figuratively be spoken of as being "born" or "created" (DM 1.48). Moreover, she is portrayed as emerging in order to effectuate or accomplish (*siddhyartham*) the acts (*kārya*) of the gods, suggesting that she arises to enable the gods to achieve their goals; their power derives through her agency.

Episode One

Medhas now recounts the first of the three main mythic exploits of the Devī. At the end of the cosmic eon, when the universe was a single ocean and Lord Viṣṇu was reclining on Śeṣa (the cosmic serpent that serves as his throne), from the dirt in Viṣṇu's ear there arose Madhu and Kaiṭabha, two fearsome *asuras*, intent on killing Brahmā Prajāpati. Noticing the *asuras*, Brahmā, whose abode was Viṣṇu's navel-lotus, with the singular sentiment to arouse the sleeping Viṣṇu, praised Yoganidrā, the divine sleep of Viṣṇu, queen of the universe, supporter of the world (*jagaddhatrī*), its maintainer and destroyer, who had made her abode in his eyes (DM 1.51–53).

Here we note that Yoganidrā is identified with the power that puts Viṣṇu to sleep, and her persona as the true supporter, maintainer, and destroyer of the universe is reiterated. The creator god Brahmā Prajāpati is powerless to awaken Viṣṇu on his own. Viṣṇu is in the grips of Yoganidrā's power, and only she can release him from his sleep. Mahāmāyā/Yoganidrā is thus already portrayed as superior in potency to both Brahmā, and Viṣṇu, two key figures in the so-called Hindu trinity. She is referred to as the destroyer of the creation (*saṃhārakāriṇī*) (DM 1.53), tacitly appropriating the role of Śiva. Brahmā is identified with Prajāpati in this episode.

Brahmā's Hymn (The Brahmā-stuti)

Brahmā commences singing a hymn of praise to Yoganidrā that reveals much about the qualities of the Devī, especially her eternal, imperishable nature. He calls her the Goddess (Devī), the Mother Supreme (*jananī parā*). He identifies her with key syllables (e.g., *svāhā, svadhā, vaṣaṭ*) uttered during Vedic sacrificial rites, and the goddess Sāvitrī herself. Her essence is the tripartite division (*tridhāmātrā*) as well as the half-syllable (*ardhamātrā*), which cannot be pronounced (DM 1.54–55).

These identifications connect the Devī intimately with the theology of sound, and the sacred utterances of Vedic *mantras*. The *ardhamātrā* is a feminine form of the *ardhamātra*, associated with the *bindu* or *anusvāra* sound at the end of the primordial Vedic hum, the *pranava*, Aum/Om. The reference to the *tridhāmātrā* and the *ardhamātrā* plays off this association, which conceives of Aum as consisting of three-and-a-half components: (1) A, the beginning sound, made by opening the mouth; (2) U, the middle; and (3) M, the end sound, made by closing the mouth, but which then fades into silence through an extended nasal hum, represented by the semi-circle or crescent moon and dot (*candra-bindu*) at the top of the written character of Aum. This final portion, which is not uttered and fades into silence, is the impotent (*sandhyā*) unutterable half component (+1/2). Aum is fundamentally a sonic vibration (*nāda*), a primordial sound, said to encapsulate Absolute Reality. These ideas are significant in Tantric metaphysics, as well as in Nāda Yoga philosophical traditions, suggesting that the DM's composer was familiar with them.[36] By equating Yoganidrā with Sāvitrī, which is the Gāyatrī *mantra* personified as a goddess, the text tacitly also references the Devī-sāvitrī or Durgā-sāvitrī that appears in the Dharmasūtra and Dharmaśāstra literature discussed in the previous chapters, and which constitute some of the earliest occurrences of Durgā in Sanskrit literature. Although she is not explicitly identified with the goddess Vāc in Brahmā's hymn, the Devī is said to be essentially sound (*svarātmikā*) (DM 1.54).

Brahmā's hymn to the Devī continues to make implicit reference (DM 1.56–57) to the Goddess as possessing the capacities of all three of the main gods of the so-called Hindu trinity, Brahmā, the creator, Viṣṇu, the preserver, and Śiva, the destroyer. It does identify these same qualities with Viṣṇu, but then notes that the Devī has subdued him with sleep (*nidrāvaśa*) (DM 1.64), thus subordinating his agency to her power. Brahmā then explicitly asks a question: Since Brahmā himself, Viṣṇu, and Īśāna (i.e., Śiva) are given bodily form through her power, who indeed could praise the Goddess adequately (DM 1.65)? This is a rhetorical motif that will recur, because if the entire creation and its primary triad of powers encapsulated by the gods are themselves manifestations through her, it implicitly asks who then is it that is praising her.

Verse 1.58 of the DM is salient, because it sings of the greatness of the Devī in no uncertain terms. She is praised as the great knowledge, science, or formula (*mahāvidyā*), and, of course, the great matrix of phantasmal reality or great illusion (*mahāmāyā*). She is great intelligence, wisdom, or insight (*mahāmedhā*), great recollection or memory (*mahāsmṛti*), and great infatuation, delusion, or bewilderment (*mahāmohā*). Significantly, it portrays the Devī in ambivalent terms, as embodying wisdom and insight, as well as delusion. The verse ends with a reinforcement of this ambivalent nature, for she is addressed as the Great Goddess (Mahādevī) and the Great Demoness (Mahāsurī). The epithet "Great Demoness" may have been discomforting to some because certain versions of the DM have the term *maheśvarī* (Great Lady, or Great Queen) instead of *mahāsurī* (e.g., Singh 1983, 13). The Devī evidently embodies the full compass of reality. This is a crucial point, because the Devī represents the embodiment of a non-dual rather than a dualistic metaphysical vision of reality. There is not really a demonic principle or power of darkness, evil, ignorance, or delusion in a perennial struggle with the power of light, goodness, knowledge, or wisdom that she represents. She is the supreme (*mahā*) principle that encapsulates both those polarities.

Her terrifying nature is further extolled when Brahmā refers to her as Kālarātrī ("Dark Night or Night of all Destroying Time"), as Great Night (*mahārātrī*), and as the pitiless night of delusion (*moharātrī dāruṇā*) (DM 1.58). The Devī's associations with the goddess Night (Rātrī), evident in the Vedic corpus and linked to Durgā as discussed in previous chapters, are clear. Brahmā describes her form as fearsome (*ghorā*) bearing a sword (*khaḍginī*), spear (*śūlinī*), club (*gadinī*), discus (*cakrinī*), conch (*śaṅkhinī*), and bow (*cāpinī*), with arrows (*bāṇa*), the *bhuśuṇḍī* (mace?) and *paridhā* (noose, lariat?) as weapons (DM 1.61). In contrast to this foreboding imagery, the Devī is also described as Śrī (i.e., the goddess Lakṣmī, or merely beneficence), as bashfulness (*hrī*), modesty (*lajjā*), intelligence (*buddhi*), prosperity (*puṣṭi*), satisfaction (*tuṣṭi*), peace (*śānti*), and patience (*kṣānti*) (DM 1.60). She is gentler than the gentle (*saumyā*), and extremely beautiful (*atisundarī*) (DM 1.62). She is the material nature (*prakṛti*) of everything, evident within manifestation's three constituent components (*guṇa-traya*) (DM 1.59). The notion that Nature or material existence (*prakṛti*) is intrinsically composed of three qualities (*guṇa*) is commonplace in epic and Purāṇic literature but is developed philosophically in the Sāṅkhya (also known as Sāṃkhya) school of Indian philosophy. Regardless of whether something is manifest or unmanifest (*sad-asad*), whatever or whenever anything is, Brahmā sings to the Devī you, who have the totality (*akhila*) as your innermost self, are the intrinsic power (*śakti*) of that (DM 1.63). Thus, the Devī is praised as the animating power (*śakti*) of all of reality.

Brahmā asks the Devī to awaken Viṣṇu and confound the *asuras* Madhu and Kaiṭabha, so that Viṣṇu's wakefulness can cause the destruction of the demons (DM 1.66–67). The goddess Tāmasī, as the Devī is here called, emerged from the eyes, nose, heart, and breast of Viṣṇu, allowing him to awaken, and she, of unknown origin, appeared before Brahmā. Viṣṇu, now awakened and seeing the ferocious demons, engaged them in battle for five thousand years. The text takes pain to refer to her as "of unknown/unmanifest birth/origin (*avyaktajanman*)," again reiterating that this is only an apparent "birth" or "manifestation," because her true nature is eternal and beyond birth. Another implication of those verses is that this battle would go on indefinitely without the Devī's deceptive intervention. Drunk with their great strength, and deluded by Mahāmāyā, the demons offered Viṣṇu a boon. Viṣṇu responded that he obviously would like to slay them. Realizing that they were tricked, and seeing that the universe was only ocean, the demons attempted to escape their fate by requesting that they be slain only where there was no water. Undaunted, Viṣṇu lifted them onto his lap and beheaded them with his discus. Medhas concludes that this was the way the Devī became manifest, appeared, or arose (*samutpanna*) when praised by Brahmā (DM 1.78).

This brief first chapter of the DM forms the first of three main mythic episodes and unambiguously glorifies the Devī as the supreme divinity, surpassing Brahmā, Viṣṇu, and Śiva, who are acknowledged as the leading gods of the male pantheon. Contrary to Coburn's claim (1984, 115), the epithet Durgā does not appear in this episode, nor does Kinsley's assertion (1986, 96) that "Durgā" rescues Brahmā in this section hold true. Instead, the Devī is explicitly referred to as Mahāmāyā, Yoganidrā, Rātrī, Kālarātrī, Tāmasī, Sāvitrī, and Śrī, among others, highlighting her multifaceted nature and powers. Some epithets, such as Śrī and Yoganidrā, link her to Viṣṇu, while others, such as Sāvitrī, connect her to Brahmā, and Kālarātrī and Tāmasī associate her with Śiva. Although Śiva is only marginally mentioned, his inclusion suggests parity with Viṣṇu in status.

In this episode, Viṣṇu's triumph over the demons Madhu and Kaiṭabha is tangentially attributed to the Devī, who wields power over him. Emerging from his body parts, she awakens him from slumber and empowers him to act, prefiguring the next episode where she manifests from the gods' combined effulgence (*tejas*). Here, Viṣṇu cannot destroy the demons without her deluding power, emphasizing a recurring motif in Viṣṇu's myths: the demons' vulnerabilities in all his subsequent victories are exploited due to the Devī's influence. As with other tales, Madhu and Kaiṭabha try to evade destruction through a loophole in their agreement with Viṣṇu. However, Viṣṇu outmaneuvers them, maintaining his cleverness while subtly affirming the Devī as the true source of their downfall. Their foolishness is portrayed as a direct result of being deluded by her power.

Although the Devī does not directly battle the *asuras* in this episode, she is depicted as both beautiful and frightening, armed with various weapons (DM 1.61), affirming her martial character. While her benign qualities are mentioned, no details of her attire or adornments are provided. Significantly, the mythic events occur during the *pralaya*, the period between cosmic cycles, before Brahmā begins creation. Yet, the Devī endures, transcending the cycles of creation and time. Observing variations among the three main episodes in the DM is instructive, should the text not have been the work of a single author but rather an amalgamation of preexisting myths and devotional hymns woven into its current form. Such a process of accretion is still evident in the addition of the so-called "limbs" (*aṅga*), and other popular hymns (e.g., the Devī Sūkta), which are regularly added before and after the main text of the DM, when it circulates on its own. It is quite common for devotees to cite verses from those texts — familiar to them through hearing recitations — thinking that they belong to the DM itself.

Episode Two or the Middle Episode

Medhas immediately launches into the next mythic episode that extols the Devī's majesty (*prabhāva*). The key features of this story, contained in Chapters 2 to 4, are without doubt the most well-known of the Devī's mythic exploits. They concern the Devī's manifestation in order to slay the buffalo demon Mahiṣa. The mythic events are retold in other Purāṇic accounts, and the battle between the Devī and Mahiṣa continues to be depicted in painting and sculpture. Medhas recounts how, in days gone by, when Mahiṣa was the chief of the *asuras* and Indra was chief of the gods, the gods and *asuras* battled for a hundred years, but the gods were defeated by the *asuras*, and Mahiṣa became the chief of all (DM 2.1–2). Some thirty of the defeated gods, led by Prajāpati, and including Sūrya, Indra, Agni, Vāyu, Candra, Yama, and Varuṇa, went to see Īśa (i.e., Śiva) and he whose banner is Garuḍa (i.e., Viṣṇu or arguably Kṛṣṇa, as depicted in the Mbh) (DM 2.3–5). This motif of the lesser gods, including Indra, who in Vedic literature is sort of the leader, being defeated in their heaven by Mahiṣa is found in the Mbh's version of the first major deed of Skanda (Mbh 3.221.52–69). There, however, Mahiṣa continues his rampage in the heavens by attacking Rudra (Śiva), who is portrayed as powerful and capable of defeating Mahiṣa. Even so, Rudra allows Mahāsena (Skanda) to perform that act. In the DM's description, Śiva and Viṣṇu, evidently great gods, are somehow differentiated from the defeated gods, which include Indra and Prajāpati, and dwell in some abode other than the heaven of the celestials overthrown by Mahiṣa. The lesser gods are displaced from power, and resort to Viṣṇu and Śiva for help. Mahiṣa does not directly challenge either of those two great gods.

The gods assert that they have taken refuge (*śaraṇa*) in Viṣṇu and Śiva and plead for assistance. The great gods, Śaṅkara (i.e., Śiva) and the discus-bearer (*cakrin*) (i.e., Viṣṇu) grow angry, and with faces furrowed and brows knotted, they, together with Brahmā and the other gods, emit fiery effulgences (*tejas*) from their mouths and bodies. This fiery splendor, which had emerged from all the gods, coalesced into a single giant mass whose brilliance filled the triple world, and became a woman (DM 2.8–12). Her mouth derived from Śambhu's (i.e., Śiva) *tejas*, her hair from that of Yama, and her arms from the *tejas* of the slayer of Madhu (i.e., Viṣṇu). Her two breasts were produced from Soma's *tejas*, from Indra's, her waist, and from the *tejas* of Varuṇa came her thighs and legs. The earth's *tejas* formed her hips, Brahmā's, her feet, and from the sun came her toes. Her fingers were from the splendor of the Vasus, her nose from that of Kubera, her teeth from Prajāpati, and her three eyes from the *tejas* of Agni. The wind's splendor produced her ears, and her eyebrows were from that of dusk and dawn (*saṃdhyā*). Indeed, whatever *tejas* was produced by any of the gods, that was Śivā ("[She who is] Auspicious") (DM 2.7– 17).

Among the noteworthy features of this section is the concept of refuge (*śaraṇa*), which we now commonly associate with the vows taken upon entering Buddhism (i.e., the Three Refuges or Three Jewels: the Buddha, the Dharma, and the Saṅgha), although it is also found in Jainism. Here, the gods resort to Śiva and Viṣṇu for refuge.[37] Brahmā is differentiated from Prajāpati here, unlike the first chapter, where they were identified with each other. Deities such as Gaṇeśa and Skanda are not mentioned. The motif of the Devī emerging through the amalgamation of the splendor of the gods likely draws its inspiration from preceding accounts. In the *Mānavadharmaśāstra* (also known as *Manusmṛti* or *Laws of Manu*; 7.3–11), the king, although appearing human, is said to be created by the brilliant energy (*tejas*) of gods such as Indra, Sūrya, Yama, Varuṇa, and Agni. Divinities inhabit his attributes (e.g., victory in his aggression, good fortune in his favor, and death in his anger). The *Manu* account parallels earlier motifs as found in the Vedic *rājasūya* consecration and initiation (Heesterman 1985, 108–27). The *tejas* emanates from deities — many traditionally identified as the *lokapāla*s (guardians of the realms) — so that the king implicitly rules over all created realms. He is also said to surpass all created beings in the brilliance (*tejas*) he exudes (Gonda 1966, 25). Similarly, the Devī is implicitly identified as a queen who presides over the triple realms. *Tejas* is akin to the majesty, aura, or glory that radiates from a person who is empowered, and analogous to the magnificence of sovereignty, the luster of gold, the glow of health and inner vitality.[38] The DM suggests that this energy, whether it is present within individuals, kings, or gods, is an abode of the Devī, an indication of her presence, and in this case, it is from where she emerges. This emergence has often been misinterpreted or construed as the "birth" or "creation" of the Devī from the collective power of the gods. For instance, Kinsley (1986, 97) incorrectly claims she was "created by the male gods and does their bidding." This appearance most certainly is not the Devī's "birth" or "creation" myth, for it is abundantly clear in the text that she exists prior to this manifestation. She is called Śivā, the feminine form of Śiva, appropriating the great god's character and name, which means "Auspicious."

Seeing her, who had arisen or been revived (*samudbhava*) — definitely not born — by their collective auric energies (*tejas*), the gods rejoiced. They now bestow on the goddess Śivā various items derived from their own possessions. The holder of Pināka (i.e., Śiva, who wields the bow Pināka), drew a spear (*śūla*) from his own (thus likely a trident), and gave it to her. Kṛṣṇa, the dark one, likely a descriptor for Viṣṇu's color, gave her a discus (*cakra*) drawn from his own. From Varuṇa she received a conch (*śaṅkha*), from the oblation eater (i.e., Agni) she got a spear or lance (*śakti*), and from the son of the Maruts (i.e., Vāyu), she was given a bow and two arrow-filled quivers. Indra, the thousand-eyed, gave her a thunderbolt (*vajra*) extracted from his own, and a bell (*ghaṇṭā*) from his elephant Airāvata. The lord of the waters (i.e., Varuṇa) gave her a noose (*pāśa*), and Yama a staff drawn from the staff of death (*kāladaṇḍa*). Prajāpati gave her a string of beads (*akṣamālā*) (possibly a reference to *rudrākṣa* beads, which derive from the *Elaeocarpus ganitrus* tree), and Brahmā gave her an ascetic's water-pot (*kamaṇḍalu*). The sun's own rays were placed in the pores of her skin, and from Kāla, she received a sword (*khaḍga*) and an immaculate shield (*carma*). The ocean of milk gave a stainless necklace (*amalahāra*), two unaging garments (*ajara-ambara*), a celestial crest jewel (*cūḍāmaṇi*), two earrings (*kuṇḍala*), bracelets (*kaṭaka*), a radiant half-moon (ornament) (*ardha-candra*), armlets (*keyūra*) for her many arms, two immaculate anklets (*nūpura*), an unsurpassed choker (*graiveyaka*), and jeweled rings (*aṅgulīyaka*) for all her fingers. Viśvakarman gave her a perfect axe (*paraśu*), various types of weapons (*astra*), and impenetrable (chain) mail (*daṃśana*). The ocean gave her garlands (*mālā*) of unwithering lotuses for her breast and head, and a truly brilliant lotus (*paṅkaja*). Himavat (i.e., the Himalayas) provided a lion (*siṃha*) as a mount, and an assortment of precious stones (*ratna*). The lord of treasure (i.e., Kubera) gave her a goblet (*pānapātra*) never empty of wine (*surā*), and the lord of all snakes, Śeṣa, who supports this earth, gave her a serpent-necklace (*nāgahāra*) bedecked with massive gems. Honored by the other gods with weapons and adornments, the Devī repeatedly roared with loud guffaws (*aṭṭahāsa*). The entire firmament (*nabhas*) was overrun with that awesome bellowing, producing a massive echo. The worlds and oceans trembled, mountains swayed, and the earth quaked. The sages (*muni*), bodies devoutly prostrate, praised her, and the delighted gods called out "Victory" (*jayā*), addressing her who rides the lion (*siṃhavāhinī*) (DM 2.19–34).

I have described this section in depth, closely paraphrasing the original text, because it offers us one of the most thorough descriptions of the appearance and form of the Devī, who is later identified explicitly as Durgā. Among the noteworthy features of the foregoing description is the prominent place that Śiva has in it. Śiva is among the great gods who is approached as a refuge when the lesser gods are exiled from heaven (DM 2.3). When angered at the bleak turn of events, the *tejas* first streams from the faces of the holder of the discus, and Śiva and Brahmā (DM 2.8–9). *Tejas* then streams from the bodies of the other gods (DM 2.10). The Devī's emergent form from the collective *tejas* of the gods is called Śivā ("[She who is] Auspicious"), and Śiva ("[He who is] Auspicious") is the first to arm her with his weapon.[39]

The Devī is beautiful but fear inspiring. Her laughter is not demure — a more becoming trait in orthodox portrayals of ideal womanhood — but loud and raucous. She quaffs an alcoholic beverage. She is explicitly named Victory (Jayā) and associated with the epithet Siṃhavāhinī ("She who Rides the Lion"). Her martial nature is evident in the weapons that she wields. Some of the weapons are akin to the ones mentioned in Brahmā's hymn in the previous episode. But other weapons (e.g., the club (*gadā*), the enigmatic *bhuśuṇḍi*, and *paridhā*) mentioned there are not replicated here, although she receives "various types of weapons" from Viśvakarman, and the noose (*pāśa*) and staff of death (*kāladaṇḍa*), could be variants on the *paridhā* and *gadā*. And while much attention is given to the Devī's clothes and ornaments here, there is no mention of those in the previous episode. She receives a celestial crest jewel (*cūḍāmaṇi*), and a head garland (*mālā*), but there is no mention of the wondrous diadem (*vicitra-mukuṭa*) or the peacock banner (*śikhipiccha-dhvaja*) from the epic hymns in this account. Instead, she holds a brilliant lotus.

The narrative continues with the *asuras*, seeing the world trembling with the Devī's laughter, stopping to take notice. Surrounded by his demon army, Mahiṣāsura, puzzled by the commotion, rushed to see the cause. He has his first glimpse of the Goddess, enormous in appearance, her thousand arms and her radiance filling the triple world in all directions. Her diadem etches the sky, her footsteps flatten the earth, and she makes the underworld shudder with the twanging of her bowstring (DM 2.34–38). This then set in motion a battle between the Devī and the enemies of the gods (DM 2.38). Here we have a very similar image of the powerful feet of the Devī crushing the earth as was found in the *Mālatī-mādhava* in the persona of Cāmuṇḍā/Karālā (see Kale 1928, 47; Coburn 1984, 136), and a foreshadowing of her feet's crushing power, which will ultimately destroy Mahiṣa. It turns out that she does have a diadem (*kirīṭa*), which still figures as an important sovereign marker, but it is no longer referred to as the wondrous diadem (*vicitra-mukuṭa*). It seems more akin to a crown atop a head, rather than something bound to the head since it etches or scrapes (*ullikhita*) the sky (DM 2.37).

The DM provides no explicit rationale for the battle. It is evidently cosmic in scope, as Mahiṣāsura now leads the gods' enemies, akin to Vṛtra in Vedic mythology, the paradigmatic *asura* traditionally defeated by Indra. Here, however, Mahiṣa has overpowered Indra and usurped his position (DM 2.2). The Devī's battle with Mahiṣa thus symbolizes a struggle for cosmic supremacy. Her appearance and demeanor leave no doubt that her purpose is warfare. The absence of a stated rationale is significant, suggesting that it was deemed self-evident, perhaps articulated in earlier accounts. This feature lies at the core of the Devī's persona and plays a key role in her rise within the Hindu tradition — a point we will revisit later in this chapter.

Intent on killing her, Mahiṣāsura, with his *asura* general, Cikṣura, and other leaders, including Cāmara, Udagra, Asiloman, Bāṣkala, Parivārita, and Viḍāla, attacked the Devī with their armies, using varieties of weapons, and millions of chariots, elephants, and horses. The goddess Caṇḍikā ("Fierce One"), her countenance unperturbed (*anāyasta-ananā*) destroyed these weapons as if in play (*līlayaiva*) (DM 2.49). To digress somewhat, modern depictions of the Devī destroying Mahiṣa frequently portray her with this sort of calm expression, although she is not depicted that way in the narrative during the actual event of his slaying. The playful nature of her behavior resonates with metaphysical notions that the motive behind divine action is pure purposeless play (*līlā*), a term typically associated with the activities of Kṛṣṇa.

The Devī hurled arms at the enemies, while her maned mount, hair matted and shaken, swept through the *asura* armies like a forest fire. Hundreds and thousands of cohorts were instantly produced by the exhalations released by the goddess Ambikā as she fought. Together with the Devī, they destroyed the hordes of *asuras*. The Goddess killed the *asuras* with her club, trident, spears, and sword, and dropped others who were beguiled (*vimohita*) by the tintinnabulation of her bell (*ghaṇṭāsvana*) (DM 2.50–55). The mysterious function of the bell as a weapon is revealed here. It is an especially appropriate attribute of the Devī because its function in battle, to bewilder or delude, aligns with the Devī's persona as Mahāmāyā, or Mahāmohā. She bound and dragged *asuras* with her noose, smashed them with her club till they vomited blood, clove them in half with her sword, pierced them with her spear, or shredded them with arrows. A grotesque scene ensued, where headless bodies and demonic forms with missing limbs or eyes still danced to the battle drum, or fought on, while others pleaded with the Devī to stop the carnage. Rivers of blood flowed through the impassable middle of the battlefield, which was piled with chariots, horses, *asuras*, and elephants that had fallen in the fray. All the while, the lion, its mane shaking, emitting a great roar, scoured for signs of life from the bodies of the enemies of the gods. The gods, delighted, showered flowers on the cohorts of the Devī (DM 2.56–68). The impassable earth, strewn with the debris of warfare and its horrific carnage evokes yet another facet of the name Durgā, which literally means "difficult passage."

With their armies destroyed, the great leaders of the *asura* hordes now attacked the Goddess. Cikṣura confronted Ambikā with a torrent of arrows, but the Devī, as if in play (*līlā iva*; *līlayaiva*) broke the arrows. She killed his charioteer and horses, severed his bow and flag, and skewered him with arrows. He attacked her with his sword, first whacking the lion on its head, and then hitting the Goddess on her left arm. The sword shattered on impact. He hurled his spear at her, but she, the goddess Bhadrakālī, flung her own, shattering it and him in the process (DM 3.1–9). With Mahiṣa's general slain, other *asura* leaders attacked Ambikā in turn. Her lion decapitated Cāmara. She slew Udagra with rocks and trees, and Karāla with her bare hands and teeth. Notable here is the demon Karāla, whose name resembles the name of the goddess Karālā in the *Mālatī-mādhava*. In Purāṇic texts, the derivation of the name of a goddess is often related to that of a demon she slays. Even the name Durgā is said to be derived from the demon Durgama later in the DM (11.45–46). So, while no explicit mention is made of the goddess Karālā, there is an implicit etymology and reference embedded in the name of the demon Karāla. Such tropes draw our attention to the many layers of the DM, and a recognition that the names of the demons, while perhaps sometimes entirely fabricated for the benefit of the narrative, may perhaps also be utilized to serve the DM's overarching purposes.

The three-eyed supreme lady (*parameśvarī*) also destroyed Uddhata, Bāṣkala, Tāmra, Andhaka, Ugrāsya, Ugravīrya, Mahāhanu, Biḍāla, Durdhara, and Durmukha (DM 3.10–19). The names of the latter two demons, Durdhara ("Unbearable" or "Irresistible") and Durmukha ("Ugly") are noteworthy for a few reasons. The prefix "dur," which can mean "difficult," also connotes something bad. It is therefore appropriately applied to *asuras* or dreadful warriors, many of whose names have negative or fearsome characteristics. The DM, as we will later note in more detail, derives the Devī's name, Durgā, precisely from such a demon *asura* named Durgama.

Seeing his armies and leaders vanquished, Mahiṣāsura, taking his own buffalo (*mahiṣa*) form, struck fear into the Devī's troops. He killed them with blows from his snout, hooves, tail, and horns. Having dropped the Pramathas ("Tormentors," a class of cohorts associated with Śiva or Gaṇeśa), he rushed to attack the Mahādevī's lion, at which point, she, the goddess Ambikā grew furious. Mahiṣa trampled the earth, shredded clouds with his horns, hurled mountains skyward, which fell back to the earth, and lashed the ocean with his tail flooding the landscape. The goddess Caṇḍikā, angered upon seeing this, resolved to slay him (DM 3. 20–27). Mahiṣa's trampling (*kṣuṇṇa, vikṣunna*) of the earth with his hooves, a motif repeated twice (DM 3.24, 3.25), is evidently set in contrast with the earth-crushing feet of the Goddess, alluded to previously.

First, she cast out her lariat (*pāśa*) and bound Mahiṣa with it, but when bound he shifted from his buffalo shape into a lion. Ambikā decapitated him, but he transformed into a shield and sword-wielding man. The Devī cut him to pieces with her arrows, but he changed into an elephant and dragged the great lion with his trunk. When the Goddess hewed off his trunk, the *asura* returned to his buffalo form. He cast mountains at the goddess Caṇḍikā, bellowed, and caused the triple world to quake. Angered, Caṇḍikā quaffed the ultimate elixir, and with ruddy eyes laughed repeatedly. With an expression intoxicatingly impassioned, she yelled out, "Fool! Roar, roar for now, while I drink ambrosia! When you are slain by me on this very spot, the gods will soon roar!" (DM 3.36). She then leapt up onto the great *asura* and, having pressed (*ākramya*) her foot onto his neck (*kaṇṭha*), pierced him with her spear. Pinned down (*ākrānta*) by her foot, thus restrained by the strength of the Devī, he came halfway out (*ardha-niṣkrānta*) from his own mouth/neck (*nija-mukhāt*). Having severed his head (*śiraś chittvā*) with her great sword (*mahāsi*), the great *asura*, halfway emerged, still fighting, was felled by the Devī. The demon army, crying out in despair, perished. The gods, enraptured, together with the great seers, praised the Devī, while the chiefs of the heavenly musicians (*gandharva*) sang, and the multitude of heavenly nymphs (*apsaras*) danced (DM 3.28–41). The motif of the Devī trampling Mahiṣa with her foot, mentioned twice (DM 3.37, 3.38), is extremely significant, because he is entirely overpowered by her without a weapon. The sword that severs his head, or the spear that pierces him, is merely the termination of his utterly humiliating defeat. And yet it is noteworthy that the verb *ākram* is used rather than the term *mardana* when describing the Devī's crushing feet. Evidently, the term Mahiṣāsuramardinī was not yet prominent at the time of the composition of the DM, even though the motif of Mahiṣa being crushed beneath her feet was unmistakably present.

I have detailed the textual account of Mahiṣa's final battle and destruction by the Devī because it becomes a dominant motif in the Devī's iconographic representations. While presenting the widely accepted translation of these passages, it is notable that many observe a disconnect between the DM's descriptions and the iconic forms. The argument for this disconnect suggests that both the myth and its artistic renditions likely developed independently or parallel to the DM, rather than directly originating from it. If the DM had been the primary influence, the imagery might align more closely with its narrative details.

It is important to note that strict correspondence between sculptural imagery and textual descriptions has rarely been the norm, even in earlier periods. Iconographers often adhered to their own established conventions, transmitted over centuries with minimal changes. Occasionally, a new iconographic form emerged, often gaining traction and replication within the region where it first appeared.

The DM's intricate depiction of Mahiṣa's demise suggests that the author might have been aware of preexisting visual or narrative traditions, though this interpretation remains speculative. Initially, Mahiṣa appears in his buffalo form, restrained by the Devī, aligning with Kuṣāṇa plaque imagery where he is depicted as a buffalo under her control, although not specifically bound by a noose. He then transforms into a lion, a transition that might symbolically echo sculptural representations of the Devī's lion mount being mistaken for the demon. Subsequently, he takes on the form of a man wielding a sword, which might reflect generalized accounts of the Devī battling a humanoid Mahiṣa. When Mahiṣa becomes an elephant, dragging the Devī's lion, this recalls the common sculptural motif of lion-elephant combat.

Finally, Mahiṣa reverts to his buffalo form, where the Goddess leaps upon him and spears him, a scene resonant with Gupta-period imagery of the buffalo demon being pierced by her spear. Conventional translations of the DM suggest that Mahiṣa partially emerges from his buffalo mouth (*mukhāt*) before being beheaded, although this depiction diverges from sculptural conventions. In most imagery, the demon is shown emerging in human form from the neck of a beheaded buffalo, where he is then pierced by the Devī's trident. This inversion of the narrative in art underscores the complex interplay between textual descriptions and iconographic traditions, revealing possible parallel but independent evolutions of the myth.

In this section of the DM, the Devī is called Caṇḍikā, Ambikā, and Bhadrakālī. She is also known by the lion-riding (Siṃhavāhinī) and the three-eyed (Trinetrā) epithets. In contrast to her composure in earlier battles, the Devī is impassioned, angry, and even intoxicated when she slays Mahiṣa. It is not clear in the narrative just what form Mahiṣa takes when he emerges halfway out of his own buffalo "mouth" (*mukhāt*). Since he is said to be still fighting, many iconographers assume reasonably that he has resumed a human form with sword and shield. Thus, the iconography often depicts the buffalo form decapitated, with the human form of a demon emerging from its severed neck. The DM, however, is conventionally thought to describe the Goddess crushing the buffalo's neck, and the demon's emergence (in an undescribed form) from his buffalo mouth, and it is this form that is beheaded by the Devī.

I suggest that we need to read/translate those DM verses somewhat differently because the conventional translation offered above does not capture the author's intent. This alternate translation, which I provide later, and in which *mukhāt* does not mean "from the mouth," but "from the fore part, or opening," along with other features in the relevant verses, better complies with subsequent iconographic renderings. We shall examine many of the variant iconographic forms in a subsequent chapter and return to correlate them with the DM's version of the destruction of Mahiṣa when those sections are translated/ interpreted differently.

Hymn of Praise by Indra and the Gods (The Śakrādi-stuti)

With the destruction of the enemies of the gods by the Goddess, the host of gods headed by Indra (Śakra) sang a hymn in her praise (DM 4.1). The hymn refers to her with an assortment of names and various epithets. These include, "[She who is] the power of the world soul" (*jagadātmaśakti*) (DM 4.2) and "She whose form incorporates the powers of the whole host of gods" (*niḥśeṣa-devagaṇa-śakti-samūha-mūrti*) (DM 4.2). Her majesty is said to be indescribable even by the Eternal Lord (*bhagavānananta*) (i.e., Viṣṇu), Brahmā, and Hara (i.e., Śiva) (DM 4.3) and she is unfathomable (*apārā*), even to Hari (i.e., Viṣṇu), Hara (i.e., Śiva), and the other gods (DM 4.6). In concert with Brahmā's hymn uttered in the first episode, in this hymn by Indra and the other gods, she is called Ambikā (DM 4.2, 4.23, 4.26), Caṇḍikā (DM 4.3, 4.24), Śrī (DM 4.4), Prakṛti (DM 4.6), Svāhā (DM 4.7), and Svadhā (DM 4.7). The Devī's ambivalent nature is evident when she is referred to as Śrī ("Grace") in the abodes of do-gooders, Alakṣmī ("Ill-Fortune") in sinful souls, Buddhi ("Intelligence") in the hearts of the learned, Śraddhā ("Faith"), and Lajjā ("Modesty") (DM 4.4).

The hymn indirectly identifies her with Brahmā's consort, through the goddess Vāc, who although not explicitly mentioned, is implied when the Devī is spoken of as having sound as her essence, and embodying the Vedic triad, the *Ṛg*, *Yajur*, and *Sāman* (DM 4.9). Her identification with Viṣṇu's consort is evident when the hymn calls her Śrī, whose only abode is the heart of the enemy of Kaiṭabha (i.e., Viṣṇu). She is explicitly identified with Śiva's consort, when she is called Gaurī, who abides with the one who has the moon as a diadem (i.e., Śiva) (DM 4.10).

Crucially, for the purposes of this study, this hymn of praise by Indra and the host of gods includes the first occurrences of the name Durgā in praise of the Devī in the DM. The half verse runs:

> *medhāsi devi viditākhila śāstrasārā durgāsi durga bha-*
> *vasāgara naur asaṅgā* / (DM 4.10)
> O Devī! You are Medhā (Intelligence or Insight); you under-
> stand (*viditā*) the essence (*sārā*) of all (*akhila*) branches
> of knowledge (*śāstra*); you are Durgā, an unconstrained
> (*asaṅga*) vessel (*nau*) on the ocean of worldly existence
> (*bhava-sāgara*) that is arduous to traverse (*durga*).
> (DM 4.10)

This verse plays upon the etymology of the word *durga*, which might simply mean something like "difficult to access," or "arduous to traverse." However, it seeks to invert the meaning, by explaining that the Goddess is an unhindered vessel or boat, capable of navigating the stormy seas of worldly existence. This image plays upon the classic symbolism of worldly existence or *saṃsāra* being akin to an ocean or a river, and salvation or liberation being located on the "far shore." We particularly associate this language with Buddhism, which speaks of the various vehicles or rafts (*yāna*) (e.g., Hinayāna, Mahāyāna, and Vajrayāna), leading sentient beings to *nirvāṇa*. It is even more significant when viewed in tandem with the preceding half-verse which identifies the Devī with insight (*medhā*). Durgā is portrayed not exclusively as a martial goddess, but as a power capable of leading one across to liberation. Moreover, she is not merely a vehicle for crossing over to deliverance but is herself unobstructed (*asaṅga*) in movement through worldly existence. She enables one to navigate the difficult waters of life's journey. The maritime imagery is worth noting, not only because it is an effective symbol, but because Durgā also continues to appeal to sailors, fishermen, and nautical travelers, who regularly take their chances upon open waters.

The hymn later includes another reference to Durgā. The full verse runs:

> *durga smṛtā harasi bhītim aśeṣajantoḥ svasthaiḥ smṛtā matim*
> *atīva śubhāṃ dadāsi* /
> *dāridryaduḥkhabhayahāriṇi kā tvadanyā sarvopakāra-*
> *karaṇāya sadā 'rdracittā* // (DM 4.16)
> O Durgā! When remembered, you dispel dread from every
> living being; when called to mind by the composed
> (*svastha*), you provide a surpassingly splendid intel-
> ligence (*mati*). O dispeller of poverty, suffering, and
> fear! Who other than you is always tender in intent to
> enact (*karaṇa*) every favor (*upakāra*)?

Here, we again note that Durgā is associated with a mental state, destroying fear when it arises, and bestowing intelligence or purity of mind on beings. Thus, Durgā's maternal qualities — she is tender-minded — are central features, offering an explanatory rationale for her actions. Her focus on this-worldly relief is again reiterated. She destroys poverty, fear, and sorrow (*duḥkha*), another term we associate frequently with Buddhism, in particular. The weakening of Buddhism on the Indian subcontinent is sometimes attributed, among other factors, to the rise in popularity of Advaita Vedānta, which absorbed many compelling features of Buddhist metaphysics. In this, the potent appeal of Śākta metaphysics is often ignored. Surely, the Devī, with her salvific promise as a refuge capable of vanquishing fear and sorrow, not to mention her persona as Mahāmāyā leading to both spiritual liberation and worldly gains, must have had enormous appeal, culling adherents who sought similar ends from doctrines such as Buddhism.

The hymn next attempts to address the seeming contradiction between the Devī's martial character and her disposition, which is described as generally benign toward all creatures. The gods explain that simply by slaying their enemies, the world is a happier place (DM 4.17). Despite this, the Goddess chooses to slay enemies in battle because death by her weapons purifies them (DM 4.18), and thus even leads those who deserve to spend much time in hell (DM 4.17) to heaven (DM 4.17, 4.18, 4.22). Hence the Devī is extraordinarily compassionate, choosing to destroy her enemies through protracted battle (DM 4.18), rather than instantly obliterating them with her enormous power (DM 4.18). Thus, Indra and the gods continue to praise the Devī, asking her for protection, offering her perfumes and ornaments, and flowers from Indra's pleasure grove (DM 4.23–26). In these verses we find the notion of struggling against or battling a deity as a form of devotion (i.e., *vidveṣa bhakti*). The notion of *bhakti* through confrontation (*vidveṣa*) is mentioned in the *Bhāgavata Purāṇa*, and is attributed to other demons, such as Hiraṇyakaśipu and Rāvaṇa, who confronted Viṣṇu or his *avatāras* (A. Bhattacharyya 2006, 132–33). The *Kālikā Purāṇa* (Chapters 60.81–135) also explains that Mahiṣa wants to die at the Devī's hand, thereby attaining salvation and permanent representation and veneration at her feet. This trait finds vivid expression in various Javanese portrayals of Mahiṣāsuramardinī, where the emerged human form of the demon is portrayed in a devotional attitude (see Knirck-Bumke et al. 2003).[40]

Suitably praised, the Goddess spoke to the gods, who were prostrated before her, saying that she would grant them whatsoever they wished. The gods replied that they did not really need anything more, since Mahiṣāsura had been killed. Since they were granted a boon, however, they wished that whenever they brought her to mind, she would dispel their problems. And they also asked that if any mortal praised her with these hymns that she would enable him to prosper with an abundance of wealth and power, through money, a wife, and so on, based on his needs. Agreeing to this request that was made by the gods on their own behalf, as well as for the welfare of the world, the goddess Bhadrakālī disappeared (DM 4.27–34).

This ends the so-called middle episode of the mythic exploits of the Devī in the DM. A couple of verses then offer a preface to the third and lengthiest episode, dealing with the slaying of the demons Śumbha and Niśumbha, and stating that while in the previous encounter with Mahiṣa the Devī had arisen from (*saṃbhūtā*) the bodies of the gods, this time she sprung up from (*samudbhūtā*) the body of Gaurī (DM 4.34–36).

Episode Three or the Final Episode

Medhas begins this story with the traditional motif of the gods having fallen from sovereignty, this time at the hands of two demons (*asura*), Śumbha and Niśumbha. Arrogant with their sense of power, they displaced Indra's rule of the triple world, and his shares in the sacrifice. They dethroned the sun, the moon, Kubera, Yama, Varuṇa, Vāyu, and Agni, leaving them defeated. Remembering the boon that the Devī had granted them, that if recalled in time of need she would end their greatest misfortunes, they resolved to seek her aid, and went to Himavat (i.e., the Himalayas), the lord of mountains, and praised the Goddess, who is Viṣṇu's *māyā* (DM 5.1–6).

Notably, this story begins with a spoiler, clarifying that this time the Devī will emerge from the body of a goddess, Gaurī, Śiva's consort, where previously she had arisen from the pooled *tejas* emanated from the bodies of the male gods. In other words, it is intent on establishing that she is present within the bodies of all the deities, both male and female, but is in essence beyond them, and that she should neither be seen as a different goddess from Gaurī, nor as exclusively identified with her. Furthermore, the Devī is identified as Viṣṇu's-*māyā*, playing off her designation as Mahāmāyā as well as Yoganidrā, the sleep of Viṣṇu. *Māyā* is an illusory power that is often associated with Asuras, who wield it (Rodrigues 2009, 469–78). Nevertheless, certain great gods also possess *māyā*, and Viṣṇu is clearly identified as having it. This *māyā* is here explained as none other than the Devī. Again, it is the lesser gods (i.e., the old Vedic gods) that have been disenfranchised from power, not the major (i.e., epic and Purāṇic) gods, Brahmā, Viṣṇu, and Śiva. The episode also firmly establishes at the outset that the Devī has acted on her promise to assist the gods in their time of need. Their misfortunes are not uncommon, and she is always there to help if remembered.

The "To That Goddess, Who" Hymn (The "*Yā Devī*" Hymn)

The gods begin to sing a hymn of praise to her. It is known for its emotionally charged refrain: "Homage to her! Homage to her! Homage to her: homage! homage!" (*namas tasyai namas tasyai namas tasyai namo namaḥ*). The hymn begins with the gods praising the Goddess as Prakṛti, and under several other names. She is Raudrā ("[She who is] of Rudra (Fury)"), Gaurī ("Brilliant"), the moon, moonlight, Kalyāṇī ("Auspiciousness"), growth, success, and

Kūrmī ("Tortoise"). She is Nairṛti ("[She who is] of Nirṛti (Death)"), Lakṣmī ("Fortune"), and Śarvāṇī ("[She who is] of Śarva (Śiva)"). Besides being identified with numerous positive qualities, such as growth and success, the Goddess notably is addressed as various feminine divinities related to Viṣṇu (e.g., Kūrmī, and Lakṣmī), and Śiva (e.g., Raudrā, Gaurī, Nairṛti, and Śarvāṇī) (DM 5.7–9).

Significantly, for the concerns of this study, she is also addressed as Durgā in a verse that runs as follows:

> *durgāyai durgapārāyai sārāyai sarvakāriṇyai /*
> *khyātyai tathaiva kṛṣṇāyai dhūmrāyai satataṃ namaḥ //* (DM
>   5.10)
> To Durgā, to She/Her who delivers through (*pārā*) what
>   is arduous to traverse (*durga*), to She/Her who is
>   the real one (*sārā*) who is the doer of everything
>   (*sarvakāriṇī*),
> To She who is renown (*khyāti*), as well as She who is black
>   (*kṛṣṇā*) [and] She who is smoky (*dhūmrā*), perpetual
>   homage!

Crucially, Durgā is again identified with a sort of deliverance through the difficulties of life, even to the far shore of spiritual salvation. She is the core, essential, or real doer of all things. In the following half verse, she is connected to dark deities, even, ostensibly, the feminine form of Kṛṣṇa, although this is most likely just a descriptive epithet.

The Devī is then described as both gentle (*saumyā*) and furious (*rudrā*) (DM 5.11), the world-support and action (*kṛti*) itself (DM 5.11). She is called the *māyā* of Viṣṇu within all creatures (DM 5.12). The Devī's ambivalent character, both benign and fierce, is made explicit. One should not gloss over the second reference to the Devī as Viṣṇu's *māyā*, within fewer than ten verses. In this second instance, the hymn elaborates upon the concept, by praising the Goddess as Viṣṇu's *māyā* within all beings (*sarvabhūta*). Although the term *sarvabhūta* could simply mean "everywhere" or "within all creation," it mostly suggests the notion of all created entities, or all creatures, since it is the locative plural *sarvabhūteṣu*. Thus, not only is Viṣṇu's *māyā* regarded as residing within all creatures, but the Goddess is identified with this principle or power — namely, that of illusion or deception. I shall return repeatedly to this theme, because despite its evidently significant place in delineating the character of the Devī, it is generally not given the attention it deserves in scholarly studies, which tend to focus on the martial or benevolent features of her persona.

This motif, which begins with the Devī as Viṣṇu's *māyā* within all creatures, becomes the paradigm for a series of some twenty verses that end with the aforementioned refrain of repeated praise or homage (*namaḥ*). The Goddess is rendered homage in many of her various forms. She is praised as consciousness (*cetana*), intelligence (*buddhi*), sleep (*nidrā*), hunger (*kṣudhā*), shadow (*chāyā*), power (*śakti*), thirst (*tṛṣṇā*), patience (*kṣānti*), birth (*jāti*), modesty (*lajjā*), peacefulness (*śānti*), faith (*śraddhā*), beauty (*kānti*), prosperity (*lakṣmī*), character (*vṛtti*), mindfulness (*smṛti*), sympathy (*dayā*), satisfaction (*tuṣṭi*), mother (*mātṛ*), and confusion (*bhrānti*) (DM 5.12–32). Like verse 5.12, which refers to the Devī as Viṣṇu's *māyā*, and which sets the tone for the litany of attributes that follow, the verses that bring the refrain of reverence to its conclusion clarify our understanding of some of what has preceded. The Goddess is praised as she who presides (*adhiṣṭhātrī*) over the senses of all creatures, as ever-present within all elements (*bhūta*), and as the Goddess who is the pervader (*vyāpti-devī*) (DM 5.33). She is the abider (*sthitā*), who has pervaded the whole creation in the form of mind/consciousness (*citi-rūpa*) (DM 5.34). These verses, when viewed in tandem with the preceding verses of homage, illustrate the enormous place given to the qualities of consciousness, from confusion to intelligence, and from bashfulness to patience. The Devī is consciousness itself, pervading every living thing created in all their mental and emotional expressions, and arguably, consciousness within the material universe itself. The hymn ends with the gods singing that just as the gods sought refuge in the past, may she, duly praised and remembered by them now, destroy their misfortunes. It also refers to how the lord of gods (*surendra*) worshipped her daily (DM 5.35–36).

The scene then shifts to the goddess Pārvatī ("[She who is] of the Mountain"), who, on her way to the river Gaṅgā to bathe, asked the gods whom they were praising. From the sheath of her body, Śivā ("[She who is] Auspicious") emerged and clarified that that hymn of reverence was sung by those who were defeated by Śumbha and Niśumbha in battle (DM 5.37–39). Medhas makes a slight explanatory aside, remarking that since Ambikā came forth from the sheath (*kośa*) of Pārvatī, she is lauded as Kauśikī. And moreover, once Ambikā/Śivā/Kauśikī emerged, Pārvatī herself became Kṛṣṇā ("[She who is] Black"), and thence known as Kālikā ("[She who is] Black") has taken up dwelling in Himāchala (i.e., the Himalayas) (DM 5.40–41). It is noteworthy that the Devī is referred to as Śivā, as she was in DM 2.17, and Ambikā, as she was in DM 2.51. Earlier, we were told that this episode would deal with the Devī's emergence from the body of Gaurī ("[She who is] Brilliant/White") (DM 4.35). Gaurī is thus identified with Pārvatī.

The Devī's emergence in this context serves to elucidate the origins and relationships of various goddesses, offering explanations for their attributes or names. This particular manifestation of the Devī, arising from the bodily sheath of Pārvatī, is called Kauśikī. Pārvatī, also known as Gaurī — names that link her to the mountain (*parvata*) and whiteness (*gaura*) — undergoes a transformation through this emergence. She loses her fair complexion, becoming Kṛṣṇā or Kālikā, both names indicating blackness, and takes up residence in the Himalayas. This links Gaurī/Pārvatī to Kṛṣṇā/Kālikā, highlighting their duality and their shared association with the Himalayas as Himavat's daughters. These verses appear to address the ambivalence regarding Pārvatī's skin color and clarify her relationship with Kālikā.

The term Kauśikī is polysemous, and its specific meaning here is ambiguous. In the Mbh, Kauśikī refers to a river, often identified with the modern-day Kośi River in Bihar. According to the Mbh, Satyavatī of the Kuśika lineage, Vyāsa's mother, transformed into the river Kauśikī, which later joined the Aruṇā River at a sacred confluence. This confluence was considered so holy that residing there for a month was said to confer benefits equivalent to those of the Aśvamedha sacrifice (Mbh III.82.123–24). In this instance, Kauśikī signifies both a semi-divine matriarch of the Bhārata lineage and a sacred river, paralleling other river goddesses such as Gaṅgā and Sarasvatī. Rivers, such as the Gaṅgā, are often symbolically tied to color transformations — dark and murky during monsoons, clear during the dry season. These shifts could have inspired symbolic associations, reflecting the changing forms or dualities of goddesses such as Pārvatī/Kālikā. This riverine symbolism deepens the understanding of Kauśikī's polyvalent identity as both a river and a divine manifestation.

In previous chapters I offered evidence and arguments for the proposal that the Chandraketugarh hairpin goddess could have represented Kauśikī, who was identified with Nidrā in the HV's Praise of Nidrā (First Stratum) (PN-s1) hymn. There Nidrā is repeatedly described as black in color. Kauśikī is credited with an abode in the Vindhyas, and with slaying the demons Sumbha and Nisumbha (not Śumbha and Niśumbha, unless this was simply a lexical error or early variant). In the Durgā Stava (DStv), the goddess is called Durgā/Kālī and is also described as dark skinned. Even so, there are comparisons to her form like the newly risen sun (v. 12), and her face like or rivalling the full moon (v. 12, 22). In the Durgā Stotra (DSto), the goddess is sometimes called Kālī, who is reddish, black, and tawny (v. 8), or ambivalently as "white one, black one" (v. 17). It may arguably offer the first instance of the name Caṇḍī for the goddess. In the Praise of Nidrā (Second Stratum) (PN-s2), Durgā and Kauśikī are identified with each other (v. 1–2), but no explicit mention is made of the goddess's color, although she is the "light of lights" (v. 26) and light itself (v. 38). Pradyumna's Hymn (PradH) from the HV repeatedly identifies the goddess as slaying Śumbha and Niśumbha (lines, 312, 364), but other than naming her Kālarātri (l. 365), there is no explicit reference to her color. Aniruddha's Hymn (AniH) from the HV refers to the goddess as Caṇḍī (l. 7), Kālī (l. 20), Durgā (lines 35, 67), and a host of other goddesses, but makes no explicit reference to her color, although Kālī is evidently dark skinned. The goddess as Durgā is also associated with the slaying of Śumbha and Niśumbha (l. 39). She is portrayed as dwelling on both the Vindhya mountains as well as Kailāsa (which is in the Himalayas). The DSto exclaims that she lives on Mount Mandara.

Thus, in this litany of hymns at our disposal, most if not all of which may have been composed before the DM, various ambiguities and seeming contradictions have emerged. Is the goddess light or dark skinned?[41] Her origins seem to have her more likely as dark skinned rather than light. And does she dwell in the Vindhyas or the Himalayas or the mythic Mandara? The hymns seem to place her more frequently in the Vindhyas. The DM's task is integrative. It attempts to fuse and solidify this array of goddesses into the persona of a single Great Goddess and therefore needs to resolve these seeming anomalies. This appears to be at the root of this somewhat complicated emergence of Ambikā/Śivā/Kauśikī from light-skinned Gaurī, transforming the light-skinned Gaurī/Pārvatī into a dark-skinned manifestation (i.e., becoming Kālikā), whose abode is also in the Himalayas. This would allow Ambikā/Śivā/Kauśikī to dwell in the Vindhyas and engage in the defeat of Śumbha and Niśumbha. However, the DM's telling of this manifestation is much more complicated. As we will later see, the goddess who slays Śumbha and Niśumbha in this telling does so in what appears to be the Himalayas. She explains that she will again manifest in the twenty-eighth *yuga* of the Vaivasvata Manvantara (in what is clearly a reference to the Nidrā myth cycle), will dwell on the Vindhya mountain, and will slay another pair of demons named Śumbha and Niśumbha (DM 11.37–38).

The narrative continues. Caṇḍa and Muṇḍa, two servants of Śumbha and Niśumbha, spotted the Goddess, and spoke to their masters of her exceptional beauty, encouraging them to abduct her. They explained that since their masters had taken possession of the finest things the worlds had to offer, such as Indra's elephant-mount, Airāvata, Brahmā's swan-yoked chariot, and so on, it seemed reasonable for them to seize this jewel of a woman (*strī-ratna*) (DM 5.43–53). The description of the divine treasures captured by these demons resonates to some degree with the description of the weapons and treasures bestowed upon the Goddess by the gods when she emerged from their collective effulgence (*tejas*) in Episode Two. Śumbha sends a demon messenger named Sugrīva to the Himalayas, to speak persuasively to the Devī. Sugrīva explains how his masters possess all the finest treasures existing in the entire triple world, and that since they regard her as a gemstone among women, she should choose either Śumbha, or his younger brother, Niśumbha, to rule as his wife (DM 5.54–65). Thus far, the narrative makes no reference to the martial nature of the Goddess. Instead, she is described primarily as extraordinarily beautiful, and it is this that lures the demons to her.

Medhas continues his narrative using a verse that makes the first mention of the name Durgā in this episode and the fourth instance in the DM thus far. It runs as follows:

> *ityuktā sā tadā devī gambhīrāntaḥ smitā jagau /*
> *durgā bhagavatī bhadrā yayedaṃ dhāryate jagat //* (DM 5.66)
> Then, thus addressed, the divine (*bhagavatī*), blessed (*bhadrā*)
> > Goddess Durgā, by whom this world is supported,
> > with a profound inner smile, intoned (*jagau*).

In this occurrence, the Devī is unequivocally identified as Durgā, as clearly as her identifications as Ambikā or Caṇḍikā. It thus seems reasonable to regard Durgā as essentially synonymous with Devī within the DM. In the verse, she is also said to support the whole world. Notably, the phrase used here (*yayedaṃ dhāryate jagat*) exactly replicates one from the *Bhagavad Gītā* 7.5, in which Kṛṣṇa describes himself to the warrior Arjuna. This does not appear to be incidental, because in the context of the BG, Kṛṣṇa is making the point that he is the ultimate source of reality.[42] While the material world is his lower nature, he possesses a higher nature that sustains the creation, and which is the source of all creatures. "Nothing at all transcends me," explains Kṛṣṇa. It is evident that Durgā is described as equivalent to Kṛṣṇa, suggesting a rivalry between the Vaiṣṇava/Kṛṣṇa and Devī (i.e., Śākta) sectarian traditions, with each attempting to claim their preferred deity as supreme.

The Devī replies to the messenger with a ruse that demonstrates her capacity to delude. She plays into the pride of the demons by agreeing that everything Sugrīva the messenger has said is true, and that Śumbha and Niśumbha are indeed lords of the triple world. She then portrays herself as weak-minded and proud. The irony and humor in this inversion is inescapable. She explains that in the past she made a promise that she would only take as a husband someone with strength equivalent to hers, and capable of defeating her in battle. She invites Śumbha or Niśumbha to hurriedly take up the challenge and win her hand in marriage (DM 5.67–70). This is the first indication in this episode that there is a martial or warring character to the Devī. There are some exceptionally telling features in this exchange that have not been adequately discussed in preceding studies of the Devī's persona. For one, the Devī is frequently associated with intelligence and a host of other positive mental qualities. In many of those same lists, undesirable qualities, such as confusion and delusion, are also regarded as her attributes. In this instance, she identifies herself as having pride (*darpa*) (DM 5.69) and as being dim-witted or silly (*alpabuddhi*) (DM 5.68). Ironically, although she characterizes herself this way, it is the demons that embody these very qualities. We are led to recognize that the Devī activates and plays upon these features of consciousness within them, qualities over which she has complete control and mastery. There is no aspect of consciousness, human, divine, or demonic, that does not derive from the Devī.

The messenger responds as if insulted. He calls her arrogant (*avaliptā*) (DM 5.71). When even the gods, headed by Indra, could not withstand the might of Śumbha and Niśumbha, how could she, a mere woman, alone (*ekākī*), do battle with them? Instead, he explains that she should simply comply and go to them rather than be taken there, dragged by the hair, stripped of respect (DM 5.71–74). The Devī again acknowledges the power of the demon brothers but reaffirms that she cannot go back on her imprudent (*anālocitā*) promise made earlier, and so urges the messenger to leave and convey the situation to Śumbha, so he may do what he must (DM 5.75–76). The narrative continues to exploit the irony of the Devī being characterized as arrogant and rash, when in fact it is the demons that display these traits. The reference to being dragged by the hair, humiliated, is repeated in several instances later (DM 6.3, 6.7, 6.19). It immediately evokes the motif of Draupadī's humiliation described in the Mbh.

Yudhiṣṭhira, the eldest of the five Pāṇḍava princes, all of whom were married to Draupadī, had just wagered, and lost her to his cousin Duryodhana in a game of dice. On Duryodhana's order, Draupadī was dragged by Duryodhana's brother, Duḥśāsana, into his presence and that of the other members of the court. There, Duḥśāsana attempted to strip off her clothing. This event was pivotal in solidifying the animosity between the Pāṇḍavas and their cousins, the Kauravas, and eventually led to a battle in which Draupadī exacted vengeance for her humiliation. The episode of Draupadī's humiliation is iconic in nature. It is depicted in lithographs and enacted in drama and dance to the present day. It plays out within the framework of devotion to Kṛṣṇa, for Draupadī prays to Kṛṣṇa for help in her plight, and he miraculously makes her *sārī* unending. Draupadī's humiliation is attenuated, because Duḥśāsana cannot disrobe her. Here, by contrast, the Goddess sets the wager of battle, and confronts her assailants single-handedly, without the intercession of a superior deity.

The messenger conveys the Devī's words to the Asura king. In response, he commands his general, the demon (*daitya*) Dhūmralocana ("Smoke Eye") and his army to drag the Goddess into his presence by her hair, and to slay anyone that steps up to her aid. Dhūmralocana confronted her on the snowy mountain, and called out his threat to the Devī, but she responded that he would have to attack her. The instant he began, Ambikā uttered a menacing hum (*huṃkāra*), which turned him to ashes. Ambikā then launched arrows, spears, and axes at the demon army. Her enraged lion-mount, roaring in anger and tossing his mane, ravaged their ranks in an instant, ripping open bellies, decapitating some with his paws, trampling them with his legs, and drinking their blood (DM 6.1–16). This is the first instance in this episode that we are made aware that the Goddess possesses weapons and has a lion mount. It is as if the narrator has assumed that the image of the Devī in her snowy mountain abode, wielding many weapons and having the lion as her mount, is evident to the audience. The reference to her snowy mountain indirectly situates her in the Himalayas ("abode [*ālaya*] of snow [*hima*]"), rather than the Vindhyas, a lower mountain range to the south, not associated with snow-capped peaks.

Śumbha, upon hearing of the destruction of Dhūmralocana and his army, next sends two powerful demons named Caṇḍa ("Fierce") and Muṇḍa ("Shorn Head") to attack her with their army, grab the Devī by the hair or tie her up, and, having killed her lion, bring her bound into his presence. The demons set forth and confronted the Goddess on the great peak of the highest mountain, where she was mounted on her lion and slightly smiling. Here again the reference to the peak of the highest mountain conveys the image of a Himalayan rather than a Vindhyan peak. They moved in on her with weapons readied, but Ambikā gave out an angry cry, and her face turned ink-black in color from wrath. Out of her forehead's knitted brows emerged Kālī, with her terrible face, who wielded a sword, noose, and an unusual skull-topped staff (*khaṭvāṅga*). She had a garland of skulls (*naramālā*), was garbed in the skin of a tiger, and had hideous shriveled skin. Her eyes were sunken and red, her tongue lolled out of her wide, gaping mouth, which uttered roars that filled the landscape. Kālī instantly descended upon the *asura* army, smashing many with blows from her body, feet, and skull-topped staff, slashing some with her sword, but mostly tossing riders, whole elephants, horses, chariots, and their weapons into her mouth, and crunching them to death with her teeth. At this point, Caṇḍa and Muṇḍa rushed at Kālī, hurling a storm of arrows and thousands of discuses, the latter streaming into her mouth like suns into a dark cloud. But Kālī only laughed terrifyingly, and then, standing atop the great lion (*mahāsiṃha*), she grabbed Caṇḍa by the hair and beheaded him, and then similarly felled Muṇḍa. The demon army fled out of fear. Kālī then picked up the heads of the two demons, and presented them to Caṇḍikā, saying with frightening laughter that she was offering to Caṇḍikā two great beasts immolated in the sacrifice of battle. The beautiful Caṇḍikā replied that since she had offered up Caṇḍa and Muṇḍa, Kālī would henceforth be renowned in the world as the goddess Cāmuṇḍā (DM 6.17–7.25).

There are other noteworthy features in the preceding scene. Most importantly, it offers an emergence narrative of the goddess Kālī. Although it is often referred to as a creation myth, Kālī is not born or created, but emerges (*viniṣkrānta*) from Ambikā (DM 7.5). Kālī is nowhere in this scene described as having black skin, but her complexion is evoked through her name (*kālī* is a feminine derivative of *kāla* (black or time)). Rather, Ambikā's face turns ink-colored (*maṣī-varṇa*) (i.e., blue-black) from anger. There seems to be some notable concern in this third or final episode with the complexion of the various goddesses involved. At the beginning of the episode, Ambikā is described as emerging from Pārvatī, who as a result becomes Kṛṣṇā ("[She who is] Black") and becomes known as Kālikā (DM 5.40–41). Ambikā becomes known as Kauśikī because she emerges from a sheath (*kośa*) of Pārvatī's body. Beyond its meaning as black, or the color of ink, *kālikā* can also refer to a flaw in gold, or a change in complexion. Both these latter meanings resonate with the scenario described, for Pārvatī undergoes a change in complexion. Ambikā is described as luminous or even yellowish (*śobhanā*) in complexion (DM 5.62), so Kālikā's blackness is like a dark flaw within the brilliance of gold. Kālikā naturally evokes identification with Kālī, since both mean "[She who is] Black." We do not know if this identification was commonly assumed at the time of the composition of the DM, but in later centuries and nowadays Kālikā is simply assumed to be another name for Kālī. As Ambikā emerged through Pārvatī, transforming Pārvatī into Kālikā in the process, so Kālī emerges from Ambikā, who is not transformed. Thus, while Kālī and Kālikā are always black, Pārvatī may be either light or dark according to the context, and Ambikā is always portrayed as light complexioned.

Kālī's appearance, with shriveled skin, sunken bloodshot eyes, gaping mouth, lolling tongue, and a garland of skulls, heads, or corpses (*nara-mālā*) offers us an image of a goddess who was probably well-known at the time of the text's composition. She wears a tiger-skin and carries a sword, noose, and the skull-topped staff. Her hideous form contrasts dramatically and purposefully with that of Caṇḍikā/Ambikā/Durgā, who is repeatedly described as a jewel among women (DM 5.45, 5.53) in beauty. In the *Mālatī-mādhava* the goddess Cāmuṇḍā is described as having a vast gaping mouth and carries a skull staff. She is dressed in elephant-, not tiger-hide, and has a necklace of skulls (Kale 1928 47; Coburn 1984, 136). In the *Gauḍavaho*, the goddess Kālī is clearly associated with severed head offerings, because her temple is full of them (v. 318).

Caṇḍikā's derivation of the name Cāmuṇḍā, which she assigns to Kālī, seems contrived. For one, why is Kālī not called Caṇḍamuṇḍā, a simple feminine form of their combined names, or Cāṇḍamuṇḍā ("[She who is] Related to Caṇḍa and Muṇḍa")? I suppose one might concede that Cāmuṇḍā is a sort of abbreviation. It does offer a precedent, in this text, that a deity may be named after a demon or demons that they slay, and thus a rationale for why a deity's name may resemble the name of something once regarded as demonic. Of course, it may be a strategy to explain how a once malevolent and thus "demonic" being has been incorporated into a benevolent divine pantheon. We have previously noted this strategy in the example of Hārītī, the once dangerous infant-slaying demoness (*rākṣasī*), who is transformed into a protector upon her conversion to Buddhism. Hārītī, of course, does not undergo a name change. It may also be a strategy through which disparate deities are linked together by being either explicitly equated with each other or ambiguously linked and identified with each other. So Durgā's identification as Caṇḍikā and Ambikā is sufficiently explicit, although there is no place where this is expressly stated. Even so, the relationship between Pārvatī and Kālī, and between Kālī and Kālikā, is ambiguous, as is that between Pārvatī and Ambikā/Caṇḍikā/Durgā. Nevertheless, the text clearly identifies Ambikā with Kauśikī, links Pārvatī to Kālikā, and identifies Cāmuṇḍā as Kālī. It seems credible that the Caṇḍa and Muṇḍa story was designed with one of its objectives precisely to identify the goddess Kālī with the goddess Cāmuṇḍā. Another of its objectives would likely be to offer a rationale for the origin of the name of the *devī* Cāmuṇḍā, whose appearance and cult predated the composition of this episode, but the etymology of whose name was not apparent. I have already discussed the preexistence (depending on the compositional date of the DM) of the name Cāmuṇḍā as the terrifying goddess mentioned in the *Mālatī-mādhava*, who was associated with human sacrifice. We have discussed the Buddhist philosopher, Bhāvaviveka's (6th century CE) pejorative critique of the comparison of Cāmuṇḍā to Tārā, because the latter granted salvific realization while the former was characterized as propitiated for mundane goals (Sarkar 2013, 419).

Moreover, Bhāvaviveka draws a distinction between the demanding style of worship necessitated by Cāmuṇḍā and the more amenable style for Tārā. This offers yet another insight into the name of the goddess Durgā, which can mean "arduous" and "difficult to access" with respect to what is needed to win her favor. Even so, the DM constructs the persona of the Devī as including Tārā-esque traits and has her granting both mundane and spiritual boons.

Creative etymological derivations are extensive in Sanskrit literature, and the DM may be displaying it here as well as in the derivation of the name of the goddess Kauśikī. Through this myth, wild goddesses, such as Kālī and Cāmuṇḍā, perhaps originally regarded as pernicious to human beings, might have been incorporated into the benevolent divine pantheon, and in the process have had their destructive personas directed away from human victims towards demonic forces that threatened the cosmic order and human welfare.

Returning to the DM narrative, Śumbha was incensed when he realized that Caṇḍa, Muṇḍa, and their armies had been devastated, and surrounded by a huge array of demon armies he now approached the Devī. Caṇḍikā filled the atmosphere with the twang of her bowstring, her lion emitted a powerful roar, and then Ambikā supplemented this noise with the sound of her bell. Kālī uttered horrific sounds that drowned out even those noises. When the demon armies encircled Kālī, the Goddess, and her lion, *śaktis* sprang out of the bodies of Brahma, Īśa (i.e., Śiva), Guha (i.e., Skanda), Viṣṇu, and Indra. The *śaktis* possessed the forms, attributes, and mounts of each of the respective male deities from which they emerged. The *śakti* of Brahmā was known as Brahmāṇī. The *śakti* of Īśa (i.e., Maheśa or Maheśvara) was Māheśvarī, and of Guha (i.e., Kumāra), Kaumārī. The *śakti* of Viṣṇu was Vaiṣṇavī, and Aindrī emerged from Indra. The Vārāha (boar) *avatāra* of Hari (i.e., Viṣṇu) produced Vārāhī, and Nārasiṃhī emerged from the Narasimha (man-lion) form. Surrounding Īśāna, they approached the Goddess. Īśāna (i.e., Śiva) spoke to Caṇḍikā, saying, "May these demons be slain quickly for my pleasure." Thereupon a horrific *śakti* of Caṇḍikā emerged from the body of the Goddess and spoke to Īśāna. She commanded him to take a message to Śumbha and Niśumbha, and the other demons, saying that if they did not return the triple world to Indra, restore to the gods their proper share of the sacrifice, and return to the underworld, but choose to fight instead, that the Devī's jackals would feed on their flesh. Since Śiva himself was sent as her messenger, this *śakti* is renowned as Śivadūtī ("[She who] has Śiva as a Messenger") (DM 8.1–27).

In this scene, some of the classes of demons, such as the Kālakas and Kālakeyas (DM 8.5), have names that are cognate with Kālikā, again suggesting a certain affinity between the deity and the demons battled against. Also, there is the notion that female forms of the major gods, known as *śaktis*, or powers, emerge from the gods themselves, and are identical to them in weapons, attributes, vehicles, and so on. While one currently tends to think of a *śakti* as a female counterpart of a male deity, a female embodiment of his power, quite surprisingly a *śakti* emerges from the Goddess herself. Implicitly, the Devī transcends gender. Even so, this *śakti* does not resemble the Goddess in form and attributes and has an appearance akin to Kālī, insofar as she is gruesome and yelps like a hundred jackals (DM 8.22). However, we note that Kālī, who had previously emerged from the Devī to slay Caṇḍa and Muṇḍa, is already present. Although Śiva attempts to assert his status by commanding the Goddess to slay the demons with the aid of the *śaktis* for his pleasure, the Devī's *śakti* emerges and commands him instead. She sends Śiva to convey her message to the demons. Leaving no uncertainty about who is in charge, she acquires the name Śivadūtī, an epithet that is often mistranslated as "Śiva's Messenger," when, in fact, it is unambiguously "She who has Śiva as a Messenger" (DM 8.27). Just as Sugrīva served as a messenger for Caṇḍa and Muṇḍa earlier in this episode, Śiva is sent to convey a message back, and is not even commanded to do so by the Devī herself but by her frightful *śakti*, leaving little ambiguity as to who is supreme.

When the demons hear the message brought by Śiva, they do not heed the Devī's advice. Instead, they directly confront Kātyāyanī, as the Goddess is here called (DM 8.28) and attack her. She playfully destroyed their weapons, and the *śaktis* of the gods, or Mātṛs ("Mothers") as they are here called (DM 8.38), along with Kālī and Śivadūtī, caused havoc as they destroyed the ranks of the demon armies. This induced the great demon Raktabīja ("Blood Seed") to enter the fray. As the weapons of the various Mātṛs struck him, the drops that fell from Raktabīja's body spawned demon soldiers exactly like him in appearance, strength, and power. Soon, bleeding copiously from the various wounds that the Mothers had inflicted, Raktabīja had filled the entire world with his demon clones. While the gods trembled, Caṇḍikā laughed and commanded Kālī to drink up the blood that fell from the demon's body and to consume the demons it had already produced. Kālī/Cāmuṇḍā began devouring the cloned, replicating demon horde. And as the Devī attacked Raktabīja, causing him to bleed profusely, Kālī drank deeply of all the flowing blood until he fell dead and bloodless to the ground. The gods were ecstatic with joy, and the Mothers danced, intoxicated with his blood (DM 8.28–62).

There is a clear rationale in this scene for Kālī's gaping mouth and her association with drinking blood. Raktabīja has intriguing symbolic connotations. His drops of blood are like a virulent infectious disease, a pandemic whose germs replicate uncontrollably and exponentially. His name conjoins the terms *rakta* and *bīja*, which can refer to female menstrual fluid and male semen respectively. These were often regarded in early Indian medical systems to be the two contributing constituents in the production of life.[43] Thus, Kālī drinks dry these very components themselves. More explicitly, Raktabīja's drops of blood, like semen, seed the production of demon clones like himself. Kālī drinks up this seed, a source of a runaway creation, the replication of endless numbers of demon spawn. She devours the clones and drinks every drop of demon-engendering seed that flows from Raktabīja's body. This blood-seed acts as an intoxicant, but remarkably, it is not Kālī but the Mātṛs who dance about, drunken on the blood that not they but Kālī has drunk (DM 8.62). This implies an intrinsic link among these goddesses, prefiguring the explicit connection that will be drawn later in the episode. The Mothers (Mātṛs) are a malleable group of female divinities in the Hindu tradition. They vary in number and in the names of the goddesses that constitute them. Here, they are depicted as female forms of the major male gods.

Kālī's capacity to drink up so much blood because the demon spawn had pervaded the entire world (DM 8.51) clearly mirrors Cāmuṇḍā's description in the *Mālatī-mādhava*, where she is lauded as having a gaping mouth capable of swallowing the seven oceans (Kale 1928 47). The Devī explicitly addresses Kālī as Cāmuṇḍā and tells her to open her mouth wide and devour all the Raktabīja clones (DM 8.52–55). Cāmuṇḍā/Kālī does so, devouring every drop of blood, every demon, and ultimately leaves Raktabīja a bloodless corpse (DM 8.60–61). The bloody intoxication of the Mātṛs (Mothers) resembles the Mbh's version (3.221.52–69) of Skanda's defeat of Mahiṣa, in which Skanda's companions kill Mahiṣa's army of demons, and then devour them by the hundreds, drinking their blood and celebrating.

When Raktabīja was slain, Śumbha and Niśumbha finally attacked the Goddess and her lion mount with their own armies. She first dropped Niśumbha and then was assaulted by the eight-armed Śumbha in a battle of cosmic proportions. Caṇḍikā, finally losing her temper, pierced him with her spear, and he fell to the ground. But by now, Niśumbha, the son of Diti, becoming ten thousand armed, hurled discuses at the Goddess. The references to Śumbha having eight arms, and Niśumbha then having ten thousand arms cannot be ignored. It is an example of the symbolic tradition of multiple limbs (arms, heads, eyes, etc.) discussed in a previous chapter. These attributes were initially associated with the Vedic Cosmic Being or creator. They were taken up by supreme deities such as Viṣṇu and the Devī, of course, in iconography (arguably among the earliest) and explicitly in hymns such as the DStv and the previous Mahiṣa-slaying episode of the DM.

One must wonder if the DM's references to Śumbha and Niśumbha and their appearance tacitly draw upon "divine" figures from rival religious traditions. After all, Tantric Buddhism had already begun to have a host of divine bodhisattvas such as Avalokiteśvara, who was represented with multiple arms, and from whom the Hindu gods and goddesses were portrayed as mere manifestations. For instance, in the *Kāraṇḍavyūha Sūtra* (c. late 4th–early 5th century CE), Maheśvara is said to have been born from Avalokiteśvara's brow, Brahmā from his shoulders, Nārāyaṇa from his heart, Sarasvatī from his teeth, the wind from his mouth, Varuṇa from his stomach, and the earth from his feet (Studholme 2002, 123). In Buddhist Tantric texts composed after the DM, Śumbha and Niśumbha are invoked positively and identified with Trailokyavijaya, a manifestation of the bodhisattva Vajrapāṇi. The secret meditative verse (*dhāraṇī*) of Trailokyavijaya invokes both Śumbha and Niśumbha to compel Maheśvara to appear and submit to Trailokyavijaya. In this conceptual framework, the goddess as Umā is regarded as the consort of Maheśvara, who is subordinated to Mahāvairocana/Vajrapāṇi (Linrothe 1999, 178–93). The ongoing jostling for supremacy among the pantheons of not just the orthodox Hindu sectarian traditions, but among all religious sects of the period, is evident.

In this part of the episode, Durgā's name again appears, and it is thus worth examining the verse closely:

tato bhagavatī kruddhā durgā durgārtināśinī |
ciccheda tāni cakrāṇi svaśaraiḥ sāyakāṃśca tān // (DM 9.29)
Thereupon, divine Durgā, destroyer (*nāśinī*) of the pain (*ārti*)
      of arduous pursuits (*durga*), irritated (*kruddhā*),
Severed those discuses and arrows with her own shafts (*śara*).

Here again, the Devī is explicitly identified as Durgā, and although it is in the context of the Devī's anger in the ongoing battle, Durgā is described as the remover or destroyer of difficulties, or the suffering associated with them.

Niśumbha again attacked Caṇḍikā, who speared him in the heart. He emerged from his pierced heart as a powerful person, urging her to stop, but the Devī, laughing resoundingly, beheaded him. Her lion, Kālī, Śivadūtī, and the Mātṛs destroyed the demons in his army (DM 9.30–39). Niśumbha's transformation and emergence calls to mind Mahiṣa's release from his buffalo form, for both demons appear to show their true identity just prior to their demise. Seeing his brother killed, Śumbha spoke to the Devī, addressing her as Durgā, saying:

balāvalepād duṣṭe tvaṃ mā durge garvam āvaha |
anyāsāṃ balam āśritya yuddhayase ya atimāninī // (DM 10.2)
O wicked (*duṣṭā*) Durgā! Do not be arrogant (*garva*), swept
      away with pride (*avalepa*) in your strength (*bala*).
You, who are so haughty (*atimāninī*), wage war by depending
      upon the strength of others.

Here the Devī is unequivocally identified as Durgā by the very demon she battles. Śumbha accuses her of being proud, arrogant, or haughty, qualities that she had used to describe herself when explaining why she took the vow to yield in marriage only to one who could defeat her in battle (DM 5.69). He even calls her corrupt/crooked or nasty/wicked (*duṣṭā*). The irony is again evident for it is he who embodies the very qualities of which he accuses the Goddess. Recognizing that he is seriously overpowered, and is losing the war, Śumbha next accuses Durgā of not fighting alone, as she had originally suggested when she had figuratively thrown down the gauntlet and invited him to battle her. This accusation that she is relying on others for help leads to perhaps the most significant scene in the episode, for it reveals, establishes, and affirms the most enduring characteristic of the Devī.

The Devī replies by saying:

ekaiva ahaṃ jagaty atra dvitīyā kā mama aparā |
paśyaitā duṣṭa mayy eva viśantyo mad vibhūtayaḥ // (DM
      10.3)
In the universe (*jagati*), I (*ahaṃ*) am indeed alone (*ekā eva*);
      what other/else (*dvitīyā*), beyond me (*mama aparā*),
      is here?
O wicked one! Behold these, my manifestations of power,
      entering in fact into me (*mayi eva*).

At that instant, all the goddesses returned to the body of the Devī, leaving Ambikā there alone. The Devī then said:

> *ahaṃ vibhūtya abahubhir iha rūpair yadā sthitā /*
> *tat saṃhṛtaṃ mayaikaiva tiṣṭhāmy ājau sthiro bhava //* (DM
> 10.5)
> When I was imminent (*sthitā*) in this world (*iha*) with my
> manifold forms, it was through my remarkable power
> (*vibhūti*).
> That has been consolidated (*saṃhṛta*) by me. I now wait alone
> in the battle. Be relentless.

The critical feature of this scene is that while Kālī and Śivadūtī had explicitly emerged from the body of the Devī, it is not only they who meld back into her. The Mātṛs, too, and the *śaktis* who seemed to have originated from the male gods, now return to the body of the Goddess. There is a certain resonance between the emergence of these *śaktis* from the gods, and the *tejas* that emanated from them when the Devī manifested in Episode Two. The *śaktis* resemble, bear the characteristics, ride the mounts, and wield the weapons of the male gods. And here they finally reenter the Devī, somewhat akin to the way in which the male gods' collective *tejas* pooled to provide the form from within which the Goddess emerged in the middle episode. Just as the gods there "equipped her" with their weapons and other items drawn from their own, here too she implicitly possesses all their weapons and attributes. It is made patently clear that she underlies the male gods and is at the basis of their power. Moreover, although she is referring to gathering up the myriad goddesses that are aiding her into a single Great Goddess, the Devī's initial words, *"ekaivāhaṃ jagati,"* evoke an Upaniṣadic monistic dictum, that there is only one Absolute, and that she is it. Implicit, too, in this scene is the notion that not only all the *śaktis* of the gods, but all *śaktis* (e.g., Śivadūtī), and indeed all other goddesses (e.g., Kālī), are only manifest forms of the one and only Great Goddess. The lion, too, seems to have vanished into the Devī, although this is not stated explicitly, and no mention is made of him in the description of the final confrontation with Śumbha. Although this observation may appear trivial or even banal, it is hardly so, because the lion is included among the cluster of "goddesses" currently worshipped in Nepal, known as the Navadurgās, a group that also includes many of the Mātṛs. The lion, too, is the Devī, a feature paralleled in the persona of the Egyptian deity Sekhmet, for instance.

Then ensued a fierce battle between the Devī and Śumbha, and she finally slew the great demon lord of the worlds with her spear. The world was soothed, and its discordant, chaotic state abated. The gods were overjoyed. The heavenly nymphs danced, and the celestial musicians sang and played their instruments (DM 10.6–28). Indra and the other gods, headed by Agni, burst into a song of praise to Kātyāyanī, as the Devī is again called (DM 11.1). This hymn is well known for its refrain "Nārāyaṇī, praise be to you!" (*nārāyaṇī namo 'stu te*) (DM 11.7–22).

The Praise to Nārāyaṇī Hymn (Nārāyaṇī-stuti)

The Devī is praised as the remover of her supplicants' pain and the queen of all that is animate and inanimate (DM 11.2). I will only highlight some of her names, epithets, and attributes in this hymn. She is the sole support of all that exists (*ādhārabhūtā*), existing in the form of earth (*mahī*) and water (*apā*) (DM 11.3). Her energy (*vīrya*) is infinite (DM 11.4), and she is the power (*śakti*) of Viṣṇu. She is the seed (*bīja*) of the whole (*viśva*), the supreme illusion (*paramā māyā*). She deludes the entire creation, and thus, verily, she can grant liberation to supplicants (DM 11.4). Indeed, all the various branches of knowledge (or the sciences, or mantric formulas) (*vidyā*) are fragments of her, and so are all the women in all the worlds (DM 11.5). She alone is mother of the world. What ultimate words are adequate to praise one who is beyond praise, who is all creation, and grants both heaven (*svarga*) and liberation (*mukti*) (DM 11.5–7)? She abides within every person's heart in the form of intelligence and is the cause of transformation through the divisions of time, the power of the evanescence of the cosmos (DM 11.7–8). She is the auspiciousness within all things auspicious; she is Sivā, accomplishing all ends (*sarvārthasādhikā*), the three-eyed Gaurī (DM 11.9). She becomes the power of creation, maintenance, and destruction, residing within the strands of material existence, the abode of those qualities (DM 11.10). She takes away the pain of all, and rescues those who take refuge in her (DM 11.11). She has the form of Brahmāṇī, Māheśvarī, Kaumārī, Vaiṣṇavī, a boar, and a man-lion. She is praised as Aindrī, Śivadūtī, Cāmuṇḍā, Lakṣmī, Lajjā, Mahāvidyā, Śraddhā, Puṣṭī, Mahārātrī, Mahāmāyā, Svadhā, Dhruvā, Medhā, Sarasvatī, Varā, Bhūtī, Bābhravī, Tamasī, and of course, as Nārāyaṇī (DM 11.12–22). It is not always clear if these are names of individual goddesses or merely epithets extolling qualities.

The "O Nārāyaṇī, praise to you!" refrain, which begins at DM 11.7, ends at DM 11.23, with a verse to Durgā:

> *sarva svarūpe sarveśe sarva śakti samanvite /*
> *bhayebhyas trāhi no devi durge devi namo 'stu te //* (DM 11.23)
> You who are endowed with all power, the lady/queen of all,
>> whose own form (*svarūpā*) is everything,
> Protect us from fears, O Goddess; O Goddess Durgā, praise be
>> to you!

The hymn continues with praises to the Devī's gentle face, adorned with three eyes, to her trident, her bell, and her sword, while addressing her as Kātyāyanī, Bhadrakālī, or Caṇḍikā (DM 11.24–27).

The hymn concludes with several telling verses. The Goddess is praised as removing afflictions when satisfied (*tuṣṭa*), but when offended (*ruṣṭa*) as destroying all wished-for desires (DM 11.28). It affirms her presence in the various bodies of knowledge (*vidyā*), in the teachings (*śāstra*) and sayings (*vākya*) requiring the light of discrimination, wherein she causes the world to swirl in darkness and attachment (DM 11.30). She protects from demons, venomous serpents, enemies, and armies of infidels (DM 11.32). The Devī is said to be worthy of praise by all who are great rulers, and those who bow in praise to her, themselves become a refuge for all (DM 11.32). The hymn ends with the gods then asking the Devī to offer protection from the fear of enemies, just as she saved them from subjugation by the demons. They ask that she be a granter of boons to the worlds (DM 11.33–34).

This hymn reaffirms many of the names, epithets, and characteristics of the Devī that were addressed in the portions of the text that precede it and emphasizes some new elements. For instance, the Devī is said to abide in the form of earth and water (DM 11.3), both components that are still utilized when constructing effigies for worship (e.g., a water-filled earthen jar). She is said to grant both heaven and liberation (DM 11.6 and 11.7), suggesting her appeal to two soteriological strands among devotees, one that quests for a heavenly rebirth, and the other that seeks spiritual emancipation (*mokṣa*). Her identity with the power of illusion (DM 11.4, 11.21, 11.30) is affirmed, as is her identification with knowledge and intelligence (DM 11.5, 11.7, 11. 30). Significantly, every woman, in all the worlds, is explicitly said to be a fragment/aspect/part (*bheda*) of her (DM 11.5). Although it seems evident that this goes for all the gods and men, too, since the Devī is repeatedly said to be all of creation, her explicit identification with all women is noteworthy. It is not always clear if the words used to praise her are names of goddesses or epithets. Some, such as Lakṣmī or Sarasvatī, simply seem to be names. Terms such as Lajjā, Śivā, Medhā, Tamasī, or Puṣṭī do circulate as the names of goddesses, rather than merely descriptive qualities such as bashfulness, auspiciousness, wisdom, darkness, or prosperity. Yet others, such as Bābhravī (possibly "[She who is] Tawny"), are somewhat enigmatic. In conjunction with the name Nārāyaṇī, the names Ambikā, Durgā, Bhadrakālī, Caṇḍikā, and Kātyāyanī appear to stand out as equivalent names for the Great Goddess, because they receive places of prominence in the hymn. It is noteworthy that all these names except for Caṇḍikā and Ambikā are the direct recipients of the *namo 'stu te* refrain. Moreover, those two names for the Goddess, Caṇḍikā and Ambikā, tend to fade in prominence over the centuries. One wonders if the hymn circulated independently prior (or subsequent) to inclusion into the DM, which utilized the less-common names Ambikā and Caṇḍikā for its narrative purposes, and that these narrative names did not endure as well as the ones that are repeated in hymnic and mantric contexts.

In many respects, the qualities for which the Devī is being praised resonate well with the characteristic qualities associated with Durgā in the preceding episodes, for the Devī is frequently spoken of as removing pain, offering protection, and serving as a refuge (e.g., DM 11.2, 11.11, 11.23, 11.28, 11.31, 11.32, 11.33, 11.34). Notably, those who are rulers are encouraged to praise her, and by so doing, themselves become a refuge (DM 11.32). This is crucial in understanding the Devī's appeal to the ruling classes, who, by turning to her for succor, may be sought out for sanctuary by their subjects. The Devī is also supplicated to become a granter of wishes not just to the gods, but to all who ask for her help. As Mircea Eliade (1971, 5) had theorized on the use of divine precedents as models for human behavior, the gods themselves set the example by successfully invoking the Devī's help to overcome their enemies and grant their wishes. They then beseech the Devī to render this option to all other beings, a wish that she grants. The proof that this was not an empty promise is unveiled closer to the end of the DM, in the actions of king Suratha and the merchant Samādhi, who have been listening to the sage Medhas's tale of the Devī's exploits.

It is worth attending more closely to DM 11.9 because something very close to it appears in an inscription that provides possible clues to the compositional date of the text. The DM 11.9 verse reads:

> *sarvamaṅgalamaṅgalye śive sarvārthasādhike /*
> *śaraṇye tryambake gauri nārāyaṇi namo'stu te //* (DM 11.9)[44]

An inscription found at the ancient Dadhimatī Mātā temple site in Rajasthan reads:[45]

> *sarvamaṅgalāmaṅgalye śive sa[ ]rthasādhake /*
> *araṇye trāṃmvake gauri [ ]rāyaṇi namo stu te //*

Pandit Ram Karna (1911–1912) adjusted this to read:

> *sarvamaṅgalamaṅgalye śive sa[rvā]rthasādhike /*
> *śaraṇye tryambake gauri [nā]rāyani namo' stu te //* (Ram
> Karna 1911–1912, Vol. XI, 304)

V. V. Mirashi (1964) convincingly argues that the inscriptional dates interpreted by Pandit Ram Karna, which placed it in the early 7th century, according to the Gupta era calendar, were incorrect, and that it probably belonged either to the Bhāṭika or Harśa eras, placing it in the late 8th or early 9th centuries. Ram Karna had interpreted the date on the inscription as the thirteenth *tithi* of the dark fortnight of the month of Śrāvaṇa in the year 289, which was assumed from palaeographic evidence to refer to the Gupta era. This works out to 608 CE. The date of this inscription is significant, because it is suggested as a *terminus ante quem*, a date before which one could reasonably place the composition of the DM. Even so, Mirashi (1964) pointed out that the inscriptional style and other factors indicate that the Dadhimatī Mātā inscription could not belong to the Gupta era. Indeed, the year was not 289, but 189, and thus could indicate the Harśa era, which would place it at 795 to 796 CE. Mirashi, however, leans more strongly towards locating the inscription in the Bhāṭika era, which was prevalent in the region at the time. Through that count the inscription would belong to 812 to 813 CE, if the year was current, or 813 to 814 CE if it had already expired. Mirashi suggests that the DM would have been composed well before this 9th century CE date for a verse to have become so popular as to be cited in the inscription. This suggests that the Nārāyaṇī hymn to the Goddess, if not the DM itself, was likely well-known at that period. This verse is also well known independently because it is still recited in isolation from the Nārāyaṇī hymn by lay devotees in rites such as the Bengali Durgā Pūjā (Rodrigues 2003, 194).

The Predicted Manifestations

Returning to the DM, the Goddess responds to the hymn of praise by acknowledging that she is indeed a boon-granter and asks the gods to choose the boon that they had in mind. They ask that she heal all the pains of the triple world and destroy their enemies (DM 11.35–36). The Devī responds with a series of predictions about how she will go about fulfilling these requests. She says that in the twenty-eighth *yuga* of the Vaivasvata Manvantara, another pair of demons named Śumbha and Niśumbha will appear. She would emerge in the house of the cowherd Nanda, by growing within the embryo (*garbhasambhava*) of Yaśodā, and then, dwelling on Vindhya mountain, she would slay those two (DM 11.37–38). Again, having descended (*avatīrya*) to earth in a very fierce form, she will kill the Vaipracitta demons, by devouring them. By so doing, her teeth will become reddened like pomegranate blossoms, and she will be praised by the gods in heaven, and human beings in the mortal realm as Raktadantikā ("She whose Teeth are Red") (DM 11.39–41). As an aside, Vipracitti is the name of a demon (*danava*), the father of Rāhu.

The Devī then foretells the event through which she will be known as Durgā. She says that on an occasion when there has been a drought, with no water for a hundred years, when eulogized (*saṃstuta*) by sages/monks/devotees (*muni*), she will arise (*sambhaviṣyāmi*) on the earth without being born from a womb. Since she will gaze at the sages with a hundred eyes, human beings will praise her as Śatākṣī ("She of a Hundred Eyes"). Then, she will support the entire world during the drought with life-sustaining vegetables produced by her own body and will thus be renowned on earth as Śākambharī ("She who Supports with Vegetables"). The next half-verses referring to Durgā read:

> *tatraiva ca vadhiṣyāmi durgama akhyaṃ mahāsuram //* (DM 11.45)
> *durgā devīti vikhyātaṃ tan me nāma bhaviṣyati /* (DM 11.46)
> Thereupon I will slay a great demon named Durgama
> Thus, my name will become celebrated (*vikhyāta*) as "the Goddess Durgā."

The Devī continues by foretelling that when she takes on a dreadful form in the Himalayas, the sages will praise her for having protected them. And when a demon known as Aruṇa causes destruction in the three worlds, she will become celebrated as Bhīmādevī ("The Terrifying Goddess"). Then, she will take on a form constituted by countless bees and will slay the demon for the welfare of the triple world and will be lauded as Bhrāmarī ("She of the Bee") (DM 11.37–50). To maintain our focus on the content of the DM, the detailed analysis of this series of predicted manifestations and the goddesses mentioned will be provided in the next chapter. Particular attention will be given to the verses that deal with Durgā.

The Devī in the DM finishes up this discourse on her future manifestations by saying that whenever demons (*dānava*) cause distress, she will manifest in bodily form to destroy them. In this she mirrors the words spoken by Kṛṣṇa in the BG, and clearly situates herself within a similar demon-destroying role. Summing up the key features of this episode, we note that it is the longest of the three episodes of the DM, spanning Chapters 5 to 11. While it primarily deals with the destruction of the demons Śumbha and Niśumbha by the Devī, it also recounts the destruction of the demons Caṇḍa and Muṇḍa by Kālī. This provides an etymological rationale for the derivation of Kālī's other name, Cāmuṇḍā. Cāmuṇḍā/Kālī is then also associated with the destruction of the demon Raktabīja. The episode contains emergence myths of the *śaktis* of the male gods, known as the Mātṛs or Mothers, as well as a *śakti* of the Devī herself, known as Śivadūtī. We know little about the cult of Śivadūtī. She could likely have originally been a goddess associated with jackals (*śivā*), and indeed been a feminine attendant or messenger associated with Śiva.[46] The DM perhaps intentionally recast her into a *śakti* of Caṇḍikā, who made Śiva into a messenger. According to the *Kālikā Purāṇa* (Chapter 63, 100-116), she is worshipped in the Durgā Pūjā and is said to have the nature of Śiva. An adept who renders her homage with devotion when hearing the howls of jackals, will obtain his desires. She is always surrounded by twelve Yoginīs, wherever she wanders. According to the *Kālikā Purāṇa*, the Yoginīs of Śivadūtī are Kṣemaṃkarī, Śāntā, Vedamātā, Mahodarī, Karālā, Kāmadā, Bhagāsyā, Bhagaśālinī, Bhagodarī, Bhagāhārā, Bhagajihvā, and Bhagā (van Kooij 1972, 128–29). Today, during the Bengali celebrations of the Durgā Pūjā, at certain high points in the ritual, women utter the *ululu*, *huluhulu*, or *ulu dhvani*, a high-pitched throaty cry that resembles the howls of jackals.

In the DM, the goddesses are strikingly independent, untethered to male deities as spouses, mothers, or daughters. The Devī is portrayed as the "mother" of all creation and consequently the mother of all gods. Even the Mātṛs — despite being referred to as "Mothers" — are not depicted as the mothers of specific deities. Although these *śaktis* emerge from the bodies of male gods and resemble them in form and attributes, they are not bound to the gods by conventional familial ties. More importantly, regardless of their origins, they all ultimately merge back into the body of the Devī, underscoring her role as their ultimate source and essence.

The DM is explicit in presenting the Devī as the singular Goddess, encompassing all other goddesses within herself. It goes further to depict her as the sole divine entity, with all gods as emanations of her being and all their powers under her control. This supremacy of the Devī is conveyed strategically, particularly through her interactions with the male gods. While she is often shown assisting lesser gods in their struggles against demons, the narrative subtly distinguishes her status from even the greatest male deities, such as Śiva and Viṣṇu. Over the course of the text, it becomes evident that the Devī is portrayed as surpassing the male gods in greatness, solidifying her position as the supreme divinity.

While Durgā is never mentioned in Episode One, she is mentioned six times in this final episode (DM 5.10, 5.66, 9.29, 10.2, 11.23, and 11.45–46). Although the Devī explains that she will emerge in a future epoch, and through killing the demon Durgama will earn the name Durgā (DM 11.45–46), earlier in that episode the demon Śumbha directly addresses her as Durgā (DM 10.2). This is extremely significant. The Devī is called by many names in the context of hymns of praise to her. These names include Ambikā, Caṇḍikā, Bhadrakālī, Kātyāyanī, Durgā, and so on. She is even referred to by these names when the *ṛṣi* Medhas is recounting his narrative of her exploits. In DM 5.66, he refers to the Devī as Durgā. Nowhere in the text is the Goddess called by a particular name — other than Devī — by any of the demons with whom she battles, except for this one instance. Śumbha calls her Durgā, which is evidently a salient reason this comes to be the dominant name for the Devī.

This narrative highlights the evolution and multifaceted persona of Durgā within the DM and its related texts. In the DM, Durgā is consistently associated with alleviating the pains of existence and guiding beings through life's difficulties, often described as a refuge and a manifestation of knowledge, insight, supreme power, and divinity (DM 4.10, 4.16, 5.10, 9.29, 11.23, and 11.45–46). While she is depicted as a warrior goddess, her martial character occupies a relatively smaller portion of her descriptions (DM 9.29, 10.2, and 11.45–46), emphasizing her salvific and transcendental qualities instead. This portrayal aligns with early textual depictions of Durgā, such as in the Durgā Gāyatrī and the Rātrī Khila, where she is primarily invoked as a protective refuge in various perilous circumstances, with little reference to her as a warrior. For instance, in the Rātrī Khila (l. 10), Durgā is depicted as auspicious, attractive, and radiant like Agni, yet no mention is made of her wielding weapons. Similarly, in the DStv, she is portrayed as a sanctuary from perils (l. 39, 51), although martial associations emerge through her identification with Kālī, Jayā, and Vijayā, goddesses linked to victory in battle.

Over time, Durgā's attributes of refuge and protection fused with the martial qualities of these goddesses, resulting in a more complex deity embodying both martial and salvific traits. This fusion becomes evident in the Mbh, where the

DStv or a related variant integrates Durgā with Nidrā, the goddess associated with the Kṛṣṇa/Kaṃsa myth. Here, Durgā appears with weapons and promises Yudhiṣṭhira victory in battle. The PN-s1, which predates the DStv's integration into the Mbh, does not mention Durgā explicitly but merges motifs of Nidrā with those of Kauśikī/Vindhyavāsinī, thereby connecting them to Kālī, Jayā, Vijayā, and Durgā. By the time the DStv is incorporated into the Mbh, this fusion is nearly complete, with Durgā firmly established as a warrior goddess who grants victory and refuge.

Later texts than the PN-s1 and arguably the DStv or unknown variant, such as the DSto, further solidify this synthesis. In the DSto, Durgā appears alongside Kālī, Caṇḍī, Jayā, Vijayā, Kātyāyanī, and Kauśikī, all connected to the Kṛṣṇa/Kaṃsa cycle. Although the hymn emphasizes Durgā's role as a universal refuge, her association with martial success is also affirmed (l. 26), as seen when she promises Arjuna victory during the Mbh war. In contrast, the PN-s2, also known as the Āryā Stava, highlights Durgā's connection to austerities and her role as a boon-giver, ruling over both material and transcendental realms. While weapons are mentioned (l. 13), the hymn de-emphasizes military triumphs, presenting the goddess as a benefactor and sovereign deity capable of granting favor across all domains.

By the time of the DM's composition, the name Durgā was most strongly associated with refuge and boon-granting, unlike goddesses such as Kālī, Ambikā, or Caṇḍikā, who are overtly tied to warfare and the destruction of demons, or Mahāmāyā and Yoganidrā, linked with illusionary power. The DM firmly identifies Durgā as the Devī, the Great Goddess, thereby imbuing her with the full spectrum of the Devī's qualities, including martial attributes. However, her enduring identity as a refuge and boon-granter remains central. This identity, conveyed through her imagery as a vessel navigating life's turbulent waters and a name associated with hard-to-access sanctuaries or dangers, points toward cross-influences from traditions such as Buddhism and Jainism, which also emphasize refuge. While much scholarship has focused on Durgā as a warrior goddess (e.g., Yokochi 2004), a symbol of kingship (Sarkar 2017), or divine sovereignty (Balkaran 2020), her persona as a compassionate protector has endured from its earliest attestations to the present day. This persona has allowed Durgā to amalgamate features of prominent goddess cults of her time, resonating with diverse devotees and addressing their myriad challenges and aspirations. This progression illustrates how Durgā's persona evolved from a refuge goddess into a powerful synthesis of martial and transcendental attributes, firmly cementing her status as the Great Goddess within the Hindu tradition, and the supreme deity in Śākta metaphysics.

The Fruits of Recitation and Hearing (*Phalaśruti*)

The DM continues with the Devī extolling the values of her own narrative of glorification. For those who praise her by singing these hymns, she will eliminate all misfortunes. To those who recount (*kīrtayiṣyanti*) the annihilation of Madhu and Kaiṭabha, the destruction of the Asura Mahiṣa, and that of Śumbha and Niśumbha, on the eighth, fourteenth, and ninth days of the lunar fortnight, as well as those who will listen with devotion to her supreme *Glorification* (*Māhātmya*), there will be no poverty, no separation from loved ones, nor will anything unfortunate happen to them, even as a result of evil acts (DM 12.1–3). Moreover, to these persons there will be no danger from enemies, scoundrels, or kings, nor ever from flood, fire, or weapons. For this reason, this *Glorification* should be recited (*paṭhita*) with focused attention and must always be listened to with devotion. Indeed, it is the supreme benediction (DM 12.4–6). This *Glorification* should placate all types of great illnesses, and the three types of natural disasters. The Devī explains that wherever it is recited properly in her abode (*āyatana*), there she is permanently established and will never desert that place. During the offering of sacrifices, in ritual worship, in the fire rites, and in the great festival, all her exploits are to be heralded and heard. When such sacrifices and worship are done, as well as the fire oblation, she indicates that she is pleased with them, regardless of whether there is understanding or not. If one filled with devotion simply hears this *Glorification* at the great autumn festival, they will be freed from ailments, and gain wealth, prosperity, and offspring through her grace (DM 12.7–12).

Not only does the DM attempt to accentuate its own virtues, but it also does so by having the Devī herself rather than the *ṛṣi* Medhas extol its benefits. There is no doubt that the DM must be recited out loud and listened to with respect, in the right contexts, at appropriate times and venues. Moreover, even listening to it is said to be just as beneficial as reciting it. This undoubtedly unleashed the tradition widely practiced today of loud, audible, public recitation of the DM, not quiet and secret, which has led to the growth in its popularity and the knowledge of some of its verses even by those not skilled in Sanskrit.

While there are obvious parallels between the DM and the BG, which it appears to mimic in various respects, the DM contrasts with the BG in distinct and telling ways. In the BG, Kṛṣṇa delivers his teachings to Arjuna, and proclaims them to be extremely mysterious (BG 18.63). Arjuna must reflect upon their meaning thoroughly and then act freely (BG 18.63). He may only share these teachings with those who are penitent and devoted, never to one who does not want to hear it, or to one who is not well-disposed toward Kṛṣṇa (BG 18.67). Kṛṣṇa does extol the value of sharing his teachings with devotion to others who are similarly devoted, saying that this pleases him above all other activities (BG 18.69). The study of the teachings is akin to sacrifice (BG 18.70), but that even hearing it recited with faith, and not criticizing it, can lead to liberation (BG 18.71). Kṛṣṇa then asks Arjuna if he has listened with his fullest concentration (BG 18.72). Sañjaya, who is reporting the conversations to Dhṛtarāṣṭra, concludes how he delights when he remembers Kṛṣṇa's words, the supreme secret, and that where Kṛṣṇa and Arjuna are, there are fortune, victory, prosperity, and righteous conduct (BG 18.78). By contrast, the DM is not presented as an abstruse and secret philosophical teaching that needs to be pondered and understood. It is simply a telling of the various exploits of the Devī. While the BG is to be shared only with willing listeners with devout orientations, the DM is to be proclaimed out loud to all and sundry. Although the recitation needs to be performed with devotion, leading to benefits for the reader, listeners, too, receive equal benefits, provided they do so with devoted dispositions. Quite importantly, they need not understand the full compass of the worship activities to satisfy the Devī, indirectly implying that they need not even understand the actual words being recited but merely know the stories of which they speak. This is a notable juxtaposition of both Tantric empowerment through the skillful performance of Sanskrit recitation, and empowerment simply through listening with devotion (*bhakti*) (DM 12.11).

The Devī goes on to list the wide assortment of benefits that accrue to reciters and listeners of the *Māhātmya* (*Glorification*). Listening to it, which tells of the Devī's manifestations and her distinction in battle, can make a person fearless. Their enemies are vanquished, they have well-being, and their family is joyful. Listening to it on any occasion with portents of sorrow, such as bad dreams, astrological conjunctions, and other omens, can bring these to an end and turn bad dreams into good ones. Children troubled by pernicious spirits become peaceful, and rifts in relationships are transformed into the strongest friendships. There is nothing comparable to this *Glorification* for vanquishing evil, because devils, spirits, and flesh-eating fiends are destroyed by its recitation. In fact, the recitation and hearing of this *Glorification*, only once, delights the Devī as much as an entire year's worth of traditional worship, day and night, such as with the best animals, flowers, offerings, incense, fragrances, lamps, feeding of Brahmins, fire oblations, and water consecrations. Extolling her manifestations and hearing about them destroys sins, confers health, and protects against evil spirits and dangers from enemies. This is because the *Glorification* deals with the Devī's destruction of demons. These praises spoken by the gods, the *ṛṣis*, and by Brahmā are said to be auspicious for the mind. The person who remembers these deeds, the Devī explains, if surrounded by fire at the outskirts or deep in the forest, or encircled by villains in a lonely place, captured by enemies, thrown into bondage, chased in the jungle by tigers, lions, or elephants, assailed by weapons in the most horrendous battle, or lashed by a wind when in a boat on the great ocean, in fact, in any terrible situation, when afflicted by pain, will be liberated from these hardships. All adversaries, lions, enemies, and villains scatter far away, through her might, if one brings her deeds to mind (DM 12.13–29).

The Goddess has left virtually no stone unturned when discussing the wide variety of grave circumstances that are remedied merely through the recitation of this *Māhātmya*. Among the many features of interest in her speech is that even though her exploits deal with the destruction of demons, hearing about her deeds has beneficial effects in many more circumstances than merely in battle with human or demonic enemies. These benefits include the mending of broken relationships and gaining wealth and offspring. The Devī explains that because her exploits concern the defeat of demons, proclaiming them has a sort of protective effect against malevolence (DM 12.22). There is an implicit form of magical agency afoot in the *Glorification*, for it serves to rectify problems and induce good fortune merely through its ritual recitation, and not through its philosophical teachings. The entire *Glorification* functions as a kind of *mantra*, a formula whose potency resides in its utterance or in the reception of its sound vibrations. The Devī offers another explanation as to how or why this sonic rite is efficacious when she points out that it produces an auspicious state of mind (DM 12.23–24).

The historical development of Durgā worship, from early Vedic references and mantric utterances to its elaboration in the DM, has some parallels with the Buddhist Prajñāpāramitā literature. The Prajñāpāramitā *sūtra*s, emerging around the 1st century BCE, were composed in varying lengths, often named by their verse count. For instance, the *Aṣṭasāhasrikā* contains 8000 verses, the *Pañcaviṃśatisāhasrikā* has 25,000, and the *Saptaśatikā Prajñāpāramitā Sūtra* mirrors the 700 verses of the *Durgā Saptaśati* and the BG, indicating the symbolic significance of this number in both Hindu and Buddhist traditions.

The 13th-century Maharashtrian poet Jñāneśvara explicitly connects these texts in his *Bhāvārthadīpikā* (*Jñāneśvarī*), a verse commentary on the BG. He writes, "The Gītā is like the goddess Bhagavatī whose praises are sung in the seven hundred hymns of the Saptashati scripture and who, by joyfully slaying Mahiṣa, the demon of illusion, brought about his liberation" (*Jñāneśvarī* v. 1645) (Pradhān 1987, 641). Jñāneśvara links the BG and DM thematically, both emphasizing liberation — through the destruction of Mahiṣa or the dissolution of delusion. Jñāneśvara also asserts that the BG condenses the 125,000 verses of the Mbh, which themselves encapsulate the Vedas (*Jñāneśvarī* v. 1640). He identifies Sañjaya's concluding words in the BG as its essence (v. 1641). Expanding the BG into 9033 verses, Jñāneśvara mirrors its 18-chapter structure. Jñāneśvara's commentary reveals that by the 13th century, the DM was widely recognized as the (*Durgā*) *Saptaśati*.

The *Prajñāpāramitāhṛdaya Sūtra*, or *Heart Sūtra*, condenses the essence of the larger Prajñāpāramitā *sūtra*s into just sixteen sentences. Often likened to a *dhāraṇī* — a mnemonic device encapsulating complex teachings — it concludes with the well-known mantric dhāraṇī: *[Om] gate gate pāragate pārasaṃgate bodhi svāhā* ("[Om] Gone! Gone! Gone beyond! Gone beyond all gones! Awakening! Verily!"). This encapsulation is emblematic of Tantric traditions, which condense extensive metaphysical teachings, such as the entirety of the Vedas, into succinct mantras, such as Huṃ or Phaṭ.

The DM emphasizes the benefits of both reciting and hearing the text, bolstering its authority by placing these assurances in the Goddess's own words. Its incorporation into the MārkP further cemented its efficacy and longevity. While no single verse explicitly summarizes the DM's substance, various verses are cited for specific purposes today. Notably, the verse inscribed on the Dadhimatī Mātā temple (similar to DM 11.9) has gained particular prominence and remains recited in ritual contexts. There are variants in how it is translated, but it may be translated thus:

> O Śivā! You, the accomplisher of all ends, are the auspiciousness in all things auspicious.
> O three-eyed Gaurī! You are a refuge! O Nārāyaṇī, salutations to you!

What stands out in this verse is the association of the Goddess — through the names Gaurī (and Śivā) and Nārāyaṇī — with both the major male deities, Śiva and Viṣṇu respectively. Moreover, the Devī's firm association with auspiciousness and her qualities as a refuge and a granter of all aims are highlighted. This verse also undercuts the capacity for the Goddess to be simply subsumed within the persona of a spouse deity such as Gaurī or Lakṣmī. She is Śivā (like Śiva) and Nārāyaṇī (like Nārāyaṇa/Viṣṇu).

The Devī in the DM asserts that a single audible recitation pleases her as much as a year of continuous *pūjās*, performed day and night (DM 12.19–21). This hyperbolic yet significant statement elevates textual recitation above traditional *pūjā* practices. *Pūjā*, often regarded as democratizing religious worship, made devotion accessible across social classes and genders, requiring no elaborate rites or knowledge of Sanskrit. It offered a simple mode of worship with nominal offerings or a concluding verse of praise. However, temple-centered *pūjās*, particularly those involving Brahmin priests, incorporated rituals such as feeding Brahmins, fire-oblations, and animal sacrifices. The DM's emphasis on Sanskritic textual recitation reasserts the primacy of the Brahminical sphere, privileging the upper three *varṇas* eligible to learn Sanskrit.

This shift is reflected in the recipients of the story: Suratha, a *kṣatriya*, and Samādhi, a *vaiśya*. Furthermore, the DM challenges temple-centric religion by stating that wherever the *Māhātmya* is audibly recited, that place becomes the Devī's permanent abode (*āyatana*) (DM 12.8). This revolutionary claim allows for the establishment of sacred spaces through sincere recitation alone, bypassing the elaborate installations traditionally requiring Brahmin ritualists. While not negating the sanctity of established temples, this allows for new *āyatana*s to be created in diverse settings, such as riverbanks and forests, simply through the act of audible recitation.

The popularity of the DM, along with its composition and prescriptions, suggests a movement to democratize worship, countering Brahmin-controlled temple-based ritualism. *Kṣatriyas* and *vaiśyas* could worship the Devī independently. Notably, the text does not exclude women or others, often disenfranchised from studying Sanskrit, from benefitting by simply hearing its recitation. While *pūjā* opened the *bhakti* path to liberation for women and lower classes, the *Māhātmya*, addressed primarily to men, diminishes *pūjā*'s efficacy compared to Sanskrit recitation, which was typically an elite rite accessible to educated, twice-born males.

This valorization has influenced practice for over a millennium. Although some women recite the DM, it remains largely a male activity. Temporary shrines (*pandal*) are often constructed for recitations, yet the DM is also recited in stairwells, home shrine rooms, temple premises, or remote settings suited for private *sādhana*. For example, many recite the DM at Banāras' Durgā Kuṇḍa temple during Navarātras, although temple authorities do not host official recitations and priests conduct their own instead. Recitation is largely personal, although Brahmins may be commissioned to perform it on patrons' behalf (Rodrigues 2003). Variations in performance abound, and the text highlights the importance of hearing the DM during the autumn Navarātra, attesting to the antiquity of this festival (DM 12.11). The autumn Navarātra remains the most elaborate Devī celebration among Hindus, with many favoring simple recitations of the DM over temple visits or elaborate *pūjās*.

Extraordinary is the pronouncement that audible recitation of her *Glorification* draws one into the Devī's presence (*sannidhi-kāraka*) (DM 12.19). While this may signify being drawn closer to the Goddess, it uses the same terminology as in the Durgā Pūjā, where the Devī is invoked and established into forms such as an earthen jar or anthropomorphic effigy for worship (Rodrigues 2003, 164). *Bhakti* had already diminished the priest's role as mediator by allowing direct worship wherever the deity was established. However, the expertise required to construct a temple and install a deity into its sanctum remained the domain of the priestly class. The DM disrupts this exclusivity, enabling anyone capable of reciting the text to invoke the Devī's presence, effectively granting them a priestly function.

The *Māhātmya* delineates a distinction between recitation and listening to the *Glorification*. Readers must demonstrate focused concentration (DM 12.1, 12.6, 12.8) and execute the recitation with precision, while listeners are expected to show devotion (DM 12.3, 12.6, 12.11) to gain the promised benefits. Proper recitation (DM 12.8) and the ability to read the entire text (DM 12.19) pose challenges for those unacquainted with Sanskrit. Consequently, the text elevates the status of those proficient in Sanskrit, particularly members of the Brahminical priestly class. Even in contemporary practice, devotees, including Brahmins, often hire skilled reciters (*pāṭha karne vālā*) to perform the text. The high esteem for accurate recitation ensures the continued significance of trained ritualists. However, the DM also emphasizes that anyone with sufficient knowledge or memorization can undertake the recitation. The Devī underscores her fondness for sacrifices, *pūjās*, fire oblations, and her great annual festival (DM 12.9, 12.10), declaring these as pivotal moments for the *Glorification*'s recitation. This highlights the DM's essential role in both individual and collective ritual worship.

The strategic merits of the *Māhātmya* are considerable, as the text prescribes contexts and occasions for its recitation, including specific lunar days and times of adversity. It promises benefits not only to reciters but also to listeners, extending its appeal across a broad audience. This inclusivity, addressing both specialists and non-specialists (*jānatā-ajānatā*, DM 12.10), those literate in Sanskrit and the illiterate, and implicitly both upper and lower classes, positions the text as universally accessible. By guaranteeing success to those in distress, the *Māhātmya* competes with traditions such as Buddhism, which similarly promised liberation from suffering (*duḥkha*, DM 12.15). The *Māhātmya* emphasizes that no philosophical erudition or moral rectitude is required; recalling the Devī's deeds is sufficient to alleviate trouble. The Goddess's aid is particularly highlighted in overcoming enemies and adversity. The text contains a significant phrase: *na teṣām duṣkṛtam kiñcit duṣkṛtotthā na cāpadaḥ* (DM 12.4). This can be interpreted as: "People will be spared not only from wicked deeds (*duṣkṛta*), but also from the consequences (*uttha*) of such deeds [even if they themselves have committed them]." Such a reading underscores the belief, still prevalent today, that the Devī's grace is accessible to all who seek her favor, including those with questionable moral standing, such as brigands.

Notably, the Devī's promises to aid individuals align closely with Durgā's persona as revealed in earlier texts. While Durgā's name appears only eight times in the narrative, she is primarily depicted as protecting from danger and alleviating hardship. This role is precisely how the Devī describes her function in the *Māhātmya*. The text does not elaborate on the mechanisms through which the Devī provides protection, eliminates fears, or resolves problems; it recounts her demon-slaying deeds but does not explicitly state that she will take up arms against an individual's enemies. Instead, it suggests that her might will cause foes to scatter. This portrayal is fully consistent with Durgā's character throughout the *Māhātmya*. The narrative's focus on her protective and problem-resolving nature offers a compelling explanation for why the DM, despite more frequent references to the names Ambikā and Caṇḍikā, is widely known as the *Durgā Saptaśatī*. It also clarifies why Durgā has become the most recognized and pervasive name for the Devī in the Hindu tradition.

Returning to the DM, Medhas continues the narrative by explaining that Caṇḍikā disappeared after uttering those promises. The gods were able to return to their places in the heavens and obtain their rightful shares in the sacrifices, while those demons that survived went back to the underworld (DM 12.30–32). Medhas summarizes some of the Devī's qualities for the benefit of king Suratha and the merchant Samādhi. Even though she is eternal, she manifests repeatedly to protect the world. She deludes the whole universe, and she begets the universe. When entreated (*yācitā*), she grants understanding (*vijñāna*), and when satisfied, she grants prosperity (*ṛddhi*). She pervades the whole creation (*brahmāṇḍa*) and is Mahākālī, in the form of the Great Death (*mahāmārī*) in the great end-time (*mahākāla*). Although unborn and eternal, she is Great Death at one time, becomes the creation, and sustains all created elements at another time. In good times, she is good fortune and prosperity, but she is misfortune during hard times, in order to bring about destruction. When praised and worshipped with flowers, incense, fragrances, and so on, she provides riches, sons, splendid intelligence, and the way to righteousness (DM 12.33–38). This reiterates the Devī's capacity to function as creator, preserver, and destroyer, namely an amalgam of the functions associated with Brahmā, Viṣṇu, and Śiva. In a manner of speaking, the DM or *Glorification* of the Goddess proper ends here, because the story now turns back to the story of the sage Medhas.

The Frame Narrative (Conclusion)

Medhas now brings the discussion back to the original reason he was approached by Suratha and Samādhi. He says that he has finished telling them the *Devī Māhātmya*, and explains that the Goddess, who is the illusory power of Lord Viṣṇu, deludes both of them and other men of discrimination. Others were deluded in the past and yet more will be in the future. Thus, it is wise to take refuge in the queen who grants enjoyment, heaven, and the final goal (*apavarga*) (DM 13.1–4).

The narrative now switches to the broader frame tale told by Mārkaṇḍeya, who explains that when the king and the merchant heard Medhas's story and advice, they set off to perform austerities, intent on receiving a vision of the Mother. Residing on a riverbank, their austerities (*tapas*) consisted of repeating the Supreme Recitation to the Goddess. They set up an image of the Devī made of earth, and offered flowers, incense, fire, and water libations. They did partial and complete fasts, with their minds focused on her, and gave her sacrificial offerings sprinkled with blood from their own limbs. After three years of such worship, Caṇḍikā Jagaddhātrī ("[She who is] the Supporter of the Universe"), pleased, spoke to them before their very eyes (DM 13.5–10). She offered them whatever they wanted. The king opted for a kingdom that would never be overrun even in another birth, as well as the return of his own kingdom after the forceful defeat of his enemies. The merchant, who is described as wise (*prājña*), disgusted with the nature of mind, chose transcendental understanding (*jñāna*), which severs attachment to concepts of "mine" and "I." The Goddess promised that the king would soon slay his enemies and get back his kingdom, and that when reborn he would become the Manu named Sāvarṇi. And as for the merchant, she told him he would receive the transcendental understanding that leads to perfect attainment (*saṃsiddhi*). So saying, she disappeared, and thus Suratha will become the Manu named Sāvarṇi (DM 13.11–17). Thus ends what is traditionally regarded as the *Devī Māhātmya* or *Durgā Saptaśati*.

These concluding sections of the DM reinforce critical aspects of the Devī's persona and her worship. The Devī is portrayed as wielding the power of delusion, enthralling the entire universe, including even those with discriminatory insight (*viveka*). This is particularly significant, as emancipatory philosophies (*darśanas*), such as Buddhism and Yoga, prioritize *viveka* as essential for liberation from false perceptions. However, the *Māhātmya* emphasizes that such liberation is impossible without the Devī's grace. The Devī is the ultimate creator, sustainer, and destroyer of the cosmos, roles traditionally attributed to Brahmā, Viṣṇu, and Śiva. While she is described as Viṣṇu's *māyā*, it is evident by this point that she is not subordinate to him, as that role represents only a fraction of her vast nature. The Devī can grant both worldly and spiritual boons, ranging from enjoyment and heaven — as seen in Suratha's divine rebirth — to spiritual liberation, arguably exemplified by Samādhi's supreme attainment. Achieving such blessings, particularly accompanied by a visible manifestation of the Goddess, demands rigorous and austere devotion. Suratha and Samādhi exemplify this dedication, undergoing three years of fasting, *pūjās*, meditative concentration, and even offerings of their own blood to secure the Devī's direct intervention.

The precise nature of the Supreme Recitation to the Goddess (*devīsūktaṃ paraṃ*) chanted by Suratha and Samādhi is ambiguous. It might refer to the *Ṛg Veda* hymn (10.125) known as the Devī Sūkta, or to one of the hymns addressed to the Goddess within the DM itself, such as those in DM 1 or DM 5. However, it cannot be the complete *Devī Māhātmya* in its current form — the full "700" verses of the *Durgā Saptaśati* — since their story is part of the text. Nevertheless, the DM strongly implies that it is the definitive Supreme Recitation to the Goddess, suitable for achieving her favor. It is reasonable to imagine that Suratha and Samādhi recited the DM as taught to them by Medhas, omitting their own frame narrative.

The use of self-offered blood in their worship is noteworthy, albeit rare today. Iconographic evidence, such as Pallava sculptures (to be discussed later), suggests the historical reality of such practices in certain regions. Similarly, Bāṇa's *Kādambarī* describes a Śabara chieftain whose arms bear scars from offering his own blood. Interestingly, Suratha and Samādhi are not depicted performing animal sacrifices, raising the question of whether the DM, by prioritizing text recitation, diminishes the emphasis on blood offerings. This shift would enable a broader spectrum of worshippers to honor the Devī, from the Brahmins, who specialized in Sanskrit recitation and typically abjured blood sacrifices, to forest-dwelling *caṇḍāla* tribes, where such practices were traditional. By doing so, the DM frames the Goddess in a way that accommodates her veneration across the full expanse of Hindu society.

The DM notably refrains from prioritizing *mokṣa* over more mundane desires, such as security, friendship, wealth, or power, aligning with the Śākta and nondual Tantric philosophy embedded in the text. As the ultimate controller of all existence, the Devī governs both desire and liberation. She simultaneously deludes and liberates, asserting that freedom from delusion is not within the control of any individual. This directly challenges self-reliant meditative paths to liberation, such as Vedānta, Yoga, Buddhism, and Jainism. Even men of great discrimination, as well as powerful gods and demons, are vulnerable to the Goddess's deluding power. Liberation under the Devī's framework is inherently paradoxical. It entails awareness of and unity with Absolute Reality, which is none other than the Goddess herself, the Supreme Matrix of Phantasmal Reality (Mahāmāyā). This realization reveals that the ultimate reality is, paradoxically, phantasmal in nature. The Goddess's ambivalence toward a person's world-affirming (*pravṛtti*) or world-denying (*nivṛtti*) aspirations has been previously acknowledged (e.g., Kinsley 1978; Balkaran 2018), but there is a deeper nuance to this portrayal. The text designates the merchant as wise, and significantly, he does not request *mokṣa*. Instead, the Devī grants him transcendent knowledge, leading to *saṃsiddhi* (perfect attainment), a state arguably distinct from *mokṣa*. These metaphysical dimensions of the Devī's nature point to Tantric notions of realization that transform one into an adept (*siddha*).[47] This subtle differentiation underscores the unique philosophical position of the DM within Hindu thought.

As an aside, the story of king Suratha is elaborated upon in subsequent *kāvya* works, such as the 13th century CE *Surathotsava* and the *Durgāvilāsa*. The former is a poetic retelling of the DM, with a focus on Suratha, although it also subsumes the Devī within Śaivism by equating her with Pārvatī. It expands upon the DM's discussion of Suratha's ascetic practices in an episode where Durgā manifests an irresistible temptress to test the king's dedication. He manages to stay focused and the phantom woman is forced to vanish after her defeat, at which point the Devī manifests to grant Suratha his wishes. In the *Durgāvilāsa*, Suratha creates a city of wonders after he successfully regains his kingdom through Durgā's help (Sarkar 2018b).

Chapter 9

Analyzing the Predicted Manifestations

The Devī's concluding response in the *Devī Māhātmya* (DM), foretelling her future manifestations, offers key insights. She predicts circumstances requiring her appearance to defeat demons, a behavior traditionally associated with Viṣṇu's descents or *avatāra* (from *ava-tṛ*). This alignment with Viṣṇu elevates her status, framing her as equivalent in the cosmic order. The sequence of her predicted manifestations is equally revealing. This chapter utilizes this framework to examine the histories and development of these earlier goddess cults that the DM amalgamated into the Devī's persona, highlighting the synthesis of diverse traditions into a unified vision of the Great Goddess. The manifestations are as Nidrā (not named, but implied), as Raktadantikā, as Śatākṣī, Śākambharī, and Durgā, arguably in the same context, as Bhīmā Devī, and as Bhrāmarī. The goddesses Śatākṣī, Śākambharī, and Durgā will be examined in the greatest detail, not just because they concern Durgā, but because the ambiguities concerning the persona of Śatākṣī point to a variety of previously discussed relationships, such as to the peacock. This provides a segue into an examination of goddess worship among Indigenous tribes, who were likely key contributors to the development of Durgā's cult. Although Durgā is just one named manifestation in the DM, her eventual identification as the Devī makes these references to divine interventions critical for understanding Durgā's broader evolution and enduring prominence.

The Manifestations

As Nidrā?

The DM situates the slaying of Śumbha and Niśumbha in the distant past, even for its audience, while also prophesying the future defeat of an identically named demon pair during the twenty-eighth *yuga* of the Vaivasvata Manvantara — the current cosmic era. King Suratha and the merchant Samādhi are described as living in the Svārociṣa Manvantara (DM 1.3), long before the Vaivasvata.

Medhas recounts these ancient events to them, further emphasizing the deep temporal layers of the narrative.

The Devī's prophesied birth through Yaśodā in the house of Nanda (DM 11.37–38) links her to the Kṛṣṇa Gopāla myth cycle. This connection implies that the DM's account of the Śumbha-Niśumbha battle predates the Kṛṣṇa/Kaṃsa/Nidrā episode, during which she later resides in the Vindhyas. The DM strategically locates her battle with Śumbha and Niśumbha on the Himālayan peaks, distinguishing it from her later Vindhyan associations and preserving the integrity of multiple mythic traditions. The *Harivaṃśa* (HV) had referred to the Devī's battle with Śumbha and Niśumbha, identifying her as Nidrā within the Kṛṣṇa birth-myth cycle and subordinating her to Viṣṇu. Evidently aware of this, the DM undermines this narrative, framing the Kṛṣṇa/Nidrā myth as a minor episode within the Devī's larger cosmic persona. Although acknowledging the HV's effort to subordinate the goddess to Viṣṇu, the DM reasserts her supremacy by presenting Nidrā as merely one manifestation of the Great Goddess, from whom all gods, including Viṣṇu, derive their power. By situating the Śumbha-Niśumbha battle in a prior cosmic framework and by tacitly linking Nidrā to Kauśikī of the Praise of Nidrā (First Stratum) (PN-s1) hymn in the *Harivaṃśa* (HV), the DM preserves and elevates the Devī's status as the ultimate source of power and divinity. This allows the DM to integrate the Kṛṣṇa birth-myth while maintaining the Devī's independent cosmic sovereignty.

As Raktadantikā

The goddess Raktadantikā ("[She who is] Red Toothed"), another predicted manifestation in the DM, is relatively obscure. She is described as devouring the Vaipracitta demons, causing her teeth to turn red like pomegranate flowers (DM 11.39–41). The Vaipracitta demons are presumably the offspring of the demon Vipracitti, father of Rāhu. However, little additional literary evidence exists about these demons, or a distinct cult associated with Raktadantikā. She is currently venerated symbolically as the pomegranate in the Durgā Pūjā, where the fruit is part of a cluster of nine plants called the Navapattrikā/Navapatrikā (see Rodrigues 2003, 45–46, 179–84). Her red teeth associate her with fierce goddesses who accept blood sacrifices. It remains unclear whether her inclusion in the Navapattrikā reflects worship traditions predating the DM or if it was influenced by the text.

Pomegranate seeds, resembling red teeth, give the fruit names such as *dantabīja* ("tooth-seed") and *raktabīja* ("blood-seed"), the latter akin to the demon slain by Kālī in the DM. Cultivated since antiquity, the pomegranate features prominently in various mythologies. In Homer's *Odyssey*, it is cultivated in the gardens of the Phaeacians and Phrygians. The fruit is also associated with Greek and Roman goddesses, such as Hera/Juno and Aphrodite/Venus, and notably with the Phrygian goddess Matar Kubileya (Greek: Kybele), whose inscriptions date to the 6th century BCE (Vassileva 2001, 51–64). Phrygia, in Anatolia (modern-day Turkey), linked Matar Kubileya to mountains, as her name translates to "Mother Goddess, She of the Mountains" (Roller 1999, 67–68), akin to the Sanskrit Mā Pārvatī.

A Greek myth involving the pomegranate provides an intriguing parallel. Dionysius castrated the demon Agdistis, whose blood and severed genitals were absorbed by the earth, giving rise to a pomegranate tree (in some versions, an almond tree). The river-god Sangarius' daughter, attracted to the fruit, concealed it in her lap and mysteriously became pregnant with Attis, portrayed as either a handsome youth or a he-goat (Kerényi 1960, 89–90). These myths share symbolic resonances with the Devī's portrayal in the DM, particularly her association with mountains and the earth. Kybele, an earth goddess, consumes Agdistis's severed organs, giving rise to the pomegranate tree, paralleling the Devī's cosmic and fertile aspects, as discussed in the next manifestation. As Yokochi (2004, 24) speculates, Hellenistic goddess cults, such as those of Nanaia (Nanā) and Kybele, may have influenced the evolution of South Asian goddess traditions. These interconnections provide fertile ground for further exploration of cross-cultural exchanges shaping goddess worship, some of which we have examined in this study.

As Śatākṣī, Śākambharī, and Durgā

Since these three goddesses Śatākṣī, Śākambharī, and Durgā are connected in the DM, we should examine them in substantial detail. They are mentioned as if the names emerged from slightly different exploits and manifestations of the Goddess, but in the same time period (DM 11.42–46).

The goddess Śatākṣī ("[She who has a] Hundred Eyes") does not appear in known literature prior to her mention in the DM. Her name is a feminine adaptation of an epithet traditionally associated with Indra. In *Ṛg Veda* 10.161, *sahasrākṣa* is usually translated as "thousand-eyed," although Griffith renders it as "hundred-eyed," possibly because while *sahasra* generally means "thousand," it can also merely signify a large number. In the PN-s1 in HV 47.46, Indra is referred to as "hundred-eyed" (*śatadṛk śakra*), linking him to the goddess Nidrā. In this context, Indra and other gods install Nidrā into the divine pantheon and accept her as a sister.

The Praise of Nidrā (Second Stratum) (PN-s2, Āryā Stava), inserted into some versions of the HV, identifies the goddess as "thousand-eyed" (*sahasranayaneti*). The DM composer, while likely familiar with the PN-s1 and the broader Kṛṣṇa/Kaṃsa/Nidrā myth cycle, either chose to omit the "thousand-eyed" epithet or adapted it to align with a distinct goddess cult associated with the name Śatākṣī. It is also possible that "Śatākṣī" simply implies "abundant eyes," emphasizing vigilance and cosmic insight, without specifying a literal number. This selective use of "hundred-eyed" rather than "thousand-eyed" suggests an intentional divergence from the PN-s2 account or an effort to integrate a preexisting cult of Śatākṣī into the theological framework of the DM.

The HV also derives a rationale for the goddess's name, Kauśikī, as related to Indra's lineage, since Indra is sometimes known as Kauśika, through his descent from Kuśika. The developing Vaiṣṇava/Kṛṣṇaite tradition, as expressed in the HV, clearly articulates its subordination of the Vedic supremacy of Indra. This stands out in the story of Kṛṣṇa lifting Mount Govardhana, wherein Kṛṣṇa demonstrates his superiority over the power of the god of the rainclouds. Kṛṣṇa protects people from the torrential rains and flooding unleashed by Indra.[48] Thus, by linking the goddess Kauśikī/Nidrā with Indra, the HV tacitly attempts to subordinate the goddess Nidrā to Viṣṇu.

The DM counters earlier Vaiṣṇava attempts to associate the Devī with Indra, offering alternative interpretations. The DM derives the name Kauśikī from *kośa* ("sheath"), explaining that Ambikā is so named because she emerged from Pārvatī's bodily sheath. While this etymology appears contrived, it is no more so than the HV's account, where Indra anoints Nidrā, installs her into her divine role, and takes her as his sister. The DM instead attributes the name Śatākṣī to the Goddess's act of gazing upon sages with a hundred eyes, dissociating her from any familial connection with the hundred-eyed Indra. This reinterpretation also tacitly undermines Indra's association with the paradigmatic Vedic struggle against Vṛtra, the "binder." Indra's battle with Vṛtra, once emblematic of the cosmic conflict between gods and *asuras*, loses prominence as other divine victories emerge in popular narratives. By the time of the DM's composition, Viṣṇu's triumphs as the Boar and Man-Lion *avatāras*, as well as Kṛṣṇa's defeats of various demons, dominate the mythological landscape. The DM situates the Devī within this evolving tradition, emphasizing her unique victories over demons and further diminishing Indra's mythic relevance.

Ṛg Veda (RV) 1.32 narrates Indra's conquest of drought by defeating Vṛtra, the demon who binds the cosmic waters. Indra, wielding the *vajra* and associated with thunder and lightning, releases these waters and ends the destructive grip of drought. The goddess Śatākṣī, however, counters drought in a markedly different way. Rather than bringing rain, she sustains life by generating vegetables directly from her body. These life-sustaining vegetative forms, not born from a womb, affirm her as Śākaṃbharī ("[She who] Supports with Vegetables"). This highlights the possibility of survival on vegetarian sustenance, implicitly elevating plant-based life as a divine provision over non-vegetarian food (i.e., life that emerges from a womb).

In a broader context, parallels may be drawn with the rise of the Chinese goddess Xi Wangmu (Queen Mother of the West), whose cult briefly waxed large during a severe drought around 3 BCE. This apocalyptic movement, characterized by ecstatic singing, dancing, zealous proselytizing, and the passing of grain stalks, reflects how goddess worship often became a refuge during times of crisis, such as droughts (Monaghan 2011, 148). While speculative, these behaviors suggest a possible cultural exchange via the Silk Road or parallel developments in goddess worship on the Indian subcontinent. The imagery of the Chandraketugarh goddess, depicted in clay tablets from the same period with stalks of grain adorning her hair, provides additional context. While I have suggested in earlier chapters that this goddess might represent the river deity Kauśikī, the association with grain and sustenance also opens the possibility that she was venerated as Śākambharī. However, our knowledge of Śākambharī prior to the DM is limited, leaving much of her earlier history obscured.

A city named Śākambharī (near Sambhar, an inland salt lake in Jaipur State, Rajasthan) served as the capital of the Chawhān (Chauhan, Cāhamāna) kings in the 11th and 12th centuries CE, highlighting the likely prominence of the goddess Śākambharī during the period of the DM's composition (Jackson 2003, 9). James Tod, an officer of the British East India Company, documented Rajasthan's history and geography in his *Annals and Antiquities of Rajast'han*, published in two volumes. Although later criticized for inaccuracies due to its reliance on bardic legends and personal observations, the work remains a key scholarly resource.

Tod recounted legends connecting Sambhar Lake to the Cāhamānas. Their lineage was said to begin with Māṇikya Rāya (Manik Rae), lord of Ajmer and Sambhar, who rose to power during the first Islamic invasion of Rajputana (Rajasthan). During this invasion, his brother Dula Rāya and Dula's seven-year-old son, Lot, were killed in battle when Dula was prince of Ajmer. The Muslims are referred to as Asuras in Tod's account. After Amber fell in 684/5 CE, Manik Rae sought refuge at Sambhar Lake, where the goddess Śākambharī appeared and granted him sovereignty over the land he could encircle in a day's ride. This area transformed into the salt-lake named after the goddess, whose statue stood on an island in the lake during Tod's time.

Manik Rae reclaimed the city of Ajmer, and his descendants, called Sambri Rao in honor of Śākambharī, formed minor dynasties. Battles with Muslim forces, detailed in Islamic chronicles, saw victories and defeats on both sides (Tod 1884, 485–92). For instance, Hursraj, a descendant who ruled from 756 to 771 CE and earned the title *ari-mardana* (crusher of the enemy) for his military successes, ultimately fell in battle to the "Asuras" (Tod 1884, 491). Tod's account, while requiring caution in interpretation, aligns Manik Rae's refuge at Sambhar Lake with the goddess Śākambharī, with the DM's portrayal of Durgā as a protector of kings, as seen in the tale of King Suratha. It underscores Durgā/Śākambharī's enduring role as a divine refuge and benefactor.

Although many scholars have typically dated the DM to the 5th, 6th, or 7th centuries, I will later argue for other compelling reasons that it was composed closer to the middle of the 8th century CE.[49] Previous scholarship accepting earlier dates for the composition of the DM could not account for the historical reality of foreign invasions into Rajasthan. A mid-8th century date for the DM recognizes that northwest India, in the century prior, was embroiled in conflicts with Muslim invaders, reportedly referred to as Asuras, based on Tod's account. Demonizing adversaries is a common wartime trope, and bardic tales of Rajput kings such as Dula Rāya, their defeats, and their subsequent victories under the banner of goddesses such as Śākambharī may have inspired the DM's narrative. The regional prominence of goddess cults in north-central and northwest India, shaped by tutelary deities such as Anāhitā, Nike, Nanā, Jayā, Vijayā, Durgā, Kālī, Kālarātri, Nidrā, and Kauśikī — worshipped and patronized by Hindu rulers who fought under their banners — likely contributed to the rise of the Goddess as the Supreme Deity associated with sovereignty and resistance to non-Hindu invaders. This theme will be revisited later in this study.

The name Śākambharī appears as early as the Durgā Stotra (DSto) (l. 17), where she is addressed together with Umā, and with the epithet, "destroyer of Kaiṭabha." Significantly, there follow various descriptors referring to her eyes ("O you of gold eyes (*hiraṇyākṣī*), deformed eyes (*virūpākṣī*), smoky eyes (*sudhūmrākṣī*)") (DSto, l. 18). Importantly, the term *virūpa* can mean many-colored, manifold, and even various, not just misshapen. Thus, it would not be unusual for the author of the DM to connect the name Śatākṣī ("[She who has a] Hundred Eyes") with Śākambharī.

The Devī's vegetative associations persist today. She is worshipped as Vana Durgā ("Durgā of the Forest") and invoked during the Durgā Pūjā ritual through a wood-apple (*bilva*) tree. She is also honored in the form of a cluster of nine plants (Navapattrikā), including plantain (*rambhā*), edible arum (*kacvī*), turmeric (*haridrā*), the *jayantī* creeper, wood-apple, pomegranate (*dāḍima/ī*), Aśoka, Māna, and rice paddy (*dhanyā*). Each plant represents a goddess, and together they embody Durgā, reflecting qualities such as nutrition, medicinal value, or symbolic resemblance to the goddess. During Navarātra, the nine-day festival for the Devī, blood sacrifices often occur, particularly at the conjunction of the eighth and ninth day, paralleling the HV's account of Nidrā receiving monthly blood offerings. Today, symbolic vegetable substitutes for blood sacrifices are common. These offerings, such as bananas, sugarcane, coconuts, or rice and lentils, often symbolize the demon slain by the Devī. The Kuṣmāṇḍā melon is a widely recognized substitute, reflecting the Devī's vegetative aspects (Rodrigues 2005, 2009).

This melon, which belongs to the Cucurbitaceae family, includes *Benincasa hispida* (Thunb.) Cogn. and other *Benincasa* varieties.[50] Widely cultivated and collected from the wild across India, the Kuṣmāṇḍā melon, also known in the West as winter melon or ash gourd, thrives on rainfall and is prized for its nutritional and medicinal properties. In Ayurveda, it is called Śreṣṭhaphala, the supreme fruit. With its waxy exterior, the melon has a long shelf life of four months or more, sometimes lasting over a year, making it invaluable during droughts or famines. Its numerous seeds, often described as eyes, are consumed for their medicinal benefits, such as treating worms. Symbolically, the term Kuṣmāṇḍā also refers to a womb just before gestation, evoking the image of a fully pregnant woman or fetus. These qualities make the Kuṣmāṇḍā melon an apt vegetative representative of the goddess Śatākṣī/Śākambharī.

Virtually any plant that provides sustenance could arguably be seen as a form of the Devī, embodying the concept of Hundred-Eyed through their seeds and replication. Śatākṣī could also symbolize the vast diversity of vegetation and its link to agriculture, highlighting the Devī's role in supporting life. During the drought referenced in the DM, survival was possible because storable, edible food sustained people and livestock — she supports the entire world (DM 11.44). This connection to survival through hardship extends to regional beliefs linking goddesses such as Śītalā and Kālī to diseases such as smallpox. In some traditions, Kālī, afflicted with smallpox as Vasūrimālā ("Garland of Pox"), scatters pox "seeds" into villages (Aiyappan 1931, 291–93). Just as disease can be seeded in hardship, the goddess, through "seeds/eyes" such as legumes, grains, and fruits, enables survival.

Since the Devī is described as gazing down on the sages/monks/devotees (*muni*) with a hundred eyes, her name "Hundred-Eyes" also has resonances with deities such as the Buddhist celestial bodhisattva Avalokiteśvara, who is often portrayed as having a hundred, a thousand, or a hundred thousand arms to reach out and help beings in distress. Avalokiteśvara means "The Lord who Looks [Down Compassionately]."[51] As his cult migrated to China and other parts of East Asia, Avalokiteśvara was transformed into the goddess Guanyin (Kannon in Japan), arguably reflecting a tendency to regard these qualities of benevolent intercession on behalf of creatures as a feminine trait, or offering a more appealing form to female devotees.[52] Although Avalokiteśvara is identified as looking down with compassion, the deity is more commonly depicted with many arms for helping than with many eyes for seeing. However, Avalokiteśvara is also described as possessing a hundred, a thousand, or even a hundred thousand eyes, with some depictions showing eyes in the palms of their hands. A notable example is the thousand-handed Avalokiteśvara in the Dazu grottoes at Chongqing, China, from the Southern Song Dynasty (1127–1279 CE), where each of the over one thousand arms has an eye in its palm. Śatākṣī epitomizes the ability to observe and respond to the suffering of all beings, aligning with this iconography of compassion and assistance.

The DM's use of the term *muni* is significant, stating that when remembered by *munis*, the Devī will manifest without being born from a womb (*ayonijā*). As she looks down (*nirīkṣyāmi*) at the *munis* with a hundred eyes, she will be called Śatākṣī (DM 11.42–43). While *muni* typically refers to sages from any tradition, particularly enlightened ones, there may be Buddhist resonances here. Siddhārtha Gautama, known as Śakyamuni ("Sage of the Śakyas"), shares this designation with his monks and other renouncers. The notion of the Devī's non-womb manifestation parallels the extraordinary births of figures such as Draupadī, born from fire, and the Buddha, who, in Sanskrit traditions, is said to emerge from Māyā's right side (*dakṣiṇa pārśva*), diverging from earlier Pāli accounts suggesting a more conventional birth (Hara 1989, 67–79). In Purāṇic explanations, conventional births render beings susceptible to Viṣṇu's *māyā*, which obscures their will and transcendental awareness (*jñāna*) (Hara 1989, 73).

There has been a long-standing identification on the Indian subcontinent of the feminine principle with trees and other forms of vegetation, arguably stretching as far back as the Indus Valley civilization. Siddhārtha Gautama's mother, named Māyā Devī or Mahāmāyā, is often portrayed in iconography as holding the branch of a Śāl tree when giving birth to him. This imagery resonates with the depictions of the so-called Yakṣī images of the same period (discussed in an earlier chapter). The Buddha's mother, Mahāmāyā, is thus symbolically linked to such *yakṣīs* or goddesses associated with trees.[53] Recent excavations and radiocarbon dating of postholes at the Māyā Devī temple in Lumbini, reputed as the Buddha's birthplace, suggest that the site may have been a tree shrine long predating Aśoka's reign (Coningham et al. 2013). This aligns with the Buddhist tradition of tree worship, seen at sites such as Bodhgaya and Anuradhapura, where the bodhi-tree remains central to veneration. Such *bodhigaras* (bodhi tree shrines) were often later accompanied or supplanted by temples housing images, yet tree shrines were significant worship sites long before Buddhism. Many of these likely centered on local goddesses, generically referred to as *yakṣīs* in Buddhist and other traditions.

The case of the Māyā Devī temple underscores the historical interplay between goddess worship and Buddhism. The parallels between Durgā's salvific persona in the DM and her role as a refuge for beings raise questions about the coincidental alignment of Durgā's epithet Mahāmāyā in the DM and the Buddha's mother's name, Māyā Devī or Mahāmāyā. Does the legendary story of the Buddha's birth from Mahāmāyā, and her death shortly thereafter, symbolically point to a tension between Buddhism's promotion of self-reliant liberation from illusion and devotion to the Supreme Matrix of Phantasmal Reality, Mahāmāyā, without whose intercession no liberation is possible?[54]

More Connections to the Peacock

Another intriguing connection to the term Śatākṣī lies in its reference to the peacock, famously called Hundred-Eyed for the eye-like patterns on its plumage. The PN-s1 mentions that the goddess Nidrā is associated with a standard or flag adorned with peacock feathers and wears bracelets made of them. In Greek mythology, the peacock is linked to the goddess Hera (Monaghan 2004, 62), who, although often portrayed as Zeus's spouse, originally appears as an independent Great Goddess akin to the Devī. In one myth, Hera assigns Argus, the hundred-eyed guardian, to watch over Io, Zeus's lover, transformed by him into a cow. When Hermes slays Argus, Hera transfers his eyes to the peacock's tail, her favorite bird (Nair 1974, 105). Hera's other symbols include the cow, cuckoo, lion, pomegranate, and poppy, and she is also often regarded as a virgin.

The parallels between Hera and Nidrā/Kauśikī are compelling. While the Argus and Io myth appears on Athenian red-figure pottery from the 6th century BCE and in plays by Aeschylus (*Prometheus Bound*) and Euripides (*Phoenician Women*) from the 5th century BCE, the Roman poet Ovid's *Metamorphoses* (1.722, c. 1st century CE) narrates the transfer of Argus' eyes to the peacock. In Roman mythology, Hera, known as Juno or Saturnia, drives a chariot pulled by peacocks (*Metamorphoses* 2.531–35). The Greeks were largely unfamiliar with the peacock — native to Asia — until Alexander's incursions into India (Miller 1997, 189–92, 311). This Hellenistic encounter may have facilitated an exchange of myths and symbols, including the association of Śatākṣī with the peacock.

Śatākṣī's links to the peacock extend beyond Hellenic influence. Indra, to whom Śatākṣī is symbolically connected, also has ties to the bird. In RV 8.1.25 and *Yajur Veda* 20.53, Indra's steeds are described as having tails like peacock plumes, and in the *Uttarakāṇḍa* (XVIII) of the *Rāmāyaṇa*, Indra transforms into a peacock to escape Rāvaṇa's wrath. Previous chapters have discussed the Devī's connections to the peacock, such as the peacock standard and bracelets mentioned in epic hymns. Here, the symbolic resonance of the peacock with Śatākṣī further underscores the Devī's multifaceted persona and her integration of varied cultural and mythological influences.

As far as the vestiges of Śatākṣī/Kauśikī/Nidrā's peacock-related cult beyond India go, the Japanese deity Kujaku Myôô, or Mahāmāyurī ("Great Peacock"), is noteworthy. Portrayed as benevolent and compassionate, Kujaku Myôô is typically depicted seated on a lotus throne atop a peacock, holding a peacock feather in one of his four arms. The term Myôô corresponds to the Sanskrit Vidyārāja ("King of Knowledge"), and Kujaku signifies a peacock. In addition to the peacock feather, Kujaku Myôô holds a lotus flower and two fruits in his other hands — one being a Bījapūraka ("Filled with Seed"), a type of citron, and the other the Fruit of Happiness (Hackin 1963, 436). The Bījapūraka has intriguing connections to the pomegranate ("seed-apple") and to the term Śatākṣī, particularly if one considers seeds as "eyes." Thus, the juxtaposition of a seed-filled fruit and the peacock strongly resonates with Śatākṣī's symbolic associations.

Kujaku Myôô is propitiated for protection from dangers, particularly during droughts, further aligning with Śatākṣī's characterization in the DM. Evidence of Kujaku Myôô's worship during Japan's Heian period (7th–8th centuries CE) coincides with the period just before the estimated composition of the DM. This suggests a possible continuity or parallel evolution of peacock and pomegranate-associated goddess cults, reflecting their enduring significance across cultural and geographic boundaries.

These Buddhist Tantric deities, associated with Shingon forms of Japanese Tantrism, were often adaptations of Hindu deities, sometimes changing gender as they migrated from India via China to Japan, as evinced in the case of Avalokiteśvara/Kuan-yin/Kannon, discussed earlier. In India, Mahāmāyurī is a Buddhist goddess, and protector of the Dharma (G. Malandra 1993, 96 ff.) Mahāmāyurī first appears in iconography at the cave complex of Ellora in India's state of Maharashtra. In the antechamber of Cave 6, she stands in *samapada-sthānaka* posture upon a lotus flower. She holds a peacock feather in her upraised right hand and a fruit in her left. There is a peacock carved to her immediate right. In the foreground there is a scribe seated at a table.[55] She is attended to by a smaller female figure. This may be her earliest extant iconographic representation. In Cave 8, she is depicted in much the same manner, but there are two flying figures that face her. The worship of Mahāmāyurī can be traced through textual evidence to at least the early 6th century CE, and she was propitiated for protection against poison, especially snakebite. Kujaku Myôô's identification as one of the Vidyārājas also evokes a link with the Devī, who personifies knowledge (*vidyā*). In the sculpture of Odisha, Mahāmāyurī may appear in groupings with Avalokiteśvara or Tārā, both of whom are Buddhist bodhisattvas characterized by their salvific natures (Donaldson 2001, 251, 254, 270, 346).

Within the context of Buddhist appropriations of Hindu deities, or their mutual interactive development, a four-armed form of Tārā, known as Durgottāriṇī Tārā ("Tārā who Transports across Arduous Paths"), offers a compelling parallel to the Hindu Durgā. Described in the *Sādhanamālā* (*Garland of [Effective] Methods*), a Tantric compendium detailing deities for meditative purposes, Durgottāriṇī Tārā is green-complexioned, clothed in white garments, and seated atop a lotus. She wields a noose, a goad, and a lotus in three hands, with her fourth hand bestowing boons through the *varada mudrā* (B. Bhattacharyya 1958, 307). Referred to as Mahāyogeśvarī, her *mantra*s are said to remove sorrow, dispel troubles, and liberate from imprisonment, bondage, and the influence of the *grahas* (luminary "graspers") (Donaldson 2001, 254; M. Ghosh 1980, 54).

An image from the 9th century, housed in the Indian Museum in Kolkata and originating from Lalitagiri in Odisha, depicts her holding a mythic blue lotus (*nīlotpala*) and a noose, adorned with a prominent hairdo and tiara (Donaldson 2001, 255). The *Sādhanamālā*, dated between the 5th and 12th centuries CE, suggests the increasing prominence of the word *durgā* during this period, with its application extending to Buddhist bodhisattvas and female Buddhas such as Tārā. The Buddhist counterparts of Durgā, including Tārā and Avalokiteśvara, share significant attributes with the Hindu Durgā: the removal of sorrow, liberation from bondage, and the granting of boons. Early Hindu textual traditions also align Durgā with the concept of refuge, often likened to a boat or raft enabling safe passage across treacherous waters. This overlap underscores the shared thematic framework and cross-cultural integration between Hindu and Buddhist traditions during this era.

Another intriguing connection between Śatākṣī and the peacock arises through the enigmatic name Kauśikī, which has various imaginative etymological interpretations. Kauśikī, the feminine form of the Sanskrit *kauśika*, refers to a snake catcher and could therefore denote creatures such as owls or pea-cocks. The peacock, believed to consume snakes and remain immune to their venom, ties symbolically to Kauśikī's potential attributes. Folklore also links the peacock's cry and dance to drought and the advent of rain — both themes closely associated with Śatākṣī. A Kuṣāṇa sculpture from the 2nd century CE, currently housed in the National Museum in New Delhi, provides further visual connections. Identified as Śrī Devī due to her stance atop a vase overflowing with lotuses (Lal 2006, 40), this figure intriguingly features an armlet shaped like a dancing peacock. This detail suggests a possible link to Nidrā/Kauśikī, described in PN-s1 (l. 44) as adorned with peacock-feathered bracelets. Earlier chapters have highlighted numerous instances in early iconography where god-desses are depicted with peacock-feather bracelets and the peacock standard, reinforcing these symbolic connections.

In modern Hinduism, the peacock is linked to the war god Skanda (Murugan), a connection that dates back to the Gupta period (5th century CE). In the DM (8.16), Kaumārī, the *śakti* of Guha (Skanda), is depicted with a peacock as her mount. The peacock is also associated with Sarasvatī, although her typical vehicle is a swan or goose. Kṛṣṇa is often shown with peacock feathers on his crown. Notably, links between the peacock and goddess worship persist in the practices of central India's largest tribal groups. This connection is critical to the story of Durgā worship, as her earliest hymns associate her with forests and mountains, traditional homes of the subcontinent's tribal populations. The PN-s2 (l. 9) explicitly mentions that the goddess is venerated by marginalized hill tribes (*barbara, śabara, pulinda*). No study of Durgā should ignore con-sideration of these groups. To explore this association further, we will examine specific rites among the Gonds and the Khonds, who are a related subgroup. These tribes, speakers of non-Āryan languages, inhabit regions including the Vindhya Mountain range, an area historically central to Durgā's mythos and cult.

Goddess Worship Among Tribals

The Gonds are central India's largest tribe and may be the largest tribal group in South Asia or even the world, with a population exceeding fourteen mil-lion. The Mughals named them Gond ("hill people") due to their mountain-ous habitats. Representing an Indigenous presence predating both Dravidian and Āryan linguistic cultures, their Dravidian language suggests they traversed such linguistic zones before settling in their current region around the 9th to 13th centuries CE. Their primary areas are western Chhattisgarh, eastern Maharashtra, and southern Madhya Pradesh, although they are spread across India and may have been more densely distributed historically. Anthropologists often classify them as Proto-Australoids (Mehta 1984; Fürer-Haimendorf and Fürer-Haimendorf 1979).

The Gonds now worship a variety of deities, such as Bara-deo (Big God, i.e., Śiva, Mahādeva), Budha-deo (i.e., the Buddha), and as well as Devī and Mātā (see Bhagvat 1968, 27–106, which this description follows) indicating their exposure to each of these religious traditions. Lingo is a type of culture-hero. Budha-deo is represented by a stone but has his abode in the Saj tree. Bara-deo is represented by a six-inch-high altar of earth. Devī and Mātā are represented by flags, one black and the other yellow, which interestingly correspond with the colors of the Nidrā's garments, emphasized in the HV account (HV 48.34–35). The black and yellow colors are sometimes associated with the colors of the tiger, or leopard, Sing-deo, who also receives some veneration, although the word "*sing* (i.e., *siṅgha*)" means a lion. A song to Budha-deo, from the Raipur region and sung in the Gondi dialect, asks:

> Of what is the staff made?
> The staff is made of bamboo
> This is the staff of god
> The staff of Mother.
> The cloth-flag,
> Of the Desai Mother,
> The Mother of the village.
> The bunch of peacock feathers
> For the Devi of the garh.
> The Devi of the royal family
> The Devi Deomagaral.
> Dhamkarati Devi
> The god Bar-deo
> The god Budha-deo
> The god Lingo
> And Sing-deo
> Honor to them.

In certain Gond worship rites, men carry yellow and black flags, beat drums, and dance while singing. The next morning, women clean the house with cow-dung, discard old earthen pots, and replace them with new ones. Rice is offered to deity images crafted as described in their songs. The Devī and Mātā are worshipped first. A goat is presented to each deity, and if it eats the grain, the offering is accepted. The goat's throat is then slit, its head offered to the goddesses, and the head and bones buried in an inner room. The festivities include sexually themed songs and licentious behavior by both sexes. Animal sacrifice features prominently in several other rites.

Bhagvat (1968, 47) observes that Gond worship typically prioritizes the Devī over male deities such as Budha-deo and Bara-deo, which he attributes to Hindu influence degrading the original male deity worship. However, the opposite may be true. Although male deities are now considered primary, the songs suggest a longstanding layer of goddess worship alongside them. For example, the cited song focuses more on the Devī (and Mātā) than on the male deities mentioned at its conclusion, even within a festival ostensibly dedicated to a male god. Elements such as peacock feather topped standards, yellow and black flags, and blood sacrifices in these rites evoke parallels with Nidrā/Kauśikī in the HV and the DM's Śatākṣī. These practices persist in thousands of villages today, but studying tribal oral traditions can only suggest and not confirm their continuity from the past.

Similar symbols and practices are found among the Khonds, a subgroup of the Gonds and one of the largest tribes in Odisha. Speaking Kui and Kuwi, both Dravidian languages, the Khonds are particularly known for their animal sacrifices. Until the early 20th century, they also practiced the Meriah, a ritual of human sacrifice extensively documented in early ethnographic studies (Bolle 1983, 37–63). While James Frazer (1984, 384–409) suggested these sacrifices were meant to ensure agricultural success, their underlying rationales were likely more intricate. Adult males were preferred as sacrificial victims, with the stipulation that they be purchased rather than seized, as this absolved the Khonds of any sin associated with the act. Human sacrifice was outlawed in the mid-19th century and substituted with buffalo and other animals, a change the Khonds viewed as a regrettable degradation of the ritual's sanctity (Bolle 1983, 49).

E. Thurston (1906) (in Bolle 1983, 51ff.) provides a vivid account of a Khond sacrificial ritual from 1837, known as the Meriah, after the sacrificial victim. The victim, purchased with brass utensils, cattle, or corn, could not be a criminal or war captive, as the Meriah had to be bought. The *pūjā* was conducted by the Zanee, a priest of any caste, through a child intermediary known as the Toomba, who was under seven years old. For a month prior to the sacrifice, the community engaged in feasting, intoxication, and dancing around the victim. On the eve of the sacrifice, the intoxicated Meriah was seated beneath or bound to a post adorned with a peacock effigy. The community danced and sang to the earth, invoking blessings for crops, seasons, and health. On the sacrificial day, the Meriah, further intoxicated and anointed with oil, was paraded around the village alongside a pole topped with peacock feathers. The procession returned to the post, situated near the village deity Zakaree Pennoo, represented by three stones and a buried brass peacock effigy.

A hog was first sacrificed, its blood filling a pit into which the Meriah was thrown and suffocated amid a cacophony of music. The Zanee cut a piece of the Meriah's flesh and buried it near the peacock effigy as an offering to the earth. Villagers took portions of the flesh to bury near their local deities and village boundaries. The Meriah's head and face were untouched, and the bones were eventually buried in the pit. A buffalo calf followed, its forefeet severed and left near the post. Women, dressed as men and armed, danced and sang around the buffalo before it was killed and eaten. The Zanee priest was dismissed with a gift of a hog or calf and rice. Barbara Boal (1997), based on extensive fieldwork, notes that under British pressure in 1846, the Khonds substituted buffalo for human sacrifice to their supreme god, Bura, and earth goddess, Tari.

However, the ritual's structure retains elements of the older human sacrifice described by earlier observers.

There are some notable parallels between this Khond ritual and what seems to be discussed in the epic hymns and the DM. One wonders if the peculiar, tribal (read, non-Āryan) appearance of groups such as the Khonds, led them to be imagined or portrayed as fearsome spirits (e.g., PN-s1, l. 45, 51), who surrounded the goddess, and who are delighted by offerings of flesh.[56] The Khonds believe in a world teeming with spirits inhabiting various natural domains. In the PN-s2, the goddess is described as venerated by savages, mountain dwellers, and barbarians (l. 9), which could refer to the prominence of goddess worship among tribes such as the Gonds. The Khonds continue to worship an earth goddess under a standard adorned with a peacock effigy and peacock feathers — symbols associated with Nidrā/Kauśikī/Durgā/Kālī in early epic hymns. This goddess is propitiated with sacrifices, originally human and later buffalo. Women play a central role, dancing and singing to music while consuming alcohol, echoing Nidrā's association with intoxicating liquor (*madhu*). The intoxication of the Meriah victim mirrors this element.

The women also dress and arm themselves as men, aligning with the warrior goddess archetype. This imagery is reminiscent of the Devī in the DM, accompanied by warriors as she slays the buffalo demon. The Zanee priest presiding over the *pūjā*, conducting rites through a child intermediary (Toomba), suggests a tribal foundation overlaid with later influences. In alternative rituals, worshippers attack a still-living victim, cutting into his stomach to let the blood flow over the deity's idol. They hack pieces of flesh from the victim, avoiding the head and bowels, and distribute these as offerings to their deities across villages (Bolle 1983, 52). This graphic and visceral imagery underscores the tribal roots and intense symbolism of these practices.

The DM associates the Devī's manifestations as Śatākṣī and Śākambharī with her later form as Durgā, who at that time will slay the great *asura* Durgama. This connection aligns Durgā with the life-sustaining and compassionate attributes of Śatākṣī and Śākambharī. Durgā's enduring association with trees and forests, as seen in her form as Vana Durgā and in the Navapattrikā rites during Durgā Pūjā, reinforces these qualities. The mythological links between these goddesses and Durgā are elaborated in texts such as the *Devī Bhāgavata Purāṇa* (7.28), where the demon Durgama features prominently. The demon Durgama's name, derived from *dur* ("difficult") and *gama* ("going, traversing"), signifies any challenging situation, paralleling the meaning of Durgā. The etymological link between the Devī and Durgama appears as contrived as the derivation of Cāmuṇḍā from the demons Caṇḍa and Muṇḍa. The frequent invocation of the Devī as Mā Durgā (Mother Durgā) or Durgā Mā suggests the possibility of the DM providing a retroactive explanation for an enigmatic and preexisting name for the goddess, which lacked a definitive origin. This reflects a broader tendency within the text to weave existing traditions into its narrative framework.

The Devī's names, such as Durgā, Caṇḍī, and Cāmuṇḍā, may originate from malevolent spirits or demons whose natures evolved into benevolent forms upon their incorporation into the divine pantheon. This pattern resonates with narratives found in Buddhist and Jain scriptures, where malevolent entities — *yakṣas*, *yakṣīs*, *nāgas*, *mahogras*, and others — reform after encountering these traditions, ultimately becoming protectors of the Dharma, the Buddha, or the Jinas. A notable example cited previously is Hārītī, a *yakṣī* infamous for devouring children to feed her own. When the Buddha intervened by hiding one of her children, Hārītī experienced the grief she caused others. She repented and became a guardian of children. Sometimes identified with Kālī, her cult spread as far as Japan, where she is known as Kishi-mojin and occasionally conflated with Kannon, the transformed Avalokiteśvara. Hārītī is typically depicted with children, carrying a child, or holding a pomegranate or cornucopia, symbolizing fertility and protection.

An early image of Hārītī from the 2nd to 5th century CE in the Peshawar Museum portrays her standing upright, holding a trident, water pot, drinking goblet, and a seated child, flanked by worshippers. This iconography parallels Tapasvinī Pārvatī, who also holds a trident and renouncer's water-pot, and Nidrā, depicted with a trident and drinking vessel. The transformation of such deities into protectors reflects the Buddhist tradition of assimilating existing gods and goddesses into their pantheon, reorienting them as guardians of the Buddha or the Dharma.

In Jainism, deities and demons were incorporated into the Jaina pantheon as supporters of the Tīrthāṅkaras ("Ford Makers"), the paramount teachers in the tradition. For instance, each of the twenty-four Jain Tīrthāṅkaras is affiliated with a so-called *yakṣa* and *yakṣī* attendant, some of whom are deities from the pantheons of other systems. Thus, Ambikā is the Yakṣī of the twenty-second Tīrthāṅkara, named Neminātha or Ariṣṭanemi. These Yakṣīs are also known as *śāsana devīs* (protector goddesses). Ambikā, also known as Kuṣmāṇḍī, Kuṣmāṇḍinī, Āmra Kuṣmāṇḍinī, or Ambā, entered the Jain pantheon by the end of the 6th century CE (M. Tiwari 1989). Her mount is a lion, and she typically holds a noose and a mango fruit (*āmra*) or sometimes a citron (*mātuluṅga*). She appears in two and four armed forms, and is mostly of a golden complexion, but occasionally dark blue or red. Two children (sometimes one), typically named Siddha and Buddha, accompany her (U. Shah 1987, 246–65).[57]

The Goddess Durgā stands out as one of the earliest deities in the Hindu pantheon to embody marked salvific qualities, paralleling those seen in Buddhist bodhisattvas and similar divine figures in the Jain tradition. It is plausible that Durgā's name originated from a once malevolent minor goddess or *yakṣī*-like being, who was transformed into a benevolent deity through the Brahmanic, Buddhist, and Jain tendencies to pacify and integrate wild or ambivalent divinities. Through her identification with the Great Goddess, Durgā merged these salvific aspects with the more complex and ambivalent characteristics of the Mahādevī, creating a multifaceted divine persona.

As Bhīmā Devī

The DM (11.46–48) refers to a manifestation of the Devī as Bhīmā Devī ("Dreadful Goddess") in the Himalayas, where she protects sages by destroying demons. Bhīmā, the feminine form of Bhīma, connects to one of the five heroic Pāṇḍava brothers of the Mbh epic. Given Bhīma's marriage to the demoness Hidimbā (or Hidimbī) and their son Ghatotkaca, it is plausible that Hidimbā herself could be referred to as Bhīmā. This identification is reinforced by the well-known Hāḍimbā Devī temple in Manali, located in the Kulu Valley of the Himalayas. This temple, dating to the 16th century, continues to support the practice of buffalo sacrifice, as noted by Ehud Halperin (2012). Devotees prefer to associate the goddess worshipped there with Hāḍimbā rather than the Purāṇic Durgā, as the former aligns better with animal sacrifice, which is less associated with the latter.

A Bhīmā Devī temple from the 9th or 10th century in Pinjore, Haryana, was destroyed in the 13th century during the Muslim invasions (Handa 2006, 153). However, the DM's mention of Bhīmā suggests the existence of a significant cult dedicated to her prior to its composition. Evidence of such a cult appears in Xuanzang's 7th-century account (Beal 1885, 113–14), which describes a Bhīmā Devī image carved from bluish-green stone, considered autochthonous by locals. This image was located on a high mountain 50 *li* (22 km) northeast of the city of Po-lu-sha. Xuanzang identified Bhīmā as the wife of Īśvara Deva, undoubtedly Śiva, and noted her reputation for attracting pilgrims from across India and all social strata. Worshippers sought her blessings and fulfilled vows when their wishes were granted. Xuanzang explained that devotees needed ardent devotion and a seven-day fast to receive a vision of the goddess, who was renowned as a boon-granter. Beal (1885, 114n106) compares this to similar claims made for Avalokiteśvara/Guanyin, whom I have previously discussed for shared salvific traits. At the mountain's base, a temple to Maheśvara stood, where ash-covered worshippers made offerings. Xuanzang's account highlights a prominent Bhīmā Devī cult with practices of ascetic purification and devotion closely aligning with those prescribed in the DM.

The origins of Bhīmā Devī's cult are undeniably ancient, as evidenced by the 190-meter-deep cave temple Xuanzang mentions, identified as the Mahāguhā or "Great Cave," within the Kashmir Smast complex on Miñjaparvata Mountain (Falk 2003, 1–18). A 5th century CE copper donation plate reveals a thriving commercial network of shops around the temple (Falk 2003, 17). The discovery of holed copper Chinese cash coins suggests the temple was situated at the edge of a trade network linking India and China during the Tang dynasty (Falk 2003, 16). Coins from the Kuṣāṇa period, Sasanian dynasty, and beyond the Ghaznavid rule (10th–12th century CE) further demonstrate the temple's enduring prominence (Ziad 2016). Seals from the Kashmir Smast depict Bhīmā Devī in a squatting posture with her legs spread, symbolizing childbirth. She is shown as full-breasted and accompanied by a jar, a trident, and a dancing figure. Intriguingly, she often lacks an anthropomorphic head, which some scholars interpret as a connection to Lajjā Gaurī, who is similarly portrayed, sometimes with a flower in place of a head, signifying her fertility associations (Khan 2002, 83–90). This iconography underscores Bhīmā Devī's deep ties to fertility and creation.

The *tīrtha* texts of the *Mahābhārata* (Mbh) explain that bathing at the *yoni* at the place of Bhīmā guarantees the reward of being reborn with golden earrings as a son of the goddess (*devyāḥ putro bhaved*) and attaining the same merits as offering a hundred thousand cows (Mbh 3.80.101).[58] Thus, the Mbh offers an early textual reference to the already renowned and evidently far more ancient site of Bhīmā Devī, whose cult the DM likely sought to assimilate into the persona of the Great Goddess.

As Bhrāmarī

The final manifestation described by the Devī is a bee form, composed of countless bees, adopted to destroy the demon Aruṇa. This act earns her the name Bhrāmarī (DM 11.48–11.50). The *Devī Bhāgavata Purāṇa* (X.10.13) expands on this myth. Bee-associated goddesses are widespread across Eurasia, although the earliest evidence of such a figure in India remains unclear. Goddesses such as Artemis and Nanā (Nanaia), whose similarities to Durgā were discussed earlier, were symbolized by bees (Sircar 1971, 20n1). Marija Gimbutas (1974, 1982) cites Porphyry (c. 234–c. 305 CE), who notes that the priestesses of Demeter, goddess of agriculture, were called *melissae* (bees). Similarly, Artemis, as the mistress of animals, was associated with the bee and worshipped in Ephesus, where her temple was likened to a beehive. These European Great Goddess associations with bees may have developed independently or through cultural interactions mirrored in the Indian subcontinent during the DM's composition. The bee's black and yellow colors resonate with the attire of Nidrā, the flying goddess who also holds a cup of liquor or honey (*madhu*).

The Bhramarāmbā Temple at Śrīśaila (Śrīparvata) on the banks of the Krishna River in Andhra Pradesh is reputed as the abode of the goddess Bhrāmarī, following her slaying of Aruṇa. The temple, one of the eighteen primary Śākta Pīṭhas, is linked mythologically to Satī, whose neck is said to have fallen there (Eck 2012, 292). The site is also significant for housing Śrī Mallikārjuna, one of the twelve self-manifested *jyotirliṅgas* ("effulgent signs") of Śiva. While the temple claims ancient origins, its prominence as a pilgrimage site predates the DM's composition. Chinese pilgrim Faxian (337–c. 422 CE), Xuanzang (602–664 CE), and Korean monk Huichao (Hyecho) (704–787 CE) all reference a monastery at Śrīśaila. Xuanzang describes it as Bhramaragiri ("Mountain of the Bee"), where Nāgārjuna, with miraculous powers, established a monastery and spent his final years (Wriggins 2004, 287n13). This evidence underscores the site's importance in the 7th and 8th centuries, aligning with the likely period of the DM's composition.

Evidently, there were notable cults dedicated to the "predicted manifestations" of the Goddess prior to the composition of the DM, which presents itself as an ancient text that accurately predicts the Goddess's future forms. However, before appraising the collective evidence garnered from the DM, earlier literary sources, and iconography, it is essential to examine materials extending beyond the early Gupta period. These iconographic artifacts may offer valuable insights into the evolution of Durgā's worship, complementing and expanding upon her mythic character as depicted in textual traditions.

Chapter 10

Korravai and Victorious Goddess Imagery

The detailed correlation of early iconography with the goddess-related epic hymns discussed in earlier chapters appears to support the argument — contrary to prior scholarship — that these hymns or their variants were composed much earlier than typically assumed. Now that the content of the *Devī Māhātmya* (DM) has been analyzed in detail, attention can shift to the iconographic depictions of Durgā, the Buffalo Demon Crusher, emerging after the early Gupta period. This analysis seeks to discern correlations among these images, the DM, and early Purāṇic and other textual material. As proposed in recent scholarship, there is reason to suspect that the DM may have originated later than the traditional 6th or 7th century CE dating. To examine this, we briefly review categories of Durgā-related imagery, particularly those depicting the goddess subduing a buffalo. While earlier images may have been associated with other names such as Kātyāyanī, Jayā, Vijayā, or Caṇḍī, the name Durgā would likely have been retrospectively applied to them. Importantly, any pre-DM images are unlikely to have been widely called Mahiṣamardinī, as the term does not appear in the DM or early Purāṇas such as the *Mārkaṇḍeya* but emerges later in Purāṇic and Tantric writings, particularly in formulaic references to the crushing of the Buffalo Demon.

This chapter focuses on Victorious Goddess (V) images, particularly those where the goddess is depicted standing atop a buffalo head. These representations, prevalent in South India during the Pallava and Coḷa periods and in Southeast Asia, are analyzed in the context of South Indian texts such as the *Cilappatikāram*, which identifies Koṟṟavai as an early Dravidian goddess. The chapter extends J. N. Tiwari's argument that Durgā/Kālī assimilates fierce regional goddesses such as Koṟṟavai, the nude Koṭavī, and Caṇḍamārī, who is adorned with human limbs. The analysis concludes with the concept of "Durgā-fication," referring to the process of merging regional goddesses into Durgā's persona, a phenomenon evident as early as the Kuṣāṇa period. This process demonstrates the gradual integration of local and regional goddess traditions into the broader framework of Durgā worship, reflecting a dynamic interplay of regional and pan-Indian religious narratives.

Victorious Goddess (V) Types

During the Pallava period, two distinct types of goddess imagery begin to emerge. The first is the Victorious Goddess (V) type, where the goddess is depicted standing atop a severed buffalo head. This corresponds to Stietencron's (2005, 115–72) type 4 and Seshadri's (1963) type II, and the term Victorious Goddess type will be used here for clarity. The second is the Anthropomorphic (A) type of the Buffalo Demon, where the demon is shown in a partial buffalo, partial human form. This corresponds to Stietencron's type 3 and Seshadri's type III. This analysis begins with a closer examination of the Victorious Goddess type.

Besnagar

Possibly one of the earliest certain representations of the Victorious Goddess type was found at Besnagar (ancient Vidiśā), in Madhya Pradesh, and now at the Gwalior Archeological Museum.[1] Besnagar is famous for its ancient stone column, erected by Heliodorus between 130 and 95 BCE. Heliodorus, a resident of Taxila and a devotee of Vasudeva, served as an envoy from the Indo-Bactrian king Antialkidas of Taxila to the court of the Śuṅga king Bhagabhadra (Holt 2012, 131). Vidiśā, the western capital of the Śuṅgas, maintained significant contact with Greek outposts in the Punjab, evidenced by the conversion of a

Figure 10.1. Victorious Goddess, 3.35 m, buff sandstone.
Besnagar, Madhya Pradesh. Accession No. 34085. *Source*: Gwalior
Archaeological Museum. Photo by the author.

high-ranking envoy to an early form of Vaiṣṇavism (Davis 2024, 255–57). This serves as one of many indications of Greek influences permeating the Indian subcontinent during the 1st to 2nd century BCE (Holt 2012, 130–31). The column, referred to in its inscription as an eagle standard (*garuḍa dhvaja*), was crowned with an image of Garuḍa, the eagle mount of Viṣṇu.

The Victorious Goddess image from Besnagar in figure 10.1 depicts the goddess in the *samapāda sthānaka* pose, standing atop a buffalo's head. The buffalo's head is carved between two seated lions facing away from the center. The goddess has six arms and wears ornaments and clothing resembling those found in reliefs from Deogarh, Mandasor, and other Gupta sites, leading R. C. Agrawala (1958, 128) to date it to the 5th century CE. The goddess's face bears a smile, her hair is styled in a topknot (*jaṭā*), and her breasts are depicted close. Her front right hand forms the *abhaya mudrā*, while the lowest left-hand rests on a rope-like girdle draped over her *dhoti*. If this dating is accurate, it indicates that later images of this type, particularly those from the Pallava region, either reflect a style prevalent in central India or were influenced by this and similar earlier imagery.

The iconography of the Besnagar image is distinctive for its period and region, while the Pallava examples, typically dated to the early 8th century CE, prominently feature a lion as the Devī's mount (*vāhana*) and often depict her riding it. In Pallava art, the buffalo-subduing goddess atop a lion becomes a defining iconographic motif. However, the two seated lions facing outward, as seen in the Besnagar piece, aligns more with late Kuṣāṇa imagery, evoking the concept of a lion throne, common in Gupta-period Jain Tīrthāṅkara depictions. Patil (1951, 96–100) suggested an even earlier date for the Besnagar image, placing it in the Kuṣāṇa period, citing its megalithic stature, posture, and voluptuous features reminiscent of the Dīdārgañj Yakṣī. Its low, pronounced girdle parallels the Chandraketugarh goddess. Regardless of whether it belongs to the Kuṣāṇa or Gupta periods, the portrayal of the goddess atop a sole buffalo head is unusual for the 5th century CE or earlier, becoming more common in the Pallava period.[2]

Notably, the Besnagar figure is not an isolated example. A 3rd century CE terracotta plaque fragment from the Sātavāhana site of Saṇṇatti (modern Karnataka) depicts a figure standing atop a buffalo head, likely representing an early Victorious Goddess. A nearby *gaṇa* attendant is also visible (Tartakov and Dehejia 1984, 303, fig. 27). This indicates that the Victorious Goddess type predates the Pallava period, although it became more prominent later. The Victorious Goddess type, showing the goddess atop a severed buffalo head, is seen throughout Karnataka at sites such as Hale Alur, Binnamangala, Nandi, Kunigal, and Kampanayura, as well as in Bikkavolu (Andhra Pradesh) (Tartakov and Dehejia 1984, 324). While many of these examples date to the 10th or 11th century, they underscore the enduring appeal of this type across the Deccan Plateau. At the Bala Brahmā temple in Ālampur (modern Telangana), a standing goddess is depicted atop two divergent lions, similar to the Besnagar figure, although the buffalo head is absent (Tartakov and Dehejia 1984, fig. 24). Divakaran (1971, 73) places the Bala Brahmā temple among the Cāḷukya structures of the mid-to-late 7th century.

These Victorious Goddess images, whether depicted with or without a lion, and commonly atop a severed buffalo head, effectively symbolize a triumphant deity standing over a subdued adversary. They align with the iconographic motif of the goddess's feet atop the buffalo's head, reinforcing her dominance. This imagery likely contributed to the eventual prominence of the term *mardinī* (crusher or destroyer of Mahiṣa), which, based on available evidence, only gained widespread use after the composition of the DM.

Notably, these images do not seem to reflect or incorporate much of the mythic narrative development associated with the goddess in textual traditions. To further explore the iconographic evolution of these depictions, including the attributes held by the goddess, we now turn to the Pallava and later Coḷa figures.

Pallava: Māmallapuram/Mahabalipuram

There are numerous examples of the Victorious Goddess Type at Māmallapuram, also known as Mahabalipuram. Māmallapuram, or ancient Mallai, Kadal-Malai, or Mamallai, was a port of the Pallava Dynasty, which ruled from their capital of Kañcipuram. The site began with work by Narasiṃhavarman I, also known as Mamalla I, who ruled from 630 to 668 CE. Most of the rock cut shrines and the renowned Shore Temple, however, were likely built or completed during the reign of his grandson, Narasiṃhavarman II, who ruled from approximately 700 to 728 CE (Romain 2011, 308).

Among the Victorious Goddess images at Māmallapuram is one carved on the outer rear wall of the so-called Draupadī Ratha. It depicts a four-armed goddess atop a buffalo head. One left hand is on her hip, and a right hand is in the *abhaya mudrā*. The shrine itself is dedicated to the same goddess, who stands in a similar posture, but atop a lotus platform as seen in figure 10.2.

There, she is flanked by devotees, two of whom are kneeling and appear to be engaged in an act of self-decapitation or drawing blood from cuts in their necks. We will explore this striking form of worship later in this chapter. In figure 10.3 one notes the large statue of a lion situated before the temple entrance, which is flanked by two female attendants. The name Draupadī Ratha is evidently a later, inappropriate designation for the Ratha, which is one of a cluster of five gigantic boulders sculpted into rock-cut shrines known as the Five Rathas.

Another image (figure 10.4), found on the right exterior wall niche (*deva-koṣṭha*) of the Trimūrti rock-cut temple, is similar to the one at the rear of the Draupadī Ratha. The goddess is in the *samabhaṅga* upright posture, bearing a bell, discus, sword, and fear-not (*abhaya*) gesture in her right hands, and holds

Figure 10.2. Goddess with worshippers making offerings of their own heads; somewhat smaller than life-size, granite. Draupadī Ratha, Māmallapuram. *Source*: Photo by the author.

Figure 10.3. Exterior of the Draupadī Ratha, with lion in front and entrance flanked by female attendants. Māmallapuram. *Source*: Photo by the author.

Figure 10.4. Victorious Goddess; somewhat smaller than life-size,
granite. Trimūrti Maṇḍapa, Māmallapuram.
Source: Photo by the author.

a shield, conch, and bow in her left hands, one of which is also in the *kaṭyava-lambitahasta* (relaxed hand on hip) posture.

A choice example of the Pallava Victorious Goddess type, as shown in figure 10.5, is found within the Ādivarāha temple (also known as the Vārahaswami temple).[3] The beautifully rendered life-sized image is to the right of the inner sanctum, which depicts Viṣṇu in his *varāha avatāra* holding aloft the goddess Bhū (or Lakṣmī as the local priest identifies her). There, the Victorious Goddess is eight-armed and stands with a straight left leg atop the buffalo's head and a bent right leg behind. This gives a slight twist to her graceful, relaxed posture. Her lowest left arm is placed by her hip, and a parrot is seated on its wrist. She carries a discus, conch, sword, shield, bow and arrow, bell, and a *śrīphala* or *bilva* (wood-apple) fruit. Like many of the Pallava images, she wears the distinctive band (*kucabandha*) across her breasts. Two kneeling male devotees with distinctive hairstyles flank her. The one on her right, who wears a large earring, appears to be drawing blood from his wrist, or inner elbow (Schmid 2011, 149), while some suggest he is readying for self-decapitation. The one on her left appears to be offering a flower. Female attendants flank these figures. One holds a bow and the other a sword. *Gaṇas* float overhead, and one carries a flywhisk. The goddess's lion and antelope are depicted in the upper corners of the bas-relief.

Tartakov and Dehejia (1984, 331) identify sixteen known Victorious Goddess images from the Pallava period. Of these, three are depicted standing

Figure 10.5. Victorious Goddess. Ādivarāha Temple interior, Māmallapuram. *Source*: Photo by the author.

atop lotuses, four stand directly on the ground, and seven stand upon the severed head of Mahiṣa. Earlier examples of this iconography have been noted at Saṇṇatti and Besnagar, as well as at Cāḷukya sites such as Ālampur. This type, prominent in South India, also appears in Southeast Asia, where it may have migrated from — or to — South India. Southeast Asian examples will be discussed later, but we will first examine additional South Indian instances, particularly under the Coḷas. Tartakov and Dehejia (1984, 330) diverge from many scholars who attribute these Pallava images to the reign of Narasiṃhavarman I (mid-7th century CE). Instead, they date all Victorious Goddess images at Māmallapuram to the reign of Rājasiṃha, Narasiṃhavarman II Pallava (c. 695–728 CE), placing their creation in the early 8th century CE.

Perhaps the most finely executed of this Pallava type, although not unambiguously assigned to the Pallavas, is found in Boston's Museum of Fine Arts, and shown in figure 10.6 (see Rowland 1953, 116. Harle (1963, 238) regarded it as early Coḷa. Seshadri (1963, 16) sees its lengthening of the form, with the goddess's elongated tubular limbs, to be a development of the later Andhra figure style. The eight-armed goddess holds a long bow, arrow, sword, shield, and discus. Behind her, there stands a trident. She delicately places her hand on her hip in the *kaṭihasta* or *kaṭyavalambita* posture. Her body, slightly turned and bent in the *tribhanga* position, has a graceful appeal not found in static, erect

Figure 10.6. Victorious Goddess; 150 × 61 × 45.7 cm, green schist
Early Coḷa period (970–1070). Accession Number: 27.171. *Source*:
Denman Waldo Ross Collection, Museum of Fine Arts, Boston. Used
with permission.

depictions. She wears the breast band (*kucabandha*), characteristic of Pallava
images.

Coḷa Images

The Victorious Goddess type continued to be popular under the Coḷas (mid-9th
to 13th century CE) and resemble the Pallava designs. In early Coḷa temples,
it was typical to place Durgā images in niches on the north side of the *ard-
hamaṇḍapa*, the smaller assembly hall adjacent to the main *maṇḍapa* (Harle
1963, 238). According to R. Nagaswamy, with whom I conversed in 2018,
this location, in which the Devī faces north, is by no means insignificant, and
its symbolic placement is explained in certain Āgamas. He explained that the
clockwise circumambulation of a Śiva temple begins with Gaṇeśa, located
in the first niche on the south side. He is the leader of the female *gaṇas*, the
mātṛgaṇas, who are the seven *mātṛkās*, which is why he is often portrayed with
them in other contexts. These *mātṛgaṇas* refer to the seven groups of phonemes
of the Sanskrit alphabet, beginning with *a*, which leads the list of vowels, *ka*,
for the first group of guttural consonants, *ca*, for the palatals, and so on with

ṭa, ta, pa, and *ya,* which leads the last or seventh group. Just as a mother gives birth to a child, these *mātṛkās* give birth to the sounds that constitute all language and therefore knowledge. Gaṇeśa represents the phonetic system, which develops into the knowledge system, symbolized by Śiva as Dakṣiṇāmūrti, the giver of knowledge, in one of the next niches. Further along one may have a Śiva and Pārvatī or a Harihara (i.e., Śiva and Viṣṇu), which represents the Absolute together with Māyā, since both Devī and Viṣṇu are associated with illusion. This is followed by Brahmā, who symbolizes Absolute realization in Vedic systems. The circumambulation ultimately culminates with Devī, who is the embodiment of all knowledge and the highest wisdom. Ultimately one enters the inner sanctum, where the *liṅga* combines the mystery of manifest (*rūpa*) and unmanifest (*arūpa*).

At Rajaraja I's renowned Bṛhadiśvara temple in Thanjavur, built in 1004 CE, there is a classic representation of this form as seen in figure 10.7. The goddess holds a conch and discus, wears a breast band, and profuse ornamentation. She holds a hand in the *abhaya* (fear-not) *mudrā.* Seshadri (1963, 16, Pl. 21) illustrates another image from there, flanked by two female attendants in *kaṭihasta,* holding fly whisks.

Another such Victorious Goddess image of note is found at the Brahmapurīśvara temple at Pullamangai (outside Pasupatikoil, nine miles from

Figure 10.7. Victorious Goddess (Coḷa Period). Bṛhadīśvara Temple, Thanjavur. *Source*: Photo by the author.

Thanjavur, on the road to Kumbhakonam) (Harle 1958). The goddess stands in a graceful *kaṭihasta* on the buffalo head and holds a sword, shield, bow, discus, and conch in various of her eight hands. Outside the niche, to the right, a devotee is depicted cutting off his head as an offering. The lion stands above. To the left, another devotee is depicted cutting flesh from his thigh, and a stag is represented above (Harle 1963, 237–46). The image is dated by a temple inscription to 918 CE, the 11th year of the Coḷa ruler Parantaka. Another similar, but probably slightly later image, is the one at Srimushanam, South Arcot District (Seshadri 1963, 17, and Pl. 21b).

The Coḷa style of image set a norm and was replicated far and wide. Late Coḷa style images are found on the large gateways (*gopuram*) of Cidambaram temple. It is noteworthy that one of these Victorious Goddess statues, located on the west *gopuram* and likely the earliest constructed of the four, bears an inscription in 12th century Tamil *grantha* script, labeling it "Durgai." The goddess, thus fairly clearly identified as Durgā, stands on a severed buffalo's head, in *kaṭihasta* posture and *abhaya mudrā*, holding a conch, discus, and bow (Balasubramanyam 1961, 27–29). A figure of the same date, also on the west *gopuram*, is labeled Tripurasundarī Devī. It is eight-armed, and has *kucabandha* (breast band), and *kirīṭamakuṭa* (crown crest), and is flanked by female attendants with fly whisks (*chauri*). Another four-armed image, dated to 1300 CE, is found on the north *gopuram*, holds a discus and conch, with other hands in *abhaya mudrā* and *kaṭihasta*. We can thus say with fair certainty that by the 12th century CE, Victorious Goddess images were being identified as Durgā, albeit not exclusively so.

Other Related Examples

An intriguing item that can be loosely categorized with the Victorious Goddess iconography is a silver rhyton housed in the Cleveland Museum of Art. A rhyton is a ceremonial vessel, often curved and designed for pouring fluids, typically featuring an animal's head at the tip of the spout. This particular rhyton combines a dignified, regal female head positioned above the head of a water buffalo. An inscription on the back of the female's neck indicates the weight of the item, written in Sasanian Pahlavi, a script and language standard used in Iran until approximately 700 CE. Martha Carter (1979, 309–25) contends that this rhyton depicts the goddess subduing the Buffalo Demon. While it may predate her identification as Durgā, the item likely references a deity with similar attributes. Carter suggests that it was produced in the Kabul Valley or near Ghazni, south of the Hindu Kush, highlighting the regional and cultural intersections present in the depiction.

Victorious Goddess type images were also produced in parts of Southeast Asia, prior to the Coḷa expansion into this region. Most notable among these for our study, because it is possibly one of the earliest in the region, is the 1.65-meter sandstone image found at Sambor Prei Kuk (Kompong Thom) in modern Cambodia. The image was found in two pieces, with the upper part of the torso in the central N1 tower and the lower part in N9 tower of the northern group, where a replica combining the two pieces is now displayed, and which I photographed in 2011 as seen in figure 10.8. Although the base is worn, a buffalo head is clearly visible in a simple style as found on images produced later. The original is on display at the National Museum of Cambodia in Phnom Penh.

Sambor Prei Kuk contains the remains of Īśānapura, the capital city of King Īśānavarman of the Chenla kingdom, who ruled from about 615 to 628 CE. Scholars, such as Philip Rawson (1967, Pl. 18), have dated the Victorious Goddess image there to the early 7th century CE or earlier, placing it potentially before the late 7th or early 8th century Pallava examples. If accurate, this dating raises the possibility of iconographic influences moving from Southeast Asia to South Asia, an often-overlooked direction. This does not suggest that the Victorious Goddess form originated in Southeast Asia, as early examples exist on the Indian subcontinent. However, the less rigid style of the Sambor Prei Kuk image, with a slightly twisting and bending body, is distinctive and may have influenced some later Pallava imagery. Even so, this style is rare in

Figure 10.8. Victorious Goddess (replica) in temple at Sambor Prei Kuk, Cambodia. *Source*: Photo by the author.

both regions, where erect (*abhaṅga*) depictions typically prevail. Such uncertainties underscore the need for caution when assigning dates and provenance, reminding us of the interconnected cultural zones where influence was multidirectional, not solely into or out of South Asia.

Who Is the Victorious Goddess?

It is natural to associate the goddess standing atop a buffalo head with Durgā, the Buffalo Crusher. The goddess's feet on the buffalo head readily evoke the term Mahiṣamardinī, as we have interpreted it. By the 12th-century Coḷa period, as seen on a gateway at Cidambaram, the Victorious Goddess was explicitly identified as Durgai (Durgā). However, earlier representations provide no definitive evidence that the Victorious Goddess was called Durgā. Intriguing aspects of the Pallava imagery prompt questions about the character of the goddess depicted. The buffalo-subduing, lion-riding, and riverine traits in earlier iconography drew comparisons with goddesses such as Nike, Anāhitā, Kybele, and Nanā, suggesting shared motifs or influences. Similarly, the portrayal of devotees offering their own blood, or possibly even severing their heads, invites further inquiry. While the DM refers to King Suratha and the merchant Samādhi offering blood from their limbs, it does not mention self-decapitation. Before exploring literary evidence concerning goddesses linked to such rituals, it is worth noting a recurring iconographic feature associated with this goddess: her deer or stag *vāhana*.

The Victorious Goddess, the Stag *Vāhana*, and Self-Mutilation

In two representative images from Coḷa temples in South India — the Brahmapuriśvara temple at Puḷḷamangai, near Paśupatikoyil, dated to the first quarter of the 10th century CE, and the Śiva temple at Puñjai, dated to the first half of the 10th century CE, both at Thanjavur — the Victorious Goddess stands atop a buffalo head, flanked by a lion and a deer (Harle 1963, 237). While the lion is firmly associated with Durgā as her *vāhana* (vehicle), the presence of the deer is both unusual and noteworthy. In the Puḷḷamangai image, the lion and deer are harnessed and saddled, and the deer is accompanied by a *bhūta* (spirit) attendant, elevating its status as an alternative vehicle of the goddess. Meanwhile, the saddled lion reinforces her identification with Durgā. This imagery suggests that by the 10th century CE, the goddess with the stag *vāhana* was linked to and identified with Durgā. In three sculptures from Bengal, Durgā is similarly depicted with both a lion and a deer (Banerji 1933, Pl. LVII, a, c, and d, cited in Harle 1963, 238n6), further substantiating this association. However, the specific connection between Durgā and the deer, a relatively lesser-known *vāhana*, requires further explanation. This raises the question: Who is the original goddess with the stag *vāhana*?

A clue derives from these and certain Pallava period images discussed above, which depict attendant devotees engaged in various forms of flesh and blood offerings. At Puḷḷamangai and Puñjai, one devotee appears to be cutting flesh from his thigh, while the other appears to be engaged in self-decapitation. At a similar type of image in the Acaleśvara shrine in the 2nd *prakāra* of Tyāgarāja temple at Tiruvārūr (dated to the last quarter of the 10th century CE) although no deer and lion are present, one devotee is offering up flesh from his thigh, while the other appears to be cutting off his head (Harle 1963, 243, fig. 3). The Varāha-*maṇḍapa* at Māmallapuram, dated to the late 7th to early 8th century CE, offers a much earlier depiction of the Victorious Goddess with a devotee likely engaged in an act of self-decapitation, and flanked by the heads of a lion and deer (see Vogel 1931, Pl. VI). The Draupadī-ratha at Māmallapuram from the same period and Tiruchirapalli's Rock Temple (lower cave) (Viennot 1957, 157), from the same or later period, also has depictions of self-mutilating, perhaps self-decapitating devotees (Vogel 1931, 540, Pl. VII). Images of some of these from Māmallapuram have been shown earlier (see figs. 10.2 and 10.5). The Vīrattāneśvara temple at Tiruttani, near Arkonam, Chottor District, is of the late Pallava period and possesses an eight-armed Victorious Goddess on a slab, flanked by devotees, one of whom appears ready to offer his head in sacrifice (Sastri 1935, 728). The Singavarman rock-cut temple also has a Victorious Goddess with a flesh-cutting figure (K. R. Srinivasan 1958, 124, Pl. LIIB). Thus, a juxtaposition of the Victorious Goddess with the deer *vāhana* and self-mutilating, even self-decapitating, devotees is evident.

Harle (1963, 240) speculates on three possibilities as to why these self-sacrificing devotees appear on imagery. First, there may be a Purāṇic myth associated with this practice, but his research uncovered no such reference. Second, they may commemorate the self-sacrifice of particularly notable devotees, but it is rare to find actual historical persons depicted within the iconography of major deities. The third possibility is that they represent an actual form of devotional practice associated with the goddess. Vogel (1931) had earlier speculated on this possibility but did not identify the goddess.

We have already noted literary sources referring to goddesses that accept blood sacrifice of animals. The early epic hymns, such as the Durgā Stava (DStv l. 34) speaks of the goddess as Kālī and Mahākālī being fond of liquor, flesh, and beasts. This could be a tacit reference to offerings of one's own flesh. In the Durgā Stotra (DSto l. 8), Kālī is described as adorned with skulls and as eternally fond of Mahiṣa's (or simply, buffalo) blood (l. 15). The skulls adornment could tacitly refer to self-decapitation, but the origin of the skulls is not explicit. The Praise of Nidrā (First Stratum) (PN-s1) sings praises to Nidrā/Kauśikī, who is constantly delighted by offerings of flesh and receives sacrifices of wild beasts (l. 51). Here, too, the flesh offerings could be inferred, although not explicitly, as a devotee's own flesh. The so-called Āryā Stava or Praise of Nidrā (Second Stratum) (PN-s2), refers to the goddess Kātyāyanī, Kauśikī, Durgā, Jayā, Vijayā, and the sister of Vāsudeva as fond of flesh and boiled rice (l. 19), another ambiguous reference to the type of flesh being offered. The goddess hymns that were inserted into the *Harivaṃśa* (HV) at a later date (likely around or even after the date of composition of the DM), such as Pradyumna's Hymn (PradH) and Aniruddha's Hymn (AniH), make no mention of any flesh offerings. In fact, in AniH (l. 37), the goddess Durgā is said to be a drinker of ghee and Soma.

We had noted that other related Near Eastern goddesses, whose cults likely influenced the conception of Durgā, also received blood sacrifices. Arədvī Sūrā Anāhitā, for instance, whose praises are sung in Yašt 5 of the *Avesta*, is described as routinely receiving sacrifices of a hundred horses, a thousand oxen, and ten thousand lambs (e.g., 5.68, 72, etc.). We also know that when Ardašīr I beheaded his enemies, he displayed their heads at her temple, as did the Sasanian king Šapur II (309–379 CE) with his executed enemies (Chaumont 1958, 159–60). Nevertheless, these were not self-decapitations, but the offering of the heads of one's vanquished foes. In worship rites to the goddess Kybele, ecstatic dances were performed by priests known as *galli*, who had performed self-castration. In both the *tauroboliums* (bull sacrifice) and *crioboliums* (ram sacrifice) performed in her honor, the blood of the sacrificial animal flowed over and purified the patron (Özkaya 1997, 97–103). In the example of Kybele's priests' castrations, we do have instances of self-mutilation as a component of goddess worship. Even so, these are examples from beyond the subcontinent.

In Xuanzang's tale of his adventure in 636 CE, he recounts nearly becoming a human sacrifice during what appears to be the autumn Navarātra celebrations. Bāṇa's *Kādambarī*, discussed in detail in a previous chapter, also speaks of Śabara tribals having self-inflicted wounds, and making human and animal sacrifices, offerings of blood and rice, and so on to Durgā/Caṇḍikā. In Bhavabhūti's *Mālatī-mādhava*, we have a description of a would-be human sacrifice to Cāmuṇḍā/Karālā. Vākpatirāja's *Gaüḍavaho* also portrays the goddess Kālī/Kālarātrī accepting human sacrifices. We therefore have numerous textual references to animal and even human sacrifices being rendered to goddesses, including Durgā, as well as offerings of one's own blood. Even so, these sources could simply be literary fictions not derived from any corresponding reality, and do not indicate anything such as self-immolation, which the Pallava and Cola reliefs appear to portray.

In the *Vetālapañcaviṃśatī* (*Twenty-five [Tales] of the Vampire*) (Tale 4), which forms part of Somadeva's *Kathāsaritsāgara* (*Ocean of Rivers of Story*), there is a tale of a Brahmin named Vīravara, who loyally served the king Śūdraka. The text is typically dated to the 11th century CE (White 1998, 306). To help prolong Śūdraka's life, which he heard was destined to end in three days, the faithful Vīravara approached his own son, Sattvavara, with a gruesome proposal. Vīravara explained to Sattvavara that he had to be killed, as an offering to the goddess Caṇḍī, and the boy conceded to this self-sacrifice for the benefit of the king's life. Accompanied by his wife, Dharmavatī, and his daughter Vīravatī, Vīravara with Sattvavara made their way to a temple dedicated to Caṇḍī, built right beside the king's palace. There, Vīravara beheaded Sattvavara, and offered his son's head to the goddess. A voice from the heavens called out and confirmed that this supreme act of sacrifice had indeed saved the king's life. Unfortunately, Vīravara's daughter, Vīravatī, was so grief-stricken at the sight of her brother's death that she died instantly. Seeing what had transpired, Vīravara's wife, Dharmavatī, bemoaned the fact that she had not beheaded herself long ago for the welfare of her king. Now that her children were dead, Dharmavatī also decided to die, perishing in the flames on the children's funeral pyre that was built and set alight by Vīravara. Thereupon, Vīravara, realizing he had paid his debt to his king by saving his life, but now having not much else to live for, since his family was dead, decided to please Ambikā with his own self-sacrifice. He sang a praise to the trident-bearing goddess, whom he addressed as Mahiṣāsuramāriṇī (notably, not Mahiṣāsuramardinī), the destroyer of the demon Ruru, Kālī, the skull-bearing goddess, Śiva, and various other epithets, and then beheaded himself. King Śūdraka, who had secretly followed the family, watched in awe their many selfless acts of sacrifice and loyalty. So thoroughly impressed by his servant's piety, the king decided to do the same, with a prayer that his own head offering might restore the life of the pious Brahmin and his family. Just as Śūdraka was about to behead himself, a voice from the heavens stopped him, proclaimed that the king had proved his courage, and Vīravara and his family were restored to life. Śūdraka eventually conferred half his kingdom on the Brahmin and his descendants, making Vīravara equal to him in power.

This story is repeated, with variations, in other narrative collections, such as the *Hitopadeśa* (iii, Katha 8) (where the goddess is called Sarvamaṅgalā), and Jayadratha's (1983) *Haracaritacintāmaṇi*, dated at the late 12th to early 13th century CE (Shibazaki 2007). There is another such story of head-offerings in the sixth tale of the *Vetālapañcaviṃśati*, which tells of Dhavala, a washerman, who cuts off his head at the shrine of Gaurī at Śobhavatī (Vogel 1931, 542). These texts almost certainly belong to a period after the 9th century CE, and perhaps even a century or two later. We can ascertain that names such as Caṇḍī, Ambikā, Sarvamaṅgalā, Kālī, and Śiva were being associated with the goddess who accepted self-sacrifice through decapitation. The name Sarvamaṅgalā resonates with the famous verse from the Nārāyaṇī Stuti embedded in the DM and found on the famous Dadhimatī Mātā inscription. The use of the term Mahiṣāsuramāriṇī, instead of Mahiṣāsuramardinī, suggests that the latter term had still not become as pervasive as it is today and as it is in later literature.

Although these accounts are works of fiction, and certainly given to hyperbole to elevate the salvific benefits of utterly selfless devotion, they repeatedly incorporate motifs that must draw upon sociocultural realities or values prevalent at the time. At the least, one could infer that the theme of self-sacrifice to goddesses, in particular, was a literary trope, conveying prevalent stereotypes or prejudices, even though self-decapitation may not have been a reality. Even so, lest we be prematurely dismissive, we do have evidence that such acts of self-sacrifice did and sometimes still do take place. Harle (1963, 243) cites some epigraphic accounts of actual self-decapitations that occurred in South India. A bas-relief on a slab from Nellore depicts a self-decapitation. The kneeling figure holds a sword in one hand and his decapitated head in the other. The inscription, dated to the reign of a late Pallava period king, records a gift of land to someone to commemorate a pious act by someone else (probably the donor's father), who cut off flesh from nine parts of his body, and finally his own head as an offering to the goddess Bhaṭārī (Krishnamacharlu 1943, cited in Harle 1963, 243). Bhaṭārī or Batari simply means "goddess" in Malaysia and Indonesia. Other such acts are recorded as late as the 13th century CE (cited in Harle 1963, 243).[4]

The Goddess Koṟṟavai

The preceding accounts of self-decapitation, fictive and real, from the 9th century CE onward, do not shed adequate light on the possible name of the Victorious Goddess depicted on the Pallava and early Coḷa reliefs. By examining much earlier Tamil literature, however, we have compelling evidence that the Victorious Goddess is most likely the ancient South Indian goddess Koṟṟavai.[5]

Koṟṟavai (pronounced Koṭṭravai) was the fearsome goddess of tribes such as the Maṟavaṉ, who inhabited the arid (*pālai*) region of Tamil country. I am primarily, but not exclusively, guided in this material on Koṟṟavai from J. N. Tiwari (1985, 229–35), and conversations in January 2018 with R. Nagaswamy, former Director of Archaeology for Tamil Nadu. This so-called *pālai* is one of five archetypal regions in Tamil literature, which include the mountains (*kuriñci*), the forests (*mullai*), the seashore, and agricultural land. The *pālai* is the wasteland, a dry desolate desert, and thus already conducive to association with the term *durga* in its earliest Sanskrit meanings of foreboding regions, which are difficult to traverse. Indeed, it is regarded as a composite of *kuriñci* and *mullai*, both also appropriately linked with the word *durga* for the aforementioned reasons. The *Tolkāppiyam*, an early Tamil grammar (c. 1st century CE for its early layers), refers to "Koṟṟavai-*nīlai*, after the victory has been won."[6] In a telling example of how Durgā's name is routinely substituted for other goddesses, the *Tamil Lexicon* (1924–36) simply renders Koṟṟavai-*nīlai* as "the theme of offering sacrifice to Durgā and worshipping her." They derive this explanation from Nacciṉārkkiṉar, a commentator on the *Tolkāppiyam*, who explains this expression means that after a battle, warriors went to pray to Koṟṟavai, the goddess of victory, and in their praises described her form (Vipulananda 1956, 254n15; Mudaliar 1964, 256, cited in J. N. Tiwari 1985, 229n62). Since Durgā in the early epic hymns is frequently praised as Jayā (conquest) and Vijayā (victory), there are obvious similarities here too with Korravai in this triumphant symbolism. The *Kuruntokai*, an early anthology of the Sangam literature, mentions a goddess Cūlī, "She who wields a spear" (*śūla*; *triśūla*, or trident). Although many scholars (including the *Tamil Lexicon*) simply identify this goddess with Durgā, because of her weapon-wielding persona, and others consider Cūlī to be Korravai (e.g., K. R. Srinivasan 1960, 21), one cannot assert with certainty that people thought of Cūlī primarily as Durgā or as Korravai at the time of the *Kuruntokai*'s composition. Cūlī appears to reflect a Śaiva influence from Sanskritic Hinduism, because Śiva is associated with the trident. Of course, we have noted that in early Gupta imagery, as well as in some of the earlier Kuṣāṇa plaques, the buffalo-subduing goddess is already portrayed with a trident. So, one cannot assume direct Śaiva influences, because the goddess may have already appropriated weapons and symbols associated with other deities. In the *Paripāṭal*, a late Sangam literary collection of seventy poems to various deities, the honorific red mark (*tiḷaka*) on a young girl's forehead is said to look like Korravai's third eye (J. N. Tiwari 1985, 229). In this instance we see the symbol of the third eye, traditionally associated with Śiva, attributed to the goddess. It is still a feature associated with Durgā today. The *Tirumurukāṟṟuppaṭai*, the first poem of the *Pattupāṭṭu* anthology, mentions Murukaṉ as the son of victorious Korravai (J. N. Tiwari 1985, 29). Here, too, there is an association with the persona of Durgā, who is eventually regarded as the mother of the Skanda, who is identified with Murukaṉ.

In the *Neṭunalvāṭai*, elderly ladies of the court, seeing the queen in grief at her separation from the king who is away at war, pray to Korravai. They call her "Mother," and pray for a quick end to the battle and the return of the king (J. Pillai 1968, 249–58). Korravai's is clearly identified by name in all the aforementioned examples, except for the *Kuruntokai*, which refers to Cūlī. So Korravai is a goddess of victory, possesses a third eye, is the mother of Murukaṉ, is referred to as "Mother," and is worshipped with post-victory rites. All these are characteristics eventually associated with Durgā. There are numerous other references in the Sangam anthologies, such as the *Puṟanāṉūṟu*, to the goddess of victory and of war, but in these she is unnamed (Diehl 1964, 313; K. R. Srinivasan 1960, 21–22). She is sometimes equated with the goddess of the forests, or as doing the *tuṇaṅkai* dance, and so on. According to the *Tamil Lexicon*, the *tuṇaṅkai* is a dance in which the arms, bent at the elbows, hit the sides, but the word also means "devil" or "festival." Evidently, the name, style, or intent of the dance is associated with celebrations of a dark nature.

This preceding so-called Sangam literature may be dated with some uncertainty to the 2nd or 3rd centuries CE (Basham 1959, 461–62; Hart and Heifetz 1999, xvi–xvii). Among the copious evidence for these dates are the references made in these anthologies to Tamil trade with the Roman and Greeks (Yāvanas), which diminished significantly by the 3rd century CE. In these texts, there is no mention of the Pallavas, a powerful dynasty in South India, who emerged by 350 CE. And the Cera king Ceṅkuṭṭuvan, who appears in these anthologies, is mentioned in the *Cilappatikāram* as being a contemporary of the Sri Lankan king Gajabahu I whose rule is dated to approximately 171 to 193 CE. This would suggest that the Cera and Coḷa kings mentioned in these early anthologies ruled from about 130 to 240 CE (Hart and Heifetz 1999, xvi–xvii). Of course, we cannot be sure that the various goddesses of war and victory or the goddesses of the forests are, in fact, Koṟṟavai, because just as the goddess Cūlī bears similar characteristics, but possesses a different name, there may have been a host of tribal goddesses, bearing various regional names, who were worshipped in those areas during this period.

In the *Puṟapporuḷ Veṇpāmālai*, a late 10th-century grammatical work, life in early Tamil society is vividly depicted. The text provides a detailed description of Koṟṟavai, the patron goddess of tribes engaged in constant cattle-raiding warfare (Pope 1899, 241–42). Surrounded by her demon entourage, she leads her warriors to attack enemy forts with such ferocity that their opponents cannot stand their ground. She holds a golden parrot and a bounding stag in her hands, while her banner prominently features a lion (Pope 1899, 237, v. 20). Wreaths, highly significant in these poems, played a key role in battle regalia. Tamil poets describe eight types of distinctive head wreaths, including those made of gold and gems, symbolizing specific military exploits (Pope 1899, 229). Crimson *veḍchi* wreaths were worn by raiders, dark purple *karanthai* by defenders, yellow *vañji* by attackers, and dark *kāñji* by the soon-to-be-defeated king and his forces. Victors wore the white-flowered *vāgai* wreath (Pope 1899, 263). Specific kings also donned unique wreaths: Cera kings wore palmyra wreaths, Pandiyan kings margosa, and Cembiyan kings *ātti* wreaths. Pope (1899, 263) identifies *veḍchi* as the "flame of the forest" blossom, *karanthai* as basil or sacred tulasi, *vañji* as a local creeping plant, and *kāñji* as elm leaves and flowers. The motif of wreaths recalls the imagery of Nike on Greek and Kuṣāṇa coins, where she flies behind a king holding a diadem. This potent motif also appears in early representations of the buffalo-subduing goddess on Kuṣāṇa plaques and Gupta reliefs.

The *Puṟapporuḷ* compares the act of defeating enemies to plowing a field, a metaphor elaborated by its commentator Naccinārkkiṉiyar. He describes how, just as a farmer harvests grain, threshes it with bulls, and offers it to the gods before sharing with the needy and family, so too does a king deal with his enemies (Kailasapathy 1968, 241). The *Puṟapporuḷ* further depicts a sacrificial celebration following battle, where demons and demonesses, revered as deities, are fed the bodies of slain enemies, and poets compose verses honoring the victorious warriors (Kailasapathy 1968, 241n5, citing *Puṟapporuḷ Veṇpāmālai*, v. 159–60). Naccinārkkiṉiyar adds grisly details, explaining how the king heaps enemy bodies, tramples them with elephants, and has their remains cooked in a large pot by a virgin priestess. The pot, filled with blood and fat, is stirred with severed body parts and offered to the gods. This grisly ritual stew, horrifyingly ceremonial, was possibly consumed by victors as part of their celebration.

While Korravai is the implied goddess of these sacrifices, earlier texts such as the *Puranāṉūru* also reference such rituals (Kailasapathy 1968, 241n8, citing *Puranāṉūru* 369, 372–73).

The battlefield rituals described suggest rulers marked victory with sacrificial rites involving the heads, blood, and entrails of enemies. These remains were ritually cooked in a vat, which stood atop a tripod formed from the enemy leaders' severed heads, replacing the traditional three stones of an oven. Stirred by virgin, post-menopausal, or barren priestesses, this grotesque concoction, which even animals would not devour — resembling a sacrificial drink — was consumed ceremonially, akin to drinking pure water in a wedding ritual.

In sum, although the *Puranāṉūru* (c. 2nd to 3rd centuries CE) does not mention Korravai, the *Purapporuḷ Veṇpāmālai*, of a much later date (c. 10th–11th centuries CE), does. It identifies Korravai as the goddess of the warring tribes who engaged in the types of previously mentioned practices (referred to in the *Puranāṉūru*), which were explained in some detail by Naccinārkkiniyar (later than the 12th century CE), a commentator on the *Purapporuḷ*. We can be sure that Korravai was either the very goddess of victory widely worshipped by warriors during the period of the compilation of the Sangam anthologies, or that by the 10th century CE she had amalgamated a host of minor goddesses of war, victory, and the forests, within her persona.

The *Cilappatikāram* (*The Ankle Bracelet*), a Tamil epic attributed to Iḷaṅkō Aṭikaḷ, offers insights into the evolution of the cult of Korravai. The narrative revolves around Kaṇṇaki, whose husband, Kōvalaṉ, is unjustly executed for allegedly stealing her anklet. In her fury, Kaṇṇaki unleashes her wrath, setting the city of Maturai (Madurai) ablaze. Her pure heart amplifies her rage, ultimately leading to her apotheosis into the fierce goddess Pattiṉi. While the precise date of the *Cilappatikāram* remains uncertain, it is generally placed in the 5th century CE (Parthasarathy 1993, 5). Even if composed slightly later, the epic predates the Pallava period imagery at Māmallapuram, providing context for the early formation and development of goddess worship in Tamil culture.

When examining the text, one finds that translators (e.g., Daniélou (1965), Parthasarathy (1993)) routinely substitute the name Durgā for other goddesses, such as Aiyai or Korravai. From my examination, there is no mention of the name Durgā in the *Cilappatikāram*. However, there are clear connections made between a deer-riding goddess and the one who slays the Buffalo Demon, as well as with fierce goddesses such as Kālī. For example, in Canto XI, the protagonist Kōvalaṉ prays to "the goddess who rides a deer" (*pāykalaippāvai*), to drive away a wood nymph, who tries to entice him. He and his wife, the epic's heroine, Kaṇṇaki, then enter a forest grove where they find a temple to Aiyai (Daniélou 1965, 76 renders this as Kālī), who has "an eye on her forehead" (Parthasarathy 1993, 118). She is described as a goddess of local bandits of that area who attack travelers and raid people in the neighboring regions.[7] The goddess expected a human sacrifice in homage for granting them victory. We here note the themes of human sacrifice, victory, and the goddess who rides a deer as a benefactress of wild tribes and brigands. In Canto XII, the couple rests in a corner of the temple to Aiyai, who is described as the goddess of hunters and of the Maravan-Eyinan tribes. They observe how one such virgin, named Cālinī (although this just means "oracle"), is possessed by the goddess Aiyai.[8] With her body hair standing on end and hands upraised she spoke to the forest-folk, who were gripped with awe:

> Herds of cattle thrive in the big villages of your foes. The meeting places of the Eyinans are in ruins. Born of the family of the Maravans, they no longer strip travelers of their possessions. They have become timid like righteous men. Unless you offer the sacrifice due to the goddess riding a stag, she won't bless your bows with victory. O men who live by plunder! If you wish to spend your days drinking palm wine, offer your sacrifice. (Parthasarathy 1993, 119–20)

As an aside, there appears to be a tension apparent between the pursuits of warfare and agriculture. The storehouses are bare because more people have been turning to agriculture (i.e., acting like peasants), perhaps with limited success in the unforgiving territory they inhabit, instead of carrying out thieving raids, which seem to have been their traditional occupation. The Eyinans are described as offering their own heads as a sacrifice, rather than be cremated upon death. Cālinī, the oracle, wearing a crescent-shaped boar tusk entwined with silvery snakes on her head, a necklace of tiger's teeth, and a short skirt of tiger-skin, then rode on a deer. Eyinan women made offerings of dolls, roosters, parrots, and peacocks at her feet, and cast black bean balls for divination. They followed her with offerings of powders, fragrant anointing pastes, boiled grain, pastries of sesamum seeds, rice cooked with meat, flowers, incense, and perfumes (Mahalakshmi 2011, 71).

The virgin oracle, Cālinī, who evidently is dressed and adorned to resemble the goddess, riding on her deer mount, prefigures the form she will take when transformed. We know that this has not yet occurred, because when gripped with the sort of prophetic, explanatory voice after her seeming trance-inducing dance, she does not speak as the goddess but admonishes everyone to bring the goddess the offerings for which she has too long been deprived. Notably, there are a variety of birds, such as roosters, parrots, and peacocks, offered to the girl. Cālinī was then taken to the temple of Anaṅku, who demands sacrifices in return for victory. She prostrated herself before the goddess "who rides a stag." It is only here that suddenly the virgin girl oracle was fully possessed and transformed into the goddess (Parthasarathy 1993, 120–21).

The description that follows serves as the standard for Korravai's appearance, for this is with whom the goddess Aiyai/Anaṅku is explicitly identified:

> The goddess wore the silver petal of the moon on her head.
> From her split forehead blazed an unwinking eye: her lips
> were coral, bright as silver her teeth, and dark with poison was

her throat. Whirling the fiery serpent as a bowstring, she bent Mount Meru as a bow. Her breasts smothered inside a bodice the venomous fangs of a snake. In her hand, piled with bangles, she bore a trident. A robe of elephant skin covered her, and over it, as Aṉaṅku, a girdle of tiger skin. Her radiant, left foot clasped a tinkling anklet, a heroic anklet her right. She is Koṟṟavai of the triumphant sword, who stood on the head of the broad-shouldered demon with two bodies. She is the goddess adored by many as Amari, Kumari, Gaurī, Samarī, the one with the trident, the blue one, Viṣṇu's younger sister, Aiyai, the red one, Durgā on the leaping stag with a sword in her large hand, Lakṣmī with a fine bracelet, Sarasvatī, the goddess of learning, the woman shining with rare gems, the ever-young virgin robed in the vesture of Kumari whom her kinsmen Viṣṇu and Brahmā, came to adore. Thus the oracle praised Aiyai. (Canto XII; Parthasarathy 1993, 120–22)

R. Parthasarathy's poetic translation, quoted here, is somewhat problematic for our purposes, because it inserts the names of goddesses that are not explicitly mentioned in the text. This would not be an issue if those epithets were unequivocally linked to the names of specific goddesses elsewhere in the text. However, in the *Cilappatikāram*, the name Durgā is never explicitly used.[9] Instead there are only references to the goddess riding the stag. J. N. Tiwari (1985, 232) replicates Parthasarathy's error, although he draws from Daniélou's (1965, 79) translation, which also calls the goddess who rides the deer Durgā, when in fact she is not identified as such. Moreover, while Parthasarathy refers to Koṟṟavai as with "the triumphant sword, who stood on the head of the broad-shouldered demon with two bodies," and Daniélou (1965, 78) renders this as "deft in swordplay, the goddess stood over a black genie with two broad-shouldered torsos," J. N. Tiwari (1985, 232) takes the leap and simply calls the goddess the "killer of the demon Mahiṣa" when there is no explicit mention of Mahiṣa in the *Cilappatikāram*. This is but another illustration of the tendency by translators to insert Durgā's name (and in this case Mahiṣa's too) when they ought not to have done so, thereby obfuscating our ability to trace the development of Durgā's cult effectively.

The *Cilappatikāram*'s portrayal of Koṟṟavai provides a compelling depiction of a fierce yet striking goddess who embodies both destructive and protective qualities. Known by names such as Aṉaṅku and Aiyai, she wields a variety of weapons — bow, arrow, sword, and spear/trident — and is adorned with symbolic ornaments such as bracelets and anklets. Her attire of elephant and tiger or lion hides emphasizes her primal and ferocious nature, while her virginity underscores her independence and autonomy as a deity. Notably, despite her fierce attributes, Koṟṟavai is not portrayed as grotesque, but rather as a formidable yet majestic figure. She is presented as a Great Goddess with multifaceted characteristics, drawing connections to both Śaiva and Vaiṣṇava traditions. Her trident links her to Śiva, while her blue complexion and identity as Viṣṇu's younger sister suggest Vaiṣṇava associations. Her connection with serpents and a third eye further align her with divine power and esoteric symbolism.

Similar motifs appear in later Sanskrit literature. For instance, Bhavabhūti's *Mālatī-mādhava* describes the goddess Cāmuṇḍā/Karālā with snakes and an elephant-hide skirt, echoing Koṟṟavai's imagery. Although Cāmuṇḍā/Karālā inspires fear with her destructive dance, she is not hideous — only terrifying in her ferocity. Likewise, the *Gaüḍavaho's* depiction of Kālī shares parallels with both Cāmuṇḍā and Koṟṟavai, emphasizing her fierce attributes while maintaining her role as a powerful and awe-inspiring deity. Importantly, Kālī in the *Gaüḍavaho* is explicitly linked to the slaying of Mahiṣa, the Buffalo Demon, drawing a clear connection to the mythology surrounding Durgā and her fierce manifestations. These observations compel us to question the arguments in some studies that speak of Kālī as originally hideous, and progressively transformed into a beautiful goddess.[10] The evidence would suggest that she was initially fierce and fear-inducing, and associated with the slaying of Mahiṣa but virginal and implicitly beautiful. Her fearsome appearance may have developed through pejorative imagery framed by traditions that abjured animal sacrifice and violence in general, such as Buddhism and Jainism.

Koṟṟavai, as depicted in the *Cilappatikāram*, exhibits traits that are clearly absorbed into the later representations of Cāmuṇḍā and Kālī. The demon upon whom Koṟṟavai stands, described as having two torsos or bodies, evokes the shape-shifting qualities associated with Mahiṣa, although he is not explicitly named as such, nor is there mention of a buffalo form in these verses. It is possible that the dualistic nature of the demon was familiar to the text's audience, leaving the details implicit. This ambiguity, however, may have contributed to later mythic expansions. These could have reimagined Koṟṟavai's adversary as two distinct demons, a single being with dual forms, or a shapeshifter capable of transforming between bodies.

After that elaborate description of Koṟṟavai/Aiyai/Aṉaṅku, the fierce but "ever-young virgin, robed in the vesture of Kumari," the *Cilappatikāram* launches into various hymns of praise that reveal more details about the goddess. She has a crescent moon in her matted locks (Hymn 3). She is the younger sister of Tirumāl (Viṣṇu) and wears golden bracelets (Hymns 4, 5, 6) (Parthasarathy 1993, 123). She is associated with the leaping stag, which is her mount (Hymns 7, 9) (Parthasarathy 1993, 124). And she is explicitly described as standing upon the black head of a wild buffalo, and killing the great Buffalo Demon, while holding a sword (Hymns 8, 9) (Parthasarathy 1993, 124). She is described with red, angry eyes, and as standing on the back of a lion, holding the conch and the discus, and as the consort of he who is adorned with the Gaṅgā in his hair (Hymn 10) (Parthasarathy 1993, 125). Her bracelets, anklets, and girdle jingle and she does a stilt dance (Hymn 12) (Parthasarathy 1993, 125). In Canto XII, Hymn 18, there is an explicit reference to blood offerings made from severed necks. Daniélou (1965, 83) renders this as severed heads. And in Hymns 19 and 20 there is again explicit reference to the marauding Eyinans making offerings of blood from their severed necks after their successful raids. In the *Kaliṅkattupparaṇi*, a 12th century CE war poem praising a Coḻa king's victory over Kaliṅga, these types of sacrifices to a goddess identified as Korravai are described at length (J. N. Tiwari 1985, 232n89; Meenakshisundaram 1969, 196–207).

Although this goddess of the hunters conveyed by the *Cilappatikāram* blends several goddesses, including Aiyai, Aṇaṅku, and others, they each seem to have, or have had, distinctive characteristics. In Canto XX, lines 35 to 40, Kaṇṇaki, angered and seeking redress for the unjust execution of Kōvalaṉ, arrives at the palace-gates of the Pāṇḍyan king. The doorkeeper tells the king:

> She is not Korravai, the goddess of victory with the fierce spear in her large hand, standing on the buffalo's neck that spurts continuous blood from its open wound. She is not Aṇaṅku, the youngest sister of the seven virgins, who made Śiva dance. She is not Kālī, who lives in the dreadful forest. She is not Durgā, who tore apart the broad chest of Dāruka. Pent up with hatred and anger at the loss of her husband, she stands at the gate, a golden anklet in her hand. (Parthasarathy 1993, 187–88)

Lest our excitement grow needlessly at the mention of Durgā, an examination of the Tamil reveals that Parthasarathy has again taken the liberty of inserting Durgā's name. Daniélou (1965, 127) translates this verse as follows:

> A woman is waiting at the gate. She is not Korravai, the victorious goddess who carries in her hand a glorious spear and stands upon the neck of a defeated buffalo losing its blood through its fresh wounds. She is not Anangu, youngest of the seven virgins, for whom Shiva once danced; and she is not Kālī, who dwells in the darkest forests inhabited by ghosts and imps. Neither is she the goddess who pierced the chest of the mighty Dāruka. She seems filled with a mad fury, suffused with rage. She has lost someone dear to her, and stands at the gate clasping an ankle bracelet of gold in her hands.

J. N. Tiwari (1985, 233) interprets this as a direct allusion to Durgā Mahiṣamardinī, although this conclusion seems unwarranted. What is evident from these verses is Korravai's association with victory, as she stands atop a severed buffalo head or neck, symbolizing a demon she has vanquished. Equipped with weapons such as a bow, spear, and sword, Korravai is also identified with figures such as Aṇaṅku, Kālī, and other demon-slaying goddesses. Kālī, for instance, is associated with remote forests and surrounded by fearsome beings. The *Liṅga Purāṇa* (1.106), dated no later than 1000 CE despite some later insertions (D. Smith 2003, 148), recounts the story of the demon Dāruka. There, Dāruka could only be slain by a woman with a beautiful face. The gods sought Śiva's help, and he directed his lovely consort, the Daughter of the Mountain, to intervene. Using her Māyā, she entered Śiva's body and formed a new body from the poison in his neck. Emerging as Kālī, she had matted hair, a blue-black neck, and a terrifying visage, born from Śiva's third eye. Terrified by her appearance, the gods fled as Kālī, adorned with a third eye, a crescent moon on her head, ornaments, and a trident, defeated Dāruka. Her fury, however, threatened to destroy the world, and Śiva had to transform into a baby boy. When Kālī suckled the infant, her anger dissipated, restoring balance (D. Smith 2003, 146).

The identification of Korravai with Kālī and the slaying of Dāruka, a demon often represented as a buffalo, extends back to the period of the *Cilappatikāram*. Although the buffalo demon is not explicitly named Mahiṣa (the Sanskrit word for buffalo), the motif of the goddess's feet upon the demon's neck or head is prominent. Korravai is also associated with both a lion and a deer as mounts, strengthening her connections with fierce, martial goddesses. In the *Cilappatikāram*, Korravai is linked to Śiva's consort and Viṣṇu's sister, suggesting familiarity with the HV's Nidrā myth cycle. This reflects efforts to subsume her supremacy within the broader pantheon by tying her to these major deities, while simultaneously asserting her identity with numerous other goddesses. The text as a whole centers on the transformation of Kaṇṇakī, a demure and virtuous woman, into the fearsome goddess Pattiṇi. Her apotheosis exemplifies the trope of a modest beautiful figure transformed by righteous fury into a terrifying force of justice and destruction. This duality helps explain why goddesses such as Korravai, who demand gruesome offerings and are associated with the battlefield, are often depicted as benign and strikingly beautiful. Their iconography captures their transformative power — at once nurturing and fearsome, embodying both the serenity and the fury of the divine feminine.

The *Maṇimēkalai* (6.50–53) another Tamil work that is contemporary with the *Cilappatikāram*, refers to Kāṭamarcelvi ("Great Lady of the Forest") and her temple, which has a sacrificial altar in its front courtyard and severed heads on tall posts surrounding it (see Schmid 2011, 150). The goddess Kāṭamarcelvi is routinely identified with Durgā in the *Tamil Lexicon*, and by early scholars as Durgā-Korravai. For instance, J. N. Tiwari (1985, 233n92) notes that K. R. Srinivasan (1960, 21) cites Kāṭamarcelvi's occurrence in the *Akanāṉūru* (345: 3–7) (2nd–3rd century CE), another Sangam anthology, and cautiously identifies her with Durgā or Caṇḍika. However, to trace the development of Durgā's cult with precision, we have noted how such repeated identifications, although suggestive and reasonable, can be misleading.

J. N. Tiwari (1985, 233) concludes that the foregoing data makes clear that Korravai was possibly the earliest and most widely worshipped goddess of the ancient Dravidian people. Her name is probably derived from the Tamil *kol*, "to kill," which is the root of words such as *korram*, "victory." And while her association with blood sacrifice and success in cattle-raiding warfare may appear to have negligible connections with fertility, the virgin priestesses that officiate at her rites may suggest some such early associations in the earlier character of the goddess. Certainly, her identification as the mother of Murukaṉ connects her with these aspects, since he was a fearsome fertility god, worshipped with blood sacrifices and orgiastic rituals involving trance dances by young girls (J. N. Tiwari 1985, 233n96).

J. N. Tiwari (1985, 234) asserts that although the Brahminic hand is already evident in the earliest Sangam poetry collections, features of the original character of Korravai seep through. He suggests that Korravai was already being subsumed by Durgā's cult, which is evident from her associations with buffalo slaying. However, there is insufficient evidence to assert that during the early Sangam period, or even at the time of the composition of the *Cilappatikāram*, Korravai was known as Durgā. Both Durgā and Mahiṣa are nowhere explicitly mentioned. Indeed, the Pallavas, Pāṇḍyas, and others, from the 7th to 10th century CE, portray a goddess with a stag as well as a lion *vāhana*. She was most likely Korravai in the eyes of most who saw and worshipped those Victorious Goddess images when they were first established. Only later did these and similar depictions come to be regarded as Durgā and subsequently reproduced as depictions of Durgā. Moreover, Korravai's acceptance of self-decapitation as a form of worship accrued to all the various goddesses with whom she was identified, particularly Kālī.

Koṭavī, the Nude Goddess

J. N. Tiwari (1985, 234) argues that the North Indian goddess Koṭavī, whose cult flourished in the early centuries of the Common Era, was most likely the South Indian goddess Korravai, whose cult had migrated north. His evidence and arguments are significant in our efforts to understand how the lion-riding goddess of north-central and northwest India, with evident resonances with Western goddesses such as Nike, Anāhitā, Kybele, and Nanā, merged with South Asian goddesses such as Kālī and Korravai. I therefore present the essence of his investigations here in some detail. Intriguingly, almost all these goddesses had a penchant for blood sacrifices and were associated with victory. V. S. Agrawala (1947–48, 151) found a variety of terracotta figures from Ahicchatra (Bareilly District, Uttar Pradesh) some dateable to between 450 and 650 CE, which he surmised might be representations of Koṭavī. The figures were of "a nude woman either moving with a bent body in a disheveled and disconsolate posture, or simply standing, with right hand drawn parallel to the body and the left akimbo" (quoted in J. N. Tiwari 1985, 220). It is difficult to know with certainty whether these figurines depict Koṭavī — her bent body evokes the image of the Tantric goddess Kubjikā — but the existence of her cult is testified to in Brahminic literature.[11] According to J. N. Tiwari (1985, 221), Koṭavi is known as Koṭarī, Koṭarā, Koṭavatī, and other similar names, and appears in various Vaiṣṇava Purāṇas as well as in the HV.

The *Mahābhārata* (Mbh IX.45.17, 30–40) lists Koṭarā as one of many Mothers (Mātṛ), wrathful deities that accompany Skanda-Kārttikeya. In the *Bhāgavata Purāṇa* (X.6.27–29) Koṭarā is described as a malicious being, in the same category as Jyeṣṭhā, Revatī, Yakṣas, Rākṣasas, Piśācas, Mātṛs, Kūṣmāṇḍas, Ḍākinis, and such. Only by a ritual recitation of the names of Viṣṇu might one be protected from their damaging actions. The *Viṣṇu Purāṇa, Bhāgavata Purāṇa*, and the HV refer to an incident in which Koṭavī intercedes to protect the demon Bāṇa. The HV tells the story in greatest detail and is closely examined by Couture (2003). Viṣṇu/Kṛṣṇa's grandson, Aniruddha, had fallen in love with Uṣā, daughter of the demon Bāṇa. When learning of their relationship, the angry Bāṇāsura imprisoned Aniruddha. Before the ensuing battle between Bāṇāsura and Viṣṇu/Kṛṣṇa, who intends to free his grandson from captivity, Kārttikeya is said to be fighting on behalf of the demon Bāṇa. Just as Kṛṣṇa is about to hurl his discus, the goddess Koṭavī appears to aid Kārttikeya. She is naked and Kṛṣṇa chides her for her immodest appearance (HV 112.49). He asks her to leave the battlefield, but she returns again on Bāṇa's behalf, pleading with Kṛṣṇa to save his life. Kṛṣṇa admonishes Bāṇa for his unmanly behavior for repeatedly soliciting her help (HV 112.99–101).

In certain editions of the HV, the imprisoned Aniruddha voices a hymn to Durgā. This hymn (AniH), not included in the critical edition, is clearly an insertion into the text, and has been discussed in an earlier chapter. What is interesting, however, is that in some versions (e.g., the Poona edition, edited by Kinjawadekar), Aniruddha begins his hymn of praise to the Devī Koṭavatī (HV II.120.1–2) (arguably the same goddess as Kotavī), while in other versions the hymn is directed to the goddess Kaumārī. Eventually, the goddess appears as Durgā, breaks his bonds, and promises that Viṣṇu/Kṛṣṇa will destroy Bāṇāsura. Evidently, this insertion illustrates the "Durgā-fication" of Koṭavatī, as well as the complex personas of these protective deities, for she is called upon by Aniruddha for protection, but also offers protection to Bāṇāsura.

The interweaving of Koṭavī into the Brahminic pantheon continues in material from the popular editions of the HV. When Kārttikeya is about to be killed by Kṛṣṇa on the battlefield, Koṭavī, called "an eighth portion of Devī" is sent by "Deva" (probably Śiva) to help him (HV II. 126.23, cited in J. N. Tiwari 1985, 223). Not only does this effectively assimilate Koṭavī into the cult of the Great Goddess as a subordinate goddess, but it situates the Goddess in a hierarchically inferior manner to Śiva, who instructs her. In the prelude to Kṛṣṇa's fight with Bāṇa, when Koṭavī intercedes, she is said to have been sent on the instructions of Rudrāṇī, by Śiva's wishes (HV II.126.106ff.). Kṛṣṇa addresses Koṭavī as "mother of Kārttikeya" (HV II.126.112). Since Bāṇa is depicted as a son of Śiva and Pārvatī, and a younger brother of Kārttikeya (II.116.16–17), and Koṭavī is the mother of Bāṇa (HV II.126.117, 120), this would imply that Koṭavī is either identical to, or an aspect of, the consort of Śiva. Of course, they are all subordinated to Kṛṣṇa in this narrative version.

In Bāṇa's *Harṣacarita* (7th century CE), Koṭavī is portrayed as wandering the fields, shaking her index finger as if tallying the dead (J. N. Tiwari 1985, 220). The *Nāyādhammakahā*, a Jain canonical text, describes a festival dedicated to the goddess Koṭṭakiriyā (in Sanskrit, Koṭṭakriyā), which J. N. Tiwari

(1985, 225) considers a variant of Koṭavī. The name Koṭṭakiriyā may mean "maker of forts" (in Sanskrit *koṭṭa*, in Tamil *koṭṭai*) or, more broadly, "maker of foreboding places," linking her to the concept of Durgā, whose name can similarly connote a fort or inaccessible refuge. Abhayadevasūri, an 11th century CE commentator on the *Nāyādhammakahā*, explicitly equates Koṭṭakiriyā with Durgā, depicted as riding the buffalo (J. N. Tiwari 1985, 225). The festival in her honor, Koṭṭakiriyā-maha, is speculated by V. S. Agrawala (1964b, 114–15; 1970, 7–10) to align with the Navarātra or Mahānavamī festival dedicated to Durgā, celebrated during the bright half of the month of Āśvina.

J. N. Tiwari (1985, 225) suggests a probable connection between Koṭṭakiriyā and Koṭavī, supported by the Jain canonical literature's antiquity. This points to a well-established cult of Koṭavī in North India during the early centuries of the Common Era, predating the compilation of these texts. However, the explicit identification of Koṭṭakiriyā with Durgā only surfaces in the 11th century CE, reflecting the gradual integration of local deities into the broader Hindu pantheon.

The *Matsya Purāṇa* (13.12ff., cited in J. N. Tiwari 1985, 225–26) references Koṭavī in an interpolated section from the early medieval period. In this account, the goddess Satī instructs her father, Dakṣa, to perform austerities at various sacred sites where she would manifest following her self-immolation, naming Koṭitīrtha as the place where she would be known as Koṭavī. While Koṭitīrtha is not a widely recognized location and lacks definitive association with Koṭavī, this mention indicates the presence of her cult and efforts to integrate it into the larger framework of the Great Goddess mythology via Satī's narrative.

Koṭavī's name (or its variants) continues to appear in later goddess-related site lists, such as the *pīṭhas*. The *Pīṭhanirṇaya* (17th–18th century CE), associated with the *Tantracūḍāmaṇi*, begins its enumeration of *pīṭhas* with Hiṅgulā (Sircar 1948, 3, 23–24). The goddess residing there is named Koṭṭarī, a likely variation of Koṭavī and Korṟavai. Hiṅgulā corresponds to modern Hinglāj, located in Balochistan, Pakistan. The site, a small mud temple situated within a cave along a riverbed, venerates a goddess referred to as Mātā or Mahāmāyā by Hindus and as Bībī Nānī by Muslims, as discussed in an earlier chapter. There is a deep circular natural water tank at the site. Significantly, some have proposed that the site of the goddess Bībī Nānī was likely chosen and dedicated to the lion-riding goddess Nanā (Nanaia), portrayed on Kuṣāṇa coins, and likely one of the crucial contributors to the persona of Durgā.[12] So, Hinglāj, in Balochistan, appears to offer intriguing intersections among the cults of Koṭṭarī (Koṭavi, Korṟavai), Nanā, and Durgā.

J. N. Tiwari (1985, 227) references a copper plate dated to around 640 CE that documents a grant by the Valabhī ruler Dhruvasena II. The plate, discovered at Bhamodra-Mohota in Gujarat-Kathiawad, records the reconfirmation of a grant initially made by King Droṇasimha on behalf of his parents to a temple dedicated to Koṭṭamahikā-devī, possibly translated as "goddess of the earthen fortress." The temple, located in Tarsamiā in the Hathab district, still exists. J. N. Tiwari (1985, 227) is confident that Koṭṭamahikā is a variant of Koṭavī and suggests that names such as Koṭṭavī, Kauṭavī, Koṭarī, Koṭarā, Koṭṭakiriyā, and Koṭṭamahikā represent the same independent popular goddess worshipped in North India during the early centuries of the Common Era. Described as a nude figure with disheveled hair and a malevolent, demonic nature, Koṭṭamahikā was later incorporated into the Śaiva pantheon, where she became associated with Durgā-Pārvatī as Śiva's consort. However, it seems plausible that she was initially linked with Kālī, a goddess with similar fierce attributes, before being fully assimilated into the Durgā-Pārvatī framework. Tiwari's use of the term "Durgā-Pārvatī" highlights this assimilation, portraying Durgā as a great goddess subsumed within the Śaiva tradition as Śiva's spouse, rather than as an independent goddess or supreme deity.

The process of acknowledging Koṭavī's independent status and simultaneously integrating her into the Brahminic scheme is also evident in the Sanskrit lexicons. Amarasiṃha's renowned *Amarakośa* (aka the *Nāmalingānuśāsanam*) (1990, 98, l. 1107), the earliest known Sanskrit lexicon dated to the 6th century CE, simply designates Koṭavī a naked woman (*strī nagnikā*). A commentary on the Jain scholar Hemacandra's 11th century CE *Abhidhānacintāmaṇi* elaborates upon Koṭavī as "an unclothed woman wandering about with disheveled hair and oppressed with deep shame" (*nagnā vivastrā yoṣid muktakeśīyāgamaḥ, koṭena lajjāvaśad yāti koṭavī*) (J. N. Tiwari 1985, 228). In both these cases, Koṭavī's nakedness induces comparisons to the goddess Kālī. The description of her hair resonates with the long, matted locks of Kālī, whose extended tongue is often explained by Hindus today as a sign of her shame. A commentary on the *Amarakośa* identifies Koṭarī (i.e., Koṭavī) with Caṇḍikā, a goddess who kills wicked demons.[13] The *Śabdakalpadruma* (1967, II, 201), a 19th century dictionary, which draws on older lexicons, cites the *Dharaṇīkośa*, which explicitly identifies Koṭavī with Durgā, who destroyed the demon Durga, equated with Koṭa.[14] It appears that Koṭa is connected explicitly via *koṭṭa* to *durga*, since both words mean a fort or a stronghold. The derivation of Durgā's name through her destruction of the demon Durga is also found in the *Brahmavaivarta Purāṇa* (57.1ff.).

Koṭavī's traits — nakedness, disheveled hair, demon-slaying prowess, and association with ominous locales — likely influenced the construction of Kālī's image. Yet, while Koṭavī, Koṟṟavai, and Kālī are depicted as fearsome, there is no indication in the sources that Koṭavī or Koṟṟavai possessed the grotesque appearance later attributed to Kālī or Cāmuṇḍā. By contrast, a more explicitly horrific characterization is found in the *Yaśastilaka*, a Jain text from the 11th to 12th century CE by Somadeva, which describes a goddess named Caṇḍamārī. Caṇḍamārī exhibits gruesome traits: she is adorned with human body parts, bathes in rivers of blood or wine, and uses excretions from corpses as cosmetics. She drinks from skulls and resides in cremation grounds. Her worship involves devotees engaging in antinomian practices, such as burning incense on their own heads, drinking their blood, and offering their flesh as sacrifice (Kinsley 1986, 117). Although not explicitly identified as Kālī, Caṇḍamārī's characteristics appear to have merged with Kālī's over time, contributing to a terrifying and macabre iconography. Interestingly, such depictions of the goddess frequently arise in texts critical of practices such as blood sacrifice, self-mortification, and especially human sacrifice. These literary sources often present these practices as abhorrent, framing the goddess in a manner that reflects their disdain for antinomian worship traditions.

The evidence collectively underscores Kālī's remarkable ability to subsume diverse regional goddess cults into her persona. Some of these, such as the cult of Korravai in South India, had substantial followings, mirrored in North India by goddesses such as Koṭavī and her variants. While J. N. Tiwari suggests that Koṭavī may have evolved from the more ancient South Indian cult of Korravai through migration, this remains uncertain. What is evident, however, is how these goddesses' attributes — malevolent, naked, with disheveled hair, inhabiting dangerous places, and venerated through sacrificial rituals often involving virgins or postmenopausal women — aligned with the multifaceted persona of Durgā/Kālī. These goddesses were propitiated by bandits, warriors, and kings seeking victory in battle, often through blood sacrifices, including human offerings.

This assimilation may have begun early if we accept the pre-HV date for the DStv or variants where Durgā and Kālī are equated, as they are in the DSto. The associations between Durgā's name and fortifications (*durga*, *koṭṭa*) also point to her role as a protector and refuge, a space where people sought shelter from invaders. Efforts to merge Durgā with Śaiva and Vaiṣṇava traditions, while simultaneously subordinating her to Śiva and Viṣṇu, further reflect her incorporation into dominant sectarian frameworks. In South Asia, Durgā maintained her portrayal as a beautiful goddess, albeit fierce in battle. However, when her worship extended to East Java and Bali, her Kālī-like characteristics became more prominent, marking a shift toward her darker, more fearsome aspects (see volume 2).

Sarkar (2017) suggests that this process of regional goddesses being amalgamated into the cult of a great goddess gestated at the time of the Kuṣāṇas, but emerged from the time of the Gupta empire, which in its expansion began to include the territories of *āṭavikarājas*, or forest kings. After the collapse of the Gupta empire, many of these tribal *āṭavika* kingdoms, which often favored patron goddesses, began to grow substantially. For example, Stambheśvarī, who in the 6th century CE was the patron deity of Tuṣṭikara, grew to be the tutelary goddess of the Śulkīs of Odisha between the 6th and 9th centuries. Inscriptional evidence attests that Śulki rulers claimed to receive their kingship from her (Sarkar 2017, 7–8). One of the necessary procedures to actualize the formation of a cohesive kingdom as its expanse absorbed regions ruled by chieftains was the development of a unifying ritual system (Kulke 1995, 234–36). An effective means of doing so was to maintain the patronage of the local religious cults, while overlaying these with a consistent ritual procedure centered on a single imperial religious cult. In this endeavor, various contenders for a great goddess, such as Kālī, Durgā, Vaiṣṇavī, Jayā, Vijayā, Kātyāyanī, Caṇḍī, Nidrā, Ambikā, Kauśikī, Pārvatī, Śrī, Bhagavatī, and so on, whose methods of worship were crafted by orthodox Brahminic ritual expertise, would prove particularly effective. Every local goddess would retain its Indigenous persona and name but be simultaneously understood as simply a particular regional manifestation of a great goddess. Examples of this process, which is still underway, would fill innumerable volumes.[15] The example of Koṭavī discussed above offers textual evidence of the absorption of various regional goddesses, including Korravaī, into that of Kālī, who is being assimilated to Durgā.

In February 2018, I observed an ongoing example of the integration and worship of diverse goddesses in Dalijoda, outside Cuttack, Odisha. A member of a royal family, now managing a bed and breakfast on his great-grandfather's former hunting lodge, oversees the worship of multiple deities on their private land. The family's tutelary goddess is Bagalamukhī, part of the Daśamahāvidyās cluster. The landlord's wife was particularly moved to discover Bagalamukhī enshrined at the lodge, as the goddess also happens to be her family's clan deity from Madhya Pradesh. Daily *pūjā*s are conducted by a priest at sunrise and sunset, with family members making efforts to attend.

Within the adjacent National Forest Reserve, previously the *rāja*'s hunting grounds, lies another shrine dedicated to Dam-damanī, the forest's protector goddess. Her primary form is an amorphous stone outcropping adorned with metallic facial features like eyes, lips, and a bindi. A hereditary tribal priest conducts daily *pūjā*s, attracting about a dozen local devotees. The landlord attributed the shrine's establishment to his great-grandfather, who reportedly dreamed of the goddess's presence there. However, the tribal priest suggested that the shrine's origins predate the *rāja*'s involvement, and the construction of the enclosure merely formalized an older tradition. Devotees see Dam-damanī not only in the stone effigy but also in the surrounding trees, reflecting an older, nature-centric worship tradition. Several trees in the grove are adorned with ribbons tied by devotees seeking boons; when their wishes are fulfilled, they return to remove the ribbons.

However, about twenty years ago a new, better-constructed temple dedicated to Vana-durgā ("Durgā of the Forest") was built right beside Dam-damanī's shrine. The *pūjā* there is conducted to an anthropomorphic image, in a much more classic manner (e.g., with an array of purifications, Sanskrit hymns, priestly *mudrās*, and sequences of offerings) by a Brahmin priest. During my few observations, almost none of the local devotees attended this *pūjā*, but it plainly receives patronage from more than just the landlord. It is evident that the new Vana-durgā temple is a Brahminic assertion that the local goddess Dam-damanī is but a particular manifestation of Durgā, the Great Goddess. The landlord scion of the former *rāja* patronized all three goddesses, Bagalamukhī, Dam-damanī, and Vanadurgā, with the sense that all these are manifestations of Devī.[16] Although I have used the term "Durgā-fication" to refer to such examples of religious colonization of minor goddess cults by the imperial cult of the Great Goddess Durgā, we do not have unequivocal evidence to assert that Durgā was a pervasive or the foremost name for the Great Goddess at the time of the composition of the *Devī Māhātmya* (DM).[17] However, I will argue that the success of the DM through its ritual narration became the mechanism through which Durgā became the dominant name for the Great Goddess.

From data found on copperplate or stone inscriptions and inscribed statuary, Sarkar (2017, 22–23) tabulated instances of wealthy private citizens or groups who patronized various goddesses in regions from Kashmir to Tamil Nadu and Mewar to Bengal; in other words, pretty much across the entire subcontinent. In her examination, Durgā's name first appears in the late 7th century CE, with numerous instances in the 8th century CE and thereafter. Mahiṣāsuramārdinī and Caṇḍī first appear in the 8th century CE. Although the list does not purport to be exhaustive, it certainly suggests that those names and epithets only began to gain widespread prominence at those time periods.

Chapter 11

The Shape-Shifting and Emerging Demon Imagery

Having examined the *Devī Māhātmya* (DM) as a foundational text that establishes the Great Goddess as the Supreme Deity in the Hindu pantheon, the previous chapter focused on Victorious Goddess (V) iconography, particularly images produced by the Pallava and Cola dynasties. These images provided insights into the integration of South Asian deities such as Korravai and Koṭavī into the persona of Kālī, later assimilated into Durgā. While the DM establishes Kālī's emanation from Durgā, as seen in texts such as the Durgā Stava (DStv) and Durgā Stotra (DSto), the Victorious Goddess imagery, featuring the goddess standing atop a severed buffalo head, aligns with the theme of the buffalo demon's defeat. However, these depictions do not explicitly align with the DM's narrative of a shape-shifting buffalo demon battling the goddess atop her lion.

In this chapter, we examine the Anthropomorphic (A) and Emergent Demon (E) iconographic types, which more closely correspond to the DM's narrative. This analysis focuses on three South Indian dynasties: the Pallavas, the Cālukyas, and the Rāṣṭrakūṭas. The Pallavas, previously discussed for their contributions to Victorious Goddess imagery, were a dominant power in east-central South India from 600 CE until their defeat by the Coḷas in the 9th century CE. The Cālukyas held sway over west-central South India from the 6th to the 12th century, while the Rāṣṭrakūṭas, who emerged in the 8th century, dominated much of the Deccan until the 10th century, overlapping with the Cālukya sphere of influence during this period (Avari 2016, 242–71). The iconographic evidence we explore suggests that the DM was likely composed around the mid-8th century CE, aligning with the stylistic and thematic developments observed in these Anthropomorphic and Emergent Demon depictions. This chapter aims to further investigate how these representations support a refined understanding of the DM's compositional history and its integration of regional goddess traditions into the overarching persona of the Great Goddess.

Anthropomorphic (A) Forms

Let us then now turn to Seshadri's third type (also Stietencron's type 3) image, in which the demon is mostly human, hence Anthropomorphic (A), but with some buffalo features, such as its head, horns, or snout. The Mukhalingeśvara Temple in Mukhalingam, from the latter half of the 8th century CE provides us with a good example (Barrett 1960, 10). In another late 8th century relief from Bhubaneshwar, the goddess steps on the backward twisted buffalo head on the *asura*'s human body and pierces his throat with her trident (Stietencron 2005, 146, Fig. 15). Seshadri (1963, 19) thinks it very probable that the Pallavas originated the anthropomorphic form, which then spread throughout South India.

Māmallapuram/Mahabalipuram

The preeminent example of the Anthropomorphic type is the large relief at the Mahiṣāsuramardinī Cave at Māmallapuram (previously known as Mahabalipuram), the dynamics of which are analyzed in Seshadri (1963, 19) and Alice Boner (1962, 238–39). Since the cave's architecture bridges the austere "Mahendra" style in its exterior and the ornate "Māmalla" style, with lion-based pillars in the interior, K. R. Srinivasan (1964) dates the cave and its reliefs to the late 7th century CE. I tend to think it may belong to the early 8th

Figure 11.1. Anthropomorphic buffalo demon in battle with the Devī;
4.0 × 2.5 m. Mahiṣāsuramardinī Cave, Māmallapuram.
Source: Photo by the author.

century CE, because this would place the Anthropomorphic type as being produced by the Pallavas, not before, but at the same period as their early images of the Victorious Goddess, who was most likely regarded as Korravai, as the textual context discussed in the previous chapter indicates.

The large relief, approximately four meters long by two-and-a-half meters high, occupies a panel at the right-hand entryway of what appears to have been a Viṣṇu temple. As shown in figure 11.1, this depiction is unique for its dynamic, narrative quality. The central focus is a slim, eight-armed goddess riding her lion into battle against the buffalo demon, portrayed as a larger-than-life human figure with a massive, crowned buffalo head. The demon leans away from the goddess's charge, suggesting a reluctant retreat, and is surrounded by his anthropomorphic military entourage, most of whom are depicted in retreat, their faces turned away from the goddess's forces. The goddess's army is composed primarily of squat, chubby *gaṇa*s. Among her companions, a kneeling female warrior is prominently positioned at the forefront, raising a sword overhead. While a bald figure appears to be falling onto her blade, it may instead be a perspectival shift in the relief's depiction, showing the figure trampled beneath the goddess's lion. This interpretive complexity is echoed at the top center of the panel, where a soldier from the demon's army battles a *gaṇa* in a scene likely intended to depict ground combat rather than an airborne conflict.

The kneeling female warrior with the upraised sword seems poised to finish off a demon lying on the ground between the buffalo demon's feet. The goddess herself, adorned in the Pallava-style breast band (*kucabandha*), wields an array of weapons, including a bow (with an arrow implied or just released), sword, bell, discus, conch, noose, and shield. The honorific status of both the goddess and the buffalo demon is signaled by their crowns and the parasols held above their heads by attendants, although the identity of the figure holding the parasol over the buffalo demon is unclear.

This relief unmistakably portrays a lion-riding goddess engaged in battle with a buffalo-headed demon. Early epic hymns such as the DStv mention Durgā and her role in slaying Mahiṣāsura, while the DSto refers to her affinity for buffalo blood. However, neither hymn references the goddess's lion. It is in later epic hymns, such as the Pradyumna's Hymn (PradH), that Durgā is explicitly depicted as mounted on a lion and slaying the *asura* Mahiṣa. This suggests that by the time of the PradH's composition, viewers familiar with the hymn — or related myths and terminology — might identify the goddess in this relief as Durgā, as well as by other names such as Kātyāyanī, Kālī, or Vijayā. Likewise, the buffalo-headed adversary would almost certainly be recognized as Mahiṣāsura. However, there is uncertainty regarding the PradH's date of composition, its geographic dissemination, and whether the artist of this relief was aware of it.

Moreover, as noted earlier, this relief does not depict Durgā "crushing" Mahiṣāsura, rendering the name commonly attributed to this cave, Mahiṣāsuramardinī Maṇḍapa, somewhat inaccurate. Tartakov and Dehejia

(1984, 291) have proposed an alternative designation: Mahiṣāsura *sainyavadha* ("the slaying of the armies of Mahiṣāsura"). A simpler, yet precise, name could be Mahiṣāsura Maṇḍapa, although this would emphasize the demon rather than the goddess. Additionally, the term Mahiṣāsuramardinī appears to have only gained widespread usage after the composition of the DM. Thus, the pivotal question remains: Was this relief carved after the DM was composed?

It seems plausible to assume that the DM inspired this panel. The narrative elements align well with the DM's second episode, recounting the Devī's battle with Mahiṣa. The panel portrays Mahiṣa as a potential shapeshifter, mid-transition between human and buffalo forms. His crown suggests he might have usurped the throne of Indra and the other displaced gods, consistent with the DM's narrative. Additionally, the relief opposite this panel depicts Viṣṇu reclining on the endless serpent Ananta/Śeṣa, possibly referencing the first episode of the DM where Brahmā awakens Viṣṇu to slay Madhu and Kaiṭabha. This juxtaposition suggests that the first two mythic episodes of the DM were recognized and connected in some way. However, the absence of a depiction of the DM's third and lengthiest episode — the slaying of Śumbha and Niśumbha — raises questions about the extent of the DM's possible influence on these panels.

It is also worth noting that in Vaiṣṇava circles, efforts to link the buffalo-slaying goddess with Nidrā were present during the insertion of epic hymns into the *Mahābhārata* (Mbh). This suggests that the thematic connection between the two episodes predates the production of these reliefs. Interestingly, the Mahiṣāsura panel introduces a novel narrative element not explicitly described in earlier iconography: a battle scene involving both the goddess's forces and those of Mahiṣāsura. This dynamic portrayal adds depth to the visual storytelling and potentially reflects evolving interpretations of the myth.

I am not convinced that the DM had been fully composed at the time these images were produced, unless the text was constructed in stages, with the first two mythic episodes circulating independently beforehand. V. S. Agrawala (1964a, 832) suggested such piecemeal construction, positing that the hymn known as the Nārāyaṇī Stuti may have been a later addition. Others argue that the final sections, dealing with the worship of the Devī and the *phala-śruti* (benefits of recitation), were also later inclusions. J. N. Tiwari (1985, 63–64, n. 11) concurs, proposing that even the Madhu and Kaiṭabha episode might not have been part of the DM when it was first inserted into the *Mārkaṇḍeya Purāṇa* (MārkP). The critical edition of the MārkP, edited by Wadekar (2011), acknowledges the DM as an insertion but offers no insights into its compositional stages.

While the DM may have been composed incrementally, the Pallava relief primarily demonstrates that myths of a lion-riding goddess battling a shape-shifting buffalo demon king were already widely circulated. The relief does not definitively point to the DM as its inspiration. For instance, the DM does not mention the prominent female warrior depicted alongside the goddess in her battle with Mahiṣa. Such accompanying warriors, such as the Mātṛkās, are found in the Śumbha/Niśumbha episode, suggesting that the DM was likely a composite work drawing from diverse iconographic depictions, rather than being the direct source for this imagery. It seems more plausible that the DM was influenced by these preexisting representations and earlier narratives, and only subsequently influenced other narrative traditions and iconography.

This iconography of the lion-riding goddess battling a buffalo-headed demon is found elsewhere near Māmallapuram, such as carved on a rock in front of the Atiraṇachaṇḍa Maṇḍapa, built by Rājasiṃha Pallava in the early 8th century, at Saluvankuppam, just two miles north of Māmallapuram proper (Tartakov and Dehejia 1984, 327, Pl. 39, 40). There are notable differences; in the Saluvankuppam image, which is about one by two meters, the goddess rides her lion sort of sidesaddle with one foot upon the ground, as if about to step off it. Mahiṣa is not just beginning to yield, but without his club he is portrayed in a stumbling flight preceded by a single fleeing and falling cohort, while both are being overrun by the goddess's entourage of *gaṇas*.

Cāḷukya and Rāṣṭrakūṭa Period Pieces
(Late 7th to Early 8th Century CE)

Pattadakal

Tartakov and Dehejia (1984) make a convincing case that the large relief at the Mahiṣāsura Maṇḍapa in Māmallapuram clearly served as an inspiration for a small panel carved on a pillar in the Mallikārjuna temple at Pattadakal, built during the reign of the Cāḷukya emperor Vikramāditya II. A temple inscription tells that it was dedicated to him by the younger of his two queens and can be dated to between 733/734 and 744/745 CE. They see this as an unusual Pallava iconographic intrusion into Cāḷukyan depictions. Indeed, there are other examples of this human body and buffalo-headed or buffalo-horned iconography from this late 7th to 8th century CE period.

Ellora

The renowned Kailāsanātha temple at Ellora, hewn from a single rock, has several depictions of what appears to be a developing narrative of the goddess slaying the demon Mahiṣa, who is part human and part buffalo. On the north wall of the entrance gateway (*gopura*), there is a depiction (as shown in figure 11.2) of an eight-armed goddess, sitting sidesaddle, in a throne-like fashion upon her lion, battling Mahiṣāsura. There are three arrows in flight released from the goddess's bow about to strike Mahiṣa's head and neck. The demon is

Figure 11.2. Anthropomorphic buffalo demon in battle with lion-riding Devī. Kailāsanātha Temple, Ellora; basalt rock.
Source: Photo by the author.

not cowering but appears ready to deliver a blow with his club to the goddess or her lion, which is trampling and mauling members of Mahiṣa's demon entourage. Among the distinctive features of this image is that the gods are portrayed viewing the battle from the heavens above, and Mahiṣa is shown with a human face and buffalo horns.

In another image (shown in figure 11.3), on the north of the *maṇḍapa*, one sees the goddess about to slay Mahiṣa, who is on his knees and gripping a sword. Not only does he have buffalo horns, but he has the long ears of a buffalo. The goddess has one foot upon the ground, but her other leg is raised, and her foot appears to be pressing down upon his neck. She is about to thrust her spear into him, while her lion devours the head of another demon to the left of the tableau. In this and the previous relief we see more clearly the sense that Mahiṣa does not merely possess a buffalo head, but that his form is transformative, changing from buffalo to human or vice versa. Between the first and second images we note two frames of the narrative, the first in which the goddess rides her lion and engages a combative and transforming Mahiṣa in battle, and the second in which she descends from her lion, presses her foot onto a defeated Mahiṣa's neck, and is about to slay him with her spear.

Figure 11.3. Anthropomorphic buffalo demon being subdued by the
Devī's foot and killed. Kailāsanātha Temple, Ellora; basalt rock.
Source: Photo by the author.

Figure 11.4. Emergent Demon type of buffalo demon, trampled and
killed by the Devī. Kailāsanātha Temple, Ellora.
Source: Photo by the author.

The Emergent Demon (E) Type

An important relief appears on the south wall of the entrance corridor of Kailāsanātha. As one can see in figure 11.4, it does not mimic the previous anthropomorphic types found in Pallava and Cālukya sites. It would belong to Seshadri's fourth type and Stietencron's type 5. Yokochi (2004, 132) classifies this as the Mediaeval type. Tartakov and Dehejia (1984, 320) call it the metamorphic type, and I, aligned with Seshadri, classify it as the Emergent Demon (E) type. In this image, the goddess stands with one foot atop the back of the neck of the severed body of the buffalo, with her other foot atop the neck of an anthropomorphic demon that has emerged from the severed torso. The demon's head is forced into an unnatural backward bend by her foot, and she plunges both her sword and her trident into his upturned breast. While the imagery is unclear, it also appears that the goddess has just released an arrow from her horizontally held bow into the face of Mahiṣa and may be reaching for her quiver. The severed buffalo head lies further to the left of the panel. The goddess is flanked by two smaller warriors.

The rock-cut caves at Ellora were excavated from the late 6th to the 10th centuries CE, with additional carving continuing into the 13th and 14th centuries CE. Among the earlier excavations, a cave likely dedicated to a goddess was carved in the early 7th century CE, alongside twelve Buddhist caves dated to approximately 600 to 730 CE (Spink 1967, 11–22). The Kailāsanātha temple is often attributed to the Rāṣṭrakūṭa king Kṛṣṇarāja I, who reigned from 756-773 CE. Inscriptions on the Baroda plates, produced forty years after his reign, mention Kṛṣṇarāja commissioning a temple at Elāpura (Ellora) that astonished both gods and architects, likely referring to Kailāsanātha (R. G. Bhandarkar 1883, 228–30).

If these dates are accurate, the development leading to the Emergent Demon representations of Mahiṣāsura seems to have begun in the second half of the 8th century CE, within the Rāṣṭrakūṭa sphere. The Kailāsanātha temple, although grander, mimicked the Virupakṣa temple at Pattadakal, built by the Cālukyas of Badami, which in turn was inspired by the Pallavas' Kailāsanātha temple at Kanchipuram (Tartakov and Dehejia 1984, 288–89). Similarly, Pallava Anthropomorphic buffalo demon motifs influenced Cālukya designs, which were later adopted and adapted by the Rāṣṭrakūṭas. The Emergent Demon type appears to have originated with the Rāṣṭrakūṭas, spreading rapidly through the Deccan and beyond (Tartakov and Dehejia 1984).

I am inclined to place the composition of the DM and its insertion into the MārkP in the mid-8th century CE, correlating its rise in popularity as a ritual text with the emergence of the Emergent Demon type iconography. However, a perplexing aspect remains: the DM's description of Mahiṣa's demise appears largely incongruent with the iconographic imagery, both historically and contemporarily. Even over a millennium since its composition, images aligning precisely with the DM's narrative are scarce. This disparity persists today, despite the DM's centrality during Navarātra and Durgā Pūjā celebrations, where its verses are repeatedly chanted and widely recognized.

There are plausible reasons for this variation between narrative and representation. Traditional image-making often adheres to established Śilpa-śāstras or meditative visualization verses (*dhyāna śloka*) used in rituals, rather than literary descriptions. Even so, the apparent disjunction warrants a closer examination of the DM's verses describing Mahiṣa's destruction. It is possible that the standard translations have perpetuated interpretations not entirely reflective of the original intent. The enduring absence of images that correspond closely to the DM's standard translations — both historically and in modern times, despite the creative reinterpretations seen in Durgā Pūjā tableaux — suggests the need for a reevaluation of these verses to discern their intended depiction.

Coburn (1991, 47) translates the relevant DM verses as follows:

> 3.37 Having spoken thus and springing up, she mounted the
>   great Asura.
> Having struck him with her foot, she beat him with her spear.
>   [40]
> 3.38 Then he, struck with her foot, came forth out of his own
>   mouth,
> Completely hemmed in by the valor of the Goddess. [41]
> 3.39 That great Asura, who had come forth halfway fighting,
>   was felled by the Goddess,
> Who had cut off his head with a great sword. [42]

The sense obtained from this translation is that the demon in the form of a buffalo is first stomped upon and speared, and because of the Devī's foot, he emerged halfway from his own buffalo mouth — it is assumed in a human form – at which point he is beheaded by the Goddess. Iconographic depictions almost never show the Goddess beheading a human demon who has emerged from the mouth of a speared and stomped-upon buffalo. That appears to be the gist of many translations, which suggests that it is certainly a reasonable rendition of the verses in question. However, let us examine them again, more closely, in the version taken from the critical edition (MārkP, 2011, 569).

> 3.37 *evam uktvā samutpatya sā arūḍhā tam mahāsuram /*
> *pādena akramya kaṇṭhe ca śūlenainama tāḍayat //*
> 3.38 *tataḥ so 'pi pada akrāntas tayā nija mukhāt tataḥ /*
> *ardhaniṣkrānta evāti devyā vīryeṇa saṃvṛtaḥ //*
> 3.39 *ardhaniṣkrānta eva asau yuddhyamāno mahāsuraḥ /*
> *tayā mahāsinā devyā śiraś chittvā nipātitaḥ //*

The first verse (3.37) is uncomplicated:

> Having spoken thus (*evam uktvā*), having leaped up (*samutpatya*), she mounted (*ārūḍhā*) the great demon (*mahāsuram*), and having trodden (*ākramya*) upon the throat (*kaṇṭhe*) with her

foot (*pādena*), she struck him (*tāḍayat*) with her spear (*śūlena*).

Coburn has entirely omitted the crucial phrase concerning her crushing the demon's throat with her foot. And clearly *mahāsura* refers to the demon in his buffalo form. The next verse (3.38) could read:

> Thereupon, overpowered (*ākrāntaḥ*) by her foot, he neverthe-less (*so'pi*) was half-emerged (*ardhaniṣkrānta*) from his own (*nija*) neck/forepart (*mukhāt*), restrained (*saṃvṛtaḥ*) by the strength (*vīryeṇa*) of the Devī.

Here, too, Coburn completely omitted the phrase that the demon is half-emerged. While the tendency is to translate *mukha* as mouth, which is the obvious and common meaning, the broader sense of that word conveys any opening at the top or the tip of an object. It can be an animal's snout, but may also be the head, upper part, forepart, or topside of something. While one might consider it a reach for me to translate it as neck or forepart, it is certainly not inappropriate when one considers this verse in tandem with the next (3.39). This is because verse 3.39 explicitly repeats the phrase *ardhaniṣkrānta* (half-emerged), and the term *mahāsura* (great demon, arguably as referring to the buffalo form from the previous verse) as if to properly explicate what had already occurred. It could read:

> That great demon (*mahāsuraḥ*) [i.e., the buffalo, whose neck had been trodden upon], having [had] his head severed (*śiraśchit-tvā*) by the great sword (*mahāsinā*) of the Goddess, that same one (*eva asau*), who had half-emerged (*ardhaniṣkrānta*), bat-tling, (*yuddhyamāno*), was made to fall (i.e., slain) (*nipātitaḥ*).

When translated this way, these verses could portray a different sequence of events. The great demon Mahiṣa, in his buffalo form (referred to as *mahāsura*), is first crushed by the Devī's foot on his throat, while she is atop him, and she assaults him with her spear. Thoroughly overpowered by the Devī, he half-emerges from his own neck. The reading I offer is that this is because he (the *mahāsura*) had been beheaded — in his buffalo form — by the Devī's great sword, and then, half-emerged and still fighting, is slain. We do not exactly know in what form he emerges, but it is generally assumed that he takes up a human form. The verses also leave the exact nature of his demise in the emer-gent form unclear. The implication from this reading is that he was attacked with her spear (or trident), then beheaded in his buffalo form with her sword, and slain (probably in his human form, which emerged from the severed neck), possibly with her spear (or trident) or sword, the two weapons that are men-tioned in the verses dealing with his demise.

If we now turn again to the Emergent Demon image from Kailāsanātha tem-ple at Ellora, we see a rendition that is quite closely aligned with these verses from the DM. The Devī is atop Mahiṣa in his buffalo form, with a foot atop his neck. The buffalo is beheaded, and its head lies to the bottom left of the relief. The demon partially emerges from the severed neck of his buffalo body, and he grasps a shield indicating that he is fighting. The Devī appears to be slaying his human form in a variety of ways. His chest is pierced by her trident and her sword, and she seems to have shot an arrow from her bow into his face. There are other depictions in which the anthropomorphic demon emerges from a partially severed neck of the buffalo, which is also consonant with this translation.

While the Victorious and Anthropomorphic types persisted, the Emergent Demon type gained prominence, and Theriomorphic depictions began to decline, although they did not disappear immediately. One of the finest Theriomorphic representations of the buffalo-slaying goddess is found in the so-called Durgā temple at Aihole, characterized by its distinctive apsidal structure. Tartakov (1997) argues that this temple, dedicated to Āditya, the sun god, was constructed between 725 and 730 CE.

Meanwhile, the Emergent Demon (E) type spread rapidly, reaching as far as modern Afghanistan. Notably, a large image of the Emergent Demon type was discovered in Vihāra 23 at Tapa Sardar, Ghazni, within a Buddhist monastic complex (Taddei 1973; 1978, 54–57). Although the image has since disappeared due to regional warfare, photographs suggest the presence of a severed buffalo head positioned near the front legs of the figure. The separately found goddess's face, featuring a composed expression, a third eye, and exquisite workmanship, indicates Indian stylistic influence and has been dated to the second half of the 8th century. This aligns with a period when a Hindu ruler in Kabul replaced Tang Chinese influence in the area (Verardi and Paparatti 2005, 440–42).

Chiara Antonini (2005, 326) speculates that the placement of the buffalo-demon-slaying goddess alongside a Buddha image within a Buddhist complex highlights her salvific role, symbolizing liberation. This suggests a blending of iconographic traditions and theological functions in a region marked by religious and cultural intersections.

The Albert Hall Museum in Jaipur displays an exemplary image of the Emergent Demon type from Ābānerī, dated by R. C. Agrawala (1958, 130) to the 8th century CE. However, I am inclined to attribute it to the 9th century for several reasons. Other Emergent Demon type images exist at Ābānerī, notably one in situ at the Chand Baori stepwell, the largest of its kind (Livingstone 2002, 38). Niches near the lowest water level, part of the stepwell's early construction phases, include depictions of Gaṇeśa and the buffalo-demon-slaying goddess in the Emergent Demon type. The stepwell is associated with King Chandra of the Nikumbha dynasty, generally dated to the 8th or 9th century. Although often placed around 800 CE, it likely belongs to a slightly later period. Local tradition links the stepwell to the goddess Harṣat Mātā, who is also associated with a nearby temple of uncertain origins. The connection of significant water sources to goddess worship is not unusual.

Cynthia Atherton (1995, 235) suggests that despite its name, the temple was likely constructed following a Vaiṣṇava Pāñcarātra metaphysical framework, highlighting the region's complex religious and political influences during the 8th and 9th centuries. Known historically as Sapādalakṣa and Śākambharī — a name linked to Durgā in the DM — the area demonstrates deep roots in goddess worship, which persists today in the reclamation of the temple for Harṣat Mātā. Atherton (1995, 234) speculates that the temple may have been commissioned by the Pratīhāra ruler Nāgabhaṭa II (c. 793–833 CE). His grandson, Bhoja I (r. 836–882 CE), arguably the dynasty's most powerful ruler, controlled a kingdom extending from Western Punjab to Bihar. Dasharatha Sharma (1957, 132) notes that Bhoja worshipped the goddess Bhagavatī, although inscriptions and coinage suggest his personal identification with Ādi-varāha, the boar *avatāra* of Viṣṇu. The Sāgartāl inscription credits him with defeating the *asuras*, likely referring to rival rulers. It is plausible that both the Chand Baori stepwell, dedicated to a goddess, and the so-called Harṣat Mātā temple, dedicated to Viṣṇu, were products of Pratīhāra patronage, possibly under Bhoja I. This timeframe supports a mid-9th century date for the Emergent Demon type buffalo-demon-slaying images, consistent with the rising influence of the DM. R. C. Agrawala (1958, 130) also references medieval images from the museum in Mathurā where the buffalo head is not entirely severed, and multiple demons appear to emerge from it, further illustrating the evolving iconography of the Emergent Demon type.

The Emergent Demon type, with the demon exiting from the severed neck of the buffalo, as reflected in the alternate translation of the DM verses I offered above, became the predominant iconographic norm. However, rare examples depict the demon emerging from the buffalo's mouth, aligning with the conventional translation provided by scholars such as Coburn. One such depiction is from the Mahāliṅgeśvara temple at Varuna in Mysore State (Seshadri 1963, Pl. 35A). Seshadri (1963, 22) notes inscriptions dating the temple to 900 CE, suggesting that by this period, the DM's descriptive verses allowed for interpretations supporting both iconographic forms. However, the beheaded buffalo form grew and remains dominant, strongly influenced by the DM's ambiguous verses. Agrawala (1966) discusses some rare examples of the Devī killing a fully human demon, with no buffalo present.

Summing up our examination, the Victorious Goddess type of the buffalo-slaying goddess dates back as early as the 3rd or 4th century CE, exemplified by the terracotta fragment from Saṇṇatti in Karnataka (Divakaran 1984, 288) and the eleven-foot, six-armed stone sculpture from Besnagar (R. C. Agrawala 1958, 126). This iconographic type proliferated during the Pallava period (early 8th century), flourished in the Coḷa sphere, and continues to the present day. Additionally, it appears in the pre-Angkorian Chenla kingdom at Sambor Prei Kuk, which inscriptional evidence dates to the 6th and 7th centuries CE (O'Reilly 2007, 112). While these Cambodian images may predate the Pallava examples, they are likely contemporaneous. The Pallavas also introduced the

Anthropomorphic type, as seen in the large relief at Māmallapuram depicting the lion-riding goddess battling a buffalo-headed human-bodied demon. This type was later elaborated by the Cālukyas (e.g., Virūpākṣa temple, Paṭṭaḍakal) and the Rāṣṭrakūṭas (e.g., Kailāsanātha temple, Ellora) throughout the 8th century CE. Kailāsanātha, which features both Anthropomorphic and Emergent Demon types, is dated to the second half of the 8th century CE, coinciding with the likely composition and insertion of the DM into the MārkP.

Prior centuries must have developed the narrative of the shape-shifting buffalo demon and the lion-riding goddess, first fully represented at Māmallapuram. Although conventionally linked to the DM, the Māmallapuram relief likely predates its composition. To substantiate the narrative's development, we turn to early Purāṇas, such as the early *Skandapurāṇa* (SP), whose oldest layers, including buffalo-slaying goddess sections, likely date to the mid-6th century CE (Bakker 2014, 4–7).

Chapter 12

Durgā in the Early Purāṇas

We have examined the portrayal of Durgā in the *Devī Māhātmya* (DM), often regarded as a late addition to the *Mārkaṇḍeya Purāṇa* (MārkP). While the MārkP is considered one of the earliest Purāṇas, the DM's composition was typically placed between the 6th and 9th centuries CE. Wendy Doniger (1988, 5) critiques the wide-ranging estimates for Purāṇic dates, with some placing the MārkP as early as 250 CE. However, it is implausible to assume that the DM was composed alongside the earliest strata of the MārkP, which is often dated to the 3rd or 4th century CE. Pargiter (1904) and Rajendra Chandra Hazra (1987, 12) date the DM to the 5th or 6th century CE but no later than the 9th century. Despite its status as an early coalescing text of the Great Goddess tradition, our detailed study casts doubt on earlier datings of the DM. Instead, I have argued for a mid-8th century composition, aligning with the views of recent scholarship (e.g., Yokochi 2004; Sarkar 2017).

I have suggested that the Durgā Stava (DStv) and Durgā Stotra (DSto), inserted into the *Mahābhārata* (Mbh), predate the DM and circulated independently before their inclusion. I place the DStv, or unknown DStv* variants, earlier than the *Harivaṃśa* (HV) and the DSto after the *Bhagavad Gītā* (BG). Their presence in Devanāgarī manuscripts suggests a North Indian provenance, marking them as late insertions. Nevertheless, I have suggested that their independent composition predates their incorporation with frame verses into the epic, which I designated as DStv+ and DSto+.

The absence of early manuscripts and critical editions complicates tracing the historical development of Purāṇic myths. Myths in any Purāṇa often have ancient cores, later expanded through insertions and additions. This chapter examines key myth cycles of Durgā and related goddesses in early Purāṇas, identifying elements later developed in the DM and noting the absence of its key features. For example, the *Varāha Purāṇa* describes the demon Ruru driving the gods from heaven, prompting them to pray to Raudrī (Kālarātrī), who defeats the demon with Rudra's aid. Similarly, the early *Skanda Purāṇa* (SP), as detailed by Yokochi, recounts Kauśikī's defeat of Sumbha, Nisumbha, and Mahiṣa. The *Devī Purāṇa* credits Umā/Vindhyavāsinī with vanquishing the buffalo demon Ghora. While these accounts emphasize the goddess's power, they also subordinate her to male deities: Raudrī acts with Rudra's assistance, Kauśikī is a manifestation of Pārvatī and thus subordinate to Śiva, and Umā/Vindhyavāsinī shares a similar fate. The DM counters this trend by portraying the Great Goddess as supreme, independent, and the ultimate refuge for the gods.

The *Varāha Purāṇa*

Typically dated between the 10th and 12th centuries, although possibly as early as 750 CE, the *Varāha Purāṇa* (VarP) contains an account of a goddess's battle with Mahiṣa (Rocher 1986, 242; Doniger 1988, 5). Kane (1930–62, vol. V, 155) argues that the VarP may present the earliest Purāṇic version of the Mahiṣa-slaying myth. It is certainly among the earliest instances of such a narrative in Hindu literature, apart possibly from the early SP, which will be discussed later. The VarP is significant because it contains no mention of Durgā, despite her later identification with the Mahiṣa-slaying myth. This omission suggests the VarP might represent an early stage in the development of the myth cycle, preceding the firm association of Durgā with this narrative. Alternatively, it could reflect regional variations where Durgā was not yet prominent. It is also worth noting that the Mahiṣa-Devī myth cycle may predate the VarP itself, having possibly circulated orally before being recorded in the text.

The VarP (90.3) establishes a hierarchy among the three principal male gods, with Nārāyaṇa/Viṣṇu as supreme, followed by Brahmā, who emerged from him, and Rudra/Śiva, who arose from Brahmā. The buffalo-slaying goddess's origin is narrated within this framework. Śiva, while sporting with Pārvatī and his *gaṇas* (cohorts), is approached by Brahmā and the gods, who plead for help against the torment caused by the demon Andhaka. Brahmā calls to mind Nārāyaṇa, resulting in the fusion of the three great gods. From their combined gazes emerges a young, beautiful goddess with dark hair, the complexion of a mythic blue lotus, and three colors — black, white, and yellow. The gods, initially unaware of her identity, inquire about her nature. She chastises them for not recognizing her as the embodiment of their three energies. Pleased, they name her Trikalā ("Tripartite"), entrust her with protecting creation, and promise that she will have multiple names, each associated with distinct achievements. At their request, she assumes three forms, each linked to one of her colors and corresponding to the three gods. The white form, associated with Brahmā, embodies the creative power and is known as Brahmā/Sṛṣṭi. The red (although earlier described as yellow) form, associated with Viṣṇu, is called Vaiṣṇavī or Viṣṇumāyā, who protects creation. The black goddess form, linked to Rudra, and later named Raudrī, represents destruction. These three goddesses then proceed to Mounts Śveta, Mandara, and Nīla, respectively, to engage in fierce austerities (90.1–36).

This account reveals that the goddess arising from the combined energies of the gods is distinct from Pārvatī, who is explicitly present alongside Śiva. However, the newly emerged goddess embodies the creative, preserving, and destructive powers of the *trimūrti* — Brahmā, Viṣṇu, and Śiva. The narrative appears to unify the cults of various goddesses under a single, overarching deity, or is attempting to cast such a preexisting deity into a new framework. Trikalā, as her name implies, is closely tied to multiplicity, with each of her forms linked to specific mythic achievements, either established or anticipated in the text. Her asceticism on mountains aligns her symbolically with Pārvatī, reinforcing her role as a powerful protector of the gods against demonic forces. While Trikalā's beauty is emphasized, her skin's comparison to the mythic blue lotus may not definitively denote a dark complexion. This description could instead serve as a literary trope, signifying her flawless and divine beauty, a common feature in classical depictions of goddesses.

The narrative next recounts some exploits of each of the three goddesses. It begins with the god Brahmā seeking out the goddess Brahmā's help when he could no longer create, and she re-entered him to reinvigorate his creativity (90.37–48). The VarP then explains that all three goddesses are actually one but arose out of Rudra. The Brahmā form is known by various names, such as Svāhā and Svadhā, Vāgīśā, and Sarasvatī.

In her Vaiṣṇavī form, while practicing austerities on Mount Mandara, the Devī created the city of Devīpura, filled with countless palaces inhabited by female forms she had generated from herself. This imagery parallels the Praise of Nidrā (First Stratum) (PN-s1), which mentions Nidrā/Kauśikī dwelling in the Vindhya Mountains and illuminating the earth with a thousand places. Similarly, the DSto situates her on Mandara, reflecting a rich and widespread tradition of goddess worship across regions. Among the goddesses referenced in the VarP are Śivadūtī, Jayā, Vijayā, and Aparājitā. The sage Nārada, captivated by the Vaiṣṇavī Devī's beauty and grandeur, relayed news of her to Mahiṣāsura, the buffalo-formed *asura* chief residing in the city of Mahiṣa. Enamored by the description of the goddess, whom Nārada described as being revered by gods, demons, and sages alike, Mahiṣāsura became obsessed with possessing her. His advisors suggested pursuing marriage through diplomacy, beginning with negotiations with her closest kin and offering gifts. Only if these methods failed would they consider battle as a last resort. However, they resolved that before seeking her hand, they must first defeat the gods, seize the heavens, and claim their harems, believing this conquest would compel the goddess to yield to Mahiṣāsura's desires (VarP 93.1–36).

Since Mahiṣa had a boon rendering him invulnerable to any male, he and his formidable army defeated Indra and expelled the gods from heaven. Mahiṣa then sent the eloquent Vidyutprabha to Mount Mandara, where the goddess resided with her female entourage, to propose marriage on his behalf. Vidyutprabha recounted Mahiṣa's origins, explaining that he was born to Princess Māhiṣmatī, who had been cursed by the sage Supārśva to take the form of a buffalo. Māhiṣmatī's curse would only end after she bore a buffalo son. The princess conceived when she drank water from the Narmadā River, unknowingly imbibing the sage Sindhudvīpa's semen, which had been spilled into the river when he was aroused by the sight of a beautiful demoness named Indumatī. Māhiṣmatī was freed from her curse upon giving birth to Mahiṣa, who grew into a powerful king and conqueror of the triple world. Vidyutprabha urged the goddess to accept Mahiṣa's proposal. In response, the goddess laughed, terrifying the messenger, who saw the entire triple world within her abdomen. Her attendant, Jayā, further unsettled Vidyutprabha by stating that her mistress had taken a vow and that neither she nor any of her divine companions were available for marriage to Mahiṣa (VarP 95.1–29).

Shortly thereafter, Nārada approached the goddess, informing her that Mahiṣa and his forces were preparing to attack, and urging her to destroy the demon lord who had usurped the gods' place in heaven. A fierce battle ensued, during which the goddess's armed retinue annihilated the demons. Eventually, Mahiṣa himself charged at the goddess, who rode a lion and wielded numerous weapons across her twenty hands. As the battle intensified, the goddess turned her thoughts to Rudra, who immediately appeared. She bowed to him, declaring that his mere presence ensured her victory. After the demons were slain or driven away, she faced Mahiṣa in a prolonged duel that lasted ten thousand divine years, as the demon alternated between attacking and retreating. The confrontation reached its climax on Mount Śataśṛṅga ("Hundred Peaks"), where the goddess trampled Mahiṣa and killed him with a spear. He was beheaded with a sword. Being killed by the goddess, Mahiṣa's soul ascended to heaven.

The gods rejoiced and sang hymns praising the goddess Vaiṣṇavī as the destroyer of Mahiṣa. They proclaimed that anyone reciting these praises would be freed from bondage and live free of threats from wild animals, thieves, or unjust rulers. Moved by their praise, the goddess offered them a boon. They requested that she fulfill the wishes of anyone who recited their hymn of praise. She granted this boon, choosing to remain at that location, while the gods departed (VarP 95.30–72).

What is noteworthy in this segment is the sense that the VarP is firmly aware of the worship of a major goddess whose abode is on mountains. A noteworthy aside is that she slays Mahiṣa atop the mountain Śataśṛṅga, which translates as "Hundred Peaks" or alternately as "Hundred Horns (*śṛṅga*)." Evidently, the abodes of goddesses in temples often situated atop remote mountain peaks that resemble buffalo horns resonates with the imagery of the goddess trampling the horned buffalo-demon. In the VarP's account, the goddess's worshippers derive from a wide and diverse social array, because the text explains that her devotees include the gods, *siddhas*, demons, and many others. Mahiṣa's story tells of a relatively benign and powerful figure, who is portrayed in a manner that provides a rationale for his warfare on the goddess. Unlike the DM's account, Mahiṣa in the VarP is infatuated with the goddess, and wishes to wed her. In the DM, the goddess leads the armies of the gods. Mahiṣāsura is both startled and angered when he sees her, with her thousand arms, sky-scratching diadem, and footsteps that cause the earth to bow. He immediately launches into battle (DM 2.35–38). The DM's version appears to be a retelling of a mythic encounter that was already known to its readers because it provides little rationale for the battle. Does the VarP present an earlier version of the Mahiṣa-slaying myth, or did it develop later as an elaboration on the DM telling?

In the VarP, the goddess battling Mahiṣa is not portrayed as the Great Goddess, much less as the supreme deity, but as the Vaiṣṇavī manifestation of Trikalā, a deity formed from the combined energies of Brahmā, Viṣṇu, and Śiva. This Vaiṣṇavī is explicitly subordinated to Śiva, evidenced by her invocation of Rudra, her obeisance to him, and her assertion that her victory depends on his presence. While Vaiṣṇavī is depicted riding a lion and wielding many weapons, there is no suggestion that these weapons are bestowed by the gods — a prominent feature in the DM.

The depiction of Mahiṣa's demise — trampled, speared, and then beheaded — aligns with motifs found in earlier iconographic forms, particularly those of the Gupta period. However, the narrative lacks the elements of shape-shifting or emergence from the buffalo's severed head, which later become central to the Emergent Demon type imagery. Interestingly, the VarP introduces the notion of Mahiṣa's human and royal origins, tracing his lineage to the cursed princess Māhiṣmatī. This royal dimension finds a parallel in the Mahabalipuram bas-relief, where honorific umbrellas are depicted over both Mahiṣa and the goddess, underscoring their regal status. One wonders if the use of honorific umbrellas in that relief might represent a symbolic evolution of the peacock tailfeather standard seen in earlier Kuṣāṇa and Gupta representations of the buffalo-slaying goddess. Notably, the Anthropomorphic type, where Mahiṣa is shown as a human with a buffalo head, as depicted in Mahabalipuram, does not appear in the VarP. However, the text's acknowledgment of Mahiṣa's human ancestry hints at evolving narrative traditions.

Mahiṣa's attraction to the goddess is sexual, which is completely ignored in the Mahiṣa episode of DM but picked up as a rationale for the actions of the demons Śumbha and Niśumbha in the DM's third episode.[1] Among the qualities attributed to the goddess in the VarP's hymn of praise sung by the gods are such notions as knowledge, success, but also nescience. She is identified as having a frightening form and is also called the great power of illusion (*mahāmāyā*). These all-encompassing and ambivalent qualities certainly are suggestive that the VarP was cognizant of tropes of a Great Goddess cult, reflected in other goddess hymns, but it attempts to frame these attributes in a manner that nevertheless subordinates the goddess to the gods, particularly Viṣṇu (she is Vaiṣṇavī), and more so, Śiva.

The VarP notably refrains from using names commonly associated with the goddess in the DM, such as Caṇḍikā, Ambikā, or Kātyāyanī. Among these, Caṇḍika is rarely found in widespread usage, and its absence is less surprising. Toward the end of the gods' hymn of praise (*stotra*), the goddess is addressed as *mahādevī* (great goddess) and *parameśvarī* (supreme goddess). She is also extolled as a refuge and a source of success in battle, with the power to free worshippers from threats such as wild animals, imprisonment, and thieves — qualities strongly associated with Durgā. Yet, the name Durgā is conspicuously absent from the VarP. This omission raises intriguing possibilities. It may indicate that the VarP predates or originates from a region removed from the widespread association of Durgā with the Mahiṣa myth. Alternatively, the text may intentionally avoid the name Durgā, perhaps to align with or emphasize its sectarian agenda. If, by this period, Durgā was increasingly equated with the supreme deity of the Hindu pantheon, the VarP might have sought to downplay her independent status, situating her instead within a Śaiva sectarian framework. The VarP does contribute to the consolidation of various goddess figures into a unified divine persona, aligning with developments that led to the Śakta-oriented Great Goddess tradition, or inadvertently acknowledging its preexistence. Clearly, its approach differs from that of the DM. Unlike the DM, which presents the goddess as the supreme and independent deity, the VarP integrates the goddess into a Śaiva context, emphasizing her subordination to Śiva while acknowledging her divine prominence. This reflects its distinct theological and sectarian priorities, suggesting a stage in the evolution of goddess worship that predates or diverges from the fully developed DM tradition.

The epithet Durgā has often been loosely applied by scholars to the Great Goddess (Devī) or other prominent goddesses such as Pārvatī, Nārāyaṇī, and Vaiṣṇavī. Maurice Winternitz, in his *History of Indian Literature* (1927, 570), describes the VarP as "not a Purāṇa in the ancient sense of the word, but rather a manual of prayers and rules for the Viṣṇu-worshippers. Despite the Viṣṇuite character of the work, it yet contains a few legends relating to Śiva and Durgā." While accurate in its characterization of the VarP as largely Viṣṇuite, there is no actual mention of Durgā in the text. In fairness, modern scholarship has advanced since Winternitz's time, and he duly recognized the importance of the goddess Trikalā and her forms, particularly Vaiṣṇavī, in shaping Durgā's mythology.

In recounting the exploits of the goddess Raudrī, the VarP tells of the demon Ruru, who with his minions conquered the heavens and drove Indra and the other gods to Mount Nīla, where Raudrī was performing fierce austerities. They thought of her as the goddess Kālarātrī ("Dark Night"), the destructive power, and pleaded with her for help. She laughed, and from her mouth countless fierce armed goddesses emerged and joined her entourage. They attacked Ruru's demon armies until only he was left to confront Kālarātrī. Ruru's magic put the gods into a deep sleep, but the goddess separated his skin (*carma*) from his head (*muṇḍa*). Since she had separated his hide from his head, she acquired the name Cāmuṇḍā. *Carma* is sometime translated as "trunk," although skin or hide is the most common translation of the term. The separation of hide from head could reasonably refer to "scalping." Her goddess minions, numbering in the millions, were hungry and asked for food. Unable to find a solution for their hunger, and concerned that they might devour her, Kālarātrī pleaded with Rudra for help. He explained that these frightening goddesses may hereafter feed on the ignorant, may steal newborns, and may possess the bodies of lustful and otherwise adharmic women. He then sang a hymn of praise to her, calling her Cāmuṇḍā, Kālī, Karālī, and Kālarātrī. Among the benefits of her worship the text mentions that a king will regain a lost kingdom if he worships Kālarātrī by fasting for a year on Aṣṭamī, Navamī, and Caturdaśī. The text explains that the three forms of the goddess correspond to the tripartite energetic constituents of creation: namely, that the white, red, and black forms correspond to the sattvic, rajasic, and tamasic natures of Brahmā, Viṣṇu, and Rudra, respectively. Listening to the origin of this tripartite power is said to be enormously beneficial, especially on the Navamī *tithi* (lunar day). Even keeping a written version of a book describing this account in one's home is said to be beneficial, freeing one from most perils and conferring the homeowner with all manner of material benefits. The account ends with Varāha stating that each of the three goddesses has boundless numbers of manifestations. He explains that Śiva produces a manifestation of himself as a spouse for each of them and is thus pleased with anyone who worships these goddesses (VarP 96.1–76).

Hazra (1987, 101) considers Chapter 99 of the VarP to be likely taken (with some modifications) from the *Padma Purāṇa* (Sṛṣṭi Khanda 34). The VarP refers to the goddess Māyā, identified as the goddess Gaṅgā, who as Vaiṣṇavī slew the demon Mahiṣa on Mount Mandara during the Svāyambhuva epoch. Then, as the goddess Nandā, she slew the demon Caitra in the Vindhya Mountains. The goddess Māyā is also equated with the goddess Gāyatrī, who has eight arms, and is said to have emerged from Avyakta ("The Unmanifest") through the body of Brahmā (VarP 99.1–7).

When analyzing the foregoing sections, we note that the VarP repeats the trope of a demon driving the gods out of the heavens. This key pervasive theme and its relationship to goddess worship will be addressed in the final chapter, which provides speculative theoretical offerings. Here, the goddess who rescues the gods is not described as beautiful or comely but appears emaciated from her fierce austerities. She is frightening and produces a host of terrifying goddesses. This goddess, Raudrī, is Kālī, who also appears in the Mbh and the hymns inserted into it (e.g., DStv l. 34 and DSto l. 9, 10). In the VarP, Kālī, also called Karālī and Kālarātrī, is identified as Cāmuṇḍā.

Pargiter (1904, xii) had suggested that the first textual mention of Cāmuṇḍā may be the DM, which he thought might have been composed much earlier than we and others now suggest. However, Cāmuṇḍā is pejoratively compared to Tārā in Bhāvaviveka's 6th century CE writing, and the earliest textual reference to Cāmuṇḍā alongside the Mātṛkās is in the *Śivadharma* (see Bisschop 2018, 156), likely from the 6th to 7th century CE. I have also argued for Cāmuṇḍā's early appearance in Bhavabhūti's *Mālatī-mādhava* and possibly here in the VarP. In fact, the VarP may provide an early identification of Cāmuṇḍā with Kālī. Both, as Raudrī, are linked to the Śaiva pantheon, hinting at the association of Cāmuṇḍā's fearsome, often shriveled form with Kālī. Before this, Kālī, like many goddesses associated with blood sacrifices, was fearsome but not depicted as hideous.

The VarP also provides an etymology for Cāmuṇḍā's frightening form that appears as contrived as similar accounts, such as in the DM. Notably, Kālarātrī is one of the Nine Durgās praised in the Devī Kavaca, the textual preface of later provenance often recited with the DM. The VarP demonstrates familiarity with an abundance of goddesses, all regarded as manifestations of a greater goddess. These forms of Raudrī are frightening, with their destructive actions, such as the death of newborns, rationalized. A sectarian agenda is evident, as Raudrī is subordinated to Rudra. All three forms of the goddess Trikala are said to emanate from Rudra, and each is paired with a Rudra manifestation. This suggests a well-developed goddess-centered tradition existed, which the VarP seeks to align within a Śaiva-oriented sectarian framework, further subordinated to a Vaiṣṇava theological structure.

Noteworthy is the reference to the hymn of praise sung by Rudra, particularly the general comments regarding the benefits of possessing a text that extols the tripartite goddess, worshipping it, and reciting it. Eventually, the DM becomes the dominant text regarded and utilized in this manner. One wonders whether the VarP was aware of the DM's existence or if it set a precedent for its emergence. I lean toward the latter, as the VarP's account of the Mahiṣa myth differs significantly from the DM. Moreover, there is no incorporation of epithets such as Durgā, Ambikā, Kātyāyanī, Kauśikī, or episodes such as the slaying of Śumbha and Niśumbha in the VarP's narrative of the goddess's exploits.

The VarP does point to days of worship, such as Aṣṭamī, Navamī, and Caturdaśī, which were evidently significant for goddess worshippers. It also mentions fasting, likely referring to various types of vowed ascetic observances (*vrata*) commonly linked to her cult. In its descriptions of the benefits for kings reclaiming their kingdoms and the material and spiritual benefits attainable, parallels arise with the stories of King Suratha and the merchant Samādhi, later elaborated in the DM. Indeed, the three episodes of the DM appear oriented toward the major deities: the first episode, where the Devī rescues Brahmā from Madhu and Kaiṭabha, aligns with Brahmā; the second, with its focus on the Vaiṣṇavī goddess and the slaying of Mahiṣa, reflects a Vaiṣṇavī orientation similar to the VarP; and the third, involving Raudrī and the slaying of Śumbha, Niśumbha, and Raktabīja with Kālī's emergence, carries a Śaiva undertone.

It is reasonable to infer that the DM ultimately serves as the epitome of the devotional and ritual text hinted at in the VarP. Despite its goddess-related insertions and hymns, the VarP fails to achieve the same level of significance. Hazra (1987, 104) dates the earliest core of the VarP to around 800 CE. He asserts that the goddess-related episodes (Chapters 90–96), although interpolated, must predate 1400 CE because verses from Chapter 99, a later interpolation aware of Chapters 90 to 96, are quoted in subsequent texts, although their earliest dates remain uncertain (Hazra 1987, 104). Our analysis suggests that the primary goddess-related material in the VarP (excluding the Chapter 99 additions) likely originates from a time preceding the composition of the DM. Mirashi's (1964) dating of the Dadhimati Inscription (c. 800 CE), which contains a near-exact replication of a DM verse, provides a *terminus ante quem* for the DM's composition. The Emergent Demon type of the buffalo-slaying goddess at the Kailāsanātha temple at Ellora (attributed to the Raṣṭrakūṭa king Kṛṣṇa I) is the first known representation of its kind. It is remarkably close in the way it parallels the DM's depiction.[2] Thus, the vicinity of circa 756 CE, the ostensible start of Kṛṣṇarāja I's reign, could provide a possible *terminus a quo* for the DM, which drew its inspiration from such images — or even that particular one — or inspired it. Were this true, it would suggest that the goddess-material from VarP was composed and circulated even earlier than that, even prior to the Anthropomorphic type that first emerges with the Pallavas.

The VarP's provenance is almost certainly North India, as its sections predominantly reference northern holy cities (Hazra 1987, 107). This suggests it may have been unaware of the iconographic and mythic developments emerging in central and southern India. The goddess-related sections appear to have been composed during the early stages of the human-buffalo mythos of Mahiṣa, prior to its depiction as an anthropomorphic buffalo in iconography. These sections also seem rooted in a Śaiva sect that maintained a degree of separation from Śākta religious texts and practices. The sect emphasized the *trimūrti* ideal and did not advocate the concept of a supreme independent Goddess, even as the text adopts "great goddess" terminology. Notably, the VarP does not employ the name Durgā or other names commonly associated with the Great Goddess in other materials we have examined.

The Old *Skanda Purāṇa* (SP)

We now turn to the old *Skanda Purāṇa* (SP), of which volumes I, IIa, IIb, III, IV, and V have been published due to ongoing efforts to prepare its critical edition. The editors of this critical edition estimate the SP was composed between the 6th and 8th centuries CE (SP I, 5). Bakker (2014, 3) summarizes their view, suggesting the text was unlikely written before the early 6th century and not much later than the 7th century. However, certain goddess-related sections may belong to the early 6th century. Prior to the critical edition's release, Hazra (1987, 165) stated, "there seems to be little in it which can be dated earlier than 700 A.D." Others, such as Doniger (1988, 5), have placed the text's composition between 700 and 1150 CE, referring to the later *Skanda Purāṇa* (SkP) Veṅkateśvara Press version, frequently cited in earlier scholarship.

The first recitation of the SP may have occurred in the mid-7th century CE during Emperor Harṣa's reign, followed by multiple recensions with additions and errors. A later manuscript dated to Caitra, Samvat 234 (namely 810/11 CE), formed the basis for more recent studies (Bakker 2014, 21). The SP, therefore, holds a position of similar — and potentially earlier — antiquity to the DM, necessitating close examination of its Devī-related myths. Yokochi

(2004) provides compelling evidence that the old SP predates the DM, making its accounts essential for further analysis. Let us now consider the relevant evidence.

The relevant chapters and verses begin with Vyāsa asking Sanatkumāra to explain how Devī, who was dark-skinned, attained fair skin (SP 34.1–2). My paraphrased summary derives from the translation by Yokochi (2004, 157–95) from the constituted Sanskrit manuscripts (2004, 200–334). Once, when frolicking on Mount Mandara, Śiva teased Umā by calling her Kṛṣṇā ("[She who is] Black"). Although he apologized, and she accepted his apology, she requested that he grant her the boon of lightening her complexion, but only after she had performed austerities (*tapas*). He agreed, and the daughter of the mountain headed to the Himalayas to find a suitably remote peak. As she began her austerities, a tiger approached. Mesmerized by her austerities, and incorrectly surmising that she could not be the daughter of Himavat (i.e., Umā/Pārvatī), the tiger decided to wait by her side and devour her after she died from her efforts (SP 34.51). When the intensity and duration of her *tapas* began to cause the cosmic order to teeter out of balance, the gods approached Brahmā and asked him for help. They requested that he grant her wishes (SP 53). Brahmā traveled to the Himalayan peak where the daughter of Himavat was engaged in her practice (SP 54). He offered her boons, and she first requested that the patient tiger, despite his bad intentions, become the leader of her cohort (*gaṇeśvara*). Brahmā granted her wish and named the tiger Somanandin. She next asked that she be given a fair complexion, radiant like gold, and thereafter be known as Gaurī ("[She who is] Fair"). She finally asked for a son, not born from a womb, who would be excellent in many ways. Brahmā promised to grant these wishes (SP 55). The son would be Skanda, upon whom the Purāṇa is centered.

Pārvatī immersed herself in the pond formed from drops of water emitted by her body during her austerities. Thereupon, she shed her dark sheath (*kṛṣṇā kośī*) and shone like moonlight. Kauśikī was produced from the skin that she shed (SP 58.2–8). Kauśikī is described as beautiful, resembling the goddess Lakṣmī, full-breasted and with a slim-waist. She has eyes like blue lotuses, and eight arms, wielding weapons, including a bow and quivers. She wears yellow robes, has a breast plate, and is called Aparājitā ("[She who is] Invincible") (SP 58.1–16). Asking Pārvatī for directions, she was told that she will be known as Kauśikī and other names, including Varā ("[She who is] Choice"), Varadā ("[She who is] a Granter of Boons"), Vareṇyā ("[She who is] Most Desired"), Durgā, and Sarvārthasādhanī ("[She who is] the Realizer of All Ends") (SP 58.20). She was told that whosoever remembers her with devotion in situations of great duress (*atidurgeṣu saṃsthita*) will be saved from dangers (*durgāṇi tariṣyanti*) (SP 58.19). She would serve as a form (*mūrtisthāna*) of Pārvatī and would be worshipped by all creatures. Then, Pārvatī provided her with a chariot drawn by lions, and bedecked with flags and bells and assigned Kauśikī to Mount Vindhya as her abode. Kauśikī flew there, saw that it was a wonderful place, with flowing waters, wild animals, flowers, trees, mountain peaks, and birds, and took up her abode on that mountain (SP 58. 17–22).

The SP offers intriguing features regarding the goddess Kauśikī, particularly her association with dark skin and the Vindhya Mountains, but contrasts with the DM version (5.37–41). In both accounts, Pārvatī originates in the Himalayas, but the details of Kauśikī's emergence differ significantly. In the DM, the gods sing a hymn of praise directed at the Devī. Unaware of the hymn's recipient, Pārvatī witnesses Ambikā emerging from a sheath (*kośa*) of her body and declaring herself the goddess being praised. As a result, Pārvatī's complexion turns black (*kṛṣṇā*), and she remains in the Himalayas in this dark form as Kālikā, "[She who is] the Black One." Ambikā, having emerged from the sheath, is celebrated as Kauśikī. This narrative offers an explanation for Pārvatī's transformation into Kālikā while also acknowledging her earlier fair-skinned form as Gaurī. However, it also acknowledges Pārvatī's fair-skinned status and name, Gaurī, for Medhas introduces the Śumbha-Niśumbha slaying episode as merely a particular occasion when the Devī emerged through the body of Gaurī. It suggests that the DM was aware of both the dark and light skinned portrayals of Pārvatī/Gaurī. It implies that on the occasion when the Great Goddess emerged through or from the light-skinned Pārvatī/Gaurī, the residue was the dark-skinned Kālikā. One cannot help but think that the DM wishes to have both Pārvatī/Gaurī, and Ambikā, who is a manifestation of the Devī as light-skinned, while relegating the dark skin to Kālikā.

Paralleling the SP, the DM derives Kauśikī's name from the term for sheath (*kośa*). However, the DM identifies the Great Goddess with Kauśikī, and subordinates Pārvatī to her (Pārvatī is transformed because the Devī emerges through or from her). By contrast, in the SP, Pārvatī is portrayed as the Devī, and Kauśikī is her creation. Kauśikī carries off Pārvatī's dark complexion and is assigned by Pārvatī/Gaurī to the Vindhya Mountains as her abode. But the SP also portrays Pārvatī as subordinate to Śiva, in dramatic contrast to the DM. When comparing the SP and the DM, we note obvious tensions between these two. The SP clearly wants to take a well-known, arguably blue-eyed — arguably, because "like a blue-lotus" is often simply used to designate distinctive beauty — yellow-robed warrior goddess, variously named Kauśikī and Durgā, who rides a chariot pulled by lions, and whose well-established cult is situated in the Vindhyas, and assimilate it to the cult of Pārvatī, thereby amalgamating and yet subordinating it to the cult of Śiva.[3] The DM, however, has a different agenda. It considers Kauśikī as a particular manifestation of Ambikā/Durgā, when the Devī emerged through Gaurī. The DM thus attempts to assimilate the Pārvatī and Kauśikī cults into its Śakti centered cult. A rationale for the scene in which the tiger sits beside the ascetic Pārvatī may be that it is a response to the pervasive iconographic motif in which Pārvatī or some goddess is depicted with a tiger (lion?) by her side.

Returning to the SP, when Vyāsa asks Sanatkumāra, the son of Brahmā, why Kauśikī was sent to the Vindhya Mountains, he is told that Vindhya had practiced austerities and won a boon from Pārvatī. Vindhya requested that the goddess stay on him forever. To fulfil his wish, she split herself in two, sending Kauśikī, who is called one half of her, to defeat demons (SP 60.1–5). When explaining which demons she was sent to kill, Sanatkumāra recounts a lengthy tale (SP 60. 17f). He begins with a story about the demons Sunda and Nisunda, who, angered with the gods for killing their kinfolk, took up austerities in Gokarṇa, intent on winning a boon from Brahmā. When deviating from the narrative to discuss the sacred founding of Gokarṇa, Sanatkumāra explains how when Indra and the gods were defeated by Vṛtra, they sought the assistance of Śiva. While looking for Śiva, they came upon a young girl, whom Viṣṇu recognized to be Pārvatī. Viṣṇu sang a hymn of praise to her, in which he called her by many names and epithets including, Umā, Bhadrakālī, Mahāgaurī, mistress of the gods, mother of the cohorts (*gaṇa*), and Kauśikī Vindhyavāsinī. He also called her Durgā, Mahāvidyā, Sarasvatī, Mahāmāyā, Gāyatrī, Lakṣmī, queen of all *yoga* masters, Satī, Brahmacāriṇī, Ṣaṣṭhī, and so on (SP 60.38–43). He sang of her beauty and mentioned that beings on earth make offerings of buffalo heads to her. He described her as riding a lion and killing demons with her sharp arrows as well as with her battle-axe. Duly propitiated, Pārvatī abandoned her form as a little girl and took up one that appeared like a heap of effulgences (*tejas*). She explained where the gods might find Śiva. Śiva appeared to the gods in the form of a deer. Brahmā established a portion of one of the deer's horns at Gokarṇa, sanctifying the site. The sacred horn played a role in Indra's defeat of Vṛtra, and the reestablishment of the gods to their rightful place.

The demons Sunda and Nisunda practiced asceticism at Gokarṇa until Brahmā granted them a boon. Since they could not be granted immortality, they chose that the only way they could die would be the unlikely scenario that they kill each other. With their boon obtained, they returned to their demon allies and decided to wage war on the gods. The demon Mahiṣa showed up in this gathering of demon chiefs and suggested that they make peace with the gods rather than attempt to overthrow them. He pointed out that the gods cannot be disunited, and that the Rākṣasas and Yakṣas would likely not lend their support to the demon army. This approach was rejected, and Sunda and his younger brother Nisunda prepared for war (SP 60. 72–130).

After successfully driving the gods from the heavens, the demon brothers departed for the foothills of the Vindhya Mountains to relax. Brahmā decided on a plan to defeat them and restore the gods to their rightful place. He produced a woman of exceptional beauty, named Tilottamā, from portions (*tila*) of various jewels. Enlisting the aid of Śiva, who was invoked on a peak of Vindhya, Brahmā had Tilottamā parade around Śiva's *liṅga*. Various faces, aspects of Śiva, sprouted from the *liṅga* in the cardinal directions, each emitting effulgence (*tejas*) into Tilottamā. The text explains that the faces emerged not because of Śiva's desire for Tilottamā, but because of his intent to fulfil the wishes of the gods. Śiva explained that this *tejas* had been stored up within him since his destruction of Kāma, the god of love. *Tejas*, incidentally, may also be translated as semen. He told the gods that this place would thereafter be called Maṇḍaleśvara, and the *liṅga* would be known as Piṇḍāreśvara.

The gods then sent Tilottamā, with various companions including pride (*darpa*), wrath (*krodha*), time (*kāla*), sexual desire (*madana*), death (*mṛtyu*), delusion (*moha*), and so on, to confront the demons (SP 62.35). When Sunda and Nisunda saw her, each was overcome by pride, sexual desire, and delusion, and longed for her. Filled with anger and jealousy, they attacked and slew each other with their clubs. The semen that spilt from their bodies produced two offspring named Sumbha and Nisumbha (the earlier variant spelling of Śumbha and Niśumbha). The oldest manuscript of the SP dated 810 CE, and another manuscript slightly younger, both render the demons' names as Sumbha and Nisumbha. Also, the oldest dated manuscript of the DM, found in Nepal and dated Nepal Saṃvat 229 (1109 CE), has the same spelling. This suggests that the original names of the demon brothers were Sumbha and Nisumbha, and not Śumbha and Niśumbha. In some manuscript versions, the two spellings are mixed, so the variation may simply be scribal (Yokochi 2004, 84). Vindhya adopted the children, who upon discovering their demon ancestry performed austerities to gain boons. Brahmā eventually granted them their requested boon, which was that they may only be killed by a virgin (*kanyā*) who is the mother of the world (*jaganmātā*) (SP 62.1–66). Almost indestructible because of this boon, the brothers then gathered up their demon allies and ousted the gods from the heavens.

Sumbha and Nisumbha returned to Vindhya to relax and celebrate their victory. There, their attendant, Mūka ("Dumbo"), encountered Kauśikī, whom he noted was a woman of extraordinary beauty but skilled in warfare. He told Sumbha about her, and the demon king, overtaken by desire, sent Mūka back to ask for her hand. Kauśikī said that she would only wed someone who defeated her in battle. Overcome by lust and delusion and spurred on by Death itself, the demon brothers, with their armies, marched over to meet the goddess in battle. Kauśikī, by means of extraordinary *yoga*, produced an army of fearsome female beings that emerged from her own body (SP 64.1–18).

The SP narrative provides a rationale for the presence of the demons Sumbha and Nisumbha in the Vindhya Mountains. According to the SP, these demons were born from the spilled seed of Sunda and Nisunda, who succumbed to the irresistible allure of Tilottamā. Crafted from fragments of gemstones, Tilottamā was made sexually irresistible through Śiva's infusion of *tejas*. Similarly, Kauśikī is described as extraordinarily beautiful. These motifs parallel Episodes Two and Three of the DM, where the Devī emerges through the collective *tejas* of Śiva and other gods to vanquish Mahiṣa. However, the treatment of *tejas* differs significantly between the two texts. In the SP, *tejas* is explicitly linked to sexual allure through Tilottamā's story, while in the DM, the Devī's sexual magnetism is notably absent in the Mahiṣa myth. Instead, it becomes central in the DM's narrative of Śumbha and Niśumbha's defeat, where Śumbha's infatuation with the Devī's beauty drives the plot, and the goddess is also referred to as a jewel of a woman.

The erotic dimensions of Tilottamā, which transfers to Kauśikī, and by extension Durgā, Pārvatī, and the other goddesses with whom she is identified, have not received the attention they deserve.[4] Perhaps this is because the Śumbha and Niśumbha episode of the DM, which acknowledges the Devī's sexual allure, has not achieved the same prominence in the public imagination as her buffalo-slaying myth. In the DM, while the Goddess is described as beautiful, Mahiṣa views her solely as an adversary, lacking the sexual attraction depicted in the VarP. However, images of the many-armed, sexually alluring goddess, often referred to as Śṛṅgāra Durgā, appear as early as the 5th century CE, but more commonly between the 6th and 8th centuries. Examples from Mandasaur, Osiān, and Ābānerī reflect this motif.

The image in figure 12.1, from Ābānerī and currently stored at the Hawa Mahal in Jaipur, illustrates this blending of allure and warrior identity. The multi-armed goddess is seated with a lion by her left foot. She is voluptuous, adjusting a large earring with two hands, her hair with her uppermost right hand, and viewing herself in a mirror held in her left hand. Two hands attach an anklet, while others hold a water pot and a decorated bell. This image could depict Pārvatī, traditionally associated with a lion and a mirror, but the multi-armed depiction and bell suggest a warrior identity. While not definitively a Śṛṅgāra Durgā, this sculpture evidences an eroticized depiction of the lion-riding goddess, predating the DM, and points to an evolving fusion of Pārvatī and Devī attributes.

R. C. Agrawala (1968, 199–201) discusses several Śṛṅgāra Durgā images, including the one illustrated here. He identifies her middle right hand as holding a parrot (*śuka*), which he associates with the goddess Ambikā (1968, 200), now often linked to the goddess Mināksī, whose abode is the great temple in Madurai. The parrot is also depicted on the wrist of Victorious Goddess images, such as those at the Ādivarāha temple in Māmallapuram, and texts describe Korravai with a golden parrot. While the parrot and water pot are not weapons, another image at the Hari Hara Temple No. 1 in Osian (near Jodhpur, Rajasthan), also discussed by R. C. Agrawala (1968, 200), is particularly revealing. This goddess is seated on a lion, attaching an anklet on her right foot, while holding a parrot, sword, arrow, shield, bow, mirror, and water pot. Dated to the early 8th century CE, this image unequivocally merges the goddess's sensual, even erotic, qualities with her martial attributes. As a lion-riding, multi-armed, weapon-bearing deity, she can be confidently identified as Śṛṅgāra Durgā. By extension, other similar but less elaborate depictions may also be regarded as representations of the same goddess.

In the SP, Pārvatī is explicitly identified as the supreme goddess (but not the independent supreme deity), with Viṣṇu's hymn linking various other goddesses to her, including Kauśikī Vindhyavāsinī, whose origin myth is provided earlier in the text, and Durgā, along with Mahāmāyā, Mahāvidyā, Bhadrakālī,

Figure 12.1. Śṛṅgāra Durgā, with multiple arms, highlights the Devī's attractive appeal (c. 8th century CE). Ābānerī, Rajasthan. *Source*: Hawa Mahal Collection, Rajasthan. Photo by the author.

Mahāgaurī, Brahmacāriṇī, and others. Mahāgaurī and Brahmacāriṇī are among the Nine Durgās listed in the Devī Kavaca, a ritual appendix of the DM. Epithets such as Mahāmāyā, Mahāvidyā, and Bhadrakālī frequently appear in the DM as titles for the Devī. This suggests the existence of prominent cults dedicated to these goddesses during the SP's composition. It is unclear whether these cults centered on a single goddess known by various names or if the SP was attempting to unify distinct goddess cults under Pārvatī. The companions accompanying Tilottamā in battle, such as delusion and arrogance, sometimes appear in the DM as personified deities, qualities of the Devī, or epithets for the Great Goddess. This provides context for the often-unattractive depiction of the Devī's cohorts — they symbolize negative emotions and psychological flaws she uses to orchestrate her enemies' defeat. The SP also depicts Pārvatī receiving buffalo heads as offerings from all over the earth, a clear indication of buffalo sacrifice being commonly associated with goddess worship during this period.

The evidence so far suggests that the SP's goddess myth cycle predates that of the DM. Mahiṣa, central to the DM, plays only a minor role in the SP — if indeed he is the same demon — merely appearing as one among various demonic lords during the time of Sumbha and Nisumbha. Additionally, the DM relocates the slaying of Śumbha and Niśumbha to an earlier cosmic cycle, possibly in the Himalayas, while predicting their destruction in the Vindhyas in a later cosmic cycle. This positioning indicates the DM's familiarity with the SP's narrative and its motifs, such as the emergence of Kauśikī and the collective massing of *tejas*, while skillfully elevating the Devī to the status of the supreme deity, transcending both Pārvatī and Śiva.

Alternatively, one could view the SP as later than and influenced by the DM, deliberately reframing the latter's account to subordinate Kauśikī/Durgā to Pārvatī and emphasizing the Sumbha and Nisumbha episode over the Mahiṣa slaying. Goddess cults associated with the Vindhyas, buffalo sacrifices, and the lion as a mount or chariot vehicle were evidently popular and influential. Earlier scholarship generally prioritized the DM's composition, working primarily with the later SkP and assuming that the DM's portrayal of the Devī as supreme was subsequently reworked by the SkP to integrate her buffalo-slaying exploits into Pārvatī's mythology under a Śaiva framework. However, this interpretation becomes less persuasive when analyzing the SP. The DM's detailed handling of the Śumbha and Niśumbha episode and the emergence of the Devī through the gods' collective *tejas* appears to draw upon the SP rather than the reverse. This position aligns with Yokochi's (2004) groundbreaking study of the SP, particularly its focus on the Kauśikī-Vindhyavāsinī myth cycle, which supports the SP's precedence and a later date for the DM.

The SP's version of Kauśikī's slaying of Sumbha and Nisumbha continues with the goddess using her yogic powers to manifest an army of goddesses and women to assist her and confront the demon armies. Some of the leader goddesses have familiar names, both benevolent and malevolent, such as Lakṣmī and Alakṣmī, while others are the names of demonesses such as Pūtanā. They lead a surprisingly substantial bevy of bird-headed troops. These include women with heads of crows, owls, swans, ducks, hawks, peacocks, and herons. As well, there were women with heads of jackals, dogs, lions, tigers, elephants, and horses. Kauśikī fashioned chariots and weapons for them and, fanned by chowries (a yak-tailed fan, which is a royal insignia), led them into battle on her own flying chariot (a gift of Pārvatī's) drawn by two lions and with a peacock-topped standard. Eventually, after graphic descriptions of the bloody fray, Sumbha and Nisumbha leapt into the sky to meet the goddess, who crushed the life out of them. The gods were thrilled and asked her in gratitude what she wished for. She said she would like to see her parents, Śiva and Pārvatī. They instantly appeared before the divine throng. Śiva appeared as radiant as the collective of everyone's *tejas*, since his *tejas* outshines all others. Kauśikī and the other gods prostrated themselves at the celestial couple's feet. Śiva then promised Kauśikī that she would be invincible, widely worshipped, would aid the gods when they were troubled, and would grant the desires of her devotees. Pārvatī intoned that Kauśikī would be worshipped by humans, gods, and sages as she herself is worshipped, and that she would enjoy this adoration because of Pārvatī's grace. So saying, they vanished. Kauśikī was then adored in a consecration rite. Indra appeared and took her as his sister, commanding her to freely wander wherever she desired, to kill demons, and offer protection. Along with the other gods, he then departed (SP 67).

The narrative offers several notable points. Among the goddesses manifested from Kauśikī is Caṇḍā, whose name is the feminine form of Caṇḍa, the demon defeated by Kālī in the DM. As noted earlier, Caṇḍā is potentially connected to the inscribed name of a *yakṣī* depicted at the Bharhut *stūpa* complex (c. 2nd–1st century BCE). This may represent the earliest visual portrayal of what eventually intersects with the Hindu goddess Caṇḍī, evolving into the Buddhist goddess Cundā, whose name has many variations, including Caṇḍā (Shaw 2006, 283). Caṇḍā also closely resembles Caṇḍī, a variant of Caṇḍikā, the main epithet of the Great Goddess in the DM, and first appears in the DSto.

Kauśikī is depicted as embodying nearly every goddess except Pārvatī, with notable associations to bird-faced goddesses, such as those linked to peacocks and owls. This resonates with the reputedly bird-faced Vindhyavāsinī at her temple in Mirzapur, as discussed earlier. These animal-faced goddesses evoke the "wolf-faced" epithet of Durgā found in the DSto. Additionally, Kauśikī's link with the lion as a chariot vehicle is significant. Unlike the SP, the DM omits the lion chariot — depicting the lion as a free-roaming beast. The SP appears aware of the hymns to Durgā in the Mbh and those in the HV, which share these features. However, the SP explicitly subordinates Kauśikī to Pārvatī and Śiva by presenting her as their daughter. It also includes Indra taking Kauśikī as his sister, a motif found in the PN-s1 (l. 47–48) but absent in the DM. The peacock standard, prominent in the Mbh hymns and early HV as well as in iconography, is featured in the SP but excluded from the DM. These elements suggest that the SP's version of Kauśikī's battle with Sumbha and Nisumbha postdates the DStv and PN-s1 and was possibly composed after the DSto and Praise of Nidrā (Second Stratum) (PN-s2). The PN-s1 (l. 49), part of the HV's core, names Kauśikī/Nidrā as the slayer of Sumbha and Nisumbha, as does the SP. However, later HV hymns, such as Pradyumna's Hymn (PradH l. 364) and Aniruddha's Hymn (AniH l. 39), adopt the spelling Śumbha and Niśumbha, as do all but the earliest DM manuscripts.

In earlier chapters, I suggested that the Chandraketugarh goddess, associated with birds such as the peacock and owl, might have been known as Kauśikī (equated with Nidrā), whose cult was prominent in the Vindhya region. It is apparent that the fame, reverence, and widespread veneration of Kauśikī as a Great Goddess predated the SP's framing of these qualities as bestowed by Śiva and Pārvatī. A significant aspect of Kauśikī's representation is her association with bird-headed and animal-headed women. The bird-headed women evoke imagery of Yoginīs, often linked to flight, while the animal-headed ones recall goddesses such as Vārāhī (boar-headed), Nārasiṃhī (lion-headed), and Vināyakī (elephant-headed). In the SP, there is only a general mention of such animal-headed goddesses. However, in the DM, Vārāhī appears tearing into demons' chests with her tusks (DM 8.34–35), and Nārasiṃhī rips apart demons with her claws. These goddesses, Vārāhī and Nārasiṃhī, are among the Mātṛs

(Mothers), *śakti*s emanating from their male counterparts, and are closely associated with Viṣṇu's animal *avatāra*s. The elephant-headed Gaṇeśa is frequently depicted alongside the Mātṛkās in sculptural representations, although neither he nor Vināyakī appear in either the SP or the DM.

The SP narrative continues, in Chapter 68, with Kauśikī allocating to different regions the various goddesses that had spawned from her in the battle with Sumbha and Nisumbha. So, Pracaṇḍā is placed in Tukhāra, Lakṣmī on Mount Kola, Jayā and Vijayā in Kauśikī's own place (probably Vindhyā), Śivā in Abhira, Bahumāṃsā in Kotīvarṣa, Vānarī in Śabara, Nirāyāsā and Citraghaṇṭā in Vārānaṣī, and so on. Some of these locations and goddess names appear to be imaginary, while others seem derived from renowned sites of goddess worship. For instance, modern-day Kolhapur is still a well-known site of Lakṣmī worship with a long-documented history. Again, this suggests the existence of a widespread cult of regional goddesses, who were being, or already were, pulled together under the rubric of a Great Goddess, Kauśikī. Citraghaṇṭā is the name of one of the Nine Durgās mentioned in the Devī Kavaca, an appendage of the DM when it circulates as an independent ritual text.

There next follows a very short description of Kauśikī's encounter with Mahiṣa, who is described as the son of Sumbha. In his buffalo shape he attacks the goddess, who grabs him by a horn and throws him to the earth. She presses down on his head while lifting him by the tail. And then she kills him by stabbing his back with her trident. This Mahiṣa episode seems very much like an insertion. For one, the entire Chapter 68 is rather short. This Mahiṣa seems to differ from the one in the Sunda and Nisunda story, where he provides cautionary advice. However, this episode is notable for its alignment with iconographic depictions of the buffalo-slaying goddess that emerged in the late Kuṣāṇa and Gupta periods and are prominently represented in the Cāḷukyan monuments of Karṇāṭaka and Andhra. Examples include the exterior rock-cut shrine I at Badami and the miniature shrine in the Bala Brahmā temple compound at Alampur (Tartakov and Dehejia 1984, figs. 17, 18). As discussed earlier, earlier iconography of the buffalo-slaying goddess depicted the act differently.

Tartakov and Dehejia (1984, 318) date a well-known tail-gripping, head-trampling image from Badami to the third quarter of the sixth century. Yokochi (2004, 20) notes that this iconographic style emerged around 500 CE, and her chapters 5.2 and 5.3 (Yokochi 2004, 133–50) extensively analyze variations of the so-called Gupta type and their origins. This correlation strongly suggests that the Mahiṣa episode was written and inserted into the SP during this period. It is unlikely that the SP's terse description of the episode served as the basis for the development of the rich Gupta and Cāḷukya iconographic traditions, as it lacks the compelling narrative detail found in the DM.

The insertion appears to connect the Mahiṣa-slaying goddess to the Kauśikī myth cycle, identifying the two as one. Given that the tail-gripping, head-trampling, body-spearing imagery predates the Emergent Demon type, first seen in the Rāṣṭrakūṭa Kailāsanātha temple at Ellora (c. 756 CE), and that the

Anthropomorphic type also emerged earlier in the Cālukyan and Rāṣṭrakūṭa spheres, it is likely that the SP composers were unaware of these later developments. This reinforces the notion that the SP's Devī myth cycle predates the DM. The Mahiṣa slaying episode, a later addition to the SP likely dates to a period after the 5th century but before the 8th century CE.

Evidently, Vaiṣṇava sectarian traditions sought to unify the diverse village, tribal, and folk goddess cults under the figure of Yoganidrā, thereby subordinating her to Viṣṇu. Concurrently, Śaiva traditions pursued a similar strategy by elevating Pārvatī as the true great goddess, although subordinate to Śiva as his wife. Both sects appear to have been contending with an independent Great Goddess–centered — or even a Goddess as Supreme Deity — tradition in which various local goddess cults were progressively unified under major goddesses such as Nidrā, Kauśikī, Bhadrakālī, Mahāmāyā, Ambikā, Durgā, and Kātyāyanī. Many of these goddesses may have originally had distinct cults, although some may have been epithets for the same deity. Blood sacrifice, particularly buffalo sacrifice, seems to have been a common feature among these goddess cults, necessitating acknowledgment of the buffalo-demon slaying mythology in efforts to assimilate them into the dominant sectarian frameworks.

Summing up Durgā's appearances in the SP (following verse references from Yokochi (2004)), we find her equated with Pārvatī in three instances (SP 29.209a, SP (Bh) 60.41a, 157.24f) and with Kātyāyanī twice (SP 29.193d, 69.14a). These identifications occur within hymns to Pārvatī, where the goddess is addressed by numerous other names and epithets. Durgā also appears in a list of names for Kauśikī (SP 58.29a) and once within a list of Lokamātṛs ("Mothers of the World") (SP (Bh) 111.4ab). Notably, Durgā's name appears alongside Gāyatrī and Sāvitrī, and elsewhere in the SP, she is again mentioned with these Vedic goddesses (SP (Bh) 60.41ab, 157.24ef).

Yokochi (2004, 17–18) reasonably suggests that Durgā retained a Brahmanical or Vedic character during the SP's composition and may not have originally been a demon-slaying warrior goddess. She further proposes that by the 6th century CE, Durgā, along with her lineage name Kātyāyanī, was integrated into the developing cult of the Warrior Goddess. Alternatively, she posits that Durgā-Kātyāyanī (a woman of the Kātyāyana lineage) may have first been associated with the buffalo-slaying goddess Mahiṣamardinī. As Mahiṣāsuramardinī evolved into the Warrior Goddess, Durgā and Kātyāyanī were absorbed as epithets, with the latter aiding in legitimizing Mahiṣāsuramardinī's status within the Brahmanical Hindu pantheon. Yokochi concludes that the ascendancy of Durgā as the dominant name for the Warrior Goddess remains to be studied but likely occurred no earlier than the 8th century CE, possibly even later.

This study of the rise of the goddess Durgā offers an opportunity to refine Yokochi's proposals. Yokochi's argument relies on the later dating of the Mbh and HV hymns. However, as argued here, if the core of the DStv or some DStv* variant was indeed composed at or prior to the HV's core, which contains the PN-s1, Durgā was already equated with Kālī, Jayā, and Vijayā, associated with the destruction of Mahiṣa, and depicted wielding many weapons. This would suggest that by the 3rd century CE, Durgā was already identified as a Warrior Goddess associated with victory in battle (DStv l. 32). Even so, verses specifically explicating Durgā in the DStv emphasize her role as a Great Goddess and, more prominently, as a protector and refuge, ensuring the safety of her devotees (l. 39–43, 50–51) and granting boons (l. 31, 35, 38). She is associated with qualities such as fame and compassion, and her ability to free devotees from delusion and even death (l. 44–47). These attributes align with those describing Durgā in the arguably earlier Rātri Khila verses, where her name also appears. These references underline Durgā's salvific origins, with her protective power tied to the recitation of her mantras and hymns.

The PN-s1 presents Kauśikī, identified with Nidrā, as its central goddess, without naming Durgā. It does not reference the slaying of Mahiṣa but associates Kauśikī/Nidrā with the slaying of Sumbha and Nisumbha (l. 49). Set within a Vaiṣṇava framework, the PN-s1 subordinates Kauśikī/Nidrā to Viṣṇu. However, the DStv+, in its frame verses, adopts the Vaiṣṇava association of Kauśikī/Nidrā through the Kaṃsa myth cycle and explicitly identifies Durgā (l. 2) as this goddess. After Yudhiṣṭhira recites the hymn, Durgā appears to him and promises victory in battle, solidifying her role as a Warrior Goddess at the time of the DStv+'s insertion into the Mbh.

This period marks the fusion of the buffalo-slaying goddess, identified as Durgā, with the Sumbha/Nisumbha slaying goddess of the Vindhyas, both linked to empowering kings. Durgā's name also features prominently in the DSto (l. 23) and its frame verses, which label the hymn the Durgā Stotra (l. 4). By the time of the DSto+'s insertion into the Mbh, Durgā was firmly established as a Warrior Goddess. In the PN-s2, Durgā is explicitly identified with Kauśikī, Kātyāyanī, Jayā, and Vijayā, embodying characteristics of refuge, boon-granting, and martial prowess. Evidence from Chinese translations indicates that the hymn, also known as the Āryā Stava, was in circulation before 703 CE, based on its earliest known manuscript (Ludvik 2006, 4–5).

The VarP does not mention Durgā, and the SP integrates her within Pārvatī's manifestations. However, with the DM, which our evidence leads us to date to the late-middle 8th century, Durgā rises to prominence as the primary name for the Great Goddess, Devī. In fact, in the DM Devī is framed as the supreme deity, with highly strategic theological features that inhibit her ability to be subsumed under other male deities. These will be discussed in greater detail in the final chapter of this study. The ascendancy of Durgā as Devī is likely reenforced by Śumbha addressing her by name in the pivotal episode where he accuses her of not fighting alone, prompting her to draw all goddesses into herself. Additionally, Durgā's association with Mahiṣa's slaying and the compelling power of that myth cycle, supported by its vivid iconographic depictions, solidifies her prominence. These temple portrayals captivate visually, while the ritual recitation of the DM ensured the widespread dissemination of Mahiṣa's destruction by Durgā.

The *Devī Purāṇa*

The *Devī Purāṇa* (DevīP) is one of the earliest of the lesser Purāṇas (*upapurāṇa*) to describe Devī worship, and has been quite influential on later prescriptive texts, such as Dharmaśāstra digests (*nibandha*) and ritual manuals (*paddhati*). We will discuss those aspects of it elsewhere. There are five known manuscripts of the DevīP, three in Devanāgarī and two in Bengali script, with major discrepancies among them (L. Gupta 2002, 247n1). Hazra (1963, vol. 2, 73) convincingly argued that the DevīP was composed near Tamralipti, in Bengal. He also conjectured that this may have taken place as early as the latter half of the 6th century CE but no later than 850 CE (1963, vol. 2, 73–79), although it has been vigorously amended with insertions.

The DevīP references Durgā in several instances, such as its detailed instructions in Chapter 72 about building and protecting fortresses (*durga*). The text mandates that Durgā, the buffalo-slayer, be installed in every fortress. The version I consulted uses the phrase *durgeṣu kārayed durgāṃ mahiṣāsuraghātinīm*, while Sarkar (2017, 206n81) cites the phrase with *mahiṣāsuramardinīm*. This discrepancy suggests that *mahiṣāsuramardinī* may not have been commonly used when the DevīP was composed. Alternatively, the term might have been standardized in later manuscripts. If the version I referenced is based on an earlier manuscript, it would reinforce the notion that the composition of the DevīP postdates the *Śivadharma* (c. 7th century CE), where the term *mahiṣamardinī* (and/or *mahiṣamardanī*) appears for the first time.

The DevīP prescribes that fortress gates be named after Durgā's various forms, such as Jayā, Kālī, and Caṇḍā, as well as Durgā (72.145–48), the inclusion of her name possibly indicating her growing prominence from a specific goddess to a synonym for the Great Goddess. It further directs that Durgā, along with deities such as the Mātṛs and Grahas, be worshipped with sacrifices (*balim datvā*, 73.58) before constructing a victorious fortress (*vijayākhyam mahāpuram*, 73.37). Daṇḍin's *Daśakumāracarita* (c. 700 CE) mentions the worship of Vindhyavāsinī at Tamralipti (Humes 1993, 203n6), suggesting a thriving goddess cult in the region. This raises the possibility that Tamralipti was the religious center responsible for producing the DevīP, although I question whether the DevīP represents a Śākta sect that held the Great Goddess as supreme. Instead, the text likely emanates from a sect that revered the goddess but placed her in a moderately subordinate role to Śiva. Tamralipti, a major center of goddess worship in early 8th century CE Bengal, would have gained further prominence through references in Daṇḍin's work. Based on these connections, it is plausible that the DevīP's core composition dates to the late 7th or early 8th century CE. Verses in the DevīP also appear to have borrowed from Bāṇabhaṭṭa's *Kādambarī* typically dated to the first half of the 7th century CE (Hazra 1963, vol. 2, 76–77). Hazra's findings convincingly suggest that the DevīP was not directly influenced by the DM. Hazra (1963, vol. 2, 76) even argues that the DevīP shows no familiarity with the DM, which is supported by its alternative telling of a buffalo-demon slaying myth. This version features the demon Ghora, who assumes the form of a buffalo (*mahiṣa*) before being killed by Umā.

The DevīP's divergence from the DM aligns it more closely with texts such as the VarP and the SP, which use the buffalo-slaying goddess narrative to subordinate her to Viṣṇu in the VarP and to Śiva and Pārvatī in the SP. Consequently, while the DevīP centers on the exploits and worship of a great goddess, it does not elevate her to the status of the Great Goddess as Supreme Deity celebrated in the DM. This interpretation is further supported by examples from the DevīP, as explored below.

In the DevīP (Chapters 2–9, 13–20; Hazra 1963, vol. 2, 28–29), King Nṛpavāhana learns of the *kāmikā vidyā*, an esoteric knowledge said to confer supreme power or ultimate liberation, from the sage Agastya. The *vidyā*'s transmission is hierarchical: from Śiva to Viṣṇu, to Brahmā, and then to Indra. Brahmā, while sharing it with Indra, advises him to worship Ādyā Śakti, recounting her victory over the demon Ghora. The narrative parallels the DM's frame story, where Medhas instructs King Suratha and the merchant Samādhi, suggesting the DM may have drawn from the DevīP or that both narratives arose independently in distinct regions. The DM ultimately gained dominance in Śākta traditions, while the DevīP resonated more with Śaiva contexts. The texts also differ in their depictions of worship. In the DevīP, sages at Agastya's hermitage worship Brahmā, Viṣṇu, Skanda, Umā, and Durgā, indicating a Śaiva-aligned pantheon. In contrast, the DM highlights the exclusive primacy of the Great Goddess in Medhas's hermitage, omitting references to male gods. These differences reflect the distinct theological orientations of the two works.

The DevīP continues by recounting that the demon Ghora received a boon from Viṣṇu ensuring only the goddess Śiva could slay him. Empowered by this boon, Ghora, alongside his son Vajradaṇḍa, conquered the triple world. When Vajradaṇḍa attacked heaven, Indra sought Viṣṇu's aid, prompting the latter to recount Ghora's origins as follows.

A demon named Dundubhi once lusted after Umā, who occupied the left half of Śiva's body. Śiva turned Dundubhi to ashes, from which Ghora emerged, inheriting his father's lust for Umā. When Ghora approached her, Umā cast him to earth but spared his life, an act for which Śiva chastised her, deeming it foolish. In anger, Umā retaliated by making Ghora invincible to the gods, enabling him to rule the triple world. Frustrated by her defiance, Śiva cursed Umā to descend to earth, where Ghora would desire her as his wife. In response, Umā vowed to slay Ghora while playfully riding a lion. Viṣṇu explained that Ghora's rule would persist until he lusted after Umā, at which point he would be vanquished by the lion-riding goddess Vindhyācala-nivāsinī.

This account insinuates the existence of a vibrant cult centered on a lion-riding Great Goddess in the Vindhya region, which the DevīP seeks to assimilate into a Śaiva framework. The narrative provides a rationale for Viṣṇu's non-intervention, as the conditions for Ghora's demise were already established. As an aside, the trope of Śiva cursing Umā to go to earth, where she is ambiguously paired with a male demonic counterpart, is central to Durgā's mythology in Java and Bali (discussed in volume 2 of this study).

In Chapter 5 of the DevīP, the god Brahmā salutes Viṣṇu and his ten incarnations, which include Kṛṣṇa, the Buddha, and Kalkin (Hazra 1963, vol. 2, 40–42). It indicates that the DevīP must have been composed after the Buddha had been incorporated into the *avatāra* scheme, which occurred after 550 CE according to Hazra (1963, vol. 2, 75, n. 178). In Chapter 6, Brahmā reminds Viṣṇu how in bygone eons the goddess Cāmuṇḍā was sent by Śiva to save Viṣṇu from peril. Viṣṇu was threatened by Kālāgni-rudra, and his son Hālāhala. Cāmuṇḍā is described as a powerful Śakti capable of creating, maintaining, and destroying the universe, and after saving Viṣṇu and being eulogized by him, she promised to help when called upon. The DevīP's reference to Cāmuṇḍā saving Viṣṇu is unusual. The name Kālāgni evokes the fires at the end time, and Hālāhala, the poison that threatens to destroy the cosmos. It is conceivable that if the DM was influenced by the DevīP, it picked up on this motif of the Devī saving Viṣṇu in its first episode concerning Madhu and Kaiṭabha, but associated this with Yogamāyā (i.e., Nidrā), who can be fierce, rather than with Cāmuṇḍā. In Chapter 81 of the DevīP, Kālāgni-rudra is puzzlingly described as identical to Kālikā, lives in Kālāgnipura, is surrounded by other Rudras, and eventually destroys the world.

Iconographic studies indicate the early occurrence of fierce (*raudra*) or savage (*ugra*) forms of goddesses, possibly referred to by Bhavabhūti as Cāmuṇḍā. However, these depictions are rarely solitary; they typically appear in conjunction with clusters of Mātṛkās, who are generally portrayed as benign figures. Examples include the Mātṛkā images from Śāmalāji, dated to the early 5th to 6th century CE. In these early representations, the savage goddess is depicted as full-bodied, beautiful, and large-bellied, with her fierce attributes subtly conveyed through details such as protruding fangs, skull ornaments, and weapons. By later periods, her form evolved into the classic emaciated figure with sunken limbs and a hollowed belly (Panikkar 1995, 56–66).

Although modern scholarship frequently identifies this fierce goddess as Cāmuṇḍā, there is no definitive evidence for this name in the period of these depictions. Textual references to Cāmuṇḍā in association with the Mātṛkās only appear with the *Śivadharma* (6th–7th century CE) (Bisschop 2018, 156). Even the DevīP, assuming an early date, does not include Cāmuṇḍā in connection with the Mātṛkās, nor does Bhavabhūti's *Mālatī-Mādhava*. The first textual correlation of Cāmuṇḍā with Mātṛkās occurs in the *Śivadharma*, underscoring her relatively late integration into this grouping.

In the DM, the Mātṛkās (or Mātṛs) appear as emanations (*śakti*) of male gods, created to combat the demon Raktabīja, whose blood generates replicas of himself. Cāmuṇḍā, however, is not listed among these Mātṛs. The frightening emanation from the Devī herself is Śivadūtī, who, unlike Cāmuṇḍā, is directly named and plays a prominent role. Śivadūtī, with her cruel laughter and association with jackals, assists the Mātṛkās, Kālī, and the Devī in battle. Given these distinctions, textual evidence suggests that the fearsome figure frequently associated with jackals and depicted alongside Mātṛka clusters in early sculptural arrays prior to the DM might align more closely with Śivadūtī rather than Cāmuṇḍā.

The DM identifies Cāmuṇḍā with Kālī, a different goddess from Śivadūtī entirely. Kālī emerged from the forehead of the Devī, whose complexion has turned dark with anger. Kālī is described as black, gaunt, with sunken eyes, gaping mouth, and lolling tongue, wielding a skull-topped staff and wearing a tiger skin and a garland of human heads. This, of course, is why the image of the *raudra* goddess with the Mātṛkās is often identified as Cāmuṇḍā, because she is often portrayed with some of these attributes. Kālī is produced to destroy the demons Caṇḍa and Muṇḍa, whom she decapitates and is thereby named Cāmuṇḍā by the Devī. In the context of the Raktabīja episode, involving the Mātṛs, the Devī, explicitly calling Kālī by the name Cāmuṇḍā (DM 8.52), asks her to drink up the blood of Raktabīja. So there is an unmistakable identification forged between Kālī and Cāmuṇḍā in this episode, and when Kālī/Cāmuṇḍā drinks up Raktabīja's blood, the Mātṛs are intoxicated with it. This too forges a connection between Cāmuṇḍā and the Mātṛs, who seem intrinsically linked. Since Śivadūtī is not well represented in later literature or iconography, the DM may have succeeded in fusing the cults of Śivadūtī, Kālī, and Cāmuṇḍā. Śivadūtī may only have been a strategic creation by the DM, as I will explain below.

To return to the DevīP, numerous instances illustrate its attempt to subordinate Viṣṇu to the great goddess while simultaneously subordinating her to Śiva. In the earlier example, Cāmuṇḍā appears as a great goddess, not the Great Goddess, to distinguish her lesser role. For instance, Brahmā advises Viṣṇu to eulogize Śiva, not Umā, for Ghora and Vajradaṇḍa's destruction. Śiva explains that Parā Śakti, abiding in his left side, will manifest in the Vindhyas, make the male gods her servants, and be attended by a retinue of unmarried goddesses. Her lion is described as comprising all the gods, goddesses, and the heavens and earth. While this description initially suggests the goddess's supremacy, the DevīP clarifies that Śiva provides her a protection formula (*rakṣā-mantra*) and sends her, along with her attendants and lion *vāhana*, to the Vindhyas. This portrayal firmly establishes Śiva's dominance, as he directs and safeguards the goddess.

This section (Chapter 7) reveals that a vibrant Śākta cult centered on a Great Goddess — possibly as Supreme Deity — flourished in the Vindhyas during the composition of this portion of the DevīP. The goddess and her lion were evidently regarded as embodying all male deities and creation itself. However, the text ultimately reduces her status by depicting her as subordinate to Śiva's authority. This pattern of elevating the goddess while simultaneously subordinating her mirrors tropes found in the PN-s1 (e.g., Nidrā) or Skanda's defeat of Mahiṣa in the Mbh.

To dupe Ghora, various empowerment rites of the type we associate with Tantric practices were performed by Nārada, such as performing a fire ritual (*homa*) with human flesh (*mahāmāṃsa*), which successfully depraved Ghora to yearn for young mountain girls living in the Vindhyas. The DevīP digresses in Chapters 9 to 12 into the description of other Tantricized practices, such as Śaiva Yoga, and the erection of a victory banner, also bestowed by Śiva, which it explains had previously been used by Durgā, Viṣṇu, and other deities. Chapter 13 recounts how Ghora's wife had been influenced by the teachings and practices of Digambara Jains, leading her to perform all sorts of vowed ascetic observances (*vrata*) and other such religious duties. So, sex-starved Ghora and his armies set out to enjoy the mountain girls in the Vindhyas, described as the home of sages and the standard assortment of foreign (*mleccha*) tribes, namely the V(B)arbav(b)ars, Pulindas, Śav(b)aras, and so on. There Ghora spotted Devī in her form as a young girl and was smitten. His first emissary, Durmukha, was killed by Vijayā. Chapters 14 to 16 describe how the Devī's attendants, Jayā, Vijayā, Ajitā, and Aparājitā, slew various demons. Jayā slew Vajradaṇḍa. Nārada sang a eulogy to the goddess, who is described as protecting Brahmā, Viṣṇu, and Śiva, and is known by a host of names, including Durgā, Śākambharī, Gaurī, Vindhyavāsinī, Kātyāyanī, Kauśikī, Jayā, Vijayā, Cāmuṇḍā, Caṇḍī, Pārvatī, Ambikā, and so on. The text emphasizes that although she does these things and takes on these forms she originates from Rudra. Ready for battle with Ghora, the Devī appeared with her lion, carried an assortment of weapons, and wore a leopard skin. So here again we note how the DevīP is instrumental in the development of the persona of a great goddess, whom it affirms is none other than all the various major goddesses it names, but whom it considers as a sort of emanation of Śiva.

Since Ghora was about to attack and kill the female attendant deities, Śiva sang a eulogy to her praising the goddess as Kālī, Bhadrakālī, Kapālinī, as well as with names of several of the female counterparts of the male gods, such as Brahmī, Kaumārī, Māhendrī, Māheśvarī, Vaiṣṇavī, and Vārāhī, akin to the Mātṛs of the DM, as well as Arundhatī, Jāhnavī, Sarasvatī, and so on (Chapter 17).[5] The battle began, and Jayā, Ajitā, and Aparājitā slew many demons (Chapters 18 and 19). Finally, Devī slew Ghora, who had taken the form of a buffalo, and all the other demons that emerged from his body (Chapter 20). Thus she, Umā/Vindhyavāsinī, who is also called Ādyā Śakti and Yoga-nidrā, became renowned as the *mahiṣa*-killer.

The DevīP's version of the buffalo-demon myth, through its use of the epithet Yoga-nidrā, demonstrates familiarity with the Vaiṣṇava Kṛṣṇa-Kaṃsa myth cycle, in which Nidrā flies off to the Vindhyas to become the virgin goddess residing there. The text incorporates the myth of the Great Goddess slaying a buffalo demon but adapts it to its own framework, naming the demon Ghora and identifying the goddess as Umā/Vindhyavāsinī, thereby subordinating her to Śiva. Umā and Śiva are depicted as bickering, reflecting their roles as husband and wife, or as Śiva/Śakti. While Umā is described as part of Śiva, evoking the Ardhanārīśvara form, the relationship implies near equality, although she remains slightly inferior. Ghora, whose name means "frightful," is presented as a rebirth of Dundubhi, a bovine demon referenced in Vālmīki's *Rāmāyana*. If the DevīP predates the DM, it suggests the presence of an advanced and integrated Śākta tradition at the time. In this context, the Great Goddess, referred to as Ādyā Śakti, is portrayed as embodying all deities. Her lion *vāhana* is depicted as an extension of her being, sharing similar divine attributes.

I am inclined to place the DevīP's narrative before the DM for several reasons. The DM seems to respond to Śaiva efforts to assimilate the Devī, rather than the DevīP reacting to the DM, whose content likely spread quickly within Śākta circles due to its ritual significance. The DM unequivocally names the buffalo demon Mahiṣa, not Ghora, making it unlikely that the DevīP would attempt to introduce an alternate name if it were composed afterward. In the DM, the Devī, manifesting through Pārvatī, slays Śumbha and Niśumbha in the Himalayas and predicts she will defeat another pair of demons with the same names in the Vindhyas in a future manifestation. This positioning clearly makes Pārvatī (Umā) a mere manifestation of the Great Goddess in the DM. By doing so, the DM decisively diminishes the possibility of regarding the Great Goddess (Devī, Durgā, etc.) as primarily Pārvatī, or even as the Śakti half of the Śiva/Śakti duality that the DevīP repeatedly emphasizes.

Another critical clue is found in the DM's version of the Mātṛkā-Raktabīja myth. After the male gods create their *śakti*s, such as Brahmāṇī, Māheśvarī, Kaumārī, Vaiṣṇavī, and Vārāhī — figures also mentioned in the DevīP but not termed Mātṛkās — the DM significantly shifts the narrative dynamic (8.21–8.27). In a pivotal moment, Śiva attempts to command the Devī, echoing the subordinating tone found in the DevīP. He instructs Caṇḍikā to slay the demons to please him. The DM, however, subverts this trope. In response, the Devī manifests her own fearsome *śakti*, Śivadūtī (also called Aparājitā, "[She who is] Invincible"), who overturns Śiva's authority. Rather than obeying his command, Śivadūtī compels Śiva to act as her messenger, ordering him to deliver a challenge to the demons on her behalf. This marks a decisive departure from the DevīP, where Śiva wields authority over the goddess. Here, even one of the Great Goddess's manifestations, Śivadūtī, asserts dominance over Śiva.

Śivadūtī subsequently joins the Mātṛs, the Devī, and Kālī in battle, where her laughter devastates the demons, and she devours them. Her appearance in the DM may have been deliberately crafted to counter theological tropes that subordinate the Great Goddess to Śiva. By creating Śivadūtī, the DM not only challenges narratives of male authority but also asserts the Great Goddess's independent supremacy. Just as male deities possess *śakti*s, the Great Goddess has her own *śakti*, affirming her status as a supreme deity rather than a mere consort or counterpart to a male god.

The DevīP is described as containing a narrative of the Śumbha-Niśumbha myth in the third of its four primary parts. However, since surviving manuscripts primarily focus on the second part — detailing the first manifestation of the Devī — the actual content of this narrative remains unknown. If recovered, it could potentially clarify whether the DevīP predates the DM. The Śumbha-Niśumbha (or Sumbha-Nisumbha in earlier variants) myth is included in the SP, which almost certainly preceded the DM. Therefore, it is plausible that the DevīP also presented its own version of the tale, likely from a Śaiva perspective that elevated the greatness of a goddess while subordinating her to Śiva.

The DevīP references what appear to be Tantric practices, suggesting that it was composed during the period when Śaiva Tantra was gaining prominence. At this time, Śaivism seems to have been asserting itself against both Vaiṣṇavism and Śāktism, leveraging its authority to prescribe and standardize worship for major deities, including the goddess. This integration suggests the inclusion of ritualists with Vedic expertise within its ranks. This trend is evident in the DevīP's Chapters 21 and beyond, where a theology of the goddess and her modes of worship are articulated. Many of these Purāṇic guidelines later influenced ritual manuals and Śāstra literature. These contributions of the DevīP to ritual and theological frameworks will be discussed in greater detail in the second volume.

Sanderson (2009) exhaustively traces, particularly through the inscriptional record, the ascendency and eventual dominance of Śaivism from the 5th to the 13th century CE in much of the Hindu world. He notes that allegiance to Śiva by far surpasses the other rival religious options, such as adoption of Buddhism or Jainism, or devotion to Viṣṇu, Sūrya/Āditya, or the Devī. This extended beyond the subcontinent, into the kingdoms of Java and Bali and the Khmer empire and the Champa in southeast Asia. For the most part, Śākta cults were absorbed by Śaivism, where they gave rise to esoteric notions fusing male (Śiva) and female (Śakti) dimensions of divinity. The great goddess within such Śaiva configurations often functioned to confer, maintain, or restore a king's sovereignty. In fact, she did so even when assimilated within Vaiṣṇava or Buddhist sectarian traditions. This trend towards progressive assimilation, combined with her capacity for sovereign empowerment, is resisted in the masterful positioning of the role of the Devī in the DM. In the next chapter, I appraise how these forces are at the heart of a theological triumph of the Great Goddess as Supreme Deity, who consolidates her victory, at least among Śāktas, through the *Devī Māhātmya*, and in the centuries following its composition.

Chapter 13

Durgā Triumphant

At this juncture, it is vital to reassess the findings on the development of the cult of Durgā, synthesizing the evidence into a broader understanding. Across a wide spectrum of textual and material sources, several consistent symbols and themes associated with the worship of Durgā and the Great Goddess tradition emerge. Among her defining attributes are her multiple arms, weaponry, lion mount, the act of subduing or crushing a buffalo demon, self-coronation with a unique diadem, peacock feather ornaments, and a peacock feather standard. While many of these elements have South Asian origins, some show intriguing parallels with goddess traditions from outside the subcontinent.

A key theme is the integration of minor goddesses into a larger unified figure within Śaiva or Vaiṣṇava frameworks, although these attempts often sought to subordinate the Great Goddess to a supreme male deity. Another recurrent motif is her role in aiding the minor gods, restoring their positions in the pantheon after being ousted by a demon adversary. This aspect emphasizes her role as a restorer of cosmic balance. Ritual devotion to Durgā frequently involves mantric hymns of praise, with the Durgā Stava (DStv) and the *Devī Māhātmya* (DM) serving as enduring liturgical texts. From early depictions, Durgā is characterized as a salvific deity, a grantor of boons, and a refuge from countless dangers. Over time, these qualities were augmented as other deities and their mythologies were subsumed into her cult, amplifying themes such as sovereign empowerment and her role as the ultimate source of authority and victory.

While prevailing scholarship often attributes the emergence of the Great Goddess as the Supreme Deity, as presented in the DM, to the amalgamation of subordinated Vaiṣṇava or Śaiva goddesses, I propose an alternative theory. An enduring Śākta tradition likely upheld the concept of an independent Great Goddess as a Supreme Deity long before these sectarian integrations. This preexisting tradition, I argue, absorbed and redefined the subordinated "great goddesses" of Vaiṣṇava and Śaiva frameworks. The DM exemplifies and perhaps even operationalizes this strategy, which remains influential today. To substantiate this perspective, I propose a theoretical framework grounded in the material analyzed. This framework explores the intersections of key themes: iconism versus aniconism, monotheism versus polytheism, ambivalent attitudes toward blood sacrifice, the sanction for sovereignty and its symbols (notably the diadem), political and religious imperialism, cross-cultural exchanges, and metaphysical concepts. These elements collectively illuminate the ascension of

Durgā as the Supreme Refuge. The DM adeptly reconciles such tensions among competing theological and cultural paradigms. It presents the Great Goddess, unequivocally identified as Durgā, as a supreme deity without directly challenging rival theological traditions, maintaining inclusivity and adaptability. Simultaneously, it democratizes worship practices, making devotion accessible to a broad audience, while preserving the authority of sacred specialists. The theoretical framework that I present in this chapter is not meant to be definitive but seeks to advance our understanding of the evolution and significance of the Great Goddess tradition in Asia.

The maritime and Silk Road trade routes, active for centuries before and after the Common Era, fostered dynamic interactions between the Indian subcontinent and regions such as Egypt, Greece, Central Asia, China, and Southeast Asia. Far from being isolated, India engaged actively with both neighboring regions and distant nations. The persona of the Great Goddess, as Durgā, and the prominence of her name likely evolved through the fusion of numerous goddesses, including Indigenous deities such as Korravai, Kālī, and Kauśikī, and foreign influences from China, Egypt, and Mesopotamia. The movement of ideas and imagery was bidirectional; for instance, multi-armed deities, a concept derived from notions of absolute divinity and perhaps riverine goddess imagery in India, influenced artistic and theological developments beyond its borders. Durgā's emergence as a dominant figure occurred amidst ongoing interactions and tensions with Śaivism, Vaiṣṇavism, Buddhism, Jainism, and other religious traditions within South Asia. However, I propose that theological and metaphysical concepts from regions outside the subcontinent also significantly shaped the development of the Hindu Great Goddess. Reassessing these interplays and the forces that preceded the "crystallization" of Durgā's cult can provide insight into deeper currents underlying the evolution of Goddess worship in the Indian religious landscape.

Early Configurations of the Lion-Riding Goddess

Although in this study we have followed the classic Indologists' pattern of first looking for the historical roots of a deity in the Vedas, our findings there have been somewhat equivocal. We can say with fair certainty that the name Durgā for a goddess of refuge appears in mantric verses in the Dharma Śāstra literature from as early as the 1st century BCE, with some hint of such verses prefigured from a few centuries earlier, in the Durgī(ā)-gāyatrī in the *Taittirīya Āraṇyaka* (TA) 10.1 and 10.2.2, where Durgā is compared to Agni. By the time of the *Baudhāyana Gṛhyaśeṣasūtra* (BGŚS 3.3), arguably composed in the first centuries CE (Lubin 2020, 43), we have clear evidence of Brahminic ritual and recitation of hymns to Durgā.

More robust data for the chronology of Durgā's origins derive from iconography, particularly through parallels with the goddess Nanā. Nanā (Nanaia,

Nanaya), discussed earlier, likely originated in Elam and first appears in Sumerian pantheon lists from the Ur III period (2112–2004 BCE) (Westenholz 1997, 58–60). Numerous textual references to her exist, but her earliest unequivocal depiction is on a document of the Babylonian king Melišpak II (1186–1172 BCE). According to the *Temple of Ishtar Inscription*, the Assyrian emperor Ashurbanipal (668–c. 627 BCE), ruler of the then-largest empire, conquered Elam and sacked Susa in circa 646 BCE. He claimed this campaign restored Nanā and other Assyrian gods, displaced to Elam 1635 years earlier (Gertoux 2015, 25–26; van Koppen 2013, 380). Despite Nanā's prominence, Ashurbanipal's name, meaning "The god Ashur is creator of an heir," underscores Assyria's devotion to Ashur and rulers' divine aspirations. Nonetheless, Nanā shared an elevated status alongside Ashur in the pantheon.

Evidence of Nanā's lion-riding cult includes a relief of a goddess atop a lion on an axe handle from the Bactria-Margiana Archaeological Complex (BMAC), or Oxus civilization (Ghose 2002, vol. 2, 31, figs. 1.41–1.44; 2006). This suggests the cult's presence northeast of the Indian subcontinent as early as the Bronze Age (c. 2300–1700 BCE). If Nanā's lion-riding tradition migrated to the Oxus from Mesopotamia, it likely interacted with Indus Valley Civilization "goddess and feline" traditions, such as the relief of a woman throttling two tigers. Unfortunately, evidence tracing the development from this period to later centuries remains scarce. Scholars, including Madhuvanti Ghose (2002, 2006), have demonstrated parallels between Nanā and the lion-riding goddess of Northwest India. To further explore Durgā's evolution into the Supreme Deity of the Hindu pantheon within Śākta metaphysics, a brief discussion of theism in Achaemenid Persia is necessary.

Monolatry, Monotheism, and Polytheism

Ancient Examples of Monolatry

The vast Assyrian empire, stretching from Egypt to parts of modern Iran, began to collapse shortly after Ashurbanipal's death, giving way to the Achaemenid Persian Empire (c. 550–330 BCE). This empire, renowned for rulers such as Cyrus II (the Great), Darius I (the Great), and Xerxes I (the Great), traces its name to its ancestral king, Achaemenes. The Behistun (or Bisitun) inscription is a key source of information, depicting Darius I with two attendants subduing rebel leaders. One rebel, the *magus* Gaumāta, lies beneath his foot, while nine others stand tethered and bound. Above, a winged disc likely symbolizes the god Ahura Mazdā, frequently referenced in the inscription (Waters 2014, 59, 61).

Ahura Mazdā, the principal deity of the Achaemenid emperors, may have derived aspects of his persona from the Assyrian god Ashur. After conquering Babylon, Ashurbanipal stated he imposed the "yoke of the god Ashur, which they had cast off" (Brinkman 1991, 61). While "throwing off the yoke" often metaphorically describes rebellion, efforts were made to elevate Ashur to the Babylonian pantheon's apex, previously held by Marduk. This mirrored the contests for political supremacy among rulers, as kings ruled as representatives or offspring of their deities. The Achaemenids adopted this imperial religious imposition, although with notable differences. Unlike the Assyrians, who worshiped diverse cult deities through temple images, early Achaemenids such as Darius I and Xerxes I favored a singular supreme deity, Ahura Mazdā.

The precise religious beliefs of Cyrus the Great remain uncertain. He was buried in an above-ground tomb, where horse sacrifices were regularly performed by the *magi*, a hereditary priestly class, often during festivals for Mithra (identified as the Sun in Greek sources) (Briant 2002, 96). In contrast, Achaemenid kings from Darius I onward were interred in cliff-carved tombs at Naqš-i-Rustam, reflecting a shift in religious practices after Cyrus. The Behistun inscription recounts Darius I's conflict with Gaumāta, a *magus* who likely upheld a form of Ahura Mazdā worship that included other deities. By Darius's reign, the Achaemenids seem to have transitioned towards monolatry — the worship of a supreme deity over others — and possibly monotheism. This suggests that Darius's battle with Gaumāta may have been a struggle between polytheism and Darius's emerging monolatrous or monotheistic views (Waters 2014, 76–80). As I shall argue, the DM engages with such tensions among monotheism, monolatry, and polytheism, warranting an exploration of monotheistic developments in regions influencing South Asia.

Ancient Examples of Monotheism

Monotheistic notions were likely not new in the region of the Achaemenid empire. The Egyptian pharaoh Akhenaten (d. c. 1336 BCE) earlier promoted monotheism centered on the Sun god Aten (Hoffmeier 2015). Hornung (2001, 87–88) describes Akhenaten's religious zeal, which included the destruction of images of other deities, especially Amun, and the erasure of theriomorphic symbols (e.g., the vulture of Mut and Amun's goose). Even plural forms of "god" were avoided. Early inscriptions reflect a shift from a distinctive theism ("there is no other god like him") to monotheism ("there is no other god but him") (Hornung 2001, 93). Donald Redford (2013, 26) unequivocally states, "The terms 'monolatry' or 'henotheism', tentative in their assessment of plurality, cannot be applied to Akhenaten's thought." The pharaoh was himself framed as uniquely linked to Aten ("unique like Aten, there being no other great one but him") (Hornung 2001, 93). Monotheistic versus polytheistic tensions were evident in the region.

Scholars often link Darius I and Xerxes I's favoring of Ahura Mazdā to Zoroastrian influence, although debates persist over whether these rulers were truly Zoroastrians. The religious tensions arising from the promotion of an imperially favored ideology within the Achaemenid empire have not been fully explored, especially in regions beyond Persia. Notably, the Achaemenid influence extended to lands beyond the Indus River, as attested by Xerxes I's inscriptions. Amélie Kuhrt (2007, 1) argues that the rise of the Macedonian and Mauryan empires on the empire's edges was partially a response to pressures from Achaemenid Persia. For over two centuries, the Achaemenids ruled an empire stretching from the Dardanelles to northwest India and often included Egypt. Considering the profound cultural impact of Hellenism after Alexander's conquests, the Achaemenid legacy warrants attention in understanding historical developments in South Asia.

A potential indication of Persian religious influence in northwest India is found in Strabo's account, quoting Aristobulous (375–301 BCE), a companion of Alexander. Aristobulous noted that the people of Taxila both cremated their dead and left them for vultures (Beckwith 2015, 177–78). While cremation is a traditional Indian practice, leaving bodies for vultures is attested as a Persian custom from the 9th century BCE, as described by Herodotus (I. 140.1–2). However, Vajrayāna Buddhists in mountainous regions such as Tibet, where wood is scarce, also practice "sky burials." This tradition may derive from Indigenous tribal defleshing rites, making it uncertain whether Taxila's practices reflected Persian influence or local customs that later shaped Buddhist postmortem traditions.

Nevertheless, to illustrate the zeal with which the early Achaemenid emperors promoted their brand of Mazdāism, it is instructive to examine a relevant inscription by Xerxes I in detail. I am utilizing the translation provided by Kuhrt (2013, 304–5). Kuhrt (2013, 152n5) notes that Auramazda (Avestan: "Ahura Mazdā") is the only deity mentioned by name in the inscriptions of Darius I and II, Xerxes I, and Artaxerxes I, while other deities are simply called "the gods." The inscription is found in multiple copies (in Babylonian, Elamite, and Old Persian).

1. A great god is Auramazda, who created this earth,
   who created yonder heaven, who created man,
   who created blissful happiness for man, who
   made Xerxes king, one king of many, one lord of
   many.
2. I (am) Xerxes, the great king, king of kings, king of
   countries containing all kinds of men, king on
   this great earth far and wide, son of Darius the
   king, an Achaemenid, a Persian, son of a Persian, an Aryan, having Aryan lineage.
3. Xerxes the king proclaims: By the favour of Auramazda, these are the countries of which I was

king outside Persia; I ruled them; they bore me tribute. What was said to them by me, that they did. The law that (was) mine, that held them (firm/stable): Media, Elam, Arachosia, Armenia, Drangiana, Parthia, Areia, Bactria, Sogdiana, Chorasmia, Babylonia, Assyria, Sattagydia, Lydia, Egypt, Ionians who dwell by the Sea, and (those) who dwell beyond the Sea, the Maka people, Arabia, Gandara, **Indus** [emphasis mine], Cappadocia, Dahae, the Scythians (Saca), who drink *haoma*, Scythians (Saca) who wear pointed hats, Thrace, the Akaufaka people, Libyans, Carians, Nubians.

4a. Xerxes the king proclaims: When I became king, there is among those countries which (are) inscribed above (one, which) was in turmoil (Old Persian *yaud*; could also mean rebellion). Afterwards Auramazda brought me aid; by the favour of Auramazda I defeated that country and put it in its proper place.

4b. And among those countries there were (some) where formerly the *daivas* had been worshipped. Afterwards by the favour of Auramazda I destroyed that place of the *daivas*, and I gave orders: 'The *daivas* shall not be worshipped any longer!' Wherever formerly the *daivas* have been worshipped, there I worshipped Auramazda at the proper time and with the proper ceremony.

4c. And there was something else, that had been done wrong, that too I put right. That which I have done, all that I have done by the favour of Auramazda. Auramazda brought me aid, until I had done the work.

4d. You, who shall be hereafter, if you shall think: 'Happy may I be (while) living, and (when) dead may I be blessed', obey that law which Auramazda has established. Worship Auramazda at the proper time and with the proper ritual! The man who obeys that law which Auramazda has established, and (who) worships Auramazda at the proper time and in the proper ceremonial style, he both becomes happy (while) alive and blessed (when) dead.

5. Xerxes the king proclaims: Me may Auramazda protect from evil, and my (royal) house, and this land! This I pray of Auramazda; this may Auramazda grant me.

Scholars have speculated extensively on the identity of the rebellious land mentioned in Xerxes I's inscription (4a) and the *daiva*-worshipping regions he suppressed in favor of Ahura Mazdā. The term *daiva*, cognate with Indo-Iranian *deva* (meaning "gods"), here refers to deities demonized by Xerxes. Possible locations include Greece, Babylonia, and Egypt — all polytheistic — or Persia itself, which traditionally worshipped Indo-Iranian gods before the Achaemenids adopted Ahura Mazdā as central (Vallat 2013, 47). Alternatively, the inscription (4b) may reflect a broader suppression of polytheistic religions in favor of promoting Ahura Mazdā as the principal deity. Xerxes, often seen as a tyrant for this suppression, may also have used Ahura Mazdā as a rhetorical frame for asserting Persian sovereignty. His language follows precedents set by Darius I in earlier inscriptions.

Pierre Briant (2002, 125–28) affirms that Darius I established a state religion with Ahura Mazdā as supreme. While many scholars believe Darius embraced Zoroastrianism, others argue he promoted a broader Mazdean tradition. Darius explicitly references the Zoroastrian concept of the Lie (*drauga*) versus the Truth (*arta*), extending it into the political sphere. As Ahura Mazdā's chosen ruler, Darius was tasked with ensuring *arta* prevailed over *drauga* in his realm. It is unclear from his inscriptions whether his victories, such as over the Śakas, were attributed merely to his devotion to Ahura Mazdā or if worship of the deity was enforced in those territories. By Xerxes I's reign, however, accepting Ahura Mazdā's worship likely became a necessary symbol of Achaemenid sovereignty (Briant 2002, 126).

The monotheistic or monolatrist focus on Ahura Mazdā under Darius I and Xerxes I began to wane during the reign of Artaxerxes II (404–356 BCE). Berossus, a 3rd century BCE Babylonian priest, reports that Artaxerxes II promoted the worship of Anāhitā, particularly through idols, in major cities. Inscriptional evidence also shows that Artaxerxes II recognized Mithra and Anāhitā, alongside Ahura Mazdā, as deities supporting his kingship. Scholars generally agree that Artaxerxes II did not introduce the worship of Anāhitā but restored marginalized cults to Mithra and Anāhitā that had been overshadowed during Ahura Mazdā's dominance. Berossus further notes the reestablishment of images for Anāhitā's worship, suggesting prior suppression of such practices (see Dandamaev and Lukonin 1989, 323).

Iconism and Aniconism

Tensions among monotheistic, monolatric, and polytheistic beliefs were also present in South Asia, although evidence emerges much later than the example of Akhenaten. *Śramana* philosophies, such as nondual Vedānta, early Buddhism, and Jainism, developed during the Upaniṣadic period and generally rejected deity worship. However, preexisting deities were later incorporated into their cosmologies, and devotional practices soon elevated the founders of

Buddhism and Jainism themselves to divine status. Atheism, polytheism, and monotheism all flourished, with polytheists often practicing monolatry centered on specific deities. Additionally, some traditions likely rejected iconography altogether. This diversity challenges views that portray theistic uniformity across cultural expressions.

I agree with Noel Salmond, who suggests that "aniconism as a stance (in binary opposition to image-affirmation) is a religious universal" (2006, 137). I propose that this binary exists even among those that embrace the same religious tradition. Moreover, the binary manifests on a spectrum, with those who might promote the intangible or formless dimensions of the divine (aniconism) at one end, to those who might favor the proliferation of representations (image-affirmation or iconism) on the other. Segments holding hegemony within cultural groups may dictate whether, or the degree to which, iconism is permitted or aniconism is enforced. I use the language of permission and enforcement because representation, through language, writing, action, and material art, for instance, is intrinsically creative and has the potential for unbridled profusion. Therefore, it is generally associated with manifestation (i.e., the embodied), and life "in the world." Aniconism, in its most extreme form, inverts all such creative vectors back to a single point. In its less extreme expression, aniconism may restrict or structure the creative iconic impulse. Aniconism is aligned with the transcendent, the pre- and post-creative, and arguably with life "of the spirit." This body/spirit, manifest/unmanifest, or immanent/transcendent dualism is rooted in a fundamental polarity within human consciousness, which plays itself out in our religious lives throughout history.

Others have explored such polarities extensively, including Lévi-Strauss's nature/culture distinction, Freud's Eros/Thanatos tension, and South Asian philosophy's *bhoga/yoga, prakṛti/puruṣa, śakti/śiva*, and multiplicity/oneness dichotomies. Simplifying the complex interplay of restraint and creativity that shapes language, ritual, and technology, I term this the iconism-aniconism impulse. Polytheism, monolatry, monotheism, and non-theism align along this spectrum, as polytheism emphasizes representation to distinguish deities, while monotheistic and nontheistic systems lean toward non-representational ideations. It is not strictly the case that polytheism necessitates iconism, for we note aniconic forms of worship in the Vedic tradition, where sacrificial fire rituals could propitiate a variety of deities without iconic representation.[1] Even so, in those cases, mantric verses, prayers, and hymns served as the "icons," enabling differentiation of one deity from another. Furthermore, devotionalism as a religious approach would favor the production of images of one's personalized beloved deity.

The tensions among monotheism (worship of a single deity), monolatry (worship of one deity above others), and polytheism (worship of many deities), alongside the tension between iconic and non-iconic worship, were central to Achaemenid Persia's religious culture. It is plausible that similar dynamics existed within the empire's spheres of influence. Greek disdain for Achaemenid monotheism (Ahura Mazdā) and aniconism (fire altars), as seen in Herodotus, might mirror sentiments that were held among the polytheistic, image-making peoples of the Indus. While the lack of material evidence of image-making on the subcontinent post-Indus Valley suggests aniconic tendencies, it is likely any image-making involved perishable materials such as wood or unbaked clay. This sets the stage for our argument regarding Durgā in the DM.

A recurring trope in Purāṇic literature is the rise of a powerful demon (*asura*) who displaces the lesser gods (*deva*) from their heavenly thrones. In Vaiṣṇava myths, Viṣṇu vanquishes such demons, while in Śaiva sources, it is Śiva. Yet, in Hindu India today, the most enduring of these narratives is that of Mahiṣāsura, defeated by the Devī — a tale immortalized in the DM and depicted in countless images across the subcontinent and beyond. Could these mythic tropes draw from historical dynamics such as those seen in Achaemenid Persia? And, if so, what accounts for the Devī's prominence as the ultimate vanquisher of the most formidable demons?

In an argument largely ignored or marginalized by scholars, N. Gopala Pillai (1937) proposed that Mahiṣāsura's defeat by Skanda, as narrated in the *Mahābhārata* (Mbh), reflects a preserved memory of Alexander's conquest of the Achaemenids and their deity. In this interpretation, Alexander (known in Indian traditions as Sikander) becomes Skanda, while Ahura Mazdā is represented by Mahiṣāsura. Pillai's theory relies on too many speculative connections between these figures, but it rightly underscores the need to consider the substantial impact of the Achaemenids and Hellenistic Empire on Indian religious and cultural developments.

The Mauryan use of inscriptions and pillars, many of which were bilingual and included Greek, likely drew inspiration from Achaemenid practices, such as the trilingual inscriptions of Darius I at Behistun (J. Finn 2011, 248–49). Similarly, Harle (1994, 22, 24) reasonably identifies Achaemenid influences in Mauryan pillar capitals, such as the lion capital, with additional potential Greek stylistic elements. These material influences point to a broader exchange of ideas during the Achaemenid and Hellenistic periods. Beyond material culture, the recurring Hindu mythic themes of polytheism triumphing over monolatry or monotheism, and of iconism prevailing over aniconism, reflect tensions that were prominent during the Achaemenid and Hellenistic eras. These themes, deeply embedded in Indian religious literature, suggest an internal wrestling with similar ideological dynamics, echoing those seen in Persia and the Hellenistic world.

Western Indologists initially struggled to identify a supreme deity in the Vedic hymns, as they anticipated finding a system akin to Greek or Roman monolatry, where one god among many held ultimate authority. Their analysis of potential candidates such as Indra or Agni proved inconclusive. To address this complexity, Max Müller (1868, 28) introduced the term kathenotheism ("one by one") to describe the unique Vedic approach. This involved elevating each deity to a supreme or unique position during its worship, effectively creating a form of serial monotheism, while the tradition as a whole remained distinctly polytheistic.

By the Upaniṣadic period, the concept of an overarching universal principle, Brahman, had become central. Brahman, prefigured in Vedic hymns such as the Nāsadiya Sukta of the *Ṛg Veda*, was presented as the singular source and essence of all divinities, who were understood as its diverse manifestations or aspects. However, it would be overly simplistic to assume that early Indian thought lacked metaphysical variety. I disagree with Müller's (1892, 76) notion that religions evolved from henotheism and polytheism to monotheism, which he regarded as the highest stage. The philosophical schools (*darśana*) of the time reflected a rich tapestry of beliefs. For example, dualistic traditions such as Sāṅkhya and Yoga coexisted with monistic Advaita Vedānta, while Buddhism and Jainism espoused non-theistic or trans-theistic worldviews, further demonstrating the complexity of pre-Achaemenid Indian intellectual and religious life.

In some respects, any potential Achaemenid influences may have bolstered tendencies toward monolatry, if not outright monotheism, during this period. It is in the Achaemenid era and its aftermath that evidence emerges of the rise of supreme deity traditions on the Indian subcontinent. While the existence of such traditions before this time cannot be definitively confirmed or denied, the period marks the development of the three dominant sectarian traditions of Indian religion today: Śaivism, focusing on Śiva (also called Maheśvara or Mahādeva, meaning "great lord or god"), Vaiṣṇavism, centered on Viṣṇu/Kṛṣṇa (also known as Puruṣottama, meaning "supreme being"), and Śāktism, devoted to the Devī, or Mahādevī ("great goddess"). Notably, while adherents may favor one tradition, Hindu practice often includes veneration of all three deities, as well as their associated divine figures, reflecting a broader inclusivity. The triadic structure of one female and two male deities in Hinduism aligns intriguingly with the triad of Anāhitā, Ahura Mazdā, and Mithra observed in later Achaemenid Persia, suggesting possible parallels or shared conceptual underpinnings in these religious frameworks.

It is challenging to determine the extent to which people on the Indian subcontinent created images for worship before contact with Hellenistic culture. Beyond the material remains from the Indus Valley Civilization, where seals with depictions of deities or symbolic forms have been discovered, there is little evidence of substantial image-making until the Mauryan period under Aśoka. It is plausible that images were crafted from perishable materials, such as wood or unbaked clay, which have not survived. At the same time, worship practices likely included aniconic approaches, such as Vedic fire rituals (*yajña*) and water-based offerings and libations (*tarpaṇa*). Additionally, deities were often venerated in natural forms, such as trees, animals, rocks, ponds, mountains, and rivers, a practice that persists in tribal communities across the subcontinent. Significantly, the period following Artaxerxes II's promotion of Anāhitā worship using idols, combined with the collapse of the Achaemenid empire and Alexander's subsequent conquest, coincides with the emergence of durable and sizeable images and inscriptions in India. This marks the beginning of a visible and enduring iconism, which may have paralleled the rise of more devotional and personal approaches to worship.

We do not know about the religious practices of the Pauravas, who battled Alexander after he crossed the Indus River into the Indian subcontinent. But according to Greco-Roman sources, not long after Alexander's death his general, Seleucus Nikator, ruler of the eastern portion of Alexander's empire, tried unsuccessfully to battle the Mauryans under Candragupta. Candragupta had already conquered the Punjab, and we are told that after obtaining a gift of 500 war elephants, Seleucus ceded the Punjab and most of Afghanistan (except for Bactria) to the Mauryan emperor (Keay 2011, 84). Legends based on questionable references claim that Candragupta converted to Jainism, eventually became a Jain renouncer, and gave up his life by committing voluntary death by starvation (*sallekhanā*).[2] While the veracity of certain claims remains uncertain, it is well-documented that Candragupta's grandson, Aśoka, carved out India's largest empire and eventually embraced Buddhism. The influence of Achaemenid administrative practices on the Mauryan Empire, including specific phrases in Aśoka's inscriptions, is widely recognized. Aśoka's initiatives to promote his faith, Buddhism, within his empire and beyond its borders echo the strategies of his Assyrian and Achaemenid predecessors. He claimed to have dispatched emissaries to distant regions, including ancient Macedon and Egypt, and even asserted that Antiochus, ruler of the Seleucid Empire, was converted to his Dharma.

Although Aśoka personally identified as a Buddhist, his concept of Dharma may not have been strictly confined to Buddhism but was likely a broader ethical framework. Nonetheless, he significantly fostered an environment conducive to the spread and flourishing of Buddhism. Aśoka's relationship with Hellenistic rulers following Alexander's conquests is well-attested and has sparked speculation regarding deeper cultural connections. For instance, some have proposed that Aśoka's grandmother (or mother) was Cornelia, the daughter of Seleucus Nikator, given to Candragupta as part of an intermarriage agreement during their peace treaty (Kosmin 2014, 33).

Legendary accounts of the Buddha's life tell of a prophecy that he would become a great wheel-turner (*cakravartin*), an ideal emperor whose chariot wheels symbolically turn freely across his unimpeded empire, itself represented as a wheel (*maṇḍala*). The Buddha, however, chose a different path, setting in motion the wheel of the Dharma (*dharmacakraparivartana mudrā*), representing a spiritual sovereignty bound by his teachings rather than political conquest. If we accept the legend that Siddhārtha Gautama, the historical Buddha, was a prince of the Śakya kingdom in the Himalayan foothills, his proselytizing successes with the Magadhan king Bimbisāra and the subsequent influence of his followers — culminating in Aśoka's reign — mark an extraordinary example of religious imperialism that extended far beyond his lifetime.

Aśoka's efforts undeniably catalyzed the spread of Buddhism beyond his empire to regions such as Sri Lanka and Myanmar. However, just as Aśokan influence reached beyond the Mauryan Empire's boundaries, earlier empires, notably the Achaemenids and the Macedonians, likely exerted significant cultural and religious influences on the Indian subcontinent. These influences would have been interwoven with the diverse religious fabric of the region, which included strains of Zoroastrian or Mazdean traditions from the Achaemenid era, Hellenistic religious concepts, remnants of the Indus Valley's religious heritage, Vedic practices, pre-Aśokan Indic philosophical schools (*darśana*), and Indigenous tribal spiritual contributions.

If Siddhārtha Gautama, the founder of Buddhism, and Mahāvīra, the founder of Jainism, were indeed princes as portrayed in legendary accounts, they mark a significant pivot in the history of South Asian sovereignties. They were heirs-apparent, who were abandoning their roles as worldly rulers in favor of religious empires. Perhaps there were others like them at the time. Vālmīki's epic, the *Rāmāyaṇa* (VRām), tells the tale of prince Rāma, who ends up in a forest exile in a hermit-like hut, albeit not quite like a full-fledged renouncer because he is accompanied by his wife and brother. Unlike Siddhārtha, Rāma returns to claim his rightful throne, after having conquered the southern kingdoms with the sword and not with religious teachings. The VRām offers a contrasting vision to the models of worldly renunciation favoring spiritual sovereignty set by the Buddha and Mahāvīra. Neither the Buddha nor Mahāvīra remained solitary ascetics. Both formed monastic communities, and the Buddha is reputed to have sent out entourages of missionaries to proselytize his teachings. Such teachings evidently continued to circulate in Magadha, and succeeded in "conquering" Aśoka, who was a true wheel-turner (*cakravartin*) in both its worldly and religious connotations.

Mauryan inscriptions stand out for their persuasive and encouraging tone, reflecting Buddhist and Jain values of nonviolence, unlike the proclamations of Achaemenid rulers Darius I and Xerxes I, or earlier Assyrian kings such as Ashurbanipal. This marks a distinct contribution of the Indic world to global civilization. Rather than depicting himself crushing adversaries underfoot, as seen in Darius's Behistun Inscription or Anubanini of Akkad's imagery much earlier, Aśoka expresses deep remorse for the bloodshed in his conquest of Kalinga, which cost over 100,000 lives. He declares that henceforth, conquest by Dhamma would be the only true victory (Rock Edict 13 in A. Sen 1956, 98–102). This vision redefined kingship, combining traditional dominion with the spiritual values of a renouncer. Unlike the Buddha, who abandoned his kingdom, Aśoka embodied a renouncer's spirit while wielding political power, exerting a righteous, dharmic influence over his empire. This anticipates ideas in the Mbh and *Bhagavad Gītā* (BG), where Kṛṣṇa, a spiritually realized king, teaches Arjuna *niṣkāma karma* — acting without attachment to outcomes. Through this philosophy, one could fulfill societal roles, even as king, and still attain liberation.

Having established the context of sovereignty and the encouragement if not imposition of imperial religious values, we now turn to the tensions concerning blood sacrifice to better understand the full compass of the DM's achievement in its construction of Durgā's persona and modes of worship.

Animal Sacrifice and Iconism

The Mauryan inscriptions reveal that large-scale animal sacrifices were prevalent throughout the empire. Aśoka himself acknowledged that, prior to his conversion to Buddhism, vast numbers of animals were slaughtered daily even within his court for preparing curry (Rock Edict 1 in A. Sen 1956, 64). Following his conversion, he prohibited animal sacrifices for worship and festival gatherings (*samāja*), where such practices were customary (Rock Edict 1 in A. Sen 1956, 64). In Rock Edict 4, Aśoka notes that for centuries before his reign, animal sacrifices were widespread, and disrespect toward *brāhmaṇas* and *sramaṇas* was common. He intriguingly suggests that the absence of sights such as temples (*vimāna*), elephants, and divine figures (*divyāni rūpāṇi*) over the past centuries would now be addressed to promote Dhamma (A. Sen 1956, 71). In Rock Edict 13, while expressing remorse over the destruction caused during his conquest of Kalinga, Aśoka warns the tribal populations (*aṭavi*) within his realm not to mistake his commitment to nonviolence as weakness, asserting that their annihilation remained a possibility if they disobeyed his rule.

These earliest written accounts of religion on the Indian subcontinent, particularly in relation to sovereignty, indicate that before Aśoka's reign, festival practices involving animal sacrifice were widespread, and meat consumption was common, especially among royal families. These records also suggest that wandering philosophers and renouncers (*sramaṇa*) were not widely respected or well-treated. Aśoka, known for his religious tolerance, adopted the title "Beloved of the Gods" (Devānaṃpiya Piyadasi), signifying his inclusive approach. While he promoted Buddhism, he did not impose monotheism or enforce his Dharma upon all subjects. Aśoka supported other religious traditions and their celebrations, provided they abstained from animal sacrifice. The aboriginal tribes within his empire seem to have been the primary potential violators of this prohibition.

I am unable to evaluate Christopher Beckwith's recent arguments (2015), which propose, for example, that the Upaniṣads and Jainism postdate Buddhism, or that some of the rock and pillar inscriptions attributed to Aśoka were authored by his father, Bindusāra. These claims, while provocative, do not challenge the thrust of my hypotheses. If anything, they underscore the tension between Buddhism's critique of animal sacrifice and the practices of what Beckwith terms early Brahmanism, in which such sacrifices were prevalent (Beckwith 2015, 90–91). Broadly, there was a clear conflict between religious traditions that endorsed animal sacrifice and those, such as Jainism and Buddhism, that strongly abjured it through their orientation toward non-violence (*ahiṃsā*).

Goddess worship, particularly, was associated with animal sacrifice, a tradition persisting in many parts of South Asia and linked to tribal communities such as the Gonds and Khonds, who were traditionally hunter-gatherers. Royal families, especially *kṣatriyas*, were encouraged to perform animal sacrifices, reinforcing traits such as physical strength, aggressiveness, and dispassion for slaughter. These Indigenous traditions of sacrifice likely blended with Achaemenid influences, particularly in the persona of the river goddess Arədvī Sūrā Anāhitā, discussed in detail in chapter 3.

Anāhitā, a boon-granting goddess described in Yašt 5 of the Avesta, frequently accepted large-scale sacrifices, including a hundred horses, a thousand oxen, and ten thousand lambs (e.g., 5.68, 72). Notably, her vibrant cult appears to have absorbed elements of the pre-Zoroastrian Persian goddess Anaïtis, herself influenced by the Mesopotamian goddess Ištar. Anāhitā likely held the position of supreme goddess within the Zoroastrian pantheon. Her worship was suppressed under Achaemenid rulers such as Darius I and Xerxes I but revived during the reign of Artaxerxes II (404–359 BCE). Similarly, her Indic analogs, with attributes potentially mirrored in deities such as Kauśikī/Nidrā and whom I have suggestively linked to the Chandraketugarh goddess, may also have faced suppression during Aśoka's rule and earlier periods.

The scarcity of durable imagery on the Indian subcontinent from the Indus Valley period until the Mauryan era suggests a prevailing sentiment against iconography among the ruling elites. This parallels the Persian aversion to imagery described by Herodotus (mid-5th century BCE) and Berosus, a Babylonian writer from Alexander the Great's time (de Jong 1997, 270–274). Vedic religious practices, centered on *yajña* (oblations in temporary fire altars), did not endorse temple building or imagery, as altars were dismantled post-ritual. Philosophical schools of the late Vedic (Upaniṣadic) period, such as Vedānta and Saṅkhya, similarly rejected material representations of deities. Artaxerxes II's rule (404–358 BCE) marked a significant shift. While Ahura Mazdā had been the supreme deity under earlier Achaemenid rulers, Artaxerxes II elevated the roles of Anāhitā and Mithra alongside Ahura Mazdā as sources of his kingship. Crucially, he initiated the establishment of images of Anāhitā across the empire, breaking with earlier Persian traditions of aniconism (de Jong 1997, 270–74).

Whatever the underlying causes of this openness to image-making may have been, Alexander of Macedon's conquest of the region would have certainly enhanced iconism. One can trace the origins of Greek sculpture to about 1000 BCE, but by the time of Alexander's death, Hellenic sculptural traditions were widely influential within and beyond his empire.[3] The Hellenistic iconographic styles both influenced and were influenced by the regions they contacted. During this period, the Mauryan dynasty introduced significant artistic and architectural developments, including the Aśokan pillars, inscriptions, pillar capitals, and large-scale representations of theriomorphic and anthropomorphic figures, such as the Dīdārgañj Yakṣī (although the latter may date to a slightly later period). Despite modern isolationist ideologies in China and India that may resist the idea of cultural exchange, historical evidence underscores extensive interactions between these regions. The Silk Road's expansion during the Han dynasty (206 BCE–220 CE) did not pioneer new connections but enhanced pre-existing trade networks that had facilitated cultural and commercial exchanges for centuries.

I do not suggest that image-making was entirely absent in South Asia until Alexander's arrival; the artifacts of the Indus Valley Civilization clearly attest to its presence. However, the scarcity of material evidence for nearly 1,500 years cannot be overlooked. Beyond the sculptures of the Indus Valley period, the subcontinent yields little apart from basic terracotta figurines, dated as early as the 5th or 6th centuries BCE. It is plausible that effigies were crafted from perishable materials such as unbaked clay or wood and intentionally destroyed after worship, a practice still observed with Vedic fire altars, sand *maṇḍalas*, and festival *pūjā mūrtis*. However, there was a marked reemergence or revitalization of durable image-making on the Indian subcontinent with the Mauryans, and this must have stood in tension with prevailing sentiments of aniconism, particularly when representing deities.[4] The great *stūpa* of Bharhut, whose intricately sculpted railings and gateways are now housed at the Indian Museum in Kolkata, is dated to around 150 BCE (Quintanilla 2007, 10, n. 11). These reliefs illustrate episodes from the Buddha's life and various Jātaka tales. Significantly, early Buddhist art, such as that at Bharhut, the railings and medallions of Sanchi (c. 100 BCE), and the Amaravati Mahācaitya, does not depict the Buddha anthropomorphically. Instead, the Buddha is symbolized — for example, by a riderless horse in the Great Departure, or through representations such as *stūpas* or his footprints.

The Bīmarān Casket, a ruby-studded golden reliquary from Afghanistan dated to the early 1st century CE, may feature the earliest anthropomorphic depictions of the Buddha. Stone sculptures of the Buddha in human form appear later, emerging from Gandhāra and Mathurā, with Mathurā already a major center of sculptural activity from the Śuṅga period (c. 150 BCE) and flourishing during the Kuṣāṇa and Gupta periods (Quintanilla 2007, 8). Although debates about the reasons for the Buddha's initial aniconic representation, as explored by Susan Huntington (1992, 111–156) and Vidya Dehejia (1991, 45–66; 1992, 157), remain unresolved, they highlight early Buddhist art's aniconic tendencies. These tensions persisted even after anthropomorphic depictions became prevalent (DeCaroli 2015).

Although early Buddhists were hesitant to depict the Buddha anthropomorphically, they were notably inclined to portray animals and female figures, reflecting a longstanding South Asian tradition dating back to the Indus Valley Civilization. Prominent examples include the so-called *yakṣīs* displayed on the Bharhut *stūpa* railings and gateways (2nd century BCE). These *yakṣīs*, some of whom bear names, were likely representations of local goddesses. For instance, the so-called Caṇḍā Yakṣī, already discussed, is plausibly an image of a regional goddess. From the Mauryan period onward, depictions of female figures, broadly classified as *yakṣīs* and often local goddesses, became relatively common. This shift marks the decline of pre-Mauryan aniconic tendencies and underscores the early prominence of goddess imagery. This continuity may extend back to the Indus Valley period, where numerous female figurines have been unearthed. The Chandraketugarh goddess figures (c. 2nd century BCE–2nd century CE) further attest to the popularity of goddess imagery during this era.

It is conceivable that, following the Indus Valley period, the production of durable images was suppressed or marginalized, but goddesses continued to be venerated using non-durable materials, a practice still evident during festivals such as Navarātra. This association between goddess worship and non-durable representations contrasts with aniconic traditions and suggests a parallel tension, akin to that between goddess worship through animal sacrifice and traditions rejecting blood sacrifice. The DM, in its promotion of offerings of one's own blood, or simply textual recitation to nondurable earthen imagery, mediated between the blood versus pacifist and iconism versus aniconism tensions. Although there is no direct evidence for early non-durable image-making practices, they likely originated in antiquity and evolved over time. Attitudes toward aniconism and temporary representations were not static. For example, despite the reluctance to create enduring anthropomorphic images of the Buddha during the Mauryan period and for some time thereafter, the Buddha has since become one of the most frequently depicted figures in the world.

Sovereignty and the Diadem

One of the earliest known examples of a diadem is found on the so-called "priest-king" steatite sculpture from the Indus Valley site of Mohenjo-daro. This diadem is a headband tied at the back of the head, with ribbon ends hanging down behind the neck. At the forehead, there is a circular inlay ornament, and a smaller, similar item is strapped to the figure's upper right arm.

In the Mycenaean civilization (15th–13th century BCE), diadems were primarily used as funerary items, a tradition possibly inherited from the earlier Minoan civilization (2000–1450 BCE) centered in Crete (Castleden 2005, 75). Mycenaean diadems, mostly found in female shaft tombs, highlight their association with status and ritual (Hood 1994, 198). During the Neo-Assyrian period (911–612 BCE), kings wore a fez-like cap with a conical top, wrapped in front with a diadem, or *kulūlu*, which had ribbons at the back. Assyrian queens were also depicted wearing diadems, further signifying their association with royalty (Gaspa 2018, 174, 314).

In Achaemenid Persia, Darius I is portrayed in the Behistun reliefs wearing a crenellated diadem, which became a defining symbol of sovereignty for Achaemenid rulers. A 2nd century CE account by Polyaenus recounts Darius I's campaign against the Śakas, highlighting the diadem's role in sovereignty and ritual. When his troops were stranded without water, Darius climbed a hill, planted his scepter into the ground, and placed his tiara and royal diadem on his robe. He prayed to Apollo — likely equated with Mithra — who answered by sending rain (Briant 2002, 239). This story further reinforces the diadem as a symbol of authority and divine connection.

The Hellenistic kings, starting with Alexander, adopted the *diadema* as an exclusive royal emblem. While some view this as rooted in Macedonian tradition, others see it as influenced by Persian practices. E. A. Fredricksmeyer (1997, 98) argues that the diadem was not exclusively a royal symbol in Macedonian tradition but was elevated to this status by Alexander. He challenges the prevalent belief that Alexander adopted the diadem from the Achaemenid rulers after the defeat of Darius III in 331 BCE. Fredricksmeyer contends that if Alexander had sought solely to legitimize his claim as the successor to the Persian Empire, he would have adopted other symbols of Achaemenid sovereignty, such as the upright tiara or the titles "Great King" or "King of Kings," which he notably did not. Instead, Fredricksmeyer (1997, 102–3) suggests that Alexander chose the diadem as a symbol of Dionysus, a deity significant to the Macedonian kings and associated with the conquest of the East. This choice resonated with both Macedonian and Persian audiences, as Dionysus had cultural and mythological importance in both traditions. The diadem subsequently became the exclusive royal insignia for Hellenistic kings, cementing its role as a symbol of sovereignty in the post-Alexandrian world (Collins 2012, 377).

The diadem's status as an ultimate symbol of sovereignty is underscored in Arrian of Nicomedia's *Anabasis of Alexander* (1st–2nd century CE). Arrian recounts an incident where Alexander's diadem was blown off his head into some reeds. A sailor swam to retrieve it, placing it on his own head to keep it dry. Although initially rewarded with a talent, the sailor was later flogged — or, in some accounts, beheaded (Collins 2012, 378). This highlights the diadem's inviolable association with kingship. In *Bibliotheca historica*, Diodorus Siculus notes that Alexander adopted the Persian diadem and other royal attire, emulating the extravagance of Asian kings (Collins 2012, 379). Collins (2012, 385) disputes the idea that Alexander's diadem was a symbol of Dionysus and instead suggests that Alexander, seeking to assert his rule over Asia, incorporated elements of Persian regalia to complement his Macedonian clothing. Regardless of its origin, the diadem's role as a supreme symbol of sovereignty established by Alexander endured through successive empires, including the Seleucids, Parthians, and Sasanians.

Among Alexander's successors (the Diadochi), Lysimachus (reigned 305–281 BCE), ruler of Thrace, minted coins featuring Athena Nikephoros ("Bringer of Victory"), depicted seated with a helmet, leaning on her shield with a spear behind her. The winged goddess Nike (Victory) stands on Athena's palm, crowning the king's inscribed name. On some coins, the "crown" is a looped diadem; on others, it resembles a leafy wreath. Although associated with Athena, Nike is often portrayed as a distinct deity, appearing alongside her, as in the Pergamon Altar frieze (c. 2nd century BCE) at the Pergamon Museum, or independently, as in the *Winged Victory of Samothrace* (c. 2nd century BCE) at the Louvre.

Nike also appears on coins of Antiochus I Soter (r. 281–261 BCE), who earned the title Soter ("Savior") after defeating the Gauls in Anatolia with sixteen Indian war elephants (Vandorpe 1995, 301). He is likely the Antiochus mentioned in emperor Aśoka's Edicts as a recipient of Buddhist emissaries. On these coins, Nike holds a wreath and palm branch, symbols of victory. Similarly, Indo-Greek king Antimachus II (r. 174–165 BCE) minted coins featuring Nike or simply the wreath, contributing to his title Nikephoros. Nike's wreath, resembling a diadem, symbolized both victory and sovereignty.

Artifacts such as the Bactrian Gold Hoard (c. 1st century BCE–1st century CE) from Tillya Tepe, Afghanistan, further highlight Nike's significance. A pair of gold clasps from Tomb VI depict Dionysus riding a panther with Ariadne, daughter of King Minos of Crete, in his arms. In Greek mythology, Ariadne was tasked with managing the labyrinth that housed the Minotaur — a creature that was part-man, part-bull, and to whom sacrificial offerings were made. These myths of the Minotaur, circulating in the region, may have influenced concepts of the shape-shifting demon Mahiṣāsura. On the same clasps, Nike hovers above Dionysus, holding a palm branch and preparing to crown him with a wreath.

Nike also features on coins of Heraios, Kuṣāṇa clan chief in Bactria (r. 1–30 CE), where the ruler is depicted on horseback, crowned by Nike, with a diadem knotted at the back (Stančo 2012, 176–77). Other rulers in the region, including Gondophares, Menander, Maues, and Azes I, also minted coins featuring Nike with a wreath resembling the Achaemenid or Hellenistic diadem (Stančo 2012, 180–81). Nike's cult, widely present in north-central and northwest India, equated her wreath with the royal diadem of sovereignty. As the winged embodiment of Victory, Nike likely resonated with or influenced goddesses such as Jayā and Vijayā (names meaning Victory) and Nidrā/Kauśikī, who, in Vaiṣṇava traditions, flies to her Vindhya abode.

With this background, supported by more evidence than cited here, we turn to the early iconographic representations of the buffalo-subduing goddess depicted on Kuṣāṇa plaques and later Gupta reliefs. I have presented substantial evidence that these depictions portray the goddess engaged in an act of self-coronation, a point extensively explored by D. Srinivasan (2022). I propose that this self-coronation involves a divine diadem, potentially referenced as the *vic-itra-mukuṭa* (wondrous diadem) in the DStv (l. 23) and possibly the crown of three discs in the Praise of Nidrā (First Stratum) (PN-s1 l. 43), although the latter may symbolize a variation of the diadem's potency. I suggest that this divine diadem serves as a symbol of divine sovereignty, distinguishing it from interpretations of the goddess holding a wreath, garland, piece of intestine, or iguana, as suggested in prior scholarship. These hymnic references may provide the only textual attestations of this significant iconographic feature, which appears prominently across a broad range of material artifacts.

It is essential to examine the motif of self-coronation within the context of prevailing religious ideologies of the time. From the Assyrians to the Achaemenids, Alexander, and the Indo-Greek rulers, the royal diadem evolved as the principal symbol of sovereignty. These rulers often formed close associations with specific deities, regarded as the ultimate source of their authority. Such associations were prominently displayed on coins, reflected in ruler names that aligned with these deities, and reinforced through policies that encouraged or, at times, coerced the adoption of their favored deities' worship. The fates of these deities were intimately tied to those of their worldly patrons. Among the Achaemenids, rulers such as Darius I and Xerxes I elevated Ahura Mazdā to a supreme position within their divine hierarchy. Beyond monolatry, there is evidence of a monotheistic drive to establish Ahura Mazdā as the sole deity. This mirrored worldly politics, where powerful emperors subdued rebellious kings, as Darius I famously did. Similarly, the minor gods, or *daivas*, associated with these rebel kings, were subordinated or obliterated by the preeminent god, paralleling the imperial domination of earthly rulers.

During the period from the 3rd century BCE to the 3rd century CE, heightened cultural exchange via Silk Road trade coincided with the composition of the Mbh and *Harivaṃśa* (HV) and saw the rise of major sectarian traditions on the Indian subcontinent. These included Śaivism, Vaiṣṇavism, Śāktism, and Buddhism, each absorbing influences from beyond the subcontinent. Buddhism enjoyed imperial patronage under the Mauryas, while Hindu sectarian traditions experienced a revival under Śuṅga rule following the Mauryan collapse.

Śākta-oriented rulers would have attributed their sovereignty to powerful goddesses such as Anāhitā, Nanā, Nike, Durgā, Kauśikī, Kālī, and Nidrā, promoting these deities as supreme. Similarly, emerging Vaiṣṇava cults and those devoted to deities such as Skanda would have sought to elevate their chosen gods within the divine hierarchy. Elevating a goddess required asserting her as the conferring agent of victory and sovereignty, as seen in the vigorous cults of Nanā, Anāhitā, and Nike. These goddesses were firmly established as central to the legitimacy of rule and success in battle.

This dynamic is vividly illustrated in the rock-cut relief at Naqš-e Rustam, where the Sasanian ruler Narseh (r. 292–301 CE) receives the diadem of sovereignty from a goddess, generally identified as Anāhitā (Anahid), the tutelary deity of his father Šapur I and grandfather Ardašir I (Daryaee 2012, 192). Similarly, Sasanian reliefs at Tāq-e Bostān depict the transfer of the royal diadem, a *cydaris*, as a symbol of kingship. In one relief, Ardašir II (r. 379–383 CE) is shown receiving the diadem either from Šapur II or Ahura Mazdā, both figures standing atop the defeated Roman emperor Julian (r. 361–363 CE). In the large cave relief (dated 590–628 CE), Khusrau II, the last Sasanian ruler, is depicted receiving the diadem from Ahura Mazdā on his right and Anāhitā on his left (Canepa 2009, 198). These depictions highlight the enduring significance of the diadem as the symbol of kingship, also evident in coinage, and the ongoing negotiation of sovereignty among Anāhitā, Ahura Mazdā, and even previous rulers. In contrast, within Hindu South Asia, the Devī ultimately emerges as the supreme bestower of kingship and triumphs as the sovereign goddess.

While the promotion of Ahura Mazdā within Zoroastrianism or Mazdaen religion often reflected an iconophobic and monolatric — if not monotheistic — disposition, the continued veneration of Anāhitā (Anahid) and Mithra (Mihr) indicates a tolerance for polytheism or religious pluralism. This duality is relevant to South Asian studies because of the significant cultural exchanges between North India and the Parthian and Sasanian empires, which followed the Achaemenid and Hellenistic periods. The Sasanian empire (224–651 CE) endured longer than other influential empires, such as the Achaemenid, Hellenistic, Mauryan, Gupta, and Kuṣāṇa kingdoms. The life of the prophet Mani (216–274 CE), despite its hagiographic embellishments, exemplifies the dynamic interplay of religious ideas in this period. Born in Babylon, Mani was exposed to Jewish and Christian teachings, traveled to the northwest fringes of South Asia where he encountered Hinduism and Buddhism, and ultimately met his demise under Bahram I, a Zoroastrian patron. Mani's experiences highlight the religious and cultural currents flowing between Rome and Pāṭaliputra, which influenced kings and laypersons alike. The South Asian motifs of multiple-armed deities and demon-slaying goddesses influenced Parthian and Sasanian depictions of Nanā as far as Sogdiana. It would be simplistic to assume that these exchanges were unidirectional. South Asian religious notions certainly traveled westward, but equally, Western empires' religious concepts influenced South Asia, shaping its spiritual and iconographic traditions.

Although there is no textual or iconographic evidence predating the Mbh to firmly associate South Asian goddesses such as Kauśikī, Nidrā, and Kālī with sovereignty, it is plausible that such ideas developed through contact with Indo-Greek goddess cults. The later emergence of these associations likely did not occur in isolation. By the time of the DStv or its DStv* variants without frame verses, there is clear textual evidence linking the goddess — named Jayā and Vijayā — with victory in battle (v. 31, 32), paralleling deities such as Nike and Nanā. In the same hymn, the goddess named Kālī is associated with animal sacrifice (v. 34), echoing Anāhitā, while as Durgā, she is connected to salvation, knowledge, compassion (vv. 44, 45), and supreme refuge (v. 39–51), traits reminiscent of the Buddha. Thus, by the composition of the DStv — and likely centuries earlier — the goddess, known as Durgā, Kālī, Jayā, and Vijayā, who is explicitly tied to the slaying of the Asura Mahiṣa (v. 29), was likely already regarded by her followers and royal patrons as the supreme deity in their divine pantheon.

What better way to portray divine sovereignty than by depicting the goddess wearing a royal diadem? Importantly, it would be no ordinary diadem of a worldly ruler but the royal diadem of the divine realm. This aligns with the DStv's reference to the goddess adorned with the "wondrous diadem" (*vicitra-mukuṭa*, v. 23). By contrast, in the PN-s1, the goddess Nidrā/Kauśikī is not described with this diadem but rather with a "crown of three discs" (v. 43). The PN-s1 appears to subordinate Nidrā/Kauśikī to Viṣṇu, depicting her ascending to the heavens where Indra and other gods, at Viṣṇu's command, perform her consecration (v. 45, 46). This stands in sharp contrast to the self-coronation imagery seen in Kuṣāṇa plaques and early Gupta art (e.g., the Udayagiri reliefs), where the goddess is shown holding what is arguably the divine sovereign diadem aloft and poised to place it upon her own head. Such imagery unequivocally establishes her as the supreme divine monarch, deriving sovereignty from no other deity. An alternative interpretation could suggest that the goddess, holding the diadem aloft, is prepared to crown an earthly ruler or another deity. However, in one of the Udayagiri reliefs, portions of the diadem rest upon her own head making the interpretation of self-coronation almost unequivocal.[5]

The Rise of Monolatry (Supreme Deity Traditions)

It is crucial to acknowledge that while the goddess Durgā/Jayā/Vijayā exhibits affinities with Near Eastern goddesses, she possesses numerous characteristics that are uniquely South Asian. These distinctions strongly suggest that traditions of goddess worship on the subcontinent predated and were not solely shaped by external influences from neighboring empires. Self-coronation with the imperial divine diadem, although a motif likely adopted in South Asia, did not endure significantly beyond the Gupta period. However, Indigenous traditions, such as the use of wreaths in heroic warrior cultures of South India, were prominent, and point to internal parallels. The attire and adornments of deities reflected contemporary South Asian fashions, shaped by both local innovation and external exchanges, such as the acquisition of silk from China. One distinctly South Asian symbol is the buffalo-demon, an Indigenous substitute for the bull, which held sacred status and was unsuitable for sacrificial representation. This contrasts with its depiction in Nike and Mithraic tauroctonies. Similarly, the peacock tail banner (*śikhipiccha dhvaja*) referenced in the DStv (v. 26) appears to be another distinctly South Asian motif, possibly paralleling the palm branch carried by the goddess Nike in its symbolism of victory and sovereignty. These motifs, including self-coronation and the peacock tail banner, found in early representations of the buffalo-subduing goddess, unequivocally signal her supremacy in the divine pantheon. Notably, the DStv and PN-s1 remain the only textual sources that explicitly reference these salient iconographic symbols of the goddess's sovereignty and claim to supremacy.

Among South Asia's most enduring symbolic contributions to religious iconography is the portrayal of deities with multiple heads and arms. As discussed earlier, and in alignment with D. Srinivasan (1997, 5), this feature initially symbolized supreme divinity, although it later came to represent the various powers or attributes of deities, including minor ones. The abundance of arms remains a central feature of the imagery of the sovereign goddess of victory, Durgā, and continues to signify her supremacy in contemporary depictions. While the motif of multiple heads and arms quickly extended to other male and female deities, I speculated that their origin may lie in the riverine symbolism of the goddess, as suggested in the Chandraketugarh goddess imagery of various hair adornments. These might evoke the headwaters of rivers emerging from treasure-granting mountain peaks, the life-sustaining waters of multiple tributaries, and the fertility of deltas, such as that of the Gaṅgā — the world's largest and among the most fertile. By the early centuries of the Common Era, multiple arms were also adopted in depictions of Viṣṇu (as Vasudeva-Kṛṣṇa) and Śiva, reflecting their competing claims to supremacy in the divine pantheon.

Durgā Triumphant

By the mid-8th century CE, Śaivism had emerged as the most widely patronized sectarian tradition among rulers in South and Southeast Asia, rivaling Buddhism, Jainism, and Vaiṣṇavism (Sanderson 2009, 44). However, I argue that the Great Goddess, Durgā, maintained her supremacy in the divine pantheon, albeit in a manner reflective of the nuanced cultural position of the feminine in South Asian societies. Textual and iconographic evidence reveals that while goddesses such as Nanā, Nike, and Anāhitā held supreme positions in central Asia and possibly the northwest of the subcontinent, their supremacy faced challenges from figures such as Ahura Mazdā and Mithra. Similarly, on the Indian subcontinent, Durgā, the buffalo-subduing goddess, contended for supremacy with deities such as Śiva, Viṣṇu, Indra, Sūrya, and Skanda.

The self-crowning, peacock-standard-bearing, buffalo-subduing imagery of Durgā on Kuṣāṇa plaques and early Gupta reliefs may signify an era when Śākta sects sought to assert her preeminence in the divine hierarchy. Textual evidence, such as the DStv, reflects this assertion. However, Vaiṣṇava-oriented epics such as the Mbh had already begun to diminish her position. For instance, the Mbh attributes the slaying of Mahiṣa to Skanda, himself a subordinate to Śiva, while the BG elevates Kṛṣṇa to supreme status. The insertion of the DStv+ into the Mbh, linking Durgā to the Kṛṣṇa-Kaṃsa cycle, alongside the HV's PN-s1, reveals efforts to subordinate the goddess Nidrā/Kauśikī to Viṣṇu, reflecting broader sectarian dynamics during this period.

These subordinating efforts paradoxically contributed to the unification of goddesses such as Nidrā and Kauśikī from the Vindhya region with Durgā, Kālī, Jayā, and Vijayā from the northwest and north-central regions into a more cohesive figure of a Great Goddess. Later configurations of texts, such as the DSto+, inserted into the Mbh, and the Praise of Nidrā (Second Stratum) (PN-s2), appended to the earlier PN-s1 in the HV, were not intended to subordinate Viṣṇu/Kṛṣṇa to the Goddess but rather to establish the opposite. These hymns extolled her as the "great goddess" (DSto v. 25; PN-s2 v. 8), celebrated her powers to grant boons, protection, and victory, yet simultaneously linked her in potentially subordinate roles to her male rivals, Viṣṇu and Śiva. In the DSto (v. 14), she is called the "youngest sister of the lord of cowherds" (i.e., Kṛṣṇa), and in PN-s2 (v. 15), she is identified as the sister of Vāsudeva and equated with Pārvatī (v. 42). This gradual diminishment of her independent supremacy paralleled the rising prominence of Vaiṣṇavism, Śaivism, and Buddhism. Over time, the goddess was increasingly associated with subordinate roles, such as the deity Kaṃsa tried to kill in the Kṛṣṇa birth myth cycle, or as Śiva's spouse in texts such as the *Caṇḍīśataka*. From the Śākta perspective, the DM played a critical role in articulating a vision that allowed the Goddess to retain or reclaim her position as the supreme deity, presenting her as the ultimate divine power in a manner that resonated with Śākta theological frameworks.

Apart from its frame tale, the DM presents three distinct episodes. The first recounts the Devī deluding the demons Madhu and Kaiṭabha, the second describes her defeat of Mahiṣa, and the third details her victory over the demons Śumbha and Niśumbha. Of these, the middle episode is the most prominent in memory, narrative retellings, and iconographic depictions. The third and longest episode serves to integrate a multitude of goddesses, who fight alongside the Devī, into her singular identity. This is most clearly demonstrated when Śumbha accuses her of not battling him alone, prompting her to absorb all the goddesses into herself (DM 10.3–5). My field studies suggest that the notion that all goddesses are one still endures widely in India today, while that is not a common assertion regarding the male gods. Followers of other sectarian traditions — and some scholars — have mistakenly regarded the middle episode as an origin myth for the Devī because it portrays her as emerging from the collective luminescence (*tejas*) of the gods to defeat Mahiṣa. However, this interpretation is almost certainly incorrect. As explained earlier, the DM explicitly describes the Devī as eternal. Before recounting her exploits in the first episode, the sage Medhas clarifies that the Devī is eternal and manifests in various forms to accomplish the gods' purposes (DM 1.47–48). He further emphasizes that while she may be described as "born in the world," she is fundamentally without beginning or end (DM 1.48).

With this clear prefatory explanation, Medhas narrates three instances of the Devī's "birth," better understood as her "emergences." In the first episode, responding to a plea from Brahmā, she emerges from Viṣṇu's eyes, where she resided as Yoganidrā (DM 1.52). Viṣṇu awakens only when "released by her" (DM 1.70), an explicit assertion of her supremacy over him. This episode responds directly to the HV's PN-s1, which attempted to subordinate Nidrā to Viṣṇu, portraying him as the source of her fame and power.

In the middle episode, the Devī does not originate from the gods' collective *tejas* but emerges from each individually. The *tejas* of Śiva forms her mouth, that of Viṣṇu her arms, and similarly, the *tejas* of other gods contribute specific aspects of her being (DM 2.13). The term *tejas* encompasses meanings such as vital power, semen, majesty, authority, and spiritual potency. This episode demonstrates that the inner power and very essence of rulership of all male gods reside in the Great Goddess. In the third episode, the gods, once again in peril, call upon the Devī for aid. She emerges from a sheath of Pārvatī's body, but crucially, this does not subordinate her to Pārvatī. Pārvatī is portrayed as unaware of the gods' praises (DM 5.38), and the Devī explains that their prayers were directed at her, not Pārvatī. Following this emergence, the Devī leaves Pārvatī transformed in color. While the first episode highlights her control over Viṣṇu, and the second her embodiment of the gods' combined potency, the third emphasizes her supremacy over all goddesses, including Pārvatī, in whom she resides.

The episodes of the Devī's power and exploits in the DM could have simply reasserted the Goddess's supremacy in the divine pantheon. However, the DM employs a crucial strategy that ensures the Devī's ultimate triumph. In Episode One, Brahmā faces a threat; in Episodes Two and Three, the lesser gods, including Indra, are driven out of the heavens. The Devī does not vanquish the demons to claim the throne herself. Instead, she emerges to restore cosmic balance, then retreats into the sacred primordium from which creation arises. The Devī's victory lies in not overtly claiming the supreme position. Instead, she restores harmony disrupted by demons who sought to usurp ultimate power. Mahiṣa seizes control of the gods and becomes Indra (chief of gods). Similarly, Śumbha and Niśumbha, inflated by their power, usurp Indra's triple world and the domains of other gods such as the Sun, Moon, Kubera, Yama, and Vāyu (DM 5.1–3). These myths critique a monolatry that approaches monotheism (or duotheism, in the case of Śumbha and Niśumbha), as demons such as Mahiṣa aim to become the sole or principal deity. The text underscores this disruption: the expelled gods wander the earth like mortals, stripped of their celestial status (DM 2.6).

The Devī's triumph is her conquest over monolatry and monotheism, and a restoration of the kathenotheistic polytheism that has characterized Hinduism from the time of the Vedas. Like a traditional Hindu wife, she does not strive to "wear the pants" in the divine household overtly, but takes a deferential role, allowing the male gods their days in the sun. Although she is the true power that underlies everything, she allows for a pluralistic divine society, in which the many different gods and goddesses reside, each receiving their share of worship. The DM's vision is no longer the Devī that crowns herself with the sovereign diadem as the paramount deity, but the Devī who is ready to depose any entity that strives to assert itself as such a singular or supreme divinity. This is a core message of the DM, which likely has contributed to its success in the religiously pluralistic Hindu world. It is vital to recognize that the DM, despite its ritual success and effectiveness, likely did not emerge from a vacuum. There must have been a robust tradition of Śākta theologians who sought to secure the primacy and paramount status of the Goddess in the face of the highly effective assimilation efforts by Vaiṣṇavas and Śaivas. It is unlikely that such a subtle construction of a supreme deity would arise simply through the amalgamation of various subordinate goddesses and manage to garner a following from Śaiva and Vaiṣṇava devotees. A close reading of the DM reveals that it does not emerge from a Vaiṣṇava or Śaiva milieu, because it simply continues to assert the primordial supremacy of the Devī, but it does so in a remarkable manner that is nonconfrontational to the other gods and goddesses. The Devī does not linger in the limelight but vanishes into a metaphysically paradoxical juxtaposition of transcendence and immanence.

From the perspective of this interpretation, Mahiṣa symbolizes any deity, principle, or power that seeks paramount or sole supremacy over the polytheistic divine pantheon. The Sanskrit word *mahiṣa* does carry the generic meaning of "great" or "powerful," and thus the wild water buffalo (*Bubalus arnee*) is an appropriate symbol of power. The similarly sounding term *maheśa* means "great lord," and soon grows to be synonymous with Śiva, while the term *mahiṣī*, the feminine form of *mahiṣa*, is routinely applied to a queen or woman of high status. This suggests that the masculine *mahiṣa* also certainly carries the more pointed connotation of "great lord," although it may have had a pejorative pun built in. Not *maheśa*, but *mahiṣa*; not a great lord but a buffalo.

Why the Devī's Slaying of Mahiṣa Supersedes Skanda's Claim

We are now better equipped to consider why the myth of the Devī's slaying of Mahiṣa, arguably first attested in the DStv, supplants Skanda's earlier attribution in the Mbh. It is plausible that these attributions coexisted, especially if the DStv predates its insertion into the Mbh, as I have suggested. Rather than seeing the Devī as overtaking Skanda's mythic conquest, it is possible that rival claims about Mahiṣa's defeat and its symbolic meaning emerged simultaneously. This interpretation assumes the narrative is metaphorical, reflecting competing human conceptions of divinity rather than recounting the literal deeds of a shape-shifting buffalo demon named Mahiṣa who overthrew the gods and took their place in the heavens.

If we accept that the elevation of Ahura Mazdā as the supreme deity under Achaemenid rulers such as Darius I and Xerxes negatively impacted *daiva*-worshipping kingdoms beyond the Indus, it is reasonable to infer that the decline of Achaemenid monotheism or monolatry was welcomed in those regions. This shift towards theistic pluralism likely began under Artaxerxes II, who supported the worship of Mithra and Anāhitā alongside Ahura Mazdā and encouraged iconographic depictions of these deities. Following the Achaemenid collapse under Darius III and Alexander's conquest, it is plausible that the Hellenistic period was celebrated for dismantling the supremacy of Ahura Mazdā and enabling a revival of polytheistic worship. Even without endorsing G. Pillai's (1937) speculative claim that Alexander (Sikander) became the deity Skanda and Ahura Mazdā transformed into the Asura Mahiṣa, it is evident that Hellenistic influence facilitated greater tolerance for polytheism and iconographic representation within the former Persian empire and neighboring regions. This cultural shift aligns with the broader reestablishment of pluralistic religious traditions after the suppression experienced during the Achaemenid era.

While the Hellenistic model encouraged polytheism, it was not entirely devoid of tendencies toward monolatry. The Greek pantheon maintained a hierarchy with Zeus at its apex, and Alexander the Great himself aspired to divine status, claiming to be the son of Zeus. In 324 BCE, he sought recognition of his friend Hephaestion as divine, received ambassadors in a manner befitting a god, and wished for his mother, Olympias (also called Polyxena), to be worshipped as a goddess. Despite sporadic worship of Alexander in cities such as Alexandria, this did not catalyze the establishment of a broad Hellenistic ruler cult (Koester 2012, 11, 37). The emergence of ruler cults gained traction primarily in Egypt under Ptolemy I, with hints of similar practices among the Seleucids (Koester 2012, 38). Seleucid King Antiochus III (223–187 BCE) formalized a state cult honoring himself and his ancestors, establishing the practice of high priestesses serving such ruler cults as a norm (Cline and Graham 2011, 156). These developments reflected state cults centered on sovereigns as divine figures within polytheistic frameworks, placing the ruler in a hierarchical but elevated position akin to a supreme deity in a pantheon.

Divine rulership in South Asia may not have been as widespread as in the Seleucid, Greek, or Roman traditions. However, the Khmer empire's 9th century CE *devarāja* cults, influenced by India, equated kings with deities such as Śiva or Viṣṇu, elevating them posthumously to divine status through assimilation with their patron deity (Higham 2004, 151). In India, the 3rd century BCE saw the rise of the Mauryan Empire and its promotion of Buddhism. Although Aśoka tolerated religious pluralism, he positioned the Buddha as the supreme "deity," advancing an incipient *bodhisattva* ideal, signaling rulers' affiliations with their tutelary deities.

This period marked the rise of supreme deity traditions with figures such as the Buddha, Viṣṇu, Śiva, Sūrya, Nanā/Anāhitā/Kauśikī, Skanda, Durgā, and Indra competing for supremacy. Royally sponsored monolatry fluctuated among kings and kingdoms, as theologians subordinated rival deities by promoting myths favoring their preferred divinities — a method that persists today. Following the Mauryas' decline and the Śuṅgas' rise, when the Mbh likely began taking shape, its Skanda/Mahiṣa myth exemplified subordination through elevation, depicting Skanda as ordered by Maheśvara to slay Mahiṣa.

Texts such as the *Vāmana Purāṇa* (VāmP) simultaneously attribute Mahiṣa's defeat to Durgā and Skanda.[6] Sarkar argues that "she [the goddess] did not borrow Mahiṣa's mythology from Skanda" and that "the goddess's association with Mahiṣa was firmly established as far back as the Kuṣāṇa period" (2017, 111). Sarkar also questions Srinivasan's claim that Skanda's Mahiṣa myth in the Āraṇyakaparvan predates the buffalo-subduing Kuṣāṇa plaques from Mathurā (D. Srinivasan 1997, 303). Agreeing with Sarkar on that point, I have proposed the DStv proper or DStv* variant, which proclaims Durgā's defeat of Mahiṣa, was likely contemporaneous with the Kuṣāṇa plaques, demonstrating a parallel claim to the victory.

Richard Mann (2001, 113) examines the early development of Skanda's cult, highlighting that in Kuṣāṇa-period Mathurā imagery, Skanda is depicted with a group of ghoulish goddesses, the Mātṛs, distinct from the Saptamātṛkā panels of the Gupta period. These early Mātṛs often have bird-like faces, emphasizing the fearsome Skanda Graha rather than the more benign Skanda Kumāra, son of Śiva. The Mbh associates the Grahas with Skanda but stops short of identifying him as one of them. However, the epic transitions Skanda's characterization from an inauspicious figure to an auspicious warrior deity. Kuṣāṇa sculptures from Mathurā reflect this evolution, depicting Skanda alone as a warrior holding a spear (Mann 2001, 118, fig. 5). These images evoke *bodhisattva* iconography from the same period. In Gandhāran depictions, Skanda consistently appears in armor, wielding his spear and often accompanied by a bird, such as a rooster. Mann (2001, 124) concludes that Skanda's martial persona likely developed in the Gandhāran and Bactrian regions of the Kuṣāṇa empire, where he assimilated traits of Hellenistic and Parthian martial deities, such as Ares/Mars and Sraoša, the latter also associated with the cock. This depiction of Skanda as the gods' commander (*senāpati*) dominated by the Gupta period. However, Skanda's transformation from a malevolent deity requiring propitiation to an auspicious warrior figure made him less feared by worshippers. Consequently, his cult was gradually subsumed into that of Śiva's (Mann 2007, 468).

Skanda's persona as a warrior god likely drew partial inspiration from the persona of would-be god-kings like Alexander and the monarchs of the Hellenistic and Seleucid empires. As *senāpati*, the leader of the gods' army, Skanda would have offered an ideal archetype for earthly rulers aspiring to divinity. Sarkar (2017) dedicates chapter 3 of her study to Skanda's displacement by the Devī as the primary slayer of Mahiṣa. She identifies the Southern Cāḷukyas as the first major dynasty to prioritize the worship of Durgā over their traditional tutelary deity, Skanda-Mahāsena. Mythologically, Durgā supplanted Skanda's role by aligning with protective figures such as the Mātṛs, who were originally associated with Skanda. By being propitiated alongside the Mātṛs, Durgā absorbed their fearsome yet protective and salvific functions. While Skanda was "tamed" and "domesticated" as Śiva's son, Durgā retained her independence. With the rise of royal celebrations, especially Mahānavamī, to ensure the prosperity of their kingdoms, Durgā secured her status as the ultimate source of sovereignty and protector of the realm.

As Mann (2007) notes, Skanda's domestication into the orthodox pantheon, achieved by distancing him from his destructive associations with the Mātṛs and Grahas, reduced his fearsome nature and, consequently, his worship. As Skanda became Kumāra, a more benign figure, he was effectively assimilated into the Śaivite pantheon, where his importance diminished in comparison to the more powerful Śiva. Patronizing Skanda/Kumāra became less appealing, especially when direct support could be sought from Durgā, who was increasingly recognized as the true source of the Mātṛs' protective power. In contrast to Skanda's pacification, Durgā progressively assimilated the cults of various goddesses, both benevolent and fearsome. Her ambivalence — being both a feared force and a boon-granting savior — ensured her enduring appeal. Sarkar (2017, 97–114) explores this evolution, noting that Durgā's link to sovereignty and the grand patronage she received in annual rituals, such as Mahānavamī and Navarātra, solidified her prominence. Efforts to assimilate Durgā into Vaiṣṇavism and Śaivism have seen limited success, partly due to her independent link with kingship and state rituals, and partly because of the enduring influence of the DM. The DM's metaphysical vision of the Devī, and its integral role in rituals, has ensured that Durgā remains a central figure in the Hindu pantheon.

Moreover, the Devī triumphs more effectively over what Mahiṣa symbolizes than does Skanda. The Devī-Mahiṣa myth, which I suggest represents the goddess's victory over oppressive monolatry or monotheism, can be interpreted as parallel to Anāhitā's rise from suppression to equality with Ahura Mazdā and Mithra under Artaxerxes II. While Anāhitā's assimilation with goddesses such as Nanā, Nike, Adroxso, Tyche, Durgā, Kālī, Kauśikī, Koṭṭavai, and Jayā marked her elevation, it did not inherently align her with the anti-monolatric allegory of the Mahiṣa myth cycle. As these various goddesses were amalgamated, often through Vaiṣṇava and Śaiva efforts to subordinate a plurality of goddesses, the emergent Great Goddess began to rival male deities for supremacy. This is strikingly depicted in Kuṣāṇa plaques and Gupta reliefs, where she is multi-armed — a South Asian emblem of divine supremacy — and engaged in self-coronation, possibly with the extraordinary divine sovereign diadem. A similar contest for divine primacy played out in the Sasanian Empire, where the rivalry between Anāhitā and Ahura Mazdā persisted from the Achaemenid to the Sasanian periods, reflecting the struggle for supremacy within their pantheon. In South Asia, parallel dynamics unfolded among deities such as Viṣṇu, Śiva, Devī, Sūrya, the Buddha, Skanda, Indra, and Brahmā, each championed by sovereign patrons seeking to elevate their preferred deity to the apex of the divine hierarchy.

In South Asia, both conquerors and the conquered may often have sought their power from or attributed their success to a tutelary goddess. Male-centered deity traditions found it advantageous to elevate a great goddess over their rival male deities, as long as that goddess was subordinated to their favored god. Śaivas identified the "great goddess" as Pārvatī or Mahākālī, while Vaiṣṇavas portrayed her as Vaiṣṇavī or Mahālakṣmī, positioning her as the consort of Śiva or Viṣṇu, respectively. This dynamic, which continues to this day, reflects ongoing sectarian strategies. Ironically, these rivalries ultimately consolidated the idea that the patron goddesses of various rulers were manifestations of a single Great Goddess, the Devī. By the mid-8th century CE, the Devī had firmly established herself as the ultimate source of sovereign power and military success across much of the Hindu world, transcending the specific male deity patronized by individual kings. However, I suggest that the concept of a Supreme Deity as the Great Goddess likely did not arise solely from these sectarian amalgamations. Instead, it seems probable that the notion of such a Supreme Deity already existed among Śākta communities, providing a theological framework into which the various sectarian-based aggregations of great goddesses were assimilated.

Powerful male rulers often sought to align themselves with male deities as their sons, *avatāra*s, or chosen representatives, but forging similar identifications with the Goddess was more challenging. At best, they could frame themselves as her servants, messengers, or spouses, although the latter risked implying an untenable superiority. For example, Rāṣṭrakūṭa rulers, borrowing from the Cāḷukyas, claimed *cakravartin* status as earthly manifestations of Viṣṇu and thus as the "husbands" or "beloveds" of goddesses such as Śrī or Lakṣmī (Inden 2000, 234). However, Śākta theologies countered such frameworks by emphasizing the Great Goddess's virginal and autonomous nature, undermining attempts to subordinate her to male deities or align her with lesser goddesses.

For instance, the persona of Skandamātā situates Skanda within a Śaiva framework by presenting the Devī as both Śiva's spouse and Skanda's mother. However, the Great Goddess tradition subverts this diminution by treating Skandamātā as one among the many manifestations of the Devī. Myths associating her with Pārvatī are thus contextualized as iterations of her broader identity as the supreme deity. In political contexts, where monarchs or dynasties promoting a particular deity as supreme were defeated by rival kingdoms or alliances, such victories were likely interpreted as expressions of the Great Goddess's power. These triumphs symbolized her support for the victors and rejection of the rival's oppressive monolatry. This idea finds a mythic parallel in the DM, where the Devī emerges through the combined *tejas* (majesty) of displaced gods to restore cosmic balance. This pooling of divine power mirrors the collective strength of alliances that toppled oppressive monarchies in historical contexts.

At the risk of affirming gender stereotypes, the Goddess may be seen to serve as an archetype of the female that is courted by rival male suitors. Just as Sītā is desired by Rāvaṇa in the *Rāmāyaṇa* (Rām), although her favor rests with Rāma, and Draupadī is the husband of the five Pāṇḍavas in the Mbh, although she is lusted after by Kīcaka and others, those princesses — women, albeit ultimately goddesses — are portrayed as having granted their favor to the epic heroes and not the villains who desire them. In later Purāṇic literature and other versions of the Rām, Rāma secures the favor of the Devī to defeat Rāvaṇa. And the DStv+, when inserted into the Mbh, becomes a hymn that Yudhiṣṭhira recites to win the favor of Durgā before his battle with the Kauravas. One is left to wonder what might have transpired if both the Kauravas and Rāvaṇa also sought the favor of the Goddess. We see instances of such tensions between rivals that both propitiate Durgā in Southeast Asian narratives, as discussed in volume 2.

A crucial contribution of the DM to the persona of the Goddess is that she does not assert a manifest supremacy over the male gods. Make no mistake, she does assert her ultimate supremacy in the DM but relegates herself in all three of its episodes, and in the descriptions by Medhas and Mārkaṇḍeya in the frame story, to a transcendent and therefore mostly concealed dimension. As the cliché states that behind every great man there is a great woman, so too, behind every successful monarch and male deity, there is a manifestation of the supreme Great Goddess. This contributes to the ultimate triumph of the Devī because she is the underlying source of sovereignty and victory, regardless of who is victorious. Her ultimate loyalties are only with whoever has propitiated her to her satisfaction. By her powers, she deludes all others into misguided actions from a misplaced sense of their source of power (i.e., their own arrogance or egotism) ultimately leading to their downfall, by not knowing that she orchestrates everything.

For Śāktas, this vision of a supreme, transcendent independent Goddess would function well in polytheistic societies, even those that endorse monolatry, but not in those that promote non-theistic doctrines (e.g., early Buddhism) or monotheism (unless the Goddess is the sole, supreme power). Perhaps, this is why the vision that developed, and was eventually articulated in the DM, proved so successful in the South Asian context. In the legendary story of the Buddha's life, prince Siddhārtha becomes the Buddha, thereby accruing the benefits of being a son of the goddess-queen Māyā. She (i.e., the queen/*yakṣī*/ goddess) dies shortly after his birth. Is this a symbolic way of pointing to more than the death of the power of illusion (*māyā*) with the teachings that lead to liberative knowledge (Buddhahood)? Is it a tacit assertion of the demise of worship of the Goddess as the supreme power of illusion (Mahāmāyā) with the ascendency of the sovereignty of the Buddha? Is it a claim to the victory of meditative self-application over sacrificial propitiation of the Devī in her remote abodes as the ultimate refuge?

We have already explored the tensions, influences, and amalgamations between Buddhism and goddess-worship traditions in earlier chapters. For instance, in the terminology of refuge, the Buddha, his teachings, and community of monks are promoted as superior to the refuge offered by often remote and inaccessible (*durga*) sites of goddess worship. Both utilize the imagery of the salvific raft upon the turbulent waters (*durga*) of life. But in the narrow theological vision of early Buddhism, which placed the Buddha at the summit in a relatively feeble divine pantheon, there was no room for a Goddess of any consequence. Although goddesses did make their way back into Buddhism through the Mahāyāna and Vajrayāna traditions, as Avalokiteśvara, Tārā, Prajñāparamitā, and so on, for the most part early Buddhism did not promote the worship of deities. Thus, the end of the "Buddhist monolatry" promoted by the Mauryas and the rise of the goddess-supporting Śuṅgas and Guptas could be symbolically seen as another defeat of a "Mahiṣa" by the Devī, represented as the Buddhist elephant being laid low by the Devī's lion (as I have heard in my field studies).

During the Gupta period, historical tensions among monotheism, monolatry, and polytheism, as well as between image worship and aniconism, echoed similar dynamics in the Sasanian empire (3rd–7th centuries). In Persia, as with the Achaemenids, there was a struggle between monolatry centered on Ahura Mazdā and a polytheistic tradition that included Anāhitā, Mithra, and other deities. The Sasanian empire's collapse coincided with the rise of Islam, which spread rapidly to the fringes of South Asia. In South Asia, this period saw parallel tensions between Buddhism and polytheistic Hinduism, particularly its goddess traditions. Xuanzang's account of his capture by zealous goddess worshippers highlights the intensity of these tensions. Despite such conflicts, Emperor Harṣa presided over a religiously pluralistic empire, although he himself shifted allegiances, initially a Śaivite and possibly converting to Buddhism later in life. These shifts reflect the competition for royal patronage between Śaivism and Buddhism during his reign. The *Caṇḍīśataka*, composed likely under Harṣa's patronage, praises the Devī but attempts to subordinate her to Śiva as his spouse, illustrating efforts to integrate Śāktism into Śaivism. This period demonstrates the significant influence and rivalry of Śāktism, Śaivism, and Buddhism, which each vied for royal support and popular devotion.

It is too facile to insinuate that the myths of the Goddess's victory over Mahiṣa are simply or solely an allegory of polytheistic Hinduism's battle with and victory over non- or quasi-polytheistic rule, and of iconism over aniconism, if these terms are understood broadly. But that is evidently a sizeable component of its meaning. And it is certainly the case that the DM and the worship of Durgā are still co-opted into rousing sentiments whenever those values are under duress. The resistance to certain metaphysical notions within Buddhist, Islamic, Jain, and Christian teachings — namely, non-theism, monolatrist sentiments, or radical monotheism — would have heightened Hindu support for Durgā and her promise of victory in the struggle against rulers who patronized such rival religious teachings.

Surely, the Śākta response to the arrival of Islam, which brought with it an iconoclastic monotheistic attitude that eventually dominated much of the subcontinent until the waning of Mughal power, would have contributed to a more fervent dependence on the Devī's promise in the DM. As noted in our earlier discussion of the goddess Śākambharī in the bardic traditions gathered by James Tod (1884), the Muslims who invaded northwest India were called

Asuras, against whom goddesses such as Śākambharī were supplicated for support. Legends aside, although they are often the building block of myths, it is beyond the capacity of this study to outline the history of the many Muslim campaigns along and beyond the Indus from the mid-600s to the mid-700s. A particularly notable campaign prior to the composition of the DM was the invasion of the Deccan by al-Ḥakam of the Umayyad Caliphate in 739 CE. An inscription (CII IV.1.23) from 740 CE speaks of his many victories but eventual defeat at Navsāri in southern Gujarat by Avanijanāśraya Pulakeśin, a viceroy of the Cāḷukya ruler (likely, Vikramaditya II) with the aid of the Rāṣṭrakūṭa prince Dantidurga. According to the inscription, al-Ḥakam had already defeated various regions including Saindhava, Kachchhēlla, Saurashtra, Chāvōṭaka, Maurya, and Gurjara, indicating that he was a foe of substance who had conquered much of the northwest.

An inscription by Dantidurga at Ellora, surmised to be from about 750 CE (Owen 2012, 132) indicates that he eventually went on to defeat the Cāḷukya king, Kīrtivarman II, and others, and acquire the status the "Beloved of Śrī" (*śrīvallabha*), an epithet of Viṣṇu. In other words, Dantidurga asserted his near divine status as Viṣṇu-like, through his bond with the goddess Śrī, the consort of Viṣṇu. It indicates the role played by goddesses in the attainment, assertion, and preservation of sovereignty, if not divinity, for various rulers of that period. The inscription also briefly records that Dantidurga performed the *mahādāna* ceremony, entailing bequeathing "great gifts" of gold and jewels to his subjects. According to Inden (2000, 245) the *mahādāna* ritual, the equivalent of the Vedic *hiraṇyagarbha* (golden embryo) *śrauta* rite, was believed to transform Dantidurga into a king of kings with a divine body, a veritable Viṣṇu on earth. An inscription by one of Dantidurga's successors testifies to him performing the *hiraṇyagarbha* ritual, a likely reference to the *mahādāna* ceremony (Owen 2012, 133n7). Dantidurga is credited by some as the initiator of the building of Kailāsanātha temple at Ellora, which was likely finished by his successor Kṛṣṇarāja I (Owen 2012, 130–36). That temple has one of the earliest reliefs of the Devī slaying Mahiṣa that closely complies with the description found in the DM, which is a contributing factor to my dating of the DM at the mid to late 8th century CE. At their height under Govinda III, the Rāṣṭrakūṭas were likely the most powerful empire on the subcontinent. Dirks (1993, 37–39) notes the Rāṣṭrākūṭa influence on the subsequent Vijayanagar empire, in which the *mahādāna* became the principal ritual of Vijayanagar polity, conducted during its principal ritual occasion, which was the Mahānavamī festival to the Great Goddess. We are led to wonder if Dantidurga's rite was conducted on such an occasion.

Although the aforementioned Cāḷukya inscription clearly states that Avanijanāśraya Pulakeśin was a devout worshipper of Maheśvara, it opens with an acknowledgment that the Cāḷukyas had been raised by the seven mothers (*sapta-mātṛ*) of the seven worlds. They also acknowledge protection from Kārttikeya (i.e., Skanda). However, it is also true that many Cāḷukya inscriptions include the phrase that they had acquired their kingdom through a boon from Kauśikī (e.g., EI 27.10, which records grants from the Cālukya ruler Amma I in the 10th century CE). A more pertinent example is an earlier grant of Maṅgi Yuvarāja (r. 672–696 CE) who makes clear that the Cālukyas attained their sovereignty from the precious beneficence of the goddess Kauśikī (*kauśikīvaraprasādalabdharājyānāṃ*) (Fleet and Temple 1891, 98–99n16, 441). This points to the crucial place of the goddess Kauśikī as the conveyor of sovereignty to Hindu rulers of the region and period, even though they expressed devotion to other deities such as Maheśvara or Kārttikeya.

The battle at Navsāri is regarded as pivotal because it marks a turning point in the Hindu struggle against early Muslim invasions and led to a series of subsequent victories by Hindu kingdoms resulting in the eventual expulsion, apart from Sindh, of the Umayyad Caliphate's incursion into India (Blankinship and Blankinship 1994, 187–91). I suggest that it is precisely these battles between polytheistic Hindus and Muslim monotheists in the first century of Islam's entry into the northwest of the subcontinent that may have fueled inspiration for the composition of the DM, particularly its frame tale of the disempowered king Suratha, and Episodes Two and Three in which the Devī defeats *asura* armies. If we know anything from our preceding examination, it is that goddesses such as Nanā were firmly associated with conferring and maintaining the sovereign power of a monarch. This was certainly the case in the northwest and north-central regions of India from the Kuṣāṇa period. And in folk tales, we hear about the defeat of such polytheistic Hindu monarchs by Muslim armies, referred to as Asuras, while folk tales, historical accounts, and inscriptions testify to the subsequent victories of these monarchs under the banner of goddesses, such as the Mātṛs and Kauśikī. Even if the composition of the narrative of the DM (in the mid- to late-8th century CE) was not robustly influenced by these social and religious realities of the mid-7th to mid-8th centuries in northwest India, the DM most certainly would have struck a chord with the polytheistic Hindus who read it. These realities may have aided in the endurance of the scripture and its success as the best-known articulation of Śākta theology.

More significantly, it offers us a compelling rationale why the Goddess wins out as the most salient divine ally in the struggle against rival religions, because we know that she does. The spread of Islam throughout the subcontinent may have played a key role in the ascendant and concomitant spread in popularity of the DM and the theology of the Great Goddess. It was yet another cycle of the rise of aniconic monolatry (in the case of Islam, radical aniconic monotheism) on the subcontinent, another manifestation of Mahiṣa and his *asura* armies displacing the lesser deities from their share of worship, with the Goddess providing the most reliable refuge and recourse in a perennial struggle. However, this is not to say that the struggle with Islamic rulers was the only factor in the rise of the Goddess. Nor it is implying that Mahiṣa unilaterally represents the aniconic monotheism of Islam. After all, the DM could be invoked meaningfully in the struggle against any other monolatric, great god traditions. As previously discussed, within any conflict with rival kings, and these were mostly among Hindu kingdoms until the early 11th century with the rise of the Ghaznavids, goddesses would often be the lineage deities of the warring Hindu rulers, even if these were patrons of Śiva or Viṣṇu. In other words, a goddess, who was understood to be a discrete manifestation of the Great Goddess, would be known as the true source of the monarch's power, particularly in battle. And nowadays, of course, Mahiṣa represents a wide array of different notions to devotees, not just a rival religio-political enemy or system.

Iconographic and Sacrificial Compromise

The DM also expresses a sort of compromise between iconographic and iconoclastic sensibilities, which may reflect preexisting modes of representation of the Goddess prior to the composition of that influential text. It also struck a compromise — albeit less effectively until more recently — against animal sacrifice. In the DM, King Suratha and the merchant Samādhi worshipped the Goddess by fasting and making blood offerings. However, they did not conduct animal sacrifices on a grand scale, preferring instead to demonstrate their devotion through drawing their own blood. They also constructed earthen images of the Devī. Such earthen images might well have been akin to types of the earthen jar effigies on low earthen altars, or anthropomorphic unbaked clay images of the Devī still used for worship during Navarātra. While these serve as iconographic representations of the Goddess, they are destroyed after the worship rituals have been completed, akin to the fate of Buddhist sand *maṇḍalas* and Vedic fire altars. As such they allude to the emergence of the Devī into manifest forms for the sake of worship, and her repeated return to her transcendent state. This mode of worship undercuts the classical temple traditions, with their permanently established abodes for deities who reside there in the form of durable images (*mūrti*) typically of stone or metal. Although temple priests may establish earthen jar forms of the Devī privately for their own worship, in my fieldwork on Durgā temples, they rarely install jar forms or anthropomorphic unbaked clay images of the Devī during Navarātra. The dominant explanation provided is that the Devī permanently resides at the temple, so there is no need to establish her there again. Moreover, it helps us to understand why there are not very many Durgā temples in India, since any "permanent residence" in a locale is somewhat contradictory to her primarily transcendental metaphysical persona.

This contrast between the iconocentric temple traditions of Goddess worship and the use of perishable imagery leads one to wonder if the latter type predates the ascendency of durable images within temples, the building of which developed in South Asia only after the period of contact with the Hellenistic empire. By contrast, the use of temporary worship sites dates to Vedic times, with *yajña* fire altars or with water oblations, both of which are promoted by the DM for the worship of the Goddess. The Buddhists too eschewed the building of temples, opting for *stūpas* in the early centuries after the Buddha's *parinirvāna*. Many of the most renowned Hindu goddess temples developed beside aniconic abodes, such as a spring or pond. An example is the Kāmākhyā Devī temple on Nilachal Hill in Guwahati, Assam, where the goddess is a *yoni*-shaped spring-fed cleft in a rock. And within other goddess temples, the central image may not be a statue, but a mask or cosmogram (*yantra*). Thus, a quasi-aniconic mode of representation persists in many goddess temples, further alluding to her transcendence.

The most distinctive representations of Durgā are in the context of her defeat of Mahiṣa in the various iconographic forms described in previous chapters. But these are rarely in temples of their own, and more often are found within subsidiary shrines of temples dedicated to other deities. However, as Kramrisch (1946 105) noted in her detailed study of the Hindu temple, the Goddess "is invoked in the bricks of which the Vedic altar is piled, and the Hindu temple is built." She asserts this from such evidence as *Taittirīya Saṃhitā* IV.2.9.4, which states "To thee, O Goddess, O Brick, let us sacrifice with oblation" (Kramrisch 1946, 105). Arguably then, the Devī is present within the very substance of the structures that house or encapsulate the context for the worship of all deities. To put it another way, Durgā's triumph as Supreme Deity derives from her capacity as the Great Goddess to claim the primordial transcendent ground from which all manifestation emerges, a characteristic that may have its roots in the most ancient of Hindu scriptures. She allows worshippers, kings, and subjects alike to worship her or any other god or goddess, in virtually any form and manner, whether or not they know of her supreme status as the true matrix of their very beings and all their activities.

It is beyond the scope of this book to trace the full sweep of the development of Durgā's worship in the centuries beyond this period. The second volume traces salient expressions of her worship in literature, symbolism, and ritual in various parts of Asia from the 8th century to the present time, eventually focusing on those expressions in the city of Banāras.

Appendix I

The Rātrī Sūkta

The Rātrī Sūkta (*Ṛg Veda* 10.127), in Sanskrit (from Müller 1849–74, vol. 6, 454–58):

rātrī vyakhyadāyatī purutrā devyakṣabhiḥ /
viśvā adhi śriyo'dhita // 10.127.01
orvaprā amartyā nivato devyudvataḥ /
jyotiṣā bādhate tamaḥ // 10.127.02
niru svasāramaskṛtoṣasaṃ devyāyatī /
apedu hāsate tamaḥ // 10.127.03
sā no adya yasyā vayaṃ ni te yāmannavikṣmahi /
vṛkṣe na vasatiṃ vayaḥ // 10.127.04
ni grāmāso avikṣata ni padvanto ni pakṣiṇaḥ /
ni śyenāsaścidarthinaḥ // 10.127.05
yāvayā vṛkyaṃ vṛkaṃ yavaya stenamūrmye /
athā naḥ sutarā bhava // 10.127.06
upa mā pepiśattamaḥ kṛṣṇaṃ vyaktamasthita /
uṣa ṛṇeva yātaya // 10.127.07
upa te gā ivākaraṃ vṛṇīṣva duhitardivaḥ /
rātri stomaṃ na jigyuṣe // 10.127.08

In English (Coburn 1984, 257–58; phrases he italicized for emphasis are not reproduced here):

1. The goddess Night approaches, illuminating manifold places with her eyes: She has put on all her glories (*śriyaḥ*).

2. The immortal goddess has filled up the broad expanse, the heights and depths; With (her own) light, she drives out the darkness (*tamaḥ*).

3. The goddess approaches, replacing her sister Dawn. May (this) darkness also disappear.

4. (May you stand) by us now, at whose coming we go to rest, Like birds to their nest in a tree.

5. To rest have gone the villagers, as have all legged and winged creatures, Even the greedy hawks.

6. Ward off the she-wolf and the wolf, ward off the thief, O Night,
    And be easy for us to get through.
7. Distinctly has the plastering black darkness come unto me.
    O Dawn, may you collect (it) like a debt!
8. Accept, O daughter of heaven, what I have presented you as if (it were a herd) of cattle,
    (Viz.) this hymn, (presented) as if to a conqueror, O Night.

Appendix II

A Powerful Queen Defeats an Arrogant Emperor

In the semi-divine princesses in the Hindu epics, such as Sītā and Draupadī, we have images of strong, even fiery, women, capable of bringing down their demonic enemies. However, these women do so through the agency of men. It may well be that their power, or *śakti*, empowers their spouses, spurring them to victory, in much the same way that a king, who propitiates Durgā and wins her favor, might feel assured of success in an upcoming battle. And we do know of the association of goddesses, such as Nike, Ištar, Athena, Nanā, Anāhitā, and so on, with victory in battle, and even the wearing of armor and the wielding of weapons. However, there are few ancient narratives of a warrior queen defeating a great emperor in battle that resonate with Durgā's encounter with Mahiṣa. Even princess Ambā, who was wronged because of her abduction by Bhiṣma, had her revenge by slaying him in the form of Śikhandi, who was born female but transitioned to a male. So, what might have served as a model for the battle between a woman and king that led to his ignoble demise?

While scouring through literary sources, I came upon in Herotodus's *Histories* an account of queen Tomyris of Massagetae, who was set upon by the Achaemenid emperor Cyrus the Great. The Massagetaeans were known to be warriors and were ruled by queen Tomyris after the death of her husband. Due to arrogance at his martial successes and the sense that he was divine, Cyrus decided to conquer Massagetae. He sent Tomyris ambassadors, to court her by pretending that he wanted to marry her, but she, recognizing that he wooed not her but her kingdom, resisted the advances. Cyrus then began his advance by building a bridge for his armies across the Araxes River. Tomyris sent him a message counselling him not to wage war, but also said that since she knew her words would go unheeded to simply choose the location of battle on his or her side of the river. All but one of his counselors recommended that Cyrus allow Tomyris to cross the river. Croesus of Lydia, the dissenting voice, recommended that Cyrus not wage war, because human rulers were not always fortunate. However, if he thought of himself as immortal, and did not heed this advice, Cyrus should cross the river and wage war on Massagetaean land. Moreover, as a kingdom at the margins, unfamiliar with Persian delights, the Massagetaeans would easily fall for a trap. By luring them into battle with a contingent of weak troops supported with sumptuous food and drink at the front line, the initial victory by the Massagetaeans would lead to a premature celebration, debilitating them, at which point they could be defeated. Cyrus opted for this strategy.

That night Cyrus had a bad dream about his fortunes, which he mistakenly interpreted not as his own defeat but as Darius's ambitions for his throne. Thereafter, he implemented the plan proposed by Croesus. A third of the Massagetaean army, led by queen Tomyris' son, Spargapises, attacked and easily defeated the forward encampment of Persian troops, and began to feast on the spoils of food and wine left behind. When they had fallen asleep after their drunken victory celebrations, they were attacked by the Persians under Cyrus. Many were slain and even more taken prisoners, Spargapises himself among the latter. Thereupon, Tomyris sent another message to Cyrus, calling him bloodthirsty and blaming the wine for the defeat of her troops. She offered him the opportunity to restore her son alive, and to leave her land content in the knowledge that he had destroyed a third of her troops. If he refused, she swore that she would give him his fill of blood. Cyrus ignored her message, and Spargapises, awakening from his drunken sleep, only then realized the full reach of the predicament. He convinced Cyrus to free him from his shackles and instantly committed suicide.

Tomyris, collecting her entire army, then attacked Cyrus. Herodotus reckoned it was the most fearsome battle that ever occurred among kingdoms outside of Greece, fought first with arrows and then hand-to-hand with swords and spears. Eventually, the Massagetaeans prevailed, and Cyrus was slain. They searched for his body among the dead and Tomyris placed his head into a skin filled with blood, saying that true to her threat, she was giving him his fill of blood. Herodotus claims to have heard many versions of the story of the death of Cyrus, but this he deemed the most believable. The story of Cyrus the Great's defeat by a valiant widowed queen surely offered a model of resistance that captured the popular imagination, as do many such David-versus-Goliath tales. The story would have been especially inspiring to those under the sway of Cyrus's even more ruthless successors, Darius and Xerxes.

If Herodotus was aware of versions of the Tomyris narratives in Greece, beyond the western fringe of the Achaemenid Persian empire, it is likely that similar versions also circulated beyond the eastern fringe, in South Asia, particularly if the battle between Tomyris and Cyrus was of the ferocity and scale to which Herodotus alludes. Although there is no scholarly consensus on what became of Massagetae, some speculate that the Jats of the Punjab are related to the Massagetaeans, which if true would offer a mechanism for the migration of the story to northwest and north-central India. In the warrior queen and son, we see resonances with the Devī as the mother of Skanda, both of whom are associated with battle. Cyrus's arrogance and pride, like Mahiṣa's, led him to battle, and one has the motif of him sending emissaries to woo Tomyris with a marriage proposal as found in certain Mahiṣa-Devī narratives. The bloodiness of Cyrus's end is especially striking in relationship to Devī/Mahiṣa imagery because he appears to have been beheaded and then placed in a skin filled with blood. We could imagine this being a container akin to a large wineskin, still bearing the appearance of the animal from which it came, such as a large goat or bull. Could such imagery have given rise to the sanguine, beheaded, half-human, half-buffalo in the Devī-Mahiṣa myth? Of course, there is little to support a direct correlation between the Tomyris-Cyrus tale and that of the Devī and Mahiṣa, which has innumerable differences. However, just as the Tomyris story continued to capture the imagination of writers and artists in the West, such as Reubens (in about 1622 CE) and Shakespeare, we can imagine that such tales circulated in South Asia and may have contributed to the narrative development of the Mahiṣa-Devī myth. After all, one also notes shared narrative tropes between the Greek and South Asian epics.

Appendix III

Peacock Angel Worship Among the Yezidis

A curious vestige of peacock worship is found in the highly syncretic religion of the Yezidis, whose supreme deity is Malak-Tāwūs, the Peacock Angel. The Yezidis, who live among the Kurdish people of Northern Iraq, have recently been lethally persecuted by the Islamic State of Iraq and the Levant (ISIL, also known as ISIS), a militant Islamic organization intent on reestablishing a global caliphate. Envisioned as male, Malak-Tāwūs is central to the character of Yezidi religion. Although he is angelic to the Yezidi, and a symbolic equivalent of the people themselves and their faith, he is viewed by neighboring groups as the devil (Iblis, Satan) himself. Thus, Malak-Tāwūs possesses an intriguing ambivalent character, as both divine and demonic. A detailed account of the ambivalent character of the peacock in the Islamic world is found in Garnik Asatrian and Victoria Arakelova (2003, 28–30). During Jamā'at, the Festival of the Assembly, held in late September, a bull is sacrificed at the shrine of Sheik 'Adi, one of the other major deities in the Yezidi pantheon. The origin of the peacock symbolism, so central to the Yezidis, is as perplexing as their origins, which some factions of Yezidis attempt to trace to Āryan ancestors (Spät 2008, 401–2).

The central cultic object of the Yezidis is the *sanjak* (flag, banner), a bronze or copper column, resembling a large candlestick, topped with a peacock. It resembles the *ārati* lamps used in the worship of the South Indian deity Murugan. Each peacock column represents a different region, which is presided over by an associated angel. Malak-Tāwūs emanated seven *sanjaks* from his own image, and each of these ultimately represents him (Nicolaus 2008, 220). During ceremonial travels, each of the *sanjaks* is carried in a parade by a certain caste of priests (Qawwāl) to all the villages within its assigned region. The Mir, the supreme leader of all Yezidis, derives his sovereign and religious authority by virtue of possessing all seven *sanjaks* (Fuccaro 1999, 17). The parade and the *sanjaks* are believed to grant spiritual fulfilment and divine protection to followers of the Peacock Angel (Nicolaus 2008, 221). The ritual worship of the *sanjak* has been kept secret and not accessible to non-Yezidis until recently. Despite the highly syncretic nature of Yezidi rites and beliefs, and the lack of certainty about their origins, the maṇḍalic nature of the *sanjaks* (e.g., presiding protectively over regions, emanating from a central deity), and their affiliation with the sovereign and his power, secrecy, and so on, resonate with many of the features of Tantric deity worship in India. The peacock banner/column offers a notable resemblance to the Nidrā/Kauśikī symbolism that we have encountered.

Timeline of Pertinent Events

25,000 BCE or earlier	Venus from Dolní Věstonice (Czech Republic)
c. 7500–5700 BCE	Çatalhöyük in Anatolia •figure 4.6: Seated "goddess" on feline throne
c. 3450 BCE	Gebel el-Arak knife handle shows a man holding two rampant lions by the neck
c. 2500 BCE	Sumerian stele from Mari, with Gilgamesh holding apart two rearing bulls
c. 2334–2284 BCE	Sargon (the Great), Akkadian king •patronized Inanna; fused her with Ištar
c. 2334–2154 BCE	Inanna-Ištar Akkadian cylinder seal depicts winged goddess with foot on lion and weapons behind shoulders
c. 2300	Anubanini petroglyph, Kermanshah province, Iran •depicts Ninni (Inanna-Ištar) delivering captives to king Anubanini
c. 2200–1900 BCE	Mature Harappa 3C period •figure 4.1a: Planoconvex tablet from Harappa, with man spearing buffalo •figure 4.1b: Female? figure choking two tigers/ lions on reverse
2112–2004 BCE	Ur III period •Nanā (Nanaia) appears in Sumerian pantheon
1766–1122 BCE	Shang dynasty in China •oracle bones suggest early worship of goddesses
c. 1507–1458 BCE	Female pharaoh Hatshepsut •linked herself to Sekhmet (lion goddess)

c. 1386–c. 1350 BCE   Pharaoh Amenhotep III
          •almost 600 Sekhmet images for funerary temple

1500–1200 BCE
(c. 1250 BCE)   Inner core of *Ṛg Veda Saṃhitā*
          •*durga* appears but in masculine as "difficult route"

1200–1000 BCE (or later) *Atharva Veda Saṃhitā*
          •*durgā* appears in feminine but as "hardships in life"

1200 BCE
or 1000 BCE   Hymns of *The Ṛg Veda Khila*
          •Rātrī Khila with praise to Durgā as a goddess, very likely an insertion from the 1st century CE

1200–800 BCE   Earliest strata of *Taittirīya Āraṇyaka*

8th century BCE   Inscriptional evidence of cult of Kybele in Phrygia

750–500 BCE   Earliest strata of *Vālmīki Rāmāyaṇa*
          •no mention of Durgā

668–c. 627 BCE   Ashurbanipal, Assyrian emperor

646 BCE   Ashurbanipal sacks Elam on command of Nanaya
          •does so to return her captured image to Uruk

c. 628–551 BCE   Reasonable dates for Zoroaster
          Earliest strata of Yašt 5 (aka Ābān Yašt) to Arədvī Sūrā Anāhitā

c. 550 BCE   Tree shrine at Māyā Devī temple in Lumbini
          •suggests pre-Buddhist goddess/*yakṣī*/tree worship

c. 550–330 BCE   Achaemenian Period

r. 549–530 BCE   Cyrus (the Great), founder of Achaemenid Dynasty
          •killed by Queen Tomyris (as per Herodotus)

r. 522- 486 BCE   Darius (I) (the Great), Achaemenian emperor
  • Behistun Inscription tells of his defeat of Gaumāta

r. 486–465 BCE   Xerxes (I) (the Great), Achaemenian emperor

c. 484–c. 425 BCE   Herodotus, Greek historian (*Histories*)

r. 404–359 BCE   Artaxerxes II, Achaemenian emperor
  • insertions into Yašt 5
  • re(?)establishes Anāhitā worship with images throughout his empire

5th–3rd century BCE   *Mānava Gṛhya Sūtra* (as per D. G. White)
  • refers to a festival of Āryā, the mother of Skanda

late 4th century BCE   The *Zhuangzi*, influential Daoist text
  • describes goddess Xi Wangmu attaining the Dao

400 BCE–100 CE   Earliest speculative date for an unknown version of the *Bṛhad Devatā*
  • Durgā mentioned as a goddess in a list of deities (but very likely an insertion)

3rd century BCE
(no later than)   Chapter 10 of the *Taittirīya Āraṇyaka* (TA)
  • so-called Durgī(ā)-gāyatrī or Durgā-sāvitrī appears here (TA 10.1.7)
  • verses with Ṛg Vedic verse to Agni addressed to the goddess Durgā (looks like an insertion)

Although Durgā, as a goddess, may appear as early as 1200 BCE in Vedic literature, those are very likely insertions from a later period. The Durgī-gāyatrī in TA 10.1.7 may be the earliest occurrence of the goddess Durgā (but as Durgī) and is possibly from about the 3rd century BCE.

356–323 BCE   Alexander (the Great) of Macedon
- crosses Indus, conquers parts of Northwest India
- initiates Hellenistic cultural influence

360–281 BCE   Lysimachus, Macedonian diadochus of Alexander
- has coins where Nike crowns victors with wreath

4th century BCE–
3rd century CE   Variable dates for the Dīdārgañj Yakṣī (figure 3.1)
- from Mauryan to Kuṣāṇa period

c. 300 BCE   Early strata of the *Dhammapada* aphorisms
- verses contrast the self and self-control as ideal refuges versus goddess-oriented refuges

c. 340–298 BCE   Candragupta Maurya (Aśoka's grandfather)

322–185 BCE   Mauryan dynasty

r. c. 269–232 BCE   Aśoka, Mauryan emperor

269–197 BCE   Attalus I, ruler of Pergamon
- promotes worship of Kybele, as Magna Mater (Great Mother) among the Romans

312–63 BCE   The Seleucids

281–261 BCE   Antiochus I Soter, Bactrian Seleucid ruler
- coins depict Nike crowning victors with wreath

3rd–2nd century BCE   Bronze hairpins from this period have axe, thunderbolt, or Nandipāda design

early 1st–
late 1st century CE   *Vasiṣṭha Dharma Śāstra* (according to Olivelle)
- lists Durgā-sāvitrī to cleanse one from sins

This is possibly the first occurrence of Durgā as a goddess; appears within a *mantra* for purification.

3rd century BCE	Maritime trade among Gaṅgā delta (Tamralipti and Chandraketugarh), north Egypt, Mediterranean, Southeast Asia, and China
200–100 BCE	Figure 3.4: Tamluk Yakṣī
250–125 BCE	Greco-Bactrian Kingdoms • contact with Chinese Han empire
r. 190–180 BCE	Agathocles, ruler of Bactria • square silver coins depict Saṅkarṣaṇa • maybe the earliest Vāsudeva-Kṛṣṇa images, but they are two-armed
2nd century BCE	Yeuzhi migrate from Ganzu province, China • eventually become the Kuṣāṇas
2nd century BCE	Emergence of Prajñāpāramitā literature • possible emergence of goddess Prajñāpāramitā
185–75 BCE	The Śuṅga period
2nd–1st century BCE	Figure 3.2: Caṇḍā (Cadā) Yakṣī from Bharhut
2nd century BCE–1st century CE	Figure 5.7a and 5.7b: Śuṅga period bronze hairpin goddess • has diadem that is tied at the back of the head
180 BCE–10 CE	Indo-Greek kingdoms
170–145 BCE	Eucratides I, Greco-Bactrian king • coins portray Nike with wreath
165–130 BCE	Menander I Soter (aka Milinda), Indo-Greek king • empire arguably extended to Pāṭaliputra • coins portray Nike with wreath • figures 5.3a and 5.3b: Drachma of Menander, showing aegis of Athena
d. 163 BCE	Marquise of Dai, Mawangdui, Hunan • associated with Buyao hairpins

c. 85 BCE	Archebius, Indo-Greek king, ruling from Taxila • coins portray Nike with wreath
1st century BCE	Sapalbizes and Arseiles, western Bactrian rulers • Nanā (Nanaia) appears as a lion on their coins
1st century BCE– 1st century CE	Figure 3.3: Chandraketugarh hairpin goddess
1st century BCE– 1st century CE	Figure 4.7: Malhār Viṣṇu (?) • arguably the first four-armed Viṣṇu image Reasonable *terminus post quem* for *Bhagavad Gītā*
c. mid-1st century BCE	Rātrī Khila verses inserted into what is sometimes called the Durgā Stava
75–30 BCE	The Kanvas in India
2nd century BCE– 3rd century CE	Han dynasty in China • hairpinning ceremony practiced
2nd century BCE– 3rd century CE	Multiple eyes, arms, and heads appear on Hindu images
247 BCE–224 CE	The Parthians in Central Asia
206 BCE–220 CE	Han dynasty in China • Silk Road trade flourishing
200 BCE–350 CE	Early strata of *Mahābhārata*
3 BCE	Apocalyptic cult to Xi Wangmu • famine, drought; stalks of grain and tokens of goddess exchanged to avert death
1st century BCE– 1st century CE	Śuṅga period Chandraketugarh hairpin goddesses
c. 30 CE	Strabo, Greek geographer and historian • says 120 ships sailed from Egypt to India annually

r. 1–30 CE   Heraios, Kuṣāṇa clan chief
- coins depict Nike crowning king with wreath

c. 30–375 CE   Kuṣāṇa period
- empire from Turfan in China to Pāṭaliputra

60 CE   *Periplus Maris Erythraei*, a mariner's manual describes Roman Egypt's trade with India

1st century CE   Clear evidence that the lion was in India and traded to Rome

c. 1st century CE   *Baudhāyana Gṛhyaśeṣasūtra*
- mentions ritual worship of Durgā

68 CE   Kāśyapa Mātaṅga and Dharmarakṣa visit China
- first Buddhist monastery (White Horse) built

c. 77 CE   Ubouzanes, Kuṣāṇa ruler
- coins with Nike crowning king with wreath

c. 127–150 CE   Kaniṣka I, Kuṣāṇa ruler
- Nanā is the most popular deity on his coinage
- Nanā likely the highest deity in Kuṣāṇa pantheon
- earliest multi-armed Śiva images on coins

1st–2nd century CE   Early Kuṣāṇa period
- two-armed goddess subduing buffalo with bare hands (Bhita); Theriomorphic type

1st–mid-2nd century CE   Likely composition period for the *Bhagavad Gītā*
- must be before the *Harivaṃśa*
- must be after four-armed Viṣṇu images common

1st–3rd century CE   Figures 4.2 and 4.3: Kuṣāṇa period sandstone and terracottas of buffalo-subduing goddess
- goddess has four arms

1st–4th century CE   Dīdārgañj Yakṣī

c. 2nd century CE   *Arthaśāstra* (refers to Chinese silk)

2nd century CE — Rabatak inscription

2nd century CE — Artemis is still worshipped in Ephesus
 • had been conflated with Sekhmet/Mus by Herodotus

1st–early 2nd century CE (latest) — Suggested composition of Durgā Stava or variants
 • without the framing verses with Kṛṣṇa/Kaṃsa myth
 • portrays goddess as four-armed

c. 2nd century CE — Figure 6.1: Kuṣāṇa mottled red sandstone plaque entitled "Durgā on Lion"
 • holds peacock tailfeather flag

180–242 CE — Ardašīr I (Indo Sasanian king) was initiated at a goddess (Anāhitā?) temple
 • first unequivocal images of Anāhitā on his coins
 • she holds circular diadem with ribbons
 • wears distinctive crown with three large projections
 • displayed severed heads of enemies at her temple
 • only Anāhitā received such offerings

c. 268 CE — Kaniṣka III, Kuṣāṇa emperor
 • Nanā holds diadem on his coin

1st–2nd century CE — Earliest strata of the *Harivamśa* (as per Hein)

late 2nd century CE — Main text of the *Harivamśa* (as per Couture)

late 2nd century CE — Praise of Nidrā (First Stratum) composed
 • replicates a verse from the Durgā Stava (so later)
 • portrays Nidrā-Kauśikī with four arms

3rd century CE — Porphyry, Platonic author of De *antro nympharum*
 • said Mithraic temples symbolized cosmic elements

c. 3rd century CE — Figure 4.4: White terracotta Buffalo-subduing goddess with lion

c. 3rd century CE	Lion begins to appear with buffalo-subduing goddess
224–651 CE	Sasanian period
r. 293–302 CE	King Narseh •probably depicted on Naqš-e Rostam relief •receives kingship from Anāhitā
r. 309–379 CE	Šāpūr II •final insertions into Yašt 5, which is committed to writing •sent severed heads of executed Christian to Anāhitā temple for display
3rd century CE	Victorious Goddess type terracotta fragment from Saṇṇatti
later than 3rd century CE	*Deutero Baudhāyana* (as per Olivelle) •"the Durgā" likely refers to the Durgā-sāvitrī
3rd–early 4th century CE	Figure 4.5: Kuṣāṇa sandstone plaque with eight-armed goddess on two lions, with sun and moon and self-coronating with wondrous diadem
3rd–early 4th century CE	Durgā Stava likely inserted into the *Mahābhārata* •with Kṛṣṇa/Kaṃsa myth in framing verses
3rd–early 4th century CE	Udayagiri, late Kuṣāṇa, pre-Gupta •figure 5.6: Cave 6B image of buffalo-subduing image (Theriomorphic type)
3rd–early 4th century CE	Udayagiri, pre-Gupta •figure 5.5: Cave 17 buffalo-subduing image (Theriomorphic type)
3rd century or 4th century CE	Bhāsa's *Bālacarita* •refers to goddess Kārtyāyanī (not Kātyāyanī), who kills the demons Sumbha and Nisumbha

320–550 CE   Gupta period

r. 379-383 CE   Ardašīr II, Indo-Sasanian king
            •had Anāhitā on coinage

4th–5th century CE   Figure 5.2: Buffalo-subduing goddess (four-armed)
            on medallion from Rājghāṭ, with aegis-like shield
            (Theriomorphic type)

c. 401/402 CE   Udayagiri
            •figure 5.4: Candragupta Cave 6A image of
            buffalo-subduing goddess (Theriomorphic type)

459–484 CE   Pērōz I, Sasanian king
            •perhaps depicted on Tāq-I Bustān relief
            obtaining kingship from Ahura Mazdā, with
            Anāhitā in secondary role
            •coins depict Nanā with four arms (Indian
            influence)

c. 5th century CE   Figure 10.1: Large Victorious Goddess type statue

c. 5th century CE   Tarumanagara inscription in Java in Pallava script
            •reveal Hinduism in West Java

5th–6th century CE   Figure 5.1: Buffalo-subduing goddess from Bhumarā
            Gupta period, Theriomorphic form

5th–6th century CE   *Mārkaṇḍeya Purāṇa* (as per Pargiter)

6th century CE   Multiplicity tradition (arms, eyes, heads) on deities
            •expands to Buddhist and Jain images

c. 6th century CE   Gopikā cave inscription describes Devī Bhāvanī and
            Kātyāyanī with foot on Mahiṣāsura's head

516 CE   Chinese translation of *Mahāmāyūrīvidyā-rājñī*
            •describes the goddess as bringer of rain, and
            protector against danger, such as snake poison

591–628 CE   Khosrow II, Sasanian king
            •perhaps depicted on Tāq-I Bustān relief
            obtaining kingship from Ahura Mazdā, with
            Anāhitā in secondary role

early 6th century CE	Goddess sections of the early *Skanda Purāṇa*
6th–7th century CE	Babylonian Talmud (Bavli), from Sasanian Babylon •intimates that Ahura Mazdā was a demon
6th–7th century CE	*Śivadharma*, likely composition date •early instance of epithet Mahiṣāsuramardanī
6th–7th century CE	Early *Skanda Purāṇa* (not the later *Skanda Purāṇa*)
6th–7th century CE	Composition of earliest strata of the *Devī Purāṇa*
r. 630–668 CE	Narasiṃhavarman I (aka Mamalla I), Pallava ruler
636 CE	Xuanzang's account of his capture and near sacrifice
6th–8th century CE	Śṛṅgāra Durgā images begin to appear •e.g., Figure 12.1: Śṛṅgāra Durgā from Ābānerī (c. 7th century CE)
7th century CE	*Viṣṇu Dharma Sūtra* (as per Olivelle) •Lists Durgā-sāvitrī among purifying *mantras*
7th century CE (first half)	*Caṇḍīśataka* composed by Bāṇa •during reign of King Harṣa •uses motif of Devī's foot on Mahiṣa •*Kādambarī* composed by Bāṇa •refers to Kātyāyanī, lion-riding, crusher of Mahiṣa
r. 672–696 CE	Maṅgi Yuvarāja, Cāḷukya king •inscriptions say he attain sovereignty from Kauśikī
c. second half of 7th century CE	Inscription from Kudarkot has dedication to Durgā
678 CE	Nanā with four arms on silver bowl from Chorasmia
7th or 8th century CE	Earliest depiction of goddess Mahāmāyūrī at Ellora
7th or 8th century CE	Arguably the first sculpture of Tārā at Ellora opposite Mahāmāyūrī image

703 CE	Yijing's Chinese translation of *Suvarṇabhāsa Sūtra* •contains the Praise of Nidrā (Second Stratum) (i.e., Āryā Stava) •dedicated to Sarasvatī
r. c. 695–728 CE	Narasiṃhavarman II, Pallava ruler (as per Tartakov and Dehejia) •rock cut shrines at Māmallapuram. •Victorious Goddess type images on rock-cut shrines •figures 10.2, 10.3, 10.4, 10.5, and 10.6 •devotees offering up blood from limbs, or self-decapitations (figures 10.2 and 10.5).
late 7th–early 8th century CE	Figure 10.8: Victorious Goddess type image at Sambor Prei Kuk, Cambodia
early 8th century CE	Figure 11.1: Large bas-relief at Māmallapuram, depicting the lion-riding Devī battling an Anthropomorphic type buffalo demon
early 8th century CE	Śṛṅgāra Durgā image from Hari Hara temple at Osian •clearly indicates the sensual appeal of the Devī
early 8th century CE	*Mālatī-mādhava*, a play by Bhavabhūti •describes a potential human sacrifice to Cāmuṇḍā
739 CE	Al-Ḥakam of the Umayyads invades the Deccan after conquering much of subcontinent's northwest
740 CE	Inscription tells that al-Ḥakam defeated at Navsāri by Avanijanāśraya Pulakeśin, a Cāḷukya viceroy •aided by Dantidurga, a Rāṣṭrakūṭa prince •Navsāri marks pivotal shift in driving out Umayyad incursion into India
c. 750 CE	Dantidurga defeats Cāḷukyas •performs major rituals gaining near-divine status

	•perhaps initiates construction of Kailāsanātha
r. 756–773 CE	Kṛṣṇarāja I, Rāṣṭrakūṭa king, Dantidurga's successor •builder of Kailāsanātha temple, Ellora
mid-8th century CE	Figure 11.2: Bas-relief of Anthropomorphic type buffalo demon battling lion-riding Devī bas-relief on Kailāsanātha temple Figure 11.3: Bas-relief on Kailāsanātha temple of Anthropomorphic type buffalo demon being sub dued by the Devī's foot and slain Figure 11.4: Bas-relief on Kailāsanātha temple of Emergent Demon type buffalo-demon being trampled and killed by the Devī
mid-8th century CE	*Gaüḍavaho* composed in Prakrit by Vākpatirāja
c. mid-8th– mid-10th century CE	Sanjaya dynasty in Java, Indonesia
second half of 8th century CE	*Devī Māhātmya* is composed and inserted into the *Mārkaṇḍeya Purāṇa*
second half of 8th century CE	Reasonably certain period after which the terms Mahiṣāsuramardinī and Mahiṣamardinī may be used for Devī trampling the buffalo demon
793–814 CE	Govinda III, Rāṣṭrakūṭa emperor •rules the most powerful empire on the subcontinent
804 CE	Inscription from Baijnāth (Kangra) •praises Durgā/Pārvatī and Śiva
812–814 CE	Dadimatī -Mātā inscription (as per Mirashi) •has a verse from the DM •*terminus ante quem* for *The Devī Māhātmya*

Notes

Chapter 1

1. Coburn noted occurrences of *durgā*, with the long terminal vowel, "*ā*," in the *Vaidika-padānukrama-koṣa*, a concordance of Vedic Sanskrit words. Cross checking all such potentially feminine forms, he found they are often the neuter plural, and "never applied to a feminine substantive nor used as a feminine epithet" (Coburn 1984, 116n103).

2. In their detailed commentarial notes, Jamison and Brereton observe that *durga* typically refers to a place that is hard to penetrate, akin to a fortress, or an undesirable location where people might wish to avoid or seek rescue from (see http://rigvedacommentary.alc.ucla.edu/). Some of these interpretations align with the idea of a refuge — a place of escape that is difficult to access and not intended as a permanent dwelling for those who reach it. Of course, some hermitage refuges are described as very pleasant.

3. The hymn under discussion is RVKh 4.2, as numbered by Scheftelowitz (1906). The hymns of *The Ṛg Veda Khila* (*khilāni*, plural) are associated with the Bāṣkala recension (*śākhā*), one of the two main surviving versions of the RV. However, only fragments of the Bāṣkala recension remain, while the RV primarily survives in the Śākala recension. Some *khilāni* are verses appended to the beginning or end of various RV hymns, but most exist as independent hymns.

4. The Rātrī Sūkta is included in Appendix I of this book for easy reference to the verses discussed.

5. Witzel (1997, 265, 268) identifies four sequential linguistic layers in the Vedic corpus. The earliest is Ṛg Vedic, though many hymns in the tenth *maṇḍala* are later additions, closer in date to the second layer: the "*mantra* language." This layer includes *The Ṛg Veda Khila* (RVKh), *Atharva Veda* (AV), *Yajur Veda* (YV) *mantra*s, and those sections of the *Sāma Veda* (SV) differing from the RV. Next is the prose of the Black *Yajur Veda* Saṃhitās, followed by the language of the *Brāhmaṇas*, which in its later period includes the *Āraṇyakas*, early *Upaniṣads*, and some early Sūtra texts, such as the *Baudhāyana Śrautasūtra*. The final layer is the Sūtra language, as seen in the *Gṛhyasūtras*, which transitions into Epic or classical Sanskrit (see also Witzel 1989, sections 4.3.2–4.35).

6. Scheftelowitz (1906, 110–11 (Adhyaya 4.2)). Verse numbers are for the purpose of discussion. The phrases placed by me in bold font are derived from RV 1.99. Note that the bold font for all select verses or phrases within the quoted Sanskrit hymns have been placed there by me for emphasis, and are not part of the original text.

7. The formats of these translations follow their sources (in this case Coburn 1984, 264–67). However, for emphasis, I have added bold font for the translated portions of the RV 1.99 verse as I did in the Sanskrit version.

8. Coburn's translation of Subharaḥ deviates from the Sanskrit of the original verse, which is Saubharaḥ. Some scholars regard Kuśika and Saubhara as separate names (e.g., Muir 1873, 425). Others regard it as referring to the hymn's composer, Kuśika Saubhara, or to Rātrī Bhāradvājī, the daughter of Bharadvāja (e.g., Müller 1892, 412; U. C. Sharma 1975, 19–20). Lubin (2020, 42) and Yokochi (1999b, 73) identify that line as a sort of Vedic-styled *anukramaṇī*, which provides information on the deity=Night, sages=Kuśika-Saurabha and Bhāradvājin, meter=Gāyatrī, and so on.

9. In the Āndhra and Dravida recensions, they take the masculine forms Durgi, Kātyāyana, and Kanyākumāri (Yokochi 2004, 17n36). Müller (1892, 412) notes that one of the commentators on this explains that the rendering of Durgā as Durgi is due to *liṅga-vyatyaya* ("sign transposition") where, since all the preceding deities are masculine, Durgā in the list following Rudra, Vināyaka, Nandi, Kārtikeya, and so on, must also be masculine.

10. The *Mahānārayaṇa Upaniṣad* is a later composition that constitutes Chapter 10 of the TA and circulates independently.

11. Muir (1873, 426n213) presents the entirety of Sāyaṇa's interpretation of the Durgā-gāyatrī and translation. Sāyaṇa succinctly states: *durgiḥ durgā* (i.e., Durgi is Durgā). When Durgī is modified to Durgā, that Gāyatrī *mantra* and variant forms are known as the Durgā-gāyatrī or Durgā-sāvitrī and are in use ritually to the present day in such rites as the Durgā Pūjā.

12. Hindu girls are still sometimes named Durgī, and there is a town in Andhra Pradesh not far from Nagarjunikonda named Durgi, known for its stone carving.

13. A full translation of BGŚS 3.3, taken from Harting 1922, is found in the Appendix of Lubin 2020.

14. Coburn (1984, 118n109) ruminates on which of the two texts that go by the name of the *Mahā-Nārāyaṇa Upaniṣad* Farquhar is dating. One belongs to the TA of the *Black Yajur Veda*, and the other is edited by a certain Colonel G. A. Jacob (1888) and associated with the AV. Since Banerjea (1956, 577) notes that Jacob's edition contains "virtually all of the TA material and some additional mantras," Coburn sees Jacob's edition as a later version of the Upaniṣad, and thus takes Farquhar's appraisal as a reasonable date for the TA passage on Durgā, regardless of which manuscript Farquhar was dating. Varenne (1960) presents a critical edition and translation of the *Mahā-Nārāyaṇa Upaniṣad* into French, placing the composition date at about the 3rd to 4th century BCE.

15. The other two parts of the *Nirukta* are the Naigama Kaṇḍa or Aikapadika Kaṇḍa, dealing with particularly difficult Vedic word forms, and the Daivata Kaṇḍa, which is concerned with deities classified according to the earthly, atmospheric, or heavenly regions.

16. Macdonell's translation is based on the B recension of the BṛDe, which is about a sixth longer than the A recension, which he judged as derivative from the B recension.

17. I have used Bühler's translation here, because it preserves "the Durgā," while placing Sāvitrī in parentheses, whereas Olivelle omits the mention of Durgā entirely and renders it as "Sāvitrī verse" (2000, 335).

18. Other texts noted in the *Dharmaśāstra-Saṃgraha*, vol. 1 (Upadhyaya (ed.) 1982), include the Laghu-Atri-Saṃhitā 3:3.17ff, which mentions the *durgāsāvitri* and the Vṛddha-Atri-Saṃhitā 3.39.9ff, where we find *durgāsāvitryā* (Kajihara 2019, 25, n.81).

19. Kajihara 2019, 25n82 lists some written variations in the commentaries, such as *durgāsāvitrī* as one word, or as *durgāḥ sāvitrī*, two words, that are explained separately.

20. For instance, the Durgā Gāyatrī variant sometimes used in the litany of the Bengali Durgā Pūjā may be this:

> *Om mahādevyai vidmahe /*
> *durgāyai devyai dhīmahi / tan no devī pracodayāt //*
> Om! Let us make the Great Goddess the aim of our knowledge,
> let us contemplate Durgā; may the Goddess impel us to that end.
> (Rodrigues 2003, 154)

21. This would be consistent with later Tantric notions of seed syllables embodying a deity, and goddesses being referred to as *mantras* or *vidyās*.

Chapter 2

1. These names for the hymns are not used rigorously by worshippers or in textual references. For instance, Durgā Stuti is frequently used to refer to either of the two hymns, although the Durgā Stotra calls itself by that name.

2. According to Coburn (1984, 267), the DStv+ is placed in Appendix I, No. 4 of the Virāṭa Parvan of the critical edition. There are seven versions of the hymn, five in one manuscript, and one in two others. They mainly derive from Devanāgarī manuscripts, with one Telugu version. They are surprisingly not found in the Bengali manuscripts, which frequently overlap with the Devanāgarī. Much of this points to a robust northwest Indian tradition of Durgā worship, but not unequivocally to its regional provenance, because of the Telugu version.

3. Unlike the DStv+, the DSto+ is found in more manuscript traditions, and is placed in the critical edition's Appendix I, No. 1 of the Bhīṣma Parvan. According to Coburn (1984, 272), both the Devanāgarī and Bengali traditions have versions, which are replicated in the Kaśmīrī manuscripts. It is more consistent in form and length than versions of the DStv+.

4. Coburn (1991, 99–117) provides the most detailed discussion on them, noting their presence in the countless versions of the DM that circulate for ritual use.

5. In contemporary contexts, Samuel Taylor Coleridge's *The Rime of the Ancient Mariner* (1798) offers a classic example, where a frame tale depicts an old sailor recounting his wretched maritime adventure to a reluctant wedding guest. The story returns to the frame, showing the guest's benefit from hearing it. Coleridge revised the poem extensively over the years (Stillinger 1992).

6. *kālīṃ raktāsyanayanāṃ raktamālyānulepanām /*
   raktāmbaradharām ekāṃ pāśahastāṃ śikhaṇḍinīṃ //
   dadṛśuḥ kālarātriṃ te smayamānām avasthitām /
   narāśvakuñjarān pāśair baddhvā ghoraiḥ pratasthuṣīm /
   harantīm vividhān pretān pāśabaddhān vimūrdhajān // (Mbh 10.8.64–66)

7. *tataḥ sumbhanisumbhau ca dānavau nagacārtiṇau /*
   tau ca kṛtvā manasi māṃ sānugau nāśayiṣyasi // (HV 47.49)

8. Yokochi (2004, 84) makes it clear that the original names for the demons were Sumbha and Nisumbha and not Śumbha and Niśumbha, which was a later development. The original names not only occur in HV 47.49, but in old manuscripts of the *Skanda Purāṇa* as well as the oldest dated manuscript of the DM, dated Nepal Saṃvat 220 (i.e., 1109 CE).

9. See, for instance, Solomon 1970, 37–38.

10. *saṃdhyā rātriḥ prabhā nidrā kālarātris tathaiva ca //* (HV 47.54)

11. For instance, Hein (1986, 296) concurs with Vaidya (1969, 1. xxxix), editor of the critical edition of the HV, who offers the date of 300 CE for the bulk of the text. J. Fitzgerald (2010, 91–92) places the HV's development within 150 and 350 CE. Sarkar (2017, 111n30) cites communication with John Brockington, who would date the HV between the 1st and 3rd centuries CE, and even into the 4th century.

12. The DStv is found in seven rather different versions in length within manuscripts consulted for the critical edition of the Mbh. These are mostly all in Devanāgarī manuscripts, but one version in Telugu (Coburn 1984, 267). By contrast, the DSto is fairly consistent (with some variant readings) and found in the Bengalī, Devanāgarī, and Kaśmirī manuscripts (Coburn 1984, 272).

13. See Yokochi 2004, 92–93n13; Sarkar 2017.

14. This is in Appendix I No. 4 of the critical edition, in version G, line 21 (see Yokochi 2004, 93n29).

15. See, for instance, Shalom 2017, especially chapter 2.

16. More than half the manuscripts add additional verses after this hymn. In the critical edition they are placed in Appendix I, No. 8. because they are not found in the southernmost manuscripts. According to Coburn (1984, 278, n. 60), the manuscript tradition here is complicated, including verses that are partially or wholly repeated as part of the meshing process. Some manuscripts simply begin a new chapter (*adhyāya*), framing the second stratum with the phrase, "*Vaiśampāyana uvāca*," indicating that he, not Viṣṇu, takes over the narration to recite the Āryā Stava ("Eulogy to Āryā"), who is called the goddess Nārāyaṇī, queen of the three worlds (Coburn 1984, 278, n. 60).

17. It is found within four inserted chapters (*adhyāya*), regarded as an expansion (*upabṛṃhaṇa*) of an episode in the HV, and placed in Appendix I, No. 30 of the critical edition. It is present in all the manuscripts except the Malayālam, Newārī, and Śāradā versions, which are the primary ones used to prepare the critical edition (Coburn 1984, 281–82).

18. The hymn is missing from the Malayālam and Newārī manuscripts — important sources for the critical edition — as well as from other versions. It is present in the Śāradā manuscript. It is placed in Appendix I 35 of the critical edition. It is typically inserted after *adhyāya* 108 in most manuscripts, but in one instance it is inserted after *adhyāya* 109. According to Coburn (1984, 284n68) there is no obvious pattern to determine the geographical source of this passage.

19. e.g., D. Srinivasan 1997; Schmid 2002; and Sarkar 2017, chapter 1, 41–69.

20. A discussion of the parallel developments in iconography of the earliest Vaiṣṇava images and those of the goddess slaying a buffalo are found in Schmid (2002, 2011).

Chapter 3

1. Since the Śuṅga dynasty was relatively short-lived and its political domain likely did not cover the expanse of the provenance of the full assortment and range of these images, terms such as "Early-Historic" or "post-Mauryan" have been suggested in lieu of their designation as Śuṅga terracottas (Ahuja 2005, 353n2).

2. Harle (1986) assigned the figure to the 1st century CE, while Asher and Spink (1989, 5–6) situate it in the Kuṣāṇa period. P. Chandra (1985, 49) dates it at the 3rd century BCE, and D. Srinivasan (2005, 360) places it in the Mauryan period.

3. Bautze (1995, 13) refers to illustrations of hairpins made of copper and bone from the period in Marshall (1916, Pl. XXIV, a and c) and Asthana (1985, nos. 91–92). The hairpin head in the shape of the inverted comb (Asthana 1985, no. 91) resembles the item frequently (mis?)-identified as a trident in the Chandraketugarh images.

4. See http://www.metmuseum.org/collection/the-collection-online/search/38518.

5. Haque (2001, 130–56) lists and illustrates several plaques or fragments from Chandraketugarh depicting such a female (e.g., Pl. B90, B93, B96, B99, C89, C91, C95, C97, C98, C101-109, C111). Although most depict her alone, there are several that situate her with attendants, and other features, such as a peacock-topped pillar (e.g., Haque 2001, 143, Pl. C89).

6. For example, see Haque (2001 240, Pl. C369; 241, Pl. C375; 242, Pl. C393; 244, Pl. C424; 246, Pl. C452, etc.).

7. Most notably, Haque Pl. C89 (2001, 143), which depicts a tall, elaborate pillar topped with a peacock, next to the goddess, and Haque Pl. C91and C97 (2001, 144), which also depict the peacock; Pl. C101 (2001, 145) depicts her with a parrot, Pl. C103 depicts her with a crane, Pl. C102 shows her with a cat (or tiger/lion cub), and Pl. C104 shows her with a fawn.

8. More recently, they have designated the image as Lakṣmī, because of its boon-granting feature.

9. I have taken the Sanskrit version of this segment of Durgā Stava from the Vulgate version of the Virāṭa Parvan based on John Smith's revision of Prof. Muneo Tokunaga's

version of the text derived from the Bhandarkar Oriental Research Institute (BORI) in Pune, and found at https://bombay.indology.info/mahabharata/apps/UR/Supp04.txt. It follows the critical edition's line numbering convention (as opposed to numbering verses) used for the Appendices. The bold font is mine, placed for emphasis to draw attention to certain phrases in the subsequent discussion.

10. Coburn (1984, 269) translates this line as, "Shining with a garment of snakes' hoods, with row(s) of threads."

11. Coburn (1984, 269) translates this as, "With your serpentine bond you shine here like Mount Mandara (itself)."

12. Derived from *The Harivaṃśa, Being a Khila or Supplement to the Mahābhārata*, critically edited by Parashuram Lakshman Vaidya, 2 vols. (Poona: Bhandarkar Oriental Research Institute, 1969–71).

13. Yokochi (2004, 96) places the HV roughly at the 4th century and the SP at the 6th or 7th century, and so is working with relatively narrow time frame in her analysis, which ignores the weapon hairpin goddess entirely.

14. Yokochi (2004, 19) points to this possibility, but is not able to develop it within her study. However, she also points to the possibility of Indian appropriation of foreign iconographic influences, such as the goddess Cybele, whose chariot is drawn by lions (2004, 117n98).

15. I had a hurried and obscured glimpse of the image along with the crush of pilgrims vying for *darśana* of the goddess around the time of the autumn Navarātra in 1990.

16. See Sengupta et al. (2007, 95) for an example (Accession Number 98.87). They note that such figures have been found in other sites, such as Vaiśālī, Kauśāmbī, and Tamluk. Other examples (C343, C344, C350–C353) are found in Haque (2001, 238, 239). There are many more images of male figures (*yakṣa*) with wings.

17. For this and details on the Kośī's proclivity for flooding, see Das (1982, 50–78).

18. Colebrooke (1858, 271), citing from the *Jātimālā* (Garland of Castes), apparently an extract from the *Rudra Yāmala Tantra*, notes the mention of Śumbhadeśa as a place. A. K. Choudhuri (1960, 19, 20, 28, 58–59, 62) notes that according to the Buddhist Saṃyutta Nikāya and Telapatta Jātaka (96), the Buddha visited Desaka in Sumbha, which he surmises is the eastern part of the Burdwan District (near Mongalkote, Bengal).

19. See http://www.devarshi.faithweb.com/catalog_2.html (website run by Devarshi Roy Choudhury, whose family lays claim to one of the earliest iterations of the Durgā Pūjā — see volume 2 of this study).

20. Its first successful ascent occurred in 1955 CE, two years after Everest was climbed by Edmund Hillary and Tenzing Norgay.

21. Enhanced satellite images of the flood zone in 2008, despite all the contemporary flood mitigation infrastructure, such as embankments, levees, and so on, are visible here: https://earthobservatory.nasa.gov/images/9075/floods-cover-bihar-india.

22. *Aṅgavijjā*, chaps. 51, 58; cited in Joshi, (1976, 61), and *Mānava Gṛhya Sūtra* 2.13–15, cited in Rana (1995, 18) (as per White 2003, 284n83, 84).

23. Boyce et al. (1989, updated 2011). Qaderi (2018, 172–73) lists some other translations for Arədvī offered by scholars, including "flow" and "She who Succeeds," while Anāhitā can mean "holy and infallible."

24. Verse references to Yašt 5 come from James Darmesteter's (1883, 52–84) translation of the *Zend Avesta* (SBE, Vol. XXIII).

25. These details derive from Boyce (1982, 60–61).

26. It must be recited only when water is in sight and is never recited before a fire or in a fire temple (Boyce 1982, 61).

27. See Rezakhani (2017, 79–80).

28. See Qaderi (2018, 188–89n115, 116).

29. For instance, Shepherd (1980).

Chapter 4

1. See Cunningham (1877, 117–18), which also includes translations by Princep and Wilson.

2. Beckwith (2015) offers intriguing arguments that the pillar and other inscriptions may not derive solely from Aśoka, but from his Mauryan predecessors, and that a few, such as at Lumbini, might even be inscriptions from as late as the Kuṣāṇa period. Even so, the thrust of my position is not affected.

3. Although lions and tigers are no longer among sacrificial animals, if they ever were despite being mentioned in the KālP, a visit to certain goddess temples today, such as the Dakshinkali (Dakṣiṇa-Kālī) Temple, near Pharping, Nepal, which I first visited in 1991 and again in 2017, provides a vivid example the goddess surrounded by cocks and goats awaiting sacrifice.

4. In the DM, she does grab the demon Mahiṣa by the neck, at which point he transforms into a lion, a human, and an elephant. Even so, Mahiṣa is a single shapeshifter, and we do not have accounts of her subduing two felines simultaneously.

5. See https://collections.louvre.fr/en/ark:/53355/cl010007467.

6. Another classification scheme is found in Mitterwallner (1976), and further discussions are found in D. Srinivasan (1997, 287–90) and Yokochi (2004, 131–32).

7. Numbers 875, 889, 993, 2037, and 2784 are six-armed. The Indian Museum also has a six-armed Mathurā specimen (No. 8622). And Harle (1969, fig. 1) mentions and displays a photograph of one from the Ashmolean Museum (O.S. 37).

8. Also see Banerjea (1956, 172, 498, Pl. xli, fig. 4).

9. On these images, see V. S. Agrawala (1958).

10. See V. S. Agrawala (1949), cited in R. C. Agrawala (1958, 123n1).

11. This image is no longer at the museum at Āmber, but I was able to track it down with the assistance of Dr. Hridesh Kumar Sharma, the Director of the Archaeology and Museum Department for the Government of Rajasthan. It is in storage at the Hawamahal, and I was granted permission to photograph it by Miss Sarojini Chanchlani, the Superintendent of the Hawamahal.

12. Yokochi (2004, 131) notes the existence of a hybrid type between the Kuṣāṇa and Gupta types, found is places such as Ellora, Elephanta, Aihole and Alampur, and belonging to the 6th to 7th centuries.

13. Most notably, in the famous seal (National Museum, New Delhi: DK 5175/143) renowned as the "proto-Śiva," the figure appears with an elaborate buffalo-horn headdress, and is surrounded by a wild buffalo, rhinoceros, tiger, and elephant. Interestingly, the elephant, tiger(?) and buffalo are also depicted on the planoconvex tablet, as is the Indian crocodile or gharial. An extensive speculative analysis of possible relationships between the Goddess and the buffalo evoked by this seal is found in Hiltebeitel (1978).

14. Tauroctony is distinguished from taurobolium, which, at least initially, referred to the hunting of a bull, but which later was associated with a sacrificial rite. Clauss (2000, 79) notes that the Mithras tauroctonies most likely were derived from those of Nike.

15. See Ionescu (2018, 164–66) for a discussion on these theories.

16. Sarkar (2017, 28–29) suggests the probability that Mithras images may have been synthesized into the Kuṣāṇa buffalo-subduing goddess imagery, due to the Kuṣāṇa's familiarity with Mithras and various other parallel iconographic attributes, which had been previously observed by D. Srinivasan (1997, 299).

17. On the myth of the Uniquely-Created Bull, see Boyce (1975, 130–46).

18. On these depictions, see Yokochi (2004) and Mitterwallner (1976).

19. On some scientific studies on the provenance of lions in South Asia, see Policardi (2024, 177–78, esp. n1).

20. The royal motif of a throne decorated similarly with lions is evident millennia later in an image from Māṭ of a Kuṣāṇa ruler, likely Vima Taktu, on display at the Government Museum in Mathurā, and dated to the early 2nd c. CE (see illustration in DeCaroli 2015, 100).

21. See the seal at https://isac-idb.uchicago.edu/id/90eec75d-0343-4a85-8810-ad0cd-cc2a081. University of Chicago, Mesopotamian Gallery, Registration Number A27903, Accession Number 2953.

22. This association between supreme deities and multiple appendages is explored in D. Srinivasan (1997).

23. This is later than that suggested by Malinar (2007, 242–71), who for other compelling reasons places it between the 2nd century BCE and the 1st century CE.

24. Schmid (2011, 121–22) notes how early Vaiṣṇava images depict Kṛṣṇa battling the horse Keśin in a manner paralleling the buffalo-crushing goddess imagery, evoking the Vedic *aśvamedha* rite in which the horse is suffocated prior to being dismembered.

Chapter 5

1. Williams (1982, 117–22) dates the Śiva temple where it is found at 520 CE to 530 CE.

2. See R. C. Agrawala (1958, 128) and Seshadri (1963, 7) for a detailed description. The panel is depicted and discussed in Banerji (1924, pl. XIV, figs. B, C), G. H. Khare (1939, fig. 72), Iyer (1969, fig. 1), Barrett (1975–1976, No. (j)), Yokochi (1999b, A1 No. 2 in Catalogue), Stietencron (2005, 140), and Kramrisch (2013, pl. XXII, fig. 64).

3. I visited the site and photographed the relevant images in 2017.

4. The number assigned to the cave in older studies is not consistent. Banerjea (1956, 72, 498) refers to it as the Candragupta II cave. Viennot (1956, 368–74) refers to it as cave VII. Both R. C. Agrawala (1958, 123) and Harle (1974, Pl. 17) refer to it as Cave VI.

5. Mitterwallner (1976, 199–207) also discusses the three Udayagiri images, with illustrations as Figs. 4–6.

6. As an aside, the Indra Jatra in Nepal begins with Yosin Thanegu, the erection of a tall pole (c. 15 meters), made from a pine tree, from which a long banner of Indra is unfurled. The festival reputedly began in the 10th century. What is evident is that the simile of the goddess's upraised arms like Indra's banner evokes that the arms are raised high.

7. Schmid (2011, 127, 128) notes Granoff's early recognition of the self-coronation motif, and aligns with the symbolism of a blood-soaked garland.

8. See http://www.metmuseum.org/collection/the-collection-online/search/38924.

Chapter 6

1. A Japanese scholar, Watanabe Kaigyoku, incorrectly indicated that the laud in Yijing's translation was taken from a Mbh hymn, although he did not make clear whether it was the DSto or the DStv. Ludvik (2004, 710–11) explored the possibilities in detail and concluded that he quite likely had the DStv in mind. This is almost certainly the case because we have already noted the many similarities between the DStv and the Āryā Stava, but even more so between the DStv and the PN-s1. If our suggested early date for the DStv (or variant) is correct, this would lend some credence to Ludvik's suggestion of the rather early 1st century date for the Āryā Stava (or variant).

2. An excellent recent study of these goddesses through a focussed examination of a Nepalese *Pañcarakṣā* manuscript is found in Kim (2010).

3. The notion of deified mantric verses parallels the cluster of Hindu goddesses known as the Daśamahāvidyās, some of whom, such as Kālī or Tārā, may be regarded as the ruler of the group (see Kinsley 1997, especially, pages 57–60). From the earliest *mantras* to the DM, Durgā has been closely connected to refuge and protection through the recitation of empowering verses.

4. See Kim (2013) for a discussion of the relief.

5. It also parallels the notion of the removal of all great faults only on the mention of the names of the five daughters (*pañca-kanyā*), namely, Āhalyā, Draupadī, Kuntī, Tārā, and Mandodarī (D. C. Bhattacharyya 1972, 90).

6. I visited this monastery in 2011, during travels in China.

7. The ancient Chinese dictionary *Erya* (j. 4, p. 40, *Sibu beiyao*-edition, reprint by Zhonghua shuju, 1989) designates the term *wangmu* as one's father's mother, or a venerable lady, and the commentary explains that she is to be honored like a king (*wang*) (cited in Seiwert, 2003, 31n18). The term could evoke her boon-granting qualities, typically associated with one's female ancestors.

Chapter 7

1. The *mardinī* variant is found in one manuscript (Bisschop 2018, 71n22b)

2. Rajendralala Mitra edition, Vol. 2 (Chapters 115–268) (1876, 214).

3. Rajendralala Mitra edition, Vol. 3 (Chapters 269–382) (1879, 133). In the vocative case, *mahāmahiṣasuramardinī* becomes *mahāmahiṣāsuramardini* (with a short i).

4. For example,

> *kauśikī siṃhamārūḍhā pārvatyāḥ paramā sutā/*
> *viṣṇornidrāmahāmāyā mahāmahiṣamardinī* // 7.2,31.89 (*Śiva-Purāṇa*, Book 7, Veṅkateśvara Steam Press (c. 1920, 584a)).

5. For example, *aparājitā bahubhujā pragalbhā siṃhavāhinī /*

> *śumbhādidaityahantrī ca mahāmahiṣamardinī* // 1,70.339 (*Liṅga Purāṇa*, Part I, Adhyāyas 1–108, Veṅkateśvara Steam Press (1906)).

6. *veṅkaṭī nāma tatraiva devī mahiṣamardinī /*
candratīrthaṃ bhadravaṭaḥ kāverīkuṭilācalau // 2,6.68 (*Garuḍa Purāṇa*, Veṅkateśvara Steam Press Edition, available at https://gretil.sub.uni-goettingen.de/gretil/corpustei/ transformations/html/sa_garuDapurANa.htm).

7. *jaya mahiṣavimardini śūlakare jaya lokasamastakapāpahare /*
jaya devi pitāmaharāmanate jaya bhāskaraśakraśiro 'vanate // 97.105 (Revakhaṇḍa of the *Vāyu Purāṇa*, Śrīkr̥ṣṇadās, Kṣemrāj (ed.): Śrīskandamahāpurāṇam. Veṅkateśvara Steam Press, Bombay: 1910 and its reprint: Siṃha, Nāgaśaraṇa (ed.): Śrīskandamahāpurāṇam. pañcama bhāga: śrī āvantyakhaṇḍam. Nag Publishers, 1986, available at https://gretil.sub.uni-goettingen.de/gretil/corpustei/transformations/html/ sa_revAkhANDa-of-the-vAyupurANa-rkv.htm).

8. *trinetrā varadā devī mahiṣāsuramardinī /*
   śivārcanaratā durgā sā me pāpaṃ vyapohatu // 1,82.108 (*Liṅga Purāṇa*, Part I,
   Adhyāyas 1–108, Veṅkateśvara Steam Press, Bombay, 1906)

9. The standard translation by J. F. Fleet for the entire inscription is found in Salomon,
   (1998, 201). The inscription reads:

   > *unnidrasya saroruhasya sakalām ākṣipya śobhāṃ rucā*
   > *sāvajñaṃ mahiṣāsurasya śirasi nyastaḥ kvaṇannūpuraḥ/*
   > *devyā vaḥ sthirabhaktivādasadṛśīṃ yuñjan phalenārthitāṃ*
   > *diśyād acchanakhāṃśujālajaṭilaḥ pādaḥ padaṃ saṃpadāṃ//*

10. This text is also discussed by Coburn (1984, 96–99) and in detail by Sarkar (2013) and
    Yokochi (2004, 143–46).

11. The Sanskrit verse reads:

    > *sadyaḥ sādhitasādhyam uddhṛtavatī śūlaṃ śivā pātu vaḥ*
    > *pādaprāntaviṣakta eva mahiṣākāre suradveṣiṇi*
    > *diṣṭyā deva vṛṣadhvajo yadi bhavān eṣā 'pi naḥ svāminī*
    > *saṃjātā mahiṣadhvajeti jayayā kelāu kṛte 'rdhasmitā*

12. The Sanskrit verse reads:

    > *huṃkāre nyakkṛtodanvati mahati jite śiñjitair nūpurasya*
    > *śliṣyacchṛṅgakṣate 'pi kṣaradasṛji nijālaktakabhrāntibhāji /*
    > *skandhe vindhyādribuddhyā nikaṣati mahiṣasyāhito 'sun ahārṣīd*
    > *ajñānād eva yasyāś caraṇa iti śivaṃ sā śivā vaḥ karotu //*

13. The Sanskrit verse reads:

    > *mā bhāṅkṣīr vibhramaṃ bhrūr adhara vidhuratā keyam āsyā 'sya*
    > *rāgaṃ*
    > *pāṇe prāṇy eva nā 'yaṃ kalayasi kalahaśraddhayā kiṃ triśūlam /*
    > *ity udyatkopaketūn prakṛtim avayavān prāpayantyeva devyā*
    > *nyasto vo mūrdhni muṣyān marudasuhṛdasūn saṃharann aṅghrir*
    > *aṃhaḥ //*

14. Yokochi (2004, 16) points out that during Bāna's time the epithet Durgā did not stand
    out among the other epithets, such as Caṇḍī (or Caṇḍikā), which may have been the
    most popular.

15. Coburn (1984, 108–9n68) considers Kālī to be a proper name, elaborated upon in the
    DM with the Devī being called by the names Kālarātri ("the night of destruction") and
    Mahārātri ("the great night"). See Coburn (1984, 111–12) for a translation of the original
    Sanskrit of Mbh 10.8.64–67, 69, presented in note 83.

16. See discussion of this work in Yokochi (2004, 146–51) and Sarkar (2017), throughout.

17. For instance, Shimkhada and Herman (2008, 151–52), and McDermott (2001, 5).

18. Chapter 2 (e.g., A. Bandopadhyaya, 2004, 496–500) and translated by Sarkar (2013,
    433–34) and Avalon and Avalon (1913, 88–93).

19. Yokochi (2004, 19, 116n92) notes that she uses the term Mahiṣāsuramardinī descriptively and retroactively from other sources, more for convenience rather than as an actual name.

20. Sarkar (2017, 97–114) dedicates all of Chapter 3 to discussing Durgā's surpassing of Skanda's feat. I concur with most of her arguments but offer an alternative rationale in the final chapter.

21. This has been highlighted by Coburn (1984, 221–30), and again by D. Srinivasan (1997), and Söhnen-Thieme (2002).

Chapter 8

1. The DM appears as Chapters (*adhyāya*) 76–88 of the critical edition of the MārkP, but as *adhyāya* 78–90 or 81–93 of other editions (see Wadekar 2011, 42).

2. The Harikṛṣṇaśarma edition translated by Coburn (1991) has 579 verses.

3. See Wadekar (2011, 42).

4. Balkaran argues for a "ring composition" for the text, where the end is anticipated in the beginning of the frame narrative (2018, 22). There are many other structural features that he sees within the text, such as a "double-helix" that brings together two seeming opposed strands of worldly (*pravṛtti*) and other-worldly (*nivṛtti*) choices central to Hindu values.

5. I have followed Coburn (1991) in allocating verse numbers to the DM. Coburn has followed the version edited by Harikṛṣṇa Śarma, published by Veṅkateśvara Press, and republished by Buṭālā and Co. In citing the Sanskrit of the DM verses, I have used the critical edition published as Vol. II of *The Mārkaṇḍeya Purāṇa*, (Adhyāyas 76-88) edited by M. L. Wadekar (2011). The critical edition of the MārkP is based on 24 manuscripts, but the DM volume is based on 50 manuscripts selected from a total of 100 that were considered. The northern versions that comprise it are as follows: two Śāradā (Ś), three Nevārī (Ñ), five Maithilī (V), six Bengali (B), two Uḍiyā (U), and seventeen Devanāgarī (D). The southern versions are: four Telugu (T), four Grantha (G), and seven Malayālam (M). The chapter (*adhyāya*) numbers of the DM in the critical edition (76-88) of the MārkP vary from those in other popular versions.

6. On this point, see Balkaran (2018).

7. Sarkar (2018a) compares the DM's treatment of the concept of *māyā* with other philosophical traditions.

8. In his discussion of the *Dhyānabindu Upaniṣad*, T. R. Ayyangar (1938, 151) notes that in Nāda Yoga, the semi-circle represents the *nāda* or nasalized vibratory hum at the end of certain seed syllables (*bīja mantra*) and is identified with the *ardhamātra*. It fades into the point of no sound, which is known as the *bindu* (drop), which is represented by the dot above the semi-circle. In Vedantic interpretations, the *ardhamātra* is equated with the *a-mātra*, or silence, and represents Absolute Reality without attributes (Nirguṇa

Brahman). Alternately, in certain yogic and Tantric systems, the *ardhamātra* corresponds to the highest Reality, but is Nāda Brahman, and is full of sound (Beck 1993, 89–90).

9. Viṣṇu, who is not named explicitly, is merely evoked through epithets (i.e., Garuḍa-banner, slayer of Madhu, discus-holder).

10. The concept of *tejas* is explored in greater detail in Whitaker (2002) and Magnone (2009).

11. Considering the evident antiquity of the *Rāmāyaṇa*, there are no references here to Rāma or to any features of the *Rāmāyaṇa* epic, even though Kṛṣṇa as an *avatāra* of Viṣṇu is mentioned.

12. Stietencron (2005, 121–30) appraises various Purāṇic variations on the Mahiṣa's relationship to the Devī. I touch on these within my discussions of each of some Purāṇas later in this study.

13. This issue arises in the old *Skanda Purāṇa* (SP), which was likely composed before the DM, and will be taken up again in our examination of that Purāṇa.

14. Van Buitenen's (1981, 99) translation of that section runs as follows:

> My material nature [i.e., Prakṛti] is eightfold, comprising the order
> of the earth, water, fire, wind, ether, mind, spirit, and ego. This is my
> lower nature, but know that I have another, higher nature which com-
> prises the order of souls; it is by the latter that this world is sustained,
> strong-armed prince. Realize that all creatures have their source
> therein: I am the origin of this entire universe and its dissolution.
> There is nothing that transcends me, Dhanaṃjaya [i.e., Arjuna]: all
> this is strung on me as strands of pearls are strung on a string.

15. For a discussion on sexual fluids in early Hinduism, see Doniger (1980), especially Chapter II.

16. Translation provided at a later point in the discussion.

17. [ ] indicates unreadable portions of the inscription.

18. In Tantric texts, the *dūtī* refers to the female ritual partner, and sometimes used synonymously with the term *śakti* (see Törzsök 2014).

19. Some enduring examples of Tantric metaphysics in her worship in Banāras are discussed in volume 2.

Chapter 9

1. Hawley (1981, 157–62) explores other symbolic dimensions of this battle through Kṛṣṇa's persona as the god of love.

2. This date has also been proposed by other recent scholars, such as Sarkar (2017) and Yokochi (2004).

3. See Pahari et al. (2022).

4. L. Chandra (1988, 18–23) surveys the origin of the name Avalokiteśvara, with earlier variants such as Avalokita-svara and Avalokita. The Chinese Kuan-shih-yin ("He who listens to the cries of the world") was the Chinese *bhakti*-oriented adaptation, popularized by Kumārajīva in the *Lotus Sūtra* in 406 CE. L. Chandra (1988, 31) points to how Avalokiteśvara's thousand arms are reminiscent of the Cosmic Puruṣa in the RV, who serves as a prototype for the thousand-armed and thousand-eyed Viṣṇu in his *viśvarūpa* form, as well as the thousand-eyed Indra and Śiva. Kuan-yin/Avalokiteśvara became an ideal deity within which other deities were assimilated, including goddesses such as Cundā/Cundī and Tārā (L. Chandra 1988, 42–43).

5. The incorporation of Buddhist goddesses into Kuan-yin/Avalokiteśvara contributed to the feminine form becoming dominant in China (L. Chandra 1988, 47).

6. See Shaw (2006, 38–61) for a discussion of Māyadevī, and on *yakṣiṇīs* in Buddhism (2006, 62–93).

7. We also know that certain male Buddhist manifestations and bodhisattvas were derived from — or at least in tandem with — feminine Hindu deities in the first place, as in the case of Mahāmāyurī, discussed earlier and below. The precise period of the emergence of Avalokiteśvara within Buddhism in India is still debated by scholars. There is some evidence that he was worshipped as early as the 2nd century CE, but it is only by the 5th century CE that his cult begins to grow prominent. He seems to have become an independent deity with attendant female figures such as Tārā and Bhṛkuṭī by the mid-6th century (Yü 2001, 9–11). Regardless of whether salvific goddesses such as Durgā were being absorbed into the Buddhist pantheon or vice versa, mutual influences are indisputable. It is possible that Śatākṣī is a feminine correlate of a compassionate figure such as Avalokiteśvara, whose persona was influential in the centuries prior to the composition of the DM.

8. Kim (2013) speculates that this may represent the inscription or recitation of a ritual text to that Buddhist goddess.

9. Consider the term *caṇḍāla*, cognate with *caṇḍa* (fierce), used to refer to marginalized social groups.

10. I viewed a standing Kuṣmaṇḍinī Yakṣī image at Sravanabelagola in 1991.

11. See also Sarkar (2017, 141) who cites references by Falk (2003) to Mbh 3.80.100–2 and 14.8.

Chapter 10

1. I viewed this image in 1991 and again in 2017. See Tartakov and Dehejia (1984, 323–24, 341, 343) and Seshadri (1963) for a discussion of this image.

2. She is sometimes identified as Kṣemaṅkarī, a benign form of Durgā.

3. It is still used today, but only opened briefly for worship for about fifteen minutes daily, when I was able to photograph it in 2018, although I had seen it on several occasions in the previous decades.

4. More recent studies on self-sacrifice imagery are Storm (2014), which examines hero stones from Mallam, Andhra Pradesh, depicting self-decapitation, and Storm (2018), which examines self-decapitation imagery at Nalgonda. While such self-immolation in Mallam was sometimes to Śiva Bhairava, they were more often to some fierce goddess (e.g., Bhaṭārī), who is eventually subsumed into the persona of Durgā. The Nalgonda hero stones likely derived from Vīraśaiva members eager for close communion with Śiva.

5. A study of the origins of Koṟṟavai is found in R. Mahalakshmi (2011), which points to the goddess's progressive assimilation with or to the great goddess of the *purāṇic* traditions (i.e., Durgā) from the 3rd century CE.

6. See J. N. Tiwari (1985, 229) citing *Tolkāppiyam*, Puṟattiṇai Iyal 59.

7. See Mahalakshmi (2011, 68–71).

8. See Mahalakshmi (2011, 69).

9. The line numbers of Parthasarathy's translation cited above vary from many standard presentations of the *Cilappadikāram*, because he draws them from commentaries. Canto XII, l. 60–74 reads:

> *kariyiṉ urivai pōrt taṉaṅ kākiya*
> *ariyiṉ urivai mēkalai yāṭṭi*
> *cilampuṅ kaḻalum pulampuñ cīṟaṭi*
> *valampaṭu koṟṟattu vāyvāṭ koṟṟavai*
> *iraṇṭuvē ṟuruvil tiraṇṭatōḷ avuṇaṉ* (65)
>
> *talaimicai niṉṟa taiyal palartoḻum*
> *amari kumari kavuri camari*
> *cūli nīli mālavaṟ kiḷaṅkiḷai*
> *aiyai ceyyavaḷ veyyavāḷ taṭakkaip*
> *pāykalaip pāvai paintoṭip pāvai* (70)
> *āykalaip pāvai aruṅkalap pāvai*
> *tamartoḻa vanta kumarik kōlattu*
> *amariḷaṅ kumariyum aruḷiṉaḷ*
> *variyuṟu ceykai vāyntatā leṉavē;*
> *uraippāṭṭumaṭai.*

10. See Shimkhada and Herman (2008, 151–52) and McDermott (2001, 5), who point to the softening of Kālī's wrathful temperament and the benign and beautified depictions she currently has in Bengal compared to the hideous and martial depictions of yore.

11. On Kubjikā and her erotic persona, and a myth concerning her bent over persona, see Dyczkowski (1995–96, esp. 127).

12. See Schaflechner (2018) and the earlier discussion on Hinglaj Devī.

13. *kotaṃ kuṭilasvabhāvam rākṣasāsurādikam rīṇati hanti (iti koṭavī)* (cited in J. N. Tiwari 1985, 228).

14. *koṭaṃ durgaṃ durayatīti) durgā/ iti dharaṇī* (*Śabdakalpadruma* 1967, II, 201).

15. A theoretical discussion of this process with some examples from Nepal, Bali, and elsewhere, is found in Gupta and Gombrich (1986). Chakrabarti (2001, 165–233) blends ethnography and textual examples from Bengali *purāṇas* to illustrate how local "non-Sanskritic" goddesses are adopted and absorbed into the Brahminic pantheon, often through the overarching figure of Durgā.

16. Several examples of this process of local and tribal deities in Odisha being assimilated to Durgā are found in Mallebrein (1999), and many of her subsequent publications. See also Schnepel's (1995) discussion of this process in the south Odishan kingdom of Jeypore. The tensions and alliances between the king and Indigenous people (*ādivāsi*) in the celebrations of Dasara in the Odishan state of Bonai, where local goddess traditions are assimilated with Durgā are examined in Skoda (2021).

17. Yokochi (2004, 152n98) cites Eschmann (1978), who discusses this process through the amalgamation of an image, typically Durgā, with the local aboriginal goddess that is undergoing what Yokochi (2004, 6) designates as "Hinduization" at the temple level. Similar processes also occur at the royal level, which is primarily characterized by its acceptance or encouragement of animal sacrifice, while the Brahminical, temple level style abjures it.

Chapter 12

1. Stietencron (2005, 124–30) discusses the erotic appeal of the goddess Durgā and the complexities of the sexual tensions with Mahiṣa.

2. Mitterwallner (1976, 208) refers to a similar small image in Cave 15, a Śaiva temple although popularly known as Daśāvatāra Cave, which contains an inscription by Dantidurga, Kṛṣṇarāja's predecessor. This may be earlier than the Kailāsanātha image. Dantidurga's inscription was likely made late in his rule and typically dated to circa 750 CE (G. Malandra 1993, 9; Owen 2012, 132). This would move the proposed approximation for the *terminus a quo* of the DM to about 750 CE.

3. The lion-drawn chariot is typically associated with the goddess Kybele.

4. Some exceptions include Stietencron (2005, 124–30) and Kinsley (1989, 20).

5. Notably absent in this list is Cāmuṇḍā, who appears as the seventh in what becomes the well-known Saptamātṛ group that emerges as early as the fifth century (Hatley 2012, 102). The name Cāmuṇḍā is used interchangeably with Caṇḍikā and Carcikā (or Carcā) in the *Brahmayāmala* (c. 7th–8th century CE) (Hatley 2007, 376).

Chapter 13

1. In alignment with this perspective, see Dehejia (1991; 1998) and DeCaroli (2015, 28).

2. I encountered these tales during travels in 1990 and 1991 to Śravaṇabeḷagoḷa, the Jain site in the state of Karnataka renowned for its colossal statue of the Jain saint Gōmmateśvara (also known as Bāhubali), where a nearby cave is reputed to be where Candragupta meditated and eventually performed *sallekhanā*.

3. On the history of Greek art, see Robertson (1991).

4. The tensions between iconism and aniconism in the pre- and post-Mauryan periods is discussed in detail in DeCaroli (2015).

5. A more contemporary portrayal of this motif is in Jacques-Louis David's painting of Napolean Bonaparte's self-coronation on display at the Louvre.

6. See volume 2.

Bibliography

Primary Sources and Translations Used

The Ābān Yašt

The Zend-Avesta, Part II: The Sīrōzahs, Yasts, and Nyāyis. 1883. Translated by James Darmesteter. Sacred Books of the East, Vol. XXIII. Clarendon Press.

The *Abhinaya Darpana*

The Mirror of Gesture: Being the Abhinaya Darpaṇa of Nandikeśvara. 1917. Translated by Ananda Comaraswamy and Gopala Kristnayya Duggirala. Harvard University Press.

The *Agni Purāṇa*

The Agni Purāṇa. 1870–1879. Edited by Rajendralala Mitra. 3 vols. Biblioteca Indica 65. Asiatic Society of Bengal.

The *Amarakośa*

Amarakośa: Maheśvara Yaṃcyā Ṭīkesaha. 1990. Varadā Buks.

Amara's Nāmalingānuśāsanam (Text). 1940. Critically Edited by N. G. Sardesai and D. G. Padhye. Oriental Book Agency.

The *Anabasis*

Arrian. 1884. *The Anabasis of Alexander; or The History of the Wars and Conquests of Alexander the Great.* Translated by E. J. Chinnock. Hodder and Stoughton.

Arrian. 2013. *Alexander the Great: The Anabasis and the Indica.* Translated by Martin Hammond. Oxford University Press.

The *Atharva Veda* (AV)

[Atharvavedasaṃhitā] = *Atharva Veda Sanhita* (Text). 1856. Edited by von R. Roth and W. D. Whitney. Dümmler,.

Atharva-veda Saṁhitā: Translated with a Critical and Exegetical Commentary by William Dwight Whitney. Revised and Brought Nearer to Completion and Edited by Charles Rockwell Lanman. 1905. 2 vols. Harvard University.

Bloomfield, Maurice, trans. *Hymns of the Atharva Veda*. 1897. Sacred Books of the East, Vol. 42. Clarendon Press.

The *Baudhāyana Gṛhyaśeṣasūtra*

Harting, P. N. U. 1922. *Selections from the Baudhāyana-Gṛhyapariśiṣṭasūtra*. J. Valkhoff.

The *Bhagavata Purāṇa*

Srimadbhagavatam. 1896. Edited and translated by M. N. Dutt. Manmatha Nath Dutt.

The *Brahmavaivarta Purāṇa*

Brahma-vaivarta-purāṇa. 1960. Ānandāśrama Sanskrit Series.

Brahma-Vaivarta Puranam. 1920, 1922. Translated by Rajendra Nath Sen. 2 parts. Sudhindra Nath Vasu.

The *Bṛhad Devatā* (BṛDe)

The Bṛhad-Devatā attributed to Śaunaka: A Summary of the Deities and Myths of the Rig-Veda. 1904. Edited and translated by Arthur Anthony MacDonell. 2 vols. HOS v. 5 and 6. Harvard University.

The *Bṛhad Tantrasāra*

Agamavagisha, Krishnanda (Bhaṭṭācārya, Kṛṣṇānanda). 1996. *Brihat Tantrasara*. Edited by Srirasikamohana Cattopadhyaya. Navabharata Publishers.

The *Caṇḍīśataka*

Mayūra. 1917. *The Sanskrit Poems of Mayūra: Introduction together with the text and translation of Bāṇa's* Caṇḍīśataka *[sic] by George Payn Quackenbos*. Translated by George Payn Quackenbos. Indo-Iranian Series, Vol. 9. Edited by A. V. Williams Jackson. Columbia University Press.

The Cilappatikāram

Shilappadikaram (The Ankle Bracelet) by Ilangō Adigal. 1965. Translated by Alain Daniélou. New Directions.

The Cilappatikāram of Iḷaṅkō Aṭikaḷ: An Epic of South India. 1993. Translated by R. Parthasarathy. Columbia University Press.

Cilappatikāram: Text, Transliteration and Translations in English Prose and Verse. 2021. Compiled and edited by K. Chellappan. Translated by R. Parthasarathy et al. Central Institute of Classical Tamil.

The Daśakumāracarita

Daśakumāracarita of Daṇḍin. 1986. Translated by M. R. Kale. Motilal Banarisdass.

De antro nympharum

On the Cave of the Nymphs in the Thirteenth Book of the Odyssey: From the Greek of Prophyry. 1917. Translated by Thomas Taylor. John M. Watkins.

The *Devī Bhāgavata Purāṇa*

Srimad Devi Bhagavatam. 1922. Translated by Swami Vijnanananda. Sacred Books of the Hindus XXVI. Sudhindra Nath Vasu.

The Devī Māhātmya (aka *Durgā Saptaśatī*) (DM)

Śrīdurgāsaptaśatī: With Hindi Commentary. 1983. Edited by Satyavrat Singh. Institute for Pauranic and Vedic Studies and Research.

Durgāsaptaśatī saptaṭīkāsaṃvalitā. [The Durgā-Saptaśati with Seven Commentaries]. 1984. Edited by Harikṛṣṇa Śarma. Butala and Company.

Coburn, Thomas B. 1991. *Encountering the Goddess: A Translation of the Devī-Māhātmya and A Study of Its Interpretation.* State University of New York Press.

The Critical Edition of the Mārkaṇḍeyapurāṇam (Devīmāhātmyam) (Adhyāyas 76–88). 2011. Critically Edited by Prof. M. L. Wadekar. Vol. II. Oriental Institute.

The *Devī Purāṇa* (DevīP)

Devī Purāṇam. 1976. First Critical Devanāgari Edition. Edited by Puspendra Kumar Sharmā. Śrī Lāl Bahādura Śāstrī Kendrīya Saṃskṛta Vidyāpīṭham.

The *Dhammapada*

The Dhammapada: The Buddha's Path of Wisdom. 1985. Translated by Acharya Buddharakkhita. Buddhist Publication Society.

The *Garuḍa Purāṇa*

Garuḍapurāṇa. n.d. Veṅkateśvara Steam Press (or a reprint thereof). Göttingen Register of Electronic Texts in Indian Languages (GRETIL). Input by members of SANSKNET-project, 2020.

The *Gauḍavaho*

Gauḍavaho: A Historical Poem in Prākṛit by Vākpati. 1887. Edited by S. Pandurang Pandit. Bombay Sanskrit Series 34. Government Central Book Depot.

The *Geographica*

Strabo. 1917–1932. *The Geography of Strabo.* 8 vols. Translated by Horace Leonard Jones. William Heinemann.

The *Haracaritacintāmaṇi*

Jayadratha. 1983. *Rājānakaśrī Jayarathaviracito Haracaritacintāmaṇiḥ* [The Haracharitacintāmaṇī by Rājānaka Jayaratha]. Edited by Śivadatta and Kāśīnāth Paṇḍurang Parab. Kāvyamālā 61. Bharatiya Vidya Prakashan.

The *Haravijaya*

Haravijaya by Ratnākara. 1982. Edited by Pandit Durgaprasad and Kashinath Pandurang Parah, with Commentary of Rājānaka Alaka, Kāvyamālā 22. Nirṇaya Sāgara Press.

The *Harivaṃśa* (HV)

A Prose English Translation of Harivamsha. 1897. Manmatha Nath Dutt. Elysium Press.

Vaidya, P. L., ed. 1969–1971. *The Harivamśa, Being the Khila or supplement to the Mahābhārata.* 2 vols. Critical Edition. Bhandarkar Oriental Research Institute.

The *Harṣacarita by Bāṇa*

Harṣa-Carita of Bāṇabhaṭṭa with the Commentary of Raṅganātha. 1958. Edited and published by Śūranāḍ Kuñjan Pillai.

The *Harshacharita of Bāṇabhaṭṭa.* 1973. Edited by P. V. Kane. Motilal Banarsidass.

The *Histories* of Herotodus

Herodotus. 2013. *The Histories.* Translated by A. D. Godley. In *Delphi Complete Works of Herodotus (Illustrated).* Delphi Classics.

The *Hitopadeśa*

The Hitopadeśa, by Nārāyaṇa. 2006. Translated by A. N. D. Haskar. Penguin Books.

The *Jñāneśvarī*

The Jnāneshvari (Bhāvārthadipikā). 1987. Translated from the Marāthi by V. G. Pradhān. Edited and with an introduction by H. M. Lambert. Vol. 1. State University of New York Press.

The Kādambarī by Bāṇa

Bāṇa, *Kādambarī*. 1883. Edited by Peter Peterson. Government Central Book Depot.

The Kādambarī of Bāṇa. 1896. Translated with occasional omissions by C. M. Ridding. Royal Asiatic Society.

Bāna's Kādambarī (Pūrvabhāga Complete). 1928. Translated by M. R. Kale. Motilal Banarsidass.

Bāṇabhaṭṭa, *Kādambarī: A Classic Sanskrit Story of Magical Transformations*. 1991. Translated with an introduction by Gwendolyn Layne. Garland Publications.

The *Kālikā Purāṇa* (KālP)

Kālikā-purāṇa. 1891. Veṅkateśvara Steam Press.

Worship of the Goddess According to the Kālikāpurāṇa. 1972. Translated by K. R. Van Kooij. E. J. Brill.

The *Kālikāpurāṇa*. 1991. Translated by Biswanarayan Shastri. 3 vols. Nag Publishers.

The *Kathāsaritsāgara*

The Kathāsaritsāgara of Somadevabhatta. 1930. Edited by Pandit Durgāprasad and Āśīnāth Pāndurang Parab. 4th ed. Pāndurang Jāwajī.

The *Kulacūḍāmaṇi Tantra*

Kulacūḍāmaṇi Tantra. 1915. Edited by Girīśa Candra Vedāntatīrtha. Tantrik Texts. Vol 4. Sanskrit Press Depository.

The Kulacūḍāmaṇi Tantra and Vāmakeśvara Tantra with the Jayaratha Commentary. 1986. Introduced, translated, and annotated by L. M. Finn. Otto Harrassowitz.

The *Kuṟuntokai*

Kuṟuntokai: An Anthology of Classical Tamil Poetry. 2007. Translated by A. Dakshinamurthy. Vetrichelvi Publishers.

The *Liṅga Purāṇa*

Liṅga Purāṇa. 1885. Edited by J. V. Bhattacharya. J. V. Bhattacharya.

The Liṅga Purāṇa. 1906. Veṅkateśvara Steam Press. Göttingen Register of Electronic Texts in Indian Languages (GRETIL). Revised by Oliver Hellwig according to the ed. Calcutta, 1960 (Gurumandal Series No. XV), Input by members of SANSKNET-project.

The Liṅga Purāṇa. 1973. Translated by a Board of Scholars. 2 parts. Motilal Banarsidass.

The *Mahābhārata* (Mbh)

The Mahābhārata. 1973–1978. Translated and edited by J. A. B van Buitenen. University of Chicago Press.

———. *Mahābhārata, Volume 2: Book 2: The Book of Assembly; Book 3: The Book of the Forest.* 1975. University of Chicago Press.

———. *Mahābhārata, Volume 3: Book 4: The Book of Virāṭa; Book 5: The Book of the Effort.* 1978. University of Chicago Press.

Mahābhārata, Book 4, Virāṭa. 2006. Translated by Kathleen Garbutt. New York University Press.

Mahabharata. 2015. Adapted and edited by David R. Slavitt. Northwestern University Press.

The *Mālatī-mādhava*

Bhavabhūti's Mālatīmādhava: With *the Commentary of Jagaddhara.* 1928. Edited with a literal English translation, notes, and introduction by M. R. Kale. Messrs Gopal Narayen & Co.

The Mālatīmādhava *of Mahākavi Bhavabhuti with the Chandrakalā.* 1954. Edited by Śrī Śesarāja Śarmā Śāstrī. Chowkhamba Sanskrit Series.

The *Mānavadharmaśāstra*

The Laws of Manu. 1886. Translated with extracts from seven commentaries by G. Bühler. Clarendon Press.

Mānava Dharma-Śāstra: The Code of Manu. Original Sanskrit Text. 1887. Edited by J. Jolly. Trubner & Co.

The *Maṇimēkalai*

Kūlavāṇikaṉ Cīttalaic Cāttaṉ. 2021. *Maṇimēkalai: Text, Transliteration, Translations in English Verse and Prose.* Translated by Prema Nandakumar et al. Central Institute of Classical Tamil.

The *Mārkaṇḍeya Purāṇa* (MārkP)

The Mārkaṇḍeya Purāṇa. 1904. Translated by F. E. Pargiter. The Asiatic Society.

Mārkaṇḍeya Purāṇa. 2011. Edited by M. L. Wadekar. 2 vols. Critical Edition. Oriental Institute.

The *Metamorphoses of Ovid*

Ovid. 2001. *The Metamorphoses*. Translated by Horace Gregory. Penguin Books.

The *Nighaṇṭu* and the *Nirukta*

The Nighaṇṭu and the Nirukta. 1920. Translated by Lakshman Sarup. 3 vols. Reprinted by Motilal Banarsidass, 1967.

The *Padma Purāṇa*

The Padma-Purāṇa, Part II. 1989. Translated and annotated by N. A. Deshpande. Motilal Banarsidass.

The *Periplus Maris Erythraei*

Schoff, W. H., trans. & ed. 1912. *The Periplus of the Erythraean Sea: Travel and Trade in the Indian Ocean by a Merchant of the First Century.*

Casson, Lionel. 2012. *The Periplus Maris Erythraei: Text with Introduction, Translation, and Commentary.* Princeton University Press.

Plutarch's *Lives*

Lives. 1860. Translated by A. H. Clough. 5 vols. John D. Morris & Company.

Lives. 1954. Translated by Bernadotte Perrin. Harvard University Press.

Selected Lives: The Lives of the Noble Grecians and Romans. 1998. Translated by Thomas North, Introduction by J. Mossman. Wordsworth Classics of World Literature. Wordsworth Editions.

The *Ṛg Veda* (RG)

Rig-Veda-Sanhitā, The Sacred Hymns of the Brahmans; Together with the Commentary of Sayanacharya. 1849–1874. Edited by by F. Max Müller. 6 vols. W. H. Allen and Co..

Griffith, Ralph T. H., trans. 1889–1891. *The Hymns of the Rigveda*. E. J. Lazarus and Co. Reprinted by Motilal Banarsidass, 1995.

Der Rig-Veda. 1951–1957. Übers von Karl Friedrich Geldner. 4 vols. Harvard University Press.

Rig Veda, A Metrically Restored Text with an Introduction and Notes. 1994. Edited by Barend A. van Nooten and Gary B. Holland. Harvard University Press.

The Rigveda: The Earliest Religious Poetry of India. 2014. Edited and translated by Stephanie W. Jamison and Joel P. Brereton. 3 vols. Oxford University Press.

The *Ṛg Veda Khila*

Die Apokryphen des Ṛgveda (Khilāni). 1906. Herausgegeben und bearbeitet von J. Scheftelowitz. M. und H. Marcus. Indische Forschungen, herausgegeben von Alfred Hillebrandt, I. Heft.

The *Śabdakalpadruma*

Śabdakalpadrumaḥ. 1819–1858. Edited by Raja Radha Kanta Deva. 5 vols. The Chowkhamba Sanskrit Series Office. Reprinted 1967.

The *Śatapatha Brāhmaṇa*

The Śatapatha-Brāhmaṇa, in the Mādhyandina-śākhā with extracts from the commentaries of Śāyaṇa, Harisvāmin, and Dvivedaganga. 1855. Edited by Albrecht Weber. Ferd. Dümmler's Verlagsbuchhandlung.

The Śatapatha-Brāhmaṇa, according to the text of the Mādhyandina School. 1882–1900. Translated by Julius Eggeling. 5 vols. Sacred Books of the East 12, 26, 41, 43, 44. Clarendon Press.

The *Śiva Purāṇa*

Śiva-Purāṇa. 1920. Veṅkateśvara Steam Press. Göttingen Register of Electronic Texts in Indian Languages (GRETIL). Input by Jun Takashima, 2001.

The *Skanda Purāṇa* (SP) (the oldest)

The *Skandapurāṇa.*Volume I. *Adhyāyas* 1–25. 1998. Critically edited with prolegomena and English synopsis by R. Adriaensen, H. T. Bakker, and H. Isaacson. Egbert Forstein, Supplement to Groningen Oriental Studies. Brill.

———. Volume IIa. *Adhyāyas* 26–31.14: The Vārāṇasī Cycle. 2005. Critical edition with an introduction, English synopsis and philological and historical commentary by Hans T. Bakker and Harunaga Isaacson. Supplement to Groningen Oriental Studies. Brill.

———. Volume IIb. *Adhyāyas* 31–52; The Vāhana and Naraka Cycles. 2014. Critically edited with an introduction and English synopsis by Hans T. Bakker, Peter C. Bisschop, Yuko Yokochi, in cooperation with Nina Mirnig and Judit Törzsök. Brill.

———. Volume III. *Adhyāyas* 34.1–61, 53–69: The Vindhyavāsinī Cycle. 2013. Critically edited with introduction and English synopsis by Yuko Yokochi. Supplement to Groningen Oriental Studies. Brill.

(SPBh) *Skandapurāṇasya Ambikākhaṇahḍaḥ.* 1988. Saṃpādakaḥ: Kṛṣṇaprasāda Bhaṭṭarāī. Mahendraratnagranthamālā 2. Mahendrasaṃskṛtaviśvavidyālaya.

The Newer *Skanda Purāṇa* (SkP)

The *Kāśī Khaṇḍa* of the *Skanda Purāṇa.* 1961. No. 20, vol. 4. Gurumandala Granthamalaya.

The *Suvarṇabhāsa Sūtra*

Suvarṇaprabhāsottamasūtra: Das Goldglanz-Sūtra, ein Sanskrittext des Mahāyāna-Buddhismus: I-tsing's chinesische Version und ihre Übersetzung. 1958. German translation by Johannes Nobel. E. J. Brill

Emmerick, R. E. 1996. *The Sūtra of Golden Light: A Translation of the Suvarṇabhāsottamasūtra.* 3rd revised ed. Pali Text Society.

The *Taittirīya Brāhmaṇa* (TB)

Taittirīya Brāhmaṇa: kṛṣṇayajurvedīyam taittirīyabrāhmaṇam śrīmatsāyaṇācāryaviracitabhāṣyasametam. 1898. Edited by Nārāyaṇa śāstri. 3 vols. Ānandāśrama Sanskrit granthāvali 37. Āpte.

The *Tantrasāra* of Kṛṣṇānanda Āgamavāgiśa

Kṛṣṇānanda, Āgamavāgiśa. *Bṛhat Tantrasāra.* 1996. Edited by Srirasikamohana Cattopadhyaya. Navabharat Publishers.

Kṛṣṇānanda Bhaṭṭācārya, *Tantrasāra.* 2004 [Bengali Year 1413]. Edited by Aśokakumār Bandopadhyaya. 9th ed.

The *Tolkāppiyam*

Tolkāppiyam: Poruḷatikāram, Purattiṇal Iyal, with Naccinārkkiṉiyar's Commentary. 1963. The South India Saiva Siddhanta Works Publishing Company.

Tolkāppiyam in English. 2000. Translated by V. Murugan. Institute of Asian Studies.

The *Vājasaneyi Saṃhitā*

The Vājasaneyi-sanhitā. In the Mādhyandina and the Kānva-śākhā with the Commentary of Mahidhara. 1852. Edited by Albrecht Weber. Ferd. Dümmler's Verlagsbuchhandlung.

The *Vāmana Purāṇa* (VāmP)

The Vāmana Purāṇa. 1968. Text Critically Edited by Anand Swarup Gupta and Others. All-India Kashiraj Trust.

The Vāmana Purāṇa (with English translation). 1968. Edited by Anand Swarup Gupta. Translated By A. Bhattacharya, N. C. Nth. V. K. Verma. All-India Kashiraj Trust.

The *Varāha Purāṇa* (VarP)

The Varāha-purāṇa (with English Translation). 1981. Edited by Anand Swarup Gupta. Critical edition. 2 vols. Translated by Ahibhushan Bhattacharya. All India Kashiraj Trust.

The *Vāyu Purāṇa*

Revakhanda of the *Vāyu Purāṇā*. 1910. Edited by Kṣemrāj Śrīkṛṣṇadās. Śrīskandamahāpurāṇam. Veṅkateśvara Steam Press. Reprinted 1986, edited by Nāgaśaraṇa Siṃha, Śrīskandamahāpurāṇam, Nag Publishers. https://gretil. sub.uni-goettingen.de/gretil/corpustei/transformations/html/sa_revAkhAN-Da-of-the-vAyupurANa-rkv.htm.

The Vāyu Purāṇa. 1960. Translated and Annotated by G. V. Tagare. Parts I and II. Motilal Banarsidass.

The *Wuyue Chunqiu*

Jianjun He, trans. 2021. *Spring and Autumn Annals of Wu and Yue: An Annotated Translation of Wu Yue Chunqiu*. Cornell University Press.

The *Xunzi*

Xunzi. 2014. *Xunzi: The Complete Text*. Translated by Eric. L. Hutton. Princeton University Press.

The *Yajur Veda*

See *The Vājasaneyi Saṃhitā*.

The *Yaśastilaka*

The Yaśastilaka of Somadeva Sūri, with the Commentary of Śrutadeva Sūri. 1916. Edited by Mahāmahopādhyāya Paṇḍit Śivadatta and Vāsudeva Laxmaṇ Śāstrī Paṇaśikar. Tukārām Jāvajī.

Handiqui, Krishna Kanta. 1968. *Yaśastilaka and Indian Culture*. Jaina Saṃskṛti Saṃrakshaka Sangha.

The *Zhuangzi*

Zhuangzi. 2020. *Zhuangzi: The Complete Writings*. Translated, introduction, and notes by Brook Ziporyn. Hackett Publishing Company.

Secondary Sources

Agrawala, R. C. 1958. "The Goddess Mahiṣāsuramardinī in Early Indian Art." *Artibus Asiae* 21 (2): 123–30.

———. 1966. "A Rare Mahiṣamardinī Relief in the National Museum, New Delhi." *East and West* 16 (1/2): 109–11.

———. 1968. "Śriṅgāra Durgā in Early Indian Sculpture." *Journal of the Bihar Research Society* 54: 199–201, plus plates.

Agrawala, V. S. 1947–1948. "Terracotta Figurines of Ahichchhatrā, District Bareilly, U.P." *Ancient India (Bulletin of the Archaeological Survey of India)* 4: 104–79.

———. 1949. "Catalogue of the Brahmanical Images." *Journal of the U. P. Historical Society, Old Series.* Vol. XXII: 102-210.

———. 1958. *Ancient India, Bulletin of the Archaeological Survey of India.* Vol. 4. Archeological Survey of India.

———. 1964a. "The Devī-Māhātmya." *Journal of Indian History* 42: 823–32.

———. 1964b. *Prācīna Bhāratiya Lokadharma* (in Hindi). Pṛthivī Prakāśana.

———. 1970. *Ancient Indian Folk Cults.* Prithivi Prakashan.

Ahmadi, Amir. 2015. *The Daēva Cult in the Gāthās: An Ideological Archaeology of Zoroastrianism.* Routledge.

Ahuja, Naman P. 2000. "Early Indian Moulded Terracotta: The Emergence of An Iconography and Variations in Style, circa Second Century BC to First Century AD." PhD diss., School of Oriental and African Studies, University of London.

———. 2005. "Changing Gods, Enduring Rituals: Observations on Early Indian Religion as seen through Terracotta Imagery c. 200 BC–AD 200." In *South Asian Archaeology 2001*, Vol. II, edited by C. Jarrige and V. Lefèvre.

Aiyappan, A. 1931. "Myth of the Origin of Smallpox." *Folklore* 42 (3): 291–93.

Ambos, C. 2003. "Nanaja — eine ikonographische Studie zur Darstellung einer altorientalischen Göttin in hellenistisch-parthischer Zeit." *Zeitschrift für Assyriologie* 93/2: 231–72.

Antonini, Chiara Silvi. 2005. "Considerations on the Image of Mahiṣāsuramardinī of Tapa Sardār." *East and West* 55 (1/4): 313–28.

Asatrian, Garnik and Victoria Arakelova. 2003. "Malak Tāwūs: The Peacock Angel of the Yezidis." *Iran & the Caucasus* 7 (1/2): 1–36.

Asthana, Shashi. 1985. "Archaeology [comprising "Indian Terracottas" and "Taxila Remains"]." In *Masterpieces from the National Museum Collection*, edited by S. P. Gupta. National Museum.

Asher, F., and W. Spink. 1989. "Maurya Figural Sculpture Reconsidered." *Ars Orientalis* 19: 1–25.

Atherton, Cynthia Packert. 1995. "The Harṣat Mātā Temple at Ābānerī." *Artibus Asiae* 55 (3/4): 201–236.

Avalon, Arthur and Ellen Avalon. 1913. *Hymns to the Goddess: Translated from the Sanskrit.* Luzac & Co.

Avari, Burjor. 2016. *India: The Ancient Past: A History of the Indian Subcontinent from c. 7000 BCE to 1200 CE.* 2nd ed. Routledge.

Avril, Ellen B., and Nora Ling-yün Shih. 1997. *Chinese Art in the Cincinnati Art Museum.* The Art Museum.

Bagchi, Prabodh Chandra. 2011. *India and China: Interactions Through Buddhism and Diplomacy.* Anthem Press.

Bajpai, K. D. 1981. "Source-Material for Indian Art-History." In *Cultural Contours of India: Dr. Satya Prakash Felicitation Volume*, edited by V. J. Srivastava. Abhinav Publications.

Bakker, Hans. 2014. *The World of the Skandapurāṇa*. Brill.

Bakker, Hans Teye. 2019. *Holy Ground: Where Art and Text Meet: Studies in the Cultural History of India*. Brill.

Balasubramanyam, S. R. 1961. "Labelled Sculptures of the Western Tower of Chidambaram Temple." *Lalitkala* 9: 27–29.

Balkaran, Raj. 2018. *The Goddess and the King in Indian Myth: Ring Composition, Royal Power and The Dharmic Double Helix*. Routledge.

———. 2020. *The Goddess and the Sun in Indian Myth: Power, Preservation and Mirrored Māhātmyas in The Mārkaṇḍeya Purāṇa*. Routledge.

Bandopadhyaya, Aśokakumār. See *The Tantrasāra of Kṛṣṇānanda Bhaṭṭācārya*.

Banerjea, Jitendra Nath. 1956 [1974]. *The Development of Hindu Iconography*. University of Calcutta.

———. 1966. *Paurāṇic and Tāntric Religion: Early Phase*. University of Calcutta.

Banerji, R. D. 1924. *The Siva Temple at Bhumara*. Memoirs of the Archeological Survey of India 16.

———. 1933. *Eastern Indian School of Medieval Sculpture*. Archaeological Survey of India.

Barrett, Douglas. 1960. *Mukhalingeswara Temple*. Bhulabhai Desai Memorial Institute Publication.

———. 1975–1976. "A Terracotta Plaque of Mahiṣāsuramardinī." *Orientalis Asia* 21: 64–67.

Basham, A. L. 1959. *The Wonder That Was India*. Grove Press.

Bautze, Joachim Karl. 1995. *Early Indian Terracottas*. Brill.

Beal, Samuel, trans. 1885. *Si-Yu-Ki: Buddhist Records of the Western World*. J. R. Osgood.

———. 1911. *The Life of Hiuen-Tsang by the Shaman Hwui Li*. Kegan Paul, Trench, Trübner.

Beck, Guy. 1993. *Sonic Theology: Hinduism and Sacred Sound*. University of South Carolina Press.

Beck, Roger. 1998. "The Mysteries of Mithras: A New Account of the Their Genesis." *The Journal of Roman Studies* 88: 115–28.

Beckwith, Christopher I. 2015. *Greek Buddha: Pyrrho's Encounter with Early Buddhism in Central Asia*. Princeton University Press.

Bhagvat, Durga. 1968. "Tribal Gods and Festivals in Central India." *Asian Folklore Studies* 27 (2): 27–106.

Bhandarkar, R. G. 1883. "The Rāshṭrakūṭa King Kṛishṇarāja I and Elāpura." *Indian Antiquary* 12: 228–30.

Bhattacharji, Sukumari. 1980. "A Survey of Sataka Poetry." In *Indian Literature* 23 (5, Facets of Poetry): 12–40.

Bhattacharyya, Ashim. 2006. *Hindu Dharma: Introduction to Scriptures and Theology*. iUniverse, Inc.

Bhattacharyya, B. 1958. *The Indian Buddhist Iconography: Mainly Based on the Sādhanamālā and Cognate Tantric Text of Rituals*. Firma K. L. Mukhopadhyay.

Bhattacharyya, D. C. 1972. "The Five Protective Goddesses of Buddhism." In *Aspects of Indian Art: Papers Presented in a Symposium at the Los Angeles*, edited by Pratapaditya Pal. Brill Archive.

Bhattacharya, J. V. See The *Liṅga Purāṇa*.

Birrell, Anne, trans.. 1999. *The Classic of Mountains and Seas*. Penguin.

Bisschop, Peter. 2010a. "Once Again on the Identity of Caṇḍeśvara in Early Śaivism: A Rare Caṇḍeśvara in the British Museum?" *Indo-Iranian Journal* 53: 233–49.

______. 2010b. "Śaivism in the Gupta-Vākāṭaka Age." *Journal of the Royal Asiatic Society*, Third Series, 20 (4): 477–88.

______. 2018. *Universal Śaivism: The Appeasement of all Gods and Powers in the Śantyadhyāya of the Śivadharmaśāstra*. Brill Open.

Black, Jeremy A., and Anthony Green. 1992. *Gods, Demons, and Symbols of Ancient Mesopotamia: An Illustrated Dictionary*. British Museum Press.

Blankinship, Khalid Yahya. 1994. *The End of the Jihad State: The Reign of Hisham Ibn ʿAbd al-Malik and the Collapse of the Umayyads*. State University of New York Press.

Bloomfield, Maurice. See The *Atharva Veda*.

Boal, Barbara M. 1997. *Human Sacrifice and Religious Change: The Khonds*. Inter-India Publications.

Bolle, Kees W. 1983. "A World of Sacrifice." *History of Religions* 23 (1): 37–63.

Boner, Alice. 1962. *Principles of Composition in Hindu Sculpture — Cave Temple Period*. E. J. Brill.

Bonazzoli, Giorgio. 1993. "Introducing Śivadharma and Śivadharmottara." *Altorientalische Forschungen* 20 (2): 342–49.

Boyce, Mary. 1975. *A History of Zoroastrianism: The Early Period*. Vol. 1. E. J. Brill.

______. 1979. *Zoroastrians: Their Religious Beliefs and Practices*. Routledge and Kegan Paul.

______. 1982. "Ābān Yašt." *Encyclopedia Iranica* I/1: 60–61.

Boyce, Mary, M. L. Chaumont, and C. Bier. 1989, updated 2011. "ANĀHĪD." In *Encyclopædia Iranica* I/9: 1003–11.

Briant, Pierre. 2002. *From Cyrus to Alexander: A History of the Persian Empire*. Translated by Peter T. Daniels. Eisenbrauns.

Brighenti, Francesco. 2016. "A 'Sulfurous' *Śakti*: The Worship of Goddess Hiṅgulā in Baluchistan." In *Soulless Matter, Seats of Energy: Metals, Gems and Minerals in South Asian Traditions*, edited by F. M. Ferrari and T. W. P. Dähnhardt. Equinox Publishers.

Brinkman, J. A. 1991. "Babylonia in the Shadow of Assyria (747–626 B.C.)." In *The Cambridge Ancient History, Volume III, Part 2: The Assyrian and Babylonian Empires and Other States of the Near East, from the Eighth to the Sixth Centuries B.C.*, edited by John Boardman. Cambridge University Press.

Brosius, Maria. 2021. *A History of Ancient Persia: The Achaemenid Empire.* John Wiley & Sons, Inc.

Bryan, Betsy M. 2005. "The Temple of Mut: New Evidence on Hatshepsut's Building Activity." In *Hatshepsut: From Queen to Pharaoh*, edited by Catharine H. Roehrig, Renée Dreyfus, and Cathleen A. Keller. Yale University Press.

Buddharakkhita, Acharya. See The *Dhammapada.*

Bühler, G., trans. 1882. *The Sacred Laws of the Āryas as Taught in the Schools of Āpastamba, Gautama, Vāsishtha, and Baudhāyana. Part 2, Vasishtha and Baudhāyana.* Clarendon Press.

Cahill, Suzanne Elizabeth. 1993. *Transcendence & Divine Passion: The Queen Mother of the West in Medieval China.* Stanford University Press.

Canepa, Matthew P. 2009. *Two Eyes of the Earth: Art and Ritual of Kingship between Rome and Sasanian Iran.* University of California Press.

Carlleyle, A. C. 1885. *Archaeological Survey of India, Report of Tours in Ghorakpur, Saran, and Ghazipur in 1877–78–79 and 80.* Vol. XXII. Office of the Superintendent of Government Printing.

Carter, Martha L. 1979. "An Indo-Iranian Silver Rhyton in the Cleveland Museum." *Artibus Asiae* 41 (4): 309–25.

Carter, John Ross, and Mahinda Palihawadana. 2000. *Dhammapada.* Oxford University Press.

Casson, Lionel. See The *Periplus Maris Erythraei.*

Castleden, Rodney. 2005. *Mycenaeans.* Routledge.

Cattopadhyaya, Cattopadhyaya. See The *Tantrasāra of Kṛṣṇānanda Āgamavāgiśa.*

Chakrabarti, Kunal. 2001. *Religious Process: The Purāṇas and the Making of a Regional Tradition.* Oxford University Press.

Chakravarti, Chintaharan. 1965. "Purana Tradition in Bengal." *Purana* 7: 160–65.

Chandra, Lokesh. 1988. *The Thousand-Armed Avalokiteśvara.* Abhinav Publications, Indira Gandhi National Centre for the Arts.

Chandra, P. 1985. *The Sculpture of India. 3000 B.C.–1300 A.D.* National Gallery of Art.

Chandra, Rai Govind. 2014. *Indo-Greek Jewellery.* Abhinav Publications.

Chattopadhyaya, Brajadulal. 2006. *Studying Early India: Archaeology, Texts and Historical Issues.* Anthem Press.

Chaumont, M. L. 1958. "Le Culte D'Anāhitā à Staxr et les premiers Sassanides." *Revue de l'histoire des religions* 153: 154–75.

Choudhuri, Aswini Kumar. 1960. *Sibi King Vessantara: His Country and Cultural Heritage.* The Little Flower Press.

Chowdhury, Sima Ray. 2002. "Style and Chronology: Problems in Evolving a Temporal Framework for the Early Historical Terracottas from Bengal." In

Archaeology of Eastern India: New Perspectives, edited by Gautam Sengupta and Sheena Panja. Centre for Archaeological Studies and Training.

Clauss, Manfred. 2000. *The Roman Cult of Mithras: The God and his Mysteries*. Translated by Richard Gordon. Edinburgh University Press.

Cline, Eric H., and Mark W. Graham. 2011. *Ancient Empires: From Mesopotamia to the Rise of Islam*. Cambridge University Press.

Clothey, Fred. 2005. *The Many Faces of Murukan*. Munshiram Manoharlal Publishers.

Coburn, Thomas B. 1984. *Devī-Māhātmya: The Crystallization of the Goddess Tradition*. Motilal Banarsidass and South Asia Books.

———. See *The Devī Māhātmya*.

Codrington, K. de B. 1926. *Ancient India to the Guptas*. Ernest Benn.

Colebrooke, H. T. 1858. *Essays on the Religion and Philosophy of the Hindus*. Williams and Norgate.

Collins, Andrew W. 2012. "The Royal Costume and Insignia of Alexander the Great." *The American Journal of Philology* 133 (3): 371–402.

Coningham, R. A. E., K. P. Acharya, K. M. Struckland, C. E. Davis, M. J. Manuel, I. A. Simpson, K. Gilliland, J. Tremblay, T. C. Kinnaird, and D. C. W. Sanderson. 2013. "The Earliest Buddhist Shrine: Excavating the Birthplace of the Buddha, Lumbini (Nepal)." *Antiquity* 87: 1104–23.

Coomaraswamy, Ananda, and Gopala Kristnayya Duggirala, trans. 1917. *The Mirror of Gesture: Being the Abhinaya Darpaṇa of Nandikeśvara*. Harvard University Press.

Corpus Inscriptionum Indicarum (CII), *Inscriptions of the Early Gupta Kings and Their Successors*. 1888. Vol. 3. Government of India, Central Publications Branch.

Couture, A. 1991. *L'enfance de Krishna: Traduction des chapitres 30 à 78 du Harivaṃśa (éd. cr.)*. Les Presses de l'Université Laval.

———. 2003. "Kṛṣṇa's Victory over Bāṇa and the Goddess Koṭavī's Manifestation in the 'Harivaṃśa.'" *Journal of Indian Philosophy* 31 (5/6): 593–620.

Couture, A., and C. Schmid. 2001. "The Harivaṃśa, the Goddess Ekānaṃśā, and the Iconography of the Vṛṣṇi Triads." *Journal of the American Oriental Society* 121 (2): 173–92.

Cunningham, Alexander. . 1877. "Inscriptions of Aśoka." *Corpus Inscriptionum Indicarum*. Vol. 1. Office of the Superintendent of Government Printing.

———. 1879. *The Stūpa of Bharhut: A Buddhist Monument Ornamented with Numerous Sculptures Illustrative of Buddhist Legend and History in Third Century B.C.* W. H. Allen and Company.

———. 1880. *Report of tours in Bundelkhand and Malwa 1874–75 and 1876–77*. Vol. 10. Office of the Superintendent of Government Printing.

Dandamaev, Muhammad A. and Vladimir G. Lukonin. 1989. *Social Institutions of Ancient Iran*. Cambridge University Press.

Daryaee, Touraj. 2012. *The Oxford Handbook of Iranian History*. Oxford University Press.

Das, K. N. 1982. "Fluvial Processes in the Kosi Catchment Basin and the Impact on Morphology of the Floodplain." In *Perspectives in Geomorphology: Essays on Indian Geomorphology*, Vol. 4, edited by H. S. Sharma. Concept Publishing.

Davis, Richard H. 1991. *Worshiping Śiva in Medieval India: Ritual in an Oscillating Universe*. Princeton University Press.

———. 2024. *Religions of Early India*. Princeton University Press.

de Jong, Albert. 1997. *Traditions of the Magi: Zoroastrianism in Greek and Latin Literature*. Brill.

De Simini, Florinda. 2016. *Of Gods and Books: Ritual and Knowledge Transmission in the Manuscript Cultures of Premodern India*. Walter de Gruyter GmbH.

DeCaroli, Robert. 2015. *Image Problems: The Origin and Development of the Buddha's Image in Early South Asia*. University of Washington Press.

Dehejia, Vidya. 1991. "Aniconism and the multivalence of emblems." *Ars Orientalis* 21: 45–66.

———. 1992. "Rejoinder to Susan Huntington." In "Aniconism and the Multivalence of Emblems: Another Look" by S. L. Huntington, *Ars Orientalis* 22: 157.

———. 1998. "The Very Idea of a Portrait." *Ars Orientalis* 28: 41–50.

———. 2013. *The Body Adorned: Sacred and Profane in Indian Art*. Columbia University Press.

Diehl, C. G. 1964. "The Goddess of Forests in Tamil Literature." *Tamil Culture* 6: 308–16.

Divakaran, Odile. 1971. "Les temples d'Alampur et de ses environs au temps des Cāḷukya de Bādāmi." *Ars Asiatiques* 24: 51–101.

———. 1984. "Durgā the Great Goddess: Meanings and Forms in the Early Period." In *Discourses on Śiva: Proceedings of a Symposium on the Nature of Religious Imagery*, edited by Michael W. Meister. University of Pennsylvania Press.

Donaldson, Thomas E. 2001. *Iconography of the Buddhist Sculpture of Orissa*. Vol. 1. Abhinav Publications.

Doniger, Wendy. 1980. *Women, Androgynes, and Other Mythical Beasts*. University of Chicago Press.

———, ed. 1988. *Textual Sources for the Study of Hinduism*. University of Chicago Press.

Dubovský, Peter. 2013. "Dynamics of the Fall: Ashurbanipal's Conquest of Elam." In *Susa and Elam. Archaeological, Philological, Historical and Geographical Perspectives*, edited by Katrien De Graef and Jan Tavernier. Brill.

Durgāprasad, Pandit, and Āśīnāth Pāndurang. See The *Kathāsaritsāgara of Somadevabhatta*.

Dyczkowski, Mark S. G. 1995–1996. "Kubjikā, the Erotic Goddess: Sexual Potency, Transformation and Reversal in the Heterodox Theophanies of the Kubjikā Tantras." *Indologica Taurinensia* XXI–XXII: 123–40.

Eastburn, Gerardo. 2011. *The Esoteric Codex: Zoroastrianism*. Lulu.com.

Eck, Diana L. 2012. *India: A Sacred Geography*. Three Rivers Press.

Eliade, Mircea. 1971. *The Myth of the Eternal Return: Cosmos and History*. Princeton University Press.

Epigraphia Indica (EI). 1892. *A Collection of Inscriptions Supplementary to the Corpus Inscriptionum Indicarum of the Archaeological Survey*. The Superintendent of Government Printing.

Eschmann, Anncharlott. 1978. "Hinduization of Tribal Deities in Orissa: The Śākta and Śaiva Typology." In *The Cult of Jagannath and the Regional Tradition of Orissa*, edited by Anncharlott Eschmann, H. Kulke, and G. C. Tripathi. Manohar.

Falk, Harry. 2001. "The Yuga of Sphujiddhvaja and the Era of the Kuṣāṇas." *Silk Road Art and Archaeology* 7: 121–36.

———. 2003. "A Copper Plate Donation Record and Some Seals from the Kashmir Smast." *Beiträge zur allegemeinen und vergleichenden Archäologie* 23: 1–18.

———. 2015. "Kushan Rule Granted by Nana: The Background of a Heavenly Legitimation." In *Kushan Histories: Literary Sources and Selected Papers from a Symposium at Berlin, December 5 to 7, 2013*, edited by Harry Falk. Hempen Verlag.

Farquhar, J. N. 1920. *An Outline of the Religious Literature of India*. Oxford University Press.

Finn, Jennifer. 2011. "Gods, Kings, Men: Trilingual Inscriptions and Symbolic Visualizations in the Achaemenid Empire." *Ars Orientalis* 41: 219–75.

Fitzgerald, J. 2010. "Mahābhārata." In *Brill Encyclopaedia of Hinduism*, vol. 2, edited by Knut A. Jacobsen et al. Brill.

Fleet, John Faithfull, and Richard Carnac Temple. 1891. *The Indian Antiquary: A Journal of Oriental Research* 20. Kegan Paul, Trench, Trübner.

Fogelin, Lars. 2015. *An Archaeological History of Indian Buddhism*. Oxford.

Frankopan, Peter. 2016. *The Silk Roads: A New History of the World*. Knopf Doubleday.

Frazer, James George. 1894. *The Golden Bough: A Study in Comparative Religion*. 2 vols. Macmillan and Co.

Fredricksmeyer, E. A. 1997. "The Origin of Alexander's Royal Insignia." *Transactions of the American Philological Association* 127: 97–109.

Fuccaro, Nelida. 1999. *The Other Kurds. Yazidis in Colonial Iraq*. I. B. Tauris.

Fürer-Haimendorf, Christoph von, and Elizabeth von Fürer-Haimendorf. 1979. *The Gonds of Andhra Pradesh: Tradition and Change in an Indian Tribe*. Vikas Publishing House.

Garbutt, Kathleen. See The *Mahābhārata*.

Gaspa, Salvatore. 2018. *Textiles in the Neo-Assyrian Empire: A Study on Textile Terminology in Assyrian Texts*. Walter de Gruyter.

Geertz, Clifford. 1993. "Religion as a Cultural System." In *The Interpretation of Cultures: Selected Essays*. Fontana Press.

Geldner, Karl Friedrich. 1951–1957. *Der Rig-Veda: Aus dem Sanskrit ins Deutsche übersetzt und mit einem laufenden Kommentar versehen von Karl Friedrich Geldner*. 3 vols. Harvard University Press.

Gershevitch, I. 1985. *The Cambridge History of Iran*. Vol. 2, *The Median and Achaemenian Periods*. Cambridge University Press.

Gertoux, G. 2015. *Abraham and Chedorlaomer: Chronological, Historical and Archaeological Evidence*. Lulu.com.

Ghose, Madhuvanti. 2002. "The Origins and Early Development of Anthropomorphic Indian Iconography." 2 vols. PhD diss., School of Oriental and African Studies, University of London.

———. 2006. "Nana: The 'Original' Goddess on the Lion." *Journal of Inner Asian Art and Archaeology* 1: 97–12.

Ghosh, Mallar. 1980. *Development of Buddhist Iconography in Eastern India: A Study of Tārā, Prajñās of Five Tathāgatas and Bhṛkuṭī*. Munshiram Manoharlal.

Ghosha, P. 1871. *Durgā Pūjā: With Notes and Illustrations*. Hindoo Patriot.

Gimbutas, Marija. 1974. *The Gods and Goddesses of Old Europe: 7000 to 3500 BC: Myths, Legends and Cult Images*. University of California Press.

Goldman, Robert P., and Sally J. Sutherland, eds. 1985. *The Ramayana of Valmiki: An Epic of Ancient India, Vol 1: Balakanda*. Princeton University Press.

Gonda, Jan. 1966. *Ancient Indian Kingship from the Religious Point of View: With Addenda and Index*. E. J. Brill.

Granoff, Phyllis. 1979. "Mahiṣāsuramardinī: An Analysis of the Myths." *East and West* 29 (1/4): 139–51.

Griffith, Ralph T. H. See *The Ṛg Veda*

Gupta, Lina. 2002. "Tantric Incantation in the Devī Purāṇa: The Padamālā Mantra Vidyā." In *The Roots of Tantra*, edited by Katherine Anne Harper and Robert L. Brown. State University of New York Press.

Gupta, Sanjukta, and Richard Gombrich. 1986. "Kings, Power and the Goddess." *South Asia Research* 6 (2): 123–38.

Haas, Dominik. 2022. "Gāyatrī: Mantra and Mother of the Vedas. A Philological-Historical Study." PhD diss., Universität Wien.

Hackin, J. 1963. *Asiatic Mythology*. Translated by F. M. Atkinson. Thomas Y. Crowell.

Halperin, Ehud. 2012. "Haḍimbā Becoming Herself: A Himalayan Goddess in Change." PhD diss., Columbia University.

Hanaway, Jr., William L. 1982. "Anahita and Alexander." *Journal of the American Oriental Society* 102 (2): 285–95.

Handa, Devendra. 2006. *Sculptures from Haryana: Iconography and Style*. Indian Institute of Advanced Study.

Haque, Enamul. 2001. *Chandraketugarh: A Treasure-house of Bengal Terracottas*. The International Centre for the Study of Bengal Art.

Hara, Minoru. 1989. "Birth of Extraordinary Persons: the Buddha's Case." In *The Yogi and the Mystic: Studies in Indian and Comparative Mysticism*, edited by Karel Werner. Curzon Press.

Harle, James C. 1958. *Pullamangal*. Bulabhai Memorial Institute.

———. 1963. "Durgā, Goddess of Victory." *Artibus Asiae* 26 (3/4): 237–46.

———. 1969. "On a Disputed Element in the Iconography of Early Mahiṣāsuramardinī Images." *Ars Orientalis* 8: 147–54.

———. 1971–1972. "On the Mahiṣāsuramardinī Images of the Udayagiri Hill (Vidiśā) Caves." *Journal of the Indian Society of Oriental Art*, New Series 4: 44–48.

———. 1974. *Gupta Sculpture: Indian Sculpture of the Fourth to the Sixth Centuries A. D.* Clarendon.

———. 1986. *The Art and Architecture of the Indian Subcontinent*. Penguin.

———. 1994. *The Art and Architecture of the Indian Subcontinent*. Yale University Press.

Harle, James C., and Andrew Topsfield. 1987. *Indian Art in the Ashmolean Museum*. Ashmolean Museum.

Harmatta, J., B. N. Puri, L. Lelekov, S. Humayun, and D. C. Sirkar. 1994. "Religions in the Kushan Empire." *History of Civilizations of Central Asia*. Vol. 2, *The Development of Sedentary and Nomadic Civilization: 700 B.C. to A.D. 250*, edited by J. Harmatta, B. N. Puri, and G. F. Etemadi. UNESCO.

Hart, George L. and Hank Heifetz. 1999. *The Four Hundred Songs of War and Wisdom: An Anthology of Poems from Classical Tamil: the Puranāṉūru*. Columbia University Press.

Härtel, H. 1992. "Early Durgā Mahiṣāsuramardinī Images: A Fresh Appraisal." In *Eastern Approaches, Essays on Asian Art and Archaeology*, edited by T. S. Maxwell. Oxford University Press.

Harting, P. N. U. See *The Baudhāyana Gṛhyaśeṣasūtra*.

Haskar, A. N. D. See *The Hitopadeśa*.

Hatley, Shaman. 2007. "The Brahmayāmalatantra and Early Śaiva Cult of Yoginīs." PhD dissertation, University of Pennsylvania.

———. 2012. "Mātṛ to Yoginī: Continuity and Transformations in the South Asian Cults of the Mother Goddesses." In *Transformations and Transfer of Tantra in Asia and Beyond*, edited by István Keul. Walter de Gruyter.

Hawley, John Stratton. 1981. *At Play with Krishna: Pilgrimage Dramas from Brindavan*. Princeton University Press.

Hazra, Rajendra Chandra. 1963. *Studies in the Upapuranas*, vols. 1 and 2. Sanskrit College.

———. 1987. *Studies in the Purāṇic Records on Hindu Rites and Customs*. Motilal Banarsidass.

Hedges, S., H. Sagar Baral, R. J. Timmins, and J. W. Duckworth. 2008. Wild Water Buffalo (*Bubalus arnee*). The IUCN Red List of Threatened Species: T3129A9615891. Last assessed June 30, 2008. http://dx.doi.org/10.2305/IUCN.UK.2008.RLTS.T3129A9615891.en.

Heesterman J. C. 1985. *The Inner Conflict of Tradition: Essays in Indian Ritual, Kingship and Society*. University of Chicago Press.

———. 1993. *The Broken World of Sacrifice: An Essay in Ancient Indian Ritual*. University of Chicago Press.

Hein, Norvin. 1986. "A Revolution in Kṛṣṇaism: The Cult of Gopāla." *History of Religions* 25 (4: 296–317).

Higham, Charles. 2004. *The Civilization of Angkor*. University of California Press.

Hill, Christopher V. 2008. *South Asia: An Environmental History*. ABC CLIO.

Hiltebeitel, Alf. 1978. "The Indus Valley 'Proto-Śiva', Reexamined through Reflections on the Goddess, the Buffalo, and the Symbolism of Vāhanas." *Anthropos* 73 (5/6): 767–97.

———. 2001. *Rethinking the "Mahabharata": A Reader's Guide to the Education of the Dharma King*. University of Chicago Press.

Hoffmeier, James Karl. 2015. *Akhenaten and the Origins of Monotheism*. Oxford University Press.

Holt, Frank L. 2012. *Lost World of the Golden King: In Search of Ancient Afghanistan*. University of California Press.

Hood, Sinclair. 1994. *The Arts of Prehistoric Greece*. Yale University Press.

Hopkins, E. W. 1909. "Gods and Saints of the Great Brāhmaṇa." *Connecticut Academy of Arts & Sciences* 15: 23–69.

Hornung, Eric. 2001. *Akhenaten and the Religion of Light*. Translated by David Lorton. Cornell University Press.

Humes, Cynthia. 1993. "The Goddess of the Vindhyas in Banaras." In *Living Banaras: Hindu Religion in Cultural Context*, edited by Bradley R. Hertel and Cynthia Ann Humes. State University of New York Press.

———. 1996. "Vindhyavāsinī: Local Goddess yet Great Goddess." In *Devī: Goddesses of India*, edited by John S. Hawley and Donna M. Wulff. University of California Press.

Huntington, Susan L. 1992. "Aniconism and the multivalence of emblems: Another look." *Ars Orientalis* 22: 111–56.

Inden, Ronald B. 2000. *Imagining India*. Indiana University Press.

Inglis, James. 1878. *Sport and Work on the Nepaul Frontier: Or, Twelve Years Sporting Reminiscences of an Indigo Planter*. Macmillan.

Ionescu, Dan-Tudor. 2018. "Mithras, Neoplatonism, and the Stars." *Acta Classica Universitatis Scientiarum Debreceniensis* 54: 161–80.

Iyer, K. Bharatha. 1969. "An Early Gupta Seal of the Mahiṣāsuramardinī." *Artibus Asiae* 31 (2/3): 179–84.

Jackson, Peter. 2003. *The Delhi Sultanate: A Political and Military History*. Cambridge University Press.

Jacob, Colonel G. A., ed. 1888. *The Mahānārāyaṇa-Upanishad of the Atharva Veda with the Dīpikā of Nārāyaṇa*. Bombay Sanskrit Series, Vol. 35. Government Central Book Depot.

Jain, Sharad K., Pushpendra K. Agarwal, and Vijay P. Singh. 2007. *Hydrology and Water Resources of India*. Springer.

Jamison, Stephanie W., and Joel P. Brereton. 2014. *The Rigveda: The Earliest Religious Poetry of India*. 3 vols. Oxford University Press.

———. n.d. *Rigveda Translation: Commentary*. http://rigvedacommentary.alc.ucla.edu/

Jha, D. N. 2023. "Rethinking the 'Golden Age': Caste, Class, and Gender in Gupta India." *Modern Historical Studies of India* 5 (1): 101–19.

Johnston, E. H. 1942. "A Terracotta Figure at Oxford." *Journal of the Indian Society of Oriental Art* 10: 94–102.

Jolly, Julius, trans. 1880. *The Institutes of Vishnu*. Sacred Books of the East 7. The Clarendon Press.

———, ed. 1881. *The Institutes of Vishṇu, Together with Extracts from the Sanskrit Commentary of Nanda Paṇḍita Called Vaijayanti*. The Asiatic Society.

Joshi, M. C. 1994. "Goddess Cybele in Hindu Śākta Tradition." In *Art, The Integral Vision: A Volume of Essays in Felicitation of Kapila Vatsyayana*, edited by B. N. Saraswati, S. C. Malik, and Madhu Khanna. D. K. Printworld.

Joshi, N. P. 1976. *Mātṛkās: Mothers in Kuṣāṇa Art*. Kanak.

Kailasapathy, K. 1968. *Tamil Heroic Poetry*. Oxford University Press.

Kaizer T. 2002. *The Religious Life of Palmyra*. Franz Steiner Verlag.

Kajihara, Mieko. 2019. "The Sacred Verse Sāvitrī in the Vedic Religion and Beyond." *The Journal of Indological Studies* 30–31: 1–36.

Kale, M. R. See *The Daśakumāracarita*.

———. See *The Harṣacarita* by Bāṇa.

———. See *The Kādambarī* by Bāna.

———. See *The Mālatī-mādhava*.

Kane, P. V., ed. 1926. *Dharma-sūtra of Śaṅkha-likhita*. Annals of the Bhandarkar Oriental Research Institute. Vol. 7 Parts 1 and 2.

———. 1930–1962. *History of Dharmaśāstra (Ancient and Medieval Religious and Civil Law)*. 5 vols. Bhandarkar Oriental Research Institute.

———. 1958. *History of Dharmaśāstra (Ancient and Medieval Religious and Civil Law)*. Vol. V, Pt. 1. Bhandarkar Oriental Research Institute.

Kapstein, Matthew. 2001. *Reason's Traces: Identities and Interpretations in Indian and Tibetan Buddhist Thought*. Wisdom Publications.

Keay, John. 2011. *India: A History*. Revised and updated. Grove Press.

Kellens, J. 1987. "AVESTA i. Survey of the History and Contents of the Book." *Encyclopaedia Iranica* III (1): 35–44.

Kerényi, Karl. 1960. *The Gods of the Greeks*. Grove Press.

Khan, M. Nasim. 2002. "Lajjā Gaurī Seals and Related Antiquities from Kashmir Smast, Gandhara." *South Asian Studies* 19 (1): 83–90.

Khare, G. H. 1939. *Mūrti Vijñāna*. Indian History Research Council, Pune.

Kinsley, David R. 1978. "The Portrait of the Goddess in the Devī-māhātmya." *Journal of the American Academy of Religion* 46 (4): 489–506.

———. 1986. *Hindu Goddesses: Visions of the Divine Feminine in the Hindu Religious Tradition*. University of California Press.

———. 1989. *The Goddesses' Mirror: Vision of the Divine from East and West*. State University of New York Press.

———. 1997. *Tantric Visions of the Divine Feminine: The Ten Mahāvidyās*. University of California Press.

Kim, Jinah. 2013. *Receptacle of the Sacred: Illustrated Manuscripts and the Buddhist Book Cult in South Asia*. University of California Press.

———. 2010. "A Book of Buddhist Goddesses: Illustrated Manuscripts of the 'Pañcarakṣā Sūtra' and their Ritual Use." *Artibus Asiae* 70 (2): 259–329.

Kiperwasser, R. 2015. "The Encounter Between the Iranian Myth and Rabbinic Mythmakers in the Babylonian Talmud." In *Encounters by the Rivers of Babylon: Scholarly Conversations between Jews, Iranians, and Babylonians*, edited by Uri Gabbay and Shai Secunda. Mohr Siebeck.

Knirck-Bumke, Krista, Gillian S. Clough, Lorraine Nelson, and Indonesian Heritage Society. 2003. *Victorious Durga: Javanese Images of the Hindu Goddess who Conquered the Buffalo Demon*. Indonesian Heritage Society.

Koester, Helmut. 2012. *History, Culture, and Religion of the Hellenistic Age*. Walter de Gruyter.

Kosmin, Paul J. 2014. *The Land of the Elephant Kings*. Harvard University Press.

Kramrisch, Stella. 1933. *Indian Sculpture: Ancient, Classical and Mediaeval*. Oxford University Press. Reprinted by Motilal Banarsidass, 2013.

———. 1939. "Indian Terracottas." *Journal of the Indian Society of Oriental Art* 7: 89–110.

———. 1946. *The Hindu Temple, Volume 1*. University of Calcutta. Reprinted by Motilal Banarsidass, 2002.

Krishnamacharlu, C. R., ed. 1943. *South Indian Inscriptions*. Vol. 7, *The Pallavas*. Archaeological Survey of India.

Kuhrt, Amélie. 2007. *The Persian Empire: A Corpus of Sources from the Achaemenid Period*. Routledge.

Kulke, Hermann. 1995. "The Early and Imperial Kingdom: A Processural Model of Integrative State Formation in Early Mediaeval India." In *The State in India 1000–1700*, edited by H. Kulke. Oxford University Press.

Kuñjan Pillai, Śūranāḍ. See *The Harṣacarita* by Bāṇa.

Lal, Krishna. 2006. *Peacock in Indian Art, Thought, and Literature*. Abhinav Publications.

Layne, Gwendolyn. See *The Kādambarī by Bāṇa*.

Lecoq, Pierre. 1997. *Les inscriptions de la Perse achéménide: Traduit du vieux perse, de l'élamite du babylonien et de l'araméen, présenté et annoté par Pierre Lecoq*. Gallimard.

Leick, Gwendolyn. 2009. *Historical Dictionary of Mesopotamia*. Scarecrow Press.

Lerner, Martin, and Steven Kossak. 1991. *The Lotus Transcendent: Indian and Southeast Asian Art from the Samuel Eilenberg Collection*. Metropolitan Museum of Art.

Lincoln, Bruce. 1986. *Myth, Cosmos, and Society: Indo-European Themes of Creation and Destruction*. Harvard University Press.

Linrothe, Robert N. 1999. *Ruthless Compassion: Wrathful Deities in Early Indo-Tibetan Esoteric Buddhist Art*. Serindia Publications.

Li Rongxi, trans., and Huili, Jung-hi Li. 1995. *A Biography of the Tripiṭaka Master of the Great Ci'en Monastery of the Great Tang Dynasty*. Numata Centre for Buddhist Translation and Research.

Livingstone, Morna. 2002. *Steps to Water: The Ancient Stepwells of India*. Princeton Architectural Press.

Lohuizen de-Leeuw, Joanna van. 1949. *The Scythian Period: An Approach to the History, Art, Epigraphy and Palaeography of North India from the 1st Century BC to the 3rd Century AD*. Vol 2. E. J. Brill.

Lubin, Timothy. 2005. "The Transmission, Patronage, and Prestige of Brahmanical Piety from the Mauryas to the Guptas." In *Boundaries, Dynamic and Construction of Traditions in South Asia*, edited by Federico Squarcini. Firenze University Press.

———. 2020. "Retrofitting a Vedic Origin for a Classical Hindu Goddess." *Journal of the American Oriental Society* 140 (1): 37–46.

Ludvik, Catherine. 2004. "A Harivaṃśa Hymn in Yijing's Chinese Translation of the Sutra of Golden Light." *Journal of the American Oriental Society* 124 (4): 707–34.

———. 2006. *Recontextualizing the Praises of a Goddess: From the Harivaṃśa to Yijing's Chinese Translation of the Sutra of Golden Light*. Scuolo Italiana de Studi sull'Asia Orientale.

Macdonell, A. A. 1900. *A History of Sanskrit Literature*. D. Appleton and Company.

———. See *The Bṛhad Devatā*.

MacDowall, David W. 2007. "Numismatic Evidence for a Chronological Framework for Pre-Kaniṣkan Art, from Kalchayan to Gandhāra." In *On the Cusp of an Era: Art in the Pre-Kuṣāṇa World*, edited by Doris Srinivasan. Brill.

Magnone, Paolo. 2009. "Tejas (and *śakti*) Mythologemes in the Purāṇas." In *Parallels and Comparisons, Proceedings of the Fourth Dubrovnik International Conference on the Sanskrit Epics and Purāṇas*, edited by Petteri Koskikallio. Croation Academy of Science and Arts.

Mahalakshmi, R. 2011. *The Making of the Goddess Koṟṟavai-Durgā in the Tamil Traditions*. Penguin Books India.

Malandra, Geri H. 1993. *Unfolding a Mandala: The Buddhist Cave Temples at Ellora*. SUNY Books.

Malandra, W. W. 1983. *An Introduction to Ancient Iranian Religion: Readings from the Avesta and Achaemenid Inscriptions*. University of Minneapolis Press.

———. 2009. "Zoroaster, ii. General Survey." *Encyclopædia Iranica.* Published July 20, 2009. http://www.iranicaonline.org/articles/ zoroaster-ii-general-survey.

Malinar, Angelika. 2007. *The Bhagavadgītā: Doctrines and Contexts.* Cambridge University Press.

Mallebrein, Cornelia. 1999. "Tribal and Local Deities: Assimilations and Transformations." In *Devi, The Great Goddess: Female Divinity in South Asian Art*, edited by Vidya Dehejia. Arthur Sackler Gallery.

Mann, Richard D. 2001. "Parthian and Hellenistic Influences on the Development of Skanda's Cult in North India: Evidence from Kuṣāṇa-Era Art and Coins." *Bulletin of the Asia Institute*, New Series 15: 111–28.

———. 2007. "The Splitting of Skanda: Distancing and Assimilation Narratives in the 'Mahābhārata' and Ayurvedic Sources." *Journal of the American Oriental Society* 127 (4): 447–70.

———. 2011. *The Rise of Mahāsena: The Transformation of Skanda-Kārttikeya in North India from the Kuṣāna to Gupta Empires.* Brill.

Marshall, John E. 1916. "Excavations at Taxila." In *Annual Report, Archaeological Survey of India 1912–1913*, edited by John Marshall. Archaeological Survey of India.

McDermott, Rachel Fell. 2001. *Mother of My Heart, Daughter of My Dreams: Kālī and Umā in the Devotional Poetry of Bengal.* Oxford University Press.

Meenakshisundaram, T. P. 1969. "The Paraṇi Poetry." In *Proceedings of the First International Conference Seminar of Tamil Studies, Kuala Lumpur, Malaysia, April 1966,* vol. 2, edited by Xavier S. Thani Nayagam, et al. International Association of Tamil Research.

Mehta, B. H. 1984. *Gonds of the Central Indian Highlands: A Study of the Dynamics of Gond Society, Volume One.* Concept Publishing.

Miller, Margaret C. 1997. *Athens and Persia in the Fifth Century BC: A Study in Cultural Receptivity.* Cambridge University Press.

Mirashi, V. V. 1964. "A lower Limit for the Date of *The Devī Māhātmya.*" *Purāṇa* 6 (1): 181–86.

———. 1974. *Bhavabhūti: His Date, Life and Works.* Motilal Banarsidass.

Mitterwallner, G. von. 1976. "The Kuṣāṇa Type of the Goddess Mahiṣāsuramardinī as Compared to the Gupta and Medieval Types." In *German Scholars on India* 2, edited by Alfred Würfel and Magdalene Duckwitz. Nachiketa Publications.

Mol, Serge. 2003. *Classical Weaponry of Japan: Special Weapons and Tactics of the Martial Arts.* Kodansha International.

Monaghan, Patricia. 2004. *The Goddess Path: Myths, Invocations & Rituals.* Llewellyn Publications.

———. 2011. *Goddesses in World Culture.* Vol 1. ABC-CLIO.

Monier-Williams, Sir Monier. 1986. *A Sanskrit-English Dictionary.* Clarendon Press.

Mookerji, Radhakumud. 1986. *Asoka.* Motilal Banarsidass.

Mosig-Walburg, K. 1982. *Die frühen sasanidischen Könige als Vertreter und Förderer der zarathustrischen Religion*. Peter Lang.

Mudaliar, S. Arumuga. 1964. "Concepts of Religion in Sangam Literature and in Devotional Literature." *Tamil Culture* 11 (3): 252–71.

Muir, John. 1873. *Original Sanskrit Texts on the Origin and History of the People of India, Their Religion and Institutions: Comparison of the Vedic with the Later Representations of the Principal Indian Deities*. Vol. 4, 2nd ed. Trübner.

Mukherjee, B. N. 1969. *Nanā on Lion. A Study in Kushāna Numismatic Art*. The Asiatic Society.

Mukhopadhyay, Samir K. 1972. "Terracottas from Bhītā." *Artibus Asiae* 34 (1): 71–94.

Mukhopadhyay, Somnath. 1984. *Candi in Art and Iconography*. Agam Kala Prakashan.

Müller, Friedrich Max. 1868. *Chips from a German Workshop, Vol. I: Essays on the Science of Religion*. Longmans, Green, and Co.

———. 1892. *Anthropological Religion: The Gifford Lectures*. Longmans Green.

———. See *The Ṛg Veda*.

Nair, P. Thankappan. 1974. "The Peacock Cult in Asia." *Asian Folklore Studies* 33 (2): 93–170.

Nebesky-Wojkowitz, Rene de. 1976. *Tibetan Religious Dances: Tibetan Text and Annotated Translation of the 'Chams Yig*. Mouton.

Nicolaus, Peter. 2008. "The Lost Sanjaq." *Iran & the Caucasus* 12 (2): 217–51.

O'Flaherty, Wendy Doniger, trans. 1981. *The Rig Veda: An Anthology*. Penguin Books.

Olivelle, Patrick. 1998. *The Early Upaniṣads: Annotated Text and Translation*. Oxford University Press.

———. 2000. *Dharmasūtras: The Law Codes of Āpastamba, Gautama, Baudhāyana, and Vasiṣṭha*. Motilal Banarsidass.

———. 2009. *The Law Code of Viṣṇu. A Critical Edition and Annotated Translation of the Vaiṣṇava-Dharmaśāstra*. HOS 73. Cambridge University Press.

———. 2010. "Dharmaśāstra: a textual history." In *Hinduism and the Law: An Introduction*, edited by Timothy Lubin, Donald R. Davis, Jr. and Jayanth K. Krishnan. Cambridge University Press.

———. 2012. "Patañjali and the Beginnings of Dharmaśāstra: An Alternate Social History of Early Dharmasūtra Production." In *Aux Abords de la Clairière: Études indiennes et compares en l'honneur de Charles Malamoud*, edited by Silvia d'Intino and Caterina Guenzi. Brepols Publishers.

O'Reilly, Dougald J. W. 2007. *Early Civilizations of Southeast Asia*. Altamira Press.

Östör, Ákos. 1980. *The Play of the Gods: Locality, Ideology, Structure, and Time in the Festivals of a Bengali Town*. University of Chicago Press.

Owen Lisa N. 2012. *Carving Devotion in the Jain Caves at Ellora*. Brill.

Özkaya, Vecihi. 1997. "The Shaft Monuments and the ‹Taurobolium› among the Phrygians." *Anatolian Studies* 47: 89–103.

Pahari, N., Mahanti, B., Banerjee, M., Mandal, K., Bhowmick, B., & Roy, A. 2022. "A Concise Review on Benincasa hispida (Thunb.) Cogn. Plant." *International Journal of Health Sciences* 6 (S6): 844–53.

Pal, Pratapaditya. 1975. *Bronzes of Kashmir*. Hacker Art Books.

———. 1986. *Indian Sculpture*. Vol.1, *Circa 500 B.C.–A.D. 700*. University of California Press.

———. 1988. "The Chowrie-Bearing Goddess on the Aśvamedha Type of Samudragupta's Coin." *Ars Orientalis* 18: 197–205.

Panikkar, Shivaji K. 1995. "The Regional Tradition of Early Medieval Sapta Mātṛkā Sculptures in Western India (Rajasthan and Gujarat)." In *Studies in Jaina Art and Iconography and Allied Subjects in Honour of Dr. U. P. Shah*, edited by R. T. Vyas. University of Baroda.

Pargiter, F. E. See *The Mārkaṇḍeya Purāṇa*.

Parpola, Asko. 1990. "Bangles, Sacred Trees and Fertility Interpretations of the Indus script relating to the cult of Skanda-Kumāra." In *South Asian Archaeology 1987* 1, edited by Maurizio Taddei. Instituto Italiano per il Medio ed Estremo Oriente.

———. 2015. *The Roots of Hinduism: The Early Aryans and the Indus Civilization*. Oxford University Press.

Parthasarathy, R. See *The Cilappatikāram*.

Patil, Devendrakumar. R. 1948. *The Monuments of the Udaygiri Hill*. Alijah Darbar Press.

———. 1951. "'Telin' or Mahisamardini from Besnagar." *Proceedings of the Indian History Congress, 11th Session, Delhi, 1948*. Indian History Congress.

Patton, Kimberley Christine. 2009. *Religions of the Gods: Ritual, Paradox, and Reflexivity*. Oxford University Press.

Patton, Laurie L. 1996. *Myth as Argument: The Brhaddevatā as Canonical Commentary*. Walter de Gruyter.

Pérez-Remón, Joaquín. 1980. *Self and Non-Self in Early Buddhism*. Mouton.

Peterson, Peter. See *The Kādambarī by Bāṇa*.

Pillai, N. Gopala. 1937. "Skanda: The Alexander Romance in India." *Proceedings of the All-India Oriental Conference* 9: 955–97. Government Press.

Pillai, J. M. Somasundaram. 1968. *A History of Tamil Literature, with Texts and Translations, for the Earliest Times to 600 A. D.* J. M. Somasundaram Pillai.

Pinch, Geraldine. 2004. *Egyptian Mythology: A Guide to the Gods, Goddesses, and Traditions of Ancient Egypt*. Oxford University Press.

Policardi, Chiara. 2024. "The Goddess on the Lion: Animal Symbolism in the Representations of the Female Warrior Deity in Kuṣāṇa and Early Gupta India." *Cracow Indological Studies* XXVI (2): 175–205.

Pope, Rev. G. U. 1899. "Extracts from the Tamil 'Purra-poruḷ Veṇbā-Mālai,' and the 'Purra-nānnūrru.'" *Journal of the Royal Asiatic Society of Great Britain and Ireland* (April): 225–69.

Possehl, Gregory L. 2002. *The Indus Civilization: A Contemporary Perspective.* Altamira.

Puri, B. N. 1994. "The Kushans." In *History of Civilizations of Central Asia,* Vol. 2, edited by J. Harmatta. UNESCO Publications.

Qaderi, Alireza. 2018. "Mesopotamian or Iranian? A New Investigation on the Origin of the Goddess Anāhitā." *Iranian Studies* 51 (2): 171–94.

Quackenbos, George Payn. 1965. *The Sanskrit Poems of Mayūra, Edited with a Translation and Notes and an Introduction Together with The Text and Translation of Bāna's Candīśataka.* AMS Press.

Quintanilla, Ronya Rhie. 2007. *History of Early Stone Sculpture at Mathura: Ca. 150 BCE–100 CE.* Brill.

Ram Karna, Pandit. 1911–1912. "Dadhimatī-mātā Inscription of the Time of Dhrūhlāna, [Gupta-] Samvat 289." In *Epigraphia Indica,* Vol. 6, edited by E. Hultzsch. Archeological Survey of India. Reprinted 1981.

Rana, S. S. 1995. *A Study of Skanda Cult.* Nag Publishers.

Rawson, Philip S. 1967. *The Art of Southeast Asia: Cambodia, Vietnam, Thailand, Laos, Burma, Java, Bali.* Frederic A. Praeger.

Redford, Donald B. 2013. "Akhenaten: New Theories and Old Facts." *Bulletin of the American Schools of Oriental Research* 369: 9–34.

Rezakhani, Khodadad. 2017. *ReOrienting the Sasanians: East Iran in Late Antiquity.* Edinburgh University Press.

Ridding, C. M. See *The Kādambarī by Bāna.*

Robertson, Martin. 1991. *A Shorter History of Greek Art.* Princeton University Press.

Rocher, Ludo. 1986. *The Purānas.* Otto Harrassowitz.

Rodrigues, Hillary. 2003. *Ritual Worship of the Great Goddess.* State University of New York.

———. 2005. "Women in the Worship of the Great Goddess." In *Goddesses and Women in the Indic Religious Traditions,* edited by Arvind Sharma. Brill.

———. 2009. "Asuras and Daityas." In *Brill's Encyclopedia of Hinduism: Regions, Pilgrimages, Deities,* edited by Knut A. Jacobsen. Brill.

Rohlman, Elizabeth Mary. 2018. "The Elusive Sarasvatī: A Goddess, a River, and the Search for the Universal in the Particular." In *The Oxford History of Hinduism: The Goddess,* edited by Mandakranta Bose. Oxford University Press.

Roller, Lynn E. 1999. *In Search of God the Mother: The Cult of Anatolian Cybele.* University of California Press.

Romain, Julie. 2011. "Indian Architecture in the 'Sanskrit Cosmopolis': The Temples of the Dieng Plateau." In *Early Interactions between South and Southeast Asia: Reflections on Cross-cultural Exchange,* edited by Pierre-Yves Manguin, A. Mani, and Geoff Wade. Institute of Southeast Asian Studies.

Rowland, B. 1953. *Art and Architecture of India: Buddhist, Hindu and Jain.* Penguin Books.

Saadi-nejad, Manya. 2021. *Anahita: A History and Reception of the Iranian Water Goddess*. Bloomsbury.

Sahai, Bhagawant. 1975. *Iconography of Minor Hindu and Buddhist Deities*. Abhinav Publications.

Salomon, Richard. 1998. *Indian Epigraphy: A Guide to the Study of Inscriptions in Sanskrit, Prakrit, and Other Indo-Aryan Languages*. Oxford University Press.

Salmond, Noel A. 2006. *Hindu Iconoclasts: Rammohun Roy, Dayananda Sarasvati, and Nineteenth-Century Polemics Against Idolatry*. Wilfrid Laurier Press.

Sanderson, Alexis. 2007. "Atharvavedins in Tantric Territory: The Āṅgirasakalpa Texts of the Oriya Paippalādins and their Connection with the Trika and the Kālīkula, with critical editions of the Parājapavidhi, the Parāmantravidhi, and the *Bhadrakālī-mantravidhiprakaraṇa." In *The Atharvaveda and its Paippalāda Śākhā: Historical and Philological Papers on the Vedic Tradition*, edited by A. Griffiths and A. Schmiedchen. Shaker Verlag.

———. 2009. "The Śaiva Age: The Rise and Dominance of Śaivism during the Early Medieval Period." In *Genesis and Development of Tantrism*. Institute of Oriental Culture, University of Tokyo.

Sarkar, Bihani. 2013. "Thy Fierce Lotus Feet: Danger and Benevolence in Mediaeval Sanskrit Poems to Mahiṣāsuramardinī-Durgā." In *Puṣpikā: Tracing Ancient India through Texts and Traditions*, Volume 1, edited by Nina Mirnig, Péter-Dániel Szántó, and Michael Williams. Oxbow Books.

———. 2017. *Heroic Shāktism: The Cult of Durgā in Ancient Indian Kingship*. The British Academy. Oxford University Press.

———. 2018a. "From Magic to Deity, Matter to Persona: The Exaltation of Māyā." In *The Oxford History of Hinduism: The Goddess*, edited by Mandakranta Bose. Oxford University Press.

———. 2018b. "The Tale of King Suratha and its Literary Reception: Texts and Translations from the Surathotsava and the Durgāvilāsa." Translated by Bihani Sarkar. *Asian Literature and Translation* 5 (1): 146–234.

Śarma, Harikṛṣṇa. See *The Devī Māhātmya*.

Sastri, K. A. Nilakanta. 1935. *The Cholas*. University of Madras.

Saxl, Fritz. 1931. *Mithras: Typengeschichtliche Untersuchungen*. Heinrich Keller.

Schaflechner, Jürgen. 2018. *Hinglaj Devi: Identity, Change, and Solidification at a Hindu Temple in Pakistan*. Oxford University Press.

Scheftelowitz, I. See *The Ṛg Veda Khila*.

Schmid, Charlotte. 2002. "Mahiṣāsuramardinī, a Vaiṣṇava Goddess?" In *Foundations of Indian Art. Proceedings of the Chidambaram Seminar on Art and Religion*. Tamil Arts Academy.

———. 2011. "Du Rite au Mythe: Les Tueuses de Buffle de l'Inde Ancienne." *Artibus Asiae* 71 (1): 115–61.

Schnepel, Burkhard. 1995. "Durga and the King: Ethnohistorical Aspects of the Politico-Ritual Life in a South Orissan Jungle Kingdom." *The Journal of the Royal Anthropological Institute* 1 (1): 145–66.

Scott, Gerry D. III. 2008. "A Seated Statue of Sekhmet and Two Related Sculptures in the Collection of the San Antonion Museum of Art." In *Servant of Mut: Studies in Honor of Richard A. Fazzini*, edited by Sue D'Auria. Brill.

Seiwert, Hubert Michael. 2003. *Popular Religious Movements and Heterodox Sects in Chinese History*. Brill.

Sen, Amulyachandra. 1956. *Aśoka's Edicts*. The Indian Publicity Society.

Sengupta, Gautam, Sima Roy Chowdhury, and Sharmi Chakraborty. 2007. *Eloquent Earth: Early Terracottas in the State Archaeological Museum, West Bengal*. Directorate of Archaeology and Museum, Government of West Bengal.

Seshadri, M. 1963. "Mahiṣāsuramardinī: Images, Iconography and Interpretations." *Journal of the Mysore University, Section A. Arts* 22 (2): 1–28, plus plates.

Shah, Umakant Premanand. 1987. *Jaina- Rūpa-Maṇḍana (Jaina Iconography)*. Abhinav Publications.

Shahbazi, A. Shapur. 1977. "The 'Traditional Date of Zoroaster' Explained." *Bulletin of the School of Oriental and African Studies, University of London* 40 (1): 25–35.

Shalom, Naama. 2017. *Re-ending the Mahābhārata: The Rejection of Dharma in the Sanskrit Epic*. State University of New York Press.

Sharma, Dasharatha. 1957. "The Imperial Pratihāras, Rāmabhadra and Bhoja, A Revised Study." *Proceedings of the Indian History Congress* 20: 123–32.

Sharma, G. R. 1960. *The Excavations at Kausambi (1957–59): The defences of the Syenaciti of the Purusamedha*. University of Allahabad.

Sharmā, Kumar. See *The Devī Purāṇa*.

Sharma, Ramesh Chandra. 1994. *Bharhut Sculptures*. Abhinav Publications.

Sharma, Umesh Chandra. 1975. *The Viśvāmitras and the Vasiṣṭhas: An Exhaustive Historical Study, Vedic and Post-Vedic*. Viveka Publications.

Shaw, Miranda Eberle. 2006. *Buddhist Goddesses of India*. Princeton University Press.

Shenkar, Michael. 2014. *Intangible Spirits and Graven Images: The Iconography of Deities in the Pre-Islamic Iranian World*. Brill.

Shepherd, Dorothy. 1980. "The Iconography of Anahita: Part I." *Berytus Archaeological Studies* 28: 47–81.

Sherrow, Victoria. 2006. *Encyclopedia of Hair: A Cultural History*. Greenwood Publishing Group.

Shibazaki, Maho. 2007. "The Role Played by Goddesses in the Haracaritacintāmaṇi." *Journal of Indian and Buddhist Studies* 55 (3): 1035–42.

Shimkhada, Deepak and Phyllis K. Herman, eds. 2008. *The Constant and Changing Faces of the Goddess: Goddess Traditions of Asia*. Cambridge Scholars Publishing.

Sims-Williams, N. 2004. "The Bactrian Inscription of Rabatak: A New Reading." *Bulletin of the Asia Institute* 18: 53–68.

Sims-Williams, N., and F. Cribb. 1996. "A New Bactrian Inscription of Kanishka the Great." *Silk Road Art and Archaeology* 4: 75–14.

Singh, Satyavrat, ed. 1983. *Śrīdurgāsaptaśatī: with Hindi Commentary*. Institute for Pauranic and Vedic Studies and Research.

Sircar, D. C. 1948. "The Śākta Pīṭhas." *Journal of the Royal Asiatic Society of Bengal, Letters* 14 (1): 1–108.

———. 1971. *Studies in the Religious Life of Ancient and Medieval India.* Motilal Banarsidass.

Skoda, U. 2021. "The Ups and Downs of Competing Power Rituals: Dasarā and Durgā Pūjā in a Former Princely State of Odisha." In *Nine Nights of Power: Durgā, Dolls, and Darbārs*, edited by U. Hüsken, V. Narayanan, and A. Zotter. State University of New York Press.

Slavitt, David. R., See *The Mahābhārata.*

Smith, Brian K., and Wendy Doniger. 1989. "Sacrifice and Substitution: Ritual Mystification and Mythical Demystification." *Numen* 36 (2): 189–224.

Smith, David. 2003. *The Dance of Śiva: Religion, art and poetry in South India.* Cambridge University Press.

Smith, J. Z. 1988. "'Religion' and 'Religious Studies': No Difference at All." *Soundings: An Interdisciplinary Journal* 31: 231–44.

Smith, Wilfrid Cantwell. 1975. "Methodology and the Study of Religion: Some Misgivings." In *Methodological Issues in Religious Studies*, edited by Robert D. Baird. New Horizons Press.

Söhnen-Thieme, Renate. 2002. "Goddess, Gods, Demons in *The Devī Māhātmya.*" In *Stages and Transitions: Temporal and Historical Frameworks in Epic and Purāṇic Literature: Proceedings of the Second Dubrovnik International Conference on the Sanskrit Epics and Purāṇas, August 1999*, edited by Brockington Dubrovnik International Conference on the Sanskrit Epics and Purāṇas Mary, Radoslav Katičić, and Hrvatska akademija znanosti i umjetnosti. Croatian Academy of Sciences and Arts.

Solomon, Ted J. 1970. "Early Vaiṣṇava Bhakti and Its Autochthonous Heritage." *History of Religions* 10 (1): 32–48.

Spät, Eszter. 2008. "Religious Oral Tradition and Literacy Among the Yezidis of Iraq." *Anthropos* 103 (2): 393–403.

Spink, Walter. 1967. "Ellora's Earliest Phase." *Bulletin of the American Academy of Benares* I: 11–22.

Srinivasa Ayyangar, T. R., trans. 1938. *The Yoga Upanishads.* Adyar.

Srinivasan, Doris Meth. 1997. *Many Heads, Arms, and Eyes: Origin, Meaning, and Form of Multiplicity in Indian Art.* Brill.

———. 2005. "The Mauryan Gaṇikā from Dīdārgañj (Pāṭaliputra)." *East and West* 55 (1/4): 345–62.

———. 2022. "Self-Coronation: India's Earliest Victors Inherit the Olympian Gesture." *Archives of Asian Art* 72 (1): 55–74.

Srinivasan, K. R. 1958. "The Pallava Architecture of South India." *Ancient India* 14: 114–38.

————. 1960. *Some Aspects of Religion as Revealed by Early Monuments and Literature of the South*. Madras University.

————. 1964. *Cave Temples of the Pallavas*. Architectural Survey of Temples, Number 1. Archaeological Survey of India.

Stančo, Ladislav. 2012. *Greek Gods in the East*. Charles University in Prague: Karolinum Press.

Stietencron, Heinrich von. 2005. *Hindu Myth, Hindu History: Religions, Art, and Politics*. Permanent Black.

Stillinger, Jack. 1992. "The Multiple Versions of Coleridge's Poems: How Many Mariners Did Coleridge Write?" *Studies in Romanticism* 31 (2): 127–46.

Storm, Mary. 2014. "An Unusual Group of Hero Stones." *Ars Orientalis* 44: 61–84.

————. 2018. "Speculation on Hindu Self-Sacrifice Imagery at Nalgonda." *Journal of Religion and Violence* 6 (2): 225–44.

Studholme, Alexander. 2002. *The Origins of Oṃ Maṇipadme Hūṃ: A Study of the Kāraṇḍavyūha Sūtra*. State University of New York Press.

Swarup Gupta, Anand. See *The Vāmana Purāṇa*.

————. See *The Varāha Purāṇa*.

Taddei, Maurizio. 1973. "The Mahisamardini image from Tapa Sardar, Ghazni." In *South Asian Archaeology*, edited by Norman Hammond. Gerald Duckworth.

Taddei, Maurizio, and Giovanni Verardi. 1978. "Tapa Sardār Second Preliminary Report." *East and West* 28 (1/4): 33–135.

Takács, Sarolta, A. 1996. "Magna Deum, Mater Idaea, Cybele, and Catullus' Attis." In *Cybele, Attis & Related Cults: Essays in Memory of M.J. Vermaseren*, edited by Eugene N. Lane. E. J. Brill.

Tamil Lexicon. 1924–1936. University of Madras.

Tartakov, Gary Michael and Vidya Dehejia. 1984. "Sharing, Intrusion, and Influence: The Mahiṣāsuramardinī Imagery of the Calukyas and the Pallavas." *Artibus Asiae* 45 (4): 287–345.

Tartakov, Gary Michael. 1997. *The Durga Temple at Aihole: A Historiographical Study*. Oxford University Press.

Thite, G. U. 1996. "On the Fictitious Ritual in the Veda." *Annals of the Bhandarkar Oriental Research Institute* 77 (1/4): 253–57.

Thurston, E. *Ethnographic Notes in Southern India*. Madras: Government Press, 1906.

Tiwari, J. N. 1983. "An Interesting Variant in the Devī-Māhātmya." *Purāṇa* 25 (2): 235–45.

————. 1985. *Goddess Cults in Ancient India*. Sundeep Prakashan.

Tiwari, M. N. P. 1989. *Ambika in Jaina arts and literature*. Bharatiya Jnanpith.

Tod, James. 1884. *Annals and Antiquities of Rajast'han: Or the Central and Western Rajpoot States of India*. Vol. 2. Brojendro Lall Doss.

Tokunaga, Muneo. 1981. "On the Recensions of the Bṛhaddevatā." *Journal of the American Oriental Society* 101 (3): 275–86.

———. 1979. "The Text and Legends of the Bṛhaddevatā." PhD diss., Harvard University.

Törzsök, Judit. 2014. "Women in Early Śākta Tantras: Dūtī, Yoginī and Sādhakī." *Cracow Indological Studies* 16: 339–67.

Ulansey, D. 1991. *The Origins of the Mithraic Mysteries: Cosmology and Salvation in the Ancient World.* Oxford University Press.

Ustinova, Yulia. 1999. *The Supreme Gods of the Bosporan Kingdom: Celestial Aphrodite and the Most High God.* Brill.

Vallat, Francois. 2013. "Darius the Great King." In *The Palace of Darius at Susa: The Great Royal Residence of Achaemenid Persia*, edited by Jean Perrot, translated by Dominique Collon and Gerald Collon. I. B. Tauris.

van Buitenen, J. A. B., ed. & trans. 1981. *The Bhagavadgītā in the Mahābhārata: Text and Translation.* University of Chicago Press.

———. See *The Mahābhārata.*

van der Geer, Alexandra. 2008. *Animals in Stone: Indian Mammals Sculptured Through Time.* Brill.

van Kooij, K. R. 1972. *Worship of the Goddess According to the Kālīkāpurāṇa: A Translation with an Introduction and Notes of Chapters 54–69.* Brill Archive.

van Koppen, Frans. 2013. "Abiešuh, Elam and Ashurbanipal: New Evidence from Old Babylonian Sippar." In *Susa and Elam. Archaeological, Philological, Historical and Geographical Perspectives*, edited by Katrien De Graef and Jan Tavernier. Brill.

Vandorpe, Katelijn. 1995. "A Sagalassos City Seal." In *Sagalassos III: Report on the Fourth Excavation Campaign of 1993*, edited by Marc Waelkens and Jeroen Poblome. Leuven University Press.

Varenne, Jean. 1960. *La Mahā Nārāyaṇa Upaniṣad.* 2 vols. Éditions de Boccard.

Vassileva, Maya. 2001. "Further Considerations on the Cult of Kybele." *Anatolian Studies* 51: 51–64.

Vaudeville, Charlotte. 1975. "The Cowherd God in Ancient India." In *Pastoralists and Nomads in South Asia*, edited by Lawerence Saadia Leshnik and Günter-Dietz Sontheimer. Otto Harrassowitz.

Vedāntatīrtha, Girīśa Candra. See *The Kulacūḍāmaṇi Tantra.*

Verardi, Giovanni, and Elio Paparatti. 2005. "From Early to Late Tapa Sardār: A Tentative Chronology." *East and West* 55 (1/4): 405–44.

Viennot, Odette. 1956. "The Goddess Mahishāsuramardinī in Kushāna Art." *Artibus Asiae* 19 (3/4): 368–73.

———. 1957. "Les reliefs sculptés de Trichinopoly." *Arts Asiatiques* 4 (2): 143–47.

———. 1971–1972. "The Mahiṣāsuramardinī from the Siddhi-Ki-Gupha at Deogarh." *Journal of the Indian Society of Oriental Art* 4: 66–77.

Vipulananda, Swami. 1956. "The Development of Tamilian Religious Thought." *Tamil Culture* 5: 251–66.

Vogel, J. Philippe. 1910. *Catalogue of the Archaeological Museum at Mathura.* Allahabad Government Press.

————. 1911. *Antiquities of Chamba State I.* Archaeological Survey of India 36. Archaeological Survey of India.

————. 1931. "The Head offering to the Goddess in Pallava Sculpture." *Bulletin of the School of Oriental Studies, London* 6 (2): 539–43.

Warder, A. K. 1983. *Indian Kāvya Literature.* Vol. 4. Motilal Banarsidass.

Warmington, E. H. 2014. *The Commerce between the Roman Empire and India.* Cambridge University Press.

Waters, Matt. 2014. *Ancient Persia: A Concise History of the Achaemenid Empire, 550–330 BCE.* Cambridge University Press.

Westenholz, J. G. 1997. "Nanaya: Lady of Mystery." In *Sumerian Gods and Their Representations*, edited by I. L. Finkel and M. J. Geller. Styx Publications.

————. 2014. "Trading the Symbols of the Goddess Nanaya." In *Religions and Trade: Religious Formation, Transformation and Cross-Cultural Exchange Between East and West*, edited by Peter Wick and Volker Rabens. Brill.

Whitaker, Jarrod L. 2002. "How the Gods Kill: The Nārāyaṇa Astra Eoisode the Death of Rāvaṇa, and the Principles of Tejas in the Indian Epics." *Journal of Indian Philosophy* 30: 403–30.

White, David G. 1998. *The Alchemical Body: Siddha Traditions in Medieval India.* University of Chicago Press.

————. 2003. *Kiss of the Yoginī: 'Tantric Sex' in its South Asian Contexts.* University of Chicago Press.

Williams, Joanna Gottfried. 1982. *The Art of Gupta India: Empire and Province.* Princeton University Press.

Winternitz, Maurice. 1927. *A History of Indian Literature.* Vol. 1. Translated by S. Ketkar. University of Calcutta.

Witzel, Michael. 1989. "Tracing the Vedic Dialects." In *Dialectes dans les Littératures Indo-Aryennes*, edited by Colette Caillat. Institute de Civilisation Indienne.

————. 1997. "The Development of the Vedic Canon and its Schools: The Social and Political Milieu." In *Inside the Texts, Beyond the Texts: New Approaches to the Study of the Vedas.* Harvard Oriental Series, Opera Minora, Vol. 2. Harvard University Press.

Wriggins, Sally Hovey. 2004. *The Silk Road Journey with Xuanzang.* Westview Press.

Yang, Bin. 2004. "Horses, Silver, and Cowries: Yunnan in Global Perspective." *Journal of World History* 15 (3): 281–322.

Yasumura, Norkio. 2013. *Challenges to the Power of Zeus in Early Greek Poetry.* Bloomsbury Academic.

Yokochi, Yuko. 1999a. "Mahiṣāsuramārdini Myth and Icon: Studies in the Skandapurāṇa, II." *Studies in the History of Indian Thought II (Indo-Shishōshi Kenkyū)* 11: 65–103.

————. 1999b. "The Warrior Goddess in the Devīmāhātmya." Chapter 3 in *Senri Ethnological Studies* 50: 71–113.

———. 2004. "The Rise of the Warrior Goddess in Ancient India: A Study of the Myth Cycle of Kauśikī-Vindhyavāsinī in the Skandapurāṇa." PhD diss., Rijksuniversiteit Groningen.

———. See *The Skanda Purāṇa*.

Yü, Chün-fang. 2001. *Kuan-yin: The Chinese Transformation of Avalokiteśvara*. Columbia University Press.

Ziad, Waleed. 2016. "'Islamic Coins' from a Hindu Temple: Reconsidering Ghaznavid Interactions with Hindu Sacred Sites through New Numismatic Evidence from Gandhara." *Journal of the Economic and Social History of the Orient* 59: 618–59.

Index

Mahāsāhasrapramardinī, Crusher/
Slayer of the Buffalo Demon
Mahiṣa compared with, 140–141
Māhātmya. See *Glorification*
Mahāvyāhṛti. *See* Mohinī
mahiṣa. *See* buffalo
Mahiṣa (demon), 272; Devī battling,
177, 182–183, 276, 333–342,
348–349; in DM, 373n4; the
goddess battling, 284–285; origin
of, 283–285; Skanda defeating,
165–167
Mahiṣamardinī, dating use of,
164–165
Mahiṣa-slaying goddess, Kauśikī
connected to, 298–299
Mahiṣāsura, 271
Mahiṣāsura (demon), 182; Devī and,
180–181; Durgā slaying, 269–270
Mahiṣāsuramardinī. *See* Crusher/
Slayer of the Buffalo Demon
Mahiṣa
Mahiṣāsuramardinī Cave, 268–269
Malak-Tāwūs. *See* Peacock Angel
Māmallapuram (Mahabalipuram),
238–242, 268–271, 279
Manasā (goddess), 140
Mānava Gṛhya Sūtra, 68
Mānavadharmaśāstra. See *Laws of
Manu*
Maṅgi Yuvarāja (king), 363
Maṇimēkalai, 258
Mann, Richard, 166, 167, 335–336
mardana. *See* crushing
Mārkaṇḍeya Purāṇa (MārkP), 26,
147, 170, 274, 281
Marshall, John, 114
Massagetae, Tomyris of, 347–349
material artifacts, earliest, 49
Mathurā, Government Museum of
Archaeology in, 80
Mathurā Museum, 82, 84
Mātṛkā-Raktabīja myth, 306
the Mātṛkās, 303–304
Mātṛs. *See* Mothers

Matsya Purāṇa, Koṭavī referred to in,
261
Mauryan dynasty, 135–136
Mauryan inscriptions, nonviolence
reflected in, 320
Mauryan pillars, 135
Mauryan rock edicts, 77
Māyā (goddess), 54
Māyā Devī (goddess), 26, 224
Mazdāism, 313
Mbh. See *Mahābhārata*
Melišpak II (king), 311
Menander I (Milinda) (king), 91, *114,
115*, 132, 167
the Meriah (sacrificial ritual),
229–230
Metamorphoses (Ovid), 225
Metropolitan Museum of Art, 54,
57–58, 61–62, 126
Mihr. *See* Mithras
Miñjaparvata Mountain, Kashmir
Smast complex on, 232
Minoan civilization, 324
Mirashi, V. V., 203
Mithra (Mihr) (Indo-Iranian deity),
72, 90–91, 312, 315, 325
Mithras (Greco-Roman god), 89–91
Mitterwallner, G. von, 123, 383n2
Modesty (Lajjā), 184
Mohenjo-daro (site), 324
Mohinī (Mahāvyāhṛti, Sāvitrī, and
Ekānaṃśā), 40–41
monolatry, 311–312, 317, 329–330,
339; Achaemenids influenced by,
318; royalty sponsoring, 334–335
monotheism, 8, 312–313, 339
Moon Cave (Candrakupa), 110
Mothers (Mātṛs) (goddesses), 335–336
Mount Kailāsa, Rāvaṇa and, 150–151
Mount Mandara, 39–40, 59, 128, 190,
283, 287, 290
Mountain of the Bee (Bhramaragiri),
234
Mt. Kangchenjunga, 67
mouth (*mukhāt*), 184, 276

Purāṇic descriptions, buffalo-subduing goddess contrasted with, 120
Purāṇic Hinduism, 136–137
Purāṇic literature, 317
Puṟapporuḷ Veṇpāmālai, 252–253
puruṣamedha. *See* human sacrifice

Qaderi, 70
Qian, Zhang, 53
Quackenbos, George, 151

Ra (sun god), 96–97
Rabatak Inscription, 86, 91, 100
Raghuvaṃśa, 66
Rājasiṃha Pallava, 271
Rājghāṭ (site), 112–116
Raktabīja. *See* Blood Seed
Raktabīja (demon), 197, 303–304
Raktadantikā (goddess), 218–219
Rām. See *Rāmāyaṇa*
Rāmāyaṇa (Rām), 25–26
Rāṣṭrakūṭa charter, 163–164
Rāṣṭrakūṭa Period, 271–273
the Rāṣṭrakūṭas, 267, 274, 279, 340
Rātrī. *See* Night
Rātrī Khila (hymn), 10, 11–12; Durgā portrayed by, 21; Rātrī Sūkta contrasted with, 13–14; TA contrasted with, 16–17
Rātrī Sūkta, Rātrī Khila contrasted with, 13–14
Raudrī. *See* Kālī
Raudrī (goddess), 281–282, 286–288
Rāvaṇa, Mount Kailāsa and, 150–151
recensions (*śākhās*), 10
recitation, 31, 34, 214–215; of DM, 209–211; of *Glorification* contrasted with listening, 212; of SP, 289
Recitation of the Caṇḍī (*Caṇḍī Pāṭha*), 170
Redford, Donald, 312
refuge. *See specific topics*
regional goddess cults, Kālī subsuming, 263

regional goddesses: Great Goddess cults amalgamating, 263; hairpins resembling weapons representing, 323–324
religious pluralism, 327
religious traditions, DM drawing on, 198
Ṛg Veda (RV): *Avesta and*, 69; Bāṣkala recension of, 367n3; Bāṣkala recension version of, 4, 12, 88, 220, 367n3; *durga* in, 9–10
Ṛg Vedic Gāyatrī *mantra*, 14–15
Ridding, C. M., 152
Rime of the Ancient Mariner (Coleridge), 369n5
"ring composition," 378n4
river goddesses, 3, 63, 67, 102–103
riverine goddesses, multiplicity convention originated with, 102–103
riverine symbolism, 66, 71, 190, 330
Rock Edict 4 (Aśokan), 321
Rock Edict 13 (Aśokan), 321
royalty, monolatry sponsored by, 334–335
Rudra (deity), 16, 282–287
Rudra/Śiva (deity), 166, 282
rulers, the goddess aligned with by, 337
rulership, divine, 334
ruling elites, against iconography, 322
Ruru (demon), 119, 249, 280, 286
RV. *See* Ṛg Veda

Śabara tribals, 153, 155–156, 158, 161, 248
sacrificial rites, during battlefield rituals, 253
Sādhanamālā. See *Garland of [Effective] Methods*
Sage of the Śakyas (Śakyamuni), 224
sages (*muni*), 223
sahasrākṣa. *See* thousand-eyed
Śaivas or Vaiṣṇavas sect, 1, 333, 337
Śaivism, 48, 146, 153, 216, 307, 318, 330. *See also* Śiva